Mecklenburg County, North Carolina
Deed Abstracts
1763–1779

by
Brent H. Holcomb, C.A.L.S. and Elmer O. Parker

Copyright 1979
By: The Rev. ilas Emmett Lucas, Jr.

All rights reserved. No part of this publication may be reproduced, stored in a retrieval system, transmitted in any form, posted on to the web in any form or by any means without the prior written permission of the publisher.

Please direct all correspondence and orders to:

www.southernhistoricalpress.com
or
SOUTHERN HISTORICAL PRESS, Inc.
PO BOX 1267
375 West Broad Street
Greenville, SC   29601
southernhistoricalpress@gmail.com

ISBN #0-89308-108-6

Printed in the United States of America

Introduction

From its formation in 1763 from Anson County, Mecklenburg included all North Carolina counties west of Anson and south of Rowan and all or portions of the present South Carolina counties of York, Chester, Lancaster, Spartanburg, Union, Cherokee, Kershaw, Laurens, Newberry and Greenville. The Indian line was surveyed in 1767, forming the western boundary of Mecklenburg County. Tryon County was formed in 1769, taking the territory west of the Catawba River. The North Carolina-South Carolina border was surveyed in 1772 cutting off present Lancaster and a portion of York County from Mecklenburg. These abstracts cover the entire period when Mecklenburg included such a large area, and going on to 1779--the first nine deed books. These were obviously compiled at a later time from smaller volumes. This explains the lack of chronological order by recording dates.

Originally, two volumes of abstracts of Mecklenburg deeds were planned. However, by the time the second volume was well under way, the first volume was out of print. The cost of soft cover offset printing has so closely approached that of hard binding that the present arrangement is more practical. In fairness to those who purchased Volume I, this volume is priced only slightly higher than Volume II would have been, and this provides the convenience of one index and binding instead of two. With this volume, still another link in early Carolina frontier land titles is provided. With the use of of Anson and Tryon deed abstracts, a thirty-year period of land transactions is now easily accessible.

My thanks to Mr. Elmer O. Parker for helping me with abstracts of Deed Books 5 and 6, and for providing the attractive maps in this edition.

Brent H. Holcomb, C. A. L. S.
Columbia, South Carolina
May 29, 1978

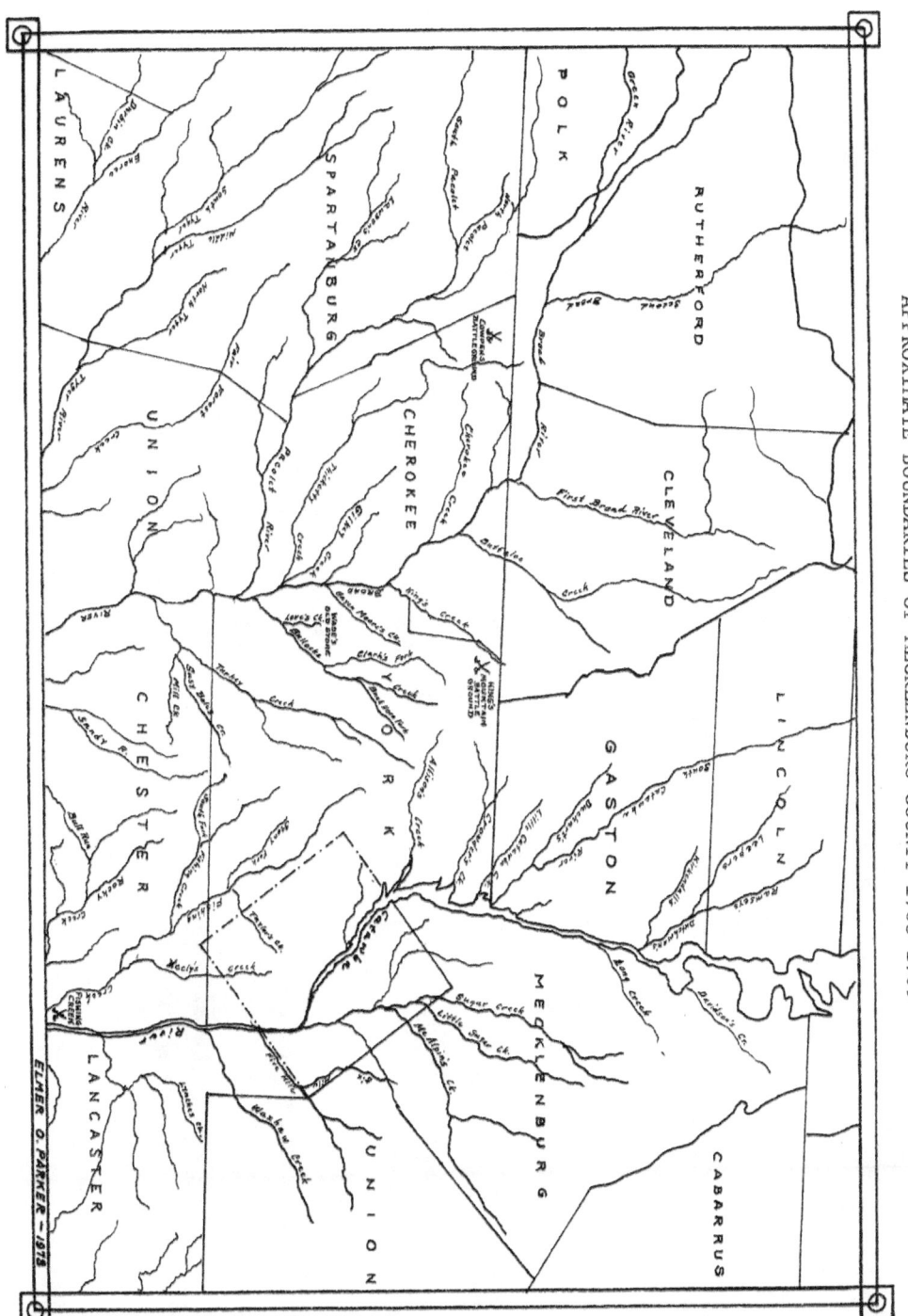

APPROXIMATE BOUNDARIES OF MECKLENBURG COUNTY 1763-1769

VOLUME I

Pp. 1-2: 12 June 1762, Robert Harris, Esqr. & wf Francis of Anson Co., to Robert Harris, Jr. of same, for ₤70 proc. money ...185 A on Dutch Buffelo Creek, a branch of Rockey or Johnston River, granted by Gov. Dobbs 18 Mar 1756...Robt. Harris (Seal), Francis Harris (/) (Seal), Wit: Thos Harris, Margaret Harris.

Pp. 2-3: 12 Apr 1763, Edmond Fanning, Esqr. of Orange Co., Town of Childsburg, to James Potts of Rowan Co., for ₤60... land on both sides Six Mile Creek, 143 A....Edmd Fanning (Seal), Wit: Jno. Brandon, Will Reed.

Pp. 3-4: 9 Dec 1762, Alexander Robinson & wf Jean of Anson Co., to John Bost (lease s5)...200 A in Anson Co., on south side Cataba River...Hindrys line...Scholar's corner...Alexander Robison (Seal), Jean Robison (/) (Seal), Wit: Robert Harris, Robert Harris, Junr.

Pp. 4-6: 22 Feb 1763, Moses Daviss & wf Jean of Anson Co., to James Walkup, for ₤20 Va. money...200 A on N side Cataba on Waxhaw Creek, by virtue of a patent 1752, conveyed from William Vaird to Robert Davis, from Robert Davis to Moses Dav<u>ies</u> ...Moses Davis (Seal), Jean Davis (Seal), Wit: Robert Davis, Robert McClenachan.

Pp. 6-9: John McKee & wf Mary of Anson Co., to John Hunter, late of sd. county, (lease s5, release ₤95)...720 A in Anson Co. on Sugar Creek, granted to sd. McKee 17 May 1754...John McKee (Seal), Mary McKee (0) (Seal), Wit: Moses Ferguson, David Hay, Moses Biggar.

Pp. 9-11: 24 June 1762, Arthur Dobbs, Gov. of NC, to James Graham of Anson Co., for ₤29 s1 proc. money...278 A on Great Coldwater Creek...Arthur Dobbs (Seal), No wit.

Pp. 12-13: 10 Dec 1762, Alexander Robinson & wf Jean of Anson Co., to John Boal for ₤29...land on S side Cataba River... Scholar's Corner...Alexander Robison (Seal), Jean Robison (/) (Seal), Wit: Robert Harris, Robert Harris, Junr.

Pp. 14-16: 21 Feb 1761, Martha Sproot of Anson Co., to James McNight of same, (lease s5, release ₤14 s10)...land on S side of Indian path from the widow Pickens to the Cataba Nation...grant to Thomas Sproot, decd, made over to his daughter Marthew by patent 3 Mar 1753, 700 A...Martha Spro<u>tt</u> (M) (Seal), Wit: Samuel Bigem or Bigger (X), Moses Ferguson, Samuel Sprott, Robert McNight.

Pp. 17-20: 20 Nov 1762, William Bigham of Anson Co., to Joseph Moore for (lease s5, release ₤24)...land on N fork of Paw Creek, granted to sd. Bigham 10 Apr 1761, 195 A...William Bigham (Seal), Wit: Moses Ferguson, Samuel Bigham, Charles Alexander.

Pp. 20-23: 20 & 21 Apr 1763, William Barnet & wf Mary of Meck., to Robert Barnet, (lease s5, release ₤20)...land on N fork Steel Creek, about a mile and a half above sd fork... William Barnet (Seal), Wit: Moses Ferguson, William Bigham, Charles Alexander.

1

VOLUME I

Pp. 24-27: 18 & 19 Apr 1763, James Graham & wf Jean or Jane of Rowan Co., to John Barnet...(lease s5, release ℔___) land on Cold Water Creek, adj. Earl Granville's line, 250 A, made by deed 21 May 1754...James Graham (Seal), Jean Graham (0) (Seal), Wit: Samuel Barnet, John Graham, Will Reed.

Pp. 27-29: 29 Jan 1763, Samuel Harris, planter, of Meck., & wf Rebecha, to John Polk, planter, of same, for ℔20 proc. money...110 A on Clear Creek...Rees Shelby's lower corner...conveyed to sd. Samuel by deed of sale 24 June 1762 by Arthur Dobbs, Gov. of NC...Samuel Harris (Seal), Rebecha Harris (X) (Seal), Wit: Adam Alexander, Saml. Harris, Robert Harris, Junr.

Pp. 29-31: 24 Nov 1762, Dobbs to Christian Ovenshine of Anson Co., planter, for ℔10 s3 d4...180 A between Dutch Buffalo and Little Coldwater Creeks...Wit: Martain Phifer, Arthur MacKay.

Pp. 31-35: 8 Mar 1763, Mary Houston, Relict & acting Executrix of L. W. & T. of David Houston of Rowan Co., to William, son of Dd. Houston of Meck., planter, for (lease s5, release ℔___)...495 A on Meck on N side Cataba...north side of McCallatis' line...both sides Buffelow Creek...granted to sd. David Houston 31 Mar 1753...Mary Houston (0) (Seal), Wit: Nathaniel Alexander, Aaron Houston, Oliver Alexander. [L. W. & T. of David Houston dated 13 Aug 1761.]

Pp. 36-39: 1 Oct 1762, Archibald Little of Anson Co., to Preston Goforth of same, (lease s5, release ℔___)...land on S side Cataba River on Crowder's Creek, known as Samuel Osborn camp, 270 A...granted to John Little by patent 3 April 1753, and from John Little & Jennet his wife to sd. Archibald Little, by L & R, 9 & 10 Dec 1755...Archible Little (Seal), Wit: Nathaniel Alexander, John Robison.

Pp. 39-42: 29 & 30 Dec 1762, Fredick Hambright of Anson Co., planter, to James Leeper of same (lease s5, release ℔34)...150 A on West side Cataba...John Kuykendall's lower corner...Fredrick Hambright (Seal), Wit: Benj. Harden, John Scoot, William Mecklemarry.

Pp. 43-46: 29 Nov 1762, Bleney Mills of Anson Co., planter, to Jacob Willhany of same, for (lease s5, release ℔50)...200 A adj. James Robisons line...Bleney Mills (Seal), Wit: John Patton, Robert Harris.

Pp. 46-49: 27 Apr 1762, Samuel Bigham & wf Mary of Anson Co., to Samuel Berryhill of same (lease s5, release   ), land on E side Cataba, on SW branch of Suggar Creek...land granted to Robert McDowell and made over to Samuel Bigham, granted 17 May 1754...Samuel Bigham (Seal), Mary Bigham (M) (Seal), Wit: Moses Ferguson, William Bigham, Samuel Bigham.

Pp. 49-52: 25 Oct 1762, Thomas Price & Elenor Alexander alias Price of Anson Co., to Andrew Erwin, late from Pa., pedlar (lease s5, release ℔55 proc. money)...land on N side Cataba River, adj. Richd. Graham, James Armor, George Rennick & Melion Hamston (?), 400 A...granted to my father William Price by patent 3 Oct 1755....Thomas Price (Seal), Elenor Alexander (Seal), Wit: Jno. Miller, Thos. Yeats, Richard Barry.

VOLUME I

Pp. 53-55: 25 & 26 Dec 1762, Hugh McKnight of Anson Co., to Hugh Hagans of same, (lease s5, release ₤32)...400 A on S side Cataba, Allison's Creek...above James Wilson's survey...granted 13 Aug 1753 to William Wilson conveyed to William McNight 19 Sept 1753...Hugh McKnight (Seal), Wit: John Coldwell, Robt. Harris.

Pp. 55-59: 18 & 19 Oct 1762, John McDowel & wf Ann of Anson Co., to William Adams, (lease s5, release ₤40 s16)...600 A on S side Cataba on Crowder's Creek, adj. Allison's survey...granted to sd. McDowel 30 Aug 1753...John McDowel (Seal), Ann McDowell (A) (Seal), Wit: John Miller, Richard Barry, Charles Moore.

Pp. 59-61: Jonathan Numan & wf Rebecca of Anson Co., to John Baird (lease s5, release ₤60)...600 A on S side Cataba, about three miles from S fork of Sd. river...granted to ad. Numan 7 Apr 1752...Jonathan Newman (Seal), Rebecca Newman ( ) (Seal), Wit: Nathl. Alexander, John Wilson.

Pp. 61-65: 10 Sept 1762, William Ratchford & wf Mary of Anson Co., to Thomas Neel for (lease s5, release ₤40)...land on S side Cataba, adj. Francis Mackelwain & John Cathy's survey between Crowder's Creek and Little Cataba...William Rachford (R) (Seal), Mary Rachford (O) (Seal), Wit: Joseph Carrel, John Carrell.

Pp. 65-69: 8 Mar 1763, Mary Houston, Relict of David Houston, decd, of Rowan Co., to Aaron Houston, son of sd. decd., (lease s5, release   )...400 A on N side Cataba, on N fork Twelve Mile Creek, formerly surveyed for William Barnet, granted to sd. David Houston 31 Mar 1753...Mary Houston (0) (Seal), Wit: Nathl. Alexander, William Houston, Oliver Alexander.

Pp. 70-73: 15 Apr 1763, Robert Miller & wf Mary of Meck., to Robert Gordan, waggon maker (lease s5, release ₤20)...200 A on N side Broad River, on middle fork Bullock's Creek, about two miles above Bullock's cabin, granted to sd. Miller 3 Sept. 1753...Robert Miller (Seal), Mary Miller (e) (Seal), Wit: Thomas Price, Thomas Jeans, Richard Barry.

Pp. 73-76: 8 & 9 Oct 1762, Andrew Allison & wf Margaret of Craven Co., SC, to William Davison of Rowan Co., NC (lease s5, release ₤5 s13)...640 A in Anson Co., on N side Indian Camp Creek, adj. William Dickey's land...granted to sd. Allison 30 Aug 1753...Andrew Allison (Seal), Margret Allison (Seal), Wit: George Davison, James Byars.

Pp. 76-80: 8 Dec 1761, Robert McDowel & wf Marthew of Anson Co., to Samuel Bigham of same, for (lease s5, release ₤2 s5)...373 A on SW branch of Sugar Creek, granted to sd. McDowell 17 May 1754...Robert McDowel (Seal), Matthew McDowell (∞) (Seal), Wit: Moses Ferguson, Joseph Clark.

Pp. 80-83: 15 & 16 Dec 1762, Rees Price & wf Sarah of Anson Co., to Mathew Nox (Knox) of same, (lease s5, release ₤29 s15)...land of E side Cataba River, near land formerly granted to James Armour and near an old Indian path, granted to sd. Price 3 Apr 1753...Rees Price (Seal), Sarah Price (Seal), Wit: Thomas Price, Richard Barry, Ann Barry.

VOLUME I

Pp. 84-86: 24 June 1762, Dobbs to Benjamin Patton of Anson Co., planter, for ₤25 d6...249 A on Buffello Creek...Wit: Martain Phifer, Wm. Powell.

Pp. 86-88: 24 June 1762, Dobbs to Caleb Blackwelder of Anson Co., for ₤50 s15 d6...151 A in Anson Co...Wit: Martain Fifer, Wm. Powell.

Pp. 88-91: 24 June 1762, Dobbs to Robert Rogers of Anson, planter, for ₤14 s9...138 A between Coddle and Buffello Creeks ...Wit: Martain Fifer, Wm. Powell.

Pp. 91-92: 3 Mar 1763, William Hull (Null?) & wf Agness of Meck., to John Crocket of same, for ₤20 proc. money...162 A on S side Waxhaw Creek...William Hull (Seal), Agness Hull (Seal), Wit: George Douglas, Joseph Pickens.

Pp. 93-94: 1 Feb 1763, Stephen White & Agness his wife of Meck., to Isaac McCullough of same, for ₤20...200 A...Stephen White (Seal), Agness White (A) (Seal), Wit: Robt. McClenachan, John Bogs, Henry Foster (?).

Pp. 95-97: 24 Nov 1762, Dobbs to Henry Matinges of Anson Co., planter, for ₤25 s6 d8...land in Anson Co....Wit: Martain Phifer, Nathan MacKay.

Page 98: Blank.
B
Pp. 99-101: 31 Mar 1763, Robert Tenan of Orange Co., NC, to John Moore of Orange Co., NC, for (lease s5, release ₤8) ...land adj. to Allen Alexander, granted to Robert Tenan 31 Mar 1753, 116 A...Robert Tenan (Seal), Wit: Nathaniel Alexander, Ebenezer Alexander.

Pp. 102-105: 10 Feb 1758, Samuel McKleveny & wf Margaret of Anson Co., to James Waughup in the Waxhaws in Anson Co., for (lease s40, release ₤60)...land on N side Waxhaw Creek, adj. Robert Caldwell's...Samuel McKlevney (Seal), Margaret McKlevney (Seal), Wit: John Pickens, William Pickens, William Henry (O).

Pp. 106-108: 1 & 2 Oct 1762, Archibald Little of Anson Co., to John Robison of same, (lease s5, release ₤70)...land on S side Cataba River on Crowder's Creek, known as Samuel Coborns camp, 220 A granted to John Little 3 Apr 1753, sold by John Little & wf Jennet 9 & 10 Dec 1755 to sd. Archibald. Wit: Nathaniel Alexander, George Alexander.

Pp. 109-111: 3 & 4 Jan 1763, John McNight of Rowan Co., to Joseph Carrel of Anson Co., (lease s5, release ₤50)...land on S side Cataba, Allison's Creek, 600 A...John McKnight (Seal), Wit: John Armstrong, Thomas Carrel.

Pp. 111-114: 9 & 10 Aug 1762, Martin Armstrong of Rowan Co., to Daniel McCartey of same, (lease s5, release ₤11)... land on N side S fork Cataba, 130 A opposite to John Armstrong's land...Martin Armstrong (Seal), Wit: Adam Butner (X), William Armstrong.

VOLUME I

Pp. 118-212: 19 & 20 Nov 1762, Allon Alexander & wf Ann of Anson Co., to Nathaniel Henderson of same (lease s5, release ₤35)...land on S fork Cataba, 450 A patented to sd. Allen Alexander 4 Sept 1753...Allan Alexander (Seal), Ann Alexander (Seal), Wit: Alexander Lewis, Rees Price.

Pp. 121-124: 10 & 11 Jan 1759, Mathies Cloues of Anson Co., to Philip Earinghart of same, for (lease s5, release ₤12)...400 A on S side Cataba, Chigles Creek, land formerly surveyed for Peter Earick...Mathies Cloues (R) (Seal), Wit: Andrew Barry, Richard Barry, Thomas Yeats.

Pp. 124-128: 22 & 23 Mar 1763, Robert Wood & wf Margaret of Rowan Co., to William Simonton of Rowan Co., (lease s5, release ₤100)...land on S side Cataba, Bullock's Creek, adj. Charles McNight and William Watsons surveys...granted to Woods 9 Sept 1753, 270 A...Robert Woods (Seal), Margret Woods (Seal), Wit: Will Reed, David Duncan, Adam Allison.

Pp. 128-132: 5 Mar 1763, Robert Leeper & wf Catherine of Anson Co., to James Crage of same, (lease s5, release ₤23) ...264 A in Anson Co....Robert Leeper (Seal), Katherine Leeper (K) (Seal), Wit: Jonathan Gullick, Samuel Craig, Thomas Neel.

Pp. 133-134: 2 Feb 1763, Robert McClenachan & wf Elizabeth of Meck., to Daniel McGloughlan of same, for ₤40... 170 A...Robert McClenachan (Seal), Eliz. McClenachan (Seal), Wit: John Boogs, John Henry.

Pp. 135-137: 5 Apr 1763, Henry Foster & wf Ann of Anson Co., to Arthur Foster of same, for s5...250 A on N side Fairforest Creek, including James McKlewain's old cabin...granted to Henry Foster 3 Oct 1755...Henry Foster (Seal), Ann Foster (Seal), Wit: Robert McClenachan, George Douglas.

Page 138: Articles of the property of Neal McCloy [?]
```
            to one Bag         ------
            to one peticot     0  5  0
            one Boulster       0 10  0
            one old quilt      0  2  6
                               ---------
                               1  1  0
```

Page 139: Blank.

Page 140: Jan. 18, 1883
          J. H. Hales Birth Dec., 2, 1853, Signed April 18, 1887.

Pp. 141-142: Blank.

VOLUME I, BOOK 2

Pp. 143-145: 17 & 18 Apr 1765, Archibald Gilleland of Rowan Co., weaver, to John Irwin of Meck., planter, (lease s5, release ₤7 s10 NC money)...300 A in Meck., on both sides of Fair Forest River between William Plummers and James Mitchels lines ...Archibald Gilleland (Seal), Wit: Robert Armstrong, James Beaty.
          [This property is in present Union County, South Carolina.]

VOLUME I

Pp. 146-149: 15 & 16 July 1765, Alexander Lewis & wf Hannah of Meck., to James Lynn of same, (lease s5, release Ŀ)...470 A on Six Mile Creek between David Houstons and Jonathan Lewis's surveys...granted to sd. Lewis 6 April 1765. Alexr. Lewis (Seal), Hannah Lewis (Seal), Wit: Benj. Lewis, Jas. Beaird.

Pp. 149-152: 1 July 1766, Moses Alexander High Sheriff of Meck., to Nathaniel Alexander for Ŀ3 s10...394 A granted 6 Geb 1754...for easy recovery of his majest's debts...Moses Alexander Sheriff (Seal), Wit: Edward Giles, Charles Alexander, William Harris.

Pp. 152-154: 9 Oct 1766, James Graham & wf Jean of Rowan Co., to Martin Phyfer of Meck., planter, for Ŀ100 proc. money...278 A on Cold Water Creek...James Graham (Seal), Jean Graham (R) (Seal), Wit: William Ray, David Speek, Jno. Phifer.

Pp. 154-156: 2 & 3 June 1766, Thomas Hawkins of Meck., to John Fondren, planter, (lease s5, release Ŀ20)...200 A on S side Cataba, on Fishing Creek...Blaney Mills's line...granted to sd. Hawkins 30 Oct 1765...Thos. Hawkins (Seal), Wit: John Thomas, Richard Sadler, Ralph Baker.

Pp. 157-158: 10 July 1766, William Howell & wf Catherine of Meck., to John Leard of same, for Ŀ40 proc. money...250 A on S side Cataba, on N side Crowder's Creek...William Howel (Seal), Catrin Howel (Y) (Seal), Wit: John Thomas, Robert Leeper, Jno. McCulloh.

Pp. 158-160: 1 Aug 1765, William Haggins & wf Mary of Waxhaw Settlement, Meck., to Thomas Coyle, for Ŀ20...land on N side Cataba, on both sides Twelve Mile Creek...adj. Land of Robert Macklehany...162 A, part of 320 A formerly of Hugh Wilson, sold to him by Mathew Gillespie 4 June 1756, made out to Gillespie by William Eadey, patented to him 620 A, 16 Nov.1752...William Haggins (Seal), Mary Haggins (R) (Seal), Wit: Robt. McClenachan, Robert Crockett, John Hagans.

Pp. 160-161: 14 July 1766, Thomas Raney & wf Agness of Meck., to John Fondren for Ŀ80...200 A on branches of Fishing Creek, part of a grant to Thomas Raney 21 Apr 1764...Thos Raney, Ann Raney (M) (Seal), Wit: John _____, Hugh H. Quin, Ben: Philips.

Pp. 161-162: 26 Mar 1766, Samuel Burnett of Waxhaw Settlement, Meck., weaver, to Joseph Crawford of same, for Ŀ24 ...376 A adj. Joseph White, granted to sd. Burnett 20 May 1754 ....Samuel Burnett (Seal), Wit: Robert Crawford, Thomas Coyle, John Lynn.

Page 163: Samuel Barten, gentleman of Meck., for Ŀ50 proc. money to Moses Alexander...sale of cattle...10 Aug 1765. Samuel Barten (Seal), Wit: John Gilmore (J), James Neel.

Pp. 163-167: 16 July 1766, William Reed & wf Mary of Meck., ordinary keeper, to John Price, planter, for (lease s5, release Ŀ93)...400 A on E side Cataba, adj. Alexander Dobbins, granted to sd. Reed 25 Feb 1754...Will Reed (Seal), Mary Reed (Seal), Wit: John Hendry, Thomas Beatey, James Way.

VOLUME I

Pp. 167-170: 4 May 1765, Geo. Augustus Selwyn of Gloucester Co., Eng., to James Stratford of Meck., planter, for ₤25 ...208 A on Crosses [?] Run, Reedy Creek, and Rockey River, on Gov. Dobbs' boundary...Wit: John Frohock, Moses Alexander. Note: Some lands may be in S. C., Henry E. McCulloch.

Pp. 171-173: 25 June 1764, Arthur Dobbs & wf Justina, to John Alexander, for ₤12 s6...123 A on Coddle Creek...Wit: John Davis, Junr., Arthur Mackay.

Pp. 173-176: 23 Sept 1765, John Sloan, Jr. to Francis Beaty, both of Meck., (lease s5, release ₤15)...220 A on Gum Branch of Long Creek, above Boyd's entry, part of 500 A granted to sd. Sloan 26 Nov 1764...adj. John Allen, Walter Davis, & Mr. Joy's lines...John Sloan (Seal), Wit: Robert Sloan, Robt. Armstrong.

Pp. 176-177: 16 July 1766, Matthew Floyd to Nicholas Leeper, both of Meck., for ₤39...land on N side Broad River, both sides Richland Creek, gr. to sd. Floyd 2 Nov 1764...Matt. Floyd (Seal), Wit: John Thomas, Samuel Robertson, Robert Leeper.

Pp. 177-178: 16 July 1766, William McKelmurry to James Leeper, for ₤30...200 A on W side Cataba River...near Frederick Hambright's lower corner...granted to sd. McKelmurry, 16 Nov 1764 ...Wm **Mackelmorry** (Seal), Wit: Robert Leeper, Matthews Armstrong, Jno. Nuckols.

Pp. 178-180: 20 & 21 Jan 1766, George Cathey & wf Margaret of Meck., to Samuel Cobrun, for ₤5...land on S fork of Second Broad River, called Cathey's Creek...George Cathey (Seal), Mar**grate** Cathey (Seal), Wit: Richd Barry, Wm. Drew.

Page 181: 15 July 1766, William How & wf Catherine of Meck., to Robert Patrick, for ₤12...50 A...William Howe (Seal), Catrin Howe (C) (Seal), Wit: John Thomas, Robert Leeper, Jno. McCulloh.

Pp. 182-183: 25 June 1764, Dobbs & wf to John Linee, for ₤51... 106 A...Wit: John Davis, Junr, Arthur Mackay.

Pp. 184-185: Nathaniel Alexander, Esqr., & wf Elizabeth of Meck., to John Martin planter, for ₤45 proc. money...390 A on N fork of Crowder's Creek, granted to sd. Alexander by deed of sale, 1 July 1754, originally granted to Robert Patterson by patent, 23 Feb 1754...Nathaniel Alexander (Seal), Elizabeth Alexander (Seal), Wit: Arthur Donaldson, Andrew Elliott.

Pp. 185-186: 28 Oct 1765, John Fondren & wf Elinore of Meck., for ₤60 to Richard Sadler...100 A on Fishing Creek, on the Waggon road that leads from Peter Kuykendalls to Charles Town, lying northward from Charles Beaty's land...granted to Edward Crafts 9 Nov 1764, conveyed to John Fondren 11 Apr 1765...John Fondren (Seal), Elinore Fondren (0) (Seal), Wit: John Thomas, John Patrick, Andrew Armour.

Page 187: 18 July 1766, John Fondren & wf Elinore to Hugh Smith, of Orange Co., NC, for ₤100...200 A on Rockey Creek, including his improvement at the cross road where the Celuda [sic] Road Crosses the South Fork Road...John Fondren (Seal), Elendor

VOLUME I

Fondren (Seal), "I saw John Fondren sign only": Will Harris, John Dunn.

Pp. 188-189: 6 May 1766, Henry Eustace McCulloh of Chowan Co., NC to George Cathey, for ₤85 sterling...land on McDowel's Creek...adj. John McDowel & John Potts land...710 A...H. E. McCulloh (Seal), Wit: John Frohock, J. McKnitt Alexander.

Pp. 190-191: H. E. McCulloh to Matthew McClure of Meck., for ₤18 sterling...120 on S fork McDowell's Creek, waters of Cataba River, adj. George Cathey...Wit: John Frohock, J. McKnit Alexander. Dated 10 May 1765.

Pp. 192-193: 18 Jan 1766, Repentance Townsend of Meck., to George McKinney, for ₤60...270 A on N side Waxhaw Creek, E side Cataba,...Robert Caldwell's line...patented 10 Apr 1761, by deed from John McCane to Repentance Townsend...Reptc. Townsend (Seal), Mary Townsend (0) (Seal), Wit: Henry Downs, Robt. McClenachan, Samuel Thompson.

Pp. 193-195: 30 Jan 1765, Thomas Moore & wf Elizabeth of the Waxhaws, Meck., labourer, to Thomas Ambrose of the same, husbandman, for ₤20...land on N side Cataba, both sides of a branch of Rain [Cain?] Creek, 57 A...Thomas Moore (Seal), Elizabeth Moore (0) (Seal), Wit: Alex. Barnett, Roger Smith, Samuel Thompson.

Pp. 195-197: 28 Dec 1764, Andrew Killen & wf Mary of Meck., to John Ramsey, late of Lancaster Co., Pa., for ₤200 s10...1162 A on S side Cataba, granted to sd. Killen 30 Sept 1749 ...1000A and 152 A granted 17 May 1754. Andrew Killen "/wrote his name Dutch/". Mary Killen (X), Wit: James McCome, James Ramesy, Henry Hendry.

Pp. 197-199: 9 & 10 Dec 1765, Peter Kuykendall & wf Mary to Alexander Love, (lease s5, release ₤40)...250 A on a branch of Fishing Creek, granted to sd. Peter 6 Apr 1765...Peter Kuykendall (Seal), Mary Kuykendall (Seal), Wit: William Watson, Samuel Davison.

Pp. 199-202: 4 July 1766, Francis Beaty & wf Martha of Meck., "Dep. Collector &c," to Robert McCord (lease s5, release ₤45)...300 A on E side Cataba, both sides of Rolls Road, adj. David McCord's, Killen's, and Hugh Beaty's...part of 640 A granted to Francis Beaty 21 Dec 1763...Francis Beatey (Seal), Martha Beatey (M) (Seal), Wit: David McCord, John Beatey.

Pp. 202-204: 20 Oct 1765, John Davison & wf Violet of Meck., to James Ker and John Murphy of same, for ₤140...land adj. Thomas McQuowns, on both sides Coddle Creek, below Joseph Tanner's bridge, land granted to Henry Hendry 27 Sept 1751... sold by the sheriff of Anson County to suit of Samuel Wilson 27 Sept 1751...sold by the sheriff of Anson County to suit of Samuel Wilson and Samuel McCrury against the goods, chattels, etc. of Henry Hendry, and brought by John Dunn, Esq. then sold to John Davison 17 Apr 1759...John Davison (Seal), Violet Davison (Seal), Wit: Thomas McQuown, Henry Hendry.

VOLUME I

Pp. 204-205: 10 Jan 1766, Thomas Barr & wf Margaret of Meck., to John Kur of same for ₤47...land on S side Cataba River, on a branch of Allison's Cr., Thomas Barr (Seal), Margaret Barr (Seal), Wit: Jno. McCulloh, Wm. Macklemory, Thomas Clark (C).

Pp. 205-206: 25 Jan 1765, John Killian of Meck., to James McCombs, late of Prov. of Pa., for ₤34...land on W side Killians Mill Creek...granted to sd. John Killian 17 May 1754...John Killian (‡) (Seal), Ann Killian (K) (Seal), Wit: James Ramsey, John Ramsey (0), Henry Hendry.

Pp. 206-209: 1 & 2 June 1765, Capt. William Haggans & wf Mary of Meck., to Thos Neel, (lease s5, release ₤35)...200 A lying below his other entry on Tar Kiln Branch...Wm. Haggins (Seal), Mary Haggins (M) (Seal), Wit: Samuel Loftain, John Neal.

Pp. 209-212: 15 & 16 July 1765, John Leppart of Meck., to George Williams (lease s5, release ₤30)...285 A originally granted to Phillip Miller, 10 Apr 1753, and afterwards conveyed to John Leppart...John Leppart (Seal), Catharine Lippert (KL), Wit: Paul Barringer.

Pp. 212-214: 18 Jan 1765, William Pickens & wf Elizabeth of Meck., to James Wahup...for ₤30...362 A formerly conveyed to William Pickens & Griffith Rutherford by King's patent...also by virtue of a deed conveyed 16 July 1759, by Griffith Rutherford & wf Elizabeth to sd. William Pickens...on W side Cataba, on Rockey Creek...William Pickens (Seal), Elizth Pickens (X) (Seal), Wit: None.

Pp. 214-215: 4 Nov 1765, George Potts & wf Ann to Adolph Reid [?], for ₤80...land on S side Fishing Creek, adj. Samuel Wilsons corner, 300 A...Goerge Potts (‡) (Seal), Ann Potts (‡) (Seal), Wit: Thomas Calhoun, Lewis Bropots [Probst?] " A Dutch name," and "A Dutch man."

Pp. 215-218: 6 & 7 May 1766, Jacob Sights to Paul Whistenhunt both of Meck., (lease s5, release ₤75)...200 A on both sides Doctor's Run, a branch of Killen's Creek, granted to Sight 23 Dec 1763...Jacob Sights (Seal), Wit: Robert Lowry, Michael Rudisale, James Wyatt.

Pp. 218-220: 15 Apr 1765, Henry Eustice McCulloh to John McDowell of Meck., for ₤90...land on Cataba River, adj. Catheys corner...H. E. McCulloh (Seal), Wit: John Frohock, Robt. Harris.

Pp. 221-223: 9 & 10 Dec 1765, Samuel Davison & wf Margaret to Alexander Love, (lease s5, release ₤220)...600 A, when surveyed in Anson, but now Meck., ...on Moses Dickeys Creek, S side Cataba, granted to Geo. Davison 9 Mar 1765, by Mathew Rowan...Samuel Davison (Seal), Margaret Davidson (Seal), Wit: William Watson, Peterkuykendall.

Pp. 223-226: 4 & 5 July 1766, Francis Beatey & wf Martha of Meck., to David McCord...300 A on # side Catabaw River on the path leading from Mathew Pattons to the ford on the Tuckasegey including the Boyling Spring...on Killens line...part of 647 A granted to sd. Beatey 21 Dec 1763...Francis Beatey (Seal), Martha Beatey (M) (Sea0, Wit: John Beatey, Robert McCord.

VOLUME I

Pp. 226-230: 8 & 9 May 1766, Joseph Harden, Surveying Granted and Partnour with John Kuykendall, Decd. of Meck., to Robert Armstrong & wf Agness (lease s5, release ₤50)...200 A on W side Cataba River...between Rodger Cooks and James Leppards...half of 400 A granted to Samuel Young made 3 Feb 1754, and conveyed to Joseph Harding and John Kuykendall by deed 4 Feb 1754...Joseph Harden (Seal), Wit: Benjamin Harden, John Price, Robert Sloan.

Pp. 330-331: 15 Sept 1765, William Davis & wf Ann of Meck., to Joseph Barnet of Parish of St. Mark, Craven Co., SC, Blacksmith, ...268 A on both sides Camp Creek in Waxhaw settlement...adj. Rodger Smiths line...granted to James Larrimore 17 May 1754...unto sd. William Davis by power of attorney...unto Andrew Pickens who executed a good deed of sale, 16 July 1754...Wm Davis (Seal), Ann Dav (Seal), Wit: John Pickens, Rodger Smith, Samuel Thompson.

Pp. 232-233: 22 Oct 1765, William Moore & wf Ann to Robert Gibley all of Meck., for ₤150...309 A on S side Cataba, on N branch of Fishing Creek, part of 400 A granted to William Watson 30 Aug 1753, conveyed to sd. Moore 21 May 1764...William Moore (Seal), Ann Moore (Seal), Wit: William Watson, James Risk, John Wilson.

Pp. 233-234: 16 July 1 66, William McCulloh & wf Elizabeth to Andrew Sprot, all of Meck., for ₤40...land on S side Catawba River, on S side Mill Creek, 230 A part of a tract granted to Robert Leeper, 20 Mar 1755...William McCulloch (Seal), Elizabeth McCulloch (Seal), Wit: None.

Pp. 234-235: I, Samuel Hughs, of Meck., North Carolina, Weaver, for ₤15 acknowledge payment by Saml Wills of Meck., Wheelwright, for a black mare, one cow & calf, yearling stter... (later mentioned as Samuel Wilson)...10 Dec 1765, Samuel Hughs (Seal), Wit: Jonathan Nusman.

Pp. 235-237: 6 May 1765, Samuel Watson of Meck., Sadler, to Robert Shaw, for ₤30...100 A on Rockey Allisons Creek...Samuel Watson (Seal), Wit: James Lusk [?], John Barry.

Pp. 237-239: 16 July 1766, George Allen & wf Sarah to William Cromikel (lease s5, release s5)...600 A on S branch of Steel Creek, on E side Cataba, near John Henrys, adj. Samuel Knoxs granted 21 Dec 1763, to Samuel Bigham...Geo. Allen (Seal), Sar. Allen (Seal), Wit: James Moor, Andr. Herron [?].

Pp. 240-242: Repeat of deed on pp. 238-239.

Pp. 242-243: 13 Feb 1766, Andrew Nutt & wf Margaret to William Barnett, for ₤25...land in Waxhaw settlement, on NE side Cataba, on the N side Waxhaw Creek, including a spring... 200 A including where sd. Andrew Nutt now lives...granted to Nutt 23 Feb ____. Andrew Nutt, Margaret Nutt. Wit: James Barnet, Samuel Thompson.

Pp. 244-245: 22 Aug 1765, John Hill & wf Jean of Meck., to Alexander Hemphill of Marlick Township, County of Lancaster, Prov. of Pa., for ₤45...1000 A formerly granted to John Killian 30 Sept 1749, conveyed by him to Jacob Brown 1 Jan ____,

then to sd. Jno Hill 20 July 1757...Philip Earnharts corner...
John Hill (Seal), Jean Hill (0) (Seal), Wit: Robert Ewart, John
Duncan.

Pp. 245-247: 7 Feb 1766 & 8 Feb 1766, Charles McLean & wf Susannah
to John Fondren, 400 A on S side Cataba, on head of
Allisons Creek, originally granted to William Watson 30 Aug 1753
...then to sd. McClean 1765...Charles McLean (Seal), Susanna
McLean (♋) (Seal), Wit: John Baber, John Venables.

Pp. 248-249: 30 June 1765, William Simonton of Roan Co., to Charles
McLean of Meck., for ₤30...land on N side Broad
River, in fork of Bullocks Creek, adj. Charles McNight, William
Watson...granted to Robert Woods 1753, then conveyed to Simonton
22 Mar 1763...William Simonton (Seal), Wit: John Wilson, James
Smith, John Venables.

Pp. 249-51: 5 Sept. 1765, William Davison of Rowan Co., planter,
to Alexander Hemphill of Martick Township, Lancaster
Co., Pa., (lease s5, release ₤100)...590 A on Mudlick Creek, S
side Cataba, Adj. William Dickeys, part of a 640 A grant __ Aug
1753, Patent #299...William Davison (Seal), Wit: Margret Moore,
John Duncan.

Pp. 251-254: 17 July 1766, John Henry & wf Martha of Meck., planter, to John Sloan of Rowan County (lease s5,
release ₤70)...land on Steel Creek, granted to sd. Henry 2 Nov
1764, adj. Barnett s line...John Hendry (Seal), Martha Hendry
(0) (Seal), Wit: Richd. Barry, Andrew Sprot, James Camaell (Camp
bell).

Pp. 254-256: _____, Thomas Moore & wf Elizabeth of Waxhaw Set-
tlement, to Alexander Barnett & Joseph Barnett,
blacksmiths, for ₤27...167 A on a branch on Cain Creek, E side
Cataba, adj. Thomas Ambrose...Thomas Moore (Seal), Elizabeth
Moore (L) (Seal), Wit: Thomas Ambrose (A), Rodger Smith, Samuel
Thompson.

Pp. 256-258: 2 Sept 1765, William Davis & wf Ann of Waxhaws,
Meck., to Rodger Smith, Yoeman, for ₤40...land on
both sides Cain Creek, E side Cataba, 100 A in the Waxhaw settle-
ment...patent made out to James Larimore 1754, sold to Andrew
Pikens, then to sd. Davis 16 July 1754...Wm Davis (Seal), Ann
Davis (Seal), Wit: John Pickens, Joseph Barnet, Samuel Thompson.

Pp. 258-   : 6 October 1765   , John Young & wf Ann of Meck.,
to Charles Hart, for ₤30...115 A in the fork of
plum Branch, Hamby's Creek, waters of Rockey River...John Young
(Seal), Ann Young (X) (Seal), Wit: Martin Phifer, and "a Dutch
Name wrote in this Place."

Pp. 259-261: 8 Nov 1765, John Young & wf Ann to Charles Hart for
₤11 [?] s10...1__ A lying in ye fork of Plum Branch
...John Young (Seal), Ann Young (X) (Seal), Wit: Paul Barringer.

Pp. 261-262: 10 Feb 1765, Dobbs & wf to William Harris of Meck.,
for ₤27 s16... 178 A on both sides McKees Creek, a
branch of Rockey River...Wit: John Davis Junr, Arthur MacKay.

VOLUME I

Pp. 263-264: 25 June 1764, Dobbs & wf to Samuel Harris of Meck., for ₤10 s10...105 A on ridges between Duck and Goose Creeks, waters of Rockey River...Samuel Harris Junr....Wit: John Davis Junr, Arthur MacKay.

Pp. 264-265: 26 June 1766, Samuel Harris & wf Margaret of Meck., to Thomas Hall for ₤10 s10...105 A (same land as in preceding deed)...land formerly conveyed to Samuel Harris Junr by Arthur Dobbs...Samuel Harris (Seal), Margaret Harris, Wit: Robert Harris Junr., Robert Harris, James [?] Harris.

Pp. 266-267: 2 Mar 1764, Dobbs & wf to David Moffit of Meck., for ₤13 s2...131 A on head branch of Rockey River...Wit: Martin Phifer, Richd. Barry.

Pp. 267-269: 25 June 1764, Dobbs & wf to Alexander Ferguson, for ₤20 s16...208 A on English Buffalo Creek, a branch of Rockey River...adj. John Conjines [?] corner...Wit: John Davis Junr., Arthur MacKay.

Pp. 270-271: 5 June 1764, Dobbs & wf to William Adams of Meck., for ₤16 s4...162 A on both sides Reedy Creek, a branch of Rockey River...Wit: John Davis, Junr; Arthur MacKay.

Pp. 272-273: 26 June 1766, William Adams & wf Angess of Meck., to George Davis of same, for ₤30 proc. money...162 A on Reedy Creek, purchased of Arthur Dobbs...William Adams (8) (Seal), Agness Adams (0) (Seal), Wit: Robert Harris, Arthur MacKay.

Pp. 274-275: 25 June 1764, Dobbs & wf to John Polk of Meck., for ₤6 s10...65 A on both sides Rockey River...Wit: John Davis, Junr; Arthur MacKay.

Pp. 276-277: 28 June 176_, John Polk & wf Elinor to John Powel, all of Meck., for ₤8 s13 d8...65 A on both sides Rockey River, purchased of Arthur Dobbs...John Polk (Seal), Elener Polk (0), Wit: Adam Alexander, Rees Shelby.

Pp. 278-280: 25 & 26 Oct 1765, James Watson & wf Jean of Rowan Co., weaver, to Robert Cochran of same (lease s5, release ₤55)...318 A on Coddle Creek, adj. Hugh [?] McKowns and including Samuel Watson improvement, granted to James Wilson 16 Nov 1764[?]...James Watson (Seal), Jean Watson (Seal), Wit: Thomas McQuown, James Neel.

Pp. 281-283: 2 Mar 1764, Dobbs & wf to Andrew Binghart, for ₤15 s18...150 A in the forks of Dutch Buffalo Creek... [later Andrew Rignhart]...Wit: Martin Fifer, Richard Barry.

Pp. 283-284: 14 Mar 1765, Hezekiah Alexander & wf Mary of Prov. of of Pa., County of NewCastle, to Moses Ferguson of Meck., for ₤15 sterling...land on both sides Allisons Creek, on W side Cataba...adj. William Patrick...patented to Hezekiah Alexander 9 Nov 1764...Hezekiah Alexander (Seal), Mary Alexander (Seal), Wit: Joseph Cannon, Moses Moore.

Pages 285-287: 3 & 4 Nov 1765, Thomas Allison of Rowan Co., to Pattrick of Nortuck Township, Lancaster Co., Pa., for (lease s5, release ₤22)...201 A on S side Cataba, between John Humphries and William Watsons land, granted 28 Mar 1756...Thomas Allison (Seal), Wit: Charles Moore, Hugh Barry, John Duncan.

VOLUME I

Pp. 287-288: 11 Oct 1765, William Bear & wf Jean of Craven Co., SC, to James Cash [?], for ₤5 proc. money...156 [?] A in Meck...William Beard (Seal), Jean Beard (0) (Seal), Wit: Jacob Gray (7), Joseph John Mungen (ʃ).

Pp. 288-289: 25 Aug 1766, John Lippard & wf Catherine of Meck., to Abraham Glimph, for ₤25 proc. money...land on waters of Dutch Buffalo Creek, patented __ Nov 1765...John Leppart (Seal), Catherine Leppart (K), Wit: Paul Barringer.

Pp. 290-291: 22 Oct 1766, Arthur McClure of Meck., to John Russel, for ₤ __, 250 A above John Wattsons on S side Broad River, granted to sd. McClure 4 Sept 1753...Arthur McClure (Seal), Wit: Robt Harris, Robert Harris, Junr.

Pp. 291-292: 10 Sept 1766, Andrew Reynhart of Meck., to Joseph Sterns, planter, of same, for ₤ __ ...112 A on Meck., on the place where Andrew Reynhart now lives, on a branch of Adams Creek...Andrew Reynhart (Seal), Hannah Reynhart (Seal), Wit: Paul Barringer, Lusart [?] Salby.

Pp. 293-294: 20 Oct 1766, John Caldwell & wf Elisabeth of Meck., to John Morrison, planter, of same, for ₤70 proc. money...land on Caldwell s Creek, granted by deed of seal 25 June 1761 [?], from Arthur Dobbs...John Caldwell (Seal), Elisabeth Caldwell, Wit: Robert Harris, William White.

Pp. 294-295: 15 Apr 1766, John Fondren & Alender his wife of Meck., to Samuel Gay, for ₤53 s6...land on branches of Fishing Creek...Nabbs corner...granted to Thomas Rayne, 21 Apr 1764...John Fondren, Alendor Fondren: Wit: Thomas Arkins [?], John Coburn.

Pp. 295-296: 6 Oct 1766, John Davis to James Davis, both of Meck., for s5, ...114 A, conveyed to John Davis by Arthur Dobbs, 24 Nov 1762...John Davis (Seal), Wit: Robert Harris, Robt. Harris Junr.

Pp. 296-297: 22 Oct 1766, David Hays Senr & Wf Jean to William McClure, all of Meck., for ₤20...land on S side Cataba River, on a branch of Sugar Creek....James Salles, formerly from the Widdow Pickens...patented 17 May 1754...David Hay (Seal), Jean Hay (Seal), Wit: Moses Ferguson, Nat: McClure, Robert Wilson.

Pp. 297-299: 14 Oct 1766, Magnus Simonson of Anson Co., lately now Mecklenburg Co., to Thomas Hollingsworth of same, for ₤50...land laid out unto John Hannah 27 Sept 1753, and sold to sd. Magnus Simonson...Magnus Simonson (Seal), Wit: Elias Hollingsworth, Joseph Hollingsworth, Thomas Cost [?].

Pp. 299-301: 15 & 16 Oct 1766, John Haggins & wf Elizabeth, planter, of Meck., to George Neel of same, (lease s5, release ₤25)...300 A on the Sedar Fork of Twelve Mile Creek, patented 20 Dec 1762...John Haggins (Seal), Elizabeth Haggins (Seal), Wit: James _____, Henry Downs [?], Thomas Conkran.

Pp. 301-304: 4 Feb 1766, John Thomason of Rowan Co., to Amos Byrd of Meck., (lease s5, release ₤50)...200 A on S fork Clarks Creek, sold by Alexander Whitely to John Thomas, formerly granted to William Sherill, 13 Sept 1749...John Thomason (Seal), Wit: James Robinson, Isaac Johnson, William Coleman.

VOLUME I

Pp. 304-306: 24 Dec 1765, William Haggins & wf Mary of the Waxhaws, husbandman, to John Drennan, late from Pa., yoeman, for ₤20...land on N side Cataba, opposite the Cataba Indians Town, part of an original grant to Robert Mukelhaney... William Hagins (Seal), Mary Hagins (0) (Seal), Wit: ____ Nutt, Robert Crockett, Samuel Thompson.

Pp. 306-308: 17 & 21 Oct 1766, John Hagins & wf Elizabeth to Thomas Cockran, all of Meck., (lease s5, release ₤10)...150 A on Cedar Branch of 12 mile Creek, granted to John Hagans 4 Nov 1764...George Nutts corner...John Hagans (Seal), Elizabeth Hagans (Seal), Wit: Hendry Downes, James Tate, Geo: Neel [lease has Lazarus Tate instead of James Tate.]

Pp. 308-312: 2 & 3 June 1766, Jacob Gardner to Thomas Parker lease s5, release ₤60)...land on S side Broad River, on Big Creek, above the mouth of the Packolate, 500 A patented to Charles McDowell, 11 Apr 1751...and another patent of sd. McDowell which at his deceased went to his daughter Rachel Eagan....George Cathey, Exr of L. W. & T. of sd. McDowell...John McDowell as attorney...Jacob Gardner (Seal), Wit: Daniel Davies, Benj. Lewis, Alexr. Lewis.

Pp. 312-313: ____ 1765, James Rian of Meck., to William Hagan, for ₤30, 150 A on ____ Branch of Twelve Mile Creek, granted ____...James Rian (Seal), Wit: James Miller, Robt. McClenachan.

Pp. 313-314: ____ 1766, Thomas McClenahan & wf Ann to Peter Culp, for ₤200...190 A on Stony fork of Fishing Creek... Thomas McClena_?_ (Seal), Ann McClelana_?_ (X) (Seal), Wit: Robert McClenachan, Fenney McClenachan.

Pp. 315-316: 10 Aug 1765, John Hackey [?] to George Hies [?] Hicks [?]...for ₤17...200 A...John Harch [?] (Seal), Wit: [Two German signatures.]

Pp. 316-317: 24 Oct 1766, Thomas Hays [?] to James Robertson, for ₤20...land on S side Pakolate River, E side Browns Creek...patented 1755[?]...Thomas ____ [?] (Seal), James Robertson, Wit: Thomas Polk.

Pp. 317-320: 12 & 13 Jan 1766, Alexander Whiteley to John Thompson, both of Meck., (lease s5, release ₤20)...200 A formerly called Roan and Anson, now Meck., patented 13 Sept 1749 to William Sherril...Alexander Whiteley (Seal), Wit: James Robinson, Isaac Johnson, William Coleman.

Pp. 320-322: 14 Oct 1766, Martha Hollingsworth of Anson Co., late called Meck., to Joseph Hollingsworth, Junr...land granted to Joseph Hollingsworth S R, on S side Broad River... Martha Hollingsworth (M) (Seal), Wit: Elias Hollingsworth, Thomas Hollingsworth, Thomas Cox.

Pp. 322-326: 18 Oct 1766, John Potts, planter, of Meck., to Henry Bullinger of Barges [Bargo?] Co., Pa., for ₤75... land on ye S fork Cataba, adj. his old survey...Francis McSwains [?] line...400 A, granted to Samuel Howard, deed bearing date 13 Oct 1756...John Pots (Seal), Mary Potts (M) (Seal), Wit: James Robinson, Andrew Coltener, Jurate; William Goodman.

VOLUME I

Pp. 326-328: 20 & 21 Jan 1765, Thomas Turner of Rowan Co., to John Armstrong of Meck., (lease s5, release ℔35)...land on S side Cataba, adj. Thomas Robinsons survey...granted to sd. Thomas Turner or his father John Turner 30 Aug 1765...Thomas Turner (Seal), Wit. William Moore, Andrew McNabb, John Fleet [Teurl?].

Pp. 329-332: 5 & 6 Sept 1766, Mathias Clemence of Granville County, SC, to Adam Meek of Meck., (lease s5, release ℔50)...land on S fork of Little River, about a mile below James Mitchells land, granted to sd. Clemence 24 Sept 1754...Mathias Clemans (M) (Seal), Wit: Nathl. Alexander, James Wallace, Robert Campbell.

Pp. 332-337: 29 & 30 Sept 1766, Francis Beaty of Meck., to James Cavil, carpenter of Rowan Co., (lease s5, release ℔ 25)...land on Mitchells Creek, on the south side of Feair Forrest Creek, on N side Tyger River...granted to Henry Fforster, 3 Oct 1755, & conveyed to sd. Beaty by L. & R. 20 & 21 Sept 1765...200 A...Francis Beaty (Seal), Wit: Robert Armstrong, James Beaty, Adam Meek.

Pp. 338-342: Blank.

END OF BOOK I, PART 2.

BOOK I, PART 3.

Pp. 343-345: 19 & 20 Oct 1765, William Moore & wf Mary of Meck., to Ephraim McLean of same (lease s5, release ℔30)...land at head of S fork Fishing Creek, adj. to branches of Turkey Creek...300 A...William Moore (Seal), Mary Moore (Seal), Wit: William Dunlop, John Wilson.

Pp. 346-347: 26 July 1766, John Macknit Alexander of Meck., to John McKee of same, for ℔15...land on head branches of ___ Creek, E side Cataba 150 A granted to sd. Alexander 9 Nov 1764...Jno. McK. Alexander (Seal), Jane Alexander (Seal), Wit: William McKinley, William Sharp.

Pp. 347-349: 20 Mar 1765, Henry Eustice McCulloh to Archibald Houston of Meck., for ℔13 sterling...325 A on Cowdle Creek...H. E. McCulloh (Seal), Wit: John Frohock, _____ Alexander.

Pp. 349-351: 18 July 1766, John Hagans & wf Elizabeth of Meck., to William White of same, for ℔40...land adj. James Miller & Thomas Patens lines, whereon James White now dwelleth ...granted to sd. John Hagans, 16 Apr 1761...John Hagans (Seal), Elizabeth Hagans (Seal), Wit: James Tate, James Linn, William Mageum.

Pp. 351-352: 16 Jan 1767, Henry Eustace McCulloh to William Alexander of Meck., for ℔35 s5...150 A...Wit: John Frohock, Thomas Polk.

Pp. 352-353: 17[?] Jan 1767, Henry Eustace McCulloch to James Forster of Meck., for ℔37...land adj. Benj. Alexander, 166 A...Wit: John Frohock, Thomas Polk.

VOLUME I

Pp. 353-354: 20 Jan 1767, Henry Eustace McCulloh to John Shields for ₤42...lands on both sides Mallerd Creek, adj. Andrew Elliott & Joseph Mitchell...185 A...Wit: John Frohock, Thomas Polk.

Pp. 354-355: 20 Jan 1767, Henry Eustace McCulloh to James Forster, merchant, of Meck., for ₤62...275 A...Wit: John Frohock, Thomas Polk.

Pp. 357-358: 16 Jan 1767, Henry Eustace McCulloh to Andrew Elliott, for ₤46 s16...land on both sides Mallerd Creek...200 A...Wit: John Frohock, Thomas Polk.

Pp. 358-359: 16 Jan 1767, Henry Eustace McCulloh to Alizabeth Mitchell, widow, of Meck., for ₤25...land on both sides Lock harth Creek, 115 A...Wit: John Frohock, Thomas Polk.

Pp. 360-362: 10 Jan 1767, Moses Alexander, Esq, high sheriff of Meck., by an Act of Parliament for recovery of debts on his majesty's plantations...estate of Robt. Welsh, for ₤17...which Stephen Houston late in the Inferior Court...200 A patented 28 Mar 1755...Moses Alexander, Sheriff (Seal), Wit: Will Harris, Robert Harris Junr.

Pp. 363-365: 10 Jan 1767, Moses Alexander, Sheriff, on est. of Robert Patterson...sold to Nathaniel Alexander...land granted 25 Feb 1754, 234 A...Moses Alexander, Sheriff, (Seal), Wit: Will Harris, Robert Harris Junr.

Page 366: 22 Jan 1767, Robert Odare & wf Susannah of Meck., to Samuel Gay, for ₤60...272 A on Turkey Creek, granted to sd. Odare __ Sept 1766...Robert Odare (R) (Seal), Wit: Zachariah Bullock, John Fondren, John Moore.
     [This land now in S.C.]

Pp. 367-9: 26 Dec 1766, Thomas Black to James Hannah, for ₤5...land on Rockey Creek, above where Thomas Kittchens now lives...204 A...Thomas Black (Seal), Wit: Ralph Baker, John Thomas, Jona. Williams or Williamson.

Pp. 369-373: 24 & 25 Oct 176_, Nathaniel Alexander & wf Elizabeth of Meck., to Francis Johnston, of Rowan Co., (lease s5, release ₤40)...275 A on N side Catawba, on middle fork of Twelve Mile Creek, granted to sd. Alexander 29 Mar 1753...Nathl. Alexander, (Seal), Elizabeth Alexander (Seal), Wit: John Gilmore (J), Geo: Alexander.

Pp. 373-374: 21 Oct 1766, John McKnit Alexander, of Meck., to Robert Kur of same, for ₤10...land on both sides Beaverdam Creek...including the Great Flat Rock...granted to Daniel Pritchard, 9 Nov 1764, conveyed by him to sd. Alexander...Jno McK. Alexander (Seal), Jean Alexander (Seal), Wit: Mat. McCluer, William Sharp.

Pp. 374-375: 12 Jan 1767, Daniel Alexander to Phillip Cansillor, both of Meck., for ₤35 proc. money...200 A on N side S fork Cataba, Below Darrick Ramsoeurs...Daniel Alexander (Seal), Wit: Will Harris, Robert Harris, Jr.

VOLUME I

Pp. 375-377: 22 Jan 1767, John Davis & wf Elizabeth of Meck., planter, to George Calhoon, of same, planter, for ₤26...land on E side CAtaba, waters of Steel Creek, adj. Samuel Knox & John Henry...James Biggers corner...granted to Samuel Knox, 400 A...John Davis (Seal), Elisabeth Davis (Seal), (N), Wit: Moses Ferguson, Robert McNight, John Fearil.

Pp. 377-378: 11 Aug 1766, Thomas Raney & wf Agnes of Meck., to William Bratton, of same, for ₤36s6, land on middle branch of S fork Fishing Creek, adj. McNabs land, part of the same tract that was conveyed to John Fondren...granted to sd. Raney 21 Apr 1764...Thomas Raney(Seal),Agnes Raney (0) (Seal), Wit: Jas Moore, Rachel Moore.

Pp. 378-380: 19 Apr 1765, Samuel Bigham & Francis Beaty of Meck., to John Buckanan of same, for ₤20 proc. money...408 A adj. W side Cataba...including the Great Island, nearly opposite to William Wilson's land...McMillen's corner...granted to sd. Bigham & Beaty, 16 NOv 1764...Samuel Bigham (Seal), Francis Beatey (Seal), Wit: Jas Beatey, Robert Armstrong, Thos Polk, Samuel Bigham, Junr.

Pp. 380-381: 19 Jan 1767, John Garven of Meck., planter, to James Muskelly, for ₤32 s10...land on Turkey Creek, land that John Garven bought of John Moore, 290 A...John Garven (Seal), Martha Garven (X) (Seal), Wit: John Thomas, Benjamin Raney, John Garvin, Junr.

Pp. 382- 383: 1 Dec 1766, Matthew Floyd & wf Sarah of Meck., to William Minter of same; for ₤500 SC money...land on N side Broad River, about 5 or 6 miles above Second Broad River from the mouth of the creek...land granted to Mathew Floyd 16 NOv 1764 ....Matt Floyd (Seal), Sarah Floyd (Seal), Wit: Theophilus Faver, John Mc Mulin (J).

Pp. 383-384: 20 Oct 1766, Henry White of Meck., to Isaac Johnston of same, for ₤25 proc. money...land Henry White purchased of John Clark, 8 & 9 April 1765, on S side S fork Cataba, bounded by the other part of the original survey now owned by John Shuford. .granted to Samuel Wilkins, 7 Sept 1751, 500 A... opposite the plantation of James Robinson, Esqr...Henry White (Seal), Wit: Samuel Sprot, William Cromall, James Cotton.

Pp. 384-385: 29 Sept 1766, Hugh Quinn of Meck., to William Yancey of same, for ₤53 s2 d6 proc. money...land in the fork of Main Broad River and First Little Broad River...200 A... Hugh Quinn (H) (Seal), Margret Quinn (M) (Seal), Wit: John Harden, Samuel Richardson, John Richardson.

Pp. 385-386: 16 Jan 1767, Jacob Summerman to Peter Summerman, both of Meck., for ₤5 sterling...land granted to sd. Jacob 19 Apr 1763, on S side S fork Cataba, 112 A...Jacob Summerman (Seal), Catharine Summerman (⊕) (Seal), "In English" written over signatures, Wit: John Dillinger,, "Two witnesses who wrote their names in Dutch."

Pp. 386-389: 22 Jan 1767, Matthew Floyd Of Meck., to Joseph Clark of same, for (Lease s5, release ₤20)...300 A, surveyed 7 Aug 1765 by William Dickson Dept Surveyor, granted 20 Oct 1765, to sd. Floyd...Matt Floyd (Seal), Sarah Floyd (Seal), Wit: none.

VOLUME I

Pp. 390-391: 5 Sept 1765, Charles Anderson & wf Elizabeth, late from Virginia, to Robert McClenachan of Meck., for ₤38...219 A on SW side Cataba River...James Miller's line... granted to Robert McClenachan 25 Sept 1754...sold to Charles Anderson 22 June 1764...Chas Anderson (Seal) Eliza. Anderson (Seal), Wit: John Smith, Jas Patton, William Hagans.

Pp. 392-394: 11 & 12 Jan 1766, Nathaniel Alexander & wf Elizabeth of Meck., to John Gullick of same, (lease s15, release ₤30)...land on S side S fork Cataba, on Little Cataba, granted to Robert Patterson 3 FEb 1754, and at deceased of sd. Patterson, Nathaniel Alexander, Exr. bought at Publick sale, from Moses Alexander high sheriff, 234 A...Nathaniel Alexander (Seal), Elizabeth Alexander (Seal), Wit: Abraham Sitton (?), George Alexander, Edward Giles.

Pp. 394-395: 18 Jan 1767, Archibald Houston & wf Margaret to Andrew Falls, all of Meck.,for ₤30...250 A on N fork of Crowder's Creek, adj. Jacob Cobruns land, William McRay (?) land...500 A originally granted 9 Nov 1764...Archibald Houston (Seal), Margaret Houston (H) (Seal), Wit: William Dickerson, Jonathan Newman.

Pp. 396-399: 25 & 26 Nov 1765, Francis Beatey & wf Martha of Meck., to Adam Crayn Jones (lease s2, release ₤26 s10)... 150 A on Sw side of S fork Cataba...granted to sd. Beatey 21 Apr 1764...Francis Beatey (Seal), Martha Beatey (M) (Seal), Wit: Robert Armstrong, James Beatey, William Moore.

Pp. 399-400: James Hanna & wf Jean if Meck., to John Wallis, for ₤26 NC money...land on S fork Fishing Creek, 300 A on branches of Turkey Creek...granted to William Moore 8 Apr 1754 ...James Hanna (Seal), Jean Hanna (0), Wit: John Thomas, Oliver Wallace, James Wallace (₮).

Pp. 401-403: 21 & 22 Oct 1766, Derrick Ramsour of Meck., planter, to Nicholas Fryday (Friday), of same, planter, (lease s5, release ₤50)...400 A on S fork Cataba, on N side of sd. fork...adj. John Armstrong...granted to John Clark, 28 Mar 1755...conveyed by Clark to Ramsour 22 & 23 Sept 1755...Derrick Ramsour (X) (Seal), Wit: Jacob Ramsour, Daniel (David?) Ramsour, and a German signature appearing to be Gottlieb Youn___).

Pp. 404-405: 6 Sept 1766, Richard Barry, son & heir to Andrew Barry, decd & wf Ann, of Meck., to Hugh Barry of same, planter, for ₤12 NC money...Land on N side Cataba, S side McDowell's Creek, where sd. Hugh Barry now lives...428 A, adj. Samuel Wilsons, granted to sd. Andrew Barry, 23 Feb 1754...Richd Barry (Seal), Ann Barry(Seal), Wit: Wm Drue, Geo Elliot, James Price.

Pp. 405-406: 9 Feb 1767, Phillip Rudisail & wf Elisabeth of Meck., to Nickles Truom (?) for ₤37...land on N side S fork (Catawba), opp. to John Armstrongs land, 130 A purchased by Rudisail from Martin Armstrong, 9 Jan 1767...Philip Rudisil (Seal), Elizabeth Rudisil (Seal),,(both signed in German); Wit: John Dillinger, and two German signatures appearing to be Jacob Erwin, Fanny (?) Dillinger.

VOLUME I

Pp. 406-408: 15 & 15 Jan 1767, Martin Tillinger of Meck., to Michael Rudisal (lease s5, release £10 NC money)...land on S side Cataba, Leeper's Creek, being the now dwelling plantation of sd. Martin Tillinger...200 A, granted to Martin Tallinger 24 Sept 1754...Martin Tillinger (Seal), Wit: John Dillinger, Lamuel Saunders, Mary Tallinger (O).

Pp. 408-410: 19 Apr 1765, David Hay and Francis Beatey of Meck., to John Buchanan of same, for £20 proc. money...540 A on both sides Steel Creek, adj. Thomas Houston's lower line, including the Reedy Fork...granted to sd. Hay & Beatey, 24 Apr 1762...David Hay (Seal), Francis Beatey (Seal), Wit: Jas Beatey, Robt Armstrong, Hugh Beatey.

Pp. 410-413: 13 & 14 Jan 1767, Robert Leeper & wf Catherine of Meck., to Robert Johnson sf same, (lease s5, release £60)...200 A on S side Cataba, below the mouth of S fork of sd. river...part of 800 A granted to sd. Leeper, 30 Aug 1753...Robert Leeper (Seal), Catherine Leeper (K) (Seal), Wit: Andrew Armour, Andrew McMillen.

Pp. 413-414: 16 Jan 1767, Andrew McMillen sf Meck., to Joseph Waddell of same, for £ 60 proc. money...land on W side Cataba...Collonel Osburns corner...300 A...Andrew McMillen (Seal), Wit: Thomas Neel, John Leard.

Pp. 414-415: 24 Sept 1766, John McCulloh to James Watson, both of NC, for £40 proc. money...land on both sides Allison's creek, adj. John McNitt Alexanders land, 315 A, part of the land sold by Andrew Allison to John McCulloh 19 & 29 Jan 1762...Jno McCulloh (Seal), Wit: Robt. Adams, John Miffitt.

Pp. 416-417: 26 Nov 1766, Thomas Clark of Meck., planter, to John Pearson, for £12...land on N branch of Allisons Creek, the NW part of a patent of 214 A granted to sd. Thomas Clark -- April 1765...Thomas Clark (C) (Seal), Wit: Alexander Nickell, James Nickell, James Reynolds.

Pp. 417-240: 19 July 1765, Benjamin Lowry of Meck., farmer, to James Brice, of same, planter, (lease s5, release two pistoles)...200 A on Back Creek, otherwise called Six mile branch of Twelve Mile Creek, adj. McKane's line...granted to sd. Lowry 6 Apr 1765...Benjamin Lowry (Seal), Wit: James Tate, James McClure.

Pp. 420-423: 17 & 20 Sept 1766, George Poff of Meck., planter, to Abraham Ahart (A. Hart), Blacksmith, (lease s5, release £12)...50 A on W side Cataba...Killians Creek...adj. Mathias Clows land...granted to Jacob Forney 21 Oct 1758...George Poff (Seal), Wit: Jacob Forney, Willm Berry.

Pp. 423-424: 16 Jan 1767, Alexander Harden of Meck., to John Carmilian of same, for £12 s10 proc. money...(name later appears to be John Carniham)...land on a branch of Turkey Creek...296 A...Alexander Harden (♋) (Seal), Wit: William Watson, John Watson, William Stephenson.

Page 425: 20 May 1766, Adam Jones Of Meck., for £80 pd. by Richard, Nathaniel, Adam Crain, & Molly Jones and delivered unto my son Richard Jones, one feather bed, etc...unto my son Nathaniel ...which William McDowell bought of Robt Leper...bought at the widow Leepers sale...son Adam Crain Jones...bought of Daniel (?) Henderson to my daughter Molly Jones...bought of Sarah Cackendell (Kuykendall)...Adam Jones (Seal), Wit: Thomas Neel, Maryan Copland (X).

    (Adam Crain Jones was a tax collector for Ninety Six District, Abbeville County, S. C. 1787.)

Pp. 426-427: 1 Nov 1766, Ephraim McLean & wf Elizabeth of Meck., to James Hanna of same, for ₤55...land on S side Cataba, River, S fork of Fishing Creek, adj. branches of Turkey Creek, 300 A...granted to William Moore, 18 Apr 1754...Ephraim McLean (Seal), Elizabeth McLean (X) (Seal), Wit: Saml Lacey, Sam (?) McCullough, John Thomas.

Pp. 427-429: 12 Jan 1767, John Welsh & wf Margaret of Meck., to Robert Blackburn, for ₤60 proc. money...200 A in Meck.,.formerly called Anson, on waters of Clarks Creek, N side S fork Cattaba, adj. William Mill, decd...Daniel Warlocks line ...granted to sd. Welsh 10 Apr 1761...John Welsh (Seal), Margret Welsh (M) (Seal), Wit: John Lust, Nicholas Welsh.

Pp. 429-430: 25 Apr 1765, John Woods Of Meck., to Jabez Evans of same, for ₤30 NC money...land adj. W side Cataba, adj. Alexander McLeans and Nicholas Leepers & James Carters lines... 300 A granted to John Woods 3 Apr 1762...sold to John Armstrong, then to Loudwick Laird, but never any forms of lease or conveyance made...John Woods (Seal), Wit: James Allcorn, John Hendry, _____ Hutchison.

Pp. 432-433: 15 & 16 Jan 1767, Andrew Cathey & wf Rebecca of Meck., planter, to Archibald Cathey of same, planter, for (lease s5, release ₤10 NC money)...300 A on E side CAtaba, below the mouth of Paw Creek...granted to sd. Andrew Cathey 21 Oct 1756 ...Andrew Cathey (Seal), Rebecca Cathey (R) (Seal), Wit: John Brandon, Christopher Brandon.

Pp. 434-436: 13 Jan 1767, Francis Beatey & wf Martha of Meck., to John Todd of same, (lease s5, release ₤25 NC money) ...200 A on Gumb Branch of Long Creek, adj. Walter Davies' land, Jeremiah Joys line...John Allen's line...granted to John Sloan Junr 16 Nov 1764, conveyed to sd. Beatey by deed...Francis Beatey (Seal), Martha Beatey (M) (Seal), Wit: Joseph Moor(e), John Beatey.

Pp. 436-438: 29 Sept 1766, James Brice, late of Meck., to Dr. Thomas Wiggins of Lancaster Co., Pa., for ₤25... land on Back Creek, otherwise called Six Mile Branch of TwelveMile Creek...purchased from Benjamin Lowry 19 July 1765...James Brice (Seal), Wit: James Kerr, Thos Carmichael, John Kerr.

Pp. 438-441: 26 & 28 Oct 1765, John Haggan & wf Elizabeth of Meck., Distiller, to James McClure if same, planter, (lease s5, release ₤20)...153 A on middle fork of Twelve Mile Creek, three miels from James McCall's...granted to John Hagan 16 Nov 1764...John Hagans (Seal), Elizabeth Hagans (Seal), Wit: James Dunn, James Tate.

VOLUME I

Pp. 441-443: 22 Jan 1767, William Minter of Meck., to Hezekiah Alexander of NewCastle County, Pa., for ₤80 NC money ...land five or six miles above Second Broad River...granted to Mathew Floyd, 16 Nov 1764, conveyed to William Minter 1 Dec 1766 ...Will Minter (Seal), Wit: Moses Alexander, Jno McK. Alexander, Wm Sharp.

Pp. 443-445: 16 Jan 1767, William Small of Meck., to Joseph Kennedy, Doctor, for ₤60...cattle, furniture, etc.... William Small (M) (Seal), Wit: Ann Neal, Hon Ogle.

Pp. 445-446: 15 Jan 1767, Henry Dillinger of Meck., to John Martin Sulls, for s5 sterling, 300 A on Leeper's Creek, granted 4 Oct 1765...Henry Dillinger (Seal), Hannah Dillinger (Seal), Wit: Lancelot Armstrong, Nickles Trum (∓), John Dillinger.

Pp. 447-448: William Green of Meck., to James Bridges of same, for ₤70 (?)...a king's patent bearing date ____, on S side Broad River, on both sides Thicketty Creek, nigh to and above Richard Millers survey...Willm Green (W), Wit: Jon Clark, Joseph Baghensmark (8), Joel Blackwell (X), Andr. Hutchins (X).

Pp. 449-452 are blank.

VOLUME I, part 4

Pp. 453-455: 14 & 15 Sept 1756, Jean McWhorter of Rowan Co., to Joseph Gillespie of Rowan Co, for ₤30proc. money... land in County of Anson...Alexander Osburn's corner...430 A... Jean McWhorter (Seal), Wit: Alexr Lewis, John Brevard.

Pp. 456-458: Repetition of some of above deed.

Pp. 458-463: 10 June 1763, Arthur Dobbs to Maurice Moore, Esqr of Prov. of NC, County of New Hanover...for ₤25 proc. money...250 A in Meck...where James Lusk now lives...Arthur Dobbs (Seal), Wit: Robt Harris, John Davis Junr.

Pp. 463-466: 4 Dec 1762, Henry Whitner of Anson Co., to Michael Whitner of same, for ₤25 NC money...133 A adj. Conrad Yother...part of two tracts of 1000 A granted to Henry Whitner 29 Sept 1750 and 28 Mar 1751...Henry Whitner (Seal), Wit: Francis Beaty, Jacob Wolfang.

Pp. 466-469: 5 Sept 1764, John Anderson of Meck., planter, to the Rev. Mr. Alexander Craighead, for (lease s5, release ₤20)...550 A on Long Creek...John Bravard's old line...John Anderson & wf Margaret....294 A granted to sd. Anderson 17 May 1754 and 257 A granted to John Bravard, Esqr. 31 Aug 1753...John Anderson (Seal), Wit: Richd Barry, Alexr Lewis, J. McKnitt Alexander.

Pp. 470-472: 5 Oct 1764, Alexr Osburn & wf Agness of Rowan Co., to Robert Findley of same, (lease s5, release ₤10) ...350 A on W side Cataba, on Little Cataba, granted to sd. Osburn 20 Sept 1754...Alexr. Osburn (Seal), Agnes Osburn (Seal), Wit: Joseph Alexander, Adlai Osburn.

VOLUME I

Pp. 472-475: 22 & 23 May 1764, Thomas Davis, carpenter of Meck., to Hugh Houston of same (lease s5, release ₤31 NC money)...130 A on Clarks branch of Twelve Mile Creek...granted to sd. Davis 23 Dec 1763...Thomas Davis (Seal) Wit: Aaron Houston, Francis Beatey.

Pp. 475-476: 24 Sept 1765, William Cleghorn & wf Lettice of Anson County, to Andrew Robinson for ₤40 proc. money... land on W side of S fork Cataba, including the mouth of Du hart Creek...150 A granted to sd. Cleghorn 24 Apr 1762...William Cleghorn (Seal), Lettice Cleghorn (X) Wit: Jas. Moore, William Moore, John Thomas.

Pp. 476-480: Peter Elliott of Parish of St. George, Province of Georgia, Indian Trader...land on Cataba River in Meck., to Alexander Lewis to sell 19 Jan 1764...Peter Elliot (P) (Seal), Wit: David Emanuel JP, Benj. Lewis.
23 &24 Apr 1764, Peter Elliott to John Miller of Meck., (lease s5, release ₤___)...150 A on N side Cataba, granted by George II, 7 Oct 1749...about 3 miles below Price's land... Alexander Lewis for Peter Elliott (Seal), Wit: Richd Barry, Hugh Barry, John McDowell.

Pp. 480-482: 6 July 1764, John Castolo & wf Ellener of Craven County, SC, to John Sellers of Meck., for ₤18 proc. money...100 A on W side Cataba, granted to Robert McClenechan 24 Sept 1754 and conveyed to John Castolo 26 Oct 1760...Thomas Williams' land...John Castolo (Seal), Wit: Thomas Janes, James Linn.

Pp. 482-486: 24 Mar 1764, Peter Club of Meck., to Jacob Sights of same, (lease s5, release ₤25)...250 A on S side Cataba, both sides Killions Creek...between Killions line and Robert Leepers old survey...granted to Samuel More 1 Sept 1753... Peter Club (Seal), Wit: Francis Beatey, James Beatey.

Pp. 486-488: 8 & 9 Aug 1764, John Humphrey of Prov. of Ga., to William Kelly, (lease s5, release ₤56)...land on N side Fishing Creek, W side Cataba...400 A granted to sd. Humphrey 3 Sept 1753...John Humphrey (Seal), Wit: Moses Ferguson, Henry Vernor, William Patrick.

Pp. 489-491: 28 Sept 1764, Maurice Moore Esqr of Brunswick Co., NC to James Stafford of Meck., planter, for ₤26 sl... purchased by Maurice Moore of Arthur Dobbs, 10 June 1763...250 A ...Maurice Moore (Seal), Wit: Robert Harris, Junr, Arthur MacKay. Rec. 28 Sept 1764 from within named James Stafford ₤26 sl proc. money...Maurice Moore., Wit: John Davis Junr.

Pp. 491-493: 13 Oct 1764, Samuel Wilson of Meck., to Jacob Hose (Hoss?) of same, for ₤130 money of NC...land on S side Clarks River, mouth of Fishers Creek...conveyed from John Parker 10 May 1760, 400 A...Samuel Wilson (Seal), Beersheba Wilson (Seal), Wit: Three German signatures (1)_____ Dillinger, (2) _____Rudisil, (3) Jacob _____.

VOLUME I

Pp. 493-494: 20 Sept 1764, John Price & wf Margaret and James Price & wf Mary of Meck., to John Black of same, for ₤25 proc. money...land on N side Cataba, 400 A on Rachel Price, deceased mother's line...land made over to John Price with James Price by virute of a patent granted to aforesaid Rachel Price, deceased aforesaid John Prices former wife and aforesaid James Prices mother 3 Feb 1754...John Price (Seal), Mary Price (X) S(eal), Wit: John Thomas, William Price.

Pp. 494-495: 21 Jan 1764, James Wilson, planter, & wf Margaret of Meck., to Robert Rudsil, of same, planter, for s5 sterling...302 A in Meck., formerly Anson Co., on a branch of Thicketty Creek opposite to Richard Millers land known by the name of Richd. Harrels(?) land...James Wilson (Seal), Margaret Wilson (W) (Seal), Wit: John Patton, Samuel Patton, James Robinson, Jas. Scott.

Pp. 496-497: 27 Aug 1764, William Crawford of Chester Co., Pa., to Thomas McCool, of Baltimore Co., Md., for ₤15 proc. money...land on N side Broad, on Turkey Creek above James Love's survey...450 A granted to Oliver Crawford 13 Aug 1753... at the death of Oliver Crawford, fell to William Crawford, heir at law...William Crawford by Adam McCooll. Be it remembered that on 12 Sept 1763 William Crawford appointed Adam McCool his lawfull attorney to sell said land...Wit: Matt Floyd, John Love, William Dickson.

Pp. 497-500: 18 & 19 July 1763, Benjamin Harden & wf Catharine of Meck., planter, to Joseph Keller (lease s5, release ₤15)...land on N side Cataba, part of a grant to William Wattson 28 Feb 1754, 200 A...conveyed by sd. Wattson to Benjamin Harden by L & R 10 & 11 July 1754...Benjamin Harden (Seal), Catharine Hardin (X) (Seal), Wit: Joseph Hardin, Jno Miller.

Pp. 500-503: 5 Oct 1764, Daniel Prichard of Meck., to John McKnitt Alexander, for ₤50...land on both sides Allison's Creek, W side Cataba...John McCullough's land...300 A...Daniel Prichard (Seal), Mary Prichard (M) (Seal), Wit: James Taggart, William McDowel, George Cathey (+). Land includes 120 A, part of the Great Flat Rock and Cedar Grove.

Pp. 503-506: 24 & 25 July 1764, John Young & wf Ann of Meck., to Paul Barringer, of same, (lease s5, release ₤40)... land adj. David Speeks line on Dutch Buffelo Creek, adj. Charles Ferguson, Martin Barringers lines...conveyed to sd. Young by Arthur Dobbs, 24 June 1762...John Young (Seal), Ann Young (+) (Seal), Wit: (Two German signatures).

Pp. 507-509: 15 & 16 Oct 1764, John Beard & wf Frances Of Meck., to Joseph Bradner, of same, (lease s5, release ₤45) ...550 A on S side Cataba River, N fork of Crowders Creek...granted to James Wahop...John Beard (Seal), Frances Beard (0) (Seal), Wit: Jonathan Newman, William Beard.

Pp. 509-513: 27 Jan 1764, Blaney Mills of Meck., planter, to James Millikan of same, planter, for (lease s5, release ₤41) ...450 A on N side Broad River, S side Fishing Creek, above William Ratchford...granted to sd. Mills 3 Feb 1754...Bleny Mills (Seal), Wit: James Rusk, Hugh Beatty, Frances Beatey.
(This land now in S. C.)

VOLUME I

Pp. 513-514: 12 Sept 1763, William Crawford of Chester Co., Pa., appoints friend Adam McCooll of Broad River in NC, attorney at law, to sell land in Anson County, N. C. 455 A granted to my deceased father 10 Aug 1753...William Crawford (Seal), Wit: John Scott, Catharine Clingan, Sworn before William Clingan, Esq., a Justice for Chester County, Pa.
    (A grant to one Oliver Crawford for 455 A, on Turkey Creek, Anson County, N. C., is found in the Land Grant Office, Vol. 2, p. 70, dated 30 Aug 1753. The property is now in S. C.)

Pp. 514-515: 16 Oct 1764, David McCarty of Meck., to Phillip Rudisall of same, for ₤37...land on N side S fork Cataba, opposite to John Armstrongs land...130 A granted to Martin Armstrong, 3 Oct 1755...Daniel McCartey (Seal), Agness McCartey (A) (Seal), Wit: 3 German signatures (1), Jacob _____, (2) _____ Hans _____ (3) Conrod (?) Manz (?).

Pp. 515-516: 15 Oct 1764, Thomas Bauford of Town of Salsbury, Rowan Co., to Edmond Fanning, attorney at law of Towns of Childsburg, Orange Co., N. C....for ₤100...land on Meck Co., on S side S fork Cataba, S side of Long Creek, 350 A granted to Andrew Nowland, 26 Mar 1755...Thos Bauford (Seal), Ann Bauford (Seal), Wit: Saml Spencer, Wm. Harrison.

Pp. 517-520: 9 May 1760, John Brown of Anson Co., to John Brandon of same, for (lease s5, release ₤20)...land in Anson County...John Brown (Seal), Ann Brown (Seal), Wit: William Kennedy.

Pp. 521-524: 4 June 1764, John Rudisilly, eldest son & heir at law of Gerick (Yorick?) Rudisilly, decd of Yourk Co., Pa., to Henry Dillinger, Waggonmaker (lease s5, release ____)... 200 A adj. Phillip Rudisily's line, granted to sd. Gerick Rudisally 20 May 1754...John Rudisally (Seal), Wit: 2 German signatures (1) Jacob Coburn (2) Jethro _____.

Pp. 524-527: 5 Dec 1763, Samuel Devenny sf Craven Co., SC, to Hamilton Ross of Meck., for ₤5 SC money (release ₤200 SC money)...400 A in that part of Anson County, now Meck., between Phifers & Wm Taylors land...granted by Gov. Dobbs...Saml. Devenny (Seal), Wit: John Pickens, Robert Allison, David Dickson, James Campble.

Pp. 527-530: 24 & 25 Nov 1764, Christian Acre of Anson Co., planter, to Peter Acre of same, (lease s5, release ₤10) ...400 A on S side Bever Dam Creek, granted to sd. Christian Acre, 31 Mar 1755...Christian Acre (+) (Seal), Wit: Hugh Beatey, Francis Beatey.

Pp. 530-534: 17 Sept 1759, Joseph McDowell & wf Mary or Margaret, of Frederick Co., Va., to John McDowell of Anson Co., NC (lease s5, release ₤20 Va. money)...land on Rocky Creek that runs into the Cataba, below Davison Creek about a mile below where the Indian path crosses the sd. creek, 400 A...granted to sd. Joseph 30 Sept 1750...Joseph McDowell (Seal), Margaret McDowell (Seal), Wit: John Walker, William Adams, J. Nocks, John Lindsey.

VOLUME I

Pp. 535-537: 6 Oct 1762, Peter Kuykendall of Anson Co., planter, to Francis Beatey of same, surveyor &c., (lease s5, release ₤20 NC money)...300 A in Anson County, on N side Broad River, on main fork of Kings Creek, adj. Samuel Findleys land... granted 4 Sept 1754 to sd. Peter Kuykendall...Peter Kuykendall (Seal), Wit: William Walton, Bleney Mills, Chas Beatty.

Pp. 537-538: 4 Feb 1763, Joseph Green of Meck., to William Hager of same, for ₤8 proc. money...land on Bever Dam Creek, a S branch of the S fork Cataba...adj. Christian Acres line...300 A granted to sd. Green 21 Oct 1758...Joseph Green & wf Mary... Joseph Green (∓), Mary Green (M), Wit: Christian Carpenter, John Thomas, German signature, appear to be GOOB _____.

Page 538: Meck., Co., N. C.Margaret Ruth do sell all my right and title to a 2 yearling and a colt., etc. to Benjamin Roberts, for ₤17...23 Nov 1763, Margaret Ruth (M), Jeremiah Ruth (Seal), Wit: Abraham Alexr., William McCullock (?).

Page 538-541: 1 Oct 1760, John Patton & wf Jane of Anson Co., to Thomas Coburn of same, (lease s10, release ₤30)... land on E side S fork Cataba adj. James Wilsons corner, 350 A... John Patton (Seal), Jane Patton (∓) (Seal), Wit: Martin Phifer, Andw Elliot, Alexr. Scott.

Pp. 542-544: 24 Nov 1762, Arthur Dobbs to David Coldwell of Anson Do., for ₤36 s2 d5...287 A on Coldwells Creek...Wit: Robert Harris.

Pp. 544-546: 19 Jan 1762, Andrew Allison of County of ____, SC, gentleman, to John McCullock of Rowan Co., NC, (lease s5, release ₤20 Va. money)...640 A in Anson County, granted to sd. Allison 30 Aug 1753...Andw Allison (Seal), Wit: Francis Beatey, Jno. Oliphant, Walter Carruth.

Pp. 547-550: 22 & 24 Jan 1763, Robert Leeper & wf Catherine of Anson Co., to Robert Harris (lease s5, release ₤22 NC money)...land on S side Cataba, 200 A...Robert Leeper (Seal), Catherine Leeper (K) (Seal), Wit: Rees Price, Alexr. Lewis.

Pp. 550-553: 18 Apr 1764, Andrew Armour of Meck., planter, to James Armour (lease s5, release ₤20)...land on S side Cataba River, between Crowder's Creek & Allisons Creek, granted to John Thomas 28 Mar 1755...conveyed to James Armour, decd...adj. James Campbels land...Andrew Armour (Seal), Wit: Samuel Bigham, Moses Ferguson, Robert Leeper.

Pp. 553-556: 25 & 26 Jan 1764, Francis Beatey of Rowan Co., surveyor to Thomas Henry of Rowan Co., cabinet maker (lease s5, release ₤30)...land on S side S fork Cataba, adj. to a survey made for Jeremiah Potts...adj. Daniel Warlocks...patented to Robert McPherson 13 Mar 1756...Francis Beatey (Seal), Wit: James Rusk, James Beatey.

Pp. 556-558: 5 May 1764, George Denny & wf Jane Of Meck., to William Henry, for ₤30...land on S side Cataba, on Allison's Creek...granted to James Armour 27 July 1755...George Denny (Seal), Jane Denny (P) (Seal), Wit: Andw Erwin, Robert Lowry, Richard Barry.

VOLUME I

Pp. 558-560: 6 Apr 1755, Samuel Young of Rowan Co., NC, to John Alexander of Anson Co., for ₤10...land on N side S fork Cataba, a branch of Clarks Creek...granted to sd. Young 31 Mar 1755...400 A...Saml Young (Seal), Wit: James Willson, Junior, James Willson.

Pp. 560-561: 12 Apr 1764, Peter Kuykendall of Meck (formerly Anson), to Andrew Hampton of same, for ₤25 proc. money...land on S side Cataba and Leeper's Creek, 150 A granted to Matthew Kuykendall 1 Apr 1750, conveyed to sd. Peter 1 & 2 March 1754...Peter Kuykendall (Seal), Mary Kuykendall (M) (Seal), Wit: Robert McDowel, William Ader, John Thomas.

Pp. 561-562: 16 Apr 1764, John Lanham & wf Comfort of Meck., to William Cleghorn of same, for ₤17 NC money, land on both sides Dutchman's Creek...Matthew Kuykendalls corner... granted to sd. Lanham 14 Apr 1759, 150 A...John Lanham (Seal), Wit: Peter Kuykendall, Robert McDowel, John Thomas.

Pp. 562-564: 1 Dec 1763, John Clark, Gent., of Meck., to James Hughey, for ₤___ land on S side Broad River, including the improvement he bought of Richd Camel (Carrol?)...south bank of Peccolet (sic) River...200 A...Jno Clark (Seal), Wit: Edmund Beard, John Davis, Edward Flentham, Robert Collins.
(This land now in S. C.)
VOLUME I, Part 4

Page 565: 1 June 1764, Robt Tate of Roan Co., NC, to John Miller of Louninburg (sic) Co., Va., for ₤15 Va. money... 300 A in Anson (now Meck), south side of Broad River, north fork of Golden Grove, adj. George Parks survey...divided tract granted to Robt Tate 30 Apr 1753...Robt Tate (Seal), Wit: Saml Young, Moses Thompson.
(This land now in S. C.)

Page 566: 1 June 1764, Robt Tate of Roan Co., NC to Willm Lyon of Albemarle Co., Va., for ₤18 Va. money...336 A in Anson (now Meck)...south side of Broad River, N fork of Pacolet River, above Chas. Bettys survey...granted to sd. Tate 1 Sept 1753...Robt Tate (Seal), Wit: Moses Thompson, Saml Young.
(This land now in S. C.)

Pp. 567-569: 28 Sept 1764, Andrew Cathey & wf Martha of Meck., to Thomas Yates of same, (lease s5, release ₤30 proc. money)...250 A on S side Cataba, adj. Abraham Scotts upper corner, granted to John Keller (?), 13 Sept 1749, conveyed to him to Jacob Brown 23 June 1757, to Andrew Cathey by sd. Jacob Brown... Andrew Cathey (A) (Seal), Martha Cathey (X) (Seal), Wit: Richard Barry, William Campbell, William Grant.

Pp. 569-571: 26 Sept 1764, Maurice Moore Esqr of Brunswick Co., NC to James Stafford of Meck., planter...land sold 10 June 1763 from Arthur Dobbs to Maurice Moore, adj. to where James Lusk now lives, 250 A...Maurice Moore (Seal), Wit: Robt Harris, Junr, Arthur MacKay.

Pp. 572-574: 11 July 1763, Alexander Dobbin of Roan Co., planter, to Hugh Carrathers (lease s5, release ₤106 NC money) ...550 A granted to sd. Dobbin 12 Mar 1754...Alexander Dobbin (Seal), Wit: Francis Beaty, John Cathey.

VOLUME I

Pp. 574-575B: 3 May 1763, James Henderson of Rowan Co., to John Walker of Anson Co., (lease s5, release £26)...land on S side Cataba, N branch of Fishing Creek, adj. Mathew Tolls survey on the N side, granted to Thomas Walker 30 Aug 1755 and conveyed by him to James Henderson 1 & 2 Dec 1755...James Henderson(Seal), Wit: Thos Yates, Hugh Barry, Richd Barry.

Pp. 575B-578: 23 & 24 Nov 1762, Moses Moore of Anson Co., planter, to Thos Black of same, planter, (lease s5, release £80 NC money)...280 A on S side Indian Creek, adj. Valentine Mauneys and land of Joseph Cloud, decd...Moses Moore (Seal), Wit: Frances Beaty, Hugh Beaty.

Page 578: 27 Nov 1762, James Young of Augusta Co., Va., to Robert Sloan of Rowan Co., NC, for £20 Va. money...land on N side Cataba, including ye mouth and both sides of Paw Creek, granted to Charles Beatey 30 Aug 1753 & conveyed to sd. Young 17 & 18 May 1762, 795 A...James Young (Seal), Wit: John Brady, John Sloan.

Pp. 579-581: 23 Nov 1762, Moses Moore of Anson Co., to Valentine Mauney of Anson Co., (lease s5, release £35)...370 A on N side Indian Creek, adj. land on Joseph Cloud, decd...170 A granted to John Moore decd, then conveyed to Jeremiah Potts, then to Moses Moore, and 200 A granted to Moses Moore 10 Apr 1761...Moses Moore (Seal), Wit: Thomas Robinson, Francis Beaty.

Pp. 581-584: 24 Nov 1762, Moses Moore of Anson Co., to Thomas Robinson, planter, of same, for £55 NC money...300 A on both sides Indian Creek, a branch of S fork Cataba, part of 600 A where sd. Moses Moore now dwells, granted 28 Mar 1755...Moses Moore (Seal), Wit: Valentine Mauney, Francis Beatey.

Pp. 584-586: 4 & 5 July 1763, John Armstrong of Meck., to Jacob Costner of same, for (lease s5, release £37 NC money)...350 A on ye south side of S fork Cataba River below ye Great Shoales...John Armstrong (Seal), Mary Armstrong, Wit: Jacob Seits, Peter Clob.

Page 587: 22 Mar 1759, William Patrick of Anson Co., to John Chittim for £18 proc. money...land on N side S fork Cataba, above ye place where Robt Leeper now lives...granted to William Patrick 3 Oct 1755, 300 A...William Patrick (Seal), Wit: John Armstrong, John Thomas.

Page 588: 14 Dec 1762, Willm Cleghorne & wf Lettice of Anson Co., to William Moore, for £35 proc. money...land on S side Cataba River, above where Saml Coburn lives...378 A granted to Judith Coburn 30 Aug 1763, and conveyed by her & her husband John Clemons, to Saml Coburn 28 Dec 1755, then to William Cleghorn 22 Nov 1758...William Cleghorn (Seal), Lettice Cleghorn (her mark obliterated) (Seal), Wit: James Moore, John Thomas, Sarah McKendrick (S).

Page 589: 14 Dec 1762, William Adear & wf Mary of Anson Co., to Wm Moore of same, for £94 proc money...land adj. Judith Coburns survey...granted to Frederick Hambright 30 Aug 1753...conveyed by Hambright & wf Sarah 28 Sept 1758...William Adear (Seal), Mary Adear (Seal), Wit: John Price, Saml Lacey, John Thomas.

VOLUME I

Pp. 590-592: 19 July 1763, Daniel Allexander of Anson Co., to John Armstrong of Meck., for s5 sterling...land on N side Cataba, on Buffelow Creek, upper side of Davis Hughstons survey... 387 A granted to sd. Allexander 12 Apr 1765...Daniel Allexander (Seal), Wit: David Rees, Moses Allexander.

20 July 1763, Daniel Allexander of Anson Co., to John Armstrong of same, for ℔11 s10 NC money...land on N side Cataba, on Buffelow Creek, 387 A granted to Nathaniel Alexander 23 Feb 1754, then conveyed to Daniel Alexander 12 Apr 1755...(same signatures and witnesses.)

    (The above appear to be Lease & Release of the same property, but there are several variants to be noted.)

Pp. 592-594: 18 Apr 1764, Andrew Armour of Meck., to James Armour of same, (lease s5, release ℔20 NC money)...540 A in Meck., beginning at a walnut standing on the bank of ye Cataba River...patented to James Armour 6 Apr 1753...Andrew Armour (Seal), Wit: Saml Bigham, Moses Ferguson, Robert Leeper.

Pp. 595-597: 22 & 23 March 1764, John Bumgardner of Meck., planter, to Matthew Clows, (lease s5, release ℔14 NC money) ...150 A on both sides Leepers Creek...granted to sd. Bumgardner 21 Dec 1763...John Bumgardner (W) (Seal), Wit: James Beaty, James Rusk.

Pp. 597-600: 1 & 2 Feb 1764, Francis Beatey of Rowan Co., surveyor, to Samuel Zicklagg of Meck., (lease s5, release ℔25 NC money)...200 A on E side Cataba, on both sides of Fools Road Gap (?) Creek...granted to sd. Beaty 19 Apr 1763...Francis Beatey, Wit: James Beaty, Thomas Beaty.

Pp. 600-601: 13 Apr 1764, Thomas Barr & wf Margaret of Meck., to Thomas Clark, of same, for ℔38...land on S side Cataba River, on a branch that runs into Dickeys Creek, 600 A... Thomas Barr (Seal), Margaret Barr (Seal), Wit: John Person (IP), Ezekiel Wallace, Robert Parks.

Pp. 601-602: 10 Apr 1764, John Anderson & wf Margret of Meck., to George Elliot, of same, for ℔30 proc. money... 360 A on S side Cataba, on Gars Creek, granted to John Bravard, 30 Aug 17__, conveyed by sd. Bravard & wf Jean to sd. Anderson 13 Sept 1758(?)...John Anderson (Seal), Margret Anderson (∞) (Seal), Wit: Richard Bery, Hugh Bery, Andrew (?) Goforth.

Pp. 603-605: 13 Jan 1764, Frances Beaty & wf Martha of Rowan Co., to Samuel Biggerstaff of Meck., planter, (lease s5, release ℔25)...400 A on head waters of Pow Creek, granted to sd. Beaty 19 Apr 1753...Francis Beaty (Seal), Martha Beaty (M) (Seal), Wit: Thomas Beaty, Samuel Beaty.

Pp. 605-608: 10 & 11 Apr 1764, Samuel Bigham & wf Mary of Meck., to George Allen (lease s5, release ℔60)...600 A on head waters of Steel Creek, E side Cataba, adj. Samuel Knoxes & John Davis' lines...granted to sd. Bigham 21 Dec 1763...Samuel Bigham (Seal), Mary Bigham (Seal), Wit: Moses Ferguson, Jas Bigham, Samuel Bigham.

VOLUME I

Pp. 608-610: 14 & 15 Mar 1762, Jacob Forney & wf Mary of Meck., Distilar, to George Potts, of same cooper, (lease s5, release ₤12 proc. money)...50 A on W side Cataba, on S side of N fork Killians Creek...granted to sd. Forney 31 Oct 1758... Jacob Forney (Seal), Mary Forney (X) (Seal), Wit: Chas Moore, Lenard (?) Killian (┌), and one German signature.

Pp. 610-613: 16 & 17 July 1763, John Brandon Esqr of Rowan Co., to Matthew Armstrong of Meck., (lease s5, release ₤30)...350 A on both sides Sugar Creek, granted to sd. Bigham 21 Dec 1764...Samuel Bigham (Seal), Mary Bigham (Seal), Wit: Moses Forgison, Jas Bigham, Samuel Bigham.

Pp. 616-617: 26 Mar 1764, Abraham Kuykendall & wf Elisabeth of Meck., to John Leinburger of same, for ₤20 proc. money...land on a branch of Hoyles Creek, commonly called Handleges(?) Creek, North of the S fork of Cataba...granted to sd. Kuykendall 21 Oct 1758, 200 A...Abraham Kuykendall (4) (Seal), Elisabeth Kuykendall (X) (Seal), Wit: Peter Kykendall, Thos Scott, John Thomas, and on German signature.

Pp. 617-619: 22 Dec 1763, Dobbs & wf Justina to Paul Barringer, for ₤11 s18...119 A in Meck Co....Wit: Nathaniel Allexander, Martin Phifer.

Pp. 619-621: 2 Mar 1764, Dobbs & wf Justina to Christopher Walbert, for ₤18...164 A in Anson Co. on Great Cold Water Creek....Wit: Richard Barry.

Page 621: 9 Jan 1764, Henry Nealy & wf Elisabeth of Meck., to William Hagar (?) for ₤35 proc. money...land on S side Cataba, 250 A granted to Jno Hagar, 27 Sept 1751 & conveyed to sd. Nearly 29 & 30 Mar 1758...Henry Nealy (Seal), Elisabeth Nearly (0) (Seal), Wit: Moses Ferguson, William Neely.

Pp. 622-624: 21 Jan 1764, Jas Davis of Meck., planter, to Jas Kerr of same, (lease s5, release ₤32 NC money)... 480 A on both sides Sugar Creek, adj. John Woods line...James David (Seal), Wit: Moses Ferguson, Samuel Zach, Andrew Armour.

Pp. 624-625: 30 Jan 1754 (sic), Thos Beaty & wf Margaret of Meck., to Abraham Scott, of same, for ₤20 proc. money...land granted to sd. Thomas Beaty 28 M.r 1755, 590 A...Thomas Beaty (Seal), Margret Beaty (Seal), Wit: Charles Beaty, John Cathy, Allxr. Lewis.

Pp. 625-626: 17 Jan 1764, Nathaniel Allexander, Justice of Co. of Meck., to George Grean of same....whereas Jas More an orphan of the age of 14 years was bound to sd. George Grean for 4 years & 4 months to learn the art and Mistery of a weaver, and he was to give sd. Jas More schooling, and necessary meat, drink, and clothing...(reason for transaction not clear) ....Nathl Allexander (Seal), George Grean (Seal), Wit: Robert Harris.

Pp. 626-628: 19 Jan 1764, Samuel Knox of Meck., to John Davis of same (lease s5, release ₤30)...500 A on ye south fork of Steel Creek...Biggers line, John Henrys line...granted to sd. Knox 19 Apr 1763....Samuel Knox (Seal), Wit: Moses Ferguson, Jas. Alexr., Robert Barnet.

VOLUME I

Pp. 628-629: 23 Oct 1763, Phillip Walker & wf Jean of Meck., to Hugh White, for ₤20 proc. money...300 A on N side Fishing Creek...Phillip Walker (Seal), Wit: Robert McClanahan, Jas Millar.

Pp. 629-630: 10 Dec 1763, Daniel McGlaughlin of Meck., to Jas Millar of same, for ₤15...170 A...Daniel McGlaughlin (&) (Seal), Wit: Robert McClanahan, William Gambell.

Pp. 630-633: 29 Nov & 30 Dec 1763, Jas Potts & wf Sarah of Meck., to William Grimes of same (lease s5, release ₤40)...land granted to sd. James Potts 230 A, 1 Oct 1758...Jas Potts (Seal), Sarah Potts (\) (Seal), Wit: Nathaniel Allexander, John Lach (?).

Pp. 633-635: 24 & 25 Mar 1764, Francis Beaty of Rowan Co., to David Watson of Meck (lease s5, release ₤24 NC money)...340 A on middle fork of Bullocks Creek, granted to Jas Armstrong 28 Aug 1753, & conveyed to sd. Beaty by deed 2 Feb 1760...Francis Beaty (Seal), Wit: James Watson, Samuel Watson.

Pp. 635-637: 10 June 1764, Margret Davison of Rowan Co., to Robert Hunter of same, (lease s15, release ₤10)...land granted to George Davison 4 Sept 1753, and by his last will & testament granted to sd. Margret...Margret Davison (D) (Seal), Wit: George Davison, John Bresson (?).

Pp. 637-639: 22 & 23 Apr 1764, Benjamin Roberts & wf Ellinor of Meck., (lease s5, release ₤55) to Thomas Houston...land on Sweringames branch, including Joseph Sweringames improvement...Benjamin Roberts (Seal), Ellinor Roberts (M) (Seal), Wit: Henry Downs, Robert Craford, Hugh Wilson.

Pp. 639-640: 5 July 1764, James Millar & wf Texanna of Meck., to Charles Anderson of same, for ₤50...170 A in Meck... Jas Millar (Seal), Texana Millar (Seal), Wit: Robert McClenahan, David Milar (?), Jno C ckett.

Pp. 641-642: 11 & 12 July 1764, Thomas Houston & wf Agness Of Meck., to Thomas Polke Esqr of same, (lease s5, release ₤28)...400 A on both sides of Steel Creek, granted to sd. Thomas Houston 19 Apr 1763...Thomas Houston (Seal), Agness Huston (/) (Seal), Wit: Nathl Alexander, Robt Harris, Junr.

Pp. 643-644: 20 Feb 1763, Thomas Mitchel to Thomas Ferral, for ₤30...half of a tract on the S side of fairforest... Thomas Mitchel (Seal), Agnes Mitchel (R) (Seal), Wit: Robert McClanahan, John Boogs.
            (This land now in S. C.)

Pp. 644-645: 2 Apr 1764, John Wilkins of Meck., to John Clark of same, for ₤20...560 A on both sides Clarks Creek, granted to sd Wilkins 21 Dec 1763...John Wilkins (₮) (Seal), Wit: William Clark, William ___ham.

Pp. 646-647: 17 Mar 1764, Casper Culp of Meck. Yoeman, to Matthew Patton, for ₤75 NC money...land on W side Cataba... adj. John Launces (?)...Casper Culp (Seal), Wit: James Patton, Ann Foster, Henry Foster.

VOLUME I

Pp. 649-651: 22 Dec 1763, Arthur Dobbs & wf Justina to Aaron
Alexander, for ₤8 s2 ...81 A on ridge between Coddle
Creek & English Buffelow Creek and the Waters of Rockey or Johnstone River...the Waggon Road leading from Capt Fifers...Wit:
Nahtl. Allexander, Martin Phifer.

Pp. 651-652: Robert Waller (Walter?) to Andrew Hampton, for ₤ s3
d5...sale of cattle, etc....Robert Waller (Seal),
Wit: William Cleghorn, Jeremiah Harrison.

Pp. 652-653: 4 Jan 1764, Robert McLehany & wf Margaret to William
Richardson, for ₤42...land granted __ Apr 1752, 150
A...Robert McLehany (M) (Seal), Margaret McLehany (⊕) (Seal),
Wit: Robert Ramsey, Samuel Dunlap, James Barnet.

Page 654: Blank.

"VOLUME IV, 3rd part"

Pp. 655-657: 16 & 17 Jan 1763, Margaret Dickey alias Margaret
Davies of Savannah, Georgia, to John Walker of Anson
Co., NC, for (lease s5, release ₤15)...land on S side Catawba,
above Geo Cathey's land, adj. George Davisons survey...granted to
sd. Margaret Dickey 23 Feb 1754, 600 A...Margaret Davies (Seal),
Wit: Joseph Earle, Jacob Coburn.

Page 658: Blank.

Pp. 659-662: 21 Jan 1757, Patrick Smith of Waterford in ye Kingdom of Ireland, to Arthur Dobbs, Gov. of N. C. in
America, for ₤600 Irish money...12,500 A in Anson County, being
subdivided from ye trace number __, surveyed by Matthew Roan,
Esqr. and bound by a tract belonging to Jno Campble of Edinton,
Merchant...Patk Smith, Wit: Arthur Smith, Phin. Riall, Edwd Smith.
City of Waterford in Ireland, &C., Arthur Smith of
sd. City, Merchant came before and swore to sd. deed 7 Mar 1763.
Thomas Miles, Mayor.

Pp. 662-665: 19 July 1763, John Davies & wf Elizabeth Of Meck., to
Matthew Patton of same, (lease s5, release ₤__)...
600 A granted to sd. Davis by pattent...on waters of Paw Creek
and Long Creek...corner of an old survey made to Walter Davies
...John Davis, Elis Davis (X), Wit: Moses Ferguson, Joseph More,
Archibald McDowel.

Pp. 666-667: 24 Nov 1762, Arthur Dobbs to James Caldwell, planter,
of Anson Co., for ₤14 s15...140 A in Anson Co...Arthur
Dobbs (Seal), by Wm Powell (?), Wit: James Harris, Robt Harris.

Pp. 667-669: 24 Nov 1762, Dobbs to John Colwell, for ₤8 s8...land
in Anson Co....first station being the place formerly surveyed for Michel Moore, 75 A...Arthur Dobbs (Seal), by Wm
Powell(?), Wit: James Harris, Robt Harris.

Pp. 669-671: 1 & 2 Aug 1763, John Caldwell & wf Elizabeth of Meck.,
to William Campbell of same (lease s5, release ₤40
NC money)...75 A...John Caldwell (Seal), Elizabeth Caldwell (Seal),
Wit: Robt Harris, Junr., Robt Harris.

VOLUME I

Pp. 672-674: 6 & 7 Oct 1763, John Burnet & wf Mary of Rowan Co., to John Patterson of same (lease s5, release ₤30) ...land on Coldwater Creek, adj. Earl Granville's line...250 A ...John Burnet (Seal), Mary Burnet (Seal), Wit: John Haggin, Martin Phifer, John Patton.

Page 674: 15 Oct 1763, John Smith of Anson, alias Meck., planter, to Mark Edwards of same, planter, for ₤10...land on N side Broad River...John Smith (Seal), Wit: John Hitchcock, Timothy Calaham (X).

Pp. 675-676: 15 Oct 1763, John Smith & wf Mary of Meck., to Daniel McCarty of same, for ₤30...150 A on N side Cataba on Island below the Tuckaford Road...granted to Joseph Harind 26 (?) Mar 1755...John Smith (Seal), Mary Smith (M) eal), Wit: Robert McClenachan, William Leonard (?), James Miller.

Pp. 676-677: 19 Aug 1763, William Cathey Of Meck., to James Ervin of Rowan Co., for ₤18 proc. money...1000 A granted to John Killion 30 Sept 1749 conveyed to Jacob Brown, 1 Jan 1754... adj. John Hills corner... William Cathey (W) (Seal), Wit: Robt Harris, Alexr Martin, John Thomas.

Pp. 677-681: 24 Nov 1762, Alexander McCulloch, Exr. of L. W. & T. of James McCulloch of Roan Co., NC, decd., to Archibald Elliot, (lease s5, release ₤33)...400 A on the S side Fishing Creek, including the old Indian camp and a tree marked IMC...granted to sd. James McCulloch, 1 Aug 1753...Alexr McCulloch (Seal), Wit: James Patton, Robt McClenachan, Jn o McCulloch.

Pp. 681-683: 24 Nov 1762, Dobbs to John Davis of Anson Co., for ₤12 s5...114 A in Anson Co., on the N side Rockey River...Arthur Dobbs by Wm Powel, Wit: Robt Harris, James Harris.

Pp. 684-686: 18 Oct 1763, Mathias Dick of Meck., & wf Mary to George Dick of same, for ₤10 proc. money...land on S side Cataba, 190 A, part of a grant to sd. Dick 3 Apr 1762... Cheges line...Mathias Dick (Seal), German signature, Wit: George Paff, and two German signatures (1) Birk _____ (2) Johannes Nagel.

Pp. 686-689: 20 & 21 Dec 1762, George Leonard Seller, planter, of Anson Co., to Francis Beatey of Rowan Co., (lease s5, release ₤50)...300 A on W side Cataba, below William Harris and Andrew McNabbs land...granted unto sd. <u>Sealer</u> 6 Apr 1753... George Leonard Seller (Seal), Wit: Jas Rush, James Beaty, Archd Gilleland.

Pp. 689-693: 13 Oct 1763, Joseph Carrel & wf Jean of Meck., to John Craig, late of same, (lease s5, release ₤40) ...350 A on W side Cataba, on the NE side Crowders Creek, below John Ligtles survey...granted to Samuel Young 29 Mar 1753... Joseph Carrell (Seal), Wit: Thomas Neal, Thomas Sprot, Samuel Craig. Also signed Jean Carrel (0) (Seal)

Pp. 693-695: 11 & 12 Aug 1762, Jonathan Lewis of Anson Co., to John Linn of same, (lease s5, release ₤70 proc. money)...500 A granted to sd. Lewis 2 Apr 1753, adj. corner of John Clarks land, on 12 mile Creek...Jonathan Lewis (Seal), Wit: John Miller, Andrew Sumrall.

32

VOLUME I

Pp. 695-698: 16 & 17 Sept 1763, Mathias Cloues & John Seigel & wf Elizabeth, both of Meck., to Jacob Forney (lease s5, release ₤12)...½ of grant of 400 A to Mathias Cloues & John Seigel 4 Feb 1754...Matthias Cloues (Seal), John Seigel (Seal), Elizabeth Seigel (X) (Seal), Wit: George Paff, and two German signatures (1) Mathias Dick(?), (2) _____ Cunntz.

Pp. 698-699: 25 Sept 1762, James Carter of Rowan Co., Millright, to John Mitchell of Salsbury, Rowan Co., storekeeper, for ₤93 proc. money...land in Anson Co., on E side Cataba, and on the path that leads to the Indian Nation, granted 9 Apr 1753 to Edward Hughes, and conveyed by him to James Carter 17 Apr 1755... James Carter (Seal), Wit: Wm Harrison, Hopkins Muse (?).

Pp. 700-703: 16 Sept 1763, Bastian Bost (Best?) & wf Katharine of Meck., to Devalt Crittes (lease s5, release ₤22 proc. money)... land on Killions Creek, a mile above Killion Junrs land, 250 A, granted unto Bastian Bost, by L & R from Matthias Cloues & Jno Sigle, 21 Aug 1754...Bastian Bost (Seal), Katharine Bost (⊕) (Seal), Wit: Jacob Forny, Georg Paff, Mathias Dick, German signature.

Pp. 703-706: 24 & 25 Sept 1762, Charles McKnight, farmer, to Samuel Watson of Rowan Co., (lease s5, release ₤20s10)... land on N fork of Fishing Creek, called the Wild Cat branch... lease says Deal branch), below George Derricks survey...Charles McKnight (Seal), Wit: Hugh McQuown, W. McKnight.

Pp. 706-708: 8 June 1763, John Hickcock of Meck., to Francis Ross of same, for ₤60 NC money...560 A granted to sd. Hichcock 31 Mar 1753...John Hickcock (Seal), Wit: William Cobun, John Barnet, John Bogs.

Pp. 708-710: 20 July 1763, William Dickson of Duplin Co., NC, planter, to Robt Harris of Meck., for ₤5 proc. money ...land between Crowders Creek and Cataba River on a branch of Mill Creek, adj. Robert Leapers and James Craigs lines...200 A granted to sd. William Dickson 22 Apr 1763...William Dickson (Seal), Wit: Robert Harris, Junr., Robt McKee, _____ Alexander (?).

Pp. 710-711: 15 July 1763, James Patton Senr of Meck., to Michael Patton of same, for ₤20 proc. money...320 A granted to Matthew Patton 3 Mar 1755 & conveyed to sd. James Patton Senr by the death of sd. Matthew Patton...James Patton (Seal), Wit: Robt McClenachan, John Seller (S).

Pp. 712-713: 19 Feb 1763, Abraham Scott & wf Margaret of Meck., to John Davison, Blacksmith, of same, for ₤45 s16 NC money...land on S side Cataba, N fork Fishing Creek, called Wild Cat Creek, granted 28 Mar 1753 to George Renicke, conveyed to sd. Abraham by deed 20 Mar 1760...Abrm Scott (Seal), Wit: Wm Price, Thos Garvin.

Pp. 713-714: 10 Dec 1762, Peter Crowel of Anson Co., & wf Catharine, to Conrod Harshea (?) of same, for ₤12...100 A in Anson Co., on Buffelow Creek, granted to Paul Barringer 27 Sept 1762...Peter Crowel (Seal), Catharine Krowl (⌒) (Seal), Wit: James Carter, Martin Harrahas (?), Daniel Littel.

VOLUME I

Pp. 714-716: 14 Jan 1764, Andrew Armour of Meck., to James Robinson of same, for ₤20...land on both sides Camp Creek, part of the Waters of the Cataba on the E side of sd. river, 400 A, granted to John Arnolpender & William Aldrey 6 Mar 1764...conveyed to James Armour 9 Dec 1754...Andrew Armour (Seal), Wit: Robt McClenachan, James Armor, William Merryhill.

Pp. 716-719: 3 & 4 June 1763, John Armstrong & wf Mary of Meck., to William Morrison (lease s5, release ₤23)...land on Kuykendalls Creek, adj. James Armstrongs corner...granted to sd. John Armstrong 23 Apr 1762, 150 A...John Armstrong(Seal), Mary Armstrong (Seal), Wit: Robert Walter, William Grant.

Pp. 719-722: 5 Feb 1757, David Parks of York Co., Pa., to David Black of Rowan Co., NC, for ₤7 s10...land in Anson Co., on Packolet River, above the place where Col Clark now lives ...granted to David Parks 27 Feb 1754, 200 A...David Parks, Wit: William Black, John Black, James Rudsil (Russal?).

Pp. 723-726: 7 & 8 July 1763, John Walker of Meck., & wf Elizabeth, planter, to John Armstrong of same, planter, (lease s5, release ₤160 NC money)...625 A on Leopards Creek...land of three surveys to John Walker...John Walker (Seal), Elizabeth Walker (Seal), Wit: Willm Morrison, Jacob Cobun, Thos Scott. (Release adds "adj. Sanders first survey").

Pp. 727-729: 12 & 13 July 1763, William Davis of Meck., to Thomas Fulton & Andw Green both of Augusta County, Va., (lease s5, release ₤30)...640 A on Fishing Creek, above Stover's (?)...Wm Davis (Seal), Wit: Will Harris, James Harris.

Pp. 730-732: Dobbs & Wf Justina to David Rees of Meck., for ₤20 s14 proc. money...207 A...Wit: Nathl Alexander, Martin Fifer.

Pp. 732-735: 17 Sept 1759, Joseph McDowel & wf Margaret of Frederick Co., Va., to John McDowel of Anson Co., NC, (lease s5, release ₤50(?))...370 A on N side Cataba, granted to Joseph McDowel 31 Mar 175_...Joseph McDowell (Seal), Margaret McDowell (M) (Seal), Wit: William Adams, ____ Cocks, John Lindsey.

Pp. 735-738: 6 & 7 Jan 1763, John Brandon of Roan Co., NC, to Thomas McKnight of Anson Co., (lease s5, release ₤70)...203 A on S side Cataba, granted to James Carter, by writ against him by John Brandon...court held for counties of New Hanover, Bladen, Onslow, Duplin, and Cumberland &C &C...Jno Brandon (Seal), Wit: Thomas Beatey, Francis Beaty.

Pp. 739-741: 28 & 29 Nov 1763, John Dickey of Rowan Co., to James Henderson of Rowan Co., (lease s5, release ₤5?), 500 A granted 3 Feb 1754...John Dickey (Seal), Wit: Wm Moore, Thos Yeats, Richd Barry.

Pp. 741-743: 3 & 4 Dec 1762, Henry Whitner of Anson Co., to Conrad Yother (?) of same, (lease s5, release ₤47 NC money) ...land on both sides S fork Cataba...to the line of sd. Henry's 1000 A tract...Henry Whitner (Seal), Wit: John Mole, Francis Beaty. (Release adds "granted to Henry Whitner 28 Mar 1751(?)").

Pp. 744-745: Blank.

VOLUME 2

Pp. 1-2: 25 ___, 176_, Arthur Dobbs, Gov. of N. C. and Justina his wife to Adam Alexander of Meck., for s_ proc. money ...102 A on both sides Goose Creek, a branch of Rockey or Johnston River...Arthur Dobbs (Seal) Justina Dobbs (Seal), Wit: John Davis Jur., Arthur MacKay. Recd. June 25, 1765 of Adam Alexander, ₺10 s4, Arthur Dobbs.

Pp. 3-4: 25 June 1764, Arthur Dobbs and Justina his wife to Samuel Erwin of Meck., for ₺28 s10...285 A on N side Rockey or Johnston River...Arthur Dobbs (Seal), Justina Dobbs (Seal), Wit: John Davis Junr., Arthur MacKay.

Pp. 5-6: 25 June 1764, Arthur Dobbs and Justina his wife to John Scott of Meck., for ₺16 s6...163 A on both sides of Coddle Creek, a branch of Rockey or Johnston River...Arthur Dobbs (Seal), Justina Dobbs (Seal), Wit: John Davis Junr., Arthur MacKay.

Pp. 7-8: 25 June 1764, Arthur Dobbs and Justina his wife to William White, for ₺16 s2...161 A on English Buffilow Creek, a branch of Rockey or Johnston River...Arthur Dobbs (Seal), Justina Dobbs (Seal), Wit: John Davis Junr., Arthur MacKay.

Pp. 9-10: 25 June 1764, Arthur Dobbs and Justina his wife to William Ross of Meck., for ₺14 s8...144 A lying on the Ridges between English Buffilow and Coddle Creek...Arthur Dobbs (Seal), Justina Dobbs (Seal), Wit: John Davis Junr., Arthur MacKay.

Pp. 11-12: 25 June 1764, Arthur Dobbs and Justina his wife to Robert McClellan of Meck., for ₺15 s4...152 A on both sides of English Buffilow, a branch of Rockey or Johnston River...Arthur Dobbs (Seal), Justina Dobbs (Seal), Wit: John Davis Junr., Arthur MacKay.

Pp. 13-14: 25 June 1764, Arthur Dobbs and Justina his wife to William Speers of Meck., for ₺4 s10....45 A on Red [?] Creek, a branch of Rockey or Johnston River...Arthur Dobbs (Seal), Justina Dobbs (Seal), Wit: John Davis Junr., Arthur MacKay.

Pp. 15-16: 25 June 1764, Arthur Dobbs and Justina his wife to Henry Philer, for ₺18 s10 ...185 A on both sides Adams Creek ...Arthur Dobbs (Seal), Justina Dobbs (Seal), Wit: John Davis Junr., Arthur MacKay.

Pp. 17-18: 25 June 1764, Arthur Dobbs and Justina his wife to Mathias Barringer of Meck., for ₺13...130 A on both sides Dutch Buffilow Creek, a branch of Rockey or Johnston River ...Arthur Dobbs (Seal), Justina Dobbs (Seal), Wit: John Davis Junr., Arthur MacKay.

Pp. 19-20: 25 June 1764, Arthur Dobbs and Justina his wife to Christian Sytes of Meck., for ₺10 s14 proc. money...107 A on both sides Dutch Buffilow Creek, a branch of Johnston or Rockey River...Arthur Dobbs (Seal), Justina Dobbs (Seal), Wit: John Davis Junr., Arthur MacKay.

Pp. 21-22: 25 June 1764, Arthur Dobbs and Justina his wife to Jacob Myers of Meck., for ₺14 s4, proc. money...142 A on both sides Dutch Buffilow Creek...Arthur Dobbs (Seal), Justina Dobbs (Seal), Wit: John Davis Junr., Arthur MacKay.

VOLUME 2

Pp. 23-24: 24 June 1764, Arthur Dobbs and Justina his wife to Charles Fisher of Meck., for ₤22 s14 proc. money...227 A on both sides Adams Creek a branch of Rockey or Johnston River...Arthur Dobbs (Seal), Justina Dobbs (Seal), Wit: John Davis Junr., Arthur MacKay.

Pp. 25-26: 25 June 1764, Arthur Dobbs and Justina his wife to James White, Junr of Meck., for ₤12 proc. money...120 A on NW side Rockey or Johnston River...Arthur Dobbs (Seal), Justina Dobbs (Seal), Wit: John Davis Junr., Arthur MacKay.

Pp. 27-29: 15 Jan 1765, Francis Beatey of Rowan Co., to Nicholas Leeper of Meck., (lease s5, release ₤60 N. C. money) ...300 A on N side Broad River, main fork of King's Creek, adj. land formerly surveyed for Samuel Finley...granted to Peter Kuykendal, 24 Sep 1759, conveyed to Francis Beatey by L & R 6 & 7 Oct 1762...Frances Beatey (Seal), Wit: Thomas Beatey, Hugh Beatey, James Beatey, Robt. Armstrong.

Pp. 30-31: 13 May 1765, Robert Cowdon, Brother and proper heir of William Cowdon of Meck., planter, to Moses Wylie of same, for ₤36 proc. money...244 A, part of a 600 A grant to William Cowdon, 3 Sep 1754, including the mouth of Cowds. Creek... Robert Cowdon (Seal), Wit: Wa. [?] Cowdon, Robert Harris Jur.

Pp. 31-34: 21 Jan 1765, Aaron Steel of Meck., to James Tate of same (lease s5, release ₤20 N. C. money)...450 A on E side Cataba in New Providence on Six Mile Creek, waters of Twelve Miles Creek, adj. James Pot's land and Jordian's survey, adj. Indians line, granted to sd. Aaron Steel, 21 Spr 1764...Aaron Steel (Seal), Wit: Hugh Beaty, James Brice, John Sloan.

Pp. 34-37: 15 Oct 1765, Francis Beatey of Roan Co., Surveyor &c., to David Stanley of Meck., (lease s5, release ₤50 N. C. money)...202 A on S fork of Cataba on Long Creek, including a Great Shoal...granted to James Armstrong, 3 Oct 1755 and conveyed unto sd. Francis Beatey by deed 2 Feb 1760...Francis Beatey (Seal), Wit: Robert Armstrong, James Beatey.

Pp. 37-39: 7 Nov 1764, Samuel Blyth of Rowan Co., to Hance McWhorter of Rowan Co., WheelWright, (lease s5, release ₤18) ...460 A on S side Cataba River, N side Fishing Creek...E of Joseph Millikan's land, granted to James Dogherty 3 Apr 1753, conveyed by him to Samuel Blyth by deeds dated 20 & 21 June 1753...Samuel Blyth, Wit: Francis Beatey, Robert Gray.

Pp. 40-42: 15 Oct 1764, David Standley of Meck., to Frances Beatey of Rowan Co., for ₤135, ...320 A on E side Cataba, adj. Robert Sloan and sd. Francis Beatey, conveyed by Benjamin Harden and John Harden to sd. David Standley, by deed 10 Nov 1758... David Standley (D) (Seal) Wit: Robert Armstrong, James Beatey.

Pp. 42-45: 7 July 1763, James McClure and Margaret his wife of Meck., planter, to James Robinson Junr of same, planter (lease s5, release ₤10)...275 A on waters of Clark's branch of Twelve Miles Creek, adj. James Dinns corner and Clarks survey...James Rions line, granted to sd. James McClure 19 Apr 1763...James McClure (Seal), Margaret McClure (Seal), Wit: Francis Beatey, Thos Beatey, Jas. Rusk.

VOLUME 2

Pp. 45-48: 24 March 1765, Francis Beatey of Rowan Co., surveyor, to Archibald Gilleland of Rowan Co., weaver, (lease s5, release ₤30 N. C. money)...190 A on Little Sugar, adj. Hugh Barry's first corner, formerly surveyed for James McConnell... Francis Beatey (Seal), Wit: Robert Armstrong, James Beatey.

Pp. 48-51: 5 Apr 1765, Fredirect Hambright and Sarah hig wife of Meck., to Rodger Cook of same, (lease s5, release ₤30 N. C. money)...200 A on W side Cataba, including Joseph Hardins and Frederick Hambrights improvements, part of a 400 A grant to Samuel Young, conveyed unto John Kuykendall, decd, then to Joseph Harden then to Frederick Hambright...Frederick Hambright (Seal), Sarah Hambright (S) (Seal), Wit: Benajmin Harden, James Leeper, John Sloan.

Pp. 51-53: 12 Apr 1765, Jacob Cook of Meck., to Michael Hoil of same, (lease s5, release ₤20 N. C. money)...200 A on waters of Beaver Dam Creek and a cattail branch of Mountain Creek, S waters of the S fork of Cataba adj. Jacob Mauneys line... granted to Jacob Cook 21 Dec 1763...Jacob Cook (Seal), [appears to be a German signature under his], Wit: Christian Simmerman (C Ŧ_, and a German signature, Ernst _____.

Pp. 53-56: 12 Jan 1765, William Patrick of Meck., planter, to Robert Armstrong, of same, Waggon maker, (lease s5, release ₤100)...400 A on Allison's Creek, adj. James Campble, land sold by Andrew Allison to John McCulloch...John Davis corner... granted to Wiliam Patrick 16 Nov 1764...William Patrick (Seal), Wit:James Beatey, John Patrick.

Pp. 56-59: 17 & 18 Apr 1765, William Falls of Meck., to Joseph Massey of same (lease s5, release ₤30 N. C. money)... land on Turkey Creek, fork of Baols Creek, 640 A, about a mile above John Bridges...granted to sd. Falls 10 Apr 1765...William Falls (Seal), Wit: Thomas Martin, Hugh Beaty, James Orman.

Pp. 59-61: 10 & 11 Dec 1764, John Sloan of Meck., Co., to Oughtery McThibben of same (lease s5, release ₤26 N. C. money) ...150 A on both sides Clark's Creek of Twelve Mile Creek, adj. James Rions line...granted to sd. Sloan 21 Apr 1764...John Sloan (Seal), Wit: Matthew Patton, Joseph Berryhil.

Pp. 61-64: 15 & 16 Apr 1765, Elizabeth Biggerstaff & Benjamin Biggerstaff, Exrs. of Samuel Biggerstaff, decd., of Meck., to William Gardiner of same (Lease s5, release ₤40 sterling) ...400 A on head waters of Paw Creek and Gum Branch, adj. Silvins and Joys lines...granted to Francis Beatey 19 Apr 1763, conveyed to Sameul Biggerstaff 31 Jan 1764...Elizabeth Biggerstaff (+) (Seal) Benjn. Beggerstaff (b) (Seal), Wit: William Erwin, William Harris.

Pp. 64-65: 1 Mar 1765, John Crockett & Margaret his wife and Archibald Crockett & Mary his wife to Robert Crockett all of Meck., for ₤100 N. C. money...528 A adj. Andrew Pickens line, Wm. Nutts line...deed dated 13 Feb 1755._.John Crockett, Margret Crockett (M) (Seal), Archd. Crockett, Mary Crockett (M) (Seal), Wit: Robt. McClenachan, John Wray [?], James Miller.

VOLUME 2

Pp. 66-68: 11 & 12 Feb 1763, Michael Oyster & Julianna his wife of Anson Co. to Mathias Lock of Rowan Co., (lease s5, release ₤60 proc. money...land in Anson Co., a mile up Robert Leepers line, adj. 50 A granted by Peter Oyster & Mary his wife to Peter Clubb...260 A granted to Peter Oyster 24 Sept 1754... Michael Oyster (Seal), Julianna Oyster (+) (Seal), Wit: Edwd Hughes, Will Reed.

Pp. 68-70: 15 Apr 1765, Robert Crockett & Jean his wife ot Meck., to Archd. Crockett for ₤50 N. C. money...264 A on N side Cataba, adj. Pickens line...by virtue of a deed 1 Mar 1765... Robert Crocket (Seal), Jean Crocket (Seal), Wit: Robert McCleanachan, James Miller., Wm. McCulloch.

Pp. 70-72: 9 & 10 Nov 1764, John McKnight of Rowan Co., Gent., to David Byers of York Co., Pa (lease s5, release ₤60 proc. money)...340 A on N side Broad River, on a fork of Turkey Creek, above Clarks path...granted to John McKnight 30 Aug 1753...John McKnight (Seal), Wit: John McCulloh, David Byers, John Armstrong.

Pp. 72-74: 4 & 5 Mar 1765, John Miller of Meck., planter, to William Henderson late from Pa., cooper, (lease s5, release ₤45)...150 A on N side Cataba, granted to Peter Elliot 7 Oct 1749, and sold to Miller by L & R 23 & 24 Apr 1764...John Miller (Seal), Wit: Richd Barry, Josias Black, John Duncan.

Pp. 75-77: 4 & 5 March 1765, Robert Miller & Rachel his wife of Meck., to John Henderson, late from Pa. (lease s5, release ₤40 proc money)...200 A adj. Wm. Price's line, part of land granted to Geo. Renick 31 Mar 1753 and 30 Aug 1753, then conveyed to Adam Meek, weaver, and by Adam Meek & wife Eliz. to James Miller by L & R 13 & 14 Jan 1759, and by Miller & wife Mary to Robert Miller 13 & 14 Apr 1764... Robert Miller (Seal), Rachel Miller (+) (Seal), Wit: Richd. Barry, George Denney, Willm. Henderson.

Pp. 77-78: 13 Apr 1765, Christian Acre & Eve his wife of Meck., to William Hager of Meck., for ₤10 proc. money....land on N branch of Long Creek abt. a mile above William Fronoburgers survey, on S side S fork Cataba, 300 A granted to Acre 10 Apr 1761...Christian Acre (+) (Seal), Eve Acre (⌒) (Seal), Wit: Richd. Barry, William Drew, John Black.

Page 79: 13 Apr 1765, William Hagar & Elizabeth his wife of Meck., to Christian Acre, for ₤ 80 proc. money, land on both sides main branch of Bever Damm Creek, a S branch of S fork Catawba, adj. sd. Acres line...300 A granted to Joseph Green 21 Oct 175_, sold to sd. Hagar 4 Feb 1763...William Heaker (Seal) Eliz. Heager (C) (Seal), Wit: Richd. Barry, William Drew, John Black.

Pp. 80-81: 30 July 1764, Thomas Clark of Meck., to Samuel Macklemory of same, for ₤19 proc. money...land on a branch on N side Allison Creek, granted to John Barr, 31 March 1753, and by his decease came to Thomas Barr and sold by him to Thomas Clark 12 Apr 1764, 300 A...Thomas Clark (X) (Seal), Wit: John Macklemurry, William Dickson.

38

VOLUME 2

Pp. 81-82: 21 May 1764, William Watson & Violet his wife of Meck., planter, to William Moore, of same, weaver, for ₤100 proc. money...309 A, on a branch of Fishing Creek above John Humphreys, part of a 400 A grant to William Watson 13 Aug 1753... William Watson (Seal), Violet Watson (Seal), Wit: William Henry, Thomas Scott.

Pp. 82-83: 14 June 1764, Rees Morgan of Meck., to William Ramsey of same, for ₤40 proc. money, 200 A granted to sd. Rees Morgan 23 Feb 1759, on W side Cataba, adj. Alexander Catheys corner...Jean Adams corner...Rees Morgan (X) (Seal), Wit: John Cathey, Henry Hendry, James Price.

Pp. 83-85: 6 Apr 1765, Samuel Bigham & Mary his wife of Meck., to William Barnet of same, for ₤10, 150 A on main branch Suggar Creek, between William Barnet's and Silvins lines, including a shole...Samuel Bigham (Seal), Mary Bigham (M) (Seal), Wit: Archd. McNeall, William Bigham, Samuel Bigham.

Pp. 86-88: 30 & 31 Dec 1764, James Russell & Jean his wife of Meck., to Robert Russell of Rowan Co., (lease s5, release ₤20)...310 A adj. Alexander Fergusons corner, on S side Little River on Antiquorum Creek... James Rusell (Seal), Jean Rusell (Seal), Wit: Martin Phifer, Jo. Phifer.

Page 89: 21 Aug 1764, Archibald Huston of Orange Co., Va., farmer, appoints Hugh Huston of New Providence in Meck. Co., N. C., farmer, lawful attorney...all that is due me from estate of David Huston...Archibald Huston (Seal), Wit: Telix Gilbert, James Thompson.

Pp. 89-90: 16 Apr 1765, Moses Moore of Meck. Co., to John Walker of same, for ₤20 proc. money, land on Cain Creek of the Second Broad River, including the Buffilow lick, 400 A, granted to Moses Moore by patent 16 Nov 1764... Moses Moore (Seal), Wit: Alexr. Lewis, Will Reed.

Pp. 90-93: 25 & 26 March 1765, John Mitchel & Eliz. his wife of Salsbury, Mercht., and John Brandon & Eliz. his wife of Rowan Co., Esqr to Samuel Allain of Meck. (lease s5, release ₤57 proc. money)...469 A on E side Cataba, which sd. Allain now lives on, half of 938 A granted to James Cartee 9 Apr 1753, sold to sd. John Mitchel 25 Sept 1762 & the above Brandon said an Execution on sd. land on record in Superior Court...John Mitchel (Seal), Elizabeth Mitchel (Seal), John Brandon (Seal), Elizabeth Brandon (Seal), Wit: James Karr, Jaohn Braly [?].

Pp. 93-96: 25 & 26 March 1765, John Mitchel & Eliz. his wife & John Brandon and Eliz. his wife To Alexander Robinson & William Robinson of Meck., (lease s5, release ₤50 proc. money) ...land on E side Cataba, on path from Cataba Nation to McDowells, half of 938 A granted to James Cartee...John Brandon (Seal), Elizabeth Mitchel (Seal), Wit: James Karr, John Braly [?].

Page 96: 13 July 1764, John Grover of Meck., planter, to Peter Culp, for ₤400 S. C. money, one negro man Burn...John Glover (Seal), Wit: Robt. McClenachan, Robert Glover

VOLUME 2

Pp. 96-98: 2 Mar 1764, Arthur Dobbs & Justina his wife to Mathias Mitchter of Anson Co., planter, for ₤17 proc. money... 170 A on Little Cold Water Creek, waters of Rockey or Johnston River...Arthur Dobbs (Seal), Justina Dobbs (Seal), Wit: Marin Phifer, Richd. Barry.

Pp. 98-100: 2 March 1764, Arthur Dobbs & Justina his wife to Abigail Shinn [Shinn?], spinster, of Meck., for ₤15s12 proc money...156 A on Little Coldwater Creek, adj. Mathias Mitchters corner...Arthur Dobbs (Seal), Justina Dobbs (Seal), Wit: Martin Phifer, Richd. Barry.

Pp. 100-101: 11 Mar 1765, Henry Eustace McCulloh of Chowan Co., Esqr., to George Alexander of Meck., for ₤20 sterling, land on both sides Rockey River, adj. Moses Alexanders corner... 520 A... H. E. McCulloh (Seal), Wit: John Frohock, Moses Alexander.

Pp. 102-103: 13 Mar 1765, Henry Eustace McCulloh to Robert Smith of Meck., for ₤22 sterling, land on N side Rockey River, adj. Harris' corner, 218 A...H. E. McCulloh (Seal), Wit: John Frohock, Moses Alexander.

Pp. 104-105: 23 Apr 1765, John Campble of Bartie Co., NC, to John McKnit Alexander of Meck., for ₤45 sterling, part of a tract granted to John Campble, 3 Mar 1745, 509 A...John Campble by Henry E. McCulloh, Wit: John Frohock, Moses Alexander.

Pp. 106-107: 27 Apr 1765, John Campble to John McKnit Alexander, for ₤10 sterling, 100 A granted to Campble 3 Mar 1745 ...John Campble (Seal), b Henry E. McCulloh, Wit: John Frohock, Moses Alexander.

Pp. 108-109: 12 Mar 1765, Henry Eustace McCulloh to Edward Giles of Meck., for ₤15 sterling, 165 A on Rockey River... H. E. McCulloh (Seal), Wit: John Frohock, Moses Alexander.

Pp. 109-112: 3 May 1765, George Augustus Selway of Co., of Gloucester, Great Britain, to James Wyley of Meck. Co., planter, whereas George II did grant 3 Mar 1745(O.S.) on Santee or Cataba tract #3...for ₤28 sterling, land on both sides Reedy Creek, waters of Rockey River, 277 A....Geo. Aug. Selwyn by Henry Eust: McCulloh; Wit: Moses Alex Ander, John Frohock.

Pp. 113-114: 15 May 1765, Henry Eustace McCulloh to Walter Hogshead of Meck for ₤20 sterling ... land on Back Creek, waters of Rockey River, 279 A...H. E. McCulloh (Seal), Wit: Robt. Harris, John Frohock.

Pp. 114-115: 17 Mar 1765, Henry Eustace McCulloh to William Wallace, of Meck., for ₤18 sterling, 162 A...H. E. McCulloh, (Seal), Wit: John Frohock, George Alexander.

Pp. 116-117: 13 Mar 1765, Henry Eustace McCulloh to Adam Meek of Meck., for ₤23...land on Rockey River, adj. Alexander's line, 222 A...H. E. McCulloh (Seal), Wit: Geo. Allen, John Frohock.

Pp. 117-118: 12 Mar 1765. Henry Eustace McCulloh to Arthur Donolson of Meck., for ₤23 sterling...228 A on E side Rocky River, adj. Moses Alexander's corner...H. E. McCulloh (Seal), Wit: John Frohock, Moses Alexander.

VOLUME 2

Pp. 119-120: 20 Apr 1765, Henry Eustace McCulloh to Jamima Sharp for ₤12 s10 sterling...land on branches of McDowell's Creek, waters of Cataba, 131 A...H. E. McCulloh (Seal), Wit: John Frohock, Jno. McKnitt Alexander.

Pp. 120-122: 25 Apr 1765, John Campbell of Bartee Co., NC, to Kern Henderson for ₤35, 423 A on waters of Mallard & Sugar Creeks...John Campbell by Hen. McCulloh (Seal), Wit: John Frohock, Jas. Alexander.

Pp. 122-124: 12 Mar 1765, Henry Eustace McCulloh to Samuel Brown of Meck., for ₤23 sterling, 239 A adj. Donaldson's new line... H. E. McCulloh (Seal), Wit: John Frohock, David Alexander.

Pp. 124-126: 16 Mar 1765, Henry Eustace McCulloh to James Wallace of Meck., for ₤28 sterling...land on waters of Coddle Creek adj. David Alexander's line, 238 A...H. E. McCulloh (Seal), Wit: John Frohock, Moses Alexander.

Pp. 126-128: 26 Apr 1765, John Campbell of Bertie Co., to Mathew Robison of Meck., for ₤24 sterling...296 A on waters of Mallard Creek...John Campbell (Seal), by Henry E. McCulloh, Wit: John Frohock, W. Hemphill.

Pp. 129-130: 3 May 1765, Henry Eustace McCulloh, to Robert Harris of Meck., for ₤5 sterling...54 A on waters of Rockey River...Henry E. McCulloh (Seal), Wit: John Frohock, Chas. Harris.

Pp. 131=132: 9 May 1765, John Campbell of Bertie Co., to Alexander Wallace of Meck., for ₤25, 242 A on Malard Creek, adj. line of land whereon Thomas Parker lives...John Campbell (Seal), by Henry E. McCulloh, Wit: John Frohock, J. McKnitt Alexander.

Pp. 133-134: 9 May 1765, John Campbell to James Alexander, of Meck., for ₤26 s10 sterling...257 A on Malard Creek ...John Campbell by Henry E. McCulloh (Seal), Wit: John Frohock, J. McKnitt Alexander.

Pp. 135-137: 16 May 1765, George Augustus Selwyn to Capt Abraham Alexander of Meck., for ₤50 sterling...land on Shugar Creek, including a mill seat, 620 A...Geo. Aug. Selwyn (Seal), by Henry Eustace McCulloh. Wit: John Frohock, Nathl. Alexander.

Pp. 138-139: 27 Apr 1765, John Campbell to John Boles for ₤10 sterling...18 A...John Campbell by Henry E. McCulloh (Seal), Wit: John Frohock, Jas. Alexander.

Pp. 140-141: 29 Apr 1765, John Campbell to Robert Crockett, of Meck., for ₤35 sterling...350 A on waters of Shugar Creek...John Campbell by Henry E. McCulloh (Seal), Wit: John Frohock, Moses Alexander.

Pp. 141-143: 26 ___ 1765, John Campbell to Moses Robison of Meck., for ₤30 sterling...305 A adj. Robert Crockett's... John Campbell by Henry E. McCulloh (Seal), Wit: John Frohock, J. McKnitt Alexander.

VOLUME 2

Pp. 143-145: 1 Mar 1765, Henry Eustice McCulloh to David Garrison of Meck., for ₤15 sterling...land on both sides Malard Creek, adj. tract of young Moses Alexander...152 A...H. E. McCulloh (Seal), Wit: John Frohock, Moses Alexander.

Pp. 145-147: 25 Apr 1765, John Campbell to William Alexander of Meck., for ₤7 sterling...75 A...John Campbell by Henry Eustace McCulloh (Seal), Wit: John Frohock, J. McKnitt Alexander.

Pp. 147-149: 23 Apr 1765, John Campbell to Alexander Brown of Meck., for ₤19 sterling, 201 A, adj. John McKnitt Alexander's corner...John Campbell by Henry Eustace McCulloh (Seal), Wit: John Frohock, J. McKnitt Alexander.

Pp. 149-151: 16 Mar 1765, Henry Eustace McCulloh of David Alexander of Meck., for ₤17 s10 sterling...land on S side Coddle Creek, adj. Abraham Cordins line...155 A...Henry E. McCulloh (Seal), Wit: John Frohock, Moses Alexander.

Pp. 151-153: 20 Mar 1765, Henry Eustice McCulloh to John Alexander of Meck., for ₤15 sterling...167 A on both sides Coddle Creek, adj. line run by George Dobbs...H. E. McCulloh (Seal), Wit: John Frohock, James Wallice.

Pp. 153-154: 17 Mar 1765, Henry Eustace McCulloh to James Gilmore of Meck., for ₤25 sterling...203 A on waters of Rockey River... H.E. McCulloh (Seal), Wit: John Frohock, Nathl. Alexander.

Pp. 155-156: 16 Mar 1765, Henry Eustice McCulloh to James Campbell of Meck., for ₤20 sterling...tract on Mallard Creek that Wm Wallice lives on...180 A...H. E. McCulloh (Seal), Wit: John Frohock, Moses Alexander.

Pp. 156-158: 23 Dec 1762, Roger Lawson of Halifax Dist., Ga., to Charles Moore of Anson Co., Schoolteacher (lease s5, release ₤25 proc. money)...1000 A on S side Broad River, Lawson's Creek, granted to Roger Lawson 23 Feb 1754...Roger Lawson (Seal), Wit: William Alexander, Robert Lowery, Richard Barry.
[This land now in S. C.]

Pp. 158-159: 26 Sept 1754, Samuel Young to John Latta, for ₤12 proc. money...300 A on S side Little River, including the place where Thomas Timings formerly lived, mouth of fair forrest...Samuel Young (Seal), Wit: John Kelso, John Kerrel (J).
[This land now in S. C.]

Pp. 159-160: 13 July 1765, William Welsh of Meck., planter, for love and good will to my loving cousins Sarah Mills & Ann Mills & Jeane Mills of Meck., 640 A on Clark's Creek, surveyed for Will---Mills, granted to William Welsh 19 Apr 1763... to Ann Mills for her part 200 A...William Welsh (Seal), Wit: James Robison, Niclas Welsh, Alexander Lockhart.

Pp. 160-161: 17 Feb 1763, John Martin Cline & Caterina his wife of Meck., to Robert Gault of same, for ₤20 proc. money...302 A on N side Cataba below Robert Ramsey's line, N side Cain Creek...John Martin Cline (M) (Seal), Caterina Cline (X) (Seal), Wit: Robert McClenachan, John Boogs, Arche. Crockett.

VOLUME 2

Pp. 161-163: 9 Feb 1765, Samuel Anderson of age of 21 years, of Meck., to Edward Williams for ₤9 proc. money..land that John Anderson lives on, W side Clarks Creek, 300 A granted 3 Sept 1763...Samuel Anderson (SA), Wit: John Wilkins (₮), Amos Byrd, William Croham.

Pp. 163-166: 11 & 12 July 1765, Alexander Lewis & wf Hannah Of Meck., to Samuel Neally, planter, of same (lease s5, release ₤40)...400 A formerly in Anson Co., now Meck., on E side Fishing Creek about 2 miles below Cobus Kirkendalls land... granted to sd. Lewis 9 Apr 1753...Alexander Lewis (Seal), Hannah Lewis (Seal), Wit: John Thompson, James Harris, Benj. Lewis.

Pp. 167-170: 1 & 2 May 1765, Danial McCarty & wf Angess of Meck., Millwright, to George Allen of same, planter, (lease s5, release ₤140)...land adj. N side Catawba, including the island below Tuckasegy ford...adj. Benj. Hardins old corner, granted to Joseph Harding 26 Mar 1755, conveyed to John Smith 12 Nov 1757, then to McCarty...Danial McCarty (Seal), Agness McCarty (A) (Seal), Wit: Francis Beaty, Agness Beaty (A), David Standley (D).

Pp. 171-174: 2 & 3 Sept 1765, Peter Duncan of Meck., School Master, to Richard Ward of same, planter, (lease s5, release s10) 320 A on both sides Little Broad River, part of 640 A including his own improvement, granted to sd. Duncan 16 Nov 1764... Peter Duncan (Seal), Wit: Jacob Ramsoeur, _____, _____ [illegible].
            [This land is in present Cleveland Co., NC, at the mouth of Wards Creek].

Pp. 174-177: 7 & 8 June 1765, John McDowell & wf Ann of Meck., to Joseph Moore, late from Pa., carpenter (lease s5, release ₤   )...part of 725 A conveyed from Eustice McCulloh to sd. McDowell 10 Apr 1765, on McDowell's Creek, waters of Cataba R...John McDowell (Seal), Ann McDowell (8) (Seal), Wit: Richd. Barry, Chas. Moore, William Berry.

Pp. 178-179: 10 June 1765, William McKenny of Craven Co., SC, & wf Barbara to James Crawford (Crofford) of Meck., for ₤180 SC money...334 A on W side Catawba adj. Casper Culp, granted to William Taylor 25 Sept 1754 & sold to sd. McKenny...Willm McKenny (M) (Seal), Barbara McKenny (0) (Seal), Wit: Robt. McClenachan, Mathew Forsyth.

Pp. 179-180: 15 July 1765, John Price & James Price of Meck., to William Price of same, for ₤10 proc. money...64 A adj. Rees Morgan, Grahm, part of grant to John Price's wife & James Price mother 30 Aug 1733 must be meant for 1753 ...James Price (Seal), John Price (Seal), Wit: John Hill, Walter Carson, James Ramsey.

Pp. 180-182: 24 Dec 1764, John McKee of Meck., to Samuel McKee of same, for ₤20...249 A, granted to William McKee, decd 26 Mar 1753...John McKee (Seal), Wit: Robt. McClenachan, John Smith (∅).

VOLUME 2

Pp. 182-183: 21 June 1765, Alexander Brown & wf Agness of MEck., to Joseph Canner of same, for ₤93... land granted to John Campble of Bertie Co., 3 Mar 1745...sold to Brown "23 April last"...201 A adj. John McKnitt Alexander...Alexander Brown (Seal), Agness Brown (A). Wit: J. McNitt Alexander, Joseph Mitchell, Moses Moore.

Pp. 183-185: 23 Apr 1765, Moses Moore of MEck., planter, to Thomas Tobinson of same, planter, for ₤20...250 A on S side Indian Creek, adj. John Moore old Corner...granted to Moses Moore 19 Apr 1763...Moses Moore (Seal), Wit: none.

Pp. 185-186: 9 July 1765, Charles Whiticar of MEck., to Robert Humphries of same, for ₤30...333 A on Buffilow Creek ...Charles Whitticar (C) (Seal), Wit: Richard Henderson, William Wilkins, James McCarty.

Pp. 186-187: 4 June 1765, Stephen White & wf Agnes of Meck., to Felex Kennedy of same, for ₤30... 25 A on E side Cataba granted to White 1753...Stephen White (Seal), Agness White (+) (Seal), Wit: Robt. Harris, Henry White [?].

Pp. 188-190: 7 & 8 June 1765, John McDowell & wf Ann of Meck., to James Moore of Stevensburgh Va., Taylor (lease s5, release ₤70 proc. money)...204 A on McDowells Cr, part of 725 A conveyed from Henry Eustace McCulloh to sd. McDowell...John McDowell (Seal), Ann McDowell (8) (Seal), Wit: Richd Barry, Chas. Moore, William Barry.

Pp. 191-193: 23 Apr 1765, George Augustus Selwyn, heir of John Selwyn decd, of Gloucester, England, to James Norris of Meck, planter, for ₤23 s10...294 A, part of tract #3, on a branch of Sugar Creek...Geo. Aug. Selwyn (Seal), by Henry Eustace McCulloh, Wit: John Ffrohock, Nathl. Alexander.

Pp. 193-196: 16 May 1763, Selwyn to Charles Alexander of Meck... part of tract #3, 100,000 A on Rockey River...for ₤12s6...157 A on Sugar Creek...Wit: John Ffrohock, Moses Alexander.

Pp. 196-198: 24 Apr 1765, John Campbell of Bartie Co., to James Clark of Meck., for ₤25...land adj. tract claimed by James Johnston, 265 A...John Campbell (Seal), by Henry Eustace McCulloh, Wit: John Ffrohock, Jno. McKnitt Alexander.

Pp. 198-200: 21 Mar 1765, McCulloh to Robert Scott of Meck., for ₤8...107 A on Rocky River...Wit: John Ffrohock, Jas. Alexander.

Pp. 200-201: 25 Apr 1765, John Campbell to William Hemphill of Meck., planter, for ₤7 s10...land on both sides Mallard Creek, part of tract #4, 88 A...Wit: John Ffrohock, Jno. McKnitt Alexander.

Pp. 201-203: 25 Apr 1765, John Campbell to John Cook of Meck., planter, for ₤15 proc. money...152 A...Wit: John Ffrohock.

VOLUME 2

Pp. 203-205: 14 May 1765, John Campbell to James & Ezekiel Alexander of Meck., for Ŀ10 sterling...111 A, Wit: John Ffrohock, W. Hemphill. about 40 A may fall into Mr. Selwyns tract.

Pp. 205-206: 14 May 1765, James Harris & wf Mary of Meck., to Samuel Harris of same, for Ŀ100 NC money...300 A on S side Packelot, Harris Creek, granted to sd. James Harris 18 Nov 1752...James Harris (Seal), Mary Harris (0) (Seal), Wit: Charles Harris, John Gullick.
[This property is in present South Carolina.]

Pp. 206-209: 14 & 16 Apr 1759, Edward Boyl of Anson Co., to Thomas Gillespie of Rowan Co., (lease s5, release Ŀ40)... land on S side Cataba, 300 A, granted to sd. Boyl 31 Aug 1753... Edward Boyl (0) (Seal), Wit: John Keer, John Cathey.

Pp. 209-210: 2 Mar 1764, Dobbs & wf to Christopher Lewis of Meck., for Ŀ15 proc. money...115 A on Great Coldwater Creek, adj. James Scott, John Patton...Arthur Dobbs (Seal), Wit: Martin Phifer, Richd. Barry.

Pp. 210-212: 9 Mar 1765, Abraham Kuykendall & wf Elizabeth of Meck., to James Young of same, for Ŀ47...land on Sw side Cataba, both sides Fishing Creek, granted 22 Apr 1763, adj. Millikin, PeterKuykendall, the place sd. Abraham now lives on... Abram Kuykendall (A) (Seal), Alisabeth Kuykendal (X) (Seal), Wit: John Richman, Abram Bougher (+).
[This property is in present South Carolina.]

Pp. 212-213: 15 July 1764, James Price & wf Mary of Meck., to William Price of same, for s1 proc. money...land on N side Cataba, 88 A granted to Price 7 Oct 174_...James Price (Seal), Mary Price (0) (Seal), Wit: John Hilf, Water Carson, James Ramsey.

Pp. 213-214: 4 Mar 1763, Andrew & Joseph Pickens of Meck., to Robert & Joseph Crawford of same, for Ŀ30...551 A conveyed to us by L. W. & T. of Andrew Pickens, Esq. on N side Waxhaw Creek...Andw. Pickens (Seal), Joseph Pickens (Seal), Wit: Robt. McClenachan, John Bogs.

Pp. 214-217: 9 & 10 July 1765, Preston Goforth, planter, of Meck., to James McAfee of same, (lease s5, release Ŀ40)... 300 A on N side S fork Cataba, on W side Clarks Creek, adj. James Wilson, Daniel Warlock...granted to Goforth 27 Sept 1753...Preston Goforth (X) (Seal), Wit: James Robinson, Mathew Wilson, Nicholas Welsh.

Pp. 218-221: 12 & 13 June 1765, Nathl. Miller & wf Elizabeth of Prov. of Ga., to John Steen of Prov. of NC (lease s5, release Ŀ40 sterling)...land on Thicketty Creek, bought of Jonathan Wilkins below William Greens, 400 A...Nathl. Miller (Seal), Elizabeth Miller (Seal), Wit: John Anderson, Dond. Fraser, Thos Trammell.

Pp. 221-224: 19 & 20 Nov 1764, Francis Beaty & wf Martha of Rowan to Aaron Biggerstaff of Meck., (lease s5, release Ŀ12) ...320 A on path that leads from Widow Biggerstaff to Derick Ramsours, on N side S Fork Catawba, granted to sd. Beaty 16 Nov 1764 ...Francis Beaty (Seal), Martha Beaty (M) (Seal) Wit: David Miller, James Tate, Hugh Beaty.

VOLUME 2

Pp. 225-227: 9 & 10 July 1765, Preston Goforth of Meck., planter, to James McAfee of same, planter, (lease s5, release ₤40)...150 A on N side S fork Catawba below the head of Tyry Harris' branch adj. James Wilson, Thomas Coburn, part of 400 A of which part was sold to John Patton, 250 A...granted to Goforth 24 Sept 1750...Preston Goforth (X) (Seal), Wit: James Robinson, Matthew Wilson, Nicholas Welch.

Page 228: 4 Mar 1765, Henry Myers of Orange Co., <u>Mylrite</u> & wf Catharine, to Peter Smith of same, (no amt. given)... land on SW side CAtaba, above Ramsours land, granted to sd. Myers 16 Nov 1760, 300 A,...Henry Myers (Seal), Caterine Myers (K) (Seal), Wit: Martin Shutts, Da. _____, Nicholas Cuntz. "all Dutch names."

END OF BOOK N^O. 5

Page 229: Book N^O. 6
in this book to page 247 is 124 deeds not proven in court then to the end   20 Do certified by S. Martin in 1777
North Carolina
Mecklenburg County
Kept P
Robert Harris.

Page 230: Blank.

Page 231: 10 Aug 1761, John Falls of Rowan Co., & Martha Clark of Anson Co...agreement...whereas John Falls intends to espouse & marry sd. Martha Clark...agreed that she keep her third part of the estate of her decd. husband John Clark...John Falls (Seal), Wit: Nathl. Alexander, Robert Harris.

Page 232: Will of William Black, 5 Oct 1763...being sick & in a Low condition of health... to son William Black, gristmill, now in partnership between him & me...to son John Black a full shute [sic] of Cloathes which I formerly wore & one colored boy 3 years old... to son in law Alexand. Osburn...unto Thomas Clining [?], one Dolar...to son in law Abraham Miller, ₤103...to nephew John Osburn, ₤1...to nephew William Osborn...unto my nephew & neice William Black & _____ [torn]...William & John Black, Exrs ...William Black (Seal), Wit: Jas. Hanna, Abraham Mill er William Black.

Pp. 233-236: Blank.

Pp. 237-238: 2 Mar 1763, Dobbs & wf to John Davis of Meck, for ₤18 s8 proc. money...184 A on the head branch of Rocky or Johnston River, the place where he now lives...Wit: Martin Fifer [signed in German], Richd. Barry.

Pp. 239-241: 18 & 19 Apr 1764, Isaac Kilough & wf Mary of Meck., to John Armstrong farmer, of same, (lease ₤80, release ₤20)...140 A, granted to Kilough 8 Mar 1764...Isaac Kilogh (Seal), Mary Kilough (M) (Seal), Wit: Adam Alexander, J. McKnitt Alexander.

VOLUME 2

Pp. 241-244: 13 & 14 Apr 1764, James Miller & wf Mary of Meck., Cordwinder, to Robert Miller of same, weaver, (lease s5, release ₤25 proc. money)...200 A on E side Catabo where sd. Robert now lives...near Wm Prices line...subdivided from 2 tracts of 300 & 200 A, granted to Geo. Renick 31 Mar 1753 & 30 Aug 1753, conveyed from Renick to Adam Meek, weaver, then from Meek & wf Elizabeth to James Miller 13 & 14 Jan 1759...James Miller (Seal), Mary Miller (Seal), Wit: Richd. Barry, Jno. Miller, Robert Ewart.

Pp. 244-247: 8 & 9 Feb 1764, Andrew Haseloup [Haslep] & wf Kathrine of Meck., to Samuel Clegge of same, (lease s5, release ₤15)...80 A granted to Thomas Robinson 4 Apr 1759, sold to Edwd Given, 22 Oct 1752...Andrew Heslop (Seal), Kathrine Heslop (*a*) (Seal), Wit: Richd. Barry, Wm Drew, John McDowell.

Pp. 247-248: 5 Mar 1764, James Dunn & wf Elizabeth of Meck., to James Johnston of same, for ₤40 proc. money...160 A on Cain Creek...James Dunn (Seal), Elizabeth Dunn (*u*) (Seal), Wit: Robt. McClenachan, John McClenachan.

Pp. 248-251: 18 Apr 1764, Mathew Patton & wf Jean of Meck., to Robert McKinley (lease s5, release ₤ 600 sterling)...400 A on Paw Creek & Long Creek, part of 600 A granted to Jno. Davis & conveyed to sd. Patton 19 July 1763...Mathew Patton (Seal), Jean Patton (*M*) (Seal), Wit: Richd. Barry, Cha. Moore, Geo. Eliot.

Pp. 251-254: 10 & 11 Feb 1764, Francis Mackelwean of Dobbs Co., & John Cathey of Anson Co., (lease s5, release ₤50)...to William Howe, land on S side Catabo, N side Crowders Creek, 750 A granted to sd. Mackelwean & Cathy 29 Mar 1753...Francis Mackilwean (Seal), Jno. Cathey (Seal), Wit: Richd. Barry, Martin Fifer [signed in German].

Pp. 255-258: 19 & 20 Nov 1755, James Armstrong & Samuel Young of Anson Co. & Rowan Co., to Joseph Kerrel of Chester Co., Pa. (lease s5, release ₤   )...land on little Catabo Creek, adj. Tyla Harris, Andrew Cathey, Henry Oneal, & Alex. Osborns lines...478 A, granted to sd. Armstrong & Young 25 Sept 1754...James Armstrong (Seal), Samuel Young (Seal), Wit: Saml Kerral (*C*), Elizth. Young (0).

Pp. 258-260: 2 Mar 1764, Dobbs & wf to Daniel Davis of Meck., for ₤10 s19 proc. money...109 A on head branches of Rockey River where he now lives...Wit: Martin Phifer, Richd. Barry.

Pp. 260-262: 2 Mar 1764, Dobbs & wf to Alexr. Lewis of Meck., for ₤14 s4 proc. money...242 A on N side of one of the head branches of Rockey River adj. to line between the 2 baronies, Gov. Dobbs & Mr. Hardin's ...Wit: Martin Phifer, Richd. Barry. Proven & rec. April Court 1764.

Pp. 262-263: 2 Mar 1764, Dobbs & wf to Rees Price of Meck., for ₤21 s16 proc. money...218 A on head branch of Rocky River, where he now lives...Wit: Martin Phifer, Richd Barry.

Pp. 264-265: 11 Mar 1763, Henry E. McCulloh to Moses Alexander, Gentm. of Meck., for ₤70 sterling...594 A on both sides Rocky River, adj. George Alexander, including a mill seat ...Wit: John Ffrohock, Nathl. Alexander.

VOLUME 2

Pp. 266-267: 13 Mar 1765, H. E. McCulloh to Charles Harris of Meck., planter, for Ł55 sterling...455 A on both sides Rocky River...Wit: John Ffrohock, Adam Meek.

Pp. 268-269: 23 Feb 1765, Henry Hendry & wf Isabel to John Davison & John Niehler of MEck., for Ł50...land on W side Coddle Creek, part of 2 surveys granted to sd. Hendry & sold by Sheriff to Mr. John Dunn, attorney, 180 A adj. Thomas McQuowns... Henry Hendry (Seal), Esbel Hendry ( ) (Seal), Wit: Thomas McQuown, Hugh McQuown.

Pp. 269-271: 6 May 1765, Geo. Aug. Selwyn to William Alexander, Jr. of Meck., for Ł19, 240 A...Wit: John Ffrohock, Edmd Fanning.

Pp. 271-273: 19 May 1765, Henry E. McCulloh to David Rees of Meck., for Ł35 sterling...land on N side Land Creek, 350 A ...Wit: John Ffrohock, Moses Alexander.

Pp. 273-274: 14 Mar 1765, H. E. McCulloh to William Alexander of Meck., for Ł12 sterling...94 A on S side Mallard Creek...Wit: John Ffrohock, James Wallace.

Pp. 275-276: 14 Mar 1765, H. E. McCulloch to Moses Alexander of Meck., for Ł14...114 A on Mallard Creek...Wit: John Frohock, James Wallace.

Pp. 276-278: 14 Mar 1765, H. E. McCulloh to Andrew Alexander of Meck., for Ł12 s10...200 A adj. Moses Alexander... Wit: John Ffrohock, Moses Alexander.

Pp. 278-279: 14 Mar 1765, H. E. McCulloh to David Alexander of Meck., for Ł20...298 A on Mallard Creek...Wit: John Frohock, James Wallace.

Pp. 280-281: 13 May 1765, John Campbell of Bertie Co., to David Russel of Meck., planter, for Ł10...93 A...John Campbell (Seal), by Henry E. McCulloh, Wit: John Ffrohock, James Neal.

Pp. 281-282: 8 Oct 1765, Edmund Fanning of Orange Co., NC, to John Mitchell of Roan Co., merchant, for Ł50...350 A on S side S fork Cataba...on S side Long Creek...Edmond Fanning (Seal), Wit: Maxl. Chambers, John ____ [German].

Pp. 282-283: 9 Aug 1765, James Anderson of Orange Co., to John Wharrey, late of Meck., for Ł100 proc. money...600 A on N side Broad, Clarks Creek...James Anderson (Seal), Wit: Edmond Fanning, Is. Edwards.

Pp. 283-284: 3 May 1765, Robert Leeper & wf Catherine of Meck., to William McCulloh of Meck., for Ł28 proc. money... 230 A on S side Catawba, S side Mill Creek, granted to Leeper 20 Mar 1755...Robert Leeper (Seal), Catherine Leeper (K) (Seal), Wit: Thomas Neal, Jno. McCulloh, John Hally [?].

Pp. 284-285: 18 Oct 1765, William Moor of Meck., to Robert Alexander of same, planter, for Ł22...land on Doctors Creek, W side Catawba, 96 A granted 10 Apr 1761 to sd. Moor...William Moor (Seal), Wit: Robert Harris, Jur.

VOLUME 2

Pp. 285-286: 14 Oct 1765, Joseph Clark & wf Margreat of Meck., to James Clark of same, for ₤50 proc. money...250 A on Alisons Creek...Joseph Clark (Seal), Margret Clark (0) (Seal), Wit: Jno. McCulloh, James Thompson.

Pp. 286-287: 14 Oct 1765, David Neal & wf Jean of Meck., to Robert Patrick of same, for ₤7 proc. money...part of a grant to sd. Neal on N side Crowder's Creek...David Neal (Seal), Jean Neal (J) (Seal), Wit: Thomas Neal, Joseph Howe.

Pp. 287-288: 14 Oct 1765, Henry Johnston of Meck., to James Thompson of same, for ₤40 proc. money...land on N side Allisons Creek, including mouth of Catabah [?] branch, 340 A...Henry Johnston (Seal), Wit: James Johnston.

Page 288: 3 Aug 1765, John Shambley of Meck, bound as apprentice to John McDowle of same, for 7 years...John Shamley (ᚺ) (Seal), John McDowle (Seal), Wit: Richd Barry, Wm Drew.

Pp. 288-289: 5 Oct 1765, John Stenson of Meck., to Joseph Green of same, for ₤30...land on N side Broad River, on Buffelow Creek, 130 A...John Steenson (T) (Seal), Wit: John Harden, John Mackelmurry, Thomas Rile[?] (0).

Pp. 289-290: 22 Aug 1765, John Neeley & wf Elizabeth of Meck., to Thomas McCulough of same, for ₤25, land on W side Fishing Creek...300 A gr. 20 Sept xxviii year of reign of George II...John Nealy (Ŧ) (Seal), Elizabeth Nealey (ᐱ) (Seal), Wit: Alex. Barnet, Robt. McClenachan.

Pp. 290-291: 14 Aug 1765, Simon Krowl & wf Betty of Meck., to Peter Kepple, for ₤40 proc. money...200 A on SW side Pee Dee, adj. Conrode Karcher [?] tract granted to Paul 27 Sept 1756...Simon Crowll (Seal), Betty Crowll (Seal), Wit: Zachary Esbell, Charles Barnhart (KB), Tho. Fletchall, Paul Barringer.

Pp. 291-292: 16 Jan 1765, Samuel Wilson & wf Sarah of Meck., to John Davison of same, for ₤45...250 A on McDowells Creek, about 1/4 mile below his own line, adj. George Cathey, Senr. granted 1 Sept 1753...Samuel Wilson (Seal), Sarah Wilson (Seal), Wit: James Aston, Hance Mec Whorter, Hen. Hendry.

Pp. 292-293: 2 Oct 1765, Lewis Road & wf Barbara of Meck., to Jacob Mires of same, for ₤107 proc. money...122 A on both sides Sherewolf Creek, a branch of Rocky River...Ludwig ___ R___ (Seal), [German signature], Mary Barbara Rottes (+) (Seal), Wit: Paul Barringer.

Pp. 294-295: 4 Sept 1765, John Wilkins & wf Rebecca of Rowan Co., to Hugh Montgomery of Burrough of Salisbury, same co., for ₤70 proc. money...640 A granted 21 Sept 1763 on both sides Clarks Creek...adj. Alex. McAllulys[?] and William Welsh, including John Andersons improvement...John Wilkins (Ŧ) (Seal), Wit: John Dunn, Wm Temple Cole, Andrew Smith.

Page 295: 1 Sept 1764, James McAffee of Meck., planter, to Alexander Harden of same, planter, for ₤42 proc. money...296 A on E side Turkey Creek, granted to sd. McAffee 6 Apr 1765...James McAffee (Seal), Wit: William Watson, Violat Watson, Will. Moor.

VOLUME 2

Page 296: 10 Mar 1764, William Taylor of Meck., to William McKinney of same, for ₤50...331 A on W bank Catawba, granted to Taylor 20 Sept 1752...William Taylor (Seal), Wit: Robt. McClenachan, Henry Keny (H).

Page 297: 8 Oct 1765, Frederick Ford of Meck., yeoman, to James McClennan, Marchant of Barkly [Berkeley] Co., SC, for ₤50...49[?] A....Fredk Ford (Seal), Wit: Robert McClenachan, Margret Crockett (M).

Page 298: 10 Oct 1765, Margaret Davidson of Roan Co., to William Grimes of Meck., for ___ ...land on S side Cataba, N fork of Turkey Creek, about 3 miles from Moses Dickeys...granted to George Davidson 31 Mar 1753...Margret Davidson (O) (Seal), Wit: John Davidson, Robert Templeton.

Pp. 299-300: 7 Sept 1765, James Harris of Meck., farmer, & wf Dinah to John Harris of same, for ₤25...293 A on S side S fork Cataba on S side Third Creek near Robert Patterson...place which sd. James purchased from Wm McConnell, granted 23 Feb 1754.... James Harris (Seal), Dinah Harris (Seal), Wit: Robert Harris, Jnr., Benj. Lewis.

Pp. 300-302: 14 & 15 Oct 1765, William Huggins & wf Elizabeth of Meck., to Charles McClean of same (lease s5, release ₤40)...land granted to Villiam Watson 30 Aug 1753 on S side Cataba, head of Allisons Creek, adj. James Wilson, sold by Watson to William McKnight 19 Sept 1753...William Huggins (X) (Seal), Elizabeth Huggins (E) (Seal), Wit: John Carr, Robert Harris.

Pp. 303-305: 1 & 2 Oct 1765, Thomas Clark of Meck., to Thomas Janes of same, planter, (lease s5, release ₤40)...300 A on W side Catabo, half of 600 A granted to John Barr 1 Mar 1753, adj. William McElmurray...Thomas Clark (C) (Seal), Wit: James Hendry, Robert Irwin.

Pp. 306-307: 12 Jan 1765, William Morrison of Meck., to David Alexander, for ₤29...150 A on Kuykendalls Creek, adj. James Armstrong...granted to John Armstrong, 23 Aug 1762, sold to sd. Morrison...Will: Morrison (Seal), Wit: John Armstrong, Robert Gesander, James Millican (M).

Pp. 307-307A: 17 July 1765, Benjamin Shaw of Meck., to Daniel Lessebee of same, for ₤27 proc. money...200 A on middle fork of Buffelow Creek, adj. Moses Moore...granted to Shaw 16 NOv 1764...Benjamin Shaw (Seal), Wit: James Thelby (Ŧ), Aaron Biggerstaff.

Pp. 307A-308: 4 Feb 1765, Allen Alexander & wf Nancy of Meck., to John Bratton of SC, for ₤65...164 A, part of a grant to Robert Tinnen 3 Mar 1753, sold to sd. Alexander 25 Feb 176L... Allen Alexander (Seal), Nancy Alexander (Seal), Wit: James Potts (I P), Henry Hendry.

Pp. 308-309: 3 & 4 June 1765, William Patrick & wf Mary of MEck., to John Hendry of same, planter, (lease s5, release ₤25)...300 A on Allisons Creek, near the Shoals & Great Cain Creek, formerly called a Mill Seat...granted 6 Apr 1767, Francis Beaty, D. Surv...William Patrick (Seal), Mary Patrick (ᛯ) (Seal), Wit: Robert Harris, Junr., Benj. Lewis.

VOLUME 2

Page 310: 16 May 1765, John McKnitt Alexander of Meck., to Thomas Ray of same, for ₤15 proc. money..land on both sides S fork Catawba, adj. Hoyles Mountain...100 A granted to sd. Alexander 9 Nov 1764...J McKnitt Alexander (Seal), Jean Alexander (Seal), Wit: Moses Ferguson, John Scott, Andrew McNab.

Pp. 311-312: 14 Sept 1764, Bartholomy White & wf Leady [Lydia] of Meck., to John Cain of same, for ₤12 s2 d10 sterling ...land on both sides Camp Creek, adj. Robert Galts, 200 A... Bartholomew White (Seal), Wit: Phillip Walker, Nathaniel Walker.

Pp. 312-314: 17 & 18 Apr 1764, Andrew Armour of Meck., planter, to John Miller, of same, carpenter (lease s5, release ₤60)...land on E side Cataba, adj. Armours old mill place, 212 A, granted to Armour 10 Apr 1761...Andrew Armour (Seal), Wit: Samuel Bigham, Robert Leeper, James Robinson.

Pp. 314-317: 14 & 15 June 1765, Jacob Agner of Meck., planter, to Nicholas Whistlehunt of same, for (lease s5, release ₤25)...400 A on a branch of Clarks Creek...part of 600 A granted to sd. Agner 21 Apr 1764...Jacob Eagner (Seal), Mary Eagner (X) (Seal), Wit: James Robinson, Moses Whitely, _____ "[a Dutch Name]".

Page 318: Blank.

Pp. 319-320: 1 Dec 1763, John Clark, Gent., of Meck., to James Hughey of same, for ₤400...land on S side Packeleot River, 800 A...Jno Clark (Seal), Wit: Edmund Beard, Robert Collins, John Davis, Edward Flintham.

Pp. 320-324: 20 & 21 Apr 1764, Samuel Bigham, Jr. of Meck. to Thomas Polk, Esqr., of same (lease s5, release ₤90) ...420 A on waters of Sugar Creek, adj. David Hays, Shelwins line, granted to sd. Bigham 21 Dec 1763...Samuel Bigham Junr (Seal), Wit: John Williams, Junr; Robert McClenachan, Richard Henderson.

Pp. 324-328: 14 & 15 Mar 1764, George Potts of Meck., cooper, to Jacob Forney, Distiller, of same (lease ₤50)...land on S side Cataba, both sides Killions Creek, 300 A adj. Killion, granted to Michael Miller 28 Feb 1754 & sold to Devault Potts, 13 Oct 1756...George Potts (Seal), Wit: Charles Moore, Leonard Killian (✓), _____ [German signature].
    15 Mar 1764, Mary Potts, widow & relict of Devault Potts, release of dower...Mary Pots (+) (Seal).

Page 328: 5 Feb 1757, David Parks of York Co., Pa., to William Black Jr. of Roan Co., for ₤7 s10...300 A on middle fork of Little River about 3 miles above Robert Millers ...David Parks (Seal), Wit: William Black, John Black, James Russell.

Pp. 329-330: 2 Mar 1764, Arthur Dobbs & wf to Robert Youart [Ewart], of Meck., for ₤13 s8 proc. money...134 A on head branches of Rockey River...Wit: Martin Phifer, Richd Barry.

Pp. 331-333: 5 July 1757, David Parks of Yourk Co., Pa., to William Black, Jr. of Roan Co., NC, for ₤7 s10... 300 A in Anson County, on middle fork of Little River...David Parks (Seal), Wit: William Black, John Black, James Russell.

51

VOLUME 2

Pp. 333-335: 20 Mar 1764, Matthew Biggar of Meck., to Robert Eliot of same, for ₺50...300 A on N side S fork Steel Creek ...Mathew Bigger(Seal), Wit: Francis McBride, Moses Bigger.

Pp. 335-338: 27 Nov 1763, James Bigger of Meck., to Mathew Bigger of same, for ₺18 proc. money...lane on N side S fork Steel Creek...300 A...James Bigger (Seal), Wit: Robert Elliot, Moses Bigger, John Bigger.

Pp. 339-341: 5 July 1764, David Black of Meck., to Thomas Flanney of same, for ₺15...land on S side Pacolet above ye place where Col. Clark lived...granted to Black 5 July 1757... David Black (Seal), Wit: Elener Black (Seal), Wit: Alexr. Thompson, Sarah Thompson.

Page 342: Blank.

Page 343: 15 Apr 1764, Hugh Robinson of Orange Co., NC to Robert McClenachan of Meck., for ₺20...land on N bank Wachaw Creek, adj. John Linn, formerly Joseph Whites, 200 A...Hugh Robinson (Seal), Wit: Alexander Lacky (⌒), John Robinson.

Pp. 344-346: 10 & 11 Apr 1764, James Campble & wf Jennet of Meck., to Andrew Campble of same, (lease s5, release ₺40) ...147 A on Allisons Cr., granted 23 Feb 1754...Jas. Campble (Seal), Jennet Campble (Seal), Wit: John Craig, Robt. Adams.

Pp. 346-347: 13 Mar 1764, Phillip Rudasul of Meck., to Jacob Rine of same, for s5, 200 A where sd. Rine now lives, part of a grant 20 Mar 1754...on Peter Hoyls creek...Phillip Rudasel (Seal), Mary Rudasel (X) (Seal), Wit: Jacob Zimmerman, Jacob Yottle (?), William _____ [all German signatures].

Pp. 347-349: 26 & 27 July 1763, James Aston & wf Mary of Rowan Co., planter, to Samuel Bigham of Meck (lease s5, release ₺31 s10)...land on both sides Rocky Sugar Creek & near the ford joining Mary McDowells & Hugh Parks, granted to sd. Aston 22 Apr 1763...James Aston (Seal), Mary Aston (A) (Seal), Wit: John Braly, David Kerr.

Pp. 350-351: 2 Mar 1764, Arthur Dobbs & wf to Peter Keeler of Anson Co., for ₺16 s12...166 A on both sides Dutch Buffalo Creek...Wit: Martin Phifer, Richd Barry.

Pp. 352-354: 15 & 16 Dec 1763, John Walker & wf Elizabeth of Meck., to William Ratchford of same, (lease s5, release ₺)...land on S side Cataba above George Catheys, adj. George Davison...granted to Margaret Dickey, alias Davis 23 Feb 1754... John Walker (Seal), Elizabeth Walker (Seal), Wit: Thos Black, John Cathey.

Pp. 354-356: 17 Jan 1763, John Cathey & wf Mary of Meck., to Banjamin Harding, Junr of same, for ₺20...land between N & S fork Cataba, granted to John Cathey 12 Mar 1753, part of 821 [?] A adj. Thomas Robinson, 200 A...John Cathey (Seal), Mary Cathey (L) (Seal), Wit: Edmd Fanning, Richard Henderson.

VOLUME 2

Pp. 356-359: 24 & 25 Nov 1763, Evan Lewis & wf Mary of Parish of St. George, Prov. of Georgia, to Hugh Shannon of Meck., (lease s5, release ₺63)...600 A on N side first branch of S fork Cataba, S side of sd. fork...Evan Lewis (Seal), Mary Lewis (M) (Seal), Wit: David Emanuel, Davis Lewis, Josiah Lewis.

Pp. 359-360: 14 Jan 1764, Alexander Nisbet of Meck.,yoeman, to Thomas Wright of same, for ₺25...150 A on E side Cataba, Kain Creek, adj. David Strain, William Moore, Alexander Nisbet (Seal), Agnes Nisbet (OO) (Seal), Wit: Robt. McClenachan, William Linn, Samuel Thompson.

Pp. 361-364: 12 & 13 Jan 1764, Isabel E. Stevens, widow of William E. Stevens, decd, & Andrew Allison & William Luckey, Exrs. to est. of sd. William E Stevens of Rowan Co., to Thomas Price of Meck...his L. W. & T. dated 30 Oct 1762...(lease s5, release ₺45 s10)...300 A on S side Cataba, granted to James Armour 29 Sept 1750 & conveyed to William Alexander 17 Mar 1753 & then to sd. Wm Esteven 8 Sept 1756....Isabel E Stevens (E) (Seal), Andrew Allison (Seal), Willm Luckey. Wit: Thomas Black, Adam Allison, Elisabeth Allison.

Pp. 364-366: 10 Dec 1763, Mathew Bigar of Meck., to Robert Elliot of same, for ₺35 or ₺40...land on N branch of McAlpins Creek, 200 A...Mathew Bigar (Seal), Wit: Samuel Coningham, Joseph Jones, Adam Allexander.

Pp. 366-369: 12 Aug 1762, Joseph Femster of Parish of St. Mark, Township of Fredericks Burg, Craven Co., SC, Carpenter, to George Bell of Parish, Twnshp, County, Prov. aforesaid, Wheel Wright (lease s5, release ₺10)...land on N side Broad River, including the place John Clark bought of John Kerr, mouth of Sandy River...300 A...Joseph Femster (Seal), Wit: Robert McClenachan, Samuel Femster.

Pp. 369-370: 25 Nov 1763, Martin Armstrong & wf Mary who formerly went by the name of Kuykendal of Meck., to Andrew Hampton of same, for ₺40...land on N side Dutchman Creek, 280 A granted to sd. Mary Kuykendall 26 Mar 1755...Martain Armstrong (Seal), Mary Armstrong (X) (Seal), Wit: Robert Walker, William Cleghorn, John Wilson.

Pp. 371-373: 14 & 15 July 1764, George Davison of Rowan Co., & wf Katherine, to Samuel Davison, for (lease s15, release ₺25)...land on S side Cataba, on Moses Dickeys Creek, including the forks of sd. creek...granted to sd. George 9 Mar 1754, 640 A...George Davison (Seal), Kathrine Davison (Seal), Wit: John Bryson.

Pp. 374-375: 14 July 1764, John Sellers & wf Elizabeth of Meck., to Charles Anderson, late from Va., but now of Meck., for 8 pistoles...100 A on W side Cataba, part of a grant to Robert McClenachan 24 Sept 1754, Adj. Thomas Williams...John Sellers (Seal), Elizabeth Sellers (L⌒) (Seal), Wit: Andrew Carswell, Daniel McCoy.

Pp. 375-376: 16 July 1764, Robert Russal of Meck., to son William, for love & good will...one black horse, two mares & colt, Nine cows, one Loom & geers...Robt. Russal (Seal), Wit: James Rusal, Robt. Black.

53

VOLUME 2

Pp. 376-378: 17 July 1764, William Dickson of Dublin [sic] Co., NC, to John Harden of Meck., for ℔5 s10 d8 proc. money...land on both sides Fishing Creek, where sd. Harden now lives...300 A granted to Dickson 23 Dec 1764...William Dickson (Seal), Wit: Robt. Harris Jr., Zaccheus Wilson.

Pp. 378-381: 24 & 25 March 1764, Joseph Davies of Rowan Co., planter, to Robert Armstrong of Meck., (lease s5, release ℔30)...land on S side Catawba, land granted to sd. Davies 17 May 1754...280 A...Joseph Davies (Seal), Wit: James Beaty, Arthur Patterson.

Pp. 381-383: 9 June 1764, Robert Alison & wf Ann of SC, to Henry Foster of Meck., for ℔200 SC money...330 A granted to Malkam Fisher 23 Feb 1754, conveyed to sd. Alison by Archibald Fisher, Exr. of Malkam 20 May 1760, on N side Cataba, island in Cataba...Robt Alison (Seal), Ann Alison (𝌶) (Seal), Wit: John Pickens, Robert McClenachan.

Pp. 384-385: 7 May 1764, John Lata & wf Elizabeth in Craven Co., SC, to John McFadien of same, for ℔20 NC money...300 A in Meck., on S side Cataba on S side Fishing Creek, adj. Jacob Foyler, ...deed from Philip Waker to sd. Lata 15 Jan 1760...John Lata (Seal), Elizabeth Latta (W) (Seal), Wit: Thos. Ferral, Robt McClenachan.

Pp. 385-387: 22 June 1764, Major Robert McClenachan, Gentleman of Meck., to Charles Anderson "Leat of the County of Lunenburg, Colony of Va.", Gent., for 38 pistoles...219 A on SW side Cataba, adj. James Miller...granted to sd. McClenachan 25 Sept 1754...Robt McClenachan (Seal), Elisabeth McClenachan (Seal), Wit: Robert McClellan, John Sellars (∽), Saml. Thompson.

Pp. 388-391: 26 & 27 June 1764, John Leech & wf Margret of Meck., to Thomas Benson of same, (lease s5, release ℔23)...land granted to James Pots 21 Oct 1758, & sold to sd. Leech, adj. Governor's line, 200 A...John Leech (Seal), Margret Leech (𝒱) (Seal), Wit: Nathl. Alexander, Napilot Johnson.

Pp. 391-393: 20 May 1764, Casper Culp of Meck., Yeoman, to James Patton of same, for ℔75 SC money...225 A adj. Cataba River...Matthew Pattons land...granted to sd. Culp 25 Sept 1754 ...Casper Culp (Seal), Wit: Matthew Patton, Ann Foster, Henry Foster.

Pp. 393-395: 20 May 1760, Archibald Fisher, Exr. of Meklam Fisher, decd, & wf Jean of Anson Co., to Robert Alison, leat of sd. county... for ℔50...land including an island in the Cataba, 300 A...Archibald Fisher (Seal), Jena Fisher (0) (Seal), Wit: Robert McClenachan, John Crocket, Mary Crocket (M).

Pp. 395-397: 5 & 6 Jan 1764, Hamilton Ross of Meck., to Cornelius Anderson of Rowan Co., (lease ℔5 SC money, release ℔300 SC money...)...400 A between Fishers & William Taylors lines ...Hamilton Ross (Seal), Wit: Henry Sloan, John Sloan.

Page 398: 2 Dec 1765, Samuel Young to Daniel Plummer, for ℔250 ....520 A granted 31 Aug 1753 to sd. Young, on S side Broad, Fairforest Creek, below the Buffalo lick, below James Means's...Samuel Young (Seal), Wit: Robert Cowdon, James Means.

VOLUME 2

Pp. 399-400: 1 Mar 1764, James Harris & wf Elizabeth of Meck., to John Carr, of same, farmer (lease s5, release Ł 23) ...land on S side Cataba, on a S branch of Allison Creek, granted to sd. Harris 23 Feb 1754...James Harris (Seal), Elizth. Harris (Seal), Wit: Robert Harris, Robert Harris Jr.

Pp. 400-401: 2 July 1764, John Polk & wf Elenor of Meck., to Charles Polk of same, for Ł30 proc. money...110 A on Clear Creek, a branch of Rockey River...Rees Shelbys corner... granted to sd. John Polk...John Polk (Seal), Ellener Polk (P) (Seal), Wit: Robert Harris Junr, Ezekiel Polk.

Pp. 401-402: 2 July 1764, John & Elenor Polk for good will & affection to our two children Charles & Ellener Polk... land we now live on, on Rockey River, also horses & negroes, household stuff...John Polk (Seal), Ellenor Polk (P) (Seal), Wit: Charles Polk, Ezekiel Polk, Robert Harris, Junr.

Pp. 402-403: 24 June 1762, Arthur Dobbs to James Plunket of Anson Co., for Ł9 s18...95 A near Buffalo Creek...Arthur Dobbs (Seal), Wit: George Miller, Arthur MacKay.

Pp. 404-405: 2 Mar 1764, Arthurs Dobbs & wf to Benjamin Brown of Meck., for Ł22 s10 proc. money...225 A on head branch of Rockey River, where he now lives...Wit: Martin Phiffer, Richard Barry.

Pp. 405-406: 2 Mar 1764, Dobbs & wf to James Slone of Meck., planter, for Ł22 proc. money...320 A on head branches of Rockey River...Wit: Martin Phiffer, Richard Barry.

Pp. 407-408: 2 Mar 1764, Dobbs & wf to Robert Youart [Ewart] of Meck., for Ł10 s12 proc. money...106 A on head branches of Rockey River...the place where he now lives...Wit: Martin Phiffer, Richard Barry.

Pp. 408-410: 4 & 5 Dec 1764, Moses Ferguson of Meck., Schoolmaster, to Hugh Carrothers of same, for (lease s5, release Ł20)...300 A on N fork Steel Creek, adj. Willm Barnets, granted to sd. erguson 19 Apr 1764...Moses Ferguson (Seal), Wit: Henery Vernor, Barbara Vernor (Z).

Pp. 410-412: 11 & 12 June 1764, Francis Beaty & wf Martha of Roan Co., to Martin Phiffer of Meck., (lease s5, release Ł72)...450 A on both sides S fork Cataba, including ye great shoals, about 2 miles below Saml. Biggerstaff, near Ramsoeurs, granted to sd. Beaty 10 Apr 1761...Francis Beaty (Seal), Martha Beaty (m) (Seal), Wit: William Draper, James Beaty, Thomas Millsaps, John Phiffer.

Pp. 413-414: 14 & 15 Jan 1765, John Sloan, Junr of Meck., planter, to John Allen of same, Shoe maker (lease s5, release Ł30)...280 A on Gum Branch of Long Creek, above Boyds land including Allens improvment, granted to Sloan 16 Nov 1764...John Sloan (Seal), Wit: Moses Ferguson, James Aston.

Pp. 415-417: 17 & 18 Jan 176_, James Ormund of Meck., planter, to Hance McWhorter of Roan County, Wheel Wright (lease s5, release ₺7 s10)...land on N side Cataba, adj. land surveyed for Rees Morgan, Richard Grahm, & Thomas Erwin, granted to Ormund 17 May 1764...James Ormund (Seal), Wit: John McCulloh, Samuel Young.

Pp. 417-418: 17 Jan 1765, Robert Cowdon, late of Meck., to Robert Elliot of Meck., farmer, for ₺10 [?], 412 A on S side Broad, N fork Golden Grove above Walter Cowdons land, granted to sd. Robert 3 Sept 1753...Robert Cowdon, Wit: Moses Ferguson, John Elder.

Page 418: Meck Co.: Samuel Sinclair of Meck., to William Reed, Inn holder, for ₺50 proc money...one negro boy 12 or 13 years old...Samuel Sinclair (Seal), Wit: John Carr, Margaret Taylor.

Pp. 418-421: John Campbell of Bertie Co., is possessed of a tract in the back of this province, granted 3 Mar 1745, to Jeremiah Joy, 1000 A on Anson County on S side S fork Catawba, gormerly granted to Elias Lagardere 3 Apr 1753, & another tract of 1000 A on S side Pedee, lower side of Browns Creek, granted to George Gould ___ Mar 1747, & 640 A in the fork of Mountain Creek, granted to sd. Gould on Jones Creek, a tract granted to Gould 25 Mar 1748... & 300 A on S side Pedee, adj. William Henry, granted 6 Apr 1750 to James McManus...power of attorney to Henry Eustace McCulloh, 10 Aug 1762...John Campbell (Seal), Wit: Robert Aarney [?], Alexr. Ford.

Pp. 421-422: I, William _____, Lord Mayor of London, do testify that John Blake being a person well known and worthy of good credit swears to the matters in the attached affadavit... 22 Nov 1763 (Hodges).

Page 422: John Blake of Middle Temple, London, Gentleman, did see George Augustus Selwyn sign the attached letter of attorney...John Blake, Sworn at the Guild Hall, London __ Nov 1763, before Wm Bridges, Mayor.

Pp. 422-425: 21 Nov 1763, George Augustus Selwyn of County of Gloucester, am entitled to 2 tracts in the province of NC, granted to John Selwyn, my late _____ deceased, known as tract #1 and Tract #3, 100,000 A each...part of tracts heretofore granted to Mary Crymble, James Huey and their assigns...whereas these tract have been settled and improved & ought to be surrendered to the crown...power of attorney to Henry McCulloh of Middlesex & Henry Eustace McCulloh of NC, to sell...G. Augustus Selwyn (Seal), Wit: John Cottrell, servant to Mr. Selwyn, John Blake of the Middle Temple London, Gentn.

Page 426: Blank.

Pp. 427-431: 1 & 2 Mar 1765, John Bumgardner of Meck., planter, to George Rees, of same, planter, (lease s5, release ₺7 s15)...150 A on a branch of Leepers Creek, adj. sd. Bumgardner, including George Rees's improvement...granted to sd. Bumgardner, 16 Nov 1764...John Bumgardner (J) (Seal), Wit: William Moor, Andw Hampton, Robert Alesander.

VOLUME 2

Pp. 431-435: 1 & 2 Oct 1765, Francis Beaty of Rowan Co., Recr of Quitrents to Robert Gordon of Meck., planter, (lease s5, release ₤15)...250 A on N side Allisons Creek, including a Shoal about 1 1/2 miles below the Cedar flatt, crossing the Beaver dam branch of Crowders Creek, granted 21 Mar 1764...Francis Beaty (Seal), Wit: Robt. Armstrong, James McMeen.

Pp. 435-439: 7 & 5 Oct 1765, William Armstrong & wf Margaret of Meck., planter, to Michael Miller of same, planter, (lease s5, release ₤60)...300 A on Keenes branch of Leepers Creek, granted to sd. Armstrong 16 Nov 1764...William Armstrong (Seal), Margrit Armstrong (X) (Seal), Wit: _____, ____ Folmer [German signatures], Benjamin Hide (BH).

Pp. 439-442: 20 & 21 Sept 1765, Henry Forster on Cataba River, late of Meck., Esq., to Francis Beaty of Meck., Recr of Quit rents (lease s5, release ₤15)...land on Mitchells Creek, S side Fairforest Creek, N side Tyger River, ad. Thomas Mitchells line, granted 3 Oct 1755, to sd. Forster...Henry Forster (Seal), Wit: Robert Armstrong, James McMeen, Hugh Beaty.
[This land now in SC]

Pp. 443-446: 14 & 15 Oct 1765, Benjamin Love of Meck., planter, to Robert Elliot & James Elliot of same, planter (lease s5, release ₤10)...280 A on N side Broad River, adj. Robert Love's including sd. Benjamin's improvement...granted to sd. Benjamin Love 5 Feb 1754...Benjamin Love (B) (Seal), Wit: Robert Armstrong, James McMeen.
(This land now in S. C.)

Pp. 446-450: 11 & 12 Sept 1765, Peter Duncan of Meck., Schoolmaster, to Thomas Black of same, planter, (lease s5, release ₤50)...320 A on both sides Little Broad River, lower ½ of 640 A granted to sd. Duncan 16 Nov 1764...Peter Duncan (Seal), Wit: Moses Moore, Thos Johnson.

Pp. 450-454: 21 & 28 Sept 1765, Thomas Gillaspie of Anson Co., to Henry Gillaspie of Rowan Co., (amt. not stated)... 300 A on S side Cataba on Humphries Creek, a N fork of Fishing Creek between Moses Deickeys & john Kukendalls...Thomas Gillespie (Seal), Wit: James Wylly, Robert Harris.

Pp. 455-458: 16 Oct 1765, Robert Tate to James Henry, for ₤33... land on S side Cataba on S fork Crowders Creek joyning David Rankins survey 360 A, granted to sd. Tate 31 Aug 1753... Robert Tate (Seal), Wit: Robert Harris, Will Reed.

Pp. 458-461: 24 & 25 Feb 1763, John Burnett of Rowan Co., & wf Mary, to John Doudle of Meck., (lease s5, release ₤23)...300 A on N side Cataba adj. John Bravard, Robert Jinnings ...John Burnet (Seal), Mary Burnet (Seal), Wit: Martain Phifer, Saml Burnet.

Pp. 461-464: 14 & 18 Aug 1765, John Clark of Roan Co., planter, to Nicholas Frye, late of Meck., (lease s5, release ₤120)...560 A where Frye now lives on both sides Clarks Creek, including John Wilkes improvement that he sold to John Clark, granted to John Wilkins 21 Dec 1763...John Clark (Seal), Wit: William Graham, James Willson, James Witherow (₮).

VOLUME 2

Pp. 464-467: 30 & 31 Aug 1765, Adam Meek & wf Elizabeth of Meck., Weaver, to John Hill of same, planter, (lease s5, release Ŀ20)...land on S side S fork Cataba on Long Creek, 340 A, granted to sd. Meek 17 May 1754...Adam Meek (Seal), Elisabeth Meek (∞) (Seal), Wit: Nathl Alexander, David Caldwell, John Giles.

Pp. 467-469: 2 Mar 1764, Arthur Dobbs & wf Justina to Andrew Reynhart of Meck., planter, for Ŀ15 s18 proc. money ...159 A in forks of Adams Creek & Dutch Buffalo Creek, branches of Rockey River...Arthur Dobbs (Seal), Justina Dobbs (Seal), Wit: Martin Phifer, Richd Barry.

Page 470: Blank.

Page 471: 19 Oct 1765, Jacob Mouney of Meck., to John Frohock of of Rowan Co., for Ŀ20...5 cows & 4 calves, one Gray Horse, one Bay mare, 20 Head of Hoggs, & one Cuteau knife...Jacob Mouney (Seal), Wit: William Alexander, Ezekiel Alexander.

Pp. 472-474: 17 Oct 1765, John McDowel of Meck., for Barnaby Eagan & wf Rachel of Va., to Jacob Gardner, late of Pennsylvania, (lease s5, release Ŀ__)...200 A on S side Broad River, where sd. Gardner now lives, on the econd Big Creek that runs into sd. river above the mouth of Pacolate, granted to Charles McDowell, decd 4 Apr 1751, & thence to his daughter Rachel Eagan, wife to sd. Barnaby Eagan...from Rachel McDowell & Geo. Cathey, Exrs. to L. W. & T. of sd. decd, 29 & 30 July 1754...Barnaby Eagan (Seal), Rachel Eagan (Seal), by John McDowell, Wit: Will Harris, Alex Macky (N).
(The will of Charles McDowell, dated 4 June 1754, is recorded in Anson Co., NC, Will Book I, pp. 2-3.)

Pp. 475-477: 16 Oct 1764, John Moore of Orange Co., NC "of the Hawfields" to John Malony of Meck., (lease s5, release Ŀ8)...160 A granted to sd. Moore 31 Mar 1753, adj. Allen Alexander ...John Moore (Seal), Wit: Henry Potts, Walter Lindsay.

Page 477: 26 Mar 1757, William Green of Anson Co., planter, to John Brian of same, planter, for Ŀ40...land on S side Broad River, on Thickety Creek, 350 A...William Green (W) (Seal), Ann Green (𝒴) (Seal), Wit: William Sharp, Will Hughes.
(This land now in S. C.)

Pp. 478-480: 7 & 8 Oct 1765, John Buchanan & wf Ann of Meck., to Jackson Neely late of same, (lease s5, release Ŀ100) ...land on Steel Creek, adj. John Hindry, Walter Davis, Samuel Knox...John Buchanan (Seal), Ann Buchanan (A) (Seal), Wit: Thos Polk, Moses Alexander, James McCall.

Pp. 481-482: 24 Feb 1762, Jonathan Wilkins of Anson Co., to Joseph Downs of same, for Ŀ5 proc. money...land on Thicketty Creek, the place he bought of Richard Miller...below William Greens, granted to Richd Miller 16 Mar 1751 (1752?)...Jonathan Wilkins (Seal), Wit: William Crittenden, William Wilkins, Francis Downs.
(This land now in S. C.)

VOLUME 2

Pp. 482-483: 28 July 1764, James Land of Craven Co., SC, to William McKeney of same, for ₤20 proc. money...340 A on both sides Rocky Creek...James Land (Seal), Wit: William Stevenson, Robt McClenachan.
    "Returned This Farr October the 6th 1767."

Pp. 484-485: 18 Sept 1776, John Ford, Esquire of Meck., to William Morris of same, for ₤10 proc money...land on waters of McCalpins Creek, adj. to & part of the tract where sd. Ford now lives...10 A...John Foard (Seal), Wit: Will Reed, Zebulon Foard.
    Meck Co.: Jany Session 1777, the within deed acknowledge in open court by the Grantor in Person.

Pp. 485-487: 18 Sept 1776, John Ford to William Morris, for ₤25 ...land on waters of McCalpins Creek, part of a survey granted to Ford by deed from Geo. Augustus Selwyn 24 Feb 1767... adj. to Buckalews corner, Culbertsons & Johnston's corner, 85 A ...John Foard (Seal), Wit: Will Reed, Zebulon Foard.
    Proven Jany Session 1777. Sam Martin, C. C.

Pp. 487-488: 30 Dec 1775, Thomas McCall of Meck., for natural love & affection to son James McCall...tract where I now live, reserving to my wife Margaret the possession of the Dwelling House...Thomas McCall (Seal), Wit: Hugh McQuown, Jas. McQuown, John McQuown.
    Proven July Sessn. 1776, by Jas McQuown; Saml Martin, C. C.

Pp. 489-490: 20 Mar 1776, Adam Carruth of Meck., planter, to John Carruth, a minor Son of James Carruth, late of Meck., decd., for natural love & affection & s10 proc. money...210 A, part of 610 A conveyed to sd. Adam by Francis Beaty, L. &. R. 7 & 8 June 1762....Adam Carruth (Seal), Wit: John Braly, John Sloan, Robert Carruth.
    Proven by grantor, July Sessn, 1776, Saml Martin, C. C.

Pp. 491-492: 7 Aug 1772, Thomas Polk of Meck., to James Walker of same, for ₤150 proc. money...481 A in 3 surveys... (1) joining Abenr Newton & Widow Allens lands...near Henry Walker, 100 A...(2) ____ A near John McElwees line...(3)...121 A granted to Thomas Polk by deed...patents dated 13 Mar 1767, 4 May 1767 (1769?), & 4 May 1769, 481 A total...Thos Polk (Seal), Wit: William Patterson, William Walker.
    Proven by William Patterson Jany Sessn 1777 Saml Martin, C. C.

Pp. 493-494: 19 Nov 1774, John Black of Meck., to William Henderson of same, for ₤20 proc. money...the NW End of a tract of 100 A including his house, 32 A...sold to Black by Henry Eustace McColoh, 15 Jan 1766...John Black (Seal), Margaret Black (Seal), Wit: John Hamilton, Archibald Coulter, Elener Black (W).
    Proven by grantors in person, Jany Sessn 1777. Saml Martin, C.C.

VOLUME 2

Pp. 495-496: 20 Jan 1777, John Johnson & wf Ann of Meck., planter, to William Irwin, for ₤15...land on waters of McAlipns Creek, including Improvements he now lives on, adj. Stevens line, 150 A...John Johnston (Seal), (Ann did not sign.). Wit: John Black, Robert Campbell.
  Proven by grantor Jan Sessn 1777. Saml Martin, C. C.

Pp. 497-498: 17 Apr 1776, Joseph Johnston of Meck., to John Black of same, for ₤20 proc. money...land on waters of McAlpins Creek, including Blacks improvements, adj. Abraham Millers line...60 A, granted to sd. Johnston __ Feb 1775...Joseph Johnston (Seal), Wit: Peter Johnston, James Osburn, Jas. White.
  Proven by James Osburn Jany Sessn. 1777. Saml Martin, C. C.

Pp. 499-500: 20 July 1774, Thomas Polk, Jereh McCafferty, & Wm Patterson of Meck., to Joseph Kennedy of same, for ₤30 proc. money...lots in Charlotte, #s 106 & 107 on the Back side of Trade Street, nearly an acre...granted to above by deed from George Augustus Selwyn, 15 Jan 1767...Thos Polk (Seal), Jeremh McCafferty (Seal), Wm Patterson (Seal), Wit: John Baret, Robert Scott.
  Proven by Robert Scott Jany Sessn 1777.

Pp. 501-502: 17 Jan 1775, William Irwin & Sarah Irwin of Meck., to Thomas Gribble of same, for ₤25...50 A on waters of McCalpins Creek...adj. to the "Old Original open line"...William Irwin (Seal), Sarah Irwin (Seal), Wit: John Hamilton, John Black, James Beaird.
  Proven by grantor Jany Sessn 1777. Saml Martin, C. C.

Pp. 503-504: 10 June 1774, John Harris & wf Elender of Meck., planter, to Jesse Harris of same, planter...land on both sides Goose Creek, granted to sd. John Harris by Abm Nesh(?) & wf Justina 15 Feb 1771, 68 A...John Harris (Seal), Elander Harris (つ) (Seal), Wit: Joseph Harris, Thomas Harris.
  Proven by Joseph Harris Jany Sessn 1777. Saml Martin, C. C.

Pp. 505-506: 13 Mar 1776, Richard Stillwell & wf Margaret (Stitewell?), to Thomas Ree, for ₤88...120 A, part of tract #2...Richd Stitewell (Seal), Margaret Stitewell (M) (Seal), Wit: Samuel Montgomery, William Smith (W). Proven by grantor, Jly Sessn 1776. Saml Martin, C. C.

Pp. 507-508: 17 Apr 1776, John Johnston of Meck., to John Black of same, for ₤20...122 A on both sides of Beard br. of McAlpins Cr....John Johnston (Seal), Wit: Peter Johnston, James Osburn, Jas White. Proven by James Osburn, Jany Sessn 1777. Sam Martin, C. C.

Pp. 509-510: 17 Apr 1777, William Starret & wf Ruth of Tryon Co., NC, to Messrs William & James McCafferty, for ₤250 proc. money...163 A on Garrisons Cr., adj. Thomas Polk, Andw Sprott, & Alexander Starret...deeded to sd. Wm from Geo. Aug. Selwyn, 9 Jan 1767...William Starret (W) (Seal), Ruth Starret (+) (Seal), Wit: Joseph Moore, Andw Sprott. Proven by Joseph Moore, April Sessn 1777, Saml. Martin, C. C.

VOLUME 2

Pp. 511-512: 28 Nov 1776, James Love & John McCackin of Meck., to John Davis of same, for ₤100 proc. money...140 A on Back Cr., of Rockey River...James Love (Seal), John McCachin (Seal), Wit: James Harris, Robert Rodgers. Proven by grantors, April Session 1777, Saml Martin, C. C.

Pp. 512-513: 3 Dec 1776, John Davis of Meck., to John McCackin, for ₤100...140 A on Back Creek...John Davis (Seal), Wit: James Harris, Robert Rodgers. Proven by Robert Rodgers Apr Sessn 1777. Sam Martin, C. MS.

Pp. 514-515: 3 Jan 1777, John Clark of Meck., to Christefor Erwin of same, for sufficient & lawfull yearly maintainance till the day of his death...130 A...John Clark (Seal), Wit: Wm Wilson, James Wilson, Proven by grantor Apr Sessn 1777. Saml Martin, C SM.

Pp. 516-517: 29 May 1776, Thos Polk, Jeremiah McCafferty & William Patterson of Meck., to Margaret Dempsey of same, for s30 proc. money..lotts in Charlotte #s 266 & 247 on S side Trade St., near an acre...deeded from Selwyn 15 Jan 1767...Thos Polk (Seal), Jeremh McCafferty (Seal), Wm Patterson. Wit: William Clark, Thos Polk.

Pp. 518-519: 12 May 1775, Thos Polk, William Patterson & Jeremiah McCafferty of Meck., to Mrs. Mary Curron of same, for s30...lotts in Charlotte, on W side of Tryon St., near an acre, deeded from Selwyn 15 Jan 1767...Wit: David McKee, DL., M. Thompson, Proven by David McKee April Sessn 1777 Saml Martin, C. Sm.

Pp. 520-522: 15 Apr 1775, Robert Crockett & wf Rachel of Meck., to Joseph Kerr, Junior of same, whereas Joseph Kerr, Senior decd, did in his lifetime purchase from Mr. John Mitchel & wf Elisabeth 362 A on waters of Long Creek, a br. of Cataba 9 Dec 1769, under mortgage & died not having devised sd. land in his L. W. & T. & did leave the following children: the sd. Joseph Kerr Jr. & 2 daughters Elisabeth Parker, wf of Isaac Parker & the sd. Rachel Crockett wf of Robert Crockett...sd. Joseph Kerr, Jr. pd to sd. Mitchel the mortgage money...land has fallen into dispute among heirs...sd. Crocketts quit their claim to land...362 A part of 12,500 A granted to Jeremiah Joy of City of London... Robert Crockett (Seal), Rachel Crockett (Seal), Wit: Wrighstut Avery, Hez.: Alexander, William Alexander, Proven by grantors April Session 1777. Saml Martin, C sm.

Pp. 523-526: 18 Oct 1776, Isaac Parker & wf Elisabeth to Joseph Kerr, Jr....quit of claims (same property as in preceding deed)...Isaac Parker (Seal), Elisabeth Parker (Seal), Wit: Mary Todd (0), Robert Carr. Proven by Robert Carr, April Session 1777. Saml Martin Csm.

Page 526:   Book No 6 by Robert Harris Register

             In this book is 144 Deeds registered Ano Dom 1777
                of which   124 is no probates of proving in Court
                and   20 has the probates registered
                in all   144 deeds herein.

Page 527-534: Blank.

VOLUME 2

Page 535: No 7: 103 deeds no certificates of probate in court
North Carolina Mecklenburg County
Registers Office Book # No 7
<u>Keept</u> by Robert Harris Publick Register
for the County aforesaid

Page 536: Book No 7
Robt Harris Register 1764 & 1765

Pp. 537-538: 25 June 1764, Dobbs & wf to Moses Alexander of Meck., for Ŀ10...100 A on Clear Creek...Wit: John Davis Junr., Arthur MacKay.

Pp. 539-540: 25 June 1764, Dobbs & wf to Moses Alexander, for Ŀ8 s6...83 A on Clear Creek...Wit: John Davis Junr., Arthur MacKay.

Pp. 541-543: 15 & 16 Aug 1764, Henry Vernor & wf Barbara of Meck., to Alexander Robertson of same (lease s5, release Ŀ___)...land on S side S fork Cataba, on a Br. of Crowder's Creek on the N side, granted to James Waughup 29 Mar 1753, & conveyed to sd. Vernor...Henry Vernor (Seal), Barbara Vernor (M) (Seal), Wit: Moses Ferguson, Robert Elliot, John Kerr.

Pp. 543-544: 24 Oct 1763, Davis Leonard of Meck., to Frederick Ford of same, for Ŀ30...39 A including the cross roads one leading to McDonnaolds ford of Cataba leading down sd. river adj. Thomas Attisons line...Davis Leonard (Seal), Wit: Thos Leonard (g), Thos Stilt (?), George Gordon.

Pp. 544-546: 23 Aug 1764, Stephen White & wf Agness of Meck., to Lodwick Laird of same, for Ŀ43, 265 A on both sides Rockey Cr...granted to sd. Stephen White's father in law Malcom Fisher 29 Feb 1754, bequeathed to sd. White & Thomas Steel, the sd. Malcom Fishers sons in law & Archibald Fisher, his natural son...Stephen White (Seal), Agness White (M) (Seal), Wit: Robt McClenachan, William Leard, Samuel Thompson.

Pp. 546-547: 14 Jan 1765, Samuel Dunlop & wf Mary of Craven Co., SC husbandman, to John Thompson of same, for Ŀ156...land on NE side Cataba, on Cain Creek 104 A...granted to sd. Dunlop 3 Apr 1752...Samuel Dunlop (Seal), Mary Dunlap (D) (Seal), Wit: Robt McClenachan, Robert Ramsey, Samuel Thompson.

Pp. 548-550: 3 &4 July 1753, John McCulloch of Rowan Co., to James Young of Meck., (lease s5, release Ŀ40)...350 A on main branch of Fishing Creek, about 2 miles below James Kuykendalls granted to sd. McCulloch 3 Feb 1754...#684...Jno McCulloch (Seal), Wit: James Dysart, Allen Alexander, John Young.

Pp. 550-551: 5 Jan 1765, Thomas Price & wf Isabella of Meck., to John Davison of Cumberland Co., Pa., for Ŀ60 proc. money..land on S side Cataba, S fork Fishing Creek, 791 Agranted to William Price decd, father to sd. Thomas Price, 30 Aug 1753...Thomas RPice (Seal), Isabella Price (i) (Seal), Wit: Abrm Scott, Joseph Scott, John Thomas.

Pp. 551-553: 31 Oct & 1 Nov 1764, Wm Sherill of Craven Co., SC St. Mark's Parish, to Jonathan Robinson of Meck., (lease s5, release ₤100)...land on S side S fork Cataba at Jumpin Run, granted to Sherill 4 Apr 1750...William Sherril (W) (Seal), Wit: James McClain, Moses Sherril, William Sherril (W).

Pp. 553-556: 28 & 29 Oct 1764, Thomas Beaty & wf Margaret & John Beaty & wf Elizabeth of Meck., to John Connelly of Chester Co., Pa., for ₤50...660 A on S side Cataba, adj. Thomas Beatys, granted to sd. Beatys 24 Sept 1754...Thos Beaty (Seal), Margret Beaty (Seal), John Beatey (Seal), Eliz: Beaty (X) (Seal), Wit: Galbreath Falls, Thomas Beatey.

Pp. 556-557: 3 Aug 1764, David Stanley & wf Hannah of Meck., to John Moore of same, for ₤61...land on N side Cataba, part of a grant to William Watson, 28 Feb 1754...sold to Benjamin Harden then to sd. Stanly 10 July 1754...David Stanlee (D) (Seal), Hannah Stanlee (H) (Seal), Wit: Jacob Mony, John Low.

Pp. 557-558: 13 Oct 1762, William McConnel of Peters---- Township, Cumberland Co., Pa., carpenter, appoints John Wilson of Rockey River, & Andrew Allison of _____ attorneys to sell property...William McConnell (Seal), Wit: Ezekiel Wallace, Saml Findlay (instrument fragmentary).

Pp. 558-560: 17 & 18 Jan 1764, William McConnel & John Wilson his attorney Both of Meck., to James Harris Junr of same (lease s5, release ₤51)...316 A granted to sd. McConnel 23 Feb 1754 on S side _____...Robert Patterson survey...William McConnel (Seal), by John Wilson Wit: Charles Harris, Robert Harris, Moses Wylie.

Pp. 560-563: 25 Oct 1764, John Wilkins & wf Rachel of Meck, farmer, to Joannah Humphries (lease s5, release ₤28)...land on S side Cataba, part of 250 A granted to Leonard Killion 30 Sept 1749, conveyed by Killion & wf Margaret to George Brown 1 Jan 1754, then to Watkins 20 July 1757...John Watkins (‡) (Seal), Rachel Watkins (+) (Seal), Wit: George Walker (W), Wm Grant, William Haggerty (H).

Pp. 563-564: 4 Jan 1765, John Moore & wf Ann of Meck., to John Garvin for ₤60, 580 A granted to sd. Moore 26 Mar 1755...on N side of a branch called by some Moores Creek...John Moore (Seal), Ann Moore (A) (Seal), Wit: William Dunlop, John Thomas, James McCord.

Pp. 564-565: 12 Jan 1765, James Millican & wf Jean to John Rendel for ₤40...land on N side Broad River, S side Fishing Creek above William Ratchford, granted to Bleny Mills 3 Feb 1754 & sold to Millican 27 Jan 1764, 400 A (end of deed mutilated).

Pp. 566-568: 26 & 27 Oct 1763, David John of Parish of St. George, Georgia, Blacksmith, to John Walker of Meck, (lease s5, release ₤__)...land on Mountain Creek, adj. Alexander McConnels, 210 A...David John (Seal), Wit: Thomas Irwin, Jacob Coburn. Georgia, Parish of ST. George: 27 Oct 1763, appeared before me David Emanuel, Thomas Irwin of the parish aforesaid, proved deed...David Emanuel J. P.

VOLUME 2

Pp. 569-570: 16 Nov 1764, Dobbs & wf to John McKnitt Alexander of Meck., for ₤13 s2 proc. money...131 A on head branches of Rockey River, where David Davis did live...Wit: Richd Barry, Martin Phifer.

Pp. 571-572: (first part missing)...patent 4 Sept 1753 to Joseph Milliken & given to William Millican...for ₤10 pd. by James Young...343 A, except 150 A that Peter Kuykendall patented ...William Millican (◯) (Seal), Wit: William Cleghorn, Moses Alexander.

Pp. 572-573: 24 Oct 1764, Andrew Cathey & wf Martha of Meck., to Abraham Scott of same, for ₤27 proc. money...land on S side CAtaba, 250 A, part of 1000 A granted to John Killion 13 Sept 1749, sold to Jacob Brown 2 Jan 1754, & sold to Cathey 20 June 1757...Andrew Cathey (X) (Seal), Martah Cathey (X) (Seal), Wit: John Tygart, John Hill.

Pp. 573-574: 16 Jan 1765, James Armour of Meck., to Andrew Armour of same, for ₤50 proc money...land on E side Cataba, granted to _____ Armour decd 6 Apr 1753, 640 A...James Armour (Seal), Wit: Moses Ferguson, Robt. Harris.

Pp. 575-576: 7 Jan 1765, Samuel Dunlap & wf Mary of SC, to William Barnet of Meck., for ₤385 SC money...313 A on N side Cataba, adj. Andrew Pickins, William Davis, & William Hood...Samuel Dunlap (Seal), Mary Dunlap (Seal), Wit: William Richardson V. D. M., Joseph Pickens, Robert Ramsey.

Pp. 576-577: 25 Nov 1764, William Cleghorn of Meck., to John Bowers of same, for ₤20...land on both sides Dutchman Creek, adj. Mathew Kuykendalls, 150 A, granted to John Lanham & sold to sd. Cleghorn...William Cleghorn (Seal), Wit: George Rutledge, Benjamin Armstrong, Mathew Armstrong.

Pp. 577-579: 16 Nov 1764, Dobbs & wf to James Meek of Meck., for ₤___...235 A on head branches ... (deed torn)...Wit: Richd Barry, Martin Phifer.

Pp. 579-581: 16 Nov 1764, Dobbs & wf to John Young, for ₤11 s10, 115 A...Wit: Richd Barry, Martin Fifer..

Pp. 581-583: 16 Nov 1764, Dobbs & wf to Paul Barringer of Meck., for ₤12s6...120 A on Dutch Buffelow Cr., adj. Charles Fishers...Wit: Richd Barry, Martin Fifer.

Pp. 583-584: 16(?) Apr 1765, John Walker of Meck., to Edmond Fanning of Orrange Co., NC, for ₤30...land on S side S fork Cataba, on both sides Little Creek, 390 A, sold by John Duhart & wf to sd. Walker, 29 Dec 1762...John Walker (Seal), No wit.

Pp. 584-586: 22 Feb 1764, Dobbs & wf to William Booth for ₤21s8 ...214 A on both sides Coddle Creek...Wit: Martin Fifer, Richd Barry.

Pp. 586-588: 25 June 1764, Dobbs & wf to John Polk of Meck., for ₤7s10...77 A on both sides mouth of Clear Creek...Wit: John Davis Junr., Arthur MacKay.

VOLUME 2

Pp. 588-589: 25 June 1764, Dobbs & wf to William Hays of Meck., for ₤26 s10...265 A on Buffelow Creek, adj. John Thompson Wit: Arthur MacKay, John Davis, Junr.

Pp. 590-591: 2 Mar 1764, Dobbs & wf to Lewis Road of Meck., for ₤12 s4...122 A on both sides Wolf Cr., a branch of Rockey River (end missing).

Pp. 592-593: 10 Feb 1765, Dobbs & wf to John Penny of Meck., for ₤15 proc. money,...150 A on both sides English Buffilow Cr...Wit: John Davis, Junr. Arthur MacKay.

Pp. 594-595: 10 Feb 1765, Dobbs & wf to Jacob Castor, for ₤7s8... 74 A on ridges between Cold Water & Dutch Buffilow Cr....Wit: Geo. Ownsby, Arthur MacKay.

Pp. 596-597: 25 June 1764, Dobbs & wf to Mark House of Meck., for ₤9s12...96 A on ridge between Adams Cr. and Dutch Buffilow. Wit: John Davis Junr Arthur MacKay.

Pp. 598-599: 10 Feb 1765, Dobbs & wf to Christian Barnhart of Meck., for ₤19s16...198 A on Little Cold Waters Cr., adj. Nicholas Cook...Wit: John Davis Jr., Arthur MacKay.

Pp. 600-601: 25 June 1764, Dobbs & wf to John Query, for ₤13... 130 A on Goose Cr., a branch of Rockey R...Wit: John Davis Jr., Arthur MacKay.

Pp. 602-603: 10 Feb 1765, Dobbs &wf to Adam Alexander of Meck., for ₤27s14...227 A on both sides Goose Creek (end mutilated).

Pp. 604-605: 25 June 1764, Dobbs & wf to William Query of Meck., for ₤10s12...106 A on waters of Goose Creek...Wit: Arthur MacKay, John Davis Jr.

Pp. 606-607: 25 June 1764, Dobbs & wf to James Harris for ___, 183 A on Clear Cr...Wit: Arthur MacKay, John Davis Jr.

Pp. 608-609: 25 June 1764, Dobbs & wf to William Huggins of Meck., for ₤9s6...93 A on Redy Cr., a branch of Rockey R... Wit: John Davis Junr., Arthur MacKay.

Pp. 610-611: 10 Feb 1765, Dobbs & wf to William Martin for ₤33s16 ...338 A, adj. William Penneys & David Russel(?)... Wit: John Davis Junr., Arthur MacKay.

Pp. 612-613: 10 Feb 1765, Dobbs & wf to Moses Shelbey of Meck., for ₤22s14...227 A on Caldwells Bever Dam branch of Rockey R., adj. David Coldwell...Wit: John Davis, Jr., Arthur MacKay.

Pp. 614-615: 25 June 1764, Dobbs & wf to John Coldwell of Meck., for ₤13s8...134 A on head of Coldwells Cr, the place where Lemmonds (Simmonds?) lived...Wit: John Davis Junr., Arthur MacKay.

Pp. 616-617: 25 June 1764, Dobbs & wf to Andrew Davis of Meck., for ₤20 s8 proc. money...204 A on both sides Redy Cr., S side Rockey R...Wit: John Davis Junr., Arthur MacKay.

VOLUME 2

Pp. 618-619: 25 June 1764, Dobbs & wf to James White of MEck., for ₤13s6...133 A on English Buffilow Cr., adj. Benja. Patton & Michael Leggits...Wit: John Davis Junr., Arthur MacKay.

Pp. 620-621: 25 June 1764, Dobbs & wf to Michael Legget, Junr., for ₤10s6...103 A on both sides Clear Creek...Wit: John Davis Jr., Arthur MacKay.

Pp. 622-623: 25 June 1764, Dobbs & wf to James Harris of Meck., for ₤28s6...283 A on both sides Redy Cr...Wit: John Davis Junr., Arthur MacKay.

Pp. 624-625: 25 June 1764, Dobbs & wf to Robert Camble of Meck., for ₤14s10...145 A on W side Coddle Cr...Wit: John Davis Junr., Arthur MacKay.

Pp. 626-627: 25 June 1764, Dobbs & Wf to Robert McMurray of Meck., for ₤6s4...62 A on S side Rockey R., both sides of the Road from Colonel Harris's to the meeting House...Wit: John Davis Jr., Arthur MacKay.

Pp. 628-630: 25 June 1764, Dobbs & wf to George Dry of Meck., for ₤13s10...135 A adj. Nicholas Corzines...Wit: John Davis Jr., Arthur MacKay.

Pp. 630-632: 25 June 1764, Dobbs & wf to Godfrey Lipe for ₤13s12 ...135 A on a branch of Dutch Buffelow Cr., Wit: John Davis ,Arthur MacKay

Pp. 633-634: 10 Feb 1765, Dobbs & wf to Nicholas Ross of Meck., for ₤30 s6...303 A on Coldwells Cr...John Davis, Arthur McKay, wit.

Pp. 635-637: 26 Jan 1765, Dobbs & wf to Turner Stafford of Meck., for ₤8...80 A on Reedy Cr... Wit: John Davis, Jr., Arthur MacKay.

Pp. 637-639: 25 June 1764, Dobbs & wf to Charles Polk of Meck., for ₤5s16...58 A in forks Goose Creek & Dutch Buffilow Cr...Wit: John Davis Jr., Arthur MacKay.

Pp. 639-641: 25 June 1764, Dobbs & wf to Nicholas Cook of Meck., for ₤34s2...341 A on Little C(oldwater?) Creek... Wit: John Davis Jur., Arthur MacKay.

Pp. 642-643: 25 June 1764, Dobbs & wf to Christopher Hardlocker, for ₤____ 105 A...Wit: John Davis Jr., Arthur MacKay.

Pp. 644-645: 25 June 1764, Dobbs & wf to Thomas Roaddy of Meck., for ₤10s16...108 A onClear Cr...Wit: John Davis Jr., Arthur MacKay.

Pp. 646-648: 25 June 1764, Dobbs & wf to James White of Meck., for ₤9s18...99 A known as Belly bentrim, on both sides Rocky R...Wit: John Davis, Jr. Arthur MacKay.

Pp. 648-650: 25 June 1764, Dobbs & wf to Charles Fisher of Meck., for ₤8...80 A on both sides Adams Cr...Wit: John Davis Jr., Arthur MacKay.

VOLUME 2

Pp. 650-652: 10 Feb 1765, Dobbs & wf to John Willson of Meck., for Ł4s8...144 A in fork of Buffelo & Great Cold Water Cr...Wit: John Davis Junr, Arthur MacKay.

Pp. 652-654: 25 June 1764, Dobbs & wf to Leonard Hartsel for Ł18s4 ...144 A on both sides Dutch Buffelow Cr...Wit: John David Junr., Arthur MacKay.

Pp. 654-656: 10 Feb 1765, Dobbs & wf to John Rodgers of Meck., for Ł28s2...281 A on ridge between Coddle Cr. & Buffelow ...Wit: John Davis,Jr. Arthur MacKay.

Pp. 657-659: 25 June 1764, Dobbs & wf to Michael Cline of Meck., for Ł10s14, 107 A on head branches of Adams Cr.... Wit: John Davis Jr., Arthur MacKay.

Pp. 659-661: 25 June 1764, Dobbs & wf to George German of Meck., for Ł8s2...81 A on both sides Rocky R...Wit: John Davis Jr., Arthur MacKay.

Pp. 661-663: 25 June 1764, Dobbs &wf to Godfrey Youte, for Ł10s16 ...108 A on both sides Adams Cr...Wit: John Davis Jr., Arthur MacKay.

Pp. 663-665: 25 June 1764, Dobbs & Wf to Mathew Stewart of Meck., for Ł10...100 A on both sides Goose Cr...Wit: John Davis, Junr, Arthur MacKay.

Pp. 665-667: 25 June 1764, Dobbs & wf to Charles Polk, for Ł8s4 ...82 A on both sides Crooked Cr., of Rocky R...Wit: John Davis Jr., Arthur MacKay.

Pp. 667-669: 25 June 1764, Dobbs & wf to Frederick Fisher, for Ł13s8 ...149 A on Ridge between Cold Water & Adams Cr... Wit: John Davis, Jr., Arthur MacKay.

Pp. 670-672: 10 Feb 1765, Dobbs & wf to John Hegler of Meck., for Ł25s10...255 A on Dutch Buffelow Cr...Wit: John Davis Jr., Arthur MacKay.

Pp. 672-674: 25 June 1764, Dobbs &wf to George Conder of Meck., for Ł10...100 A on a branch of English Buffelow Cr... Wit: John Davis Jr., Arthur MacKay.

Pp. 674-676: 25 June 1764, Dobbs & wf to Robert McMurray of Meck., for Ł15s10...155 A on S side Rocky River Wit: John Davis,Jr., Arthur MacKay.

Pp. 676-678: 25 June 1764, Dobbs & wf to William Wadington, for Ł6s6...63A on S side Rocky River...Wit: John Davis, Jr., Arthur MacKay.

Pp. 678-680: 25 June 1764, Doobs & wf to Henry Goldman of Meck., for Ł10s2...101 A on Little Coldwater Cr., adj. John Adam Blackwelders...Wit: John Davis, Junr., Arthur MacKay.

Pp. 681-682: 25 June 1764, Dobbs &wf to John Rodgers of Meck., for Ł8s4...82 A on both sides English Bufilow Cr...Wit: John Davis Jr., Arthur MacKay.

VOLUME 2

Pp. 683-684: 25 June 1764, Dobbs & wf to Moses Camble of Meck., for Ŀ6s2...61 A on ridges between English Buffilow & Cowdle Cr...Wit: John Davis,Jr. Arthur MacKay.

Pp. 685-686: 10 Feb 1765, Dobbs & wf to Samuel Patan, for Ŀ9s4...292 A between Buffalo Cr. & Coddle Cr....Wit: John Davis Jr., Arthur MacKay.

Pp. 687-688: 25 June 1764, Dobbs & wf to Peter Gizer, of Meck., for Ŀ10s2...101 A on both sides Rockey River...Wit: John Davis Jr., Arthur MacKay.

Pp. 689-690: 25 June 1764, Dobbs & wf to John Flemming of Meck., for Ŀ13... 130 A on ridges between English Buffelow & Coddle Cr...Wit: John Davis Jr., Arthur MacKay.

Pp. 691-692: 10 Feb 1765, Dobbs & wf to James Doherty of Meck., for Ŀ10 proc. money...100 A on the three mile branch of Rockey R....adj. James McClain...Wit: John Davis Junr., Arthur MacKay.

Pp. 693-694: 25 June 1764, Arthur Dobbs & wf to John Hughes of Meck., for Ŀ12s10...103 A on Ridges between English Buffalo & Coddle Cr., waters of Rockey R...on waggon road leading to Captain Fishers...Wit: John Davis Junr., Arthur MacKay.

Pp. 695-696: 2 Mar 1764, Dobbs & wf to Richard Reynolds of Meck., for Ŀ16s6...163 A on both sides Great Cold Water Creek...Wit: Martain Fifer, Richard Barry.

Pp. 697-698: 25 June 1764, Dobbs & wf to John Bost of Meck., for Ŀ22s6...223 A on both sides Adams Cr, adj. Caleb Blackwelders...Wit: John Davis Jr., Arthur MacKay.

Pp. 699-700: 25 June 1764, Dobbs & wf to George Crawford of Meck., for Ŀ23s14 proc. money...237 A on Reedy Cr. of Rocky R...Wit: John Davis Junr., Arthur MacKay.

Pp. 701-702: 25 June 1764, Dobbs & wf to Hugh Carothers of Meck., for Ŀ10s4 proc. money...102 A between English Buffalo & Coddle Cr...Wit: John Davis Junr., Arthur MacKay.

Pp. 703-704: 25 June 1764, Dobbs & wf to Jacob Rickey of Meck., for Ŀ24s8 proc. money...264 A on both sides Dutch Buffalo Cr...Wit: John Davis Junr., Arthur MacKay.

Page 705: 11 Apr 1765, Edward Crofts of Meck., to John Fondren, for Ŀ28 proc. money...land on waters of Fishing Creek on waggon road that leads from Kuykendalls to Charles town, north of Charles Baities, granted to Crafts 9 Nov 1764...Edward Crafts (Seal), Wit: James Hanna, William Price, John Thomas.

Pp. 706-707: 15 Apr 1765, Robert Crockett & wf Jean of Meck., to John Crockett of same, for Ŀ50...264 A including his own dwelling by virtue of a deed 1 Mar 1765...adj. Andw. Pickens on Waxaw Cr., conveyed by William Nutt...Robert Crockett (Seal), Jean Crockett (Seal), Wit: Robert McClenachan, James Miller, William Mecullah.

VOLUME 2

Pp. 707-710: 8 & 9 Apr 1765, Col. John Clark to Henry White for £200...500 A on S fork Cataba...granted to Samuel Wilkins 21 Sept 1751...John Clark (Seal), Wit: Robert McClenachan, Robert Quall (Q), Samuel Thompson.

Pp. 710-713: 7 & 10 Mar 1765, Allexander Osburn & wf Angess of Roan Co., to Matthew Bigger of Meck (lease s5, release £120)...530 A on W side Cataba, including the mouth of Crowders Creek between Cathys land & sd. river, granted to sd. Osburn 16 Nov 1764...Alexr Osburn (Seal), Agnus Osburn (Seal), Wit: Samuel Gingles, Adlai Osburn, Thomas Rees.
(This land now in S. C.)

Pp. 714-715: 25 Oct 1759, John Hamer, sheriff of Anson Co., to John Brandon...on 4th Tues. in Feb 1759 in Supreme Court at Wilmington, County of New Hanover, Bladen, Onslow, Duplin, & Cumberland...John Brandon recovered against James Carter of Rowan Co., £119...625 A on W side Cataba, below the Tuckeyseegey ford ...Jno Hamer (Seal), Wit: John Dunn, John Baily (Baity?).

(The remaining pages in the volume are fragmentary.)

Pp. 715-717: 16 ___ 1765, Alexander Lewis, Sheriff of Meck., to Abraham Alexander...on 15 Oct 1763(?) at Superior Court of Wilmington, for £119s16 proc money...against James Carter, good & chattles...667 A on S fork Catawba...Alexander Lewis Sheriff (Seal), Wit: Nathl. Alexander, Adam Alexander.

Pp. 717-719: 15 & 16 Apr 1765, Daniel Alexander of Meck., Joiner, to James Alexander of same, planter, (lease s5, release £20s5)...79 A granted to sd. Daniel 24 June 1762...Daniel Alexander (Seal), Wit: Nathl Alexander, Martin Fifer, signed in German.

Pp. 719-720: 15 Apr 1765, George Renick & wf Mary, to Lenard Killion, for £35...275 A on Killions Cr, adj. Forney's plantation...George Renick (Seal), Mary Renick (Seal), Wit: William Jones, Abraham Kuykendall (A).

Pp. 720-721: 28 Jan 1765, Robert Ramsey of Meck., to George White of same, for £40...200 A on both sides Cain Creek, granted 3 Feb 1754...Robert Ramsey (Seal), Margaret Ramsey (X) (Seal), Wit: Robert McClenachan, ___uel Thompson.

Pp. 722-724: 22 & 23 ___ 1765, Benjamin Alexander & wf Susannah, to Andrew Meek of _____ Prov. of Maryland, (lease s5, release £37)...land on _ side Cataba, on Fishing Creek, adj. Benjamin Lewis, granted 9 Nov 1764...Benjamin Alexander, Susannah Alexander (ℓ) Wit: Nathaniel Alexander, Moses Fergus___, __ses Meek.

VOLUME 3

Pp. 1-4: 1 Aug & 6 Oct 1767, William Graham & wf Jean of Meck., to James Bell of same, for £70...237 A, land granted to Graham __ Dec 1763, granted to James Pots 21 Oct 1758, and Samuel Ziklegg 25 Feb 1754...James Potts & wf Sarah by deed 21 Oct 1758, & Samuel Zikleg & wf Jean 11 Sep 1758 (1759?) [chain of title very confusing]...also states granted to James Pots 25 Feb 1754...William Grhame (Seal), Jean Grhame (0) (Seal), Wit: Francis Harris, Robt. Harris.

VOLUME 3

Pp. 4-5: 21 Jan 1768, James Hannah of Meck, to Nathaniel Henderson of Creven Co., SC, for ₤___ proc. money...land on Rocky Creek, above the place where Charles Kitchen now lives...200 A... James Hannah (Seal), Wit: Richard Henderson, Jno. Nicholes.

Pp. 5-7: 15 Jan 1768, David Reed & wf Rebecca of Meck, to James Hetherington of same, for ₤35 NC money...land on N side Broad R, E side Turkey Creek on Susannah Boals branch, between Robert Dicksons & Robert Harpers lines...conveyed by John McMillen to David Reed, granted to McMillen 6 Sept 1766, 200 A...David Reed (Seal), Rebecca Reed (X) (Seal), Wit: Robert Harper, Alexd. Harper. Proven Jan. Term 1768.

Page 7: 8 Dec 1767, Samuel Rotch Of Meck, to John Springstell of same, for ₤10...cow, horse, pewter dishes & plates, tea cattle (?), frying pan ...Samuel Roch (Seal), Wit: Abraham Alexander. Proven Jan. term 1768.

Pp. 8-9: 11 Jan 1768, Robert Leeper & wf Katherine Of Meck., to Andrew Armour of same, for ₤100...land on W side Cataba on Mill Creek, part of 3 tracts adj. McCullochs line, James Craigs line, 430 A...Robert Leeper (Seal), Catrine Leeper (K) (Seal), Wit: Hugh Wallace, Andrew Pattrick, Proven Jan. Term 1768.

Pp. 9-11: 9 Nov 1767, William Moore & wf Mary of Meck., to Adam Whisenant, for ₤51...300 A on Indian Creek that empties into Leonards fork, above Thomas Robertsons line, granted to sd. Moore L6 Nov 1764, adj. harphills line...William Moore (X) (Seal), Mary Moore (X) (Seal), Wit: none. Proven Jan. term 1768.

Pp. 11-14: 3 Dec 1767, David Mackey of SC, planter, to Jean Irwin, relict of Hugh Irwin, decd (lease s5, release ₤20)... 230 A on waters of S fork Catabo River, at the forks of fishing Creek Road...David Mackey(Seal), Wit: John Cathey, Ebenezer McAin, John Cathey, Junr. Proven Jan. term 1768.

Pp. 14-15: _____ 1767, Adam Wisenant of Meck, to Nicholas Wisenant, for ₤5...land on waters of long creek, 300 A where sd. Nicholas now lives...granted to sd. Adam 30 Oct 1765, adj. Hager ...Adam Wisenaunt (Seal), Wit: James Forsyth, Wm. Harris, Proven Jan. term 1768.

Page 16: 4 Sept 1768, Timothy Whill (?) of Meck., to James Foster of same, for ₤15...cattle and one dish...Timothy Whill (Seal), Wit: [German signature]. Proven Jan. term 1768.

Pp. 17-18: 13 June 1766, James Hannah of Meck to Robert Robertson, for ₤40...land on S side Fishing Creek, adj. Wm Hagerties & James Youngs lines...300 A, granted to Hannah 13 Oct 1765 ...James Hannah (Seal), Jean Hannah ( ) (Seal), Wit: Ralph Baker, Henery Williams. Proven Jan. term 1768.

Pp. 18-21: 20 & 21 Nov 1767, Jacob & David Ramsour of Meck, to Henry Holdman, Jr. of same, (lease s5, release ₤___) ...320 A on N side S fork & E side Clarks Creek, granted to Samuel Beason 30 Sept 1749, & conveyed to John Ramsour, Carpenter, 13 & 14 June 1754 & by sd. Jacob Ramsour as Exr. and legatee and sd. David as legatee...Jacob Ramsour (Seal), David Ramsour (Seal), Wit: Will Reed, Jacob Crosimore (Cresimore?), Proven Jan term 1768.

VOLUME 3

Pp. 22-25: 14 & 17 Apr 1759, Edward Boyl of Anson, to Thomas Gillespy of Rowan Co., (lease s5, release ₤40)...300 A on N side S fork Cautabo on hurts creek about 3 or 4 miles above Murles...Edward Boyl (G) (Seal), Wit: John Keer, John Cathy. Proven 24 May 1759 by John Cathey, Jas. Hasell.

Pp. 25-26: 7 Sept 1767, Charles Hart & wf Klera of Meck, to Mathias Beaver, for ₤200...(later says Mathias Barringer)... 250 A on both sides Dutch Buffelow Creek, grant made by Gov. of SC, 13 Aug 1762, & since by the extention of the line hath fallen into NC, enrolled at Auditors office at Wilmington 28 Apr 1767... Charles Hart (π) (Seal), Kelra Hart (K) (Seal), Wit: John Phifer, Caleb Phifer, Andrew Sits(?). Proven Jan. term 1768.
    [Grant to Charles Hart, SC Colonial Grants, Vol. 10, p. 298, dated 30 Aug 1762; Plat in Volume 7, p. 258, dated 30 Sept 1756, on Dutch Buffalo, a branch of Rockey River...vacant on all sides...Jno Carmichael, Dep. Sur. SC Council Journal, Vol. 25, p. 350, dated 7 Sept 1756, lists Charles Hart as applying for 250 acres on family right, indicating that there would be he and three others in the family. His name appears again on the same list for 200 acres. This may be an error, however.]

Pp. 26-27: 29 Jan 1767, Henry Eustace McCulloh to John Fields of Meck, school master, for ₤30 proc. money...land adj. Carradines corner...152 A...Henry E. McCulloh (Seal), No wit. Proved Jan. term 1768.

Pp. 28-29: 29 Dec 1767, Robert Harris of Meck, to William Sharp of same, for ₤80...land on Harrises creek of Fairforest, adj. John Parks, Bullocks, 250 A granted 6 Oct 1767...Robt. Harris (Seal), Susannah Harris (Seal), Wit: James McElwain, James Mays. Proven Jan. term 1768.

Pp. 29-30: 18 Feb 1767, Godfrey Lipe of Meck to Lennard Starens for ₤34...136 A on Dutch Buffalo Creek...John Go---- Lipe [german signature], Barbara Lipe (B) (Seal), Wit: Samuel Patton, John Fifer, and one German signature. Proven Jan. term 1768.

Pp. 30-33: 1 & 2 Dec 1767, Benjamin Lewis of Meck, Gent. to James Murphy of same (lease s5, release ₤102 s10)...450 A in Meck & perhaps falling into SC...on head of S fork Fishing Creek, adj. Mathew Clement...granted to sd. Lewis, 31 Mar 1753...Benj. Lewis (Seal), Wit: James Hannah, John Martin, Richard Saddler. Proven Jan. term 1768.
    [This land wholly in present SC.]

Pp. 34-35: 10 Sept 1767, John McMullin of Meck., to David Reed of same, for ₤70...land on N side Broad River, E side Turkey Creek on Susy Boals branch, adj. Robert Dickson...200 A granted to sd. McMullin 26 Sept 1766...John McMillan (Seal), Wit: Matt. Floyd, William McMillan, Proven Jan. term 1768.

Pp. 36-37: 14 Dec 1767, Samuel Gay of Meck., planter, to Thomas Rayne of same, for ₤10...200 A on Fishing Creek, adj. McNaub, granted to Thomas Rayne 21 Apr 1764...Samuel Gay (S) (Seal), Wit: John Taggert, Hugh Brattain.

VOLUME 3

Pp. 37-40: 21 & 22 Oct 1767, Amos Byrd & wf Sarah of Meck., weaver, to Philip Anthony of Township of Lyon, Northampton Co., Pa., (lease s5, release ₤90)...200 A in Meck., formerly called Anson & Rowan Counties, on S fork Clarks Creek, N side Cataba... part of 400 A that Alexander Whitely sold to John Thomasson & then to sd. Byrd, granted to William Sherrill, 13 Sept 1749... Amous Byrd (Seal), Sarah Byrd (𝓛) (Seal), Wit: _____, George _____, Jacob _____ [all German signatures]. Proven Jan term 1768.

Pp. 40-43: 12 & 13 Jan 1767, John Walker of Meck., Gent., to William Berry of same, (lease s5, release ₤25)...250 A on a branch of Mountain Creek, adj. Alexander McConnel, granted to David John 17 May 1754 & deeded to Walker 26 & 27 Oct 1763...John Walker (Seal), Wit: Jacob Coburn, Benj. Grubb, Alexander Gilleland. Proven Jan. term 1768.

Pp. 44-45: 20 Jan 1768, David Alexander of Meck., to Zacheus Wilson of same, for ₤50...land on S side Coddle Creek, subdivided from McCulloh's tract or NE Barony, on the Great Road ...155 A...David Alexander (Seal), Sophia Alexander (*) (Seal), Wit: Moses Alexander, Geo. Alexander. Proven Jan. term 1768.

Page 45-7: ___ 1766, James Armstrong & wf Elisabeth of Meck., to Samuel Rankin, for ₤50...land on W side Cautaba on Cookindols Creek...225 A granted to sd. Armstrong 2 Oct 1751...James Armstrong (A) (Seal), Elisabeth Armstrong (Seal), Wit: Andrew Hampton, Hace McWhorter. Proven Jan. term 1768.

Pp. 47-48: 20 Sept 1767, Henry Plyler of Meck., planter, to Henry Forrer (?), of same, for ₤35 s7...185 A on both sides Adams Creek, adj. Charles Fisher...Henry Blarlord (Seal) [German signature, probably Plyler]. Wit: Paul Barringer. Proven Jan term 1768.

Pp. 48-49: 14 Jan 1768, Josiah Black of Meck., to John Henderson of same, for ₤__, land on No branches of Cautabo, adj. John Hendersons, ____ A...Josiah Black, Wit:Richd Barry, Hugh Barry, Ann Barry. Proven Jan. term 1768.

Pp. 50, 51 & 52: 16 July 1767, John Walker of Meck., planter, to Alexander Gilleland, for ₤20...202 A, granted to sd. Walker 26 Sept 1766 on a branch of Crowder's Creek at Coburn's corner...John Walker (Seal), Wit: James Gordon, Robert Spurlock, John Robertson. Proven Jan. term 1768.

Pp. 50-51: 21 Dec 1767, Samuel Dobrun of Meck, to William Ray of same, for ₤50...272 A granted to sd. Cobrun 16 Nov 1764 on both sides N fork Crowders Creek...adj. Jacob Coburn... Samuel Coburn (d) (Seal), Wit: Richd Barry, Jacob Coburn, Hugh Barry. Proven Jan. term 1768.

Pp. 52-53: 16 Jan 1768, Joseph Jolley of Meck., cooper, to John Jones of same, planter, for s20...land on S side Thicketty Creek, part of tract granted to sd. Jolley 14 Spr 1767... Joseph Jolley (Seal), Wit: Henry Clark, Nath. Clark, Henry Kar. No prov. date.

VOLUME 3

Pp. 53-54: 16 Jan 1768, Joseph Jolley of Meck., cooper, to William Jolley, planter for s20...land on N side Thicketty Creek, part of 640 A granted to Joseph 14 Apr 1767, 400 A...Joseph Jolley (Seal), Wit: Henry Clark, Nathl. Clark, Henry Kar.

Pp. 54-58: 12 & 13 July 1765, William Welsh of Meck., to Nicholas Welsh of same, planter, (lease s5, release ₤40)...170 A adj. S fork Cataba on S bank, adj. James Sprots [?], corner, Joseph Milikons line, Thomas Potts...granted to sd. William by Aventon Sherrill 22 Jan 1756, granted to sd. Sherrill 28 Mar 1755 ...William Welch (Seal), Sarah Welch (S) (Seal), Wit: James Robertson, Alexander Lockart, Jonathan Robertson, William Dismunt (0), Proven Jan. term 1768.

Pp. 58-59: 7 Jan 176_, Thomas Ray of Meck., to Pattrick McDade of same, for ₤40...land on both sides S fork Cataba...100 A surveyed for John McKnitt Alexander...Thomas Ray (Seal), Wit: William Moore, David Alexander, Jacob Johnson. Proven Jan. term 1768.

Pp. 59-62: 9 & 10 Nov 1765, George Pope & wf Christiana of Rowan Co., to Matthias Probst of Lyon Township, Northampton Co., Pa., (lease s5, release ₤32)...325 A on an E branch of Clarks Creek about a mile N of Paul Anthony's place...granted to sd. pope 6 Apr 1765...George Pope (Seal), Christina Pope (X), (Seal), Wit: _____ Anthony [German signature], _____ [German signature], Jacob Quantone. Proven Jan. term 1768.

Pp. 63-64: 8 Sept 1767, Rodger Cook of Meck., to Frederick Hambright of same, planter, for ₤135...200 A adj. W side Cataba, including Joseph Hardens improvement where sd. Cook now lives... part of 400 A conveyed by Samuel unto John Kykendole decd, & then to Joseph Hardin, then to Rodger Cook...Rodger Cook (Seal), Wit: Benjamin Harden, James Anderson, James Cook, Abraham Lundes, George Lamkins. Proven Jan. term 1768.

Pp. 64-65: 19 Aug 1767, Leonard Dozer & wf Mary of Meck., to John Stroud of same, for ₤ ___, land on S side Cataba, adj. John Learges former line...290 A, granted to John Large 25 Sept 1754...Leonard Dozer (Seal), Mary Dozer (Seal), Wit: John Dozer, Leonard Wel [Uel?], (X). Proven Jan. term 1768.

Pp. 65-66: 11 Apr 1768, Hugh White of Meck., to Thomas McCulloh of same, for ₤11...land on E side Fishing Creek, adj. sd. Hugh White...Hugh White (Seal), Wit: George Gill, John Davis. Proven April term 1768.

Pp. 67-68: 9 Apr 1768, Adam Sides & wf Susannah of Meck., to George Sides of same, for ₤100 NC money...land on S side Cutabo, a N branch of Leonards Creek, 200 A adj. Lawrence Snapp...Adam Sides (Seal), Susanna Sides (X) (Seal), Wit: James Abernathy, Jacob Seids. Proven April term 1768.

Pp. 68-69: 5 Dec 1766, John Thomas & wf Jean of Meck., to John Read of same, for ₤62...land on S fork CAutabo, on Stoney branch, near John Beatys above the plantation John Little lived on, 100 A...granted to Charles, Thomas Beaty 31 Mar 1753, conveyed by them to sd. John Thomas 1 & 2 Dec 1754...John Thomas (Seal), Jean Thomas (Seal), Wit: Wm Dickson, John Fondren, Jo Dickson. Proven April term 1768.

VOLUME 3

Pp. 69-71: 6 July 1767, William Dickson of Duplin Co., NC to John Gorden of Halifax Co., Va., for Ŀ7 s10...land on Rocky fork of Fishing Creek, James Kuykandal corner, Prices line, Andrew Lucky's [?] corner...400 A granted to sd. Dickson 3 Dec 1763... Wm Dickson (Seal), Wit: John Thomas, John Fondren, Jo. Dickson.

Pp. 71-73: 9 Aug 1767, James Armstrong of Meck., to James Hanna of same, for Ŀ20...72 A on S side Fishing Creek at Vanon[?]s corner...adj. plantation where sd. Hanna now lives, formerly property of James Kuykendol & willed to his daughter Elisabeth, wife of sd. James Armstrong...James Armstrong (Seal), Wit: John Taggart, James Young, John Richman [?], Proven April term 1768.

Pp. 73-74: 23 April 1767, Thomas Beaty of Meck., to Thomas Morgan of same, for Ŀ40...250 A on both sides Humphries Creek, a branch of Fishing Creek, adj. 3 lines of Peter Kuykendol...Williams line...Thomas Beaty (Seal), Margaret Beaty (Seal), Wit: Thos Yeats, David Cherry, J___ Stallings (Ŧ), Proven April term 1768.

Pp. 74-75: 4 April 1768, Robert Morris & wf Mary of Crevan Co., SC, to George Gill of Meck., for Ŀ172 s10...land on N branch of S fork Fishing Creek...adj. Robert Brows, & John Davises lines...Robert Morris (Seal), Mary Morris (∩) (Seal), Wit: Robert Brown, Samuel Porter, Proven April term 1768.

Pp. 75-77: 18 Jan 1768, Martin Armstrong & wf Mary of Meck., to Robert Gabby of same, for Ŀ100...land on S side Cataba, on a branch of fishing creek, 260 A, Humphries branch...granted to sd. Armstrong 25 Sept 1766...Martin Armstrong (Seal), Mary Armstrong (X) (Seal), Wit: Abraham Kuykendol (8), William Haggarty (H), James Young. Proven April term 1768.

Pp. 77-79: 1 Sept 17__, Thomas Houston & wf Agnes of Meck., to Hugh McKain of same, for Ŀ130...350 A on Swearingham's branch of McCallpins Creek...by virtue of L & R, 23 Apr 1764... Thomas Houston (Seal), Agness Houston (1) (Seal), Wit: Henry Downs, Thos Harris, Joseph Kennady. Proven April term 1768.

Pp. 79-81: 4 Jan 1766, John Bahanon & wf Ann on Meck., to John Faris & James Faris of Meck., for Ŀ40...480 A on W side Cataba, opposite Wm Wilson, including the Great Island... granted to Samuel Bigham & Francis Beaty 16 Nov 1764, & then sold to sd. Bohannon 19 Apr 1765...John Bochanan (Seal), Ann Bohannan (A) (Seal), Wit: Joseph Carrol, Walter Davis, Proven April term 1768.

Pp. 81-82: 14 Mar 1768, Robert Harper of Prov. of SC, to David Stevenson of Meck., for Ŀ5 sterling...land on waters of Turkey Creek, north side of Morrises Mill branch...200 A granted 6 Sept 1766...Robert Harper (Seal), Mary Harper (Seal), Wit: Saml. Gay (S), James Stephenson. Proven April term 1768.

Pp. 82-85: 21 & 22 Mar 1767, James Stafford planter, of Meck., to William Adams, of same, for (lease s5, release Ŀ180) ...250 A on Rocky Creek adj. James Harris...James Stafford (Seal), Wit: Robert Harris, Moses Alexander.

VOLUME 3

Pp. 85-87: 16 Mar 1767, John Miller & wf Hannah of Meck., to Samuel Wilson of same, for ₤40...land granted to James Armor by L & R 16 July 1752, then to sd. Miller by L & R 10 Aug 1757, 315 A adj. John Price, Alexander Cathey...also land granted to Andrew Armour patented 10 May 1761, adj. to above tract...John Miller (Seal), Hannah Miller (Seal), Wit: John Alexander, Benjn. Willson Proven. April term 1768.

Pp. 88-89: 11 Apr 1768, Joseph Keller of Meck., planter, to John Richey of same, for ₤40...200 A on E side Catab, adj. John Richey, Millers, McCords...granted to William Watson 28 Feb 1754, sold to Benjamin Harden, then to sd. Keller...Joseph Keller (Seal), Wit: Francis Beaty, John Scott, James Richey.

Pp. 89-93: 27 & 17 Sept 1767, Niklos Frey of Meck., to Stofal Sigmon, late of Meck., (lease s5 release ₤20)...200 A where sd. Stofal now lives...granted to sd. Frey 21 Sept 1766... Nickles Frey (NF) (Seal), Magdalena Frey (⊙) (Seal), Wit: Matthias Barringer, Johannes _____ [German siganture] _____ [German signature]. Proven April term 1768.

Pp. 93-94: 28 July 1767, Richard Reynolds & Elisabeth of Meck., to Isaac Shine of same, for ₤60...163 A on Great Cold Water Creek...granted 20 Mar 1764...Richard Reynolds(Seal), Elisabeth Reynolds (X) (Seal), Wit: Martain Fifer, David Rees. No proving date.

Pp. 95-96: 9 Apr 1768, William Minter of Meck., to James Miles of Craven Co., SC, for ₤100...land on Turkey Creek, between Mathew Floyd & James Miles...granted to Minter 25 Apr 1767...William Minter (Seal), Martha Minter (X) (Seal), Wit: David Reed, William Johnston. Proven April term 1768.

Pp. 97-99: 7 Dec 1767, Elijah Massey of Kent Co., Maryland, to Thomas Huff of Rowan Co., NC, Carpenter, for ₤24 s10 ...land which Massey purchased of John Thomas, then Anson Co., adj. Henry Johnston, on S side Cataba, 448 A...Elijah Massey (Seal), Wit: Saml. Thompson, James McZachlin, Jonathan Huff.
    7 Dec 1767, Elijah Massey appoints Adam Torrance & George Davison of Rowan Co., NC lawful attorneys...attested to by Deus Delaney, Clk. Kent County. Entered in Meck., 19 Augt 1768.

Pp. 99-100: 22 Feb 1768, Hugh Beaty of Meck., planter, to John Sloan of same, planter, for ₤40...350 A on Paw Creek, land where he now dwells...adj. to land that Francis Beaty sold to Robt. McCord, Tools road, John Cathey...granted to sd. Hugh Beaty 6 Apr 1765...Hugh Beaty(Seal), Wit: James Beaty, Francis Beaty. Proven April term 1768.

Pp. 100-102: 14 Mar 1768, Roger Cook of Meck., to Frederick Hambright of same, for ₤15...92 A on S side Cataba, adj. Cunningham, Cathey...granted to sd. Cook 30 Oct 1765...Roger Cook (Seal), Wit: William Moore, George Lamkin, Saml. Price. Proven April term 1768.

VOLUME 3

Pp. 102-104: 9 Apr 1768, David Reed & wf Rebecca of Meck., to William Minter of same, for ₤100...land on Susannah Bowls Branch of Turkey Creek...granted to Reed 22 Apr 1767...David Reed (Seal), Rebecca Reed (X) (Seal), Wit: James Miles, William Johnston, Proven April term 1768.

Pp. 104-105: 24 Feb 1767, Geo. Aug Selwyn to John Black of Meck., for ₤2 s10...58 A...Wit: Tho Frohock, William Ffrohock. Proven April term 1768.

Pp. 105-107: 8 Apr 1768, Charles McLean of Meck., to John Willson of same, for ₤10 proc. money...land on S side Cataba, on a branch of Fishing Creek adj. Wm Watson, 100 A, part of 171 A granted to sd. McLean 16 Apr 1765...Charles McLean (Seal), Wit: Robert Irwin, John Jordan, Proven April term 1768.

Pp. 107-109: 18 July 1767, Edward Williams, farmer, to Nicholas Fry of Meck., for ₤20 proc. money...300 A on W side Clarks Creek, S side N fork Cataba...Edward Williams (Seal), Wit: Matthas Barringer, Amos Bird, Samuel Willson. Proven April term 1768.

Pp. 109-110: 1 Nov 1767, John Black of Meck., to James Cunningham, planter, for ₤30...64 A adj. Frederick Hambright, adj. land conveyed by Capt. Benjamin Harden to Francis Beaty...granted to sd. Black 28 Oct 1765...John Black (0) (Seal), Wit: Robert Sloan, Hugh Barry, Jno. Patton. Proven April term 1768.

Pp. 110-112: 1 Feb 1768, Jacob Miller of Crevan Co., SC, to Edward Given of Meck., for ₤50...240 A on E side Cataba, granted to Miller 27 Sept 1753...Jacob Miller (Seal), Wit: John Cathey, Jean Irwin, Samuel Given.

Pp. 112-116: 21 & 22 Jan 1767, William Watson planter, & wf Velate [Violet], of Meck., to John Ross of same, planter, (lease s5, release ₤800...400 A on main fork Turkey Creek, adj. George Davison, Richard Berry, granted to sd. Watson 13 Oct 1765 ...William Wattson (Seal), Vilatt Wattson (Seal), Wit: Charles Moore, Vilatt Duncan, Geo. Ross. Proven April term 1768.

Pp. 116-117: 13 Feb 1767, Geo. Aug Selwyn to John Clark of Meck., for ₤6 s_...130 A from tract #3...Wit: Tho Frohock, William Frohock. Proven April term 1768.

Page 118: 12 Feb 1768, Phillip Shearmann of Meck., to Dietrich Grairel [?] of same, for ₤6...a Black horse Colt 2 yrs. old...Phillip Shearmann, (Seal), Wit: William Grairel (WK), George Grairel (+), Proven April term 1768.

Pp. 119-120: 5 Apr 1768, Joseph Breedmore & wf Margaret of Meck., to James Moore, of same, for ₤12...land on W side Catabo, S side Beaver Dam Creek, 100 A...Joseph Bredmor (Seal), Margaret Bradner (Seal), Wit: James Campbell, Jno. McCulloh. Proven April term 1768.

Pp. 120-123: 9 Apr 1768, Alexander Lockart & wf Ann of Meck., to Jacob Pennington of Barkley [Berkeley] Co., SC (lease s5, release ₤300)...300 A on S side Broad River, on Kings River, adj. William Fergusons, granted to Lockart by patent 23 Feb 1754 ...Alexander Lockard (Seal), Ann Lockart (A) (Seal), Wit: Nicholas Welch, John Boyd.

VOLUME 3

Pp. 124-125: 14 Apr 1768, John Welch of Meck., to Hugh Quinn of same, for ₤100 proc. money...land on S side Broad River, on Crooked Creek, below Robert McAfersons survey...200 A, granted to John Alexander 24 Sept 1754...John Welch (Seal), Wit: Moses Alexander, Nicholas Welch. Proven April term 1768.

Pp. 126-127: 10 Apr 1768, John Anderson of Meck., to Hugh Nelley of same, for ₤20...200 A on Stoney fork of Fishing Creek, including Crabtree bottom...adj. Robert McClelland...John Anderson (Seal), Wit: William Neely, Henry Neeley.

Pp. 127-131: 26 & 27 July 1767, Matthias Clows of Meck., to Voluntine Krotz (lease s5, release ₤), 159 A on both sides Leepers Creek, granted to Clows by John Bumgarner 22 Mar 1764, granted to sd. Bumgarner 21 Dec 1763...Matthias Clows (M) (Seal), Wit: Gasper Clue, Johannes _____ [German signture], Samuel Saunders. Proven April term 1768.

Pp. 131-135: 29 & 30 1768, Christop Guire of Meck., to Peter Kries of same, (lease s5, release ₤)...150 A on W side Cataba on a branch of Middle Creek, granted to sd. Guies [?], 30 Oct 1756...Christoph Guiss (Seal), [Signed in German], Wit: Jacob Eberhart, Franz Mayr [German], _____[German].

Pp. 136-139: 10 June 1767, John Alexander & wf Elizabeth of Meck., to John Welch of same (lease s5, release ₤50)...200 A on S side Broad, both sides Crooked Creek below Robert Mcaferson, granted to Alexander 24 Sept 1754...John Alexander, (Seal), Elizabeth Alexander (A) (Seal), Wit: Nicholas Welch, James Foster. Proven April term 1768.

Pp. 140-141: 12 Nov 1767, Josiah Roberts & wf Mary of Meck., to James Carr of same, for ₤5...163 A on waters of Sugar Creek, sold by Henry E. McCulloh 14 Jan 1767...Josiah Roberts (+) (Seal), Mary Roberts (+) (Seal), Wit: Tho Polk, James Forsyth. Proven April term 1768.

Pp. 141-142: James Foster of Meck., appoints Thomas Polk & Moses Alexander to recover from William Goforth, _____ Lee & Andrew Neil, who are indebted to me...7 March 1768...James Foster (Seal), Wit: Richard Henderson, John Williams, Jr., John Fondron, Proven April term 1768.

Pp. 142-143: 16 July 1768, Hugh Pollock of Meck., Cordwinder, to James Foster, merchant, for s5...300 A on Henry River, being the S fork of Catawba including the mouth of Clubb Creek, granted to Polock 26 Oct 1767...Hugh Pollock (Seal), Wit: David Rees, Ezekiel Polk. Proven July term 1768.

Pp. 144-147: 24 Jan 1766, Moses Alexander, Sheriff of Meck., to John Fondren... a writ of fiery Facies issuing out of Inferior Court & Pleas & WS, 13 Jan 1766, on est. of Hugh Smith, including slaves & land...for ₤8 s9 recovered by James Wallace...200 A on Rockey Creek...Moses Alexander Shr. (Seal), Wit: Willm Ratchford, Jno. Sartain.

Pp. 147-148: 15 July 1768, John Hogan of Meck., to Moses Alexander, for ₤20...150 A on flat branch of Twelve Mile Creek, in New Provedence adj. James McClure, John Clark, & James Linn...John Hogan (Seal), Wit: John Nuckols, John Fifer, Proven July term 1768.

VOLUME 3

Pp. 149-150: 16 Mar 1767, Andrew McMillen Of Meck., to Moses Quarles of same, for ₤41...land on Wolf Creek that runs into Kings Creek, E side Broad...150 A granted to McMillan 1766...Andrew McMillen (Seal), Wit: Jenry Smith, John McMillen. Proven July term 1768.

Pp. 151-152: 15 July 1768, William Willson of Meck., to Moses Alexander of same, for ₤60...land on S side Broad in forks of Brows [sic] Creek, formerly surveyed for Edward McNeal, 302 A...William Wilson (Seal), Wit: John Buchanan, John Fifer. Proven July term 1768.

Pp. 152-154: 21 June 1768, William Black of Meck., to James Hannah of same, for ₤100...land on S side Broad River, on middle fork of little river about 3 miles from Robert Millers plantation adj. Cochrans ... 300 A, part of a grant to David Park 3 Feb 1754...William Black (Seal), Wit: Ralph Baker, Jabes Evans, David Adrian. Proven July term 1768.

Pp. 154-156: 22 June 1768, Benjamin Davidson of Meck., to John Beard of same, planter, for ₤5...land on both sides Little Cataba, adj. Samuel Gingles & John Beard, granted to sd. Davidson 26 Oct 1767...Benjamin Davidson (Seal), Wit: Hugh Barry, Frances Beaty, Proven July term 1768.

Pp. 156-157: 18 June 1768, George & Mary Huie of Meck., to George Dur [Den?] of same, for ₤30...100 A on E side Buffelow Creek...George Huiess [?] (German signature), Mary Huie (M) (Seal), Wit: John Ffifer. _____ (German siganture), Jacob _____ (German signature).

Pp. 157-158: 7 Apr 1767, Henry Smith of Meck., to John Russel of same, for ₤40...land on E side Broad River, above Wm Loves patent, including an improvement bought of Michael Taylor ...granted to sd. Smith 30 Oct 1765...Henry Smith (Seal), Ema Smith (A) (Seal), Wit: Thomas Chadwock, Nath: Clark, Reyderius Clark. Proven July term 1768.

Pp. 159-160: 6 June 1768, John Orr of Meck., to Alexander McCarter of same, for ₤14...160 A granted to sd. Orr 26 Oct 1767 on So branch of N fork Tyger River, adj. Alexander Vernon, Jno Miller & James Miller...John Orr (Seal), Wit: James McElwain, Esqr., George Story, William Young. Proven July term 1768.

Pp. 160-162: 17 May 1768, Robert Leeper & wf Katherine of Meck., to David Gordon of same, for ₤125...land adj. Cobus Cockendell [Kuykendall], below George Catheys on Rocky fork of Fishing Creek, granted to Leeper 30 Aug 1753...Robert Leeper (Seal), Cathrine Leeper (K) (Seal), Wit: Thomas Neel, Robert Harris, Matthew Armstrong. Proven July term 1768.

Pp. 162-164: 12 July 1768, David Huddleston, planter, to Meck., to John Armstrong, of same, for ₤30...350 A on S branch of Reynolds Creek, commonly called Camp branch, granted 10 Apr 1761 to sd. Huddleston...David Huddleston (OH) (Seal), Wit: Zach Bullock, William Huddleston. Proven July term 1768.

VOLUME 3

Pp. 164-166: 4 Dec 1767, Benjamin Phillips & Thomas Rayney of Meck., to John Fondren of same, for ₺7 s10...land on Fishing Creek, adj. John Thomas, 109 A granted to sd. Phillips & Rainey 26 Oct 1767...Benjamin Phillips (Seal), Rachel Phillips (Seal), Tho. Raney (Seal), Wit: John Taggart, John Moore. Proven July term 1768.

Pp. 166-167: 18 June 1768, Jacob Moyart & wf Margaret Of Meck., to George Huie of same, for ₺35 s10...140 A on both sides Dutch Buffelo Creek... Jacob Moyar (Seal), Margaret Moyar (Seal), Wit: John Fifer, [Also two German signatures].

Pp. 167-169: 19 Sept 1767, Moses Ferguson of Meck., Schoolmaster, to Samuel Bigham, Senr. of same, for ₺15...500 A on Steel Creek, adj. Samuel Knox, & Chronical [?], originally Bighams ...Moses Ferguson (Seal), Wit: Samuel Bigham, John Whitesill. Proven July term 1768.

Pp. 169-170: 6 June 1768, Moses Ferugson to Samuel Bigham Sr. for ₺50 [?]...200 A on Steel Creek, adj. Hugh Parks, James Carter, & Samuel Bigham...Moses Ferguson (Seal), Wit: Samuel Bigham, John Bigham, Jos: Lee. Proven July term 1768.

Pp. 171-172: 20 Apr 1766, John Macilmurry of Meck., to John Patton of same, for ₺100 [later says James Patton]...land on S side Allisons Creek, adj. Joseph Harden...240 A...John Macklemurry (Seal), Wit: Jno McCulloh, William Byers, John Willson. Proven July term 1768.

Pp. 172-174: 13 July 1768, John Fondren of Meck., to Peter Kuykendall of same, for ₺65...land on waters of Fishing Creek adj. Thomas Hawkins, 200 A granted to John Elliot 20 Sept 1766, & another tract on Fishing Creek adj. Dickies line...200 A, granted to Thomas Hawkins 13 Oct 1765...John Fondren (Seal), Wit: Zach Bulloch, Robert Harris, Proven July term 1768.

Pp. 174-175: 14 Mar 1768, Tobias Adcock of Meck., to James McKee, for ₺20...200 A adj. W side Cataba, granted 26 Oct 1767 to sd. Tobiah Adcock, adj. Benjamin Hardan...Tobias Adcock (Seal), Ann Adcock ( ) (Seal), Wit: John Scott, William Chronow. Proven July Term 1768. Robert Harris.

Pp. 175-179: 3 July 1768, William Welsh of Meck., to George Shipe of same, for (lease s5, release ₺23)...250 A on E side Clarks Creek, granted to sd. Welsh 15 Nov 1762...about a mile east of Direct Ramsours...William Welch (Seal), Wit: Will Reed, Daniel Hudson. Proven July term 1768. Robert Harris.

Pp. 179-183: 11 & 12 July 1768, Walter Davis & wf Rebecah of Meck., to Moses Ferguson of same, for (lease s5, release ₺ 100)...370 A on W side Cataba on Rocky Allisons Creek near William Patricks land in big Allisons Creek...granted to sd. Davis 16 Apr 1765...Walter Davis (Seal), Rebecah Davis (R) (Seal), Wit: Robert Ferguson, William McCulloh, Joseph Billings. Rec. July Term 1768, Robert Harris.

VOLUME 3

Pp. 183-184: 22 Mar 1768, John Hardan of Meck., to James Hannah of same, for ℔___ proc. money...205 A on fishing Creek between James Hannas and James Youngs, adj. Cobus Kuykendalls, Hardans line...granted to sd. Hardan 25 Apr 1767...John Hardan (Seal), Wit: James Wallace, John Fondren. Proven July Term 1768. Robert Harris.

Pp. 185-186: 16 July 1768, Thomas Polk and Abram Alexander of NC to James Forsyth of Meck.,for ℔3s10 proc. money... the sd. Polk & Alexander being Commissioners in trust from the Hon. Henry Eustace McCulloh Esq. as agent for George Augustua Selwyn, Esqr...lot adj. the Court House and prison of Meck. County in Charlotte on the NE side of Trade St. and SE side of the Court House frontings...Thos Polk (Seal), Abraham Alexander (Seal), Wit: Joseph Carrol, David McMichen, Jurates. Proven July Term 1768.

Pp. 186-188: 4 Nov 1767, Jacob Caster & wf Christian of Rowan Co., to George Plat of Meck., for ℔20 proc. money...74 A on Ridge between Coldwater and Duch Buffalo Creeks...deeded to sd. Caster by Arthur Dobbs & wf Justina 13 Feb _____...Jacob Castor (⌒) (Seal), Cristina Caster (+) (Seal), Wit: John Ffifer, John Fields. Proven July Term 1768.
END OF BOOK NO. 8

BOOK NO. 9

Pp. 189-192: 12 Jan 1767, George Augustus Selwyn of Glocester Co., Kingdom of Great Britain(as son & heir of John Selwyn decd), to Moses Ferguson of Meck.,...King George II, did grant of 3 Mar 1745 (O.S.) 100,000 A on waters of Santee or Catawba, on Johnson or Rockey River, called tract #3...by letter of attorney __ Feb 1763...for ℔30, part of tract #3, on Sugar Creek, adj. Samuel Carrol, John Carson & John Newman, 305 A...Geo: Augustus Selwyn (Seal), by Henry E. McCulloh. Wit: John Ffrohock, Thomas Polk.
The Clerks record of the probate of this deed is lost. Test. Wm B Alexander Clk.

Pp. 193-196: (Copied by order of Octobert Court 1807).
12 Jan 1767, Geo. Aug. Selway to Moses Ferguson... repeat of preceding deed.

Page 197: Geo. Aug. Selwyn to William McRee, for ℔55...270 A, Wit: John Ffrohock, Thomas Polk. Dated 12 Jan 1767.

Page 198:_____, 1767, Selwyn to John Kerr of Meck., for ℔60... 370 A.

Page 199: 11 Jan 1767, Selwyn to John Carson of Meck., planter, for ℔20...2__ A near Tygarts place... Newmans and Fergusons lines....

Page 200: 9 Jan 1767, Selwyn to John McKelwee of Meck., planter, for ℔30...300 A adj. Garrison.

Page 201: 13 Jan 1767, Selwyn to James Ormond, planter, for ℔17 ...160 A adj. James Steel.

Page 202: 7 Jan 1767, Selwyn to Henry Verner of Meck., for ℔36 ...305 A on McKnights Creek, adj. Kerr.

VOLUME 3

Page 203: 9 Jan 1767, Selwyn to James Moore of Meck., planter, for ₤14...140 A on Garrisons Creek.

Page 204: 7 Jan 1767, Selwyn to David(?) Kennedy of Meck., for ₤23...210 A on waters of Sugar Creek, adj. Kennedy and John Buchanan.

Page 205: 5 Jan 1767, Selwyn to Thomas Polk of Meck., planter, for ₤150... 1493 A on Garrisons spring branch. Wit: James Foster, John Ffrohock.

Page 206: 10 Jan 1767, Selwyn to Thomas Polk Esqr., of Meck., planter, for ₤14...143 A. Wit: John Ffrohock, James Stafford.

Page 207: 5 Jan 1767, Selwyn to Thomas Polk of Meck., planter, for ₤30s10...257 A on waters of Sugar Creek...Wit: John Ffrohock, James Forster.

Page 208: 7 Jan 1767, Selwyn to William Orr of Meck., for ₤6... 230 A on head waters of Sugar Creek, Wit: John Ffrohock, Thomas Polk.

Page 209: 9 Jan 1767, Selwyn to William Wilson, planter, of Meck., for ₤24...220 A adj. Moses Steel, Alexr. Starret, & Garrison on waters of Sugar Creek.

Page 210: 9 Jan 1767, Selwyn to William Wilson, planter, of Meck., for ₤20...200 A on both sides Sugar Creek.

Page 211: 20 Jan 1767, Selwyn to David Davis, planter, of Meck., for ₤18...242 A in both sides of Kings Branch, adj. Robert Campbell.

Page 212: 6 Jan 1767, Selwyn to Robert Elliot of Meck., planter, for ₤52...410 A on waters of Sugar Creek, adj. Henry Varner.

Page 213: 16 Jan 1767, Selwyn to John Johnston of Meck., planter, for ₤22s10...227 A on waters of McCappins Creek adj. John Culbertson.

Page 214: 7 Jan 1767, Selwyn to Alexander Starrit of Meck., planter, for ₤19...159 A adj. Garrison, Sprott, Wilson & William Starret.

Page 215: 8 Jan 1767, Selwyn to Ann Alexander of Meck., planter, for ₤30...302 A on waters of Sugar Creek.

Page 216: Selwyn to James Flannakan, 13 Jan 1767...for ₤25 sterling...240 A on Kings Branch, adj. Daniel Hudson....

Page 217: 7 Jan 1767, Selwyn to James Orr, Senr of Meck., planter, for ₤ 60...545 A adj. John McNils line, adj. Nath Orr, Abram Alexander.

Page 218: 7 Jan 1767, Selwyn To David Kennedy of Meck, planter, for ₤ 46...land on head waters of Sugar Creek below the meeting house, 310 A....

VOLUME 3

Page 219: 14 Jan 1767, Selwyn to David Parks of Meck., planter, for ₤32...321 A on head waters of Reedy Creek, adj. John Allen.

Page 220: 9 Jan 1767, Selwyn to William Beatey of Meck., planter, for ₤26 s5 ...271 A adj. Allen, Collins, & Thomas Polk.

Page 221. 14 Jan 1767, Selwyn to James Clark of Meck., planter, for ₤25...251 A adj. David McKey.

Page 222: 7 Jan 1767, Selwyn to William McCulloch, planter, for ₤ 26...237 A on both sides Sugar Creek, adj. Samuel Carroll, Robert Elliott.

Page 223: 23 Jan 1767, Selwyn to Jeremiah Routh of Meck., planter, for ₤10 s10...110 A adj. Gov. Dobbs line on Goose Creek.

Page 224: 12 Jan 1767, Selwyn to Ezekiel Wallace of Meck., planter, for ₤32...337 A on both sides of Campbells Creek adj. Robert Parks, Margaret Alexander, & James Sparks.

Page 225: 9 Jan 1767, Selwyn to Cutbert (?) Nicholson of Meck., planter, for ₤15...130 A on West branch of Sugar Creek adj. "Boundry line."

Page 226: 19 Jan 1767, Selwyn to John Newell Of Meck., planter, for ₤13...130 A on Goose Creek including his own improvements, near his own house.

Page 227: 13 Jan 1767, Selwyn to Margaret Donaldson of Meck., planter, for ₤16...160 A on head of Kings Creek adj. John Tay (Lor?).

Page 228: 14 Jan 1767, Selwyn to James Way of Meck., planter, for ₤23...227 A on the four mile creek adj. Henry Downs, Thomas Harris.

Page 229: 15 Jan 1767, Selwyn to Walter Beatey of Meck., planter, for ₤24...240 A on head waters of Campbells Creek, waters of McCappins Creek adj. Robert Sparks.

Page 230: 7 Jan 1767, Selwyn to David Garrison of Meck., planter, for ₤ 30...250 A on W side Abram Alexanders Mill Creek adj. Ebenezer Newton, Andw. Sprott, Alexander Starrett, William Wilson, & John McKelwee.

Page 231: 14 Jan 1767, Selwyn to Thomas Harris of Meck., planter, for ₤ 13...140 A on both sides 4 mile creek adj. James Ways.

Page 232: 8 Jan 1767, Selwyn to Alexander Campbell of Meck., planter, for ₤ 32...360 A on waters of Sugar Creek adj. James Norris, Morgan Alexander.

Page 233: 14 Jan 1767, Selwyn to John Flannigan of Meck., planter, for ₤18 sterling...190 A on waters of McCappins Creek near Flannagins place.

VOLUME 3

Page 234: 14 Jan 1767, Selwyn to Jean Flannagan of Meck., Widow, for ₤ 28...280 A on both sides McCappins Creek.

Page 235: 16 Jan 1767, Selwyn to David Moore of Meck., planter, for ₤12...117 A on McCappins Creek adj. Governours line.

Page 236: 7 Jan 1767, Selwyn to Evenezer Newton of Meck., planter, for ₤23...240 A on waters of Sugar Creek adj. Thomas Polk, David Garrison, George Allen, John McKelwee...near the Race paths.

Page 237: 13 Jan 1767, Selwyn to James Tate of Meck., planter, for ₤ 24...220 A on both sides four mile creek adj. James Johnston, Henry Downs, & John Ramsey.

Page 238: 12 Jan 1767, Selwyn to John Cooper Of Meck., planter, for ₤12 s10...138 A on Kings Branch adj. Robert Campbell, Kings line.

Page 239: 14 Jan 1767, Selwyn to John Parks of Meck., planter, for ₤ 30...290 A on waters of Sugar Creek and McCappins Creek.

Page 240: 7 Jan 1767, Selwyn to Nathan Orr of Meck., planter, for ₤ 50...440 A on Abram Alexanders Mill Creek, the head waters of Sugar Creek adj. William Orr.

Page 241: 5 May 1765, Selwyn to George Allen of Meck., for ₤16 ...157 A on both sides McKees branch, a fork of Reedy Creek near the Governors line.

Page 242: 10 Jan 1767, Selwyn to George Allen of Meck., planter, for ₤34...420 A on E side Sugaw Creek adj. Thomas Polk, William Alexander.

Page 243: 8 Jan 1767, Selwyn to Hugh Barnet of Meck., planter, for ₤ 19...190 A adj. Mrs. Campbells line, on waters of Sugar Creek.

Page 244: 8 Jan 1767, Selwyn to Robert Barnet of Meck., planter, for ₤ 17 s10...184 A on waters of Sugar Creek near Hugh Barnets, adj. Peter Garrison & others.

Page 245: 22 Jan 1767, Selwyn to John McCord of Meck., planter, for ₤10...108 A on head waters of Sugaw Creek adj. Thomas Kennedy & Mary McKee.

Page 246: 7 Jan 1767, Selwyn to Thomas Kennedy of Meck., for ₤ 26...243 A on waters of Sugar Creek adj. Barnet, McCord branch.

Page 274: 8 Jan 1767, Selwyn to Samuel Carroll of Meck., planter, for ₤ 28...280 A on both sides McKnights Creek waters of Sugaw Creek adj. William McCulloch, Henry Varner.

Page 248: 7 Jan 1767, Selwyn to Nathan Orr Junr of Meck., planter, for ₤ 28...260 A on Head waters of Abram Alexanders Mill Creek adj. Nathan Orr, Sr.

VOLUME 3

Page 249: 18 Jan 1767, Selwyn to Robert Campbell of Meck., for ₤ 20 sterling...200 A on both sides Kings Branch, adj. John Cooper & David Davis ...the Old Tradying Path....

Page 250: 24 Jan 1767, Selwyn to Robert Lockart of Meck., planter, for ₤16 sterling...160 A on both sides of McCappins Creek adj. James Ormond.

Page 251: 17 Jan 1767, Selwyn to Zebulon Alexander of Meck., planter, for ₤ 30 sterling...336 A on both sides Sugaw Creek.

Page 252: 13 Jan 1767, Selwyn to John Ramesy of Meck., planter, for ₤ 30 sterling...312 A on waters of 4 Mile Creek adj. Thomas Black.

Page 253: 13 Jan 1767, Selwyn to Thomas Dearmond of Meck., planter, for ₤ 11 sterling...107 A on both sides McCappins Creek on a Stony Hill between James Hull[?] and Thomas Dearmonds.

Page 254: 9 Jan 1767, Selwyn to John Starr of Meck., planter, for ₤ 24 sterling...240 A on McCappins Creek including his own improvement.

Page 255: 15 Jan 1767, Selwyn to John Black of Meck., planter, for ₤ __ sterling...100 A on waters of McCappins Creek including his own improvement.

Page 256: 16 Jan 1767, Selwyn to James McElwee of Meck., planter, for ₤ 12 sterling...129 A on waters of McCappins Creek adj. James Clark, including James Halls old place.

Page 257: 15 Jan 1767, Selwyn to William Pickens of Meck., for ₤ 10 sterling....101 A on McCappins Creek including his own improvement.

Page 258: 10 Jan 1767, Selwyn to Thomas Dearmond of Meck., planter, for ₤ 15 sterling...182 A on both sides McCappins Creek adj. William Flannagan.

Page 259: 6 Jan 1767, Selwyn to John Swann of Meck., for ₤3 sterling...534 A on McMichells Creek.

Page 260: 9 Jan 1767, Selwyn to John Allen of Meck., planter, for ₤ 50 sterling...546 A on waters of Sugaw Creek adj. Hezekiah Alexander & Joseph Sample.

Page 261: 9 Jan 1767, Selwyn to Joseph Priest of Meck., planter, for ₤ 20 sterling...226 A on branches of Sugaw Creek adj. John Newman.

Page 262: 14 Jan 1767, Selwyn to John Holloway of Meck., for ₤ 41 s5 sterling...425 A on waters of McCappins Creek adj. John McClure including Henry Pearsons old place.

Page 263: 7 Jan 1767, Selwyn to John Garrison of Meck., planter, for ₤ 50 sterling...400 A on waters of Sugaw Creek adj. Moses Steel.

VOLUME 3

Page 264: 19 Jan 1767, Selwyn to William Roberts of Meck., planter, for ₤ 17...176 A on the 4 mile branch including his own improvement.

Page 265: 21 Jan 1767, Selwyn to Robert Burns of Meck., planter, for ₤ 20 sterling....200 A on W side Sugaw Creek on a Ridge above Ezara Alexanders land...Flannagans open line.

Page 266: 13 Jan 1767, Selwyn to John McClure of Meck., planter, for ₤ 38...308 A on W side Sugaw Creek adj. Joseph Galbreath & John Henry.

Page 267: 8 Jan 1767, Selwyn to Joseph Kennedy of Meck., planter, for ₤ 28...242 A on both sides Four mile Creek above his house....

Page 268: 12 Jan 1767, Selwyn to Joseph Galbreath of Meck., planter, for ₤40 sterling....470 A on both sides Sugaw Creek adj. Samuel Carrol, William McCulloch, John McClure.

Page 269: 16 Jan 1767, Selwyn to Thomas Black of Meck., for ₤ 12 sterling...127 A on waters of 4 mile creek including his own improvement.

Page 270: 9 Jan 1767, Selwyn to William Starrett of Meck., planter, for ₤ 16 sterling...163 A on both sides Garrisons Creek adj. Thomas Polk, Andrew Sprott, & Allexander Starrett.

Page 271: 18 Jan 1767, Selwyn to Moses Steel of Meck., planter, for ₤23...236 A on waters of Sugaw Creek including his own Improvements.

Page 272: 13 Jan 1767, Selwyn to Henry Downs Esquire of Meck., planter, for ₤22...410 A on 4 mile creek adj. Samuel Nelson, Moses Craig, James Way.

Page 273: 14 Jan 1767, Selwyn to Jonathan Buckelew of Meck., planter, for ₤ 17...163 A on waters of McCappins Creek adj. James Clark.

Page 274: 10 Jan 1767, Selwyn to Abraham Miller of Meck., planter, for ₤ 24...241 A on McCappins Creek including his own improvements.

Page 275: 4 Jan 1767, Selwyn to William Pickens of Meck., planter, for ₤ 13 sterling...162 A on Beards Branch of McCappins Creek.

Page 276: 9 Jan 1767, Selwyn to John Dearmond of Meck., planter, for ₤ 15 sterling...144 A on both sides McMichells creek.

Page 277: 18 Jan 1767, Selwyn to William Flannagan of Meck., for ₤ 24 sterling...242 A on both sides McCappins Creek adj. Thomas Dermond.

Page 278: 8 Jan 1767, Selwyn to John Ford of Meck., for ₤ 37 sterling...392 A on waters of McCappins Creek.

Page 279: 14 Jan 1767, Selwyn to Richard Buckelew of Meck., for ₤ 45 sterling...465 A on waters of McCappins Creek.

VOLUME 3

Page 280: 9 Jan 1767, Selwyn to William Black of Meck., for Ł 14 sterling...147 A on McCappins Creek adj. Abraham Miller.

Page 281: 7 Jan 1767, Selwyn to David Hynes of Meck., for Ł 26... [later called David Haynes]...214 A on waters of Sugaw Creek adj. John Garrison.

Page 282: 15 Jan 1767, Selwyn to John Black of Meckl., for Ł 13 sterling...137 A on waters of McCappins Creek adj. Thomas Johnson.

Page 283: 9 Jan 1767, Selwyn to John Starr of Meck., planter, for Ł 8 sterling...81 A on McCappins Creek known as Loftons Bottom.

Page 284: 9 Jan 1767, Selwyn to John Starr of Meck., for Ł 23 sterling...230 A on waters of McCappins Creek including his Own Improvements.

Page 285: 8 Jan 1767, Selwyn to Isaac Edwards of Meck., Esquire, for Ł 25...190 A on waters of Sugaw Creek adj. Robert Elliot, William McCulloch.

Page 286: 10 Jan 1767, Selwyn to Isaac Edwards Esqr., of Meck., for Ł 13 sterling...115 A on both sides McMichells Creek.

Page 287: 6 Jan 1767, Selwyn to Andrew Sprot of Meck., for Ł 25... 203 A on E side Garrisons Creek adj. Thomas Polk, ___ Starret & others.

Page 288: 9 Jan 1767, Selwyn to James McCracken of Meck., planter, for Ł 16 sterling....168 A on head branches of Sugaw Creek adj. Robert Elliot.

Page 289: 8 Jan 1767, Selwyn to William Exevyor[??] of Meck., for Ł 22 s10....225 A on waters of Reedy Creek adj. Gov. Dobbs line.

Page 290: 14 Jan 1767, Selwyn to Arthur Alexander for Ł 20 sterling...268 A on Sugaw Creek adj. Samuel McClery.

Page 291: 7 Jan 1767, Selwyn to John Neel of Meck., planter, for Ł 45 sterling...414 A on Neel's branch on S side Reedy Creek of Rockey River, adj. James Wyley.

Page 292: 8 Jan 1767, Selwyn to Ezra Alexander of Meck., planter, for Ł 20 sterling...200 A on both sides Sugaw Creek.

Page 293: 12 Jan 1767, Selwyn to Robert Parks of Meck., planter, for Ł 45 sterling...432 A on waters of McCappins Creek.

Page 294: 14 Jan 1767, Selwyn to John Parkes of Meck., planter, for Ł 30...295 A on waters of Sugaw Creek.
[deed marked through]

Page 295: 19 Jan 1767, Selwyn to Thomas Houston of Meck., planter, for Ł 6 sterling...85 A on 4 mile Creek.

Page 296: 8 Jan 1767, Selwyn to Robert Robinson of Meck., for Ł 21 sterling...212 A on Reedy Creek adj. Thomas McCall.

VOLUME 3

Page 297: 8 Jan 1767, Selwyn to Margaret Alexander of Meck., widow, for ₺ 25...250 A on McCappins Creek adj. Alexander Campbell.

Page 298: 19 Jan 1767, Selwyn to John Beates of Meck., planter, for ₺ 10 sterling...130 A on Kings Branch adj. Margaret Donaldson, David Davis.

Page 299: 9 Jan 1767, Selwyn to William Hairston[?] of Meck., planter, for ₺ 10 sterling...100 A on Trips[?] branch.

Page 300: 12 Jan 1767, Selwyn to Robert Parks of Meck., palnter, for ₺ 20 sterling. 200 A on Campbells Creek, waters of McCappins Creek adj. Ezekiel Wallace & Henry Mitchell.

Page 301: 14 Jan 1767, Selwyn to James Maxwell of Meck., planter, for ₺ 10 sterling...177 A on Reedy Creek.

Page 302: 7 Jan 1767, Selwyn to John Neal of Meck., for ₺ 15 sterling...141 A on waters of Reedy Creek adj. his own old corner.

Page 303: 19 Jan 1767, Selwyn to Elijah Alexander for ₺ 21 sterling...232 A on both sides Sugaw Creek.

Page 304: 9 Jan 1767, Selwyn to John Springsteen of Meck., planter, for ₺ 24...284 A on waters of Sugaw and McMichells Creeks.

Page 305: 13 Jan 1767, Selwyn to Alexander Eakee of Meck., planter, for ₺ 21...205 A on waters of 4 mile creek adj. James Johnston, Samuel Nelson, & Henry Downs, Esqr.

Page 306: 12 Jan 1767, Selwyn to John Newman of Meck., planter, for ₺ 20 sterling...200 A on waters of Sugaw Creek adj. Henry Varnor, Samuel Carroll.

Page 307: 14 Jan 1767, Selwyn to William Steel of Meck., planter, for ₺ 17 sterling...167 A on waters of McCapins Creek near John Swans, on E side of his meadow branch.

Page 308: 9 Jan 1767, Selwyn to James McCord of Meck., planter, for ₺ 12 sterling...137 A on waters of Sugaw Creek adj. Joseph Lee, James Moore.

Page 309: 19 Jan 1767, Selwyn to John Buchanan of Meck., for ₺ 37 sterling...375 A on head branches of Sugaw Creek adj. Andrew Herion & Mr. Campbells boundry lind.

Page 310: 9 Jan 1767, Selwyn to William Henry of Meck, planter, for ₺ 15 sterling...175 A on McMichells Creek adj. David Davis, John Swann.

Page 311: 11 Jan 1767, Selwyn to Charles Alexander of Meck., planter, for ₺ 14 sterling...139 A on both sides Sugaw Creek adj. his own lines.

Page 312: 22 Jan 1767, Selwyn to Peter Garrison of Meck., planter, for ₺ 16...163 A on waters of Sugaw Creek adj. Robert Barnet, Arthur Garrison.

VOLUME 3

Page 313: 14 Jan 1767, Selwyn to Josiah Roberts of Meck., planter, for ₤ 17...163 A on waters of Sugaw Creek.

Page 314: __ Jan 1767, Selwyn to John Henry of Meck., planter, for ₤ 32 sterling...260 A on E side Sugaw Creek adj. Joseph Galbreath, John McClure.

Page 315: __ Jan 1767, Selwyn to John Henry of Meck., for ₤ 15 sterling...150 A on waters of Sugaw Creek adj. Joseph _____.

Page 316: 16 Jan 1767, Selwyn to Jane Craighead of Meck., Widdow, for ₤ 27...260 A, adj. Nathan Orr.

Pp: 317-318: 15 Jan 1767, Selwyn to Abraham Alexander and Thomas Polk of Meck., Esqrs. & John Frohock of Rowan Co., Esqr., 360 A, part of tract #3, for ₤ 90 proc. money. Wit: Math. McClure, Joseph Sample.

Pp. 318-321: By the King, a proclamation....Whereas Complaint Hath been _?__ by the several Nations and Tribes of Indians Bordering upon our Colonies & Plantations....that settlements are being made on their land and conveyences illegally being made...no grants to be made in Indians territory....16 July 1767.
    WHEREAS a Partition Line has been Run between the Westren[sic] frontier of this Province and the Cherokee Hunting Grounds, beginning at Reedy River, where the South Carolina and Cherokee Dividing Line Terminates Ruvving the North Course to Tryon Mountain of the Blue Ridge of Mountains, supposed to be sixty nine miles from the said River...all person settling beyond this line to remove themselves...no land will be granted within one mile of the aforesaid line....William Tryon.
    [The termination point on the Reedy River is in present Laurens County, South Carolina. This proclamation line forms a large part of the present boundary between Spartanburg and Greenville counties, S. C.]

Page 322: __ Jan 1767, Selwyn to William Smith of Meck., planter, for ₤ 17 sterling...162 A on McCappins Creek, adj. Abraham Miller, John Star.

Page 323: 13 Jan 1767, Selwyn to William Smith of MEck., planter, for ₤12 sterling...121 A on waters of McCappins Creek adj. Flannakin.

Page 324: __ Jan 1767, Selwyn to David Black of Meck., planter, for ₤ 14 sterling...145 A adj. W. Small.

Page 325: 16 Jan 1767, Selwyn to Andrew Rea of Meck., planter, for ₤ 21 sterling...200 A on waters of Four mile Creek adj. the Boundry Line, & Henry Downs.

Page 326: 19 Jan 1767, Selwyn to Robert Robb of Meck., planter, for ₤ 15 sterling...153 A on waters of McCappins Creek including his own Improvements.

Page 327: 4 Jan 1767, Selwyn to John McGinty of Meck., planter, for ₤ 32 sterling...321 A on waters of Sugaw & McAppins Creek adj. Alexander McGinty.

VOLUME 3

Page 328: 21 Jan 1767, Selwyn to John Rea of Meck., planter, for ₤ 30 sterling...306 A on waters of Four mile Creek adj. Andrew Rea, Moses Craige, & the Bounding line.

Page 329: 14 Jan 1767, Selwyn to Mary McKee, widow of Meck., for ₤ 33...331 A on waters of Sugaw Creek adj. David[?] Kennedy.

Page 330: 20 Jan 1767, Selwyn to Arthur Garison of Meck., planter, for ₤ 18...186 A on head waters of Sugaw Creek on the Old Trading Path near his field.

Page 331: 12 Jan 1767, Selwyn to John Parks of Meck., planter, for ₤ 18...190 A on waters of McCappins Creek adj. Margaret Alexander, Ezekiel Wallace.

Page 332: 14 Jan 1767, Selwyn to Joseph Lee of Meck., Silver Smith, for ₤ 18 sterling...185 A on waters of Garrisons Creek adj. James McCord, John Henry.

Page 333: 15 Mar 1767, Selwyn to Noble Osburn of Meck., for ₤ 15 sterling...158 A on waters of McCoppoins Creek.

Page 334: 19 Jan 1767, Selwyn to Patrick Williams of Meck., planter, for ₤ 14 sterling... 143 A on both sides 4 mile branch including his own Improvements.

Page 335: 12 Jan 1767, Selwyn to William Brown of Meck., planter, for ₤ 14 sterling....145 A on the Dividing Ridge between Shugaw Creek and McMickells Creek.

Page 336: __ Jan 1767, Selwyn to Alexandr. McGinty of Meck., planter, for ₤ 8 sterling...91 A on waters of Reedy Creek & McCappins Creek. Prov. Oct. 1767.

Page 337: 8 Jan 1767, Selwyn to Thomas Gribbill of Meck., planter, for ₤ 22 sterling...220 A on watters of McCoppins Creek adj. Richard Buckellew. Prov. Oct. 1767.

Page 338: 13 Jan 1767, Selwyn to James Johnston of Meck., planter, for ₤ 12 s10 sterling...120 A on waters of Four mile Creek adj. Samuel Nelson, John Ramsey. Proven October Term 1767.

Page 339: 19 Jan 1767, Selwyn to Alexander McGinty of Meck., planter, for ₤ 15 sterling...172 A adj. George Allen. Prov. Oct. Ct. 1767.

Page 340: 11 Jan 1767, Selwyn to John Frohock of Rowan Co., for ₤ 10 sterling...185 A on waters of 4 mile Creek known by the name of Saml. Lofton's Improvements. Wilmington, 27 Apr 1767, Acknowledged before M. Howard, Cf. Just. Wit: Thos Frohock, William Ffrohock. Note in margin: University land sold to John Stewart by Adlai Osborn Commissioner &c. July 31 1795 for ₤ 70 0 5 for 202 acres See plat No. 6.

VOLUME 3

Page 341: 7 Jan 1767, Selwyn to John Frohock of Rowan Co., for ₤ 16 sterling...327 A on waters of 4 mile Creek including his own Improvements. Wit: John Frohock, William Frohock. Wilmington, 27 Apr 1767, Acknowledged before M. Howard Chf. Just. Note in margin: University land sold to James Osborn in 1795 by Adlai Osborn Commissioner for ₤ 102 for only 303 A, see plat No. 16.

Page 342: 9 Jan 1767, Selwyn to John Frohock, for ₤ 5 s2...102 A on waters of Sugar Creek adj. John McClure & the Boundry line. Wilmington, 27 Apr 1767, Acknowledged before M. Howard Chf. Just.

Page 343: 10 Jan 1767, Selwyn to John Frohock, for ₤ 8...160 A on both sides Rockey Run, waters of McCoppins Creek. Wilmington, 27 Apr 1767, Acknowledged before M. Howard Chf. Just.

Page 344: 10 Jan 1767, Selwyn to John Frohock, for ₤ 9...167 A on waters of McCoppins Creek adj. James Holland. Wilmington, 27 Apr 1767, Acknowledged before M. Howard Chf. Just.

Page 345: 7 Jan 1767, Selwyn to John Frohock, for ₤ 8 s4...124 A on head waters of Reedy Creek adj. Nathan Orr Junr. Wilmington, 27 Apr 1767, Acknowledged before M. Howard, Chf. Just.

Page 346: 6 Jan 1767, Selwyn to John Frohock, for ₤ 16...317 A on Head waters of Sugaw Creek adj. John Buchanan, Miss Pennelope McCulloh's, James Orr & Nathan Orr. Wilmington, 27 Apr 1767, Acknowledged before M. Howard Chf. Just.

Page 347: 6 Jan 1767, Selwyn to John Frohock, for ₤ 6...118 A on waters of McMichaels Creek. Acknowledged before M. Howard, Chf. Just. 27 Apr 1767, Wilmington.

Page 348: 13 Jan 1767, Selwyn to John Frohock for ₤ 6 s5...125 A on both sides McMichells Creek. Wilmington, 27 Apr 1767, Acknowledged before M. Howard, Chf. Just. Note in margin: University land on both sides McMichaels Creek sold to Archabald Alexander by Adlai Osburn Commissioner 31 July 1795 for ₤ 61 10 0 for 147 acres---see Plat No. 5.

Page 349: 7 Jan 1767, Selwyn to John Frohock for ₤ 12...117 A on the Dividing Ridge between Sugaw and McMichells Creek near James Wilsons survey. Wilmington, 27 Apr 1767, Acknowledged before M. Howard, Chf. Just. In margin: University land...sold to Thos Kilpatrick by Adlai Osborn Commissioner 31 July 1795 for ₤ 40 1 0.

Page 350: 5 Jan 1767, Selwyn to John Frohock for ₤ 14... 290 A on waters of Sugaw Creek adj. John Buchanan, Andrew Heron, Joseph Sample, James Orr...Wilmington, 27 Apr 1767, Acknowledged before M. Howard, Chf. Just. Margin: Sold to James Maxwell by A. O. Commr. of the University for 296 acres.

Page 351: 6 Jan 1767, Selwyn to John Frohock, for ₤ 9...183 A on a branch of McCoppins Creek adj. James Parks line. Wilmington, 27 Apr 1767, Acknowledged before M. Howard, Chf. Just.

Page 352: 8 Jan 1767, Selwyn to John Frohock, for ₤ 17...145 A on waters of McCoppins Creek adj. John Holloway. Wilmington, 27 Apr 1767, Acknowledged before M. Howard, Chf. Just.

VOLUME 3

Page 353: 17 Jan 1767, Selwyn to John Frohock, for ₤ 60...850 A and 350 A over and above laid out for a Town and Town Common on waters of Neals and Garrisons Creeks adj. Thos Polk, James McCord, Joseph Galbreath. Wilmington, 27 Apr 1767, Acknowledged before M. Howard, Chf. Just.

Page 354: 6 Jan 1767, Selwyn to William Reed of Meck., planter, for ₤ 45 sterling...358 A on Wilsons Mile Creek below Willsons Saw mill. Proven April Term 1768.

Page 355: 23 Feb 1767, Selwyn to Robert Brown of Meck., planter, for ₤ 15 sterling...125 A on waters of McCalpins Creek adj. John Starr. Rec. April term 1768.

Page 356: 19 Jan 1767, Selwyn to Moses Craige of Meck., planter, for ₤ 10 s10 ster....111 A adj. Thomas Harris, James Way, Mr. Downs, John Rea on waters of 4 mile Creek. Rec. July term 1768.

Page 357: 6 Jan 1767, Selwyn to Joseph Sample of Meck., Blacksmith, for ₤ 30 sterling...270 A on Abm. Alexanders Mill Creek adj. Abraham Alexander, John McNit Alexander. Rec. Oct. term 1769.

Page 358: 15 May 1765, Selwyn to Thomas McColl of Meck., planter, for ₤ 55...485 A adj. James Wyley, a corner of the place John Neel lives on. Rec. Jan. term 1770.

Page 359: __ Jan 1767, Selwyn to Joseph Sample, for ₤ 17 sterling ...176 A on waters of McCoppins Creek Including his own Improvements. Rec. Jan Term 1770.

Page 360: 19 Jan 1767, Selwyn to Joseph Sample for ₤ 15 sterling ...151 A on waters of McCoppins Creek & the mill branch. Rec. Jan. term 1770.

Page 361: "H. E. McCulloh Power of Attorney to John Frohock--page 170."

Pp. 362-363: Henry Eustace McCulloh of the Province of North Carolina, Barrister, appoint John Frohock of Rowan County, my lawful attorney to receive all debts...5 Apr 1767...Henry E. McColloh (Seal), Wit: Lewis DeRosset, James Waller. Wilmington, 27 Apr 1767, Acknowledged before M. Howard,Chf. Just. N. C. Rowan County, Registered in Book no. 6, page 173. Test. John Beaty, Register.

END OF VOLUME III.
N. B. Beginning with page 197, all deeds bear the notation Mutatis mutandis.

VOLUME 4

Pp. 1-2: 21 May 1767, Robert Dickson of Duplin Co., N. C. to Alexander Dickson of same, for ℒ 20 proc. money...220 A on E side Turkey Creek & No side of Susy Boles branch adj. his own & David Reeds, granted to sd. Dickson 25 Sept. 1766...Robert Dickson (Seal). Wit: Wm. Dickson, Joseph Dickson.

Pp. 2-4: 21 May 1767, Robert Dickson of Duplin County, planter, to Joseph Dickson of same for ℒ proc. money...land between the Cattauba and Broad rivers on a branch of Allisons Creek, granted to Robert Dickson 24 Dec. 1763...Robert Dickson (Seal). Wit: Wm. Dickson, Alexander Dickson.

Pp. 4-5: 21 May 1767, Robert Dickson of Cuplin County to Edward Dickson of same for ℒ 60 proc. money...land on E side of Moores Creek, a branch of Broad River, granted to sd. Robert Dickson 19 apr. 1763...Robert Dickson (Seal). Wit: Wm. Dickson, Joseph Dickson. Proven July Term [year not given]

Pp. 5-7: 27 Jan. 1767, Henry Eustace McCulloh to Edmond Bearing for ℒ 40 proc. money...220 A on a branch of Back Creek...Henry E. McCulloh (Seal). Wit: John Ffrohock, J. McK. Alexander. Proven July Term, 1767.

Pp. 7-8: 27 Jan. 1767, McCulloh to William Alexnader of Meck., Black Smith, for ℒ 6 proc. money .60 A adj. Ezekiel Alexander on head branches of Mallard Creek...Proven July term 1767.

Pp. 9-10: 15 Jan. 1767, McCulloh to Matthus McClure of Meck., planter, for ℒ 5 s10...land on a branch of McDowells Creek, 110 A...Proven July Term 1767.

Pp. 10-11: 21 Jan. 1767, McCulloh to Andrew Bowmar (Bowman?) of Meck., for ___ proc. money...315 A... Proven July Term 1767.

Pp. 12-13: 21 Jan. 1767, McCulloh to James Peal of Meck., planter, for ℒ 112 proc. money...land adj. George Cathey, John McDowell, 625 A...Proven July Term 1767.

Pp. 13-14: 21 Jan. 1767, McCulloh to John McDowell of Mecklenburg Co., for ℒ 9 s 4...land adj. the Barrony line, 92 A...Proven July Term 1767.

Pp. 15-16: 28 Jan. 1767, McCulloh to John Wallace of Meck., planter, for ℒ 11 s 12...116 A adj. Gilmours(?) corner... Proven July term 1767.

Pp. 16-17: 21 July 1767, John McKnitt Alexander of Meck., to John Scott of same, for ℒ 5...200 A, the contents of a patent to sd. Alexander 20 Oct. 1765...John McKnitt Alexander (Seal), Jane Alexander (Seal). Wit: John Alexander, Joseph Cameron, Jacob Gardner. Proven July Term 1767.

Pp. 17-18: 2 Jan. 1767, John McKnitt Alexander of Meck., to William Thompson of same...for ℒ 60...land on head branches of Rockey or Johnston River, 131 A...Jno. McK. Alexander (Seal), Jane Alexander (Seal). Wit: William Sprot, Jno. Alexander. Proven July Term 1767.

Volume 4

Pp. 19-20: __ Jan. 1767, John Campbell by Henry E. McCulloh to John Wallace of Meck., for Ł 3 proc. money of NC...land on Mallard Creek, in Tract No. 4...Proven July Term 1767

Pp. 20-21: 21 Jan. 1767, Campbel by McCulloh to William Johnston of Meck., planter, for Ł 56 s 4...land on both sides Mallard Creek, 240 A...Proven July Term 1767.

Pp. 22-23: 27 Jan. 1767, Campbell to James Clark of Meck., planter, for Ł 3 s4 proc. money...land on head waters of Mallard Creek adj. his former survey, 37 A...Wit: Thomas Polk, Jno. McK. Alexander. Rec. July term 1767.

Pp. 23-25: 27 Jan. 1767, Campbell to Archibald Robinson of Meck., planter, for Ł 7 proc. money...land on head branches of Sugar Creek adj. Crocket, John Campbell's Barony Line, Robinson's former survey...80 A. Wit: John Ffrohock, Jno. McK. Alexander. Rev. July term 1767.

Pp. 25-27: __ Jan. 1767, Campbell to Kairns Henderson of Meck., planter, for Ł 13 proc. money...land on Head Branches of Mallard Creek, at or near Robisons line, 106 A & tract of 46 A...Wit: John Ffrohock, Jno. McK. Alexander [No rec. date]

Pp. 27-28: 27 Jan. 1767, Henry E. McCulloh to Denis McAfall of Meck., planter, for Ł 10 s 10 proc. money...land on McDowells Creek, adj. McMachan, 130 A...Wit: John Ffrohock, Jno. McK. Alexander. [No rec. date].

Pp. 29-30: 27 Jan. 1767, Henry E. McCulloh to John Dysart of Meck., planter, for Ł s 19 proc. money...land on Stoney Creek, at the Great Road, 185 A...Wit: John Ffrohock, Moses Alexander Rec. July term 1767.

Pp. 30-32: __ Jan. 1767, Campbell to Benjamin Alexander of Meck., planter, for s 38 proc money...land adj. Richard Robison's corner, in the Barrony line, 38 A...Wit: John McK. Alexander, Thomas Polk. [No rec. date]

Pp. 32-33: __ Jan. 1767, Campbel to Hugh Barnet of Meck., planter, for Ł3...land on head branch of Sugar Creek, adj. Mr. Selwin's line...Wit: John Ffrohock, Jno. McK. Alexander. Rec. July term 1767.

Pp. 34-35: 28 Jan. 1767, Campbell to Robert Crocket of Meck., for Ł 9 s 10 proc. money...78 A on a branch of Sugar Creek & another tract of 44 A on head branch of Sugar Creek adj. his own former survey...Wit: John Frohock, Jno. McK. Alexander Rec. July term 1767.

Pp. 36-37: 16 Jan. 1767, H. E. McCulloh to Benjamin Alexander of Meck., planter, for Ł 9 s 14 proc. money...land on both sides Mallard Creek, 391 A...Wit: John Frohock, Jno. McK. Alexander. Rec. July term 1767.

Pp. 37-39: 16 Jan. 1767, H. E. McCulloh to Benjamin Alexander of Meck., for Ł35 s 19...157 A on both sides Lockarts Creek... Wit: John Ffrohock, Thomas Polk. Rec. July term 1767.

Pp. 39-40: 16 Jan. 1767, H. E. McCulloh to George Ross of Meck., planter, for ____...land adj. James Alexander,

Volume 4

Ezekial Alexander, 110 A...Wit: John Ffrohock, Thomas Polk. Rec. July term 1767.

Pp. 41-42: 27 Jan. 1767, H. E. McCulloh to David Wilson of Meck., planter, for ₤ 60 proc. money...land adj. William Erwin, 215 A...Wit: John Frohock, Moses Alexander. Rec. July term. 1767.

Pp. 42-44: 26 Jan. 1767, J. E. McCulloh to Nathaniel Irwyn of Meck., planter, for ₤ 69 proc. money...land on N side Coddle Creek, on a branch of Rockey River, adj. corner of the tract Isaac Stanford lived on, adj. James Martin...Wit: John Ffrohock, Moses Alexander. Rec. July term. 1767.

Pp. 44-45: 26 Jan. 1767, H. E. McCulloh to Charles Harris of Meck., planter, for ₤ 6 proc. money...67 A...Wit: Moses Alexander, John Ffrohock, Rec. July term 1767.

Pp. 45-47: 20 Jan. 1767, Campbell to Isaiah Parker of Meck., planter, for ₤ 50 proc. money...land adj. Russell, John McK. Alexander, 300 A...Wit: John Allen, John Frohock. Rec. July term 1767.

Pp. 47-48: 28 Jan. 1767, H. E. McCulloh of James Martin of Meck., for ₤ 56 proc. money...land on Ostains branch, adj. David Reese, 224 A...Wit: John Frohock, Archbald Houston. (No. rec. date.)

Page 49: John Haggans of Mecklenburg Co., planter, to Thomas Polk, for ₤ 25 horse; for ₤ 12 watch; one waggon...for payment of a Note due 20 Sept. next...26 July 1767. John Hagans (Seal). Wit: Moses Alexander. Rec. July term 1767.

Pp. 49-51: 23 July 1767, John Moore of Meck., to Richard Henderson of Granville Co., N. C., for ₤ 20 proc. money...land on S fork Fishing Creek adj. Edward Lacey, James Moore on the waggon road...300 A...John Moore (Seal). Wit: John Dunn. Rec. July term 1767.

Pp. 51-52: 23 Jan. 1767, Selwyn to Capt. Abraham Alexander of Meck., for ₤ 20 proc. money...land adj. his other survey...108 A...Wit: Ezekiel Alexander, John Ffrohock. Rec. July term 1767.

Pp. 53-55: 27 Apr. 1767, Campbell to William McCulloh of Meck., for ₤ 28 sterling...land on Sugaw Creek, 347 A adj. Barony line...Wit: John Ffrohock, Ezekiel Alexander. Rec. July term 1767.

Pp. 55-57: 26 Apr. 1767, Campbell to William Carr, for ₤ 18 sterling...200 A surv. for William Alexander...Wit: John Frohock, Moses Alexander.

Pp. 57-61: 14 & 15 Jan. 1767, William Gardner of Meck., planter to Thomas Richey of same, cordwinder (lease s5, release ₤ 20 NC money)...400 A. on waters of Paw Creek adj. Mr. Selwyn & Joy lines, Maclaine, granted to Francis Beaty 19 Apr. 1763, & conveyed to Samuel Biggerstaff, then to Gardner...William Gardner (Seal). Wit: John Scott, Moses Scott. Rec. <u>January</u> term 1767.

Volume 4

Pp. 61-64: 16 & 17 Jan. 1767, John Scott of Meck., to Moses Scott of same, planter, for (lease s5, release ₤ 20 N.C. money)...100 A on both sides Long Creek, part of 300 A granted to sd. John Scott, 10 Apr. 1767...John Scott (Seal). Wit: John Henry, James Richey. Rec. July term 1767.

Pp. 64-65: 5 Jan. 1767, John Connelly of Rowan Co., planter, to John Reid of Meck., planter for ₤ 57 s10...land on S side Cataba River adj. Thomas Beaty, 660 A...John Connelly (Seal). Wit: Robert Cherry, Archibald Little. Rec. Jan. term 1767.

Pp. 66-67: 21 June 1766, Daniel Warlick, planter & wf Maria Barbar of Meck., to Tetter Havener of same, for ₤ 25...300 A granted to Warlick, 3 Apr. 1752 adj. Samuel Wilson, including sd. Tetter Haveners House...Daniel Warlick (Seal), Maria Barbara Warlick (C) (Seal), Wit: William Sims, ___ [German signature] ___ [German signature] Johan Ritzhaupt. Rec. Jan. term 1767.

Pp. 67-68: 7 Aug. 1766, Ewings Hathley of Meck., planter to Hugh Quin, for ₤ 26 proc. money...200 A on main Broad River below the Mouth of Buffalow Creek...Ewings Hatherly (E) (Seal). Wit: Samuel Richardson, John Fondren. Rec. Jan. term 1767.

Pp. 69-70: 30 Dec. 1765, Robert Davis & wf. Mildridge of Meck., to George Davis of same, for quitrents to them pd... land on N side Cataba on S branch of Twelve Mile Creek, 1/2 mile from the Pee Dee, granted 26 Mar. 1755...Robert Davis (Seal), Mildred David (M) (Seal). Wit: George Davis, John Davies, Sarah Davies. Rec. Jan. term 1767

Pp. 70-73: 13 & 14 Jan. 1767, Jacob Wishenhunt of Meck., to Bryan Connelly of same, planter, for (lease s5, release ₤ 13 proc. money)...land on both sides Mulls fork, a branch of Elk Creek, 450 A...Jacob Wishenhunt (X) (Seal). Wit: Jacob Eagner, Matthew Wilson, John Connelly. Rec. Jan. term. 1767.

Pp. 74-77: 5 & 6 Jan. 1767, John Reed & wf Martha of Meck., to David Cherry & Robert Cherry, planters, of same (lease s5, release ₤ ___)...land on S side Cataba below the mouth of Davisons Creek, 275 A...John Reed (Seal), Martha Reed (Seal). Wit: John Connelly, Archibald Little. Rec. Jan. term 1767.

Pp. 77-79: 22 & 23 Sept. 1766, George Brown & wf Eve of York Co., Pa., to Robert Watkins & Francis Coot of Frederick Co., Md. (lease s5, release ___)...950 A on S side Katawba River and on Killians Creek, granted to Leonard Killian 30 Sept. 1749, conveyed to sd. Brown by L & R 1 & 2 Jan. 1754...George Brown (Seal), Eve Brown (E) (Seal). Wit: Absolem Bonham, ___ [German signature], Thomas Hill. Rec. Jan. term. 1767.

Pp. 80-81: 2 Feb. 1767, H. E. McCulloh to Alexander Monteith of Rowan Co., planter, for ₤ 55 s10 proc. money...land adj. to where the Widow Sharp now lives, George Cathey, 253 A... Thomas Frohock, William Frohock. Wit: Proven by William Frohock, in Salisbury Dist., N. C. before Edmd Fanning.

Pp. 81-82: 2 Feb. 1767, H. E. McCulloh to Henry Monteeth of Rowan Co., for ₤ 20 proc. money...land adj. tract that Robert Miller formerly lived on, adj. tract Beard now lives on, 462 A Same wit. and recordings as preceding deed.

Volume 4

Pp. 82-83: 2 Feb. 1767, H. E. McCulloh to William Robinson of Prov. of N. C., planter, for Ł 45 s 10 proc. money...land adj. Widow Sharp, George Cathey, on Sharps branch, 225 A... Wit: Thomas Frohock, William Frohock. Proven Salisbury Dist., before Edmd Fanning, 25 Sept. 1767.

Pp. 84-86: 8 & 9 Jan. 1767, Samuel Allen & wf Patience of Meck., Wheelwright to Francis Beaty of same, (lease s 5, release Ł 42 NC money)...202 A on E side Catawba on the branches of Beaver Dam Creek, adj. Alexander Dobbins old corner, sd. Allens corner, Beaty's corner...part of tract of ___ A granted to sd. Allen 24 Apr. 1762...Samuel Allen (Seal), Patience Allen (P) (Seal). Wit: James Beaty, John Beaty. Rec. Jan. term (1767).

Pp. 87-89: 7 & 8 Oct. 1762, William Hagarty & wf. Sarah of Anson Co., to Thomas Rutledge of Augusta Co., Va., (lease s5, release Ł 26 s10)...land on a branch of Fishing Creek, below Robert Leepers survey, 300 A, granted to the sd. Hagarty, 30 Aug. 1753...William Hagarty (H) (Seal), Sarah Hagarty (S) (Seal). Wit: John Beatty, Robt. Lowry, Richd. Barry. Rec. Jan. term. 1767. [For reference to the grant to William Hagarty, see my North Carolina Land Grants in South Carolina, II, p. 10]

Pp. 89-90: 21 Jan. 1767, James Scott of Meck., to Valentine Weaver of same, for Ł 7 s 10...77 A on both sides Great Cold Water Creek, a branch of Rockey River...James Scott (Seal). Wit: Martin Phifer, William Hays. Rec. Jan. term. 1767.

Pp. 91-92: 20 Aug. 1766, Jacob Kline & wf Catharine of Meck., to Jacob Tagget of same, for Ł 15 NC money...130 A about one mile above Paul Barringer's land on Lick Creek, granted to sd. Kline 9 Nov. 1764...Jacob Kline (J) (Seal), Catharine Kline (+) (Seal). Wit: Jno Phifer, William Hay, Caleb Rufer(?). Rec. Jan. term 1767.

2d part No 10 Book No. 10

Page 93: 24 Mar. 1767, Robert Walker [Waller?] to John Russel, for Ł 80 proc. money...431 A on Coddle Creek, conveyed by Arthur Dobbs to sd. Robert Walker, by deed 25 June 1764... Robt Walker (Seal), Fromey[?] Walker (Z) (Seal), Wit: A. Nash. "I saw Francis Walker sign only. RBT. Harris Jur." The Clerks record of the probate of this deed is lost.

Pp. 94-95: 27 Jan. 1767, H. E. McCulloh to David Rees of Meck., for Ł 3...land adj. Wallace, Campbell, 63 A...Wit: Jno. McK. Alexander, George Alexander. [No rec. date]

Pp. 95-97: 20 Apr. 1767, Ulrick Crowder of Meck., to George Leonard Sealer of same, for (lease s5, release Ł 60)...land on both sides middle Branch of Killions Creek, adj. Francis Beaty's line, it being the plantation which the sd. George Leonard Sealer now lives on including the improvements, 240 A, granted to Peter Sealer, decd. 10 Apr. 1761...Ulrick Crowder (Seal). Wit: Michael Rudisill [German signature], Martin Shutts. [No rec. date.]

Pp. 97-100: 12 Mar. 1767, John Potts & wf Mary of Meck., to Margaret Willson, daughter of Samuel Willson of same, for

Volume 4

(lease s5, release ₺ 30)...350 A on S side of S fork Catawba River, adj. Warlick, granted 30 Aug. 1753 to Samuel Hayard decd the said John Potts being Heir at Law to said Land and Tennements...John Potts (Seal), Mary Potts (M) (Seal). Wit: Benj. Willson. Rec. April term 1767.

Pp. 101-102: 25 June 1764, Arthur Dobbs & wf Justina, Gov. of NC, to James Russell of Meck., for ₺ 7 s 12 proc. money... 76 A on W side English Buffelow and waters of Rockey or Johnson [sic] River, place where he now lives adj. Benjamin Pattons line... Wit: John Davis Jurn., Arthur MacKay. Proved by oath of John Davis Junr., 21 Sept. 1764 before Maurice Moore.

Pp. 103-104: 28 Mar. 1767, John Clark of Meck., to Thomas Puliam of same, for ₺ 120...land on S side Green River, on both sides of White oak Creek, S side Warriors Branch by the Indian path, 640 A...John Clark (Seal). Wit: William Chames (?), Samuel Richardson, Philip Henderson (X). [No rec. date]

Pp. 104-105: 4 Mar. 1767, Moses Campbell of Meck. & wf Agness to Robert Campbell of same, for ₺ 16 proc. money... 60 A between English Buffalow and Coddle Creek...Moses Campbell (M) (Seal), Agness Campbell (C) (Seal). Wit: Robert Rogers, Wm. Scott. [No rec. date]

Pp. 106-108: 19 & 20 Feb. 1767, James Tate of Meck., "Phlm." to Francis Beaty of same, Collector, (lease s5, release ₺ 30) ...land on both sides Hickory Creek, above Beatyes other Lands including the forks of said Creek, granted to sd. Tate 30 Oct. 1763...James Tate (Seal). Wit: James Beaty, William McClain. Rec. Apr. term 1767.

Pp. 109-110: 9 Mar. 1767, Moses Moore of Meck., to Aaron Moore of same, for ₺ 20...land on both sides "Broad River second", 300 A granted to Moses Moore 30 Oct. 1763...Moses Moore (Seal). Wit: Jos. Nicholas, James Wylly. Rec. Apr. term 1767.

Page 110: Joseph Crawford of Meck., for ₺ 40 pd. by William Brown & William Linn of same...a Still Holding 120 Gallons... 20 Apr. 1767...Joseph Crawford (Seal), Wit: John Robison. Rec. April term 1767.

Pp. 111-112: 23 April 1767, George Alexander of Meck., to Alexander Kilpattrick of same, for ₺ 150 proc. money...land granted 25 Sept. 1766, on S side Green River on both sides White Oak Creek, 300 A...Geo. Alexander (Seal). Wit: Samuel Richardson. Rec. Apr. term 1767.

Pp. 112-113: 6 Oct. 1766, Adam Alexander & wf. Mary to John Cuthberson of same, for ₺ 30 proc. money...land on both sides Goose Creek, a branch of Rockey or Johnson River, 102 A, granted by deed from Arthur Dobbs, 25 Jan. 1764...Adam Alexander (Seal), Mary Alexr. (M) (Seal), Wit: Moses Shelby, Robert Harris Junr. Rec. April term 1767.

Pp. 113-114: 21 Apr. 1767, John Crocket & wf Margaret of Meck., to Benjamin Ford of same, for ₺ 30...100 A on ___ of Twelve Mile Creek on the Waggon Road, granted 16 Nov. 1764... John Crocket (Seal), Margaret Crocket ( ) (Seal). Wit: William McCarter, Daniel(?) McCay, Martha McCay (O), Rec. Apr. term 1767.

Pp. 115-118: 19 & 20 Jan. 1767, James Millican of Meck., to Alexander Love of same (lease s5, release Ł 30)...100 A on the waters of Fishing Creek adj. Dickies, Davison & Blaney Mills, granted to Millican 13 Oct. 1765...James Millican (M) (Seal). Wit: William Moore, Hugh Davis (X). Rec. April term 1767.

Pp. 118-119: 22 Nov. 1766, Rebecah Kuykendall of Meck., to James Williamson of same, for Ł 40...land on S. side Cuttaba River, on the waters of the So fork of Fishing Creek 300 A, adj. John Kykendal, Raineys line, granted to sd. Rebecah Kykendal 16 Nov. 1764...Rebecah Kykindal (R) (Seal). Wit: None. [No rec. date] [For reference to the within mentioned grant, see my North Carolina Land Grants in South Carolina, II, p. 55].

Pp. 119-120: John McClean of Meck., for Ł 20 N.C. money pd. by George Alexander...Horses branchded IG and FP...John McLean (I) (Seal). Wit: Nath Laird, John Irwin. Rec. Apr. term. 1767.

Pp. 120-123: 4 & 5 Mar. 1767, Adam Crain Jones & wf Mary of Meck., planter, to John Beard (lease s5, release Ł 67)...land on SW side S fork Catawba, next below Hugh Berry's Entry, and the land of John Armstrong decd, near the waggon ford including an improvement made by Wm. McDowell and the said Adam Crain Jones, granted to Francis Beaty 21 Apr. 1764, and by sd. Beaty & wf Martha to sd. Adam Crain Jones... Adam Crain Jones (Seal), Mary Jones(X) (Seal). Wit: James Beard, Alexander Robertson, Hugh Irwin. Rec. April term 1767.

Pp. 124-126: 25 June 1764, Arthur Dobbs & wf Justina to James Russell, for Ł 8 s 8 proc. money...84 A on both sides English Buffalow Creek adj. Michael Ligget Junr...Wit: Arthur Mackay, John Davis Junr., Proven before Maurice Moore.

Pp. 126-127: 6 Jan. 1767, David Standley of Meck., to David Ramsour of same, for Ł 45 proc. money...202 A on the S side S Fork of the Cataubo River on Long Creek, granted to James Armstrong 3 Oct. 1755 and conveyed to Francis Beaty and from him to David Standley...David Standley (D) (Seal). Wit: Jacob Ramsour, Elisabeth Thallman (X). Rec. 2 Sept. 1767.

Pp. 127-129: 19 Mar. 1765, H. E. McCulloh to John Wallace of Meck., for Ł 18 sterling...land on waters of Rockey River adj. James Wallace, 172 A...Wit: John Ffrohock, Geo. Alexander. Rec. Apr. term 1767.

Pp. 129-130: 26 Jan. 1767, H. E. McCulloh to William Gardner, planter, for Ł 37 s 17 proc. money... 163 A adj. Robertson's... Wit: John Ffrohock, Moses Alexander.

Pp. 131-132: 27 Jan. 1767, John Campbell to Thomas McClure of Meck., for Ł 17 s 1 proc. money...280 A on Mallard Creek adj. Barony line...Wit: John Frohock, Jo. McK. Alexander. Rec. Apr. term 1767.

Pp. 132-133: 27 Jan. 1767, H. E. McCulloh to Henry Sadler of Meck., for Ł 3 s 10 proc. money...34 A adj. Andrew Elliot, John Desar...Wit: Moses Alexander, John Frohock. Rec. Apr. term 1767.

Volume 4

Pp. 133-134: 26 Jan. 1767, H. E. McCulloh to Levinas Houston of Meck., for ₺ 91 s 16 proc. money...land adj. Hogshead lived on, 250 A...Wit: John Frohock, Robert Harris. Rec. Apr. term 1767.

Pp. 135-136: 27 Jan. 1767, H. E. McCulloh to Sevinis(?) Houston of Meck., planter for ₺ 10 s 10...210 A adj. tract he lives on...Wit: Robert Harris, John Frohock. Rec. April term 1767.

Pp. 136-137: 26 Jan. 1767, H. E. McCulloh to James Gardner of Meck., for ₺ 3 s 3...73 A adj. Charles Harris, Saml Brown, William Gamon(?)...Wit: John Frohock, Will Alexander. Rec. Apr. term 1767.

Pp. 138-139: 26 Jan. 1767, H. E. McCulloh to William Wallace of Meck., planter, for ₺ 7 s 1 proc. money...71 A adj. William Wallace...Wit: John Frohock, William Alexander. Rec. Apr. term 1767.

Pp. 139-140: 21 Apr. 1767, John Robertson of Meck., to William Suin(?) of same, for ₺ 20 proc. money...200 A granted 9 Nov. 1764 on the E side Cataubo River below Gidion Thompsons including an Impvt...John Robinson. Wit: Robert Harris, Jr., William Alexander. Rec. Apr. term 1767.

Pp. 140-142: 22 Apr. 1767, Adam Alexander & wf Mary of Meck., to James Willson of same, for ₺ ___...270 A on Goose Creek, sold by Arthur Dobbs 10 Feb. 1765 to sd. Alexander...Adam Alexander (Seal), Mary Alexander (M) (Seal). Wit: Will Harris, Robert Harris. Rec. April term 1767.

Pp. 142-143: 7 Dec. 1766, Thomas McCall & wf. Margaret of Meck., planter to James McCall for ₺ 50 proc. money...184 A on Reedy Creek on McKinleys Branch...sold by Selwyn to McCall 15 May 1765...Thomas McCall (Seal), Margaret McCall (8) (Seal). Wit: James Maxwell, Andrew Eliott, James McCaul. No rec. date.

Pp. 143-145: 10 Nov. 1766, Samuel Clegge & wf Jean of Meck., to Robert Henderson of same, for ₺ 25 s 10 proc. money... land granted to Francis Beaty 17 Apr. 1763 and sold to sd. Clegge by L & R 2 Feb. 1764, 200 A on E side Cataubo River on both sides Tools Road adj. Gideon Thompson, George Elliott, on Gau Creek...Samuel Clegge (O) (Seal), Jean Clegg (O) (Seal). Wit: Jonathan Clark, William Cathey (W), James Cathy (I). Rec. Apr. term 1767.

Pp. 145-148: 25 Jan. 1767, John Moore & wf Ann of Meck. to John Rockey of same (lease s 5, release ₺ 90)...200 A on E side Catawba, half of 400 A granted to William Wattson 8 Jan. 1754 and conveyed by Watson to Benjamin Harden, then to David Stanley, then to sd. Moore, adj. Patton...John Moore (Seal), Ann Moore (A) (Seal), Wit: Hugh Barry, John Barry, Thomas Richey. [No rec. date]

Pp. 148-151: 3 & 4 Mar. 1767, James Forden & wf Ann of Meck., Waggon Maker, to James Scott of same (lease s5, release ₺ 24).. 200 A on Beaver Dam Creek adj. sd. Gorden & McCallister, granted to Thomas Jenas 9 Nov. 1764 & part of another patent to Gorden 30 Nov. 1765...James Gorden (Seal), Ann Gordon ( )(Seal)

Volume 4
Wit: John Taggart, Archibald Cathy. Rec. Apr. term 1767.

Pp. 151-153: 26 Nov. 1766, Robert Harris & wf Margaret of Meck., farmer to John Wallace, son to Hugh Wallace of same, for Ł 20 proc. money...land between Crowders Creek and Catawba adj. Robert Leeper, James Craig, 200 A granted to William Dickson 22 Apr. 1763...Robert Harris (Seal), Margaret Harris (Seal). Wit: James Craig, John Harris [No rec. date]

Pp. 153-154: 18 Apr. 1767, George Crawford of Meck., to Robert McCurry of same, for Ł 5...land on both sides Reedy Creek, a branch of Rocky River, 237 A granted to sd. Crawford 5 June 1764...George Crawford (Seal), Elenor Crawford (Seal), Wit: James Harris, Robert Harris Jr., Rec. Apr. term 1767.

Pp. 154-155: A list of Goods and Chattles made by Moses Campbell to Robert Campbell by virtue of a Bill of Sale for Ł 15 proc. money... [cattle etc.]... 4 Mar. 1767...Moses Campbell (M) (Seal). Wit: Wm. Scott, James Scott. Returned this farr to the Deputy Recr. Oct. 1767.

Pp. 155-156: 19 Oct. 1767, John Armstrong & wf Mary of Meck., to John Boldridge of the Government of Pennsylvania and Co. of Lancaster, for Ł 50 proc. money...land on both sides Lipards Creek, granted 8 Oct. 1751 to Robert Leperd and conveyed to Hance Adam Snider 25 Feb. 1754 & by Snider & wf Sarah to John Walker then by Walker & wf Ellenor to John Armstrong, 150 A... John Armstrong (Seal), Mary Armstrong (Seal). Wit: Patrick McDavid, John Cunningham, William Moore. N. B. John Boldridge is to pay Quit Rents from 1765. Rec. Oct. term 1767.

Pp. 157-158: 19 Oct. 1767, John & Mary Armstrong to John Boldridge, for Ł 32 s 10 proc. money...land on E side Leepers Creek, adj. Clutes(?) line, Bostain Bosts line...Hance Adam Sniders line...granted to Hance Adam Snider, 125 A conveyed to John Walker & by him and wife Elizabeth to Armstrong. [same signatures and wit.] Rec. Oct. term 1767.

Pp. 158-159: 19 Oct. 1767, Bostan Best & wf Lesecat(?) of Meck., to John Baldridge of Lancaster Co., Pa., for Ł 50 proc. money...250 A on branches of Leepers Creek near Buffalo Branch, granted to sd. Best, 200 A...Boston Bess, Liestat Best (O) (Seal). Wit: Patrick McDavid, Nathaniel Ewing, William Moore. [No rec. date]

Pp. 159-163: 22 Oct. 1766, Francis Beaty & wf Martha of Meck., to Henry Pollinger of Berks Co., Pa., (lease s5, release Ł 180)...600 A on S side Catawba on Fishers or Haywards Creek adj. line of Samuel Hayward decd, granted to Francis Macklewean 17 May 1754, conveyed to Francis Beaty by L & R, 15 & 15 Aug. 1762...Francis Beaty (Seal), Martha Beaty (M) (Seal). Wit: John Beaty, Martin Colter, John Shuford, "wrote in Dutch." Rec. Oct. term 1767.

Pp. 163-164: 24 Feb. 1767, Selwyn to John Kerr of Meck., for Ł 4 s 10 sterling...land on Sugar Creek adj. Joseph Price & his own line, 98 A...Wit: Thos. Frohock, William Frohock. Rec. Oct. term 1767.

Pp. 164-165: 24 Feb. 1767, Selwyn to Martha Sprott of Meck., for Ł 6 sterling...land adj. John Barnet, 123 A...Wit: Thos Frohock, Wm. Frohock. Rec. Oct. term 1767.

Volume 4

Pp. 165-167: 24 Feb. 1767, Selwyn to David Parks of Meck., for Ŀ 2 sl...land on waters of Reedy Creek adj. his own & Walter Kerr, 40 A...Wit: Thos. Frohock, Wm. Frohock. Rec. Oct. term 1767.

Pp. 167-168: 24 Feb. 1767, Selwyn to John Davis of Meck., for Ŀ5 s 10 sterling...land on waters of Sugar Creek adj. Elijah Alexander, McElroy, 50 A...Wit: Thos Frohock, Wm. Frohock. Rec. Oct. term 1767.

Pp. 167-169: 24 Feb. 1767, Selwyn to Matthew Crewsell of Meck., for Ŀ 7 s 15 proc. money...155 A adj. his own line... [same wit as preceding]. Rec. Oct. term 1767.

Pp. 170-171: 24 Feb. 1767, Selwyn to John Dearmand of Meck., for Ŀ 5 sterling...land on waters of Sugar Creek adj. Zebulon Alexander, 105 A... [same wit as preceding] . Rec. Oct. term 1767.

Pp. 171-172: 24 Feb. 1767, Selwyn to Michael Barker for Ŀ45 land adj. Martha Sprott, 88 A... [same wit as preceding] Rec. Oct. term 1767.

Pp. 173-174: 24 Feb. 1767, Selwyn to James Sprott of Meck... land on waters of Kings Creek, adj. to the Kings line, 80 A.. [same wit as preceding] Rec Oct. term 1767.

Pp. 174-176: 1 Apr 1767, Selwyn to Hezekaih Alexander of Meck., for Ŀ 20...land adj. John McKnitt Alexander on branch of Abm. Alexanders Mill Creek, a branch of Sugar Creek adj. John Allens line, 300 A...Wit: John Frohock, Felix Kenan [No rec. date.]

Pp. 176-181: Anson County, N.C. 5 & 6 May 1760, Thomas Wright & wf Martha to David Adams, for L 53...land on Bear Creek, a fork of Cain Creek, which was Thomas Wright's old place, 134 A...Thomas Wright (T) (Seal), Martha Wright (M) (Seal). Wit: William Barr, James Gambell, John Bunten. Rec. Oct. term. 1767.

Pp. 180-182: 28 Sept. 1767, John Crawford of Anson Co., to Joab Mitchell of Meck., planter, for Ŀ 40 proc. money...land on both sides S fork Packolet, 300 A granted 25 Sept. 1766 to said Crawford...John Crawford (Seal). Wit: Alexr. Lewis, John Fondren. Rec. Oct. term 1767.

Pp. 182-185: 31 Aug. 1767, James Alcorn & wf Katrin of Meck., to Thomas Neilly of same, for s 5...land on s fork Steel Creek adj. Walter Davis, above Bigers & Knox...bought of John Henty, patent dated 21 Dec. 1763...James Alcorn (Seal), Catren Allcorn (A) (Seal). Wit: Thomas Polk, Saml. Wilson. Rec. Oct. term 1767.

Pp. 185-187: 21 Oct. 1767, Capt. Benjamin Harden of Meck., to Francis Beaty of same, for Ŀ 200...318 A adj. W side Cataba below the Tuckasegey ford, 118 A granted to Harden 15 Nov. 1762 & land adj. John Cathey, 200 A conveyed from John Cathey & wf Mary to Harden 17 Jan. 1763...Benjamin Harden (Seal). Wit: James Beaty, Henry Ferguson. Rec. Oct. term 1767.

Volume 4

Page 188: 31 Aug. 1767, James Allcorn & wf Katren of Meck., to Thomas Neely for s5...350 A granted to Walter David 19 Apr. 1763 on waters of Steel Creek adj. John Henry, John Buchanan's surveys...James Allcorn (Seal), Catren Allcorn (Seal). Wit: Thos Polk, Saml. Wilson. Rec. Oct. term 1767.

Pp. 189-190: 15 July 1767, James Miller of N. C. Cordwinder to Thomas Garril, planter, for ₤ 29...land granted to Miller 6 Apr. 1765, 300 A upon Armour Creek adj. Morgan & McCullough.. James Miller (Seal). Wit: John Cathey, Chas. Moore, Robert Miller. Rec. Oct. term 1767.

Pp. 190-193: 24 & 25 Sept. 1767, Francis Beaty & wf Martha of Meck., Collector & C. to John Harden of same (lease s5, release ₤ 50)...land on main fork of Kings Creek, next to the land of John Kuykendall decd, being the place formerly surveyed for John Moore next above sd. Kuykendall, granted to Beaty 19 Apr. 1763... Francis Beaty (Seal), Martha Beaty (M) (Seal). Wit: Robert Armstrong, Hugh Beaty, Benjamin Harden. Rec. Oct. term 1767.

Pp. 193-195: 20 Oct. 1765, Andrew Killion Sr. & Andrew Killion Jr. of ___ Co., N. C. to John Kinkaid, Shoemaker of Charlotta Co., Va. for ₤ 92...850 A on S side Cataba, granted to Killion Jr. 30 Sept. 1749...Andw Killian Sr. (Seal), "His name was Writen Dutch." Andw Killian Jur. (X) (Seal). Wit: Andw. Dunn, John Ramsey (M), Henry Hendry.

Pp. 195-199: [N.B. There is an error in the original pagination here.] 15 Oct. 1767, John Gullick of Meck., to Josiah Alexander of same, for ₤ 40...163 A on waters of Rockey River, adj. Alexander Osburn, Robt. Bravard, granted to sd. Gullick 3 Apr. 1752...John Gullick (Seal). Wit: Thos. Harris, Amos Alexander, Alexr. Lewis. Rec. Oct. term 1767.

Pp. 199-201: 20 Oct. 1767, Francis Beatey, of Meck., Collector, to Capt. Benjn. Harden of same, for ₤ 100 NC money... 300 A on Noble Creek, waters of Broad River including a great bottom, granted to sd. Beatey 6 Apr. 1765...Francis Beaty (Seal), Wit: James Beaty, Henry Ferguson. Rec. Oct. term 1767.

Pp. 201-202: 21 Oct. 1767, John McKnitt Alexander of Meck., to Margaret Conaldson, Widdow, of same, for ₤ 31...land on waters of long Creek adj. Matthew Patton, Francis Beatey, 300 A...Jno. McKnitt Alexander (Seal), Jean Alexander (Seal). Wit: William Thompson, Joseph McKinley, Thomas Bullion. Rec. Oct. term 1767.

Pp. 202-204: 21 Oct. 1767, Alexander Lockart of Meck., to Robert Wilson of same, for ₤ 45...land on W side Broad River, on both sides Abbysons [sic] Creek, 510 A granted to Samuel Gilkey 11 May 1753 & since conveyed by sd. Gilkey to sd. Alexander Lockart (Seal). Wit: Jno. McK. Alexander, ___ [torn]. Rec. Oct. term 1768 [sic]

Pp. 204-205: 11 Nov. 1765, William Anderson & wf Elloner of Meck., to Nathaniel Ervin of same, for ₤ 45 proc. money... land granted to sd. Anderson 16 Nov. 1764 in a fork of Hoils Creek a little above William Smith's land...William Anderson (W) (Seal), Elliner Anderson (O) (Seal). Wit: William Moore, John Armstrong, David Alexander. Rec. Oct. term 1767.

Volume 4

Pp. 205-208: 20 Oct. 1767, James Lynn & wf Sarah of Meck., Distiller, to Thomas Wallis of same, (lease s5, release ₤20) ...land on both sides Six Miles Creek, 500 A conveyed from Jonathan Lewis, the lower part of the trak [sic]...James Linn (Seal), Sarah Linn (Seal). Wit: James Gibson, Isaiah Fitten. Rec. Oct. term 1767.

Page 208: 4 April 1768, John Buchanan of Meck., Taylor, to Hez. Alexander, for ₤ 35...several horses and cattle (described) ...John Buchanan (Seal). Wit: Thos. Polk, James Jack. Prov. April term 1768.

Pp. 209-212: 30 & 31 Dec. 1765, James Wilson of Meck., planter, to James Withrow of same (lease s5, release ₤ 30 NC money)...250 A in Mecklenburg formerly Anson Co., including where Joseph Clark cut down some Trees between, Sprots, James Robinsons & Sherills lines, granted to said Wilson 4 Oct. 1753...James Wilson (Seal). Wit: John Patton, Thos Cohune, Jacob Wilson. Proven Oct. term 1767.

Pp. 212-214: 9 & 10 Sept. 1767, James McAfee of Mecklenburg Co., to Jacob Crissimore of same, (lease s5, release ₤ 100 proc. money)...James McAfee & wf Margaret...230 A on Clarks Creek, conveyed to the sd. Jas. McAfee by a deed from Saml Beson 27 Feb. 1756...James McAfee ( ) (Seal), Margaret McAfee ( ) (Seal). Wit: Thomas Cohune, Will Reed. Prov. Oct. term 1767.

Pp. 214-218: 14 & 15 Sept. 1767, Francis Beaty & wife Martha of Meck., Collector & C., to Thomas Little of same (lease s5, release ₤ 100)...450 A on Little Creek situated between John Beateys & Lawlers Old Places where Collo. Osbeans [Osburns] old Entry Law & on W side Catawba River, a little below the old Road that lead from John Beateys to Thomas Anderson old mill Place... granted to said Francis Beaty, 36 Nov. 1757, being the Land whereon the sd. Thomas Little now Dwells...Francis Beatey (Seal), Martha Beatey (M) (Seal). Wit: James Beatey, Archibald Cathey, Ralph Fleming. Prov. Oct. term 1767.

Pp. 218-221: 19 & 20 Feb. 1767, James Harris & wf Mary of Meck., to James Byers & William Curry Gentn., of same (lease s5, release ₤ 30)...300 A in Mecklenburg County (formerly Anson), on S side Packolat on a branch of Fairrist [sic] that runs into the North side of said Fair Forest Creek, granted to said James Harris 10 Nov. 1752...James Harris (Seal), Mary Harris (O) (Seal). Wit: John Graham, Thos. Harris. Prov. Oct. term 1767.
(This land now in S. C.)

Pp. 221-222: 7 Aug. 1767, Henry Smith of Meck., to William McMullan of same, for ₤ 40...part of a tract of land pattented in the Name of William Love of 400 A, 3 Sept. 1753, and since conveyed by John Love Heir to sd. William Love, unto Henry Smith...190 A...Henry Smith (Seal), Amy Smith (A) (Seal). Wit. Henry Clark, Matt. Floyd, George Gibson, Prov. Octr. Term 1767.

Pp. 223-224: 3 Jan. 1767, John Love of Meck., to Henry Smith for ₤ 37...land on both sides Broad River, including the Improvement Henry Smith now lives on, 400 A granted to William Love, 3 Sept. 1753...John Love (Seal), Martha Love (Seal).

Volume 4

Wit.: Nathl. Clark, William McKown. Prov. Oct. term 1767.
(This land now in S. C.)

Pp. 224-226: 9 & 10 Sept. 1767, James McAfee & wf. Margaret of Meck., to Jacob Crissimore of same, (lease s5, release Ł 50 proc. money)...235 A adj. Thomas Cohune, John Bradley, conveyed to sd. McAfee by Preston Goforth 10 July 1765... James McAfee ( ) (Seal), Margaret McAfee (M) (Seal). Wit: Thomas Cohune, Will Reed. Prov. Oct. term 1767.

Pp. 227-229: 9 & 10 Sept. 1767, James McAfee & wf Margaret of Meck., to John Bradley of same (lease s5, release Ł40)... 225 A adj. James Wilson, Thomas Cohune, Daniel Warlock... James McAfee (M) (Seal), Margaret McAfee (M) (Seal). Wit: Robert Blackburn, Will. Reed. Prov. Oct. term 1767.

Pp. 229-232: 15 & 16 Oct. 1767, Jonathan Robinson of Meck., to Phillip Anthony of same, for (lease s5, release Ł 60 proc. money)...600 A on S side S fork Catawba, adj. Jumping Run, granted to William Sherell 24 Apr. 1750...Jonathan Robinson (Seal). Wit: Will Reed, John Franklin, Isaac Johnson. Prov. Oct. term 1767.

Pp. 232-233: 22 Oct. 1767, Robert Wilson to Jacob Gardner, for [page torn] ...several tracts (1) 335 A on W side Broad River, being the upper division of a patent to Samuel Gilkey, 1753 adj. Robert Wilson, William Johnston (2) 428 A granted to Samuel Gilkey as above and conveyed to Alexander Lockert... Robert Wilson. Wit: Jno McK. Alexander, Robert Harper. Prov. Oct. term 1767.
(This land now in S. C.)

Pp. 233-234: 1 Sept 1767, Thomas Jarrel & wf Mary of Meck., to Aaron Alexander of same, for Ł 38...land on Armours Creek, adj. Morgan, McCullouh, granted to James Millar, 6 Apr. 1765 and conveyed to sd. Thos. Jarrel 15 ___ 1767... Thomas Jarrel (T) (Seal), Mary Jarrel (M) (Seal). Wit: Bartholomew Johnson, James Alexander, Andrew Downs (A). Prov. Oct. term 1767.

Pp. 235-236: 4 Sept. 1767, James Campbell & wf Jennet of Meck., to Thomas Nesmith of same, for Ł 47 proc. money...land on a Branch of Allisons Creek including in the Waggin [sic] Road, adj. John McKnitt Alexander, 230 A granted to sd. Campbell 16 Nov. 1764...James Campbell (Seal), Jenet Campbell (Seal). Wit: Jno McCulloh, Andrew Campbell. Prov. Oct. term. 1767.

Pp. 237-239: 7 Aug. 1767, George Smith of Rowan Co., planter to Conruth [?] Barns late of Mecklenburg Co., for (lease s5, release Ł20)...350 A where sd. Barns now lives, on a branch of Elik Crik including sd. Barns one improvement, granted to George Smith ___ Oct. 1765...George Smith in Dutch (Seal), Cadarina Smith (O) (Seal). Wit: Mathias Barringer, "A Dutch Name," Arthur Lockhart. Prov. Oct. term 1767.

Pp. 240-241: 22 Sept. 1767, Benige Pennington & wf Elizabeth of Meck., to James McClennan of same, for Ł50...land on W side Cataba on a Branch of Allisons Creek, 187 A...Beanige Penenton (+) (Seal), Elizabeth Penentown (+) (Seal). Wit: William Stevenson, John Potts, William Watson. Prov. Oct. term. 1767.

Volume 4

Pp. 242-245: 15 & 16 Sept. 1767, James Lynn & wf Sarah of Meck., Distiller, to Aaron Houston of same, (lease s5, release ₤ 30)...100 A, part of 470 A granted 6 Apr. 1765 to Alexander Lewis, conveyed to James Lynn 16 July 1765...James Lynn (Seal), Sarah Lynn (+) (Seal). Wit: William Gillespie, Isaia Fitten. Prov. Oct. term 1767.

Pp. 245-246: 20 Mar. 1767, William King & wf Mary Ann of Meck., to Andw. Nutt of same, for ₤ 40 proc. money...155 A, part of tract of 640 A on both sides Waggon Road & on N side of the Waxhaw Creek, adj. George McCamey...William King (Seal), Mary Ann King ( ) (Seal). Wit: Samuel Lofton, John McCulloh, William McCulloh. Prov. Oct. term 1767.

Pp. 246-248: 2 May 1765, Matthew Patton & wf Rebecca of Meck., Yeoman, to James Patton Esqr., of same, for ₤ 80 money of South Carolina...225 A on W side Catawba, part of 987 A sd. Culp now Dwelleth on, adj. John Lance...Matthew Patton (Seal), Rebecca Patton (Seal). Wit: Robert McClenackan, Robt. Patton, Prov. Oct. term 1767.

Pp. 249-251: 12 & 13 Aug. 1766, Samuel Allen of Meck., Wheel Wright, to John Giles of same (lease s5, release ₤ 37 s 10)... 250 A, on E side Catawba, part of 938 A granted to James Carter & John Linn Esqrs, 9 Apr. 1753, and conveyed by them to Edward Hughs & against conveyed by sd. Hughs of James Carter, and conveyed by a Sheriffs deed to John Brandon Esqr., then to Samuel Allen, on the branches of Bever Dam Creek adj. Richard Robinsons land...Samuel Allen (Seal). Wit: Samuel Bigham Senr., Samuel Bigham. Prov. Oct. term 1767.

Pp. 252-254: 27 & 28 Aug. 1767, Thomas Clark & wf Agness of Meck., planter to Matthew Russel of same (lease s5, release ₤85)...300 A on both sides Long Creek on E side Catawba, adj. Francis Beatey, John Anderson, originally granted to John Kennedy, 18 Nov. 1757 & conveyed by John Kennedy & wf Elizabeth to sd. Thomas Clark...Thomas Clark (C) (Seal), Agness Clark (A) (Seal). Wit: Ralph Fleming, Robert Campbell, Francis Beatey, Prov. Oct. term 1768.

Pp. 255-256: 19 Oct. 1767, Thomas Little & wf Elizabeth of Meck., to John Kilpatrick of Rowan Co., for ₤ 70 NC money... 225 A on W side Catauba River, on the branches of Little Creek, granted to Francis Beatey for 450 A, 26 Nov. 1764... Thomas Little (Seal), Elizabeth Little (O) (Seal). Wit.: Archibald Little, Wm. Ramsey, Henry Hendry. Prov. Oct. term. 1767.

Pp. 256-259: 5 & 6 Oct. 1767, Bryan Connelly & wf Mary of Rowan Co., planter, to Gabriel Fry of Prov. of Pennsylvania, planter, (lease s5, release ₤ 65)...450 A in Meck. Co., on both sides of Mulls fork a branch of Elk Creek, being a tract of land made over by Jacob Wishinhunt by deed 1766 to sd. Connelly...Bryan Connelly (Seal), Mary Connelly (X) (Seal). Wit: Matthias Barringer, "A Name Write in Dutch,", John Els (O) Prov. Oct. term 1767.

Pp. 260-261: 8 May 1767, George Lamkin of Meck., to James Johnston of same, for ₤ 111 s 4 d 8...sale of slaves (named)... George Lamkin (Seal). Wit: William Lamkin, Henry Hendry Junr., Henry Hendry. Prov. Jan. term 1768.

Volume 4

Page 262: 11 June 1765, Walter Davis & wf Rebecah of Meck., to James Alcorn of same, for s5 sterling...land on waters of Steel Creek adj. John Hendry, John Bauhannons Surveys...Walter Davis (Seal), Rebecah Davis (Seal). Wit: Thos Polk, John Davis, James Armour. No rec. date given.

Page 263: 28 Jan. 1767, H. E. McCulloh to John McKnit Alexander of Meck., for L 18 proc. money...land on head branch of McDowels Creek in Tract No. 4... 270 A...Henry E. McCulloh (Seal). Wit: John Frohock, Robert Harris. Prov. Oct. term. 1767. Enroled in the Office of the Auditor General at Newbern 7 Dec. 1770. per Charles Herron Audr.

Pp. 264-265: 11 June 1765, Walter David & wf Rebecah to James Alcorn, for L 36 ... [release of land on p. 262] ..350 A..

Pp. 266-269: 12 Oct. 1767, John Bradley & wf Martha of Meck., to Henry Holdman Sr., of same (lease s5, release L 63 proc. money)...225 A adj. James Willsons, Thomas Cahoon, Daniel Warlock...sold to Bradley by L & R by James McAfee & wf Margaret...John Bradley (J) (Seal), Martha Bradley (O) (Seal). Wit: Will Reed, Jacob Ramsour. Prov. Jan. term 1768.

Pp. 269-270: 25 Dec. 1764, John Hendry & wf Martha of Meck., to James Alcorn, late of same, for L 40...land adj. Walter Davis, Bigger, Knox...400 A...John Hendry (Seal), Martha Hendry (O) (Seal). Wit: John Elder, John Bahanon. Prov. Jan. term 1768.

Pp. 271-272: 28 Aug. 1767, James Armour & wf Jennet of Meck., to James Alcorn of same, for L 26 proc. money...land on S side Catabo, on a south branch of Beaver Dam Creek adj. James Campbell, 400 A, part of a tract granted to sd. James Armour by Andrew Armour...James Armour (Seal), Jennet Armour (Seal). Wit: John McCulloh, Thomas Neel, James Davis. Prov. Jan. term 1768.

Pp. 272-273: 18 Jan. 1768, Aaron More & wf Rachal of Meck., to Peter Carpenter of same, for L 50 proc. money...land on both sides of Indian Creek, S branch of S Fork of ye Cautabo including his own Improvement, 200 A granted to Aaron Moor, 23 Oct. 1758...Aaron Moor (O) (Seal), Reachel Moor (+) (Seal). Wit: Vallentine Mauny, Robert Proclus. Prov. Jan. term 1768.

Pp. 273-274: 21 Jan. 1768, Benjamin Alexander of Meck., to James Foster of same, for L 17 proc. money...land on waters of Bullocks Creek on the hed branches of Betts Creek, 200 A... Benjamin Alexander (Seal), Susanah Alexander (O) (Seal). Wit: Richd Barry, Jon. Nickols, Hugh Barnet. Prov. Jan. term 1768.

Page 275: 20 July 1767, Samuel Coborn of Meck., planter to William Wray for L 50...300 A on both sides Catheys Creek or South fork of Second Broad River, granted 6 Apr. 1765 to George Cathey and conveyed to sd. Coborn...Samuel Coborn (Seal). Wit: Richard Barry, Hugh Irwin, Thomas Dickson. Rec. date absent.

Pp. 276-278: 15 Jan. 1765, Walter Carruth of Rowan Co., Esquire, to Robert Woods of Rowan Co., for (lease s5, release

Volume 4

L 6)...land on S side Inoree River next below Benjamin Gordons survey, granted to sd. Carruth 28 March 1755... Walter Caruth (Seal). Wit: James Henderson, Nicholas Leeper, Francis Beaty. Rec. July term 1767.
(This land now in Laurens or Newberry County, S. C.)

Pp. 278-282: 20 & 21 Apr. 1767, Walter Davies of Meck., planter to James Brown of same, (lease s5, release L 30)... land on head waters of Gum branch of Long Creek, adj. Mr. Joy, granted to sd. Davies 16 Nov. 1764 adj. to land that Francis Beaty sold and conveyed to John Todd...Walter Davies (Seal). Wit: Richard Barry, William Gardner, James Allen. Prov. July term 1768.

Pp. 282-285: 22 & 23 May 1767, Benjamin Shaw of Meck., planter, to Francis Beaty of same, (Lease s5, release L 41 NC money)...400 A on the muddy fork of Buffelow Creek, granted to sd. Shaw 26 Sept. 1766...Benjamin Shaw (Seal). Wit: Hugh Beaty, John Beaty. Rec. date not given.

Pp. 286-287: 13 July 1767, Frederick Fishar & Sevely Fishar of Meck., to Martin Fisher of same, for L 5 procl. money... 149 A on the Ridges between Cold water and Adams Creek, granted to Frederick Fisher by Arthur Dobbs 25 June 1764...Frederick Fishar (Seal), Sevely Fishar (Seal). Wit: Robert Rodgers, Jacob Fishar (IF), John Ffifer. Prov. July term 1767.

Pp. 287-288: 24 Dec. 1766, John Bowers of Meck., to Samuel Johnson of same, for L 50 proc. money...land on both sides Dutchman's Creek including the plantation whereon he now lives adj. Matthew Kuykendals, 156 A granted to John Lanham and to Glaghorn by deed from him, then to the sd.. Bowers... John Bowers (Seal). Wit: William Moore, George Rutledge. Prov. July term 1767.

Pp. 289-292: 21 & 22 Nov. 1766, John Grindal & wf Esther of Meck., planter to Alexander Love of same, for (lease s5, release L 70 NC money)...400 A, on N side Broad River and S side Fishing Creek including the said Creek above William Ratchfords, granted to Blaney Mills 3 Feb. 1754, and conveyed 26 & 27 Jan. 1764 to James Millikan and then to John Grundel 12 Jan. 1765...John Grundal (Seal), Esther Grundel (O) (Seal). Wit: William Sharp, George Dicky. Prov. July term 1767.
(This land now in S. C.)

Pp. 292-293: 13 June 1767, Edward Lacy Junr. & wf Jane of Meck., to Robert Bratton of same, for L 62 NC money...land on S side Cataba River on the head waters of Turkey Creek near Robert Ewarts, 200 A granted to Lacey 28 Oct. 1765... Edward Lacey (Seal), Jane Lacey (Seal). Wit: Samuel Gay (.), David Reed, Ralph Crofer(?), Prov. July term 1767.

Pp. 294-297: 15 & 16 July 1767, Francis Beaty & wf Martha of Meck., Collector & C., to John Todd Junr., Weaver of same (lease s5, release L 37 s 10)... land on branches of Gum Branches of Long Creek adj. tract originally granted to John Davies, on E side Cataba, between Jeremiah Joys and said river, including some of the waters of Paw Creek, granted to Archibald McClaine 10 Apr. 1761 and conveyed to Francis Beatey 14 Apr. 1767...Francis Beaty (Seal), Martha Beaty (M) (Seal),

Volume 4

Wit: Joseph Moore, Hugh Beaty, John Beaty. Prov. July term 1767.

Pp. 298-299: 20 July 1767, Capt. Moses Moore of Meck., to Hugh Irwin of same, for L 100 NC money...land on Mudy fork of Bufelow Creek...Moses Moore (Seal). Wit: John Tagerty, James Steen. Prov. July term 1767.

Pp. 299-303: 24 Mar. 1767, Joseph Armstrong of Meck., planter to George Rutledge of same (lease s5, release L 50 NC money)... two parcels of land: 150 A on S side Cataba adj. James Armstrong old line, granted to James Armstrong decd., 23 Feb. 1754 and 75 A part of another tract of said James Armstrong Land on Kuykendalls Creek, granted to sd. James Armstrong decd 30 Aug. 1753, 300 A...Joseph Armstrong (Seal). Wit: John McElroy, Samuel Johnson, James Rutledge. Prov. July term 1767.

Pp. 303-306: 24 & 25 Feb. 1767, Thomas Reynold to Thomas Reynolds, Jr., (lease s5, release L 50 proc. money)...land on both sides Indian Creek, adj. Henry Reynolds, John Reynolds, part of Thomas Reynolds survey of 600 A, 250 A granted to said Thomas Reynolds Senr., 30 Aug. 1753...Thomas Reynolds (X) (Seal), Wit: Will Reed, John Hudson (O). Prov. July term 1767.

Pp. 307-309: 29 Dec. 1766, John Carrel & wf Mary of Meck., to James Hanna of same, for L 50...land between the main Forke and Stoney fork of Fishing Creek, 150 A, formerly the property of James Kuykendall and willd to the said Mary his daughter now the wife of said John Carrel...John Carrol (Seal), Mary Carrol (X) (Seal). Wit: Joseph Carrol, John Price, Robert Leeper.
(This land now in S. C.)

Pp. 309-213: 22 & 23 May 1767, James Kelly of Meck., to Francis Beaty of same, Dept. Collector (lease s5, release L18 NC money)...200 A on both sides of the Shoaly Branch of Mudy fork of Buffelow Creek, including the three Forks a few poles above Benjamin Shaws old land and near Francis Beateys, granted to sd. Kelly 26 Sept. 1766...James Kelly (I) (Seal). Wit: Hugh Beaty, John Beaty. Prov. July term 1767.

Page 313: 20 July 1767, Jacob Forney & wf Mary of Meck., to Karot Will [probably Gerhardt Will] of same, for L 119 NC money...land on S side Cataba River, on middle fork of Killions Creek above Wm. Berrys Land whereon he now lives, formerly belonging to Leonard Killion 320 A...Jacob Forney (Seal), Mary Froney (X) (Seal). Wit: Leonard Saylor (LS), James Abernathy. Prov. July term 1767.

Page 314: 8 Apr. 1765, Jasper Hover & wf Margaret of Meck., to John Farmer of same for L 10 proc. money...land on E side Cataba River opposite William Habertys, 89 A...Gesper Hover (Seal), Margaret Hover (V) (Seal). Wit: Joseph Moore, William Lewing, William Dunlop. Prov. July term 1767.

Pp. 315-316: 1 July 1766, Samuel Humphries of Granvil Co., North Carolina to John Davidson of Rowan Co., for L 25 proc. money...land on W side Catawba on the south branch of Crowders Creek near the Waggon ford, 160 A granted to said Humphries

Volume 4

28 Oct. 1765...Saml Humphries (Seal). Wit: Richard Henderson, John Williams, Jr. Prov. July term 1767.

Pp. 316-317: 7 May 1767, William Sims of Meck., to James Henderson of same, for L 40 proc. money...land on E side S fork Cataba, 200 A, granted 25 Apr. 1767...William Sims (Seal). Wit: John Fondren, David Porter. Prov. July term 1767.

Pp. 317-318: 23 July 1767, Thomas Hooper of Granville Co., South Carolina to John Stanford of Meck., for L 50...land in Meck. Co., including a large Island at the Ninety Nine Islands, 150 A granted Apr. 1767...Thomas Hooper (LS). Wit: William Sharp, Jno. Sartain. Prov. July term 1767.
(This land now in S. C.)

Page 319: 22 July 1767, Joseph Clark & wf Elizabeth of Meck., to Jeremiah Ruth of same, for L 40 proc. money...200 A on N side of the river above the Cheroke [sic] path, granted to sd. Joseph Clark 26 Sept. 1766...Joseph Clark (LS), Elizabeth Clark (X) (LS). Wit: James Way. Prov. July term 1767.

Pp. 320-321: 25 Sept. 1766, William Hendry & wf Esabella of Meck., to John Venables of Meck., for L 65 proc. money...land on S side Cataba River on a fork of Allisons Creek adj. Thomas Dickson, James Wilson & William Mackelmurry, 300 A... William Hendry (Seal), Esabella Hendry (Seal). Wit: Charles McClean, John McCulloh, Susana McClean (S). Prov. July term 1767.
(This land now in S. C.)

Pp. 321-322: 10 ___, 1767, Thomas Hooper of Prov. of S. C. to Mathew Floyd of Meck., for L 53 s 13 d 4 proc. money...land on S side Broad River being the place the said Hooper formerly lived on, at the mouth of Enos Hoopers Creek, 160 A granted 25 Sept. 1766...Thos Hooper (Seal). Wit: William McMillin, John McMillin, John McGunagle (?). Prov. July term 1767.

Pp. 323-324: 6 Feb. 1767, Robert Alexander & wf Mary of Rowan Co., to James Millican of Meck., for L 30...96 A on Doctors Creek on W side Cataba including his own improvement, granted to William Moore 10 Apr. 1761...Robert Alexander (Seal), Mary Alexander (Seal). Wit: Jacob Nichols, Samuel Johnston, Joseph Erwin. Prov. July term 1767.

Pp. 324-327: 16 & 17 July 1767, Thomas Hendry & wf Isabella of Meck., Carpenter & Jointer to Zacheus Ruth of same, millwright (lease s5, release L 40 NC money)...land on both sides Long Creek near the land that Francis Beaty purchased of James Armstrong now David Stanlys place...granted to Francis Beaty 14 Apr. 1761 and conveyed to sd. Thomas Hendry...Thomas Hendry (Seal), Isabella Hendry (Seal). Wit: James Cook, James Cook, James Henderson. Prov. date not given.

Pp. 328-329: 20 July 1767, Joseph Harden of Meck., planter, to Allsey Watson of same, for L 5 proc. money...land on waters of Fishing Creek, 84 A adj. Robert Gabby, James Watson, granted 26 Sept. 1766...Joseph Harden (Seal). Wit: William Watson, Thomas Scott, James Davidson[?] ( ). Prov. date absent.

Pp. 329-330: 16 March 1767, John Elliot of Meck., to John

Fondren of same, for ₺ 30 proc. money...100 A on waters of Fishing Creek adj. Thomas Hawkins... John Elliot (Seal), Wit: William Dickson, James Hanna. Prov. July term 1767. (This land now in S. C.)

Pp. 330-331: 21 Aug. 1766, James Thomson of Meck., to John Thomson of Rowan Co., for ₺ 20 proc. money...land on S side Cataba River on a North branch of Allisons Creek known by the name of the Calabash branch, 170 A, part of a grant to Henry Johnson 1 Sept. 1753, conveyed to sd. James Thomson... James Thomson (Seal). Wit: Robert Adams, Jno McCulloh. Rec. date absent.
(This land now in S. C.)

Pp. 331-335: 23 & 24 Oct. 1765, James Davies & wf Margaret of Meck., planter, to James Johnston of same, planter, (lease s5, release ₺)...300 A on both sides Sugar Creek adj. John Davises Mill place, James Davies, granted to John Davis, 15 Nov. 1762 and part of 500 A granted to James Davies 16 Nov. 1764...James Davies (Seal), Margaret Davies (V) (Seal). Wit: Thomas Polk. Prov. July term 1767.

Pp. 335-336: 3 ___ 1767, Denny Dyer of Craven Co., S. C., Taylor, to Leonard Dozer of Meck., for ₺ 30 proc. money... 290 A on S side Cataba River, adj. John Large, granted to John Large 25 Sept. 1754, and conveyed by L & R...Dennis Dyer (D) (Seal). Wit: John Cathey, Mary Cathey (X), Leonard Wil. Prov. July term 1767.

Pp. 337-339: 14 May 1767, Hugh Berry & wf Jannet of Meck., to David McMickan of same (lease s5, release ₺ 100 proc. money)... land above Moses Biggers Cabin, granted 20 Dec. 1763 to Hugh Barry, 360 A...Hugh Berry (Seal), Jannet Barry (X) (Seal). Wit: Joseph Waddel, John Bigger (S). Rec. date absent.

Pp. 340-341: 10 Jan. 1767, John Campbell of Bertie Co., Esquire to John Frohock of Rowan Co., for ₺ 10 proc. money... 122 A adj. Alexr Wallace...John Campbell (Seal) by H. E. McCulloh. Wit: Thos Frohock, William Frohock. Acknowledged Wilmington, 27 Apr. 1767. In margin: University Land. 122 acres Alexr. Taceys old place on Mallard Creek sold to Alexr Wallace by Adlai Osborn for ₺ 40 in 1795.

Pp. 341-342: 24 Feb. 1767, Selwyn to John Frohock of Rowan Co., for ₺ 12 s 10 sterling...200 A...Geo. Aug: Selwyn by Henry McCulloh. Wit: Thom: Frohock, William Frohock. Prov. Wilmington 27 Apr. 1767.

Pp. 343-344: 18 Jan. 1767, Henry Eustace McCulloh to John Frohock of Rowan Co., for ₺ 40 Proc. money...land adj. Gov. Dobbs including James Miskellys old Improvement, 140 A... Wit: John Mouat, B. McCulloch. Prov. Wilmington, 27 Apr. 1767.

Pp. 344-345: 2 Feb. 1767, H. E. McCulloh to John Frohock of Rowan Co., for ₺ 90 proc. money...land on waters of McDowells Creek, adj. John McDowell, George Cathey, 350 A...Wit: Thomas Frohock, William Frohock. Prov. Wilmington, 27 Apr. 1767. In margin: University land: sold by Math. McClure by Adlai Osburn in 1795 for University.

Volume 4

Page 346: 3 Feb. 1767, Henry Eustace McCulloh to John Frohock of Rowan Co., for ₤ 50 proc. money...326 A [in margin "Supposed joining Coddle Creek] Wit: Thomas Bell, Felix Kenan. Prov. Wilmington, 27 Apr. 1767.

Pp. 347-348: 1 Feb. 1767, H. E. McCulloh to John Frohock, for ₤ 60 proc. money...land adj. to tract James Martin live upon, 280 A...Wit: Thomas Frohock, William Frohock. Acknowledged at Wilmington, 27 Apr. 1767.

Pp. 348-349: 3 Feb. 1767, H. E. McCulloh to John Frohock, of Rowan Co., for ___ proc. money...152 A adj. William Erwyn... Wit: Thomas Bell, Felix Kenan. Acknowledged at Wilmington 27 Apr 1767.

Page 349: 3 Feb. 1767, H. E. McCulloh to John Frohock of Rowan Co., for ₤ 30 proc. money...land adj. James Martin, 198 A. Wit: Thomas Bell, Felix Kanan. Acknowledged at Wilmington 27 Apr. 1767.

Pp. 350-351: 1 Feb. 1767, H. E. McCulloh to John Frohock, for ₤ 100 proc. money...land adj. John Miller, McDowells Creek, 475 A...Wit: John Mouat, B. McCulloh. Acknowledged at Wilmington 27 Apr. 1767.

Pp. 351-352: 1 Feb. 1767, H. E. McCulloh to John Frohock, 240 A part of the tract old Robt Miller lived upon...Wit: John Mouat, B. McCulloh, Acknowledged at Wilmington 27 Apr. 1767... in margin: [part of a tract sold to Martin Steel in 1795 for ₤ 20].

Pp. 352-354: 1 Feb. 1767, H. E. McCulloh to John Frohock of Rowan Co., for ₤ 100 proc... 473 A... Wit: Thomas Bell, Felix Kenan. Acknowledged at Wilmington, 27 Apr. 1767.

Pp. 354-355: 1 Feb. 1767, H. E. McCulloh to John Frohock of Rowan Co., for ₤ 100 proc. money...land on E side N fork McDowells Creek, adj. James Pelle(?), 432 A... Wit: Thomas Frohock, William Frohock. Acknowledged at Wilmington 27 Apr. 1767. [in margin: University 432 A sold to Hugh Terrence for ₤ 409 in 1795].

Pp. 356-357: 1 Feb. 1767, H. E. McCulloh to John Frohock of Mecklenburg Co., for ₤ 40 sterling...200 A adj. Governors line...Wit: Tho. Frohock, William Frohock. Acknowledged at Wilmington 27 Apr. 1767. [in margin: ___ for ₤ 125 in July 1795].

Pp. 357-359: 1 Feb. 1767, H. E. McCulloh to John Frohock of Meck., for ₤ 40 sterling...land adj. corner of tract Joseph Hobles now lives upon, 190 A...Wit: Thomas Frohock, William Frohock. Acknowledged at Wilmington 27 Apr. 1767. [in margin: McClures old place, sold to Joseph Moore in 1795 for ₤ 40].

Pp. 359-361: 11 Aug. 1767, Andrew Campbell & wf Jean of Meck., to Matthew Floyd of same, for ₤ 30...land on both sides Loves Creek on E side Broad River adj. above Pauls Land, 195 A granted to Andrew Campbell 26 Sept. 1766...Wit: Henry Smith, Abraham Smith, Thomas Chadwick...Andrew Campbell (Seal), Jean Campbell (Seal). Prov. Oct. term 1767.

Volume 4

Page 361: 10 Aug. 1767, William Smart & wf Isabella of Meck., to John Mitchel of Rowan Co., for L 100...land on E side of Main South fork of Camp Creek 400 A...William Smart (Seal), Isabel Smart (Seal). Wit: James Forsyth, as to the Husband, Alexander Dobbin. Prov. Oct. term 1767.

Pp. 362-363: 14 Sept. 1767, Henry Potts & wf Margaret of Rowan Co., planter, to Thomas Cook of Rowan Co., for L 75 proc. money...land on N side Cataba River and on the forked meadow Creek, being the place where sd. Henry Potts, lately dwelt adj. Alexr Osborn granted to sd. Henry Potts 16 May 1754, 535 A...Henry Potts (Seal), Margaret Potts (X) (Seal). Wit: Waltr. Lindsey, William Crown. Prov. by Walter Lindsey at Salisbury 23 Sept. 1767, Edmd. Fanning.

Pp. 363-366: 22 Sept. 1755, John Clark of Anson Co., to Burrel Grigg of same...(lease s5, release L 75 Va. money)... land on S side S fork Cataba at the Rockey Ford, adj. George Shoofoot, half of 1000 A that Clark bought of Samuel Wilkins.. Jno Clark (Seal). Wit: Israel Robeson, Wm. Wilkins, William Green (W). Prov. at Salisbury, Sept. Term 1767, Edmd Fanning.

Pp. 366-367: 22 July 1767, Matthew Floyd of Meck., to William Yancy of same, for L 50 proc. money...land in the fork of Broad River and First Little Broad River, 200 A...Matt Floyd (Seal), Sarah Floyd (Seal). Wit: William Sharp, James Steen. Prov. July term 1767.

Pp. 367-371: 24 & 25 Feb. 1767, Thomas Reynolds of Meck., to Henry Reynolds of same (lease s5, release L 40 proc. money)... 247 A on both sides Indian Creek, granted to Thomas Reynolds for 600 A 30 Aug. 1753...Thomas Reynolds (+) (Seal). Wit: Will Reed, John Hudson (O). Prov. July term 1767.

Pp. 371-372: 3 Apr. 1767, Andrew Campbell of Meck., to Mary Johnston of Rowan Co., for L 26 proc. money...200 A on Loves Creek, waters of Broad River adj. Thomas Price and John Wade, adj. to land the said Campbell now lives on... Andw Campbell (Seal). Wit: Jas. Craige, Barth. Lewis, Balentine Beard, Peter Johnson. Prov. July term 1767.
(This land now in S. C.)

Pp. 372-374: 22 July 1767, Ebenezer Alexander, planter of Meck., to Aughtrey McKiblin, for L 8 s 10 proc. money...116 A on Courtneys Branch a fork of Six Mile Creek, adj. William Lofton, Courtney, granted to sd. Alexander 6 Apr. 1765... Ebenezer Alexander (Seal). Wit: Aaron Houston, Geo. Alexander. Prov. July term 1767.

Pp. 374-377: 25 & 26 Feb. 1767, Thomas Reynolds Senr. of Meck., to John Reynolds of same (lease s5, release L 15 proc. money)...land on both sides Indian Creek adj. Thomas Reynolds Junr., 100 A, part of 600 A granted to sd. Thomas Reynolds 30 Aug. 1753, Thomas Reynolds (+) (Seal). Wit: Will Reed, Thomas Reynolds Junr. Prov. July term 1767.

Pp. 377-378: 6 Apr. 1767, Samuel Lusk to Samuel Neelley, both of Meck., for L 10 proc. money...300 A on E side of the branch that runs into Fishing Creek below the Saluda path... Samuel Lusk (Seal). Wit: James Patton, Robert Patton, Jane Patton. Prov. July term 1767.
(This land now in S. C.)

Volume 4

Pp. 378-379: 18 Dec. 1767, Thomas Beatey of Meck., to Thomas Rainey of same, for L 25...300 A on S side of Cataba River below the South forks of Fishing Creek, below John Kuykendall's land, granted 26 Mar. 1755 to sd. Thomas Beatey...Thomas Beatey (Seal). Wit: ___ Moore, ___ Young [torn]. Prov. Jan. term 1768.
(This land now in S. C.)

Pp. 380-381: 20 Apr. 1767, Samuel Porter of Meck., to Edmond Lee of same, for L 24...land granted 25 Sept. 1766 on both sides Fishing Creek above Smiths land by the Indian line... Samuel Porter (Seal). Wit: Robt Morris, Archd. Elliot (AE), William Neelly, Henry Neily, John Anderson. Prov. July term. 1767.
(This land now in S. C.)

Page 381: Patrick Grims of Meck., do make free & publick sale of a Baymair to William Irwyn(?)...10 June ___ ...Patrick Grims (O), Testus: David Wilson, Jean Wilson. Prov. July term 1767.

Pp. 381-384: 16 & 17 July 1767, William Armstrong & wf Margret of Meck., to John Kenor of same (lease s5, release L 10)...100 A on both sides of Kenors branch of Leepres Creek, granted to sd. Armstrong, 16 Nov. 1764...William Armstrong (A) (Seal), Marget Armstrong (M) (Seal). Wit: [Name in Dutch,]___ Saunders, ___ Sailor (2). Prov. July term 1767.

Pp. 385-387: 16 Apr. 1767, Robert Ramsey & wf Margaret of S. C., Craven County to Archibald McDowell of Meck., (lease s5, release L 100)...300 A granted to sd. Ramsey 1 March 1753 known by the name of the Large Cane Braek[sic] on the fork of the south fork of the Twelve Mile Creek above the Indian Path...Robert Ramsey (Seal), Margaret Ramsey (+) (Seal). Wit: Richd. Barry, James Ramsey, Alexdr. Nisbet.

Pp. 387-390: 30 Dec. 1766, James Moore of Meck., to John Moore of same (lease s5, release L20)...land on waters of the S fork of fishing creek, 137 A granted to sd. James Moore 28 Oct. 1765...James Moore, Rachel Moore (M). Wit: Benjamin Rainey, Samuel Rainey, Ralph Baker. Prov. July term 1767.
(This land now in S. C.)

Pp. 390-392: 24 Sept. 1766, Ephraim McClain of Meck., to John Davison of Rowan Co., for (lease s5, release L 30)... land on N side S fork Fishing Creek adj. his own and Andrew McNabbs lines, granted to sd. McClain 16 Nov. 1764, 500 A... Ephr McLean (Seal). Wit: John Moore, Saml. McCullough, John Thomas. Prov. July term 1767.
(This land now in S. C.)

Pp. 392-395: 10 & 11 July 1767, Jacob Egner & wf Mary of Meck., to Lorance Markle of same, (lease s5, release L 100)... land on both sides Pinch Gut, adj. his own line including George Hovers improvement, granted to sd. Egner 21 Apr. 1764.. Jacob Egner (Seal), Mary Egner (+) (Seal). Wit: Will Reed, ___ [German signature], Nicholas Wisenhunt (+). (Probate date missing).

Pp. 395-396: 20 Oct. 1765, Thomas Price & wf Isabel of Meck., to Alexander Baldridge of same, for L 81...two traxts on S side Cataba...300 A granted to James Armour 29 Sept. 1750,

Volume 4

then conveyed to William Alexander, ___ July 1755, then to William Steven 9 July 1756, then by Andrew & William Luckey Exrs. of Est. of William Steven 13 Jan. 1764...and 100 A adj. James Armour, granted to George Cathey 29 March 1753, 17 July 1755 and conveyed to William Stevens... Thomas Price (Seal), Isabell Price ( ) (Seal). Wit: ___ Denney, ___ Patton, ___ Hendry. Prov. July term 1767.

Pp. 397-398: 18 Dec. 1766, Conrade Povey & wf Magdalen of Meck., to Jacob Setsner of same, for Ł ___ ... 196 1/2 A granted to Boby [Poovey] 21 Apr. 1764...Conrade Povey (+) (Seal), Magdelen Povey (O) (Seal). Wit: Martin Fifer, Matthias Barrenger, Two Names Wrote in Dutch. Prov. July term 1767.

Pp. 399-400: 23 Feb. 1767, George Augustus Selvy to Jas. Holland of Meck., for Ł 5 sterling...100 A...Wit: William Frohock. Acknowledged at Salisbury 12 Mar. 1767.

Pp. 400-401: 13 Aug. 1767, Simot Hort & wf Margaret of Meck., to Andrew Sites of same, Cooper, for Ł 62...granted 25 Sept. 1766...Simon Hort (Seal), Margret Hort (1) (Seal). Wit: John Ffiter, "A Name Wrote in Dutch", Henry Sties. Prov. Jan. term. ___.

Pp. 401-402: H. E. McCulloh to James Wyley & William ___ both of Meck...said James Wyley & William Alexander, dated 27 Jan. 1767...land on both sides ___, 393 A. Wit: John Frohock, J. McK. Alexander. [Deed in poor condition]. Prov. Jan. term 1768.

Pp. 403-406: 21 & 22 ___ 1766, John Walker of Meck., to Nathl Henderson of same, (lease s5, release Ł 15)...530 A on W side North fork of Fishing Creek, granted to David Emanuel 31 Mar. 1753, and conveyed to John Walker 11 Jan. ___. John Walker (Seal). Wit: Jno Muckols, Adam Baird. Prov. Jan. term 1768.
(This land now in S. C.)

Pp. 406-407: John Stallinger of Meck., Disteller to John Pifer [sic] for s5(?) my goods, chattles, household, viz. at one James Clarks and George Catheys two Baggs and 5 Bushell of wheat one cooper Jointer, etc. [long list of items].. John Stollinger (Seal) (O). Wit: John Field, John Penny. Prov. Jan. term 1768.

Pp. 407=408: 11 Jan. 176_, John Dill of Meck. to John Tagert of same, for Ł 50 proc. money...250 A on W side Broad River, granted to sd. Dills, ___ Apr. 1767. John Dill (N) (Seal). Wit: ___ Sims, ___ Richardson, ___ Richardson. Prov. Jan. term [1768].

Pp. 409-410: 21 Dec. 1767, Charles Gillham of Meck., to Ezekiel Gilham of same, for Ł 10...land on E side Bullock Creek, part of 248 A granted 26 Sept. 1766...Charles Gilham (Seal), Elizabeth Gilham (O) (Seal). Wit: Thomas Gilham, William Sharp. Prov. Jan. term 1768. (This land now in S.C.)

Pp. 410-411: 4 Dec. 1767, John Lineberger & wf Esbel of Meck., to Ludwick Lineberger of same, for Ł 60 proc. money... land on a branch of Hoiles Creek, commonly called Standleys a N branch of S fork Cataba River, adj. corner formerly

Volume 4

James Arm___, granted by deed to sd. John Lineberger by one Abraham Kuykendall 26 Mar. 1764...John Lineber (Seal), Seville Lineberg __ (Seal), Wit: John Ritzhoup, Jacob Castner. Prov. Jan. term [1768].

Pp. 412-413: 16 Jan. 1768, John Richman of Meck., to Joseph Wishard of same, for ₤ 50 proc. money...land granted 4 Nov. 1758 on S side Cataba River... John Richman (Seal), Sarah Richman (S) (Seal). Wit: William Moore, James Young, Mary Armstrong (+). Prov. Jan. term 1768.

Pp. 413-414: 19 Oct. 1767, Thomas Richey of Meck., to James Richey of same, for ₤ 20...land on head branches of Paw Creek adj. McClain, 200 A, part of a tract granted to Francis Beatey 19 Apr. 1763...Thomas Richey (Seal). Wit: Joseph Kerr, Hugh Beatey, David Miller. Prov. Jan. term 1768.

Pp. 415-417: 21 ___, 1767, Thomas Robinson of Meck., to Elizabeth Biggerstaff of same, for ₤ 35...300 A on the first large Creek above the ___ path on N side Second Broad River, granted 16 ___, 1764...Thomas Robinson (Seal), Wit: ___ McCasland, ___ Biggerstaff. Prov. Jan. term [1768].

Pp. 417-420: 29 May 1767, Thomas MacKnight of Rowan Co., to George Ewing of Meck., (lease s5, release ₤ 47 s __) ...200 A on South fork of the Catabo...Thomas MacKnight (Seal). Wit: ___ Beaty, ___ Glen (O). Prov. Jan. term 1768.

Pp. 421-424: 8 & (May 1767, James Robinson Junr. of Rowan Co., to John Robinson of Rowan Co., (lease s5, release ₤ 10)... 275 A in New Providence, on the Waters of Clarks branch of Twelve Mile Creek adj. James Dinn, Clark, granted 19 Apr. 1763 to James McClure, and by him & wf Margaret unto sd. James Robinson Junr. 7 & 8 ___ 1763...James Robinson (Seal). Wit: Joseph Gillespy, ___ Braly. Proven Jan. term 1768.

Pp. 424-426: 10 ___, 17__, Francis Travish of Meck., Black Smith to Joseph Gabby of same, for ₤ 50 proc. money...land on both sides Fishing Creek joining between William Watson and Patrick Duncan, granted 25 Apr. 1767 to sd. Travish... Francis Travers (Seal). Wit: William Watson, [Ro]bert Gabbie Rec. Apr. term 1768.

Pp. 426-428: 24 ___, 176_, Samuel Bigham of Meck., Farmer, to Dennis McCormick of same for ₤ 30...200 A on the Head Waters of Jean Armours Creek, adj. Samuel Knox, Bigham... Samuel Bigham (Seal). Wit: Moses Ferguson, James Pursley. Prov. Apr. term 1768.

Pp. 428-430: 12 Feb. 1767, George Augustus Selwyn to Robert Mexwell, for ₤ 4 s 5...82 A...Wit: Tho Frohock, William Frohock. Rec. Apr. term 1768.

Page 430: Elizabeth Hoghead of Meck., Widow, for ₤ 74, to Alexander Wallace a certain parcels of goods, cattle, etc. [enumerated] 18 Apr. 1767...Elizabeth Hoghead (Seal). Wit: Benjamin Alexander, John (?) McLilly. Rec. July term 1768.

Pp. 430-436: 19 & 20 Feb. 1768, Peter Harper of Tenecum Township, Bucks Co., Pa., Yeoman to Thomas Salter of City of Philadelphia, Merchant, (lease s5, release ₤ 250)...600 A on S side S fork Cautabo River on N side of South Fork of Fishing Creek and another tract of 120 A on No fork of Indian Creek...Peter Harpell (Seal). Wit: Peter Knight, James(?) Moor, John Britton, Thomas Britton. Proved by Francis Moor, at Newbern NC, 26 July 1768.

Pp. 436-437: 18 June 1768, Peter Bumgarner & wf Mary of Meck., to Miles Abernathy of same, for Ł 85 NC money... 200 A on a branch of Killians Creek...Peter Bumgarner (Seal), Mary Bumgarner (1) (Seal). Wit: John Armstrong, Robt Abernathy. Rec. July term [1768]

Pp. 437-439: 15 ___, 1768, Matthew Floyd of Meck., to Daniel Warlock, Frederick Wise, Orpan Ashybranner, Peter Stotler, Peter Summy & Teter Havener, for Ł 10...land on S side S fork Cataba River adj. Peter Stotler & Jonathan Potts lines including a School-House, 50 A, granted to sd. Matthew Floyd, 26 Oct. 1767...Matt: Floyd (Seal). Wit: Jno McKnit Alexander, Henry Smith. Rec. July term [1768].

Pp. 439-440: Hugh Barry of Meck., for Ł 200 pd by David McMickin & Samuel Bell of same...horses and cattle [enumerated] 30 Sept. 1767...Hugh Barry (Seal). Wit: ___ Campbell, ___ TT Floyd. Rec. July term 1768.

Pp. 440-442: 1 Dec. 176_, James Cunningham of Meck., Planter, to Francis Beaty of same, for Ł 30...100 A, near Capt. Benjamin Hardens and ___ old places, adj. John Armstrong deceased, granted to sd. James Cunningham 26 Oct. ___... James Cunningh [am]. Wit: Robert Sloan, Hugh Beatey. Rec. July term 1768.

Pp. 442-443: 30 Sept. 176_, Hugh Batty of Meck., planter, to Joseph Carroll, for Ł 300...360 A between waters of Paw Creek and Sugaw Creek, adj. ___ & James McCallen...Hugh Barry (Seal). Wit: Andw Campbell, Amtt: Floyd. Rec. July term 1768.

Pp. 443-445: 11 Apr 176_, Jacob Eberhart of Meck., to Peder Stuts of same, for Ł ___ proc. money...land on branches of Clarks Creek adj. Bost, granted to Eberhart ___ Oct. 17__, 400 A...Jacob Eberhart (Seal), [German sign.] (+) (her mark) (Seal). Wit: Matthias Barringer, ___ (German signature) ___ Crund(y). Rec. July term 1768.

Pp. 445-447: Robert Caldwell & wf Margaret of Meck., to Samuel Lessly, for Ł 20 s 11 d 4 current money of aforesaid Prov., 175 A on N side Waxhaw Creek, part of a patent for 501 A to Robert Caldwell in 1754...Robert Caldwell (R) (Seal). Wit: Jas. Cook, James Waughup. Rec. July term 1768.

Page 447: 30 Sept. 1767, Hugh Barry of Meck., to Thomas Carroll of same, planters, for Ł 100 proc. money, "my plantation in the county of Mecklenburg"... Hugh Barry (Seal). Wit: Adnw Campbell, Matt: Floyd. Rec. July term 1768.

Pp. 448-450: 28 ___ 1768, Richard Sadler of Meck., to David Adrion of same, for Ł 30 current money of NC, 400 A on S side North fork of Tyger River on Jameys Branch, at Francis Wilsons cor., part of a granted to Richard Sadler 24 Oct. 1767 Richard Saddler (Seal). Wit: [Jose]ph Baker, [J]ohn Sadler. Rec. July term 1768.

End of Book No. 10

Volume 4

Page 451: Book No. 11   Searched Febry 20, 1796 for Millings old big Place.

Pp. 451-452: 9 Apr. 1769, John Franklin of Tryon Co., yeoman, to William Sharp of Rowan Co., for ₤ 5 s 10 proc. money, 200 A on both sides of Cubb or Clarks Creek, S side Green River about two miles from the mouth of sd. Creek, patented by John Franklin 22 Dec. 1760...John Frankline (Seal). Wit: John Potts, Jonathan Robinson.

Pp. 453-454: 10 Apr. 1769, James Crawford of Tryon Co., yeoman, to William Sharp of Rowan Co., for ₤ 5 s 10 proc. money, 100 A in Tryon County on both sides of Green River between Whitesides & Reynolds land, patented by James Crawford, 22 Dec. 1768...James Crawford (X) (Seal). Wit: John Potts, Jonathan Robinson.

Pp. 455-460: 3 & 4 Feb. 1769, Archibald McDowell of Meck., to Alexander McCown of Craven County, South Carolina, for ₤ 300 current money of NC (lease & release), 300 A in Craven County, SC on both sides Fishing Creek... Archibald McDowell (Seal). Wit: Wm. Davis, John Davis, Wm. Scott. Rec. April term 1769.

Pp. 460-462: 17 July 1768, Bartholomew Dawson of Meck., to John Cooper of same, for ₤ 8 proc. money, 190 A on South fork of Fishing Creek, adj. Rotten (Roden or Rhoden), Alexander, Bound, John Dennis...Bartholomew Dosson (B) (Seal). Wit: Robert Campbell, William Pattrick. Rec. April Court 1769.

Pp. 462-464: 19 Apr. 1769, Adam Carruth of ___ NC to Ambrose McCee (McKee) of ___, N.C. for ₤ 33 proc. money, 164 A on both sides a small branch of North fork of Steel Creek on E side Catawba River, patented to Adam Carruth, 27 Apr. 1767... Adam Carruth (Seal), Elizabeth Carruth (E) (Seal). Wit: John Dickey, Jno. McK. Alexnader. Rec. April term 1769.

Page 465: 14 Apr. 1769, about 18 months ago Andrew McNabb (then of Meck., now of Tryon County) brought from Thomas Polk a request for ₤ 17 proc. receipt of Quit Rents and sd. receipt was lost...14 Apr. 1769, Francis Beaty (Seal). Wit: John Scott, Thomas Richey. Rec. Apr. term 1769.

Pp. 466-467: 5 Sept. 1768, Samuel Patton & wf Anna of Meck., to Martin Fifer (Pfifer), Esq. of same, for ₤ 100 proc. money, 292 A whereon he now lives, on the ridge between Buffaloe Creek and Coddle Creek, waters of Rocky or Johnston River... Samuel Patton (Seal), Anne Patton (A) (Seal). Wit: James Russell, Benjamin Patton, John Pfifer. Rec. April term 1769.

Pp. 467-469: 10 Jan. 1769, John Fields and wf Sarah of Meck., to Martin Pfifer Esq. of same, for ₤ 40 s 11 NC money, 152 A adj. Abraham Caradine, James Wallace, Samuel Brown...John Field (Seal), Sarah Field (X) (Seal). Wit: John Pfifer, David Alexander. Rec. April Court 1769.

Pp. 469-470: 20 Feb. 1768, William Donaldson of Cumberland County, Penn., planter to Archibald Crocket of NC, planter, for ₤ 80 proc. money, 234 (232) A on N side Six Mile Branch, part of 450 A patented by William Donaldson, 14 May 1755...

Volume 4

Wm. Donalson (Seal), by Thos Polk. Wit: Moses Alexander, Samuel Loftain. Rec. Apr. term 1769.

Pp. 471-472: 12 Apr. 1769, James Cook of Meck., & wf Lucy to John Gordon of same, for ₤ 5 proc. money, 100 A in Meck Co., adj. McClure, the tract whereon sd. John Gordon now lives... Jas Cook (Seal), Lucy Cook (Seal), Wit: Jacob Gray (I), Charles Miller. Rec. Apr. term 1769.

Pp. 472-473: 7 Jan. 1769, Philip Tillinger & wf Mary to William Tankersley of same, for ₤ 25 current money of NC, A on both sides South branch of Leopard Creek...Philip Tillinger (Seal), Mary Tankersley (X) (Seal). Wit: George Pooff, Peter Club (P), John Tillinger. Rec. Apr. term 1769.

Pp. 474-475: 28 Jan. 1767, John Campbell of Bertie Co., NC to David Russell of Meck., planter, for ₤ 5 proc. money, 50 A. on head branches of Long Creek in sd. John Campbell's Barrony, being a part subdivided from Tract #4...John Campbell (Seal) by Henry E. McCulloh. Wit: John Frohock, Jno. McK. Alexander. Rec. Oct. term 1767.

Pp. 475-477: 24 Jan. 1769 James Wyly & William Alexander of Meck., to Andrew Robinson, Blacksmith, of same, for ₤ 125 proc. money, 392 A on both sides Back Creek, near John Allen, original deed from Henry Eustace McCulloh to James Wyly & William Alexander, 27 Jan. 1767...James Wyly (Seal), William Alexander (Seal). Wit: John Pfifer, James Way. Rec. Apr. term 1769.

Pp. 478-479: 16 Feb. 1769, William Cronicle of Meck., Ordinary Keeper, for ₤ 200 proc. money, 150 A joining on the E side of the Catawba River at the Tuckasegy Ford, including an Island & Cronicle's improvements, adj. John Richeys corner, said land granted to Joseph Harding, by patent 26 Mar 1755... William Chronicle (Seal). Wit: John Beatey, Archibald McNeall. Rec. Apr. term 1769.

Pp. 480-481: 22 Mar. 1768, James Hanna of Meck., to Oliver Wallace of same, for ₤ 30 proc. money, 150 A on waters of South fork of Fishing Creek, adj. land bought of Ephraim McClain (McLean), John Wade's corner by the Waggon Road, Benjamin Philips corner, Samuel Rainey's line, Balls line, patented to James Hanna, 25 Sept. 1766...Jas Hanna (Seal). Wit: David Adrian, William Hanna, Joseph Wallace. Rec. April term 1769.

Pp. 482-485: 9 & 10 Jan. 1769, William Simms of Meck., yeoman, to James Houston of same, farmer (lease ₤5, release ₤ 100 proc. money), 245 A, part of a grant to James Alexander and Conveyed by Him to James Dunn 10 Feb. 1759...adj. Wm. Givens.. William Simms (Seal). Wit: James Tate, Aron Houston, John Neichler. Rec. April term 1769.

Pp. 485-487: 30 Mar. 1769, William Ross & wf Elizabeth to Hezekiah James Balch of Meck., for ₤ 50 proc. money, 88 A on the ridges between English Buffaloe and Coddle Creek at head of Walker's Run...William Ross (Seal), Elizabeth Ross (M) (Seal). Wit: Thomas Neely, Francis Harris, Robt. Harris. Rec. Apr. term 1769.

Volume 4

Pp. 487-491: 6 Apr. 1769, Boston Cline of Meck., planter to John Leufever of same, (lease s5, release Ł 20), 350 A where John Leufever now lives at branches of Lyelus(?) Creek, granted to Boston Cline, 28 Apr. 1768...lease has Jacob Cline signing, release has Boston Cline "wrote in Dutch", Margaret Cline (X). Wit: Matthias Barringer with a Dutch name. Rec. Apr. term 1769.

Pp. 491-493: 27 Feb. 1768, Nicholas Frye of Meck., to William Deel of same, for Ł 25, 400 A on both sides a branch of Clarks Creek at Matthias Barringers corner, granted to Nicholas Frye __ Apr 1767...Nicholas Frey (NF) (Seal), Leasalet Frey (O). Wit: Matthias Barringer and "Two Witnesses who wrote their names in Dutch." Rec. April Court 1769.

Pp. 493-495: 12 Jan. 1769, Jacob Egner & Mary Egner of Meck., to Henry Bullinger of same, for Ł 30 currency money of Prov. of Virginia & Ł 1258 proc. money of NC, a bargain and sale to them made by James Robinson of same, 400 A on South fork of Catawba River which runs into Clarks Creek above Gum Log Ford about a mile, patented by James Robinson 27 Sept. 1751... Jacob Egner (Seal), Mary Egner (X). Wit: Robert Blackburn, "A Dutch Name" Rec. April Court 1769.

Pp. 495-497: 12 Jan. 1769, Jacob Egner & Mary Egner of Meck., to Henry Bullinger of same, for Ł 107 proc. money of NC, 200 A, the East part of 600 A granted to sd. Egner 21 Apr. 1764, extending from Carnahan's old line to tract bought from James Robinson...Jacob Eagner (Seal), Mary Eagner (X) (Seal). Wit: Robert Blackburn & a "Dutch name." Rec. April term 1769.

Pp. 497-498: 4 Feb. 1769, John McKee of Meck., to David Davis of same, for Ł 33 s 10, 150 A on head branches of Paw Creek on E side Catawba, adj. James Davis, James Moore, conveyed to McKee by John McKnitt Alexander, 9 Nov. 1764, and then by conveyance to John McKee, 26 July 1766 [apparently granted to Alexander 9 Nov. 1764 and sold to McKee 26 July 1766] ...John McKee (Seal), Hannah McKee (X) (Seal). Wit: John Hendry, John Garrison. Rec. April term 1769.

Pp. 499-500: 20 April 1768, Joseph Jolly to Thomas Wade of SC, merchant, for Ł 15 proc. money, 160 A part of a larger grant to Jolly on Thicketty Creek including his plantation where he now lives...Joseph Jolly (Seal). Wit: Henry Smith, Thos. Chadwick, Rec. Apr. Term 1769.

Pp. 501-502: 9 Feb. 1769, John Hendry & wf Martha of Meck., to James Pursley of same, for Ł 72 proc. money, 270 A on S side Allisons Creek including an Indian path, granted to John Hendry, by deed from William Patrick 6 Apr. 1765... John Hendry (Seal), Martha Hendry (O) (Seal). Wit: David Davies, Jos. Lee. Rec. April term 1769.

Pp. 502-506: 29 July 1768, John Fisher of Meck., to Jacob Miller of same, planter, (lease s5, release Ł 20 sterling), 400 A where Jacob Miller now lives on head branches of Widner's Creek and South fork branches, adj. Widner's line, patented to John Fisher, 25 Apr. 1767...John Fisher (Seal). Wit: Matthias Barringer and two who wrote their names in Dutch. Rec. April term 1769.

Pp. 507-509: 19 Apr. 1769, John Neal of Meck., to John Lusk of same, for ₤ 40 proc. money, 130 A on McCapins Creek adj. surveys made for Smith & Credenton...John Neel (Seal). Wit: Henry Downs, Samuel Loftain, Thos Neel. Prov. April term 1769.

Pp. 509-511: 30 March 1769, Matthias Barringer of Meck., to Martin Herkey of same, for ₤ 40 proc. money, 130 A on both sides of Buffalow Creek, a branch of Rocky or Johnston River, at Matthias Bevers, granted to Matthias Barringer by indenture, 25 June 1764...Matthias Barringer (Seal), Market Barringer (X) (Seal). Wit: Paul Barringer & two who wrote in Dutch. Rec. Apr. term 1769.

Pp. 511-514: 4 Dec. 1768, John Buchanan & wf Ann of Meck., to John Kinkead of Cumberland Co., Pa. for ₤ 80 proc. money, 350 A on west side of Catawba River on Mill Creek, being part of 1000 A granted to Robert Leeper, adj. lands of Leeper sold to William McCulloh...John Bouchanan (Seal), Ann Bouchanan (N) (Seal). Wit: Robt Irwin, Hugh Stuart, Andrew Leaney. Rec. April Court 1769.

Pp. 514-516: 8 June 1767, Archibald Houston & wf. Margaret of Meck., to James Price of same, shoemaker, for ₤ 30 current money, 250 A on N fork Crowders (Creek) on S side Catawba River adj. John Martin...Archibald Houston, Margaret Houston (M). Wit: William Ree, Samuel Patton, Samuel Pickens. Rec. April term 1769.

Page 517: 15 Oct. 1769, James Cook of Meck. & wf. Lucy to Jacob Gray of same, for ₤ 5 proc. money, 125 A where Jacob Gray now lives....James Cook (Seal), Lucy Cook (Seal). Wit: John McNilley, Benjamin Cook. Rec. Oct. term 1769.

Pp. 518-519: 10 Sept. 1769, John Penny & wf Margaret of Meck., to Martin Fifer of same, for ₤ 128 S 16 proc. money, 150 A on English Buffalow Creek, a branch of Rocky or Johnston River.. John Penny (Seal), Margrt Penney (Seal). Wit: Archibald Houston, Peter Johnston, James Rees. Prov. Oct. term 1769.

Pp. 519-520: 18 Apr. 1769, James David of Tryon Co., planter, to Arthur Patterson of Meck., for ₤ 70 proc. money, 200 A on waters of Shugar Creek between lands of James Johnston and Robert McClary, formerly conveyed by John Davis to James Davis.. James Davies. Wit: John Davies, Samuel McCleary. Rec. Oct. term 1769.

Pp. 520-521: 1 Sept. 1769, David Wilson & wf. Jane of Meck., to Joseph Scott of Orange Co., N.C. for ₤ 124 s 10 proc. money, 215 A on S side Coddle Creek a branch of Rocky River, adj. corner of tract where Nathaniel Erwin lives... David Wilson, Jane Wilson. Wit: John Pfifer, John Penny, Martin Fifer. Rec. Oct. term 1769.

Pp. 521-522: 12 Aug. 1769, Leonard Starring & wf Anna Catharine of Meck., to Peter Kaler of same, for ₤ 32 proc. money, 136 A on a branch of Dutch Buffalow, the waters of Rocky or Johnston River...Lennard Staring (LS), Anna Catharine Starring (ACS). Wit: John Pfifer, George Tucker (G), Martin Fifer. Rec. Oct. term 1769.

Pp. 522-523: 16 Oct. 1769, James Cook of Meck. & wf Lucy to John McNeally of same, for ₤ 5 proc. money, 200 A where John McNeally now lives...Jas Cook (Seal), Lucy Cook (Seal). Wit: Jacob Gray (₤), Benjamin Cook. Rec. Oct. term 1769.

Pp. 523-525: 10 Aug. 1769, Thomas Polk of Meck., to Samuel Jack of Meck., for ₤ 5 proc. money, 400 A on both sides of McCalpins Branch of Sugar Creek adj. William Alexanders corner Ezekiel Alexander's line, being full patent granted to Thomas Polk, 22 Dec. 1768...Thos Polk (Seal). Wit: John Davis, William Johnston. Rec. Oct. term 1769.

Pp. 525-526: 24 Aug. 1767, Arthur Alexander & wf Rachel of Meck., to Samuel McClery for d 4 proc. money, 60 A on waters of Sugar Creek, part of a grant by patent to sd. Arthur Alexander, adj. King's line...Arthur Alexander (Seal), Rachel Alexander (R) (Seal). Wit: Robert McClery, Ezra Alexander. Rec. Oct. term 1769.

Pp. 526-527: 1 Aug. 1769, Archibald Cathey of Meck., to Andrew Cathey for ₤ 250 NC currency, 300 A on the E side Catawba River, below the mouth of Paw Creek, granted to sd. Archibald Cathey by patent 21 Oct. 1768...Archibald Cathey (Seal). Wit: James McCord, John Henry. Rec. Oct. term 1769.

Pp. 528-529: 24 Feb. 1767, Henry Eustace McCulloh, Esqr., to William Hill, planter, for ₤ 12 proc. money, 240 A on head branches of McDowell's Creek in Mr. McCulloh's NW Barrony in Tract #4...adj. Bowmans line... Wit: William Frohock, Wm. Giles. Proved by William Giles, 12 Sept. 1769.

Pp. 529-530: 22 Feb. 1767, Henry Eustace McCulloh, Esq. to George Cathey of Meck., for ₤ 10 proc. money, 160 A on waters of McDowell's Creek at Cathey's former line...adj. Matthew McClure's survey, and 50 A adj. Robinson's survey, adj. Peel's corner. Wit: William Ffrohock, Wm. Giles. Prov. by William Giles, 12 Sept. 1769.

Pp. 531-532: 6 Oct. 1767, Robert McCashland & wf Agness of Meck., to James Byers of Rowan Co., for ₤ 50 proc. money, 220 A adj. the E side of Catawba River, adj. Francis Beateys upper line including a Great Bent or Turn of the River, granted by patent to sd. McCashland, 21 Dec. 1763...Robt McCasland (Seal), Agness McCasland (Seal). Wit: Aaron Biggerstaff, Henry Wright. Rec. Oct. term 1769.

Pp. 532-533: 18 Sept. 1769, Nathaniel Johnston of Meck., to John Garrison for ₤ 20 proc. money, 180 A on Mallard Creek, adj. Alexanders, Clarks, granted by patent to sd. Johnston, 22 Dec. 1768...Nathaniel Johnston (Seal). Wit: John Bouchanan, David Davison. Rec. Oct. term 1769.

Pp. 534-536: 3 Mar. 1769, John Miller of Meck., to Alexander Lewis, Getn., for ₤ 22 s 8 d 6 proc. money to be paid with interest by 13 Oct. next...two tracts on E side Catawba River (1): 315 A adj. John Price, Alexr. Cathey, granted to James Armour by L & R 16 July 1752, being the plantation John Miller now lives on (2) 212 A adj. above plantation & Mill place, at Mill Creek, granted by patent to Andrew Armour 10 Apr. 1761, and conveyed to sd. Miller...Jno. Miller (Seal), Hannah Miller (Seal). Wit: Henry Hendry, Jane Irwyn, Peter Stewart. Rec. Oct. term 1769.

Volume 4

Pp. 537-539: 28 Jan. 1767, John Campbell of Bertie Co., N. C. to John McKnitt Alexander, for ₺ 10 proc. money, tree tracts containing 250 A (1) 100 A on head branches of Millard's Creek including John Stallings old improvement, adj. late Gov. Dobbs Barryony (2) 60 [16] A on head branches of Mallards Creek, adj. John Boals and (3) 134 A on Joseph Cannons line, adj. Joys barrony line below the five springs. Wit: John Ffrohock, Robt. Harris. Rec. July term 1769.

Pp. 540-541: 21 July 1769, John Fondren, planter, of Tryon Co., to Hugh Stuart of Meck., for ₺ 65 proc. money, 200 A on waters of Rocky Creek in Tryon Co., including the Cross Roads where Celuda [Saluda] Road corsses the South fork road that leads to Charles Town, granted 6 Oct. 1765...John Fondren (Seal). Wit: William Goforth, John Conner. Rec. July term 1769.

Pp. 542-546: 21 May & 1 June 1769, Thomas Polk of Meck., to John White of Rowan Co., for (lease s5, release ₺ 47 s 10), 200 A on E side Catawba River "Between the Widder Armours and the Catawba Indians District" granted to sd. Polk 9 Nov. 1764.. Thos Polk (Seal). Wit: William Orr, Joseph Kennedy. Rec. July term 1769.

Pp. 546-548: 19 July 1769, John McKnitt Alexander of Meck., Taylor, to Hezekiah Alexander of same, blacksmith, for ₺ 80 proc. money, 300 A, part of granted to John Selwyn Esqr., 3 Mar. 1745 (O.S.) commonly called Tract #3... Jno McKnitt Alexander (Seal). Wit: James Baird, Abigail Alexander. Rec. July term 1769.

Pp. 548-549: 5 May 1768, Oliver Willey (Wyly) of Meck., to Benjamin Wilson, for ₺ 68 current money, one Negro fellow named Warrick...Oliver Willey (Seal). Wit: Richd Barry. Rec. July term 1769.

Pp. 549-551: 30 Jan. 1769, Samuel Harris of Meck., to his daughter Mary Wylie of same, and her two sons Oliver, the eldest, and Moses, the youngest, heir of her by her intermarriage with Moses Wylie, late deceased for affection and s 5 sterling, a female Negro slave called Kate...Saml Harris (Seal). Wit: John Harris, William Harris. Rec. July term 1769.

Pp. 552-553: 25 Feby 1769, George McWhorter & wf Elizabeth of Meck., to James Waughope of same, for 19 1/2 A of exchange, between each party, 19 1/2 A on S side of Waxhaw Creek in Meck., granted by Patent 3 Feb. 1754... George McWhorter (Seal), Elizabeth McWhorter (Seal). Wit: James Davis, John Curry. Rec. July term 1769.

Pp. 553-554: 21 Feb. 1769, James Waughope & wf Margaret to George McWhorter, 19 1/2 A of exchange, 19 1/2 A on N side Waxhaw Creek, granted by patent 4 May 1754...James Waughop (Seal), Margaret Waughop (Seal). Wit: James Davies, John Curry. Rec. July term 1769.

Pp. 555-557: 18 Mar. 1769, William Campbell and wf Jean of Meck., to Andrew Bones, for ₺ 50 proc. money, 75 A on Black Creek, a branch of Rocky River, granted to & conveyed from Arthur Dobbs Esqr., to John Campbell, by deed of sale, 24 Nov. 1762 and by him to William Campbell by L & R 2 Aug. 1763...

Volume 4

William Campbell ( ) (Seal), Jane Campbell ( ) (Seal). Wit: Robert Harris Junr., Robt. Harris. Rec. July term 1769.

Pp. 557-560: 19 July 1769, David Hays Junr & wf Jennet of Meck., to Moses Hays, son of John Hays decd. for ₤ 8 proc. money, 180 A on the dividing ridge between Paw Creek and Sugar Creek, where he lives, between where David Hays Senr. and David Hays, Junr., Part of two tracts, one of 560 A patented to Samuel Young, 27 Mar. 1754, the other granted to David Hays 22 Dec. 1768...David Hays (Seal), Janet Hays (O) (Seal). Wit: David Hay, Joseph Moore, Rec. July term 1769.

Pp. 560-562: 27 Feb. 1768, William Donaldson of Cumberland Co., Pa. to H Barnet of Meck., for ₤ 80 proc. money, 225 A on North side of West fork of Twelve Mile Creek granted by patent to sd. Davidson, 16 May 1754...Willm Donaldson by Thos Polk. Wit: Moses Alexander, Samuel Loftain. Rec. July term 1769.

Pp. 562-564: 24 Sept. 1768, James Howard of Meck., planter, to Robert Evans of same, for ₤ 44 proc. money, a certain tract in Meck., Co. on both sides of the north fork of Pacolet...James Howard. Wit: John Fondren, Hugh Quinn (X). Rec. July term 1769.

Pp. 564-567: 24 Sept. 1768, Zebulon Alexander & wf Hannah of Meck., to Hugh Barnet for ₤ 38 proc. money, 400 A on waters of Twelve Mile Creek in New Providence, adj. James McClure tract, about a mile from James Dunns land, James Rions corner... Zebulon Alexander (Seal), Hannan Alexander (Seal). Wit: Saml Loftain, Andrew Neel, John Clark. Rec. July term 1769.

Pp. 567-569: 18 July 1769, Thomas Beatey of Rwaon? Co., to William Latta of same, merchant, for ₤ 30 proc. money, 200 A on E side Catawba River about half a mile above John Beatey's ford between Thomas Beateys land and Robert McCashlands survey, where Robert Givens formerly had an Entry, granted to Francis Beaty 26 Nov. 1757, conveyed to Thomas Beaty by L & R, 21 & 22 Sept. 1762...Thomas Beatty (Seal). Wit: Ricd Barry, James Beatey, James Palley. Rec. July term 1769.

Pp. 570-571: 20 July 1769, James Orr Senr. of Meck., farmer, to Joseph Alexander of same, Minister of the Gospel, for ₤ 75 proc. money, 200 A, part of a grant to John Selwyn 3 Mar. 1745 (O.S.)...sold to sd. Orr, 7 Jan. 1767... James Orr (Seal). Wit: Thos. Polk, Geo. Allen. Rec. July term 1769.

Pp. 572-573: 20 July 1769, Peter Garrison of Meck., to William Sample of same, weaver, for ₤ 30 proc. money, 163 A part of a grant to John Selwyn near Kennedys corner...Peter Garrison (Seal). Wit: Thos Polk, Geo. Allen. Rec. July term 1769.

Pp. 574-575: 30 July 1769, Abraham Pfaister(?) of Meck., planter, to Matthias Mitchell of same, for ₤ 20 proc. money, and in consideration of the discharge of ₤ 56 s 5 of like money which I owe him, now conveyed several horses, cows, calves, hogs, etc., and improvements in my dwelling house at Cold Water. Abraham Pfaister (D) (Seal). Wit: Wm. Temple Coles, Peter Kittle. Rec. July term 1769.

Pp. 575-579: 19 Jan. 1769, Aaron Houseon, Planter, and wf. Margaret of Meck., to John Neichler, yeoman of same, for ₤ 48 current money, 300 A on waters of Coddle Creek near Hugh Parks, adj. Snoddy McKown, granted to Aaron Huston, 16 Nov. 1764...Aaron Houston (Seal), Margaret Houston (Seal). Wit: James Tate, James Houston, William Simms. Rec. July term 1769.

Pp. 579-581: 9 Dec. 1769, John Mitchell, Merchant & wf Elizabeth of Rowan Co., to Moses Moor of Meck., for ₺ 26 proc. money, 260 A on both sides Long Creek, part of 12,500 granted to Jeremiah Joy, late of London... Wit: Jno McKnitt Alexander, Isaac Mitchell. Rec. Jan. term 1770.

Pp. 581-583: 9 Dec. 1769, John Mitchell & wf Elisabeth to Joseph Cannon of Meck., for ₺ 40 proc. money, 303 A on waters of Long Creek, adj. Moses Moores corner, Falkners line, Wm. Henrys line, Wm. Sampels line, part of 12,500 Barony of Jeremiah Joy...Wit: Jno. McKnitt Alexander, Isaac Mitchel. Rec. Jan. Term 1770.

Pp. 583-585: 9 Dec. 1769, John Mitchel & wf Elisabeth to William Sample for ₺ 50 proc. money, 288 A on waters of Long Creek adj. Joseph Cannon, Henry, Bradley, Irwin, part of 12,500 barony of Jeremiah Joy...Wit: Same as preceding. Rec. Jan. term 1770.

Pp. 585-587: 9 Dec. 1769, John Mitchel & wf Elisabeth to John Cannon of Meck., for ₺ 18 proc. money, 200 A on waters of Long Creek adj. William Samples, James Bradleys, Crockets, part of 12,500 barony of Jeremiah Joy...Wit: Same as preceding. Rec. Jan. term 1770.

Pp. 587-588: 9 Dec. 1769, John Mitchel & wf Elisabeth to John McEntire of Meck., for ₺ 50 proc. money, 440 A adj. Bradley, Kerr, part of 12,500 barony of Jeremiah Joy. Wit: Isaac Mitchel, Jno McKnitt Alexander. Rec. Jan. term 1770.

Pp. 589-590: 9 Dec. 1769, John Mitchel & wf Elisabeth to David Hays, for ₺ 20 proc. money, 245 A adj. John McEntire. Wit: Same as preceding. Rec. Jan. term 1770.

Pp. 590-592: 9 Dec. 1769, John Mitchel & wf Elisabeth to John Boal of Meck., for ₺ 18 proc. money, 252 A on both sides of a branch of Sugar Creek, adj. Crocket, McRee. Wit: Same as preceding. Rec. Jan. term 1770.

Pp. 592-593: 9 Dec. 1769, John Mitchell & wf Elisabeth to John McRee of Meck., for ₺ 26 proc. money, 230 A on Barony Line, adj. Boal,. Wit: Same as preceding. Rec. Jan. term. 1770.

Pp. 594-595: 9 Dec. 1769, John Mitchell & wf Elisabeth to Alexander Mitchell of Meck., for ₺ 50 proc. money, 418 A on both sides a branch of Sugar Creek on Barony line, adj. John McRee. Wit: Same as preceding. Rec. Jan. term 1770.

Pp. 596-597: 9 Dec. 1769, John Mitchel & wf Elisabeth to James Reid of Meck., for ₺ 85 proc. money, 557 A adj. James Kerr. Wit: Same as preceding. Rec. Jan. term 1770.

Pp. 598-599: 9 Dec. 1769, John Mitchel & wf Elisabeth to John McCord of Meck., for ₺ 25 proc. money, 330 A adj. Mitchel,

Allin, then down Spring branch...Wit: Same as preceding. Rec. Jan. term 1770.

Pp. 600-601: 9 Dec. 1769, John Mitchell & wf Elisabeth to Culbert Nichelson of Meck., for Ł 9 proc. money, 72 A on waters of Sugar Creek...Wit: Same as preceding. Rec. Jan. term 1770.

Pp. 601-603: 9 Dec. 1769, John Mitchell & wf Elisabeth to Thomas Richey of Meck., for Ł 5 proc. money, 34 A on waters of Sugar Creek adj. Culbert Nicholsons, McCord. Wit: Same as preceding. Rec. Jan. term 1770.

Pp. 603-605: 9 Dec. 1769, John Mitchell & wf Elisabeth to William Robeson of Meck., for Ł 6 proc. money, 54 A on a small branch of Sugar Creek adj. Alexander Mitchel, John McCord. Wit: Same as preceding. Rec. Jan. term 1770.

Pp. 605-606: 9 Dec. 1769, John Mitchell & wf Elisabeth to James Allen of Meck., for Ł 38, 250 A adj. John McCord. Wit: Same as preceding. Rec. Jan. term 1770.

Pp. 607-608: 9 Dec. 1769, John Mitchell & wf Elisabeth to Joseph Kerr of Meck., for Ł 45, 362 A on waters of Long Creek a branch fo Catawba River on the barony line. Wit: Same as preceding. Rec. Jan. term 1770.

Pp. 608-610: 9 Dec. 1769, John Mitchell & wf Elisabeth to James McGin of Meck., [consideration not given] 223 A on waters of Sugar Creek & long Creek, adj. Joseph Kerr, James Reed, McEntire. Wit: Same as preceding. Rec. Jan. term 1770.

Pp. 610-611: 9 Dec. 1769, John Mitchell & wf Elisabeth to Robert Kerr of Meck., for Ł 12 proc. money, 125 A on barony line. Wit: Same as preceding. Rec. Jan. term 1770.

Pp. 612-163: 9 Dec. 1769, John Mitchell & wf Elisabeth to Robert Kerr of Meck., for Ł 71, 420 A on a long branch of long creek adj. James Bradley, John McEntire. Wit: Same as preceding. Rec. Jan. term 1770.

Pp. 613-615: 9 Dec. 1769, John Mitchell & wf Elisabeth to Robert Kerr of Meck., for Ł 15 proc. money, 1,000 A on both sides Kerr's branch of Long Creek, waters of Catawba River. Wit: Same as preceding. Rec. Jan. term 1770.

Pp. 615-617: 9 Dec. 1769, John Mitchell & wf Elisabeth to James Bradley of Meck., for Ł 60, 477 A on waters of Long Creek adj. Smith, Kerr, John McEntire, Irwin, Samples, Henry. Wit: Same as preceding. Rec. Jan. term. 1770.

Pp. 617-618: 9 Dec. 1769, John Mitchel & wf Elisabeth to John McKnitt Alexander of Meck., for Ł 15 proc. money, 222 A on N bank of Long Creek, adj. Henry, Erwin, Smith. Wit: Max Chambers, Isaac Mitchell, John Dunn. (No rec. date)

Pp. 619-620: 9 Dec. 1769, John Mitchell & wf Elisabeth to William Henry of Meck., for Ł 40 proc. money, 300 A on both sides of Long Creek, adj. Alexander, Erwin, Joseph Cannon, Smith. Wit: Isaac Mitchell, Jno. McKnitt Alexander. Rec. Jan. term 1770.

Volume 4

Pp. 621-622: 9 Dec. 1769, John Mitchell & wf Elisabeth to Jemima Sharp of Meck., for ₤ 12 proc. money, 138 A on both sides of Long Creek adj. Jos Cannon, Edward Irwin, Hobb. Wit: Same as preceding. Rec. Jan. term 1770.

Pp. 622-624: 9 Dec. 1769, John Mitchel & wf Elisabeth to Edward Erwin of Meck., for ₤ 68 proc. money, 320 A on both sides Long Creek, adj. Alexander Henry, Cannon, Sharp. Wit: Same as preceding. Rec. Jan. term 1770.

Pp. 624-625: 9 Dec. 1769, John Mitchell & wf Elisabeth to James Scott of Meck., for ₤ 20 proc. money, 185 A on waters of Long Creek and Garr Creek, adj. Smith, Patton. Wit: Same as preceding. Rec. Jan. term 1770.

Pp. 626-627: 9 Dec. 1769, John Mitchell & wf Elisabeth to John McKnitt Alexander of Meck., for ₤ 45, 377 A on both sides Long Creek adj. John Smith. Wit: Same as preceding. Rec. Jan. term 1770.

Pp. 628-629: 9 Dec. 1769, John Mitchell & wf Elisabeth to Charles Patton Meck., for ₤ 14 proc. money, 120 A on both sides of Garr Creek, adj. barrony line. Wit: Same as preceding. Rec. Jan. term 1770.

Pp. 629-631: 9 Dec. 1769, John Mitchell & wf Elisabeth to Beary McCoy of Meck., for ₤ 14 proc. money, 151 A on both sides of Garr Creek adj. James Scot, Alexander, Doherty, Patton. Wit: Max Chambers, Jno McKnit Alexander. Rec. Jan. term 1770.

Pp. 631-632: _____ 1769, John Mitchell & wf Elisabeth to John Doherty of Meck., for ₤ 18 proc. money, 185 A on both sides Garr Creek adj. John Smith, Barony line. Wit: Jno McKnitt Alexander, Isaac Mitchell. Rec. Jan. term 1770.

Pp. 633-634: 6 Mar. 1770, John Mitchell & wf Elisabeth to Isaac Lewis of Meck., for ₤ 80, 290 A on Lewis Branch, adj. James Barr, Beaver Dam Branch. Wit: Reese Price, James Barr. Rec. date not given.

Pp. 634-636: 3 Sept. 1768, John Mitchel & wf Elisabeth to Matthias Beaver of Meck., for ₤ 140 proc. money, 262 A on both sides Dutch Fuffalo Creek, adj. Gov. Dobbs line. Wit: John Phifer, Samuel Patton. Rec. July term 1770.

Pp. 636-637: 16 July 1770, Paul Barringer & wf Antis of Meck., to Nicholas Kress of same, for ₤ 100 proc. money, 171 A on Dutch B Creek at David Spreech's line, Charles Forgusons conveyed by L & R from John Young 24 & 25 July 1764, to sd. Young by Deed from Arthur Dobbs, 24 June 1762...Paul Barringer (Seal), Antis Barringer (X) (Seal). Wit: John Barringer, Georg Seil [German signature]. Rec July term 1770.

Pp. 637-638: 16 July 1770, Paul Barringer & wf Antes to Nicholas Kress of same, for ₤ 50 proc. money, 123 A on waters of Dutch Buffalow Creek, a branch of Rocky or Johnstons River, adj. Charles Foguson, Martin Binegar, David Spechs [sic] conveyed by deed from Arthur Dobbs, 16 Nov. 1764, Paul Barringer (Seal), Antis Barringer (X) (Seal). Wit: John Barringer, Georg Seil [German signature]   Rec. July term 1770.

Volume 4

Pp. 639-640: 18 July 1770, Thomas Polk of Meck., to Major Temple of same, for Ł 30 proc. money, 150 A on waters of Shuggar Creek adj. & between Mary McKee, Thomas Polk, including James Patterson's house, adj. Alexander, granted to Polk by patent 4 May 1769...Thos Polk (Seal). Wit: Abrm. Alexander, Thoms. Kennedy. Rec. July term 1770.

Pp. 640-641: 18 July 1770, Thomas Polk of Meck., to Major Temple of same, for Ł 25 proc. money, 85 A on waters of Shugar Creek adj. Abrm. Alexander, Mary McKee, granted to Polk by deed from H. E. McColough, 25 Feb. 1767. Wit: Adam Aleander, Mary McKee, granted to Polk by deed from H. E. McColough, 25 Feb. 1767, Wit: Adam Ale^{x}ander, Thomas Kennedy. Rec. July term 1770.

Pp. 642-643: 18 Dec. 1769, John Mitchel & wf Elisabeth of Rowan Co., to Thoms Wallis of Meck., for Ł 20 proc. money, 200 A on Rocky River including the improvement where William Young formerly dwelled, part of 12,500 granted to Ambrose Harding...Wit: John Shields, John Smith. Rec. July term 1770.

Pp. 643-645: 13 June 1770, Robert McKinley of Meck., to William McKinley, farmer of same, for Ł 5, 200 A on Paw Creek, part of 600 A granted to Robert McKinley, 18 Apr. 1764... Robert McKinley (2) (Seal). Wit: John Scott, David Davis. Rec. July term 1770.

Pp. 645-646: 20 Feb. 1770, Sarah Duckwalk of Meck., to Thoms. Black of same, for Ł 100 current, one mutallot wench named Rachel, one black mare, one gold ring, one pair of silver buttons, one large bell, one chince gown & apron, one new holand shift, one red cloak and Black silk handkerchief, and all other utensils that were left in the possession of Samuel Gordon...Sarah Duckwalk (X). Wit: Jams. Black, Jams. Black. Rec. July term 1770.

Pp. 647-648: 21 Mar. 1770, James Foster, Merchant of Charlotte Town in Meck., to Thoms Polk of same, for Ł 150, (1) 450 A on Indian Creek a south branch of S fork Catawba adj. Thoms. Ranolds, David Hedelstons [Huddlestons] (2) 240 A adj. Benjamin Alexander, John Sheilds (3) one house 30 foot front on Tryon St., and ninety back (4) two other tracts, one on Indian Creek on the north fork including Welches hunting camp, and another on both sides of Camp Creek below Nich Welches land... Jams Foster, Thoms Polk. Wit: Andrew Lock, John Rogers. Rec. July term 1770.

Pp. 649-650: 6 June 1770, George Colquehoon of Meck., to Charles Colquehoon, for love and affection, 220 A at Thomas Polks line, 400 A granted to Samuel Knox and conveyed to George Colquehoon on South fork of Steel Creek... George Calhown (O) (Seal). Wit: Thoms. Polk, John White. Rec. July term 1770.

Pp. 650-651: 16 Apr 1770, Samuel Bigham Senr of Meck., to William Hag of same, for Ł 30 proc. money, 250 A on E of the Catawba River on S side Paw Creek, adj. John Giles, being the moiety of 500 A granted to Bigham 21 Dec. 1763...Samuel Bigham (Seal). Wit: John Moore, John Scott. Rec. July term 1770.

Volume 4

Pp. 652-653: 5 Sept. 1769, John Farmer of Meck., to Samuel Knox and Moses Ferguson of same, for ₤ 50 sterling, tract on E side Catawba adj. Buchanan, Bigger, Walker, granted to Farmer 29 Apr. 1768...John Farmer (Seal). Wit: Richd. Barry, John Davison, Matt McClure. Rec. July term 1770.

Pp. 654-655: 20 Dec. 1769, John Frohock, Thoms. Polk Esqr., and George Allen all of Meck., to John Allen of Meck., for s 5 sterling, Lot #11 in town of Charlotte on E side Traid [sic] St., granted to Abraham Alexander, Thomas Polk, John Frohock...Wit: Ann Higgison, James Carter. Rec. July term 1770.

Pp. 656-657: 5 Jan. 1768, John Anderson of Meck., to John Caldwell of same, for ₤ 80 proc. money, 233 A on Anderson Creek a branch of Rocky River, conveyed from Arthur Dobbs Esqr., 10 Feb. 1765...John Anderson (Seal). Wit: Robt Harris, Robert Harris Junr. Rec. July term 1770.

Pp. 658-659: 18 July 1770, Mathew Patton of Meck., blacksmith, to William Moore of same for ₤ 90 proc. money, 200 A on waters of Long Creek and Paw Creek, part of 600 A granted by John Davis 10 Apr. 1761, conveyed to Mathew Patton, 19 July 1763, adj. Robt McKinley...Mathew Patton (Seal), Jane Patton (0) (Seal). Wit: Joseph Moore, George Elliot. Rec. July term 1770.

Pp. 660-663: 14 Jan. 1769, Samuel Knox & wf Mary of Meck., planter to Samuel McCrum of same, planter, for (lease s 5, release ₤ 120 NC money) 400 A on E side Catawba River, and on head waters of Jane Armours Creek, adj. McCormick...Samuel Knox (Seal), Mary Knox (0) (Seal). Wit: Thos Polk, Moses Alexandr. Rec. Jan. term 1770

Pp. 664-665: _____ 1720[sic] Thomas Polk, Abram Alexander & George Allen to William Elliot of same, for s 90 proc. money, lot #31 in Charlotte on E side of Small Street in the No. Square...Wit: Joseph Kennedy, Thos. Harris. Rec. Jan. Court 1770.

Page 666: 31 Dec. 1720[sic] John Ogle of Meck., to James Harris of same, for ₤ 5 proc. money, 300 A at Leggets upper corner...John Ogle (0) (Seal). Wit: Jams. Cook, Magel(?) Crocket. Rec. Jan. Court 1771.

Page 667: 3 Augt. 1770, Thos Stone of Craven County, S. C. to James Cook of Meck., for ₤ 5 proc. money, 300 A at Robert Davis line...Thos Stone (Seal). Wit: Jacob Greay (I), Willm Foster (X). Rec. Jan. term 1771.

Pp. 668-669: 18 Dec. 1769, John Mitchell & wf Elizabeth to Charles Harris of Meck., for ₤ 30 proc. money, 147 A on Rocky River on the Barony lien, part of 12,500 A granted to Ambrose Harding...Wit: Jno McK. Alexandr, John Braly. Rec. July term 1770.

Pp. 670-671: 1 May 1769, John Bravard & wf Jeane (Jane) of Rowan Co., to Bartholomew Johnston of Meck., for ₤ 30, 200 A on waters of Davisons Creek adj. Andw Lynn, decd., James McCleland, Mathew McKorkle, granted to John Brevard, 26 Nov. 1757...John Bravard (Seal), Jane Bravard (Seal). Wit:

Robert Doudle, Hugh Bravard, Alexandr. Young. Rec. July term 1770.

Pp. 672-673: 15 Dec. 1770, David Flough of Meck., saddler, to Daniel McKimmins of same, planter, for Ł 104 proc. money, 197 A on both sides McKees branch of Reedy Creek, waters of Rocky River, near the Governours line deed to Flough by Oliver Wyly, 29 July 1768, and to Wyly by George Allen, 27 July 1767, and to Allen by George Augustus Selwyn, 5 May 1765...David Flough (Seal). Wit: Mathew Harris, Robert Harris. Rec. Jan. term 1771.

Pp. 674-675: 15 Jan. 1770, Thoms Polk, Abrm Alexander & Geo. Allen of Meck., to Aaron Huston of same, for Ł 2 proc. money, Lot #12 in Charlotte on E side Trade St., Wit: Isaac Yelton, Robert Burns. Rec. July Term 1770.

Page 676: 27 Dec. 1770, John Ofle of Meck., to Michel Ligget Senr. of same, for Ł 5 proc. money, 300 A adj. lines of William Ligget...John Ogle (O) (Seal). Wit: Jams. Cook, Jas. Harris. Rec. Jan. Court 1771

Pp. 677-678: 14 July 1770, John Doudle & wf Elenor of Meck., to Robert Doudle of same, for Ł 1, 100 A a part of the tract whereon John Doudle now lives, adj. land of Barth. Johnston, Mathew McKorkle, granted to James McClellan, 17 May 1764, and made over to John Burnet...John Doudle (2) (Seal), Elinor Doudle (O) (Seal). Wit: Barth. Johnston, Jams. Doudle, Abram Yelton. Rec. July term 1770.

Pp. 679-680: 12 Apr. 1770, John Black & wf Margaret of Meck., to William Irvin, for Ł 100 proc. money, 137 A on waters of McCalpins Creek, adj. land of Francis Johnson, deeded from George A. Selwyn, 15 Jan. 1767...John Black (Seal), Margaret Black (Seal). Wit: James Wyly, William Harris, Rec. Jan. Court 1771.

Pp. 681-682: 4 Nov. 1770, William Queery, Cooper & wf. Margaret of Meck., to Thos Willson, weaver, of same, for Ł 105 proc. money, 106 A on waters of Goose Creek, a branch of Rocky or Johnstons River, conveyed to William Queery by Arthur Dobbs 25 June 1764...William Query (Seal), Margret Query (SelaO). Wit: Jas. Willson, Robert Harris Junr. Rec. Jan. term 1771.

Pp. 682-684: 6 Sept. 1769, John McKnit Alexander of Meck., to James Slone or Slown of same, for Ł 18 proc. money, 130 A on head branches of Mallard Creek, including John Stalfingers old improvement, adj. Gov. Dobbs baroney, deed to Alexander from John Campbell by H. E. McCulloh, 20 Jan. 1767.. Wit: John Smith, John Patteson, William Thompson. Rec. April term 1770.

Pp. 684-686: 7 Jan. 1771, William Hagans & wf Mary of Meck., to James Dunn of same, farmer, for Ł 190 proc. money, 250 A on both sides Clarks Branch of Twelve Mile Creek adj. lines of James Dunn, granted to James Ryan by patent 19 Apr. 1763, and conveyed to Hagans 13 Jan. 1764...William Hagans (Seal), Mary Hagans (Seal). Wit: Henry Downs, Jams Huston, John Hagans. Rec. Jan. term 1771.

Volume 4

Pp. 686-688: ___ Apr. 1771, David Davis & wf Elisabeth of Meck., to Francis Herring (Herron), of same, for ₤ 20, 142 A on W side Kings Branch & on both sides of the Trading Road, part of tract deed to Davis from Geo. A. Selwyn, 12 Jan. 1767.. David Davis (Seal), Elisabeth Davis (Seal). Wit: Jams. Kenneday, William Alexander. Rec. April term 1770.

Pp. 688-690: 10 Mar. 1770, William Irwin & wf Sarah of Meck., to Robert Harris Junr of same, for ₤ 180 proc. money, 225 A on waters of Reedy Creek adj. Gov. Dobbs line, adj. Joseph Harris, deed to Irwin by Selwyn, 9 Jan. 1767...William Irwin (Seal), Sarah Irwing (&) (Seal). Wit: William Harris, James Wyly. Rec. April term 1770.

Pp. 690-692: 20 May 1764, James Davis & Francis Beatey of Meck., to John Davis of same, for ₤ 10 proc. money, 600 A on N branch of Steel Creek, above John Henry's lick, granted to Davis & Beaty, 21 Apr. 1764...James Davis (Seal), Francis Beatey (Seal). Wit: John Beatey, Thomas Palley. Rec. April term 1770.

Pp. 692-695: 24 Oct. 1765, James Davis & wf Margret of Meck., to Robt McCleery of same, planter, for ₤ 10 s 15 NC money, 126 A on NW side of Shuggard Creek adj. McCleery, James Davis, the north end of 600 A granted to John Davis, 15 Nov. 1762 and conveyed to James Davis by L & R, 21 & 22 Oct. 1765... James Davis (Seal), Margt Davis (X) (Seal). Wit: Robert Gerret (X), Abigel McCleary, Thos Polk. Rec. April term 1770.

Pp. 696-697: 23 Oct. 1765, James Davis & wf Margaret of Meck., to Robert McCleery of same, for s 5 sterling (apparently lease to above deed)...Wit: Thos Polk, Major Temple.

Page 698: 14 Apr. 1770, Thomas Coyl of Meck., to Willm Hagans of same for ₤ 40 good money of NC, horses, cattle & sheep...Thoms. Coyl. Wit: John Hagans. Rec. April term 1770.

Pp. 699-700: 1 July 1771, John Garison of Meck., to William Sawyers Senr of Lancaster Co., Pa., for ₤ 60 Pa currency, 400 A on the waters of Shugar Creek adj. land of Moses Stell, full contents of a deed to John Garison 7 Jan. 1767...John Garison (Seal), Hannah Garison (H) (Seal). Wit: Ezekiel Alexander, Thos McClure. [No rec. date]

Page 701: Blank

Page 702: Book XIth, Robert Harris Register.

Page 703-704: 24 Feb. 1767, George Augustus Selwyn to Zebulon Alexander of Meck., for ₤ 5 sterl., 100 A, part of 100,000 A known as Tract #3...Wit: Thos Ffrohock, William Ffrohock. Rec. Oct. term 1767.

Pp. 704-705: 24 Feb. 1767, Selwyn to Abram (Abraham) Alexander of Meck., for ₤ 6 s 5 sterling, 125 A on waters of Sugar Creek adj. Samples, Allen, Widow Alexander, Thomas Polk, David Kenedy, Col. Frohock, Part of Tract #3. Same wit. as preceding. Rec. Oct. term 1767.

Page 706-707: 24 Feb. 1767, Selwyn to Andrew Sprot of Meck., for ₤ 3 s 15 sterling, 78 A, part of Tract #3, adj. Starret, Joseph Lee, Same wit. as preceding. Rec. Oct. term 1767.

Pp. 707-708: 24 Feb. 1767, George Augustus Selwyn to John Barnet of Meck., for ₤ 4 sterling, 83 A part of Tract #3. Same wit. as preceding. Rec. Oct. term 1767.

Page 709-710: 24 Feb. 1767, Selwyn to Timothy White of Meck., for ₤ 10 sterl., 200 A adj. John Holloway, part of Tract #3. Same wit. as preceding. Rec. Oct. term 1767.

Pp. 710-711: 24 Feb. 1767, Selwyn to Abraham Miller of Meck., for ₤ 7 sterling, 155 A on waters of McCalpins Creek, tract #3. Same wit. as preceding. Rec. Oct. term 1767.

Pp. 712-713: 24 Feb. 1767, Selwyn to John Parks of Meck., for ₤ 4 s 12 sterling 92 A part of 100,000 A. Same wit. as preceding. Rec. Oct. term 1767.

Pp. 713-714: 24 Feb. 1767, Selwyn to Noble Ozburn (Osburn) of Meck., for ₤ 6 sterling, 135 A part of Tract #3. Same wit. as preceding. Rec. Oct. term 1767.

Page 714-716: 24 Feb. 1767, Selwyn to John McElwee of Meck., for ₤ 5 s 10 sterling, 115 A (80 A and 35 A). Same wit. as preceding. Rec. Oct. term, 1767.

Pp. 716-717: 24 Feb. 1767, Selwyn to David Garrison of Meck., for ₤ 8 s 10 sterling, 170 A adj. James Willson, John McElwee, part of Tract #3,... Same wit. as preceding. Rec. Oct. term 1767.

Page 717-719: 24 Feb. 1767, Selwyn to Thomas Harris of Meck., for ₤ 2 s 10 sterling, 50 A near John Ramseys, part of Tract #3. Same wit. as preceding. Rec. Oct. term 1767.

Pp. 719-720: 24 Feb. 1767, Selwyn to John Ford of Meck., for ₤ 4 s 10 sterling, 90 A adj. Richard Buckelews, Culberson, Johnson, David Moore, part of Tract #3...Same wit. as preceding. Rec. Oct. term 1767.

Page 720-721: 24 Feb. 1767, Selwyn to Robert Barnet of Meck., for ₤ 10 sterling, 200 A part of 100,000 A. Same wit as preceding. Rec. Oct. term 1767.

Pp. 722-723: 24 Feb. 1767, Selwyn to William Hannagen of Meck., for ₤ 3 sterling, 67 A by the Road that leads from Dearmons Saw mill to Steel Creek, part of Tract #3. Same wit. as preceding. Rec. Oct. term 1767.

Pp. 723-724: 12 Feb. 1767, Selwyn to John Neel of Meck., for ₤ 3 s 10 sterling, 70 A adj. his own and John Parkes survey, part of 100,000 A...Same wit. as preceding. Rec. Oct. term 1767.

Pp. 724-725: 24 Feb. 1767, Selwyn to William Black of Meck., for ₤ 5 sterling, 110 A. part of Tract #3. Same wit. as preceding. Rec. Oct. term 1767.

Pp. 726-727: 14 Oct. 1768, John Allen & wf Agness of Meck., to Henry Mitchell of same, for ₤ 20 proc. money, 297 A on both sides of Back Creek, and subdivided from McCulloh's south east Barony in Tract #4, granted to John Allen by deed from H. E. McCulloh 3 May 1765...John Allen (Seal), Anges Allen (X) (Seal). Wit: Isaac Harland, Robert Harris, James Alcorn. Rec. Oct. term 1768.

Pp. 729-729: 9 Jan. 1768, John Harden & wf Elisabeth of Meck., to James McAfee of same, for Ł 45, 300 A on both sides Kings Creek that flows into Broad River near the Road of John Kuykendall, granted by patent to John Harden. 19 Apr. 1763... John Harden (Seal), Elisabeth Harden (X) (Seal). Wit: Rene Julien, John McElmorry, Jacob Randall. Rec. Oct. term 1768.

Pp. 730-731: 8 Oct. 1768, Willm Carson & wf Mary of Meck., to Amos Alexander of same, for Ł 38 proc. money, 200 A on Armours Creek adj. Morgan, Price and Downs land, granted to Carson 6 Apr. 1765...Walter Carson (Seal), Mary Carson (M) (Seal). Wit: Jno Cathey, John Martin, Aaron Alexander. Rec. Oct. term 1768.

Pp. 732-733: 25 June 1768, John Colson of Anson County, NC to James Minis (Minzes) of Cumberland Co., N.C. for Ł 20 proc. money, 150 A on ear a branch of Richardsons Creek, including Vill Smiths "folly," part of grant to John Colson, 25 Apr. 1767...John Collson (Seal), Mary Collson (M) (Seal). Wit: Willm Colson, George Read, John Stuart (X). Rec. Oct. term 1768.

Pp. 734-735: 6 Aug. 1768, Andrew Hampton & wf Katherine of Meck., (formerly Anson) to Benjamin Hider of same, for Ł 20 proc. money, 200 A on N side Broad River between Thomas Johnsons and Ephraim McClains, granted to Andrew Hampton (Seal), Catharine Hampton (X) (Seal). Wit: John Ritzhaupt, Davis Alexander, William Swinny. Rec. Oct. term 1768.

Pp. 736-737: ___ 1768, William Adams of Meck., yeoman, to John Smith of same for Ł 5 s 10 proc. money, 200 A on both sides Cedar Creek, waters of Broad River, above William Ray's land adj. Young's mountain, granted to sd. Adams 26 Apr. 1768.. William Adams (Seal). Wit: Thomas Price, Wm. Sharp. Rec. Oct. term 1768.

Pp. 737-738: 16 July 1768, John Doherty of Meck., to Charles Gilham of same, for Ł 20 proc. money, 140 A on both sides Bullocks Creek, E side Broad River adj. Dunlap, Bell, Sharp, granted to sd. Doherty, 29 Apr. 1768... John Doherty ( ) (Seal). Wit: William Sharp, James Scott. Rec. Oct. term 1768.

Pp. 739-740: 10 May 1768, Robert Barnett of Meck,. planter, to David Vance of same, for ₤ 25 proc. money, 310 A on each side of Catawba River on waters of Steel Creek and Sugar Creek, at William Barnett's old corner, adj. Robert McRee, Zaccheus Willson, including 300 A patented to Robert Barnett, 26 Oct. 1767, and 10 A including where David Vance now dwells part of SE part of William Barnetts land which he conveyed to Robert Barnett...Robert Barnett (Seal). Wit: Zacheus Wilson, William Bigham Rec. Oct. term 1768.

Pp. 740-741: 24 Aug. 1768, William Adair of Meck., planter, to Michael Rudisalo of same, for Ł 60 proc. money, 400 A on both sides Long Creek adj. Frederick Hamright, on S side S fork Catawba, about a mile above Jacob Hoyls plantation, granted to William Adair, 27 Mar. 1755...Wm Adair (Seal). Wit: John Moore, Sal. Moore, James Williamson. Rec. Oct. term 1768.

Pp. 742-743: 24 Aug. 1768, Frederick Hambright & wf Sarah of Meck., to William Patterson, of same, for ₤ 10 proc. money, 92 A adj. west side of Catawba River, by James Cunningham, Beaty, Cathy, Barnet, conveyed by Hambright to Patterson, by deed bearing same date as this; part of 200 A granted to Roger Cook, 30 Oct. 1765, and conveyed to Hambright 14 Mar. 1768... Frederick Hambright (Seal), Sarah Hambright (X) (Seal). Wit: Ralph Felmming, Hugh Beaty, Francis Beaty. Rec. Oct. term 1768.

Pp. 744-745: 10 Oct. 1768, Robert Campbell of Meck., to Francis Armstrong of same, Planter, for ₤ 15 proc. money, 200 A. on W side Catawba River between South fork and Main River on both sides Leeper's Waggon Road, adj. Francis Beaty, Widow Leeper, John Armstrong, decd., granted to Campbell 26 Oct. 1767...Robert Campbell (Seal). Wit: James Beaty, John Huggins. Rec. Oct. term 1768.

Pp. 745-746: 18 June 1768, Elisha Thompson of Meck., yeoman, to William Sharp of same, for ₤ 10 proc. money, 400 A on Middle fork of Tyger River, including the Shoals, adj. Thomas Penny, granted to sd. Thompson, 29 Apr. 1768... Elisha Thompson (Seal). Wit: Alexander McCarty, Joseph Kellar. Rec. Oct. term 1768.

Pp. 747-748: 24 Aug. 1768, Frederick Hambright & wf Sarah to William Patterson, for ₤ 90 proc. money, 200 A adj. W. side Catawba and Joseph Harden, Roger Cook improvements, part of 400 A granted to Samuel Young and conveyed to John Kuykendall, decd., and Joseph Harden, then to Hambright, then to Roger Cook, then to Hambright...Frederick Hambright (Seal), Sarah Hambright (8) (Seal). Wit: Ralph Fleming, Hugh Beaty, Francis Beaty. Rec. Oct. term 1768.

Pp. 749-750: 8 June 1768, Zachariah Routh & wf Elizabeth of Meck., to Michael Hoyle of same, for ₤ 100 proc. money, 200 A on both sides of Long Creek a South branch of Catawba River, a little above the Great Falls near the land of Francis Beaty, purchased of James Armstrong, now David Staly(?), granted to Francis Beaty, 14 Apr. 1761, conveyed to Thomas Henry, then to Routh...Zachariah Routh (Seal), Elizabeth Routh (X) (Seal). Wit: Frederick Hambright, John Th___ (torn) Rec. Oct. term 1768.

Page 751: 26 July 1768, Joseph White of Anson Co., NC to John Clark of Meck., for ₤ 40 proc. money, 200 A on N fork of Pacolet adj. Margaret Campbell, granted to White ___...Joseph White (Seal). Wit: Saml Spencer, Heza. Russ. Rec. Oct. term 1768.
[For an exact reference and description of the above grant and plat, see my N.C. Land Grants in S.C., Volume II, p. 84.]

Pp. 752-753: 11 Aug. 1768, Jacob Cobron of Meck., planter, to Henry Vernon of same, planter, for ₤ 60 proc. money, 317 A (except so much as interlocks with Andrew Falls land) on both sides of the North Fork of Crowders Creek, between lines of

Volume 4

William Ray & Andrew Falls, granted to Coborn, 6 Nov. 1764... Jacob Cobron (Seal). Wit: Charles McLean, John Walker, William Sims. Rec. Oct. term 1768.

Pp. 753-755: 6 Oct. 1768, Aaron Alexander of Meck., to Benjamin Cohorn, for £ 7 S 10, 100 A on E side Catawba River, being the tract whereon Alexander now lives, adj. John Martin, crossing the Meadow branch, part of grant to Jas Miller, 6 Apr. 1765 and conveyed to Thomas Jarrel, 6 Apr 1765, then to Aaron Alexander, 1 Sept. 1767...Aaron Alexander (Seal). Wit: Jno Cathey, Alexandr. Lewis. Rec. Oct. term 1768..

Pp. 755-756: 1 Aug. 1768, Robert Bishop of Craven County, S. C. to William Sisson of Meck., for £ 275 South money, 100 A on N side Pacolet River, "concluding" the plantation where Bishop did live, part of 200 A granted to Bishop, 26 Sept. 1766...Robert Bishop (Seal), Elizabeth Bishop (E) (Seal). Wit: Edward Bishop, Aron Springer (X). Rec. Oct. term 1768.

Pp. 757-758: 26 Dec. 1767, Amos Alexander of Meck., to Benjamin Cohorn (Cohron) of same, for £ 17 s 10, 100 A on E side Catawba River on waters of Armour's Mill branch, at a corner to Ramsays, Down, Miller, granted to Thomas Jarrel, 25 Apr. 17__, conveyed to Alexander 7 Nov. 1767...Amos Alexander (Seal). Wit: Jno Cathey, Alexander Lewis. Rec. Oct. term. 1768.

Pp. 759-760: 13 Oct. 1768, William Sharp of Meck., to Henry Shepherd of Craven Co., S. C. for £ 5 proc. money, 200 A on the waters of Bullocks Creek on the head of Stephenson's Branch, granted to William Sharp, 6 Oct. 1765... William Sharp (Seal). Wit: Jno McK. Alexander, Wm. Givens. Rec. Oct. term 1768.

Pp. 760-761: 7 Sept. 1768, Jno McNitt Alexander of Meck., to Saml Thompson of S. C. for £ 6 s 6 currency money, 200 A on waters of Turkey Creek on both sides of Morris' Mill Creek, by a small graveyard, granted to Alexander 30 Oct.1765, Jno McKt. Alexander (Seal). Wit: William Henry, James Cannon. Rec. Oct. term 1768.

Pp. 762-763: 3 Sept. 1768, John McNitt Alexander of Meck., to John Riggs of same, for £ 4 s 18 proc. money, 200 A on both sides Turkey Creek at Hugh Simpsons, Kolb, Morris, Moore, McBrayer, Hillhouse, Campbell, granted to John Riggs & John McNitt Alexander, 26 Oct. 1767...John McNitt Alexander. Wit: James Cannon, William Semple. Rec. Oct. term 1768.

Pp. 763-764: 24 Sept. 1768, John Walker of Meck., to Samuel Richardson of Meck., for £ __ s 10 proc. money, 157 A on east side of Broad River, granted to Walker 27 Apr. 1767...John Walker (Seal). Wit: William Sims, Robert Campbell (R). Rec. Oct. term 1768.

Pp. 765-766: 18 Dec. 1768, John McCulloh of Meck., to James Armour of same, for £ 10 s 5, 60 A between Allison's Creek and Beaver on a branch called Camp Run, including Armour's improvements, adj. Clintons entry...John McCulloh (Seal). Wit: James Campbell, James Duff. Rec. Oct. term 1768.

Pp. 766-767: 7 Dec. 1768, James Simral & wf Violet of Meck., to Jennet Irwin of Rowan Co., NC, for £ 50 proc. money, 200

Volume 4

A on N side Broad River on McDowel's Creek, about half a mile above Hugh Verrys survey, including the fork of the Creek, granted to James Simral, 25 Apr. 1767...James Simral (Seal), Vilet Simral. Wit: John Cathy, James Byares(?). Rec. Oct. term 1768.

Pp. 768-769: 29 Sept. 1768, James Clark of Meck., to Hezekiah Pigg of same, for Ł 50 lawful money, 1__ A on main Broad River adj. below John Stanford, to the foot of a mountain, granted Apr. 1767...James Clark (X) (Seal). Wit: Isom Peeples (X), William Sharp. Rec. Oct. term 176[8].

Pp. 769-770: 10 Sept. 1768, Moses Ferguson of Meck., to Thomas Polk, Esqr., of same, for Ł 100 current money, 305 A on waters of Sugar Creek adj. Carrol, John Carson, John Newman, on the Boundary line...Moses Ferguson (Seal). Wit: Thomas Kenedy[?], Nathaniel Irwin. Rec. Oct. term 1768.

Pp. 770-771: 23 Sept. 1768, John Riggs of Meck., to John McNitt Alexander of same, for Ł 5 proc. money, 200 A on both sides of Turkey Creek, granted to Riggs and Alexander, 27 Sept. 1766...John Riggs (I) (Seal). Wit: James Cannon, William Sample. Rec. Oct. term 1768.

Pp. 772-773: 8 Sept. 1768, John Brandon Esq. of Rowan Co., N.C. to John McNitt Alexander of Meck., for Ł 5 s 10 proc. money, 640 A on N side Kings Creek near Collins line, patented by John Brandon 20 Apr. 1768...John Brandon (Seal). Wit: Hez: Alexander, Walter Carouth, James Graham. Rec. Oct. term 1768.

Pp. 773-774: 10 Aug. 1768, James Adear & wf Mary of Meck., to Absolom Waters of same, for Ł 80 proc. money, 200 A on W side Catawba River, which he lives on, near the upper end of the island, granted to Adear, 21 Dec. 1763... James Adear (E) (Seal), Mary Adear (E) (Seal), Wit: Andrew Hampton, Benjamin Hider, Samuel McC[anley?]. Rec. Oct. term 1768.

Pp. 775-776: 12 Oct. 1768, James Alexander & wf Elizabeth and Ezekiel Alexander & wf Martha of Meck., to Arthur Dickson of same, for Ł 60, 111 A on one of the branches of Sugar Creek adj. John Buchannon, granted to James & Ezekiel Alexander out of John Campbells barony, by deed...James Alexander (Seal), Ezekiel Alexander (Seal), Martha Alexander (X) (Seal). Wit: Robert Irwin, John Buchanan, Wm. Flenniken. Rec. Oct. term 1768.

Pp. 777-779: 5 May 1768, William Ross of Meck., & wf Elizabeth to James Ashmore of same, for Ł 25 proc. money, 56 A lying on the ridges between English Buffalo and Coddle Creek...William Ross (Seal), Elizabeth Ross (Seal). Wit: Martin Phifer, John Ffifer. Rec. Oct. term 1768.

Pp. 779-783: 5 Aug. 1768, James Wyly Esqr., High Sheriff of Meck., to John Mitchell of Rowan Co., for his bid of Ł 415 s 10 proc. money, part of 12,500 A on branches of Johnston and Santee Rivers in Meck., known as Tract #1, adj. tracts belonging to James McCulloh, and Mrs. Penelope McCulloh by virtue of a fiere facias from the Superior Court for the District of Wilmington, Nov. 1768, for Ł 275 against Ambrose Harding, late of Dublin, Councellor at Law...Wit: John Dunn, Wm. Temple Coles. Rec. Oct. term 1768.

Volume 4

Page 784: 16 Oct. 1768, Abraham Stephens of Meck., to Alexander McKee, bill of sale, his book accounts, two beds, pails, pots, a gray Mare branded W, etc...Abram Stevens (Seal). Wit: Moses Ferguson, Jonathan Newman. Rec. Oct. term 1768.

Pp. 785-789: 5 Aug. 1768, James Wyly Esqr. High Sheriff of Meck., to John Mitchell of Rowan Co., for ₺ 460 s 5 proc. money, tract #4, part of 12,500 A on branches of Pee Dee and Santee Rivers, patented to Jeremiah Joy, 3 Mar. 1745. Wit: John Dunn, Wm. Temple Coles. Rec. Oct. term 1768.

Pp. 789-790: 14 Sept. 1768, Abraham Stevens of Meck., to John Tagert of Meck., for ₺ 10, bill of sale for one bay horse, "being the horse I lent to William Bogan at last July Court to Ride Home"...Abraham Stevens (Seal). Wit: Will Reed, Jas Way. Rec. Oct. term 1768.

Pp. 790-791: 13 Apr. 1768, Richard Barry & wf Ann of Meck., to Francis Ross, of same, for ₺ 20 proc. money, 350 A on waters of Turkey Creek and north side Davison's Branch, near William Wattson, James Afee(?), granted by patent to Richard Barry, 25 Sept. 1766...Richd Barry (Seal), Ann Barry (Seal). Wit: William Wattson, George Denny, William Drew. Rec. Oct. term 1768.

Pp. 791-792: 25 Aug. 1768, William Boggan, late of Meck., planter, to Thomas Wade Esqr., of Craven County, S.C., for ₺ 60 proc. money, 250 A on N side Broad River on Howards Creek...Wm Boggan (Seal). Wit: John Wade, Jurat: Wm McKown. Rec. Oct. term 1768.

Pp. 793-794: 20 Aug. 1768, William Boggan, planter, late of Meck., to Thomas Wade of Craven Co., S.C., for ₺ 30 proc. money 200 A on West branches of Bullocks Creek...Wm Boggan (Seal). Wit: John Wade, Jurat., William McKown. Rec. Oct. term 1768.

Pp. 794-795: 12 Sept. 1768, Thomas Roddy & wf Hanah of Meck., to Michael Ligget, planter, for ₺ 45 proc. money, 108 A on both sides of Clem Creek, on a branch of Johnston or Rocky River adj. Michael Ligget, part of a grant to Francis Roddy by Arthur Dobbs & wf Justina 25 June 1764...Thomas Ready (Seal) Hannah Raidy (X) (Seal). Wit: Adam Alexander, William Gordon. Rec. Oct. term 1768.

Pp. 795-797: 20 July 1768, David McMickons & wf Mary of Meck., to Hugh Harron, planter, of same, for ₺ 100 proc. money release, 360 A on E side Catawba River, adj. Matthew Knox, granted to McMickon...David McMickon (Seal), Mary McMicken (Seal). Wit: Archd. McNeal, Matthew Knox. Rec. Oct. term 1768.

Page 798: 19 July 1768, David McMikon & wf Mary of Meck., to Hugh Harron...lease of preceding deed. Rec. Oct. term 1768.

Page 799: 2d part of Book No. 12 50 deed herein.

Pp. 799-800: 13 Sept. 1767, Hugh Berry & wf Jean and Andrew Pattrick all of Meck., to John Bohannon, Taylor, of same, for ₺ 30, 167 A on South side of Crowders Creek adj. Nathaniel Henderson, granted by patent to Hugh Berry & Andrew Pattrick, 28 Oct. 1765. Hugh Barry (Seal), Jean Barry (Seal), Andrew Pattrick (Seal). Wit: Matt Floyd, Joseph Carrel. Rec. July term 1768.

Volume 4

Pp. 800-801: 23 June 1768, Abram Clemons of Meck., to James Howard of same, for ₤ 50 proc. money, land on which Clemons now lives on S side Pacolet...Abram Clemons (Seal). Wit: John Fondron, William Willcocks. Rec. July term 1768.

Pp. 801-802: 7 July 1768, James Alexander & wf Elisabeth of Meck., to William Alexander, blacksmith, of same, for ₤ 15 proc. money, 50 A on one of the branches of Mallard Creek, part of tract James Alexander lives on, granted to him from John Campbell...Wit: Robt Irwin, Ezekiel Alexr., Arthur Dickson. Rec. July term 1768.

Pp. 803-805: 7 June 1766, William Raynolds & wf Hannah to George Julian of same, for ₤ 40, 300 A on Kings Creek and Braod River, granted to William Raynolds, 13 Augt. 1753... William Reynolds (X) (Seal), Hannah Reynolds (X) (Seal). Wit: Matt Floyd, John McGradgn (X). Rec. July term 1768.

Pp. 805-806: 9 Apr 1768, William Wattson, Esqr., of Meck., to John Willson of Meck., for ₤ 20, 300 A on South side Catawba River, on waters of Fishing Creek adj. McLean, granted to William Watson, 25 Apr. 1767...William Watson (Seal). Wit: James Ross, Violet Wattson. Rec. July term 1768.

Pp. 807-808: 21 Mar. 1768, Benjamin Phillips, yeoman & wf Rachel of Meck., to Joseph Boggs of same, for ₤ 60 current money, 260 A part of 400 A, granted to Phillips 25 Apr. 1767.. on Main Fishing Creek adj. John Hardin, William Dickson, William Haggartis, James Hannas, James Young...Benja. Phillips (Seal), Rachel Phillips (Seal). Wit: Andrew McNall, Jno Wallace, Robert Day. Rec. July term 1768.

Pp. 809-810: 15 Jan. 1768, Benjamin Phillips and Thomas Rainey of Meck., to Isaac Killough of same, for ₤ 7 s 10 proc. money, 300 A on waters of Fishing Creek at Gordons line, adj. James Wallace, Fondron, part of a patent to Phillips and Rainey 25 Oct. 1767...Benja. Phillips (Seal), Thos Rainey (Seal), Rachel Phillips (Seal), Ann Raney (0) (Seal). Wit: Andrew McNabb, John Wallace. Rec. July term 1768.

Pp. 811-812: 21 June 1768, John Handle(R), farmer & wf Catharine of Meck., to Peter Leinberger, blacksmith, of same, for ₤ 2, 200 A on E side Kennels Creek patented 10 Apr. 1761 to sd. Handle...John Handle ( ) (Seal), Catherine Handle ( ) (Seal). Wit: David Jinkins, David Handle (D). Rec. July term [1768.]

Pp. 812-817: 12 May 1768, Abner Grigg Sen. of Dinwiddie Co., Va. to Jonathan Robertson of Meck., for ₤ 160 proc. money, 500 A on South fork of Catwba River, at the Rocky ford, adj. John Shoefoot, patented by Samuel Watkins, 27 Sept. 1751, conveyed to John Clark...Abner Grigg (X) (Seal). Wit: John Wright, Jesse Grigg, Alexr Lewis. Rec. July term 1768.

Pp. 817-818: 12 Apr. 1768, John Clark of Meck., to Andrew Kilpatrick, for ₤ 200 proc. money, 400 A on South fork of Pacolet at Hutchins corner, patented by John Clark... John Clark (Seal). Wit: Ephm Ledbetter, Wm. Marchbank, James Howard. Rec. July term 1768.

Pp. 818-819: 19 Apr. 1768, Thomas Harrod, planter of Meck.,

to John Beard of same, for ₺ 25 proc. money, 200 A on both sides of Broad River, adj. Ezekiel Smith, granted to Harrod, 25 Apr. 1767...Thomas Harrod (Seal). Wit: David Miller, James Rickey. Rec. July term 1768.

Pp. 820-821: 30 July 1768, John Hardan, planter, of Meck., to John Fondren of same, for ___, 300 A on both sides of this high shore branch of Kings Creek, adj. James Fannings late survey, near Stephen Phillips path, patented 26 Oct. 1767... John Hardan (Seal). Wit: Richard Berry, Zach Bullock, Abram Alexander. Rec. July term 1768.

Pp. 821-823: 5 Sept. 1768, Robert Watkins of S. C. to John Hill of Meck., for ₺ 50, 350 A part of 700 A purchased by sd. Watkins and Francis Cost of George Brown of York County, Prov. of Maryland [sic] 3 Sept. 1766, on S side Catawba River on Killions Creek...Robert Watkins (WR) (Seal). Wit: John Dover, John Stroud (X). Rec. Oct. term 1768.

Pp. 823-824: 7 Nov. 1767, Thomas Gerrel (Jarrel) & wf Mary of Meck., to Amos Alexander of same, for ₺ 10, land on waters of Mill Branch on E side Catawba River adj. Ramsey, granted to Jarrel, 25 Apr. 1767...Thomas Gerrel (X) (Seal), Mary Gerrel (X) (Seal). Wit: Aaron Alexander. Jurat: Bartholomew Johnston. Rec. Oct. term 1768.

Pp. 824-826: 11 Oct. 1768, Peter Club, Planter, and wf Margaret of Meck., to Michael Master of same, for ₺ 30 proc. money, 100 A on W side Catawba River and Leepers Creek, part of two tracts granted to Peter Club, 1 Feb. 1758...Peter Club (PC) (Seal). Wit: John Dunn. Rec. Oct. term 1768.

Pp. 826-828: 13 June 1768, David Standlee & wf Hannah of Meck., to Hugh Jenkins of same, for ₺ 320, two tracts 202 A conveyed to him by Francis Beaty 16 Oct. 1762 and 200 A patented by Standley 26 Feb. and enrolled in the Auditors General Office at Wilmington, 28 Sept. 1766...David Standley (D) (Seal), Hannah Standlee (H) (Seal). Wit: David Jinkins, Samuel Johnston. Rec. Oct. term 1768.

Pp. 828-829: 6 July 1767, William Dickson of Duplin Co., NC to John Fondren of Meck., for ₺ 7 s 10 proc. money, 100 A on waters of Fishing Creek adj. William Henry, John Thomas and sd. Fondren, where Fondren now lives, part of 640 A granted to Dickson 25 Sept. 1766...Wm. Dickson (Seal). Wit: John Thomas, Jo: Dickson, Edward Crofts. Rec. July term 1767.

Pp. 830-831: 9 Jan. 1768, Bartholomew Johnston & wf Mary of Meck., to John Martin of same, for ₺ 35 proc. money, 230 A on E side Catawba River, adj. James Miller, Down, Patented by Johnston 26 Sept. 1766...Bartholomew Johnson (Seal), Mary Johnson (X) (Seal). Wit: Benjamin Cochran(?), Adam Alexander. Rec. Oct. term 1768.

Pp. 832-833: 11 Jan. 1769, Joseph Sample, yeoman of Meck., to Wi-liam Sharp, of same, for ₺ 6 s 10 proc. money, 200 A on both sides of Lawsons fork of Packelet, adj. John Alexander granted to Sample 22 Dec. 1768...Wit: Hugh Pollock, Jno Smith. Rec. Jan. term 1769.

Pp. 834-835: 17 Aug. 1768, Joseph Cannon, Cooper, of Meck., to James Cannon of Meck., for ₺ 5 proc. money, 150 A on N side

Volume 4

Main Borad River adj. below Matthew Floyds, patented by Joseph Cannon, 22 Apr. 1767...Joseph Cannon (Seal), Ann Cannon (Seal). Wit: William Henry, Jno McK. Alexander. Rec. Jan. term 1769.

Pp. 836-837: 15 Oct. 1768, Jacob Gardner, Planter, of Meck., to William Johnston of same, for ₤ 5 proc. money, tract on E side Catawba River on head branches of Mallard Creek, a branch of Rocky River adj. William Johnsons old survey, where he now lives, adj. Isaiah Parker, Wallace, patent granted to Jacob Gardner, 29 Apr. 1768...Jacob Gardner (Seal). Wit: Jno. McK. Alexander, Sarah Thompson (X). Rec. Jan. term 1769.

Pp. 837-838: 21 Oct. 1768, John McMillan, planter, of Meck., to John McKnitt Alexander of same, for ₤ 30 proc. money, 100 A on E side Broad River, on both sides of Bullocks Creek, adj. Smith, Hartness, Stephenson, Armstrong, Riggs, granted to McMillan, 25 Apr. 1767...John McMillan (Seal). Wit: Matt: Floyd, Henry Smith. Rec. Jan. term 1769.

Pp. 838-840: 2 Jan. 1769, Robert Wilson, planter of Meck., to John McKnitt Alexander of same, for ₤ 5 proc. money, 100 A on E side Broad River on both sides Moore's Creek adj. McKinney, Floyd, granted to Robert Wilson, 1768...Robert Wilson (Seal). Wit: Henry Smith, Jacob Gardner. Rec. Jan. term 1769.

Pp. 840-841: 29 Oct. 1766, Benjamin Alexander of Meck., to William Sharp of same, for ₤ 5, 146 A on both sides Bullocks Creek adj. Daniel Richardson, William Sherill, Zachariah Bell, patented by Benjamin Alexander, 27 Sept. 1766...Benjamin Alexander (Seal), Susannah Alexander (Seal). Wit: William Alexander, George Reed. Rec. Jan. term 1769.

Pp. 841-842: 13 Jan. 1769, James Walker, Planter of Meck., to Francis Ross, planter, of same, for one negro Fellow, bill of sale for 50 head of cattle...James Walker (I) (Seal). Wit: Wm. Farr, Willm Harris. Rec. Jan. term 1769.

Pp. 842-843: 11 Jan. 1769, John Buchanan & wf Ann of Meck., to Joseph Howe of same, for ₤ 50 proc. money, 167 A on S side Crowders Creek adj. Nathaniel Henderson...John Buchanan (Seal), Ann Buchanan (X) (Seal). Wit: Thos Polk, Jno Huey. Rec. Jan. term 1769.

Pp. 844-845: 10 Jan. 1769, James Harris & wf Mary of Meck., to James Vernon & John Nicoll of S. C., for ₤ 50 proc. money, 640 A on S side of Broad River on Fair Forest Creek...James Harris (Seal), Mary Harris (X) (Seal). Wit: Robt Harris, Jean Branham (X). Rec. Jan. term 1769.

Pp. 846-847: 28 Nov. 1768, Samuel Zicklegg of Meck., to Francis Beatey of same, for ₤ 40 proc. money, 80 A on W side Catawba River adj. Haslip, Gideon Thompson...Samuel Zicklegg (O) (Seal). Wit: Ralph Fleming, James Cunningham, John Beatey. Rec. Jan. term 1769.

Pp. 847-849: 27 July 1767, George Allen & wf Sarah of Meck., to Oliver Wylie blacksmith of same, for ₤ 90, 157 A on both sides of McKow(?) Branch a fork of Reedy Creek near the Governor's line, conveyed to Allen by Selwyn...Geo: Allen (Seal), Sarah Allen (Seal). Wit: Sam Harris, James Harris. Rec. Jan. term 1769.

Volume 4

Pp. 849-851: 29 July 1768, Oliver Wylie, blacksmith of Meck., to David Flough, of same, saddler, for ₤ 90 proc. money, 157 A on both sides of McKee's branch...[same land as preceding deed] Wit: Adam Alexander, William Brown. Rec. Jan. term 1769.

Pp. 851-852: 13 May 1768, John Warnock, storekeeper, of East Nottingham, Cecil Co., Md., to James Foster, power of attorney to receive of John Smith, ₤ 43 s 17 d 6 due by his bill and book debt, John Hendrie, McMar__, Thomas Burk, John Corbely... John Warnock. Wit: Robert Burns, Thos Gilleland, Jeremiah Gatchell. Ack. before Jno. Macky, Cecil County 5 Nov. 1768. Rec. Jan. term 1769.

Pp. 852-853: 12 Nov. 1765, John Barnet of Meck., to David Robinson and Hugh Barnet of same, for ₤ 100, all right and title to all bills, bonds, dues, etc., John Barnet (Seal). Wit: William Alexander, Jas. Alexander. Rec. Jan. term 1769.

Pp. 853-854: 3 Jan. 1769, Francis Ross, planter of Meck., to Robert Cowan, planter, of same, for ₤ 40 procl. money, 200 A on the main Branch of Turkey Creek above James Walker's survey, being a grant to Francis Ross, 25 Apr. 1767... Francis Ross (Seal). Wit: John Tagert. Rec. Jan. term 1769.

Pp. 854-856: 11 Jan. 1769, Samuel Wilson, planter of Meck., to David Wilson (son of Samuel) planter, of same, for ₤ 5 proc. money, 283 A part of 600 A patented to Samuel Wilson 26 Sept. 1751, on McDowell's Creek adj. Benjamin Wilson, also 14 A part of 400 A patented to Samuel Wilson 1 Sept. 1753... Samuel Wilson (Seal), Margret Wilson (Seal). Wit: David Wilson, James Ramsey. Rec. Jan. term 1769

Pp. 856-858: 11 Jan. 1769, Samuel Wilson, planter, of Meck., to Benjamin Wilson (son of Samuel), for ₤ 5 sterl. 340 A consisting of tracts of 100 A part of 600 A patented to Samuel Wilson 26 Sept. 1751 on McDowell's Creek; 240 A part of 400 A patented to Samuel Wilson 1 Sept. 1751(?)...Samuel Wilson (Seal), Margaret Wilson (Seal). Wit: David Wilson, James Ramsey. Rec. Jan. term 1769.

Pp. 858-859: 9 Jan. 1769, William Bishop Glover of Meck., to James Stevenson of same, for ₤ 65 proc. money, 140 A on a branch of Turkey Creek granted 30 Oct. 1766...William Glover Bishop (Seal), Lucy Bishop (X) (Seal) Wit: Robt Harper, Saml Guy (S). Rec. Jan. term 1769.

Page 860: 3 Jan. 1769, John Portman, Junr., of Meck., to Elijah Wells of same, for ₤ 25, 130 A on both sides of Packolet River, adj. McWhorter...John Portman (P) (Seal). Wit: Simcock Cannon, Russell Cannon (X), John Portman Sr. (J). Rec. term 1769.

Pp. 861-862: 25 Nov. 1768, Richard Hix, planter of Meck., to Simcock Cannon, planter of same, for ₤ 10, 187 A on W side Broad River at James Fannins, adj. Robert Sponey Caleys, granted to Hix by Gov. Tryon of NC...Richard Hix Jr. (X) (Seal). Wit: John Haney, Russell Cannon (X), Richd Hix Senr. Rec. Jan. term 1769.

Volume 4

Pp. 862-863: 29 Dec. 1768, Daniel Lizzenbey of Meck., to Woolrick Carpenter, planter, of same, for s 5 sterling, 200 A on the Shoal Branch of Modey [muddy] fork of Buflow Creek adj. Moses Moore, granted to Benjamin Shaw and conveyed to Lizzenby...Danniel Lizzenbey (O) (Seal). Wit: Thomas Black, John Moore. Rec. Jan term 1769.

Pp. 863-865: 7 Jan. 1769, David Davis of Meck., to Nathaniel Miller of same, for L 35 proc. money, 200 A on South branch of North Fork of Tygar River above Robert Millers land, patented to David Davis 25 Sept. 1766...David Davis (Seal). Wit: James Lewis, Jonathan Potts. Rec. Jan. term 1769.

Pp. 865-867: 7 May 1767, Michael Dickson & wf Sarah to David Davis of Meck., for L 10 proc. money, 120 A patented to Dickson 22 Apr. 1763 on a small branch on the South side of Crowders Creek below the Mouth of Beaver Dam Creek... Michael Dickson (Seal), Sarah Dickson (D) (Seal). Wit: William Sprot (N), Samuel Clony. [No rec. date given]

Pp. 867-870: 27 & 28 Nov. 1768, Hugh Carithers, farmer, of Meck., to John Carithers of same, (lease s 5, release L 40 proc. money)...300 A on N fork of Steel Creek adj. William Barnet...Hugh Carithers (S) (Seal). Wit: Alexander Wallace, W. Hemphill. Rec. Jan. term 1769.

Pp. 871-872: 6 Jan. 1769, John Kelsy of Meck., to Moses Foster of same, for L 40, 200 A on N fork of Fair Forest below John Wilson...John Kelso (Seal). Wit: Samuel Wimpson?, James Mayes. Rec. Jan. term 1769.

Pp. 873-874: 10 Aug. 1765, William Wright of East Cullen Township in Chester Co., Pa. to James Wright on Wrights Creek on N side Broad River in Anson Co., for L 50 Pa. money, 600 A bounded upon Wrights Creek...William Wright (Seal), Wit: Moses Wright, Japheth Morton, Edward Millikin. Rec. Jan. term 1769.

Pp. 874-875: 31 May 1768, George Cox, millwright, of Meck., to Francis Adams of same, for L 55 proc. money, 400 A on E side Broad River on both sides Kings Creek about two miles about Dover's Mill seat..George Cox (X) (Seal), Elizabeth Cox (S) (Seal). Wit: James Watson, Damist McClenry(?). Rec. Jan. term 1769.

Pp. 876-877: 27 Oct. 1768, Thomas Williams of Meck., to James Watson of same, for L 60 proc. money, 200 A on both sides a branch of Bullocks Creek... Thomas Williams (Seal). Wit: Francis Adams, John Laughlin. Rec. Jan. term 1769.

Pp. 877-878: 31 Oct. 1768, William McClure, storekeeper of Baltimore Co., Md. to Robert Harris Junr. of Meck., power of attorney...William McClure (Seal). Wit: James Foster. Rec. Jan. term 1769.

Pp. 879-880: 21 Dec. 1768, Adoph Reip, yeoman, of Meck., to Derrick Ramsour of same, for L 5 s 10 proc. money, 60 A granted to Reip 29 Apr. 1768, on E side South fork of Catawba River...Adulp Reip (Seal). Wit: Jacob Ramsour, Henry Hollman. Rec. Jan. term 1769.

Volume 4

Pp. 881-882: 20 Oct. 1768, Derrick Ramsour, yeoman, of Meck., to William Sharp of same, for ₤ 8 s 10 proc. money, 360 A granted to Ramsour by patent 29 Apr. 1768, on both sides Pinch Gut Creek waters of Broad River adj. Peter Duncan, Willis, Sharp...Derrick Ramsour (X) (Seal). Wit: Henry Hollman, Jacob Ramsour. Rec. Jan. term 1769.

Pp. 882-884: 12 Jan. 1769, Henry Hollman, yeoman, of Tryon Co., to William Sharp of Meck., for ₤ 5 s 10 proc. money, 200 A patented to Hollman, 22 Dec. 1768, on South fork of White Oak below James Blyth and above Joel Blackwell...Henry Hollman (Seal). Wit: Joseph Sample, Eza Alexander. Rec. Jan. term 1769.

Pp. 884-885: 21 Oct. 1768, Peter Havener, yeoman, of Meck, to Henry Hildebrand of Meck., for ₤ 8 s 10 proc. money, 300 A patented to Havener 29 Apr. 1768, on both sides Howard's Creek below Nicholas Friday, including the Shoals... Teter Havener (Seal). Wit: ___ [German signature], ___ [German signature], William Sharp. Rec. Jan. term 1769.

Pp. 886-887: 9 Jan. 1769, John Stroud of Meck., to Archibald Little of same, for ₤ 45 proc. money, 200 A patented by John Large, 25 Sept. 1754, and conveyed to James Armour, then to Dennis Dyer, by L & R 24 Aug. 1755, then to Leonard Dozer, 3 Mar. 1767, then to John Stroud 10 Dec. 1768, on S side Catawba, on Johnston's Creek adj. William Haggers...John Thomas...John Stroud (X) (Seal), Martha Stroud (P) (Seal). Wit: William Hecker, John Reid. Rec. Jan. term 1769.

Pp. 888-889: 25 Mar. 1769, William Sharp, yeoman, of Rowan Co., to John King of same, for ₤ 5 10 proc. money, 300 A patented to Sharp 26 Oct. 1767, on both sides Suck Creek. Wm. Sharp (Seal). Wit: John Hankins, Walter Sharp. Rec. April term 1769.

Pp. 890-891: 11 Feb. 1769, John McElwee and wf Jean of Meck., to William Walker of Derry Township, Lancaster Co. Pa., for ₤ 110, 200 A granted to Henry Esutace McCulloh by deed 9 Jan. 1767, lying both sides Sugar Creek adj. David Garrison... John McElwee (Seal), Jean McElwee (O) (Seal). Wit: Thos. Polk, Jurate: Henry Walker. Rec. April term 1769.

Pp. 892-894: 28 Feb. 1768, James Karr of Meck., to Thomas Polk of same, for s 5 sterling, 480 A granted to James Davis, 14 Nov. ___ on both sides Sugar Creek including the mouth of Starets Creek adj. John Woods lower line...James Karr (Seal). Wit: Benjamin Alexander, Susannah Alexander. Rec. Apr. term 1769.

VOLUME 5

Pp. 1-3: 16 May 1775, Thomas McCall, planter, of Meck., to Henry E McCulloh of Halifax Co., N. C. for ₤117-17-1 proc.... mortgage for 485 A joining James Wyley's...where John Neel lives... near McKinleys...crossing Reedy Creek...Thomas McCall (Seal), Henry E. McCulloh (Seal), Wit: John Ffrohock, Jno. McKnitt Alexander. (No rec. date.).

Page 4: 11 Jan 1767, William Flaniken of &c. to Henry E. McCulloh for ₤ 63-6-0 proc. money...mortgage 242 A joining Thomas Dearmond's...Wm Flenniken (Seal), Henry E. McCulloh (Seal), Wit: John Ffrohock, Thomas Polk. (No rec. date)

Page 5: 15 May 1765, William McCulloh of &c. to Henry E. McCulloh ₤ 60-2-0 proc. money...mortgage of 347 A at the Boundary line between Mr. Selwyn & Mr. Campbell...William McCulloh (τ) (Seal), Henry E. McCulloh (Seal), Wit: John Ffrohock, James Alexander. (No rec. date)

Page 6: 17 March 1765, David Alexander to Henry E. McCulloh for ₤ 39-15-0 proc. money...mortgage 155 A jointing tract Abm Caradine lives on...David Alexander (Seal), Henry E. McCulloh (Seal), Wit: John Ffrohock, Saml Brown (S). (No rec. date.)

Page 7: 16 March 1765, Robert Smith to Henry E. McCullof for ₤ 50 proc. money...mortgage 218 A on Rocky River joining Charles Harris' tract...Robert Smith (Seal), Henry E. McCulloh (Seal), Wit: John Ffrohock, Moses Alexander. (No rec. date).

Page 8: 20 March 1765, James Campbell to Henry E. McCulloh for ₤ 44 proc. money...mortgage 180 A on Coddle Creek at Wm Wallaces ...James Campbell (IC) (Seal), Henry E. McCulloh (Seal), Wit: Moses Alexander, John Ffrohock (No rec. date.).

Page 9: 3 Feb 1767, Alexander Montieth to Henry E. McCulloh for ₤ 44-10-0 proc. money...mortgate of 225 A joining Widow Sharps tract...George Catheys...crossing Sharps branch...Alexander Montieth (Seal), Henry E. McCulloh (Seal), Wit: John Ffrohock, William Ffrohock.

Page 10: 3 Feb 1767, Henry Montieth to Henry E. McCulloh for ₤ 70 proc. money...mortgate 462 A joining place where Robert Miller lives...Henry Montieth (Seal), Henry E. McCulloh (Seal), Wit: John Ffrohock, William Ffrohock. (No rec. date).

Page 11: 3 Feb 1767, William Robinson of Rowan County, to Henry E. McCulloh for ₤ 55-10-0 proc. money.-.mortgage 253 A joining where Widow Sharp now lives...George Cathey's....William Robison (Seal), Henry E. McCulloh (Seal), Wit: John Frohock, William Ffrohock. (No rec. date.)

Page 12: 18 Jan 1767, James Foster to Henry E. McCulloh for ₤ 97-10-0 proc. money...mortgage 275 A lying on both sides the Trading Path known by the name of the Sassafras field...James Foster (Seal), Henry E. McCulloh (Seal), Wit: John Ffrohock, Thomas Polk. (No rec. date).

Page 13: 17 Jan 1767, Andrew Elliott to Henry E. McCulloh for ₤ 46-16-0 proc. money....mortgage 200 A on west side Mallard Creek...Andrew Elliot (Seal), Henry E. McCulloh (Seal), Wit: John Ffrohock, Thomas Polk (No rec. date).

VOLUME 5

Page 14: 17 Jan 1767, John Sheals to Henry E. McCulloh for Ł 42-18-6 proc. money...mortgage 185 A joining Robert Elliot's, Mitchell's line...John Shields (Seal), Henry E. McCulloh (Seal), Wit: John Ffrohock, Thomas Polk (No rec. date).

Page 15: 17 Jan 1767, Benjamin Alexander to Henry E. McCulloh for Ł 127-13-0 proc. money...mortgage 391 A on Mallard Creek...Benjamin Alexander (Seal), Henry E. McCulloh (Seal), Wit: John Ffrohock, Thomas Polk (No rec. date).

Page 16: 17 Jan 1767, George Ross to Henry E. McCulloh for Ł 25-14-6 proc. money...mortgage 110 A joining James Alexander's...George Ross (Seal), Henry E. McCulloh (Seal), Wit: John Ffrohock, Thomas Polk. (No rec. date).

Page 17: 18 March 1765, William Wallace to Henry E. McCulloh for Ł 39 proc. money...mortgage 162 A joining David Alexander's near Cowdle Creek...William Wallace (Seal), Henry E. McCulloh (Seal), Wit: John Ffrohock, George Alexander. (No rec. date).

Page 18: 20 Jan 1767, James Maxwell to Henry E. McCulloh for Ł 46-8-0 mortgage 176 A joining Dobb's...Robert Morrison's, James Wyly's...James Maxwell (Seal), Henry E. McCulloh (Seal), Wit: John Ffrohock, Thomas Polk. (No rec. date).

Page 19: 26 Jan 1767, Robert Lockart to Henry E. McCulloh for Ł 41-5-0 proc. money...mortgage 160 A adjoining James Ormond's on McCalpins Creek...Robert Lockart (Seal), Henry E. McCulloh (Seal), Wit: Ezekiel Polk, John Ffrohock. (No rec. date).

Page 20: 23 Jan 1767, Peter Garrison to Henry E. McCulloh for Ł 32...mortgage 163 A...Peter Garrison (Seal), Henry E. McCulloh (Seal), Wit: John Ffrohock, John Ffifer. (No rec.date).

Page 21: 20 Jan 1767, Wm Roberts to Henry E. McCulloh for Ł 44 proc. money...mortgage 126 A...Wm Roberts (Seal), Henry E. McCulloh (Seal), Wit: John Ffrohock, Adam Alexander (No rec. date).

Page 22: 23 Jan 1767, John McCord to Henry E. McCulloh for Ł 27 proc. money...mortgage 108 A adj. Mary McKee's, David Kennedy's, McCord's branch...John McCord (Seal), Henry E. McCulloh (Seal), Wit: John Ffrohock, Thos. Polk (No rec. date).

Page 23: 22 Jan 1767, John Rea to Henry E. McCulloh for Ł 83-3-6 ...mortgage 306 A on the Boundary line...John Rea (Seal) Henry E. McCulloh (Seal), Wit: John Ffrohock, Thos. Polk (No rec. date).

Page 24: 21 Jan 1767, Arthur Garrison to Henry E. McCulloh for Ł 48-16-0 proc. money...mortgage 186 A...Arthur Garrison (Seal), Henry E. McCulloh (Seal), Wit: John Ffrohock, David Robison (No rec. date).

Page 25: 18 Jan 1767, John Allen to Henry E. McCulloh for Ł ____ ...mortgage 546 A on Sugaw Creek adj. Hezekiah Alexander, near Abraham Alexander's Mill Dam...Joseph Samples...John Allen (Seal), Henry E. McCulloh (Seal), Wit: John Ffrohock, Thomas Parker. (No rec. date).

VOLUME 5

Page 26: 21 Jan 1767, David Davis to Henry E. McCulloh for ₤ 63-17-6 proc. money...mortgage 242 A on boundary of Selwyn tract adj. Robert Campbell...David Davis (Seal), Henry E. McCulloh (Seal), Wit: John Ffrohock, Richard Henderson. (No rec. date).

Page 27: 7 Jan 1767, William Reed to Henry E. McCulloh for ₤ 90-7-0- proc. money...mortgage 358 A on Wilson's Mill Creek ...Will Reed (Seal), Henry E. McCulloh (Seal), Wit: John Ffrohock, Thomas Polk. (No rec. date).

Page 28: 29 Jan 1767, Alexander McGinty to Henry E. McCulloh for ₤ 75 proc. money...263 A consisting of 172 A adj. George Allen's and 91 A on waters of Reedy Creek and McCalpin's Creek... Alexr. McGinty (Seal), Henry E. McCulloh (Seal), Wit: John Ffrohock, Thomas Polk (No rec. date).

Page 29: 11 Jan 1767, John McGinty to Henry E. McCulloh for ₤ 87-4-0...mortgage 321 A adj. Alexander McGinty...John McGinty (Seal), Henry E. McCulloh (Seal), Wit: John Ffrohock, Thomas Polk. (No rec. date).

Page 30: 20 Jan 1767, Patrick Williams to Henry E. McCulloh for ₤ 31 proc. money...mortgage 143 A...Patrick Williams (Seal), Henry E. McCulloh (Seal), Wit: John Ffrohock, Thomas Polk. (No rec. date).

Page 31: 28 Jan 1767, Robert Robb to Henry E. McCulloh for ₤ 42 proc. money...mortgage 153 A...Robert Robb (Seal), Henry E. McCulloh (Seal), Wit: John Ffrohock, Thomas Polk (No rec. date).

Page 32: 27 Jan 1767, John Bates to Henry E. McCulloh for ₤ 30 proc. money...130 A adj. Margaret Donaldson's, Davis', King's Branch...John Bates (U) (Seal), Henry E. McCulloh (Seal), Wit: John Ffrohock, Thomas Polk (No rec. date).

Page 33: 20 Jan 1767, John Newell to Henry E. McCulloh for ₤ 33-13-8 proc. money....mortgage 130 A...John Newell (Seal), Henry E. McCulloh (Seal), Wit: John Ffrohock, Thomas Polk (No rec. date).

Page 34: 9 Jan 1767, John Taylor to Henry E. McCulloh for ₤ 74-7-8 proc. money...mortgage 75 A adj. Margaret Donaldson, David Hays...John Taylor (Seal), Henry E. McCulloh (Seal), Wit: John Ffrohock, Thomas Polk (No rec. date).

Page 35: 20 Jan 1767, Joseph Sample to Henry E. McCulloh for ₤ 85-6-0 proc. money...mortgage 176 A...Joseph Sample (Seal), Henry E. McCulloh (Seal), Wit: John Ffrohock, Thomas Polk (No rec. date).

Page 36: 20 Jan 1767, Elijah Alexander to Henry E. McCulloh for ₤ 66-13-0 proc. money...mortgage 232 A on East side Sugaw Creek...Elijah Alexander (Seal), Henry E. McCulloh (Seal), Wit: John Ffrohock, Thomas Polk (No rec. date).

Page 37: 20 Jan 1767, John Buchanan to Henry E. McCulloh for ₤ 98-17-0 proc. money...375 A adj. Herrons, Campbells...John Buchanan (Seal), Henry E. McCulloh (Seal), Wit: John Ffrohock, Thomas Polk. (No rec. date).

VOLUME 5

Page 38: 17 Jan 1767, David Moore to Henry E. McCulloh for Ł 30-18-0 proc. money...mortgage 117 A adj. Gov. Dobbs boundary line...David Moore (√) (Seal), Henry E. McCulloh (Seal) Wit: John Ffrohock, Thomas Polk. (No rec. date).

Page 39: 17 Jan 1767, Andrew Rea to Henry McCulloh for Ł 52-6-0 proc. money...mortgage 200 A on waters of Four Mile Creek adj. Henry Downs...Andrew Rea (Seal), Henry E. McCulloh (Seal), Wit: John Ffrohock, Thomas Polk (No rec. date).

Page 40: 9 Jan 1767, Joseph Kennedy to Henry E. McCulloh for Ł 65-9-4 proc. money...mortgage 242 A...Joseph Kennedy (Seal), Henry E. McCulloh (Seal), Wit: John Ffrohock, Thos Polk. (No rec. date).

Page 41: 8 Jan 1767, Thomas Kennedy to Henry E. McCulloh for Ł 65-13-0 proc. money...mortgage 243 A on McCords branch... Thomas Kennedy (Seal), Henry E. McCulloh (Seal), Wit: John Ffrohock, Thomas Polk (No rec. date).

Page 42: 8 Jan 1767, John Garrison to Henry E. McCulloh for Ł 106-10-0 proc. money...mortgage 400 A adj. Moses Steel's ...John Garrison (Seal), Henry E. McCulloh (Seal), Wit: John Ffrohock, Thomas Polk. (No rec. date).

Page 43: 8 Jan 1767, David Kennedy to Henry E. McCulloh for Ł 56-8-0 proc.money...mortgage 210 A adj. David Kennedy...about four poles from the Meeting House...David Kennedy (Seal), Henry E. McCulloh (Seal), Wit: John Ffrohock, Thomas Polk (No rec. date).

Page 44: 14 Jan 1767, William Smith to Henry E. McCulloh for Ł 75-13-6 proc. money...mortgage 283 A consisting of 162 A on McCalpins Creek adj. William Smith, Miller, Starr and 121 A on McCalpins Creek adj. Flannikins...William Smith (Seal), Henry E. McCulloh (Seal), Wit: John Ffrohock, Thomas Polk (No rec. date).

Page 45: 14 Jan 1767, Alexander Eakin to Henry E. McCulloh for Ł 54-6-0 proc. money...mortgage 205 A adj. Nelson, Down's, Johnston's...Alexander Eakin (Seal), Henry E. McCulloh (Seal), Wit: John Ffrohock, Thomas Polk (No rec. date).

Page 46: 14 Jan 1767, John Ramsey to Henry E. McCulloh for Ł 82-5-6 proc. money...mortgage 312 A on Four Mile Creek, adj. Thomas Black's...John Ramesy (Seal), Henry E. McCulloh (Seal), Wit: John Ffrohock, Thomas Polk. (No rec. date).

Page 47: 14 Jan 1767, James Tate to Henry E. McCulloh, for Ł 59-10-0 proc. money...mortgage 220 A adj. James Johnston, Down's...James Tate (Seal), Henry E. McCulloh (Seal), Wit: John Ffrohock, Thomas Polk (No rec. date).

Page 48: 14 Jan 1767, James Johnston to Henry E. McCulloh for Ł 31-4-6 proc. money...mortgage 120 A adj. Samuel Nelson... James Johnston (I) (Seal), Henry E. McCulloh (Seal), Wit: John Ffrohock, Thomas Polk (No rec. date).

Page 49: 14 Jan 1767, John McClure to Henry E. McCulloh for Ł 96 proc. money...mortgage 380 A on Sugaw Creek where sd. John McClure now lives...John McClure (Seal), Henry E. McCulloh (Seal), Wit: John Ffrohock, Thomas Polk (No rec. date).

VOLUME 5

Page 50: 13 Jan 1767, John Henry to Henry E. McCulloh for ₤ 108-10-0 proc. money...mortgage 250 A on east side of Sugaw Creek adj. John McClure's, said Henry's; 150 A adj. the above tract and Joseph Lee's...John Hendry (Seal), Henry E. McCulloh (Seal), Wit: John Ffrohock, Thomas Polk (No rec. date).

Page 51: 13 Jan 1767, John Hill to Henry E. McCulloh for ₤ 48-18-0 Proc. money...mortgage 190 A adj. Robert Park's, Ezekl. Wallace's...John Hill (Seal), Henry E. McCulloh (Seal), Wit: John Ffrohock, Thomas Polk. (No rec. date).

Page 52: 13 Jan 1767, Robert Parks to Henry E. McCulloh for ₤ 171-5-0 proc. money...mortgage 662 A consisting of two parcels 200 A and 462 A joining Ezekiel Wallace, Henry Mitchell on Campbells Creek...Robert Parks (Seal), Henry E. McCulloh (Seal), Wit: John Ffrohock, Thomas Polk. (No rec. date).

Page 53: 13 Jan 1767, John Cooper to Henry E. McCulloh for ₤ 36-19-0 proc. money...mortgage 138 A adj. Robert Campbell's... John Cooper (Seal), Henry E. McCulloh (Seal), Wit: John Ffrohock, Thomas Polk. (No rec. date).

Page 54: 13 Jan 1767, William Brown to Henry E. McCulloh for ₤ 38-9-2 proc. money...mortgage 145 A including plantation and improvements...Willm Brown (X) (Seal), Henry E. McCulloh (Seal), Wit: John Ffrohock, Thomas Polk. (No rec. date).

Page 55: 10 Jan 1767, William Black to Henry E. McCulloh for ₤ 40 15-0...mortgage 147 A joining Abraham Miller's..."including the Dam Mill, Plantation & other Improvements...." William Black (Seal), Henry E. McCulloh (Seal), Wit: John Ffrohock, Thomas Polk. (No rec. date).

Page 56: 13 Jan 1767, Joseph Galbreath to Henry E. McCulloh for ₤ 113-19-6 proc. money...mortgage 420 A joining William McCulloh, Samuel Carroll's, John McClure's...Joseph Galbreath (Seal), Henry E. McCulloh (Seal), Wit: John Ffrohock, Thomas Polk. (No rec. date).

Page 57: 13 Jan 1767, John Newman to Henry E. McCulloh, for ₤ 53 proc. money...mortgage 200 A joining Henry Vernon's on waters of Sugaw Creek...Moses Townsend's and John Carson's...John Newman (Seal), Henry E. McCulloh (Seal), Wit: John Ffrohock, Thomas Polk (No rec. date).

Page 58: 10 Jan 1767, John Dearmond to Henry E. McCulloh for ₤ 37-7-8 proc. money...mortgage 144 A on west side of McMichells (McMichael?) Creek...John Dearmond (Seal), Henry E. McCulloh (Seal), Wit: John Ffrohock, Thomas Polk. (No rec. date).

Page 59: 12 Jan 1767, Abraham Miller to Henry E. McCulloh for ₤ 64-18-0 proc. money...mortgage 241 A by school house...and the creek...Abraham Miller (Seal), Henry E. McCulloh (Seal), Wit: John Ffrohock, Thomas Polk. (No rec. date).

Page 60: 11 Jan 1767, John Springsteen to Henry E. McCulloh for ₤ 27-13-6 proc. money...mortgage 284 A on waters of Sugaw Creek...John Springsteen (Seal), Henry E. McCulloh (Seal), Wit: John Ffrohock, Thomas Polk (No rec. date).

VOLUME 5

Page 61: 9 Jan 1767, John Swann to Henry E. McCulloh for _____ ... mortgage 534 A on a Creek near William Henry's...John Swann (H+) (Seal), Henry E. McCulloh (Seal), Wit: John Ffrohock, Thomas Polk. (No rec. date).

Page 62: 12 Jan 1767, John Carson to Henry E. McCulloh for ℔ 54-7-6 proc. money...mortgage 203 A on boundary line near John Taggart's place...Newman's, Fergusons...John Carson (W) (Seal), Henry E. McCulloh (Seal), Wit: John Ffrohock, Thomas Polk. (No rec. date).

Page 63: 10 Jan 1767, William Henry to Henry E. McCulloh for ℔ 45 proc. money...mortgage 175 A including a plantation and improvements joining David Vance's...William Henry (O) (Seal), Henry E. McCulloh (Seal), Wit: John Ffrohock, Thomas Polk (No rec. date).

Page 64: 10 Jan 1767, John Starr to Henry E. McCulloh for ℔ 122 proc. money...mortgage 150 A including plantation where John Starr now lives...John Starr (Seal), Henry E. McCulloh (Seal), Wit: John Ffrohock, Thomas Polk (No rec. date).

Page 65: 10 Jan 1767, William Houston to Henry E. McCulloh for ℔ 30-10-0 proc. money...mortgage 110 A joining Mr. Campbells barony line...William Houston (W) (Seal), Henry E. McCulloh (Seal), Wit: John Ffrohock, Thomas Polk. (No rec. date).

Page 66: 10 Jan 1767, John McElwee to Henry E. McCulloh for ℔ 80-19-0 proc. money...mortgage 300 A on Sugaw Creek joining David Garrisons...William Alexander's...John McElwee (Seal), Henry E. McCulloh (Seal), Wit: John Ffrohock, Thomas Polk. (No rec. date).

Page 67: 10 Jan 1767, Ebenezer Newton to Henry E. McCulloh for ℔ 65-14-6 proc. money...mortgage land adj. David Garrison, John McElwee, Thomas Polk, John Allen (acreage not given)...Ebenezer Newton (Seal), Henry E. McCulloh (Seal), Wit: John Ffrohock, Thomas Polk. (No rec. date).

Page 68: 10 Jan 1767, Joseph Priest to Henry E. McCulloh for ℔ 53-9-0 proc. money...226 A joining John Newman's, Nicholson's ...Joseph Priest (IP) (Seal), Henry E. McCulloh (Seal), Wit: John FFrohock, Thomas Polk. (No rec. date).

Page 69: 8 Jan 1767, James Orr to Henry E. McCulloh for ℔ 143-15-6 proc. money...mortgage 545 A by main road joining Joseph Sample's, John McKnitt's, Nathan Orr's...crossing the creek...Jeames Orr (Seal), Henry E. McCulloh (Seal), Wit: John Ffrohock, Thomas Polk. (No rec. date).

Page 70: 21 Jan 1767, Isaiah Parker to Henry E. McCulloh for ℔ 50 proc. money...mortgage 300 A joining Alexander Brown's, Russell's, John McNitt Alexander's...Isaiah Parker (O) (Seal), Henry E. McCulloh (Seal), Wit: John Ffrohock, Thomas Polk (No rec. date).

Page 71: 16 Jan 1767, William Pickens to Henry E. McCulloh for ℔ 27-7-4 proc. money...mortgage 101 A...William Pickens (Seal), Henry E. McCulloh (Seal), Wit: John Ffrohock, Thomas Polk. (No rec. date).

VOLUME 5

Page 72: 10 Jan 1767, Culbert Nicholson to Henry E. McCulloh for
Ł 33-10-6 proc. money...mortgage 131 A on the boundary
line...joining Priest's, Joy's...Culbert Nicklson (Seal), Henry
E. McCulloh (Seal), Wit: John Ffrohock, Thomas Polk. (No rec. date).

Page 73: 10 Jan 1767, James McCord, to Henry E. McCulloh for Ł 39-
19-2 proc. money...mortgage 137 A joining James Moore,
Joseph Lee...James McCord (Seal), Henry E. McCulloh (Seal), Wit:
John Ffrohock, Thomas Polk. (No rec. date).

Page 74: 10 Jan 1767, James Moore to Henry E. McCulloh for Ł 38-
7-4 proc. money...145 A mortgage on Garrison's Creek,
adj. Thomas Polk's line...Jas More (Seal), Henry E. Mcculloh
(Seal), Wit: John Ffrohock, Thomas Polk. (No rec. date).

Page 75: 9 Jan 1767, Thomas Gribble to Henry E. McCulloh for Ł
57-0-6 proc. money...mortgage 220 A on McCopins Creek,
adj. Richard Buckellew...Thos Gribble (Seal), Henry E. McCulloh
(Seal), Wit: John Ffrohock, Thomas Polk. (No rec. date).

Page 76: 16 Jan 1767, John Black to Henry E. McCulloh for Ł 33-11-
0 proc. money...mortgages 127 A...joining Johnston's...
John Black (Seal), Henry E. McCulloh (Seal), Wit: John Ffrohock,
Thomas Polk. (No rec. date).

Page 77: 17 Jan 1767, Thomas Black to Henry E. McCulloh for Ł 33-
11-0 proc. money...mortgage 127 A...Thomas Black (Seal)
Henry E. McCulloh (Seal), Wit: John Ffrohock, Thomas Polk. (No
rec. date).

Page 78: 17 Jan 1767, John Johnston to Henry E. McCulloh for Ł
59-3-6 proc. money...mortgage 227 A joining Culbert Nicholson's...John Johnston (Seal), Henry E. McCulloh (Seal), Wit:
John Ffrohock, Thomas Polk. (No rec. date).

Page 79: 17 Jan 1767, James McElwee to Henry E. McCulloh for Ł
33-5-0 proc. money...mortgage 229 A...James McElwee
(Seal), Henry E. McCulloh (Seal), Wit: John Ffrohock, Thomas Polk.
(No rec. date).

Page 80: 15 Jan 1767, Joseph Lee to Henry E. McCulloh for Ł 48-
13-0 proc. money...mortgage 185 A...Josh. Lee (Seal),
Henry E. McCulloh (Seal), Wit: John Ffrohock, Thomas Polk. (No
rec. date).

Page 81: 16 Jan 1767, David Black to Henry E. McCulloh for Ł 37-
8-0 proc. money...mortgage 145 A joining William Small's
...David Black (Seal), Henry E. McCulloh (Seal), Wit: John Ffrohock, Thomas Polk. (No rec. date).

Page 82: 16 Jan 1767, William Beatty to Henry E. McCulloh for Ł
72-1-6 proc. money...mortgage 271 A "In the line of
Allen's Cabbins" by the Forks of Reedy Creek, by Thomas Polk's
place...William Betty (Seal), Henry E. McCulloh (Seal), Wit: John
Ffrohock, Thomas Polk. (No rec. date).

Page 83: 16 Jan 1767, Walter Beatey to Henry E. McCulloh for Ł
65-2-6 proc. money...mortgage 240 A joining Spark's...on
Campbell's Creek...Walter Beaty (Seal), Henry E. McCulloh (Seal),
Wit: John Ffrohock, Thomas Polk. (No rec. date).

VOLUME 5

Page 84: 16 Jan 1767, William Pickens to Henry E. McCulloh for ₺ 43-15-0 proc. money...mortgage 160 A (note in margin reads 162 A)...William Pickens (Seal), Henry E. McCulloh (Seal), Wit: John Ffrohock, Thomas Polk. (No rec. date).

Page 85: 12 Jan 1767, George Allen to Henry E. McCulloh for ₺ 97-15-6 proc. money...mortgage 420 A joining Alexander's... Geo. Allen (Seal), Henry E. McCulloh (Seal), Wit: John Ffrohock, Thomas Polk. (No rec. date).

Page 86: 15 Jan 1767, William Still to Henry E. McCulloh for ₺ 44 proc. money...mortgage 167 A on east side of John Swann's meadow branch...William Stutt (Seal), Henry E. McCulloh (Seal), Wit: John Ffrohock, Thomas Polk. (No rec. date).

Page 87: 15 Jan 1767, James Clark to Henry E. McCulloh for ₺ 62-5-0 proc. money...mortgage 251 A joining David McKee's... James Clark (I) (Seal), Henry E.McCulloh (Seal), Wit: John Ffrohock. (No rec.date).

Page 88: 15 Jan 1767, Arthur Alexander to Henry E. McCulloh for ₺ 65 proc. money...mortgage 268 A joining Samuel McClary's ...Ezra Alexander's...the boundary line...Arthur Alexander (Seal) Henry E. McCulloh (Seal), Wit: John Ffrohock, Thomas Polk. (No rec. date).

Page 89: 15 Jan 1767, John Holloway to Henry E. McCulloh for ₺ 110 18-9 proc. money...mortgage 425 A joining McClure's... John Holoway (I) (Seal), Henry E. McCulloh (Seal), Wit: John Ffrohock, Thomas Polk. (No rec. date).

Page 90: 15 Jan 1767, Jane Flanagan to Henry E. McCulloh for ₺ 121-9-6 proc. money...mortgage 280 A on McCalpin Creek...Jane Flinnaken (O) (Seal), Henry E. McCulloh Wit: John Ffrohock, Thomas Polk. (No rec. date).

Page 91: 15 Jan 1767, Jonathan Buckilew to Henry E. McCulloh for ₺ 44-13-6 proc. money...mortgage 163 A on McCappins Creek joining Clark's...Jonathan Buckelew (O) (Seal), Henry E. McCulloh (Seal), Wit: John Ffrohock, Thomas Polk. (No rec. date).

Page 92: 15 Jan 1767, Richard Buckelew to Henry E. McCulloh for ₺ 116-5-0 proc. money...mortgage 465 A...Richard Buckelew (Seal), Henry E. McCulloh (Seal), Wit: John Ffrohock, Thomas Polk. (No rec. date).

Page 93: 15 Jan 1767, Josiah Roberts to Henry E. McCulloh for ₺ 41-14-6 proc. money...mortgage 163 A on waters of Sugaw Creek...Josiah Roberts (X) (Seal), Henry E. McCulloh (Seal), Wit: John Ffrohock, Thomas Polk. (No rec. date).

Page 94: 15 Jan 1767, James Way to Henry E. McCulloh for ₺ 60 proc. money...mortgage 227 A on the creek joining Henry Down's, Thomas Harris, Moses Craig's...James Way (Seal), Henry E. McCulloh (Seal), Wit: John Ffrohock, Thomas Polk. (No rec. date).

Page 95: 14 Jan 1767, James Ormond to Henry E. McCulloh for ₺ 43-8-0 proc. money...mortgage 160 A on the Road...crossing the creek, adj. James Steel's...James Ormond (Seal), Henry E. Mc-Culloh (Seal), Wit: John Ffrohock, Thomas Polk. (No rec. date).

VOLUME 5

Page 96: 14 Jan 1767, James Flannakin to Henry E. McCulloh for Ł 61-16-0 proc. money...mortgage 240 A adj. D. Hudson's... Jas. Flenniken (Seal), Henry E. McCulloh (Seal), Wit: John Ffrohock, Thomas Polk. (No rec. date).

Page 97: 14 Jan 1767, Moses Craig to Henry E. McCulloh for Ł 29-6-0 proc. money...mortgage 111 A joining Thomas Harris, James Way, Mr. Downs...Moses Craig (X) (Seal), Henry E. McCulloh (Seal), Wit: John Ffrohock, Thomas Polk. (No rec. date).

Page 98: 16 Jan 1767, Walter Kerr to Henry E. McCulloh for Ł 46 proc. money...mortgages 182 A in the forks of a branch... Walter Kerr (WK) (Seal), Henry E. McCulloh (Seal), Wit: Ezekiel Polk, John Bouchonan (Buchanan). (No rec. date).

Page 99: 23 Jan 1767, Robert Burns to Henry E. McCulloh for Ł 51-10-0 proc. money...mortgage 200 A above Ezra Alexander's ...along Flannakin's open line...Robert Burns (R) (Seal), Henry E. McCulloh (Seal), Wit: James Foster, Robert Irvin. (No rec. date).

Page 100: 14 March 1767, John Clark to Henry E. McCulloh for Ł 13 proc. money...mortgage 130 A...John Clark (Seal), Henry E. McCulloh (Seal), Wit: John Ffrohock. (No rec. date).

Page 101: 25 March 1767, Timothy White to Henry E. McCulloh for Ł 29 proc. money...mortgage 200 A....Timothy White (Seal), Henry E. McCulloh (Seal), Wit: John Ffrohock, Jno. Mck. Alexander. (No rec. date).

Page 102: 21 Feb 1767, Robert Brown to Henry E. McCulloh for Ł 32-11-0 proc.money...mortgage 175 A...Robert Brown (Seal) Henry E.McCulloh (Seal), Wit; John Ffrohock, Will: Alexander. (No rec. date).

Page 103: 25 March 1767, David Garrison to Henry E. McCulloh for Ł 17 proc. money...mortgage 170 A joining James Wilson's ...Will: Wilson, McElwee...David Garrison (Seal), Henry E. McCulloh (Seal), Wit: John Ffrohock, Jas. Edwards. (No rec. date).

Page 104: 13 March 1767, Noble Osburn to Henry E. McCulloh for Ł 32-4-8 proc. money...mortgage 158 A...Noble Osburn (O) (Seal), Henry E. McCulloh (Seal), Wit: John Ffrohock, Geo: Alexander. (No rec. date).

Pp. 105-108: Blank.

Page 109:

Jno Mitchell Deed for the ___?___ of Joy's Barony is in page & in Do. for Do in is page 2d. which he did in 1770 to release himself of the Quitrents for Ambrose Hardens Barony Surveyed & Plated by Jno Braley and J Mc Alexander.

NB: in page 53 a Deed from Jno Frohock to Daniel Alexander for 326 Acres joining on the South side of Coddle Creek
Query how come Jno Frohock to the fee simple thereof

Pp. 110-111: 20 July 1770, Thomas Polk, Abraham Alexander of Meck. & John Ffrohock of Rowan Co., to Josiah Alexander of

Meck. for L 2-10-0 proc. money...lot #2 in town of Charlotte, on South side of Trade Street...Thos Polk (Seal), Abrm. Alexander (Seal), John Ffrohock(Seal), Wit: James Evans, William McCulloh. Rec. July term 1770.

Pp. 111-117: 1 April 1770, John Mitchell & wf Elizabeth of Salisbury, Rowan Co., Merchant, to Andrew Mitchell of Lancaster Co., Pennsylvania, for L 100 proc. money...13 tracts containing 13,189 A consisting of (1) 110 A on waters of Rocky River on the Barony line joining Moses Andrews, Archibald Ramsey's (2) 230 A exclusive of 189 A to James Finley, on the Barony line adj. Archibald Ramseys, John Finleys, Thomas Shields, John Sheilds, Dysarts (3) 190 A on the Barony line adj. Wallis, James Dysarts, John Shields, Joseph Patterson, Caleb Barr (4) 100 A adj. Caleb Barr, James Barr, Samuel Hughes, Mr. Chambers, Joseph Patterson (5) 76 A on the Barony Line adj. McQuiston, Robert Moffet (6) 20 A on E side of Lewis' Branch adj. Barrs, Pickens, Lewis (7) 97 A adj. Thomas Shields, McCuistons, Patterson (8) 440 A adj. Samuel Pickens, Samuel Willsons, John Gilmores, crossing Rocky River, Leneys, Andersons, Joseph Pattersons, Robert Harris (9) 896 A on the Barony Line adj. Isac(?) Lewes, Samuel Pickens, crossing Clarks Creek, Samuel Willson, Newman, Wallis, Thos Fergusons (10) 597 A on Barony line adj. James Carruth's, Jo Wallis, John Gillmores, Robert Smiths survey on Milky Run, near Rocky River, Charles Harris (11) 90 A joining John Gilmores, Jas. Gilmores, Robert Smiths, crossing Rocky River, Newmans (12) 12 A adj. Wilson, Gilmore, Newman, Saml Wilson (13) 31 A adj. James Dysarts, John Shields, the said 13 tracts made out of 12,500 A granted to Ambrose Harding, Esqr., councillor at Law in Dublin and sold to John Mitchell under the hand of James Wyly, Esq., High Sheriff, 5 Aug 1768...John Mitchell (Seal), Elizabeth Mitchell (Seal), Wit: John Dunn, William Nesbit. Rec. July term 1770.

Pp. 117-121: 1 April 1770, John Mitchell & wf Elizabeth of Salisbury, to Andrew Mitchell of Lancaster Co., Pa., for L 158 proc. money...tracts on waters of Long Creek and Sugar Creek (1) 1100 A on the Barony line and Garr Creek adj. Charles Patton, James Scott, Daniel Floy, Erwin, Shog, James Cannoh, Moses Moore (2) 50 A on Long Creek & the Barony line adj. Moses Moore (3) 50 A on Long Creek adj. William Samples, William Henry, James Hannon (4) 80 A on Garr Creek adj. John Doherty and the Barony line, Mr. Coys(?), Charles Patton (5) 70 A on both sides Garrs Creek adj. John Doherty's, Mr. Coy's(?), near Alexander's (6) 50 A adj. Bradley's, Mr. Henry's, John Smith's (7) 30 A adj. Bardleys, Kerr's (8) 60 A on Barony line adj. John Boles (9) 14 A adj. McKees on Barony line (10) 18 A adj. Mitchell's, Reed's, Crocket's (11) 80 A adj. James Kerrs, McGuins (12) 1150 A on Long Creek adj. John McEntire's, James McGuire's, Joseph Kerr's on the Barony line, Robert Kerr's, Alexander's, John Smiths, by the Great Road (13) 69 A on Barony line adj. Alexander's, Doherty's, (14) 150 A adj. John Cannon's, Crockets, James Bradleys, John McEntires, David Hays (15) 30 A on Barony line adj. Joseph Karr's, James Allen's (16) 200 A on branches of Sugar Creek adj. Jno. McEntires, Hays, Crockets, James Reeds, Robert McEntires, McGuins containing in the whole 3,201 A, part of 12,500 A granted to Jeremiah Joy, late of London and sold to John Mitchell by James Wyly High Sheriff of Meck, 5 Aug 1768...Wit: John Dunn, William Nesbet. Rec. July term 1770.

VOLUME 5

Pp. 122-123: 3 Sept 1768, John Mitchell & wf Elizabeth of Salisbury, to Christian Sides of Meck., for Ł 18 proc. money... 67 A in Mecklenburg Co. (formerly Anson) on both sides of Dutch Buffalo Creek adj. Andrew Sides, Gov. Dobbs, being part of 12,500 A sold to John Mitchell by James Pickett, Esqr. High Sheriff of Anson Co., 10 Aug 1768...Wit: Samuel Patton, Mathias Binben(?) (German signature). Rec. July term 1770.

Pp. 124-125: 3 Sept 1768, John Mitchell & wf Elizabeth of Salisbury, to John Buzzard of Meck., for Ł 150 proc. money 202 A in Meck., on both sides of Dutch Buffalo Creek adj. Fite Gorright; also 177 A adj. above containing in the whole 379 A being part of 12,500 A...Wit: Samuel Patton, Matthias Binber(?) (German signature). Rec. July term 1770.

Pp. 126-127: Abm Alexander, Thos Polk & George Allen of Meck., and John Ffrohock of Rowan Co., to William Barnett of Meck., for Ł 2 proc. money...lot #89 in town of Charlotte on West side Tryon St., formerly deeded to them by Henry E. McCulloh as attorney for George Augustus Selwyn, 15 Jan 1767...Wit: Isaac Jetton, Robt. Burns. Rec. April term 1770.

Pp. 127-128: 22 Aug 1768, Wm Lawing of Meck., to Samuel Ziklagg of Meck., for Ł 25 proc. money...125 A on East bank of Catawba River adj. Thos Thomsons, granted to Wm Lawing 16 Nov 1761... William Lawing (Seal), Jane Lawing (X) (Seal), Wit: John Moore, Matthew Run (M). Rec. Jan. term 1770.

Pp. 129-130: 18 Dec 1769, John Mitchell & wf Elizabeth to Thomas Shields of Meck., for Ł 70 proc. money...465 A on Rocky River joining McCuistons, Joseph Pattersons, Saml Pickens, part of 12,500 A granted to Ambrose Harding, Esq...Wit: Joseph Patterson, Robert Moffet. Rec. April term 1770.

Pp. 130-132: 18 Dec 1769, John Mitchell & wf Elizabeth to Robt. Moffett of Meck., for Ł 50 proc. money...290 A on Rocky River adj. John Shields, Dunn's branch, part of 12,500 A granted to Ambrose Harding, Esq. Wit: Thomas Shields, Josh. Patterson. Rec. April term 1770.

Pp. 132-133: 14 Feb 1770, John Mitchell & wf Elizabeth to Josh. Patterson of Meck., for Ł 15 proc. money...196 A on Rocky River adj. Caleb Barrs, Chambers, Joh Shields, part of 12,500 A...Wit: Thos Shields, Robert Moffett. Rec. April term 1770.

Pp. 134-135: 18 Dec 1769, John Mitchell & wf Elizabeth to James Dysart of Meck., for Ł 20 proc. money...231 A on Rocky River in the NW corner of the Barony, part of 12,500 A... Wit: Saml Pickens, Jas Gilmore. Rec. April term 1770.

Pp. 135-137: 9 Dec 1769, John Mitchell & wf Elizabeth to Joseph Iher Junr. of Meck., for Ł 15 proc. money 374 A on head branch of Sugar Creek adj. John Boal's, part of 12,500 A ...granted to Jeremiah Joy...Wit: Charles Harris, John McK. Alexander. Rec. April term 1770.

Pp. 137-138: 18 Dec 1769, John Mitchell & wf Elizabeth to Josh. Patterson of Meck., for Ł 40 proc.money...312 A on Rocky River adj. Samuel Pickens, Thos Shields, part of 12,500 A granted to Ambrose Harding...Wit: Thos Shields, Robt Moffet. Rec. April term 1770.

Pp. 139-140: 13 April 1770, Hugh Park & wf Margaret of Rowan Co., to David Reed his son-in-law for 10 shillings proc. money...150 3/4 A on waters of Rocky Sugar Creek adj. Mary McDowells, Saml Bingham, Hugh Parks, 112 A of which was granted to Hugh Park 9 Nov. 1764, 38 3/4 A part of 615 A granted to Hugh Park 23 Feb 1764...Hugh Park (Seal), Margt. Park (X) (Seal), Wit: John McDowell, Edward Maloney. Rec. April term 1770.

Pp. 140-142: 20 March 1770, Charles Pollock of Meck.,farmer, & wf Mary to Thos Martindale of same, for L 20 proc. money...82 A on both sides of Crooked Creek, a branch of Rocky or Johnston River, purchased by Charles Pollock from Gov. Arthur Dobbs...Chas. Pollock (Seal), Mary Pollock (Seal), Wit: John Culverson, John Williams (X). Rec. Jan term 1770.

Pp. 142-144: 7 April 1770, John Dean of Craven County, S. C. to Henry Stokes of Anson Co., N. C. for L 26 current money...200 A on both sides of Waxhaw Creek adj. Willm Beards... ...John Dean (Seal), Wit: John Barnet, Wm Davies, John Currey. Rec. April term 1770.

Pp. 144-145: 15 Oct 1768, Joseph Crawford and wf Agness of Meck., to Samuel Flanekin of same for L 25 current money... 250 A on N side Waxhaw Creek adj. Robt Davies...Joseph Crawford (Seal), Agness Crawford (?) (Seal), Wit: John Black, John Flannaken. Rec. Arpil term 1770.

Pp. 146-147: 12 March 1770, David Davies of Meck., to Elijah Davies of same for L 30...100 A, part of 100,000 A called Tract No. 3 on both sides of King's branch, conveyed from George Augustus Selwyn, 17 Jan 1767...David Davies (Seal), Eliza. Davies (Seal), Wit: James Sprot, Robt Campbell. Rec. April term 1770.

Pp. 147-149: 12 March 1770, Thos Sprott of Meck., to William Barnett of same, for L 20 proc. money...356 A on both sides of Sugar Creek, part of a grant to Thos. Sprott, 24 April 1762...Thos Sprot (Seal), Wit: Archd. M'Neall, Peter Johnston. Rec. April term 1770.

Pp. 149-151: 16 Jan 1771, David Kennedy & wf Martha of Meck., to John Montgomery of same, for L 85 proc. money... 210 A, part of 100,000 A ca-led Tract No. 3, bought from George Augustus Selwyn, on waters of Sugar Creek, adj. John Buckhannon's ...David Kennedy's...David Kennedy (Seal), Martha Kennedy (M) (Seal), Wit: Waitstill Avery, James Reed, John Montgomery. Rec. Jan. term 1771.

Pp. 152-153: 18 Dec 1769, John Mitchell & wf Elizabeth of Salisbury, to John Shields of Meck., for L 25 proc. money ...205 A, part of 12,500 A granted to Ambrose Harding, Esqr, conveyed to Mitchell by James Wyly, Sheriff, 5 Aug 1768, adj. McCuistons, Robt Moffett, Mos Andrews, John Finleys...Wit: Thomas Wallas, John Smith. Rec. Oct. term 1770.

Pp. 153-154: 31 March 1770, Jacob Richey & wf Catherine of Meck., to Adam Wolcher of same for L 25 proc. money...100 A on Dutch Buffalow Creek of Johnston's or Rockie River, part of

254 A conveyed to Jacob Richey by Arthur Dobbs & wf Justina, 25 June 1764...Jacob Richey (X) (Seal), Cathrine Richey (X) (Seal), Wit: John Pifer, Hugh Polock, George Crosley. Rec. Oct. term 1770.

Pp. 155-156: 13 Aug 1770, John Taylor Senr of Meck., to Abraham Taylor of same, for L 40 proc. money...land on waters of Suga (sic) Creek adj. the place whereon the sd. John Taylor now lives, part of 275 A granted to sd. Taylor 8 Jan 1767 by deed from Geo. Augustus Selwyn by atty. Henry E. McCulloh...John Taylor (Seal), Wit: Will Reed, Robert Campbell. Rec. Oct. term 1770.

Pp. 156-157: 24 Aug 1770, George Augustus Selwyn Esq. to James Robison of Meck., for L 10 proc. money...100 A on waters of Reedy Creek in Meck., surveyed and laid off in a deed of surrender executed by Selwyn to his Majesty, 24 Apr 1767, adj. Thomas McCall's...Geo. Augustus Selwyn (Seal), by John Ffrohock. Wit: Exekiel Wallace, Willm. Steel. Rec. Oct. term 1771.

Pp. 158-159: 31 Aug 1768, Henry Funt Pistenbustill and wf Saffey of Meck., to John Barnet Miller of same, for L 60 proc. money...364 A on branch of Dutch Buffalo adj. Waddell's, Brandon's, Gov. Dobb's...Henry Funt Pistenbustill (Seal), Suffey Pistenbustill (X) (Seal), Wit: Georg Smitz, Paul Berringer. Rec. Oct. term 1770.

Pp. 159-160: 1 Jan 1770, William Nutt & wf Agness of Meck., to John Crockett of same, for L 20 proc. money...162 A on South side of the Waxhaw adj. land Nutt lives on patented to Nutt 5 Apr 1753...William Nutt (Seal), Agness Nutt (\/\) (Seal), Wit: John Nutt, Wm Moore, Kathrine Nutt (O), Rec. Oct. term 1770.

Pp. 161-162: 8 March 1770, Thomas Polk, Abraham Alexander, & George Allen of Meck. & John Frohock of Rowan Co., to William Hooper Esqr. of New Hanover County, N. C. for 40 shillings proc. money...lots #140 & 199 in the town of Charlotte, on N side Tryon St., conveyed by Henry E. McCulloh Esqr. for George A. Selwyn 15 Jan 1767...Wit: Hen Walker, Robt Burns. Rec. Oct. term 1770.

Pp. 162-163: 24 Aug 1770, John Frohock of Rowan Co., to Daniel Alexander of Meck., for L 106 proc. money...326 A on South side of Codle Creek, conveyed to Frohock by Henry E. McCulloh 3 Feb 1767...John Ffrohock (Seal), Wit: John Black, James Maxwell. Rec. Oct. term 1770.

Pp. 164-165: 15 Oct 1770, William Nutt & wf Agness to Alexander Cairns of Craven County, S. C. for L 5 proc. money ...30 A part of a tract surveyed to Nutt by James Carter...Willm Nutt (Seal), Agness Nutt (\/) (Seal), Wit: John Barnet, Denis Titus, John Crockett. Rec. Oct. term 1770.

Pp. 165-166: 16 June 1770, John Cathey of Meck., to Henry Hendry Jr. of same, for L 12-10-0 proc. money...55 A on North side of Catawba River, adj. John Cathey's, part of a grant to Cathey 13 Oct 17--...John Cathey (Seal), Mary Cathey (u) (Seal), Wit: Jane Irvin, Henry Hendry Senr. Rec. Oct. term 1770.

Page 167: 24 Aug 1770, Henry Eustace McCulloh Esqr. to Daniel Alexander for L 5-12-0 proc. money...56 A on waters of Mallard Creek, reserved and laid off to McCulloh to his Majesty 24 Apr 1767 (beginning about half a mile south of William Alexander's corner, being the dividing Ridge between Mallard and Back Creek, including the old Meeting house road)...Wit: John Black, Willm. Alexander. Rec. Oct. term 1770.

Pp. 168-169: 17 Oct 1770, William Flanniken of Meck., to Peter Johnston of same, for Ł 20 proc. money...67 A on waters of McCurpins(?) Creek beginning Flanniken's corner by the path that leads from Dearmond's old Saw Mill to Steel Creek... Wm Flanniken (Seal), Wit: Thomas Dearmond, David Smith. Rec. Oct. term 1770.

Pp. 169-170: 1 May 1770, Samuel Knox of Meck., planter, to Moses Swann of Lancaster Co., Penn., planter, for Ł 125 Proc. money of NC...400 A lying south west of a small path leading to Widow Armor's from Johneys Town in Mecklenburg Co., granted 19 Apr 1763...Saml Knox (Seal), Mary Knox (O) (Seal), Wit: James Tagart, Saml Berryhill. Rec. Oct. term 1770.

Pp. 171-172: 24 Aug 1770, George Augustus Selwyn to Robert Robinson of Meck., for Ł 5 proc. money...50 A on waters Reedy Creek, Wit: Willm. Alexander, Wm Steel. Rec. Oct. term 1770.

Pp. 172-174: 13 Aug 1770, Andrew Nutt & wf Margaret of Meck., to John Barkley of St. Mark's Parish, Craven Co., S. C., for Ł 325 current money of S. C....155 A part of 640 A granted to Wm King on both sides of the Waggon Road & on N side of Waxhaw Creek, adj. George McCamey's lines...Andw Nutt (Seal), Margt Nutt (✓) (Seal), Wit: Wm Davies, Jno Barnet, David Conyers. Rec. Oct. term 1770.

Pp. 174-178: 20 July 1770, James Wyly Esqr. High Sheriff of Meck., to John Bigger...whereas by an Act of Parliament passed in the 5th year of the reign of King George II, for recovery of debts...the sum of Ł 3-12-0 proc. money was levied against the estate of James Biggar, which Thos Polk Esqr. lately recovered in Court of P & QS held at the court house in Charlotte, also Ł 2-10-6 awarded Polk as damages, sold under a writ of fieri facias for Ł 63-7-8 proc. money...640 A on E side Catawba River opposite the mouth of Crowders Creek, granted to sd. James Biggar 21 Dec 1763... James Wyly (Seal), Wit: Bromfield Ridley, Robert Harris Junr. Rec. Oct. term 1770.

Pp. 178-180: 21 Aug 1770, George Schöcher Senr of Township of Macuny, County of North Hampton, Prov. of Pa., yeoman, to George Schtöcher Jr. of Anson County, N. C., for Ł 200 Pa. money ...193 A on W side Catawba River joining Casper Culp, part of a patent to Robert McClenninghan, 25 Feb 1754, conveyed to Thomas Land, then by Thomas Land & wf Eleanor, 6 Oct 1768 to sd. George Schtocher the Elder...Görg Stoscher (German signature) (Seal), Wit: Two German signatures. Rec. Oct. term 1770.

Pp. 180-183: 5 Oct 1771, George Crowell & wf Jamima to William Weatherford of Anson Co., for Ł 43 proc. money... 80 A on a branch of the river...George Crowel (X) (Seal), Jamima Crowerl (X) (Seal), Wit: Joseph Moore. Rec. Oct. term 1771.

Pp. 183-184: 11 Sept 1771, Andw. Williams of Williamtown by Andw Woods his attorny of Rowan Co., to Charles Perviance of same, for Ł 45 proc. money paid to the sd. James Woods, 200 A in Meck. on Long Creek on E side Catawba River adj. Jeremiah Joy, granted to Andrew McCalin, 10 April 1761...Archibald McClain by his atty. Jas. Woods (Seal), Wit: Samuel Jack, Th: Polk. Rec. Oct. term 1771.

Pp. 185-187: 20 Sept 1770, Robert Sloan of Rowan Co., to Charles Mason of Meck., for L 30 proc. money...200 A on E side of Catawba River on waters of Paw Creek adj. lands of John Sloan, granted to sd. Robert Sloan, 29 April ___ ...Robert Sloan (Seal), Wit: Joseph McKinley, Joseph Galbreath, Jurate. Rec. Oct. term 1771.

Pp. 187-189: 15 Oct 1771, James Bradley of Meck.- farmer, to Francis Bradley of same, farmer, for L 25 proc. money...200 A, part of 477 A conveyed by John Mitchell to sd. James Bradley, 9 Dec 1769, on waters of Long Creek adj. John McEntire, Sample...James Bradley (O)(Seal), Hannah Bradley (Seal), Wit: Sophia Garner (↶), Jurate, Jno. McK. Alexander. Rec. Oct. term 1771.

Pp. 189-190: 4 June 1771, William McCorkle and wf Ester of Meck., to Thomas Presley of same, for L 20...200 A on waters of North fork of the Waxhaw Creek including Humphrey Yarborough's improvements & joining lands of John Davis, ___ Beards, patented 16 Dec 1769...Wm McCorkle (Seal), Ester McCorkle (E) (Seal), Wit: John Davies, Henry Yarbrough, John Crockett. Rec. Oct. term 1771.

Pp. 191-192: 10 Oct 1771, John Ford & wf Katharine of Meck., to John Robinette of same, planter, for L 50 proc. money...102 A on waters of McCarpins Creek, part of a larger survey conveyed to Ford by A. Selwyn, 8 Jan 1767...John Ford (Seal), Catherine Ford (Seal), Wit: William Smith, John Hall. Rec. Oct. term 1771.

Pp. 193-194: 25 Aug 1770, Peter Kealer & wf Anamore of Meck., to George File of same, for L 65 proc. money...136 A on a branch of Dutch Buffalo Creek, waters of Rockie or Johnson's River ...Johann Petter Köslr (German signature) (Seal), Anna Morr (AM) (Seal), Wit: ___ (German signature), Paul Barringer. (No rec. date).

Pp. 194-195: 15 Oct 1770, William Nutt & wf Agness of Meck., to Alexander Carins of Craven Co., S. C. for L 600 SC money...272 A the plantation the sd. Wm Nutt now lives on and on the Waxhaw Creek...William Nutt (Seal), Agnes Nutt (✓) (Seal), Wit: Jno Barnet, Denis Tuts, Jno Crocket. Rec. Oct. term 1770.

Pp. 196-197: 6 Jan 1770, John Crocket & wf Margaret of Meck., to William Moore of same, for L 20...162 A on S side of Waxhaw Creek joining William Nutt, by virtue of a deed dated 1 Jan 1770...Jno Crocket (Seal), Margaret Crocket (M) (Seal), Wit: William Nutt, John Nutt, Katrine Nutt (O). Rec. Oct.term 1770.

Pp. 198-201: 12 & 13 Oct 1770, Moses Ferguson & wf Martha of Tryon Co., N. C. and Samuel Knox and wf Mary of Meck., to Francis Johnston and Joseph Johnston, both late of Meck (lease s10, release L 140)...400 A on E side Catawba River and SE side of path leading from Jean Armour's to the Catawba Nationa, patented 6 Apr 1765...Moses Ferguson (Seal) Martha Ferguson (Z) (Seal), Samuel Knox (Seal), Mary Knox (O) (Seal), Wit: Thos. Neely (X), Hugh Neely, Alexandr. Johnston. Rec. Oct. term 1770.

VOLUME 5

Pp. 201-204: 12 & 13 Nov 1769, John Brandon & Elizabeth Brandon of Rowan Co., to Michael Goodman of Meck., (lease s5, release Ł 100)...580 A on S side of Yadkin River and both sides Buffalow Creek about 12 miles above Charles Hart's...John Brandon (Seal), Elizabeth Brandon (Seal), Wit: Matthew Lock, Matthaus Müssler(?) (German signature), John Pifer. Rec. Oct. term 1770.

Pp. 205-210: 17 & 18 June 1769, Michael Christman of Meck., to Rev. Samuel Suther of same, (lease sl, release Ł 50 proc. money)...125 A on waters of Dutch Buffalo and N side of Rocky River adj. George Tucker's, Conrod Carloh, Michael Chambers...Michael Christman (MG) (Seal), Elizabeth Christman (O) (Seal), Wit: Lorentz Lingell(?) (German signature), Cunrad Carlah (KC), Jurate, George Tucker (D). Rec. Oct. term 1771.

Pp. 211-212: 10 Apr 1777, Andrew Downs & wf Ann of Meck., to Benjamin Maxwell of same, for Ł 50 proc. money... 150 A granted to Downs 22 Dec 1768, on E side of Catawba River on waters of Millers Creek adj. James Maxwell, Walter Carson & Benjamin Cocheran...Andrew Downs (X) (Seal), Ann Downs (X) (Seal), Wit: John Maxwell, Richard Morrow, Thos. Martin. Rec. April Sessn. 1777.

Pp. 213-214: 10 Apr 1777, Andrew Downs & wf Ann of Meck. to James Maxwell of same for Ł 54 proc. money...200 A granted to Downs 21 Apr 1764, on the waters of Davisons Creek & Millers Creek near the widow Givens and a Dutchman's land...Andw Downs (X) (Seal), Ann Downs (X) (Seal), Wit: John Maxwell, Richd. Morrow, Thos Martin. Rec. April term 1777.

Pp. 215-216: 12 Apr 1777, John Scott of Meck., to James and Patrick Scott of Tryon Co., for Ł 50...80 A on E side Catawba River adj. Scott's old line and John Smith's land granted to John Scott"12th A. D. 1773"...John Scott (Seal), Wit: William Chronicle, Wm. Chronicle Jur. Rec. April Sessn. 1777.

Pp. 216-217: 12 Apr 1777, John Scott of Meck., planter, to James & Patrick Scott of Tryon Co., for Ł 150 proc. money ...200 A on E side Catawba River including mouth of Long Creek and adj. Joseph Hardin, Moses Scott, granted to John Scott A. D. 1775...John Scott (Seal), Wit: William Crroncill, Wm Chronicle Junr. Rec. April 1777.

Pp. 218-219: 16 Apr 1777, John Cathey Senior of Meck., to John Cathey Jr. of same, for Ł 400 proc. money...571 A on waters of Paw Creek...John Cathey (Seal), Wit: Sam Martin. Rec. April Sessn .1777.

Pp. 220-221: 14 Oct 1773, Robert McClellan & wf Rebecca of Meck., to John Farr of same, for Ł 57-10-0 proc. money... two parcels containing 152 A on both sides of English Buffalo Creek, a branch of Rocky or Johnson River...Robert McClellan (Seal), Rebecca McClellan (M) (Seal), Wit: Robert Rodgers, Charles Curry. Rec. April Sessn 1777.

Pp. 221-223: 8 Apr 1777, Adam Carruth of Meck., to Walter Carruth of same, for Ł 20 current money...215 A on waters of Paw Creek, part of land said Carruth now lives on, on the division line between said Adam Carruth and James Carruth decd lands, being part of 630 A granted to Francis Beaty 23 Apr 1762, and conveyed by him &c....Adam Carruth (Seal), Wit: Peter Johnston, John Carruth. Rec. April sessn 1777.

Pp. 224-225: 28 March 1777, Samuel Roach of Meck., to John Philip Weeks of same, for ₤ 40...100 A granted to John Jack and conveyed to Roach, lying on both sides of Sugar Creek adj. lands of Elijah Alexander, Samuel Jack, John Davis ...Samuel Roach (Seal), Wit: Ezekl. Polk, John Weeks (X). Rec. April Sessn. 1777.

Pp. 226-227: 25 Oct 1776, William Moore & Rebecca his wife of Meck., to Alexander Cairns of same, for ₤ 50... 162 A on S side of Waxhaw Creek adj. lands of sd. Cairns... William Moore (Seal), Rebecca Moore (X) (Seal), Wit: Robert Ramsey, David Lethen, Daniel Cairns. Rec. April Sessn. 1777.

Pp. 227-229: 4 Apr 1776, Robert Moore & wf Martha of Meck., planter, to Joseph Wilson of same, for ₤ 40 proc. money ...190 A on Rocky River adj. lands of Mr. Chambers, Thomas Shields, being part of 12,500 A granted to Ambrose Harding, Esq. and sold to John Mitchell by James Wyly High Sheriff, and by him conveyed to Robert Moore, 13 Feb 1769...Robert Moore (Seal) Martha Moore (X) (Seal), Wit: Stephen Alexander, Alexr. Lewis. Rec. April Sessn 1777.

Pp. 229-230: 14 Nov 1775, Samuel Carroll of Meck., to William Patterson of same, for ₤ 200 proc. money...200 A on both sides of McNight's Creek waters of Sugar Creek adj.William McCulloh, Henry Vernon... Saml Carroll (Seal), Wit: Thos Polk, James Reed. Rec. Jan. term 1776.

Pp. 231-232: 16 Oct 1776, Henry Talley of Meck., to William Polk of same, for ₤ 50 proc. money...70 A on N side of Rocky River, said land deeded by Talley by Agner Nash, 25 March 1772...Henry Tally (H) (Seal), Wit: Eph. Brevard, Thos. Alexander. Rec. July term 1777.

Pp. 232-233: 3 Oct 1776, Thomas Polk of Meck., to Ezekiel Polk of same, for ₤ 300 current money of NC...100 A on S. E. side of Big Sugar Creek adj. John Barnett's, Selwyn's lines, Thomas Polk's; also 60 A adj.; also 100 A on middle fork of Sugar Creek adj. Alexander and Samuel McCleary, John Barnet's, Burns, the Waggon Road...Thos Polk (Seal), Wit: Eph. Brevard, Will Polk. Rec. July term 1777.

Pp. 234-235: 10 March 1777, Jemima Sharp (widow) of Meck., to Joseph Maxwell of same, for ₤ 45 current money... 131 A on branches of McDowell's Creek being a parcel subdivided from Mr. McCulloh's N. W. Barony in Tract #4, near late Gov. Dobb's Barony, deeded by McCulloh to Jemima Sharp, 20 Apr 1765...Jemima Sharp (△) (Seal), Wit: James Cannon, Jno. McKnitt Alexander. (No rec. date.)

Pp. 235-237: 16 July 1777, JohnBowhanon & wf Ann of Prov. of Ga. to William Hay of Meck., for ₤ 40 proc. money...200 A on head branches of Mallard Creek adj. McClery's, Wallace's... John Bowhanon (Seal), Wit: Alexander Wallace, Ezekiel Alexandr. Rec. July term 1777.

Pp. 237-239: 15 July 1777, Samuel Berryhill of Meck., planter, to Joseph Berryhill of same, planter, for ₤ 10 proc. money...18 A on waters of Sugar Creek part of 76 A granted 4 May 1769...Samuel Berryhill (Seal), Wit: Jeremh. McCafferty, Wm. McCafferty. Rec. July term 1777.

Pp. 239-240: 18 Jan 1770, Thomas Polk, Richard Barry and George Allen of Meck., to Abraham Alexander of Meck., for ₤ 3 proc. money...lot #9 on E side of Trade St. in Town of Charlotte, Wit: John Springstree, Saml Wilson. Rec. July Term 1777.

Pp. 241-242: 3 May 1777, Archibald McDowell of Meck., to Michael Ligget of same, for ₤ 300 currency of NC...310 A on N side Catawba River on South fork of Twelve Mile Creek above an Indian path...Archibald McDowell (Seal), Wit: Sam Martin. Rec. July term 1777.

Pp. 243-244: 13 June 1777, Richard McCree of Meck., planter, to James McNeely of same, blacksmith, for ₤ 113 proc. money...150 A between Little Sugar Creek and Rocky Sugar Creek adj. John Hunter's, Adam Carruth, part of 394 A granted to Richard McCree 19 April 1763...Richard McRee (Seal), Wit: Robert Beatey, John Clark. Rec. July term 1777.

Pp. 244-245: 16 Oct 1772, Moses Scott & wf Sarah of Meck., to John Heitower of Lunenburg Co., Va., for ₤ 80 proc. money ...100 A on E side Catawba River near the Tuckaseege Ford, granted to John Scott 10 Apr 1761...Moses Scott (Seal), Sarah Scott (X) (Seal), Wit: George Lamkin, Wm Alston, John Scott, George Lamkin. Rec. July term 1777.

Pp. 246-247: 7 April 1777, Margaret Givens of N. C. to William Givens her son for ₤ 200 current money of NC...300 A on E side of Catawba River adj. lands of Matthew McCorkle and a Dutchman, granted to sd. Margaret Givens, 19 Apr 1763...Margaret Givens (C) (Seal), Wit: John Givens, Thos McCorkle. Rec. July term 1777.

Pp. 248-249: 2 Oct 1775, Josiah Alexander of Meck., to Aaron Alexander of same for ₤ 70...130 A on a branch of Rockey River, adj. James Sloan's old corner, Standford's line...Josiah Alexander (Seal), Wit: Samuel Davis, John Garrison. Rec. July term 1777.

Pp. 249-251: 5 Feb 1777, Matthew Russell & wf Jane of Tryon Co., to Joseph McCane of Meck., for ₤ 42 proc. money... 180 A on S side of Long Creek originally bounded by lands of John Anderson, John Kennedy and Hugh McCracken, part of 200 A deeded by Francis Beaty to Russell, 26 Nov 1757...Matthew Russell (Seal), Jane Russell (U) (Seal), Wit: Jno Wilson, Robert McOntire. Rec. July term 1777.

Pp. 252-253: 10 July 1775, Edward Givens of Meck., to William Coldwell of same, for ₤ 50 proc. money...242 A on E side of Catawba River granted to Jacob Miller 27 Sept 1753 and conveyed to Givens...Edward Givens (O) (Seal), Wit: William Graham, Jane Carson, Thos. Givens. Rec. July term 1777.

VOLUME 5

Pp. 254-255: 8 Feb 1777, John Garrison of Meck., to Ezekiel Alexander of same, for ᛒ 300 proc. money...267 A part of Tract #3 deeded from Selwyn to Jane Craighead and by her son Robert Craighead to John Garrison...John Garrison (Seal), Hannah Garrison (X) (Seal), Wit: James Alexander, John Lockerd, David Alexander. Rec. July term 1777.

Pp. 256-257: 2 Sept 1772, John Springsteen Junr. of Meck. to Richard Springsteen of same, for ᛒ 132 proc. money... 350 A on a branch of McCalpins Creek called Swearingams Branch, including Joseph Swearingam's improvements...deeded to John Springsteen Junr by Hugh McKain and patent dated 23 Dec 1763...John Springsteen (Seal), Wit: Henry Downs, Henry Downs Junr., Benjamin Ormond. Rec. July term 1777.

Pp. 258-259: 21 Aug 1772, Hugh McCain of Meck., to John Springsteen Junr for ᛒ 135 proc. money...350 A on Swearingams Branch, granted to Benjamin Roberts 23 Dec 1763, and a title from Roberts to Thomas Houston and from him to Hugh McCain...Hugh McCain (Seal), Eleanor McCain (Seal), Wit: John Springsteen, Henry Downs. Richard Springsteen. Rec. July term 1777.

Pp. 260-261: 10 Oct 1773, Thos Polk, Robert Elliott & Jeremiah McCafferty of Meck., to Abraham Alexander, for s 15 proc. money...half an acre, lot #87 in Charlotte...Wit: Hez: Alexander. Rec. July term 1777.

Pp. 261-263: 17 April 1775, Josiah Alexander of Meck., to Aaron Alexander of same, for ᛒ 130 proc. money...163 A on waters of Rocky River, adj. Alexander Osburns line, Robert Brevards, deeded to Alexander from John Gullick, 15 Oct 1767... Josiah Alexander (Seal), Wit: James Jack. Rec. July term 1777.

Pp. 263-265: 16 July 1777, Arthur Starr and wf Hannah of Meck., to Abraham Miller of same for ᛒ 100 proc. money...52 A on S. E. side of McCalpins Creek beginning at a corner of a tract of 240 A formerly surveyed for John Starr, adj. Widow Osburns corner, granted to John Starr...Arthur Starr (Seal), Hannah Starr (Seal), Wit: Will: Reed, John Seman. Rec. July term 1777.

Pp. 266-267: 4 Jan 1777, William Hagans of Meck., to John McCain of same, for ᛒ 30...150 A on waters of Twelve Mile Creek on the Tar Kill branch near the path from Hagans to John Kings, near Wm McCuloh's Mill Road...Wm Hagans (Seal), Wit: Archd. Crockett, Wm. McCulloh, J. F. Slemon. Rec. July term 1777.

Pp. 268-269: 6 Oct 1774, Alexander Crockett of Augusta Co., Va., to William Haggins of N. C. for ᛒ 5...202 A on North branch of Waxhaw Creek...Alexander Crockett (Seal), Wit: Andw. Crocket, Wm. Thompson, James Crockett, Rec. July term 1777.

Pp. 269-271: 16 July 1777, Arthur Starr of Meck & wf Hannah to Abraham Miller of same for ᛒ 112 proc. money...100 A on SE side McCalpins Creek part of 240 A conveyed to John Starr decd from Selwyn by Henry E. McCulloh, and John Starr died intestate and Arthur Starr being his eldest son hath power to convey to Miller...Arthur Starr (Seal), Hannah Starr (Seal), Wit: Will Reed, John Seman. Rec. July term 1777.

Pp. 272-273: 3 Nov 1774, Moses Shelby and wf Isabel of Meck., to James Ross of same for ᛒ 75...93 A on Reedy Creek of

VOLUME 5

Rocky or Johnston River, conveyed to Arthur Dobbs to William Huggins, 20 Oct 1765...Moses Shelby (Seal), Isabel Shelby (Seal) Wit: Oliver Wiley, Mary Wiley. Rec. July term 1777.

Pp. 274-275: 13 July 1777, William & Samuel Bigham, farmers, of Meck., to Joseph Hart, planter, of same, for Ł 20 procl. money...100 A on waters of Paw Creek adj. John Giles corner & Steens, Andrew Catheys line, granted to William and Samuel Bigham...William Bigham (Seal), Samuel Bigham (Seal), Wit: Robt Irvin, Frans. Moore. Rec. July term 1777.

Pp. 276-278: Blank

Page 279: Book 15th
            Laird Harris Anno Christi 1771

Pp. 280-282: 16 ____ 1771, Andrew Armor of ____ to Thomas Polk for Ł 190 proc. money...640 A on E side of Catawba River formerly property of James Armor, granted to him 6 Apr 1753... Andrew Armor (Seal), Wit: William Paterson, Samuel Bigham. Rec. April term 1771.

Pp. 282-284: 18 Dec 1769, John Mitchell & wf Elizabeth of Rowan Co., to John Finley of Meck., for Ł 25 proc. money ...198 A on Rocky River-..adj. John Shields, part of 12,500 A granted to Ambrose Harding, Esq., and sold to sd. Mitchell by James Wyly Sheriff...Wit: James Gilmer, Samuel Pickens. Rec. April term 1771.

Pp. 284-286: 18 Dec 1769, John Mitchell & wf Elizabeth of Rowan Co., to James Finley for Ł __ proc. money...189 A adj. James Dysart, part of 12, 500 A granted to Ambrose Harding... Wit: Samuel Pickens, James Gilmore. Rec. April term 1771.

Pp. 286-289: 3 Sept 1768, John Mitchell & wf Elizabeth of Salisbury to Andrew Sites, of Meck., for Ł 70 proc. money...178 A on both sides of Dutch Buffalo Creek, adj. Matthew Bevor, Gov. Dobbs...Wit: Stephen Pots;(German signature)_____. Rec. April term 1771.

Pp. 289-290: 17 Jan 1770, William Alexander of Meck., to Samuel Jack of same, for Ł 12 proc. money...40(?) A on Mc-Alpines Creek adj. Mathews Biggers, granted to William Alexander 6 Apr 1765...William Alexander (Seal), Wit: Adam Alexander, Hez: Alexander. Rec. April term 1771.

Pp. 290-292: 18 Apr 1771, Alexander & William Sterret and Abigail & Ruth their wives of Meck., for Ł 25 proc. money... 500 A on McAlpines Creek adj. mouth of Four Mile Creek above Matthew Biggers land, granted to William Sterret 21 Dec 1763... Alexander Sterret (Seal), Abigail Staret (X) (Seal), William Starret (Seal), Ruth Staret (X) (Seal), Wit: Thos Polk., Andrew Robison. Rec. April term 1771.

Pp. 292-294: 19 Apr 1771, Robert Burns & wf Mary of Meck., to Hugh Montgomery of Rowan Co., for Ł ____...111 A on waters of Shugar Creek being part of land subdivided from Mr. John Campbell's Barony in Tract #4, deeded to James & Ezekiel Alexander by H. E. McCulloh, 14 May 1765...Robert Burns (Seal), Mary Burns (X) (Seal), Wit: Jno Scott, John Springsteen. Rec. April term 1771.

VOLUME 5

Pp. 294-295: 26 March 1771, Aron Alexander and wf Mary of Meck., to John Pfifer of same, for Ł ___ proc. money...56 A on waters of English Buffalo and Rocky or Johnston's River known as Samuel Paton's place...Aron Alexander (Seal), Mary Alexander (X) (Seal), Wit: Robert Smith, Joseph Scot, Samuel Patton. Rec. April term 1771.

Pp. 295-297: 3 Sept 1768, John Mitchell & wf Elizabeth of Salisbury to Fight Gorright of Meck., for Ł 35 proc. money ...144 A on both sides of Dutch Buffaloe Creek on Mathias Beaver's line, John Buzzard's survey, part of 12,500 A sold to him by James Pickett, Esqr., Sheriff, 10 Aug 1768...Wit: Max: Chambers, John Linn (X). Rec. April term 1771.

Page 298: 29 March 1771, James McCord Senior of Meck., deed by gift to James McCord Junior of N. C., all his goods, chattles and household stuff...James McCord (Seal), Wit: Thomas Polk. Peter Johnston. (No rec. date)

Pp. 299-300: 27 Dec 1770, William Small of Meck., planter to Hannah McCree of same, for Ł 19 proc. money...60 A on waters of Six Mile creek and both sides of the Waggon Road leading to Charles Town, being a tract formerly granted to John McCree since deceased...adj. James Lynn's line, Haggins....William Small (W) (Seal), Wit: W. Avery, Wm. Henry (W), William Lemmond. Rec. April term 1771.

Pp. 301-302: 18 Apr 1771, Thomas Polk Esquire of Meck., planter, to John Robinson for Ł 325 (?) proc. money...640 A on E side Catawba River granted to James Armor, Decd 4 Apr 1763... Thos Polk (Seal), Wit: Thomas McCaul, Andrew Robison. Rec. April term 1771.

Pp. 303-304: 1 April 1771, William Harris of Meck., to John Warden of same for Ł 28 proc. money...145 A on waters of Clear Creek...William Harris (Seal), Wit: Thos Walker, Robert Harris Jur. Rec. April term 1771.

Pp. 304-305: 22 March 1771, James Connor of Meck., to James McCaul of same, for Ł 17 proc. money...one bay horse, a natural pacer, branded H on the mounting shoulder...James Connor (Seal), Wit: John Wylie, Isaac Brandon. Rec. April term 1771.

Pp. 305-307: 17 April 1771, James Wilson of Meck. & wf Jane to James Orr, late of Penn., weaver, for Ł 75 proc. money...51 A on Goose Creek, part of a tract conveyed to James Wilson by Adam Alexander...James Wilson (Seal), Jane Wilson (X) (Seal), Wit: James Harris, Will: Harris. Rec. April term 1771.

Pp. 307-309: 18 Jan 1770, Abraham Alexander, Thomas Polk, and George Allen of Meck., to Robert Stuart of same, for Ł 2 proc. money...lot 97 on S side Traid St. in Charlotte ...Wit: Saml Wilson, John Springsteen. Rec. April term 1771.

Pp. 309-314: 12 April 1771, James Connor of Meck., to James McCaul of same, for Ł 6 proc. money...90 A a tract called No. 2, adj. John Finley on waters of McCrees Creek... James Connor (Seal), Wit: Elias Alexander, Thom: McCaul. Rec. April term 1771.

Pp. 314-315: 15 July 1771, Robert Barnet & wf Catherine of Meck. to John Neely of same for L 50...250 A on N fork Steele Creek, granted to William Barnet 24 April 1762 and conveyed to Robert Barnet 20 April 1763...Robert Barnet (Seal), Catern Barnet (X) (Seal), Wit: James Elliot, Thomas Neely. Rec. July term 1771.

Pp. 316-317: 14 May 1771, Hugh Barnett of Meck., to Andrew Crocket planter, of same, for L 80 proc. money... 225 A on West fork of Twelve Mile Creek, being half of a grant to William Donelson conveyed to Barnett 27 Feb 1768...Hugh Barnet (Seal), Elizabeth Barnett (E) (Seal), Wit: Archd. Crockett, John Wilson, John McKain. Rec. July term 1771.

Pp. 317-319: 26 Dec 1770, Martin Pfifer and wf Margaret of Meck., to William Black of Orange Co., N. C. for L 47 proc. money...152 A, adj. Abraham Caradine's, James Wallace's, Samuel Brown's...Martin Pfifer (Seal), Margaret Pfifer (M) (Seal), Wit: John Pfifer, James Rees, Joseph Scot. Rec. April term 1771.

Pp. 319-321: 26 Jan 1769, James Menzen to Titus Leany for L 100 ...150 A including Willis Smith's Folly near a branch of Richardson's Creek...James Menzen (X) (Seal), Wit: George Baker (B), Titus Leany (T), Thos. Chadwick. Rec. July term 1771.

Pp. 321-323: 18 May 1771, Robert Elliot of Meck. to James Elliot, for L ____ proc. money...200 A on waters of Steel Creek, part of 300 A granted 19 April 1763...Robert Elliot (Seal), Wit: Peter Johnston, David McCree. Rec. July term 1771.

Pp. 323-325: 15 July 1771, James Dyzart & wf Margaret of Meck., to Hugh Hamilton of same, for L 45 proc. money... 231 A adj. Barony line...sold by James Dyzert by John Mitchell, 18 Dec 1769...James Dyzart (Seal), Margaret Dysart (M) (Seal), Wit: James Harris, _____.(Isaeri Snford?). Rec. July term 1771.

Pp. 325-326: 19 Feb 1771, Zebulon Weathers of Meck., planter, to Livinus Houston of same, for L 3-5-0...one Red Cow, Whitish Billy croft in the off Ear, one spotted Beach & one White cow croft in the near Ear and one ____ cow croft.... Zebulon Weathers (Z) (Seal), Wit: Hez: Alexander, William Alexander. Rec. July term 1771

Pp. 326-327: 14 July 1771, Robert Elliot of Meck., to William Elliott of same, for L 60 proc. money...100 A on waters of Steel Creek, part of tract ____ 19 April 1763...Robert Elliot (Seal), Wit: William Walker, David McCree. Rec. July term 1771.

Pp. 328-330: 7 Jan 1771, William Bigham & wf Sarah of Meck., planter, to Robert Brownfield of same, planter, for L 60 proc. money... ____ hundred acres on branches of Beaver Dam Creek on West side of Hugh Park's, part of grant to Bigham 23 Dec 1763 (four acres including ____ New Meeting House the Graveyard and Spring on north side only excepted)...William Bigham (Seal), Sarah Bigham (Seal), Wit: Robert Brownfield, Jur; Samuel Bigham. Rec. July term 1771.

VOLUME 5

Pp. 330-331: 15 July 1771, William Elliott of Meck., to Walter Davis of same, for ₺ 100...100 A on waters of Steel Creek, being part of a grant to James Biggar 19 April 1763... William Elliot (Seal), Wit: David Vance, Henry Walker. Rec. July term 1771.

Pp. 332-333: 28 June 1771, Thomas Polk, Abraham Alexander & Robert Elliot of Meck., to William Paterson of same for s 40 proc. money...lot #23 on S side Elliot St. in Charlotte... Thos Polk (Seal), Wit: Joseph Moore, James Carruth. Rec. July term 1771.

Pp. 333-335: 10 Feb 1770, Thomas Polk, Abraham Alexander & George Allen of Meck., to William Paterson of Meck., for ₺ 2-1-0- proc. money...lot #21 on W side Tryon St. in Charlotte ...Wit: Henry Walker. Robert Burns. Rec. July term 1771.

Pp. 336-337: 24 Aug 1770, George Augustus Shelwin to Thos Polk of Meck., for ₺ 6 proc. money...60 A on waters of _____...Wit: John Ford, John Hendry. Rec. July term 1771.

Pp. 337-339: 24 April 1770, Joseph Carroll and Thomas Carroll, both of Tryon Co., to Joseph Clark of same, for ₺ 85...300 A adj. lands and a survey made for James McConnal, on waters of Sugar Creek and Paw Creek, granted to Hugh Berry 14 April 1761 and conveyed to sd. Carrolls...Joseph Carrol (Seal) Thomas Carrol (Seal), Wit: Jno Scote, Andrew Armor. Rec. July term 1771.

Pp. 339-341: 10 Feb 1770, Abraham Alexander, George Allen of Meck., John Frohock of Rowan Co., to Thomas Polk of Meck., for ₺ 3 proc. money...lot no. 1 in S corner from the Court House on Tryon St. in Charlotte...Wit: Hen Walker, Robert Burns. Rec. July term 1771.

Pp. 341-343: 3 Sept 1768, John Mitchell & wf Elizabeth of Salisbury to John Culp of Meck., for ₺ 20 proc. money... 123 A on both sides Dutch Buffaloe, part of 12,500 A conveyed by James Pickens Sheriff of Anson Co., 10 Aug 1768...Wit: John Braly, Georg Barringer(?) (German signature). Rec. July term 1771.

Pp. 343-345: 3 Sept 1768, John Mitchell & wf Elizabeth to George Barringer of Meck., for ₺ 50 proc. money...175 A on both sides Dutch Buffalow Creek...Wit: John Braly, John Culp (K). Rec. July term 1771.

Pp. 346-347: 10 July 1771, William Bigham Jr. of Meck. to Andrew Herron of same, for ₺ 75 proc. money...300 A on Rocky Sugar Creek, part of two grants to William Bigham Jr....William Bigham (Seal), Wit: Peter Johnston, Samuel Bigham. Rec. July term 1771.

Pp. 348-349: 24 Aug 1770, George Augustus Shelwin to Thomas Polk Esquire of Meck., for ₺ 17 proc. money...175 A on waters of Sugar Creek surveyed and laid off and reserved by him in deed of surrender...adj. William Wilson, John Garrison, McElwee, Henry Wilson...Wit: John Foard, John Hendry. (No rec. date).

VOLUME 5

Pp. 350-352: 10 Aug 1776, John Black & wf Jean of Meck., to John Jetton of same, for Ł 30...400 A on N side Catawba River adj. Rachel Price's mother's line, McCulloh's LIne, granted to Rachel Price, 3 Feb 1754, and conveyed by her heirs viz: John Price, Margaret Price, James Price & wf Mary, 28 Sept 1764...John Black (O) (Seal), Jean Black (O) (Seal), Wit: Abraham Jetton, John Potts (O). Rec. July term 1771.

Pp. 353-355: 19 July 1771, John Jetton & wf Elizabeth of Meck., blacksmith, to Lewis Jetton of same, for Ł 5 proc. money...200 A part of grant to Rachel Price, 3 Feb 1754 (same land in preceding deed)...John Jetton (Seal), Elizabeth Jetton (Seal), Wit: Abraham Jetton, Isaac Jetton. Rec. July term 1771.

Pp. 355-357: 12 July 1771, William Johnston of Meck., planter, to William McClure of same, planter, for Ł 15 proc. money...97 A on Mallard Creek at William Johnston's former survey, near Parker's corner...part of a grant to Jacob Gardner, 29 Apr 1768, conveyed to sd. Johnston...William Johnston (Seal), Mary Ann Johnston (M) (Seal), Wit: Elizabeth McElwee (O), Jno. Mck. Alexander. Rec. July term 1771.

Pp. 357-358: 25 Apr 1771, James Forsyth of Tryon Co., to Thomas Polk of Meck., for Ł 18...lot #10 on E side Main St., called Trade St., adj. Abraham Alexander's lot, John Allen's lot in Charlotte...James Forsyth (Seal), Wit: Alex Martin, Ezek. Polk. Rec. July term 1771.

Pp. 358-360: 12 Apr 1771, Thomas Polk of Meck., to Alexander Stuart of same, for Ł 55 proc. money...285 A on waters of Sugar Creek and Mcmichal Creek adj. Henry Walker, William Alexander, James Morris land, granted to sd. Polk 4 May 1769...Thos Polk (Seal), Wit: Robert Elliot, William Pattson. Rec. July term 1771.

Pp. 361-363: 20 July 1771, Thomas Polk Esquire of Meck., to Jeremiah McCafferty of same, for Ł 18 proc.money...lot #10 on Trade St. between Capt. Abraham Alexander's lot # 9 & mr. John Allen's lot #11 in Charlotte...Wit: Peter Johnston, Andrew Greer. Rec. July term 1771.

Pp. 363-365: 10 Jan 1771, James & Sarah Tom of Meck., planter, to James Douglass of same, yeoman, for Ł 40 proc. money...200 A on both sides of Long Creek, including Miller's improvement...John Anderson's line, granted to James Tom, 26 Dec 1766...James Thom (Seal), Sarah Thom (O) (Seal), Wit: John Boyd, William McKirly, William Ramsey. Rec. July term 1771.

Pp. 365-366: 15 July 1771, Samuel Knox & wife Mary of Meck., to James Blackwood of same, for Ł 100...300 A on E side of Catawba River adj. Armors Creek, Samuel M----, John Price's... Samuel Knox (Seal), Mary Knox (O) (Seal), Wit: James Boyd, Robert Harris Jur. Acknowledged in open court (no date).

Pp. 366-368: 8 Oct 1771, John Moore & wf Anna of Tryon Co., to Moses Scott of Meck., for Ł 60 proc. money...86 A in Meck. on E side Catawba River including John Thompson's improvements, granted to John Moore, 17 Nov 1764...John Moore (Seal), Anna Moore (A) (Seal), Wit: James Scott. Rec. Oct. term 1771.

End of Volume 5.

VOLUME 6

Abner Nash's Deeds herein in 1771
Book No. 16

Register's Office Kept by
Robert Harris, Public Register
of
Mecklenburg County
containing Eighty Seven Deeds & Two Cleans(?)
Two Deeds more in one Quire of paper.

Pp. 1-3: 5 Feb 1771, Abner Nash & wf Justina, for ₤ 25 proc. money, to James Harris, 153 A...A Nash (Seal), Justina Nash (Seal), Wit: Clement Nash, Proved before Richd. Henderson, 9 Feb 1771.

(N. B. All deeds from pp. 4-95 are noted *Mutatis Mutandis* and are proved 9 Feb 1771 before Richd. Henderson, by Clement Nash, the only witness.)

Page 4: 5 Feb 1771, Abner Nash & wf Justina, for ₤ 17 s 10 proc. money to Adam Alexander, 120 A in Tract #2 adj. James Harris, Moses Shelby.

Page 5: 5 Feb 1771, Abner Nash & wife Justina, to John Han____, for ₤ 7 proc. money, 68 A in Tract #2.

Page 6: 5 Feb 1771, Abner Nash & wife Justina to Adam Alexander, of Meck., for ₤ 17 s 10, 120 A adj. John Harris, Moses Shelby.

Page 7: 5 Feb 1771, Abner Nash & wife ustina to Samuel Harris, for ₤ 6 proc. money, 55 A on middle Fork of Clear Creek.

Page 8: 5 Feb 1771, Abner Nash & wife Justina, to Samuel Harris, for ₤ 6 proc. money, 65 A adj. Samuel Harris, Moses Shelby.

Page 9: 5 Feb 1771, Abner Nash & wife Justina to James Harris, 70 A in tract #2, for ₤10 proc. money, adj. to corner of re-survey of sd. Harris.

Page 10: 5 Feb 1771, Abner Nash & wife Justina to Jas Harris, for ₤ 5 proc. money, 40 A adj. James Harris.

Page 11: 5 Feb 1771, Abner Nash & wife Justina to John Culberson, for ₤ 5 proc. money, 82 A.

Page 12: 5 Feb 1771, Abner Nash & wife Justina, for ₤ 45 proc. money, to Robt Smith, 205 A (entire deed stricken).

Page 13: 5 Feb 1771, Abner Nash & wife Justina, for ₤ 17 s 10 proc. money, 117 A on Bear Creek.

Page 14: 5 Feb 1771, Abner Nash & wife Justina to James Tindsley(?), for ₤ 20 proc. money, 140 A on the head waters of the So. branch of Caldwells Creek adj. James Morrisons old Survey.

Page 15: 5 Feb 1771, Abner Nash & wife Justina, to David Moore, for ₤ 23 (?) proc. money, 155 A adj. William Blair.

Page 16: 5 Feb 1771, Abner Nash & wife Justina to David Moore, for ₤ 10 proc. money, 114 A in Tract #2, adj. Shelvin, Stilwell.

VOLUME 6

Page 17: 5 Feb 1771, Abner Nash & wife Justina to Samuel Smith, for L 4 proc. money, 36 A on the south Branch of Duck Creek.

Page 18: 5 Feb 1771, Abner Nash & wife Justina to William Morris, for L 12 proc. money, 120 A in tract #2, on N side Whiteoak Branch.

Page 19: 5 Feb 1771, Abner Nash & wife Justina to Oliver Wylie, for L 25 proc. money, 122 A in Tract #2, adj. to his house.

Page 20: 5 Feb 1771, Abner Nash & wife Justina to Caleb Barr, for L 4 proc. money, 32 A adj. McCulloh in a Tract called the Welch Tract.

Page 21: 5 Feb 1771, Abner Nash & wife Justina to William Harris, Esqr., for L 19 proc. money, land in Tract #2, 240 A adj. old survey of sd. William Harris.

Page 22: 5 Feb 1771, Abner Nash & wife Justina, to William Harris, Esqr., for L 15 proc. money, 112 A in Tract #2, adj. Seldwins line.

Page 23: 5 Feb 1771, Abner Nash & wife Justina, to Robert Glass, for L 15 proc. money, 120 A in tract #2, on S side Goose Creek.

Page 24: 5 Feb 1771, Abner Nash & wife Justina to Robert Glass, for L 10 proc. money, 50 A in Tract #2, on the East side of Middle fork of Goose Creek.

Page 25: 5 Feb 1771, Abner Nash & wife Justina, for L 20 proc. money, 210 A in Tract #2, to William Limmond.

Page 26: 5 Feb 1771, Abner Nash & wife Justina, for L 8 proc. money, to John Query, 73 A NW of the Inprovements of sd. John Query.

Page 27: 5 Feb 1771, Abner Nash & wife Justina, to John Query, for L 4 proc. money, 38 A in Tract #2, on S side Querys Branch.

Page 28: 5 Feb 1771, Abner Nash & wife Justina, to Samuel Harris, for L 55 proc. money, 178 A in Tract #2, on S side McCees Creek, adj. William Harris corner.

Page 29: 5 Feb 1771, Abner Nash & wife Justina to Daniel Davis, for L ___ proc. money, 84 A in the Welch Tract, on N side N fork of Beaver pond Creek adj. Edwards.

Page 30: 5 Feb 1771, Abner Nash & wife Justina, to Daniel Davis, for s 20 proc. money, 44 A in the Welch Tract, on N side Middle fork of Beaver Dam Creek.

Page 31: 5 Feb 1771, Abner Nash & wife Justina, to William Querey, for L 4 proc. money, 30 A in Tract #2.

Page 32: 5 Feb 1771, Abner Nash & wife Justina, to John Moffet, for L 16 proc. money, 123 A in Welch tract.

Page 33: 5 Feb 1771, Abner Nash & wife Justina, to James McCall, for L 5 proc. money, 34 A in Tract #2 at the Bottle Spring.

VOLUME 6

Page 34: 5 Feb 177, Abner Nash & wife Justina, to James McCall, for ₤ 35 proc. money, 182 A in Tract #2 on S side Goose Creek.

Page 35: 5 Feb 1771, Abner Nash & wife Justina to James Slone, for ₤ 5 proc. money, 20 A adj. John Edwards.

Page 36: 5 Feb 1771, Abner Nash & wife Justina to James Sloan, for ₤ 34 proc. money, 266 A.

Page 37: 5 Feb 1771, Abner Nash & wife Justina, to Andrew Morrison for ₤ 16 proc. money, 170 A in the Welch Tract on S side North fork of Beaver Pond.

Page 38: 5 Feb 1771, Abner Nash & wife Justina to Samuel Standford, for ₤ 20 proc. money, 226 A in the Welch Tract, adj. Capt. Lewis.

Page 39: 5 Feb 1771, Abner Nash & wife Justina to Isaac Stanford, for ₤ 20 proc. money, 172 A in the Welch Tract.

Page 40: 5 Feb 1771, Abner Nash & wife Justina to James Dysart, for ₤ 25 proc. money, 167 A in the Welch Tract on S side Rocky River, adj. Baroney line, Thomas Wallace.

Page 41: 5 Feb 1771, Abner Nash & wife Justina, to John Carry, for ₤ 10 proc. money, 110 A in the Welch Tract on S fork Rockey River.

Page 42: 5 Feb 1771, Abner Nash & wife Justina to Hugh Caragan, for ₤ 4 proc. money, 60 A adj. John Query.

Page 43: 5 Feb 1771, Abner Nash & wife Justina, to Hugh Carragan for ₤ 8 proc. money, 78 A in Tract #2, on S side Crooked Creek.

Page 44: 5 Feb 1771, Abner Nash & wife Justina to James Wilson, for ₤ 8 proc. money, 45 A in Tract #2 on S side Goose Creek.

Page 45: 5 Feb 1771, Abner Nash & wife Justina to John Harris, for ₤ 5 proc. money, 46 A in Tract #2 on S side Goose Creek.

Page 46: 5 Feb 1771, Abner Nash & wife Justina to William Henderson, for ₤ 6 proc. money, 70 A in Tract #2, on S side Crooked Creek.

Page 47: 5 Feb 1771, Abner Nash & wife Justina to John Johnston, for ₤ 16 proc. money, 100 A in Tract #2, on the Middle fork of Goose Creek.

Page 48: 5 Feb 1771, Abner Nash & wife Justina to John Polk, for ₤ 5 proc. money, 35 A in Tract #2, adj. to a tract of John Polk.

Page 49: 5 Feb 1771, Abner Nash & wife Justina, to James Harris Junr, for ₤ 25 proc. money, 229 A in Tract #2.

Page 50: 5 Feb 1771, Abner Nash & wife Justina, to George Crowell, for ₤ 10 proc. money, 80 A in Tract #2.

VOLUME 6

Page 51: 5 Feb 1771, Abner Nash & wife Justina, to Samuel Crowell, for ₤ 10 proc. money, 48 A, Tract #2.

Page 52: 5 Feb 1771, Abner Nash & wife Justina, to Beadig Howell, for ₤ 10 proc. money, 68 A in Tract #2.

Page 53: 5 Feb 1771, Abner Nash & wife Justina, to Richard Stitwell (Stilwell?), for ₤ 6 proc. money, 58 A in Tract #2.

Page 54: 5 Feb 1771, Abner Nash & wife Justina, to Matthew Stewart for ₤ 4 proc. money, 45 A in Tract #2.

Page 55: 5 Feb 1771, Abner Nash & wife Justina to Matthew Stewart for ₤ 4 proc. money, 35 A in Tract #2 on the south banks of Paddle Creek.

Page 56: 5 Feb 1771, Abner Nash & wife Justina to Thomas Hall, for ₤ 10 proc. money, 104 A in Tract #2.

Page 57: 5 Feb 1771, Abner Nash & wife Justina, to Thomas Hall, for ₤ 5 proc. money, 46 A in Tract #2, adj. sd. Thomas Hall.

Page 58: 5 Feb 1771, Abner Nash & wife Justina, to James Walker, for ₤ 50 proc. money, 222 A in Tract #2.

Page 59: 5 Feb 1771, Abner Nash & wife Justina to Matthew Walker, for ₤ 14 proc. money, 92 A in Tract #2, on S side of Crooked Creek.

Page 60: 5 Feb 1771, Abner Nash & wife Justina to David Caldwell, for ₤ 10 rpco. money, 104 A in Tract #2 on SE side of Caldwell's Creek.

Page 61: 5 Feb 1771, Abner Nash & wife Justina to Robert Morrison, for ₤ 10 proc. money, 87 A in Tract #2 on S side of McKee's Creek.

Page 62: 5 Feb 1771, Abner Nash & wife Justina to Robert Morrison, for ₤ 35 proc. money, 260 A on SE side Reedy, Creek adj. William Wiley.

Page 63: 5 Feb 1771, Abner Nash & wife Justina, to James Morrison, for ₤ 20 proc. money, 154 A in Tract #2 on Caldwells Creek.

Page 64: 5 Feb 1771, Abner Nash & wife Justina, to James Morrison, for ₤ 5 proc. money, 90 A in Tract #2.

Page 65: 5 Feb 1771, Abner Nash & wife Justina to James Morrison, for ₤ 29 proc. money, 157 A on S side Reedy Creek, adj. James Staffords.

Page 66: 5 Feb 1771, Abner Nash & wife Justina to John Wyly for ₤ 10 proc. money, 210 A in Tract #2 on the head branch of Clear Creek.

Page 67: 5 Feb 1771, Abner Nash & wife Justina to John Wyly, for ₤ 20 proc. money, 102 A adj. sd. Wyly.

Page 68: 5 Feb 1771, Abner Nash & wife Justina to John Morrison, for Ł 5 proc. money, 20 A in Tract #2 adj. Caldwell.

Page 69: 5 Feb 1771, Abner Nash & wife Justina to John Morrison, for Ł 5 proc. money, 30 A in Tract #2, adj. Moses Shelby.

Page 70: 5 Feb 1771, Abner Nash & wife Justina to John Morrison, for Ł 25 proc. money, 230 A in Tract #2 adj. Harris.

Page 71: 5 Feb 1771, Abner Nash & wife Justina to Alexander Lewis, for Ł 7 s 10 proc. money, 56 A in the Welch Tract near the Barony Line.

Page 72: 5 Feb 1771, Abner Nash & wife Justina to James Barr, for Ł 7 s 10 proc. money, 53 A in the Welch Tract adj. Cary(?).

Page 73: 5 Feb 1771, Abner Nash & wife Justina to John Edwards, for Ł 15 proc. money, 141 A in the Welch Tract.

Page 74: 5 Feb 1771, Abner Nash & wife Justina to Moses Shelby, for Ł 7 s 10 proc. money, 22 A in Tract #2, adj. sd. Moses Shelby.

Page 75: 5 Feb 1771, Abner Nash & wife Justina to Moses Shelby, for Ł 7 s 10 proc. money, 40 A in Tract #2, near the head of Thompsons Run.

Page 76: 5 Feb 1771, Abner Nash & wife Justina to Moses Shelby, for Ł 38 proc. money, 328 A.

Page 77: 5 Feb 1771, Abner Nash & wife Justina to Francis Glass, for Ł 10 proc. money, 103 A in Tract #2 on S side of a branch known as Wild Colt.

Page 78: 5 Feb 1771, Abner Nash & wife Justina to William Blair, for Ł 22 proc. money, 127 A on S side Goose Creek.

Page 79: 5 Feb 1771, Abner Nash & wife Justina to Charles Polk, for Ł 10 proc. money, 144 A in Tract #2, adj. SW corner of his former survey.

Page 80: 5 Feb 1771, Abner Nash & wife Justina to Charles Polk, for Ł 10 proc. money...45 A on S side Duck Creek.

Page 81: 5 Feb 1771, Abner Nash & wife Justina to Charles Polk, for Ł 10 proc. money, 74 A on N side Duck Creek.

Page 82: 5 Feb 1771, Abner Nash & wife Justina to Charles Polk, for Ł 10 proc. money, 73 A in Tract #2 on S side Goose Creek.

Page 83: 5 Feb 1771, Abner Nash & wife Justina to William Wylie, for Ł 30 proc. money, 150 A in Tract #2 on N side McKees Creek, adj. Samuel Morrison.

Page 84: 5 Feb 1771, Abner Nash & wife Justina to John Warden, for Ł 8 proc. money, __6 A on the Dividing Ridge between Clear Creek and Duck Creek.

Page 85: 5 Feb 1771, Abner Nash & wife Justina to William Harris, for Ł 16 proc. money, 145 A in Tract #2.

VOLUME 6

Page 86: 5 Feb 1771, Abner Nash & wife Justina to William Robb, for ₺ 24 proc. money, 154 A in Tract #2 adj. Benjamin Cockren.

Page 87: 5 Feb 1771, Abner Nash & wife Justina to Rees Price, for ₺ 5 proc. money, 42 A in the Welch Tract.

Page 88: 5 Feb 1771, Abner Nash & wife Justina to David Moffat, for ₺ 6 proc. money, 87 A in the Welch Tract.

Page 89: 5 Feb 1771, Abner Nash & wife Justina to David Moffat, for ₺ 6 proc. money, 48 A in the Welsh Tract.

Page 90: 5 Feb 1771, Abner Nash & wife Justina to Thomas Smith, for ₺ 8 proc. money, 77 A in Tract #2 on the waters of Duck Creek.

Page 91: 5 Feb 1771, Abner Nash & wife Justina to William Thompson, for ₺ 10 proc. money, 88 A in the Welch Tract adj. to sd. Thompson.

Page 92: 5 Feb 1771, Abner Nash & wife Justina to William Thompson, for ₺ 30 proc. money, 377 A in the Welch Tract.

Page 93: 25 March 1772, Abner Nash to Oliver Wylie, for ₺ 4 proc. money, two tracts of 47 A in Tract #2 on waters of Clear Creek, and the other tract, 20 A. Wit: R. Smith, Rec. Jany. Sessn. 1778.

Page 94: 25 March 1772, Abner Nash to William Blair, for ₺ 4 proc. money, two tracts: total 96 A in Tract #2, Wit: R. Smith. Rec. Jany Sessn. 1778.

Page 95: 1 Jan 1772, Abner Nash to Benjamin Brown, for ₺ 10 proc. money, two tracts, total 370 A in the Welch Tract adj. Joseph Yeward. Wit: R. Smith. Rec. Jany Sessn. 1778.

Pp. 96-98: 4 Sept 1779, Archabald Henderson of Meck., to Pattrick Knox of same, for ₺ 3250...300 A, part of a patent to Patrick Elliot, and conveyed by him to George Renicks, 14 April 1752, by Renix to John Black, 23 (?) Oct 1754, and by Thos. & Josiah Black, heirs of sd. John to sd. Henderson; also 73 A, part of 200 A granted to Geo. Renicks, 30 Aug 1753 and conveyed by John Renick, son of George Renick, 17 June 1776 to A. Henderson... Archibald Henderson (Seal), Wit: Saml Blith, William Henderson. (No rec. date).

Pp. 98-99: 13 July 1779, Robert Beaty of Meck., to Mathew Robison, for ₺ 200...305 A on branches of Beaverdam, adj. Thomas Grier which he bought of John Davis, Mr. James McRees, part of 450 A granted to Frances Beaty decd., 21 Dec 1763, and part of 210 A conveyed to Francis Beaty by L & R, 8 Jan 1767 by Samuel Allen and sd. 305 A was willed to sd. Robert Beaty by sd. Francis ...Robert Beaty (Seal), Wit: Joseph Moore, Hugh Polk, Robert Slater.

Pp. 100-101: 15 Nov 1774(?), John Long of Meck., to Daniel Sanders for ₺ 25 proc. money, land on E side Cataba River, adj. William Lowing and Samuel Claig, including his improvements, 150 A granted to sd. Long, 30 Jan 1773...John Long (Seal), Agnis Long (O) (Seal), Wit: Beaty McCay, Justie Bent.

VOLUME 6

Pp. 102-106: Blank.

Pp. 107-108: 22 Apr 1772, William McClure & wf Elizabeth of ____, to Isaac _____, _____ on E side Cataba River, granted 17 May 1764, 100 A...Wit: Richard Mason, William Sims, Prov. April term 1772. (deed in very poor condition).

Pp. 108-109: 4 March 1772, John Hamilton of Meck., to John Harris, for Ł 25...John Hamilton (Seal), Wit: ____ Prov. April term 1772. (pages torn).

Pp. 109;153: 20 Apr ____, William Barnet, farmer, to Abraham Barnet, for Ł 10, land granted 26 March 1775, to Joseph Harding, including an Island...William Barnet (Seal), Margaret Barnet, Wit: John Lahiff, Jurate.

Page 110: (fragment of a deed from Abner Nash).

Pp. 111-113: 10 Jan 1771, James Harris & wf Mary of Meck., planter, to David Hough of same, Sadler, for Ł 27 proc. money, land on Clear Creek, adj. Adam Alexander, sold to sd. Harris by Arthur Dobbs, 24 June 1762...James Harris (Seal), Mary Harris (O) (Seal), Wit: Charles Harris, James Maxwell, Prov. April term 1772.

Pp. 113-115: 4 Dec 1771, Francis Beaty of Meck., planter, to Matthew Russel, planter, for Ł 40 proc. money...200 A on S branch of Long Creek, adj. John Anderson & Hugh McCrackin decd., and sd. Russel, granted to F. Beaty, 26 Nov 1757...Francis Beaty (Seal), Wit: James Beaty, John Beaty, Jurate. Prov. April term 1772.

Pp. 115-117: 1 Feb 1770, Thomas Polk, Abraham Alexander and George Allen of Meck., & John Frohock of Rowan Co., to William Still of Rowan Co., for Ł 2 proc. money...lot in Charlotte, #33 on N side of Tryon St., near half an acre bought from Selwyn, 15 Jan 1767...Wit: Isaac Yelton, Robert Bourns. Prov. April term 1772.

Pp. 117-119: 18 Apr 177-, David McCord of Meck., planter, to Robert Shipley, for Ł 30, 185 A adj. sd. McCord, Barnet, John Richey, part of 640 A granted by Beaty to sd. McCord ...David McCord (Seal), Anne McCord (A) (Seal), Wit: ____rd Shipley, jurate. Prov. April term 1772.

Pp. 119-121: 22 Apr 1772, James Tate & wf Ann of Meck., planter, to James Simson, of Rowan Co., for Ł 90 proc. money 220 A on both sides Four Mile Creek adj. James Johnston, Henry Downs, John Ram(sey?), bought of Selwyn 16 Jan 1767...James Tate (Seal), Ann Tate (A) (Seal), Wit: ____ Sims, ____Ramsey, ___Ross. Prov. April term 1772.

Pp. 121-123: 1 Feb 1772, James Dunn of Meck., to Andrew Dunn of same, for Ł 5, land on both sides Clerks branch of Twelve Mile Creek, 200 A granted to James Ryan, and conveyed to William Haggars, then to Dunn, granted 19 Apr 176-, and conveyed to Haggars, 13 Jan 1764, and to Dunn 7 Jan 1771...James Dunn (Seal), Wit: Henry Downs, Joseph Robeson, Henry Downs Junior, Jurate. Prov. April term 1772.

Pp. 123-126: ____ 177-, Ezekiel Alexdr. of Meck., to Brice Miller, of same, for Ł 50 proc. money, all that part of sd. Alexanders land which is out of the Indian Boundarys and contained in his Paton (sic) Lines, 207 A granted to sd. Ezekiel 6 Apr 1753... Ezekiel Alexdr. (Seal), Wit: Archd. Neall, jurate; Wm. Flaniken, Elias Alexander. Prov. April term 1772.

Pp. 126-128: 17 Feb 1772, John Wilson of Meck., Yeoman, to William Wilson, planter, for 10 pistols, 127 A on waters of Sugar Creek, adj. John Lusk, John Sloan, John Wilson & Brice Miller, granted to John Wilson 29 Apr 1768...John Wilson (I) (Seal), Wit: Barry Janes, Hugh Wilson, Jurate. Rec. Apr. term 1772.

Pp. 128-131: 16 Dec 1771, Bardig Howel to Peter Kizer, for Ł 7, 68 A in Tract #2...Bardig Howel (BH) (Seal), Wit: John Polk, Jurate. Rec. April term 1772.

Pp. 131-133: 12 Sep 177-, Peter Johnston of Meck., to John Miller, for Ł 10, 200 A on waters of Twelve Mile Creek, including the Big Glade and Calhouns improvements he now lives on, granted to Johnston, 4 May 1769...Peter Johnston (Seal), Wit: Francis McCaul, Jurate; Matthew Holly (X), Rec. April term 1772.

Pp. 133-135: 3 Feb 1772, John McWhorter & wf Mary of Rowan Co., to John Brown of same, for Ł 30...land on S side of his lands & e side Cataba, adj. Henry Potts...John McWhorter (Seal), Mary McWhorter (Seal), Wit: Alexr. Osburn, Samuel Gingles, Jurate. Rec. April term 1772.

Pp. 135-137: 1 Apr 1772, Peter Kizer to Joseph Garret, for Ł 9 proc. money...68 A in Tract #2...Peter Kizer (P) (Seal), Wit: ___ Polk, Jurate. Rec. April term 1772.

Pp. 137-140: 21 Oct 1771, Joseph Howel & wf Margaret to William Murphy, for Ł 10, land in Tract #2...Joseph Howel (Seal), Margaret Howel (Seal), Wit: John Carothers. Rec. April term 1772.

Pp. 140-143: 26 Jan 1772, Samuel Crowel & wf Elizabeth to Thomas Dove for Ł 23 s ___, 48 A in Tract #2...Samuel Crowell (Seal), Elizabeth Crowel (B) (Seal), Wit: (torn), Rec. Apr. term 1772.

Pp. 143-144: 21 Aug 1772, George Hise & wife Mary of Meck., to John Lewis Beard of Rowan Co., for Ł 104...land on both sides ___, 142 A...George Hiss (Seal), Mary Hise (M) (Seal), Wit: Daniel Little, James Robinson. Prov. 12 Sept 1772 before Richard Henderson.

Pp. 144-146: 10 March 1772, Thos Polk, Abraham Alexr & Robert Elliott of Meck., to James Foster, for L ___ Proc. money, 10t #5 on S side Traid (sic) St., in Charlotte, from Selwyn deed 15 Jan 17__, Wit: Adam Alexander, William Paterson. Rec. July term 1772.

Page 147: Omitted in numbering.

Pp. 148-149: 11 July 1770, Lennard Hartsel & wf Ester of Meck., to Paul Berringer of same, for Ł 200...182 A on both sides Dutch Buffalo Creek, a branch of Johnstons River...Linnard Hartsel (Seal), Easter Hartsell (X) (Seal), Wit: John PHifer, Moses Stroher(?), Rec. July term 1772.

VOLUME 6

Pp. 149-151: 10 June 176-, John McKnit Alexander and wife of Meck., to Francis Beaty, Collector, for L 35...land on S side Long Creek, adj. Hugh McCra----, Walter Davis, John Allen, 200 A granted to sd. Alexander, 9 Nov 176-...John McKnit Alexander (Seal), Jean Alexander (Seal), Wit: James Palley, Wm. McAdau(?). Rec. July term (1772).

Page 151: Matthew McCorkel of Meck., for love and affection to son Thomas(?). (Pp. 150-160 are badly mutilated, and apparently some pages are missing).

Page 152: 21 April 1772, James Cook(?) & wife to Jacob Gray, 150 A....

Page 153: see deed page 109.

Page 154: Ann Alexander to Elias Alexander...Wit: David Rees, _____ Campbell.

Pp. 154-157: 30 May(?) 1772, Matthew McCorkle to Thomas McCorkle for s 5, 400 A part of land granted to Edward Givens, 1751, and conveyed 1752, conveyeance recorded in Anson County... Matthew McCorkle, Jean McCorkle. Rec. July term 1772. (For this deed mentioned see may Anson County NC Deed Abstracts, Vol. I, p. 13)

Pp. 157-158: 11 July 17--, Joseph Starrans and wife Catharine of _____ Meck., to Moses Stricken, the place where _____ Starrans now lives, on a branch of Adam_____...Joseph Starr__ (IS), Catherine Starrans (R), Wit: _____ Berringer, _____ Phifer. Rec. July term (1772).

Pp. 158-160: John Shields & wf Margaret to David Bradford, 10 Oct 1771, for _____ proc. money...land adj. McCuistions, Moses Andrews, John Finley, 205 A, part of a grant to Ambrose _____, indenture under the hand and seal of _____ in the County of Rowan, 18 Dec 1769...John Sheilds (Seal), Margaret Shields (Seal), Wit: _____ Sheilds, Agnes Shields (A), Rec. July term 1772.

Pp. 160-163: 23 Aug 176_, John Hughes & wf Sarah to James Scott, 123 A on the Ridges between English Buffaloe and Coddle Creek, waters of Rocky or Johnstons River, adj. James Scott, Capt. Phifer...Thomas Hughes (O) (Seal), Sarah Hughes (+) Wit: Wm Scott, Robt Campbell.

Pp. 163-164: 21 Aug 1767, Thomas Polk of Meck., to Joel Harlan, for L 94...land including Thomas Do_____ old Improvemetn, 257 A deed bearing date 5 Jan 1767...Thoms Polk (Seal), Wit: Zebulon Alexander, Elijah Davis. Rec. July term 1772.

Pp. 165-166: 7 Jan 1771, Francis Beaty of Meck., to Jabez Evans of _____, for L 50...land granted to sd. Beaty 21 Apr 1764...Francis Beaty (Seal), Wit: James Palley, Robert Beatev, Wallace Beaty. Rec. July term 1772.

Pp. 167-168: 22 July 1772, John Price Senr of Meck., to Isaac Price his own Son of same, for tender Regard, Love and Good will...189 A, granted to John Price 13 Apr 1752...John Price (Seal), Wit: _____ Davis, _____ Price. Rec. July term 1772.

Pp. 169-171: _____ 1771, Hugh Barry & wf Margaret of Meck., to Richd. Barry of same, for ₤ 60...land on which the said ___ Berry now Lives, 428 A on the E side of the Long Draft, adj. Saml Wilson(?), granted to Andrew Barry, 23 Feb 1754, and conveyed to the sd. Hugh Barry by the said Andrew Barry son and Heir of the said Andrew Barry decd., by deed 16 Sept 1763...Hugh Barry (Seal), Margaret Barry (M) (Seal), Wit: ___, ___ Wilson, ___ Elliott. Rec. July term 1772.

Pp. 171-173: 10 Feb 1769, John Mitchell & wf Elizabeth of Salisbury, Rowan Co., to Anthony Ross, for ₤ 45 proc. money...land adj. Robert Anderson, 130 A, part of land granted to Ambrose Harding Councellor at Law in Dublin, and by Indenture under the Hand and Seal of James ___ High Sheriff of Meck., 5 Aug 1768...Wit: George Ross, Joseph Ross, Jurates; Benj. Milner. Rec. July term 1772.

Pp. 173-176: 10 Feb 1769, John Mitchell & wf Elizabeth of Salisbury, Rowan Co., to James Dysart, for ₤ 10 proc. money...land adj. William Young, part of a grant to Ambrose Harding...(Same wit.) Rec. July term 1772.

Pp. 178-180: 10 Feb 1769, John Mitchell & wf Elizabeth of Salisbury, to David Bradford, for ₤ ___ proc. money, 330 A, part of a grant to Ambrose Harding, etc....Rec. July term 1772.

Pp. 181-182: 6 July 1772, Henry Fashparmon & wf Cristiana of Meck., to John Patterson of same, for ₤ 33 proc. money, land on the Long Run of Cold Water Creek, 100 A, granted 10 Nov 17__... Henry Fashpermon (Seal), Christiana Fashpermon (Seal), Wit: John Phifer, Jurate; Martin Phifer, Martin Phifer Junior. Recd 6 July 1772 ₤ 33. Rec. July term 1772.

Pp. 183-184: 18 July 1772, John Price Senr of Meck., to John Price Junior, son to the sd. John Price, for Tender Regard, Love and Good Will...211 A on E side Cataba River, opposite the Mouth of the South fork of sd. River granted to sd. John Price 13 Apr 1752...John Price (Seal), Wit: John Davis, Isaac Price. Rec. July term 1772.

Pp. 185-186: 25 June 1772, Robert Sloan of Meck., planter, to Francis Beaty Jr., of same, for ₤ 100...200 A on both sides of Paw Creek, adj. Cathey, Beaty, part of 795 A granted to Charles Beaty, 31 Aug 1753 and conveyed to James Young, 17 & 18 May 1762, and conveyed to sd. Robert Sloan by Young, 27 Nov 17--...Robt Sloan (Seal), Wit: John Beaty, Abram Berryhill, Wm Wadow (McAdow?). Rec. July term 1772.

Pp. 187 & 190: 20 July 1771, James Clark of Meck., to William Clark, of same, for ₤ 20 proc. money....land on Mallard Creek, adj. Benjamin Alexander, granted to James Clark, 22 ___ 1768...James Clark (Seal), Wit: John Garrison, Thomas Alexander. Rec. July term 1772.

Pp. 188-189: Blank.

Pp. 190-192: 28 Sept 1770, David Garrison of Tryon Co., to Thomas Polk of Meck., for ₤ 20 proc. money, land between James Wilson, William and John McClure (sic)...William Wilsons line, 170 A...David Garrison (Seal), Wit: Peter Johnston, Adam Alexander, Jurate. Rec. July term 1772.

VOLUME 6

Pp. 192-194: 18 Jan 1770, Abrm. Alexander, Thomas Polk and Richard Berry of Meck., to William Elliott of same, for s 30 proc. money, lot in Charlotte, near half an acre, by deed from Selwyn, 15 Jan 1767...Wit: Saml Wilson, John Springstan, Jurate.

Pp. 194-196: 16 July 17--, James C-ok & wf Lucy(?), to John Howey, for ₺ 5, 231 A adj. Jacob Gray, John M----...Wit: John McNealy, ____. Rec. July term 1772.

Pp. 196-198: ____ July 1772, Robert McCree of Meck., to Zacheus Wilson of same, for s __ proc. money, land adj. Indian line, granted ____ Apr 1767...Robert McCree (Seal), Wit: William Alexander, Robert Harris. Rec. July term 1772. (deed mutilated).

Pp. 198-199: 12 June 17--, Henry Stokes of Anson County to ____ of South Carolina...to William Beard...Henry Stokes (Seal), Wit: Jas Cook, Edward Curry. Rec. July term (1772). (deed mutilated).

Pp. 199-201: 16 Apr 17--, Abraham Alexander, Thos Polk, and ____, to William McCulloh, for s 30 proc. money, lot in Charlotte, on S side Tryon St., near half an acre...Wit: Robert Harris. Rec. July term (1772).

Page 202: End of Book no 17th or 17th Book.

Page 203: ____ 1772, William Martin of __ to Hug McCree, for ₺ 122 s 10 proc. money, William Martin and wf Mary... land in Meck. Co., 338 A adj. William Tanner, David Rees, conveyed to sd. Martin by deed 10 Feb 1765 from Gov. Dobbs...Willm Martin (Seal), Mary Martin (Seal), Wit: John Fifer, Archibald Houston, Robert Rodgers. Rec. Jan. sess. 17--.

Pp. 204-205: 19 Jan 1775, James Carruth of Meck., to Thomas Knighten for ₺ 70 proc. money, granted to sd. Carruth 27 Dec 1768, 200 A on waters of Paw Creek adj. Adam Carruth, John Sloan...James Carruth (Seal), Margeret Coruth (x) (Seal), Wit: John Sloan, Reuben Ross (R). Rec. Jan. Term 1775.

Pp. 205-206: 20 Feb 1775, Abner Nash of Hallifax Co., NC, to Daniel Davis of same, for ₺ 8 s 9 proc. money, 169 A on waters of Beaver Dam Creek in the Welsh Track (sic) adj. Alexander Lewis... A. Nash (Seal), Wit: R. Smith. Rec. Jan Sessn. 1775.

Pp. 207-208: 17 Jan 1775, Robt Irwin & wf Mary of Meck., to Thomas Spencer of same, for ₺ 40 money of NC, land on N fork of Steel Creek, adj. Robt Bigham, Samuel Bigham, Robt Wilson, 100 A...Robt Irwin (Seal), Wit: James Joiner, Richard Brown, Charles Carson. Rec. Jan. Sessn. 1775.

Pp. 208-210: 25 Nov 1772, Abner Nash of Hallifax Co., to Thomas Wilson of Meck., for ₺ 1 proc. money...15 A on waters of George Creek, James Willsons lines, in all 21 acres... A. Nash (Seal), Wit: R. Smith. Rec. Jany Sessn. 1775.

Pp. 210-211: 18 Jan 1770, Thos Polk, Abrm Alexander & George Allen of Meck., to Francis Herron of same, for ₺ 25 proc. money...lot #50 on Et side Tryon St....Wit: Alex Martin, Saml Mason. Rec. Jan. Sessn 1775.

VOLUME 6

Pp. 212-213: 17 Aug 1773, John Barnet of Meck., to William Barnett of same, for ₤ 40 proc. money...land on main Sugar Creek including the plantation he now lives on, part of 2 tract granted to sd. John Barnet...John Barnett (Seal), Wit: Luke Mitchener, Will Reed. Rec. Jan. Sessn. 1775.

Pp. 213-214: 18 Oct 1774, Zaccheus Wilson & wf Frances to Georg Calhoun Jun., all of Meck., for ₤ 65...land on S side Suggar Creek adj. Robt Wilson, Zacheus Willson, 130 A... Zaccheus Willson (Seal), Franciss Wilson (O) (Seal), wit: Robert Irvin, David Wicks. Rec. Jan. Sessn. 1775.

Pp. 214-215: 10 Feb 1769, John Mitchel & wf Elizabeth of Salisbury, Rowan Co., to Nathaniel Gilmore of Meck., for ₤ 10 proc. money...277 A, part of grant to Ambrous Harding.... Wit: Samuel Wilson, James Gilmore. Rec. Jan. Sessn. 1775.

Pp. 216-217: 5 Feb 1771, Abner Nash & wf Justina to John McCracken for ₤ 20 proc. money...land in Tract #2, 160 A... Rec. date not given.

Pp. 218-219: 22 Apr 1774, David Vance of Meck., to James Herron, both of Prov. of N. C., for ₤ 25 proc. money, 103 A and 3/4 agreeable to a survey now made on E side Cataba River on waters of Steel Creek, adj. Robt Irwin...N. B. It is agreed that the sd. James Herron pay the Quit Rents that is & shall become due to the King from the date of the Patent granted to Robt Barnet 26 Oct 1767...David Vance (Seal), Ruth Vance (Seal), Wit: Robert Irwin, James Carothers. Rec. Jan. Sessn. 1775.

Pp. 220-221: 26 Mar 1773, Samuel Bigham Senr of Meck., to John Bigham of same, for ₤ 85...land adj. Ambrose McKees, 200 A...Saml Bigham (Seal), Wit: Robt Irwin, James Whitsell. Rec. Jan. sessn. 1775.

Pp. 221-222: 13 May 1773, Abraham Alexander of Meck., to Whitstill Avery of same, for ₤ 10 proc. money, lot in Charlotte, 1.2 lot #9(?), on Tryon St., adj. Jeremiah McCafferty, Lot #10...Wit: Jno McK. Alexander. Rec. Janry. Sess. 1775.

Pp. 223-224: 19 Jan 1775, John Sloan of Meck., & wf Jean to Thomas Knighten for ₤ 60 proc. money, 90 A on both sides Paw Creek adj. Mason, David McCord, McKenley, granted to sd. Sloan 13 Jan 1773...John Sloan, Jean Sloan (O), Wit: James Carruth, Rebecca Ross (R). Rec. Jan. Sess 1775.

Pp. 224-227: 5 June 1773, William Black of Chitam(sic) Co., NC, to Daniel Davies, for ₤ 22 proc. money...90 A in the Welsh Track, on the S side middle fork of the Beaver pond Creek... Willm Black (Seal), Wit: R. Smith, George Alexander. Rec. Jan. term 1775.

Pp. 227-229: 4 Nov 1772, Abner Nash to James Frazer of Meck., for ₤ 21 proc. money...259 A on waters of Beaver Dam Creek, on the Barony Line...Wit: R. Smith. Rec. Jan. Sess 1775.

Pp. 230-231: 10 Feb 1769, John Mitchel & wf Elisabeth of Salisbury, Rowan Co., to Robert Moore, for ₤ 10 proc. money... land on E side Rocky River adj. James Barr, Thomas Sheites, 190 A, granted to Ambrose Harding, Esqr....Wit: Saml Wilson, James Gilmore. Rec. Jany Sessn. 1775.

VOLUME 6

Pp. 231-233: 17 Jan 1775, Robert McKindley of Meck., to William McKindley for ℔ 5 proc. money...land on both sides Paw Creek, part of 600 A granted to John Davis 10 Apr 1761, and sold to Matthew Patten 19 July 1763, then to sd. Robert McKindley 18 Apr 1764, 200 A...Robert McKindley (X) (Seal), Wit: David Davies, Justis Beech. Rec. Jan. Sessn 1775.

Pp. 233-237: 7 Jan 1775, Mathew Biggar & wf Mary of Craven Co., South Carolina, planter, to Joseph McCinlev of Meck., (s5 sterling lease; ℔ 83 release)...406 A in Meck., adj. John Biggers East line, opposite the mouth of Crowders Creek...Mathew Bigger (Seal), Mary Bigger (X) (Seal), Wit: John Bigger, William McRee, James Bigger. Rec. Jan. Sessn. 1775.

Pp. 237-238: 10 Feb 1769, John Mitchell & wf Elizabeth of Salisbury to Robert Andrew of Meck., for ℔ 10 proc. money land adj. Dyzart crossing Rocky River, James Dyzart, 248 A, part of a grant to Ambrose Harding...Wit: James Wilson, James Gilmore. Rec. Jan. Sessn 1775.

Pp. 239-240: 10 Feb 1769, John Mitchell & wf Elizabeth to Moses Andrew of Meck., for ℔ 20 proc. money, 305 A adj. John Gindley, part of a tract granted to Ambrose Harding...Wit: Patrick Carr, Joseph Patterson. Rec. Jan. Sessn. 1775.

Pp. 241-242: 17 Aug 1773, Abgal Shin of Meck., to Joseph Shinn of same, for ℔ 15 proc. money...land on Little Cold Water branch of Rocky or Johnstons River, adj. Matthias Mitchell, 156 A...Abigail Shinn (Seal), Wit: Matthäus ____ (German signature), Isaac Shinn, Matthias Mitchell. Rec. Jan. Sessn 1775.

Pp. 242-243: 17 Jan 1775, Zacheus Wilson to Robert Wilson, both of Meck., for ℔ 2 proc. money, 151 A adj. to an old survey of sd. Zacheus...N. B. It is agreed that sd. Robert Wilson pay the Quitrents that are and shall become due from the date of the Pattent 25 Apr 1776(sic)...Wit: Andrew Greer, Robt Harris. Rec. Jan. sessn 1775.

Pp. 244-245: 12 Jan 1775, George Calhoun of Meck., to Samuel Calhoun, son to sd. George, for ℔ 100....land on E side Cataba River on the Steel Creek adj. Saml Knox, John Hendres, James Biger, granted to Samuel Knox, and sold to John Davis, 180 A...George Calhoun (Seal)(C), Elisabeth Calhoun (◡◠) (Seal), Wit: Ann Brown, Wm Kerr. Rec. Jan. Sessn. 1775.

Pp. 245-247: 4 Aug 1774, John Carothers of Cumberland Co., Pensylvania, to Robert Carothers of Meck., for ℔ 10 proc. money...150 A on waters of north fork of Steel Creek adj. William Barnet...John Carothers (Seal), Wit: James Palley, Agnes Palley (S), Rec. Jan. Sessn. 1775.

Pp. 247-249: 25 March 1772, Abner Nash to Benjabin Brown of Meck., for s 40 sterling, 23 A on waters of Beaver pond Creek...Wit. R. Smith. Rec. Jan. Sessn 1775.

Pp. 249-251: 5 March 1772, Abner Nash to Daniel Davis of Meck., for ℔ 8 proc. money...51 A on the middle fork of Beaver Dam Creek, waters of Rocky River...Rec. Jan. Sessn 1775.

Pp. 252-253: 30 Jan 1770, John Mitchell & wf Elizabeth of Salisbury, to Maxwell Chambers of Meck., for ₤ 20 proc. money, land on both sides Rocky River, part of a grant to Ambrose Harding, adj. Ramsey, 420 A...Wit: John Dunn, Christopher Beckman. Rec. Jan. Sessn. 1775.

Pp. 253-255: Abner Nash to Robert Slone, 25 Oct 1772, land on waters of Rocky River, Davis Creek adj. David Slone, 100 A...Rec. Jan. Sessn. 1775.

Pp. 255-257: 12 Jan 1775, Daniel Davis of Meck., to William Osborne of same, for ₤ 30...land conveyed from William Black to sd. Davis 5 June 1773, conveyed from Abner Nash, to sd. William Black 5 Jan 1771, on Beaver Dam Creek a branch of Rocky River, two tracts...Daniel Davis (Seal), Wit: John Davis, John Osborne. Rec. Jan. Sessn. 1775.

Pp. 258-260: 20 Oct 1772, William White & wf Margret of Prov. of NC, to Isaac Sellers of Meck., for ₤ 140...158 A on S side Rocky or Johnstones River, conveyed by Arthur Dobbs to sd. William White 29 June 1762...William White, Margrate White (X), Wit: Andrew Barns, James White Senr (X). Rec. Jan. Sessn. 1775.

Pp. 260-262: 18 Jan 1775, James Finny of Meck., Carpenter, to Georg Findley of same, for ₤ 40 proc. money...land in Tract #2 on head waters of McRee Creek...James Finney (Seal), Wit: Alexander Finney, Isaac Sellers. Rec. Jan. Sessn. 1775.

Pp. 262-264: 13 Aug 1774, William Penny & wf Elisabeth of Meck., to Caleb Pfifer, for ₤ 60 proc. money...land adj. Dobbs line, 65 A conveyed to sd. Penny by Henry Eustace McCulloh, 26 Feb 1767...William Penney (Seal), Elisabeth Penney (Seal), Wit: John Pfifer, Jason Frissell, James Killpatrick. Rec. Jan. Sessn. 1775.

Pp. 264-266: 18 Jan 1775, Benjabin Cochrean to John Miller for ₤ 23 proc. money, 36 A in Tract #2 on waters of Camp branch a branch of Clear Creek...Benjain Cochrean (Seal), Wit: Alexander Finney, Isaac Sellers. Rec. Jan. Sessn.1775.

Pp. 266-268: 1 Apr 1775, John Whitsill of Meck., to Thomas Nealy Junior of same, for ₤ 100...land granted 4 May 1769 on waters of Steel Creek adj. Mathew Knox's...John Whitsell (Seal), Rachel Whitsell (R) (Seal), Wit: Robt Irwin, Jurate; Thomas McGee, Rec. April Sessn. 1775.

Pp. 268-270: 1 Apr 1775, Samuel Bigham Senior, planter to Thomas Nealy Junior, farmer for ₤ 100...land on waters of Steel Creek adj. Frances Moore, 83 A, part of 500 A granted to Moses Furgoson, 26 Sept 1766, and conveyed to Samuel Bigham Sr.... Saml Bigham (Seal), Wit: Robt Irwin, Thomas McGee. Rec. April Sessn 1775.

Pp. 270-272: 20 March 1763, James Campbell of Meck., to Henry Eustace McColloh of Hallafax Co., for ₤ 44 proc. money, land on the South Branch of Cawdle Creek, adj. Wm Wallace, 180 A...James Campbell (IC) (Seal), Wit: Moses Alexander, John Frohock. Rec. April Sessn. 1775.

Pp. 273-274: 16 Apr 1771, Thomas Polk, Abraham Alexander and Jeremiah McCafferty and Richard Barry of Meck., to Patrick Jack of same for s 55 proc. money, lot in Charlotte, #s

VOLUME 6

130 & 133...Wit; James Way, Joseph Kennedy. Rec. April Sessn 1775.

Pp. 274-275: 20 March 1772, Thos Polk, Abrm Alexander & Wm Patison of Meck., to Robt Wilson, for ₤ 1 proc. money, lot #99 in town of Charlotte, on S side Tryon St., near half an acre... Wit: R. Smith, Jurate. Rec. April Sessn 1775.

Pp. 276-277: 25 May 1770, James McClure of Meck., to Wm Givins of same, for ₤ 20 proc. money, land on both sides Heder(?) Fork of Twelve Mile Creek above Robert Ramseys lands, adj. John McColloh, 300 A...James McClure (Seal), Wit: Henry Downs, Thomas Black, Frances Downs. Rec. April Sessn. 1775

Pp. 277-278: 17 Feb 1775, Abner Nash to James Wilson of Meck., for s 30 proc. money, land on waters of Goose Creek, in Tract #2, 159 A...by power of attorney, Thos Polk (Seal), Wit: Isc. Alexander, David Hough, Jurate. Rec. April Sessn 1775.

Pp. 279-280: 15 Dec 1774, Robt Creaghead of Meck., to John Gerrison of same, for ₤ 200 proc. money...land granted by deed from Selwyn to Jean Creaghead, part of Tract #3, adj. Nathan Oar, 267 A...Robt Creaghead (Seal), Hannah Creaghead (O) (Seal), Wit: George Mitchel. Rec. April sessn 1775.

Pp. 280-282: 29 March 1773, William Patton of St. Marks Parish, Craven Co., S. C., to Alexander McKee of Meck., by grant 16 May 1754 under the hand of Mathew Rowan President of the Council, 300 A on Shuggar Creek below his other plantation in Meck., form the sd. Thomas Patton left to William Patton by will, Willm Patton (Seal), Elizabeth Patton (E) (Seal), Wit: Willm Carson, Andw. Foster, Wm. Berryhill. Rec. April sessn 1775.

Pp. 282-284: 29 March 1773, William Patton & wf Elisabeth of Craven Co., SC to Alexander McKee, land granted 6 Apr 1753 to Thomas Patton 241 A on the south fork of Shuggar Creek, for ₤ 52...Rec. April sessn 1775.

Pp. 284-285: 19 Apr 1775, John McColloh of Meck., to William Givins of same, for ₤ 50...land on the Ceder Fork of Twelve Mile Creek including the sd. William Givins Grist Mill, granted to the sd. John McColloh, 5 May 1769...John McColloh (Seal), Wit: None. Ack. in Court April Sessn 1775.

Pp. 286-287: 24 Oct 1773, Patrick Jack of Meck., to Robt McGough of same, for ₤ 60 proc. money...land on both sides McCalpins Creek, adj. Robt Eliot, Samuel Jack, being the land whereon the sd. Patrick Jack now dwells, 150A...Patrick Jack (Seal), Wit: James Tate, Saml Jack, Edward Sharp. Rec. April Sessn. 1775.

Pp. 287-288: 12 May 1775, David McCord of Meck., to Robt Mitchell of same, for ₤ 10 proc. money...112 A on the E side of the Catauba River, on a small branch of Paw Creek, granted to Mathew Brown 11 Dec 1770...David McCord (Seal), Anne McCord (Seal), Wit: Robert McCord. Rec. April Sessn. 1775.

Pp. 288-289: 10 Oct 1773, Thos Polk, Abrm. Alexander & Jeremiah McCafferty of Meck., for ₤ 10 proc. money, lot in Charlotte, #s 84 & 92, near half an acre...Wit: James Foster, Samuel Jack. Rec. April Sess 1775.

VOLUME 6

Pp. 290-292: 26 Oct 1776, Joseph McKindley of Meck., planter, to James Brown, now of the County and Prov. afsd., farmer (tanner?), for L 110 proc. money...land on E side Cattaba River adj. Bigger, opposite the mouth of Crowders Creek, 406 A granted to Moses Bigger 6 Apr 1765...Joseph McKindly (Seal), Elizabeth McKindly (J) (Seal), Wit: Saml Chambers, Francis Johnston. Rec. April Sess. 1777. Prov. by Saml Chambers.

Pp. 293-295: 10 Feb 1769, John Mitchel & wf Elizabeth of Salisbury, to Patrick Carr, for L 40 proc. money...land on both sides Coddle Creek, 230 A, granted to Ambrose Harding...Wit: Samuel Wilson, James Gilmore, John Turner, Thomas Shields. Rec. April Sessn 1777.

Pp. 296-297: Blank.

Page 298: Book No. 18th. Patrick Jacks deed is in this book.

Pp. 299-300: 17 Nov 177-, William Smith of Meck., to Henry Eustace McCulloh of Rowan Co., land on McCalpins Creek adj. Abraham Miller, John Star...William Smith (Seal), Wit: Robt Brownfield, Thos Polk. Rec. April Term 1774. Prov. by Thos Polk.

(Pp. 299-325 are in poor condition.)

Pp. 300-302: 18 Oct 176-, William Wallace of Meck., Black Smith, to John Sconnel, Late of the Province ___, for L 25 proc. money...land adj. Will. Wallace, 71 A...wm Wallace (Seal), Sarah Wallace (g) (Seal), Wit: torn. Prov. by David Rees. Rec. date torn.

Pp. 303-304: 23 April 1771(?), John McKnitt Alexander of Meck., to Hezekiah Alexander of same, for L 100 proc. money land on both sides Long___ adj. John Smith, 70 A, part of 12,500 A granted to Jeremiah Joy late of ___ 5 Aug 1760...Jno Mck Alexander (Seal), Wit: ___ Wyly. Ack. in open court, ___ 1774.

Pp. 305-306: 28 Sept 1773, Samuel Jack & wf Francis of Meck., to William Smith of same, for L 120 proc. money, land on waters of Suggar Creek, 200 A...Samuel Jack (Seal), Francis Jack (Seal), Wit: John Flenniken, John Davis. Rec. April term 1774. Prov. by John Flenniken.

Pp. 306-307: 10 Feb 1769, John Mitchel & wf Elizabeth to James Wallis of Meck., for L 10 proc. money, land adj. Thomas Forguson, 227 A, part of a grant to Ambrose Harding, Wit: Adam Alexander, Robert Harris Jur. Rec. April Court 1774. Prov. by Adam Alexander.

Pp. 307-308: 16 May 1769, John McKnit Alexander to Nath__ Johnston of Meck., for L 15 proc. money...land adj. sd. Alexander, near Mallard Creek...Jno McKnitt Alexander (Seal), Jane Alexander (Seal), Wit: Sophia Gardner (O), William Johnston. Rec. April term 1774. Prov. by William Johnston.

Page 309: 23 Apr 1774, James Bell of Charlotte Town to James Russell of Meck Co., for L 50 proc. money, lot #s 88 & 96 on W side Tryon St...James Bell, Wit: James Martin (?), ___ Avery. Rec. April term 1774.

VOLUME 6

Pp. 310-312: 25 May 1773, Jane Flaniken of Meck., to Hezekiah Alexander of same, for ₤ 105...part of a tract granted to John Selwyn, 3 Mar 1745 (O.S.), and conveyed by Henry Eustance McColloh attorney for George Augustus Selwyn, heir of sd. John, 13 May 1773 mortgage was redeemed...Jane Flaniken (J) (Seal), Wit: Sarah(?) Flaniken. Rec. April term 1774.

Pp. 312-313: 10 July 1773, Thos Polk, Abm Alexander & Jeremiah McCafferty of Meck., to Robert Harvey, lot #81 in Charlotte on S side Tryon St., Wit: Zebulon Alexander, Joseph Scott. Rec. April term 1774. Prov. by Zebulon Alexander.

Pp. 313-315: 21 Jan 1773, David Moore of Meck., & wf Anna to Jonathan Buccaloo of same, for ₤ 38 proc. money land on waters of McCaupins Creek, adj. Sitwell (Stitewell?), David Moore (M) (Seal), Anna Moore (#) (Seal), Wit: John Ford, Wi-liam Lemmond. Rec. April term 1773. Prov. by John Ford.

Pp. 315-316: 19 Nov 1773, Abraham Caradine of Meck., planter, to Sarah Alexander, widow of Col. Moses Alexander deceased of same, for ₤ 130, land adj. John Alexander, 254 A... Abraham Caradine (Seal), Wit: Adam Alexander, John Jones. Rec. April term 1773. Prov. by Adam Alexander.

Pp. 316-317: 18 Aug 1773, William Barnet of Meck., to Thomas Barnet, son of sd. William, for ₤ 20 proc. money, land on both sides Sugar Creek adj. Selwyns line, granted to sd. William Barnet 31 Mar 1753...William Barnett (Seal), Margaret Barnet (Seal), Wit: John McRee, John Johnston. Rec. April term 1774. Ack. in open court.

Pp. 317-318: 10 Feb 1770, Francis Beatey of Meck., to John Beaty of same, for ₤ 180, 361 A on E side Cataba, the land where the sd. Francis Beaty now dwells, conveyed by David Standly to Francis Beaty by deed 15 Oct 1764, and part of 640 A granted to sd. Francis Beatey, 21 Dec 1763...Francis Beatey (Seal), Wit: James Tate, James Palley, James Beatey. Rec. April term 1774. Prov. by James Beatey.

Pp. 318-319: 17 Oct 1773, Thos Polk, Abrm Alexander & Jeremiah McCafferty of Meck., for ₤ 50 proc. money, lot in Charlotte #88 & 96, on W side Tryon St., Wit: Saml Jack, Jas. Foster. Rec. April term 1774. Prov. by Saml Jack.

Pp. 319-320: 28 Sept 1773, Samuel Jack & wf of Meck., to William Smith of same, for ₤ ___ proc. money, land on waters of Sugar Creek, adj. tract where he now lives, 40 A...Samuel Jack (Seal), Francis Jack (Seal), Wit: John Fleniken, John Davis. Prov. by John Flenniken, April term 1774.

Pp. 320-321: 2 Nov 1772, Andrew Crockett of Meck., to Archibald Crockett for ₤ 100 proc. money, land on waters of Six Mile Creek adj. James Potts, William Donaldson, James Tate & Brice Miller, 140 A...Andw Crocket (Seal), Mary Crocket (1) (Seal) Wit: Frans Bassett, John Wilson, Wm McCulloh. Prov. by John Wilson April term 1774.

Pp. 321-322: 6 Apr 1773, Thos Polk of Meck., to Henry Vernor of same, farmer, for ₤ 75 proc. money, land on head waters of Sugar Creek adj. Samuel Carrot, John Carson, John Newman

3-- A...Thos Polk (Seal), Wit: Jas Foster, Wm Pottesory. Ack. in open Court April term 1774.

Pp. 322-323: 12 June 1772, Andrew Crockett & wf Mary of Meck., to Hugh Barnet of same, for Ł 20 proc. money, land adj. Donaldson, 81 A...Andrew Crocket (Seal), Mary Crocket (Seal), Wit: Andrew Neel, John Moore. Prov. by John Moor, April term 1774.

Pp. 323-324: 12 July 1771, Samuel Bigham of Meck., to William Porter of same, for Ł 60 proc. money...land on waters of Rockey Sugar Creek including his own improvements, above Samuel Bighams house...Samuel Bigham (Seal), Wit: William Bigham, Samuel Bigham, Peter Johnston. Ack. in open court April term 1774.

Pp. 324-325: 12 Jan 1773, John Hall & wf Elizabeth of Meck., to Thomas Wilson of same, for Ł 9 proc. money, land on S side Goose Creek, 34 A...John Hall (Seal), Elizabeth Hall (+) (Seal), Wit: Robt Colbrith (+). Prov. by Robt Colbrith, April term 1774.

Pp. 325-326: 21 Dec 1773, Andrew Crocket & wf Mary of Meck., to John Sturgeon of same, for Ł 20 proc. money...land on SW fork of Twelve Mile Creek adj. Archibald Crockett, sd. Sturgeon granted to William Donaldson, 16 Mar 1754, 225 A...Andrew Crocket (Seal), Mary Crocket (Seal), Wit: Arem(?) Crocket, John Wilson, William Miller. Prov. by John Wilson, April term 1774.

Pp. 326-327: ____ 1772, Richard Rains & wf Lucy of Meck., to John Springsteen Junior of same, for Ł 30 proc. money, land in Charlotte, lot #2, near half an acre...R. Raines (Seal), Lucy Raines (Seal), Wit: Thos Polk, Richard Springsteen. Prov. by Richard Springsteen April term 1774.

Pp. 327-328: 18 Jan 1774, Thomas Polk of Meck., to John Carson of same, for Ł 160...land on waters of Sugar Creek adj. David Hays, conveyed to Samuel Bigham by pattent 21 Nov 1760 to sd. Polk by deed 1 April 1764...Wit: ____, Jas McCafferty. Ack. in open court April term 1774.

Pp. 328-329: 18 Aug 1773, William Barnet of Meck., to Thomas Barnet, son of sd. William, for Ł 100 proc. money...land adj. James Sprotts, William Barnett, John McDowell, 356 A...William Barnet (Seal), Margaret Barnet (Seal), Wit: ____ McRee, Peter Johnston. Ack. by sd. Barnet & wf in open court April term 1774.

Page 329: 16 May 1769, John McKnitt Alexander of Meck., to Nathaniel Johnston of same, for Ł 34 proc. money, land on Mallard Creek, branch of Rockey Rier, 100 A granted to sd. Alexander by John Campbell & Henry E. McCulloh his attorney...Wit: Robt Miller (Patk? Miller), William Johnston. Prov. by Johnston April term 1774.

Page 330: 13 Jan 1774, Thos Polk of Meck., to John Leman of same, for Ł 20 proc. money, land on waters of McCapins Creek, adj. James Flanican, Wit: John Gibbons, Andw Rea. Prov. by Andw Read, April Court 1774.

Page 331: 11 March 1773, George Alexander & wf Margaret of Meck., to Hugh McKnight of same, for Ł 60 proc. money, land in Berkley County, <u>South</u> Carolina, on the North fork of Pacolett River

on both sides joining below his other survey, 307 A...George
Alexander (Seal), Margaret Alexander (Seal), Wit: Robt Smith.
Ack. in open court, April court, April Court 1774.

Pp. 332-333: 17 Sept 1772, Margaret Loftin & Samuel Loftin of
Meck., to Jacob Secrist of same, for L 40 proc.
money, land on both sides of Six Mile Creek adj. Donaldson, Benjamin Lowry, John McCarnes(?), 200 A...Margaret Loftin (Seal),
Samuel Loftin (Seal), Wit: William Harans, James Houston, James
Houston. Prov. by James Houston, April Court 1774.

Pp. 333-334: 22 Aug 1772, John Jackson More & wf Marv of Meck.,
to Joseph Hobbs of same, for L 22 proc. money...
land on branches of McDowells Creek adj. Aaron Alexander, John
Jittons, McCullohs baroney line, granted to sd. Moor, 22 Dec 1768
...John Jackson More (Seal), Mary Moore (+) (Seal), Wit: Thos
McCullough, John Kersey (I), Prov. by Thos McCulloh, Apr. Court
1774.

Pp. 334-335: 26 Oct 1773, Thos Polk, Abm Alexander & Jeremiah
McCafferty of Meck., to Adam Alexander of same,
for L 49 proc. money, lot # 13 on E side Tryon St., near half
an acre...Wit: Saml Jack, Jas Foster, Prov. by Jas Foster,
April Court 1774

Pp. 336-337: 15 Apr 1774, Thos Polk, Jeremiah McCaffertv & Wm
Patteson of Meck., to James Karr of Rowan Co., for
s 20 proc. money, lot #175 on W side Tryon St., in Town of
Charlotte...Wit: _____ Alexander, David McRee. Prov. by Isaac
Alexander, April Court 1774.

Pp. 337-340: 15 May 1767, Joseph Semple & wf Jennet of Meck., to
Robert Harris Senr, Moses Alexander, Paul Barringer,
Henry Downs & John McKnitt Alexander, Trustees of Town of _____
County of Meclinburg(sic), for L 60 proc. money, land on both
sides of Abram Alexanders Mill Creek, a branch of Sugar Creek, adj.
Semple, Alexander, crossing the bigg Savanah and Great Road, 100
A by deed of same from Selwyn, 6 Jan 1767...Joseph Semple (Seal),
Jennet Semple (N) (Seal), Wit: Robert Harris Junr, William Harris
(X), John Tagert. Prov. by William Harris, July Court 1774.

Pp. 431-432: 21 Apr 1774, James Foster of Meck., to Sarah Alexander, for L 70 proc. money, land adj. Ben Alexander,
166 A granted to James Foster, 17 Jan 1767, bv deed from Selwyn...
James Foster (Seal), Wit: Tho Polk, I. Alexander. Prov. by Isaac
Alexander, July Court 1774.

Pp. 343-344: 20 May 1774, Michel Goodnight of Meck., & wife Marv
to John Pifer of same, for L 105 proc. money of NC...
190 A near the three mile branch, waters of Rocky River, conveyed
to sd. Goodnight from James McClean 1 May 1764, from Arthur Dobbs,
24 June 1762 (for completion see pp. 346-347).

Page 345: (deed fragmentary), Matthew McCormic to Thomas McCorkel,
one sorrel mare and negro, 30 May 1772...Matthew McCormic, Wit: Edward Givens (O), Robert Doudle, Henry Hendry. Rec.
July term _____.

Pp. 345-346: 22 July 1772, Mrs. Ann Alexander of Meck., to Elias
Alexander, for L 20 proc. money...part of 100 A

VOLUME 6

belonging to Geo. Augustus Selwyn, conveyed 8 Jan 1767....

Pp. 346-347: (end of deed pp. 343-344)...Michel Goodnight (M) (Seal), Marry Goodnight (M) (Seal), Wit: Samuel Patan, George Goodnight (G). Prov. by Samuel Pattan, Octr. Sessn. 1774.

Pp. 348-350: 21 Apr 1774, James Foster of Meck., to Sarah Alexander of same, for ᵯ 100...275 A granted to sd. Foster by deed from Selwyn, 17 Jan 1767...James Foster (Seal), Wit: Thomas Polk, Is. Alexander. Prov. by Isaac Alexander, July term 1774.

Pp. 350-352: 10 Feb 1769, John Mitchel & wf Elizabeth of Salisbury, to James Gilmore of Meck., for ᵯ 15 proc. money... 148 A granted to Jeremiah Joy late of London, and sold to sd. Mitchel...Wit: Samuel Wilson (X), Nathanal Gilmor. Prov. by Samuel Wilson, July Court 1774.

Pp. 352-354: 10 Feb 1769, John Mitchel & wf Elizabeth to Nathanal Gilmore of Meck., for ᵯ 50 proc. money...265 A near Rocky River, by indenture 3 Aug 1768 from Ambrose Harding, Wit: Samuel Wilson (X), James Gilmore. Prov. by Samuel Wilson, July Court 1774.

Pp. 354-355: 18 July 1774, Daniel Alexander of Meck., planter, to Stephen Alexander, planter and son of Sd. Daniel, for natural love & affection, land on W side Coddle Creek, 168 A... Daniel Alexander (Seal), Wit: Will Alexander, Benjabin Alexander. Prov. by Willm Alexander, July Court 1774.

Page 356: 8 July 1771, Cunrad Garlaugh & wf Mary of Christopher Goodman, planter, for ᵯ 40 proc. money, land on N side Duch Bufflow Creek running into Rocky River, 100 A granted 26 Oct 1767 to sd. Cunrad Garelaugh...Cunrod Garelaugh (KC) (Seal), Mary Garelaugh (X) (Seal), Wit: Leonard Hartsell, Michal Glance (M), Samuel Suther Junr. Prov. by Leonard Hartsel, July Court 1774.

Pp. 357-358: 10 Feb 1769, John Mitchel & wf Elizabeth to Samuel Wilson of Meck., for ᵯ 8 proc. money, 105 A...Wit: James Gilmer, Nathaniel Gilmor. Prov. by James Gilmor, July Court 1774.

Pp. 358-359: 9 June 1774, Edward Black & wf Rebaca of Prov. of Georgia, to William Philips, for ᵯ 70 sterling, 250 A on W side of Richardsons Creek, granted to sd. Black 9 Apr 1768 ...Edward Black (Seal), Rebacca Black (C) (Seal), Wit: Reubin Phillips July Court 1774.

Pp. 359-361: 15 Aug 1772, John Wilson of Meck., to James Shanks for ᵯ 58 proc. money, land on E side Catawba River on both sides of McCaupins Creek, adj. Benjabin Roberts, Thomas Hustons, Wm Steratts, Hugh Wilson, Mr. Baxter, including the mouth of four mile Creek, granted to sd. John Wilson, 30 Apr 1768...John Wilson (I) (Seal), Mary Wilson (M), Wit: Henry Downs, Hugh Wilson, Robt Cample. Prov. by Robt Camble, July Court 1774.

Pp. 361-364: 9 Nov 1773, William Harris of Parish of St. Pauls, Prov. of Georgia, to John Mountgomery, Late of Prov. of Pensylvania, for ᵯ 300 proc. money, three tracts in Meck., on waters of McRees Creek, granted to sd. Willm Harris, 278 A granted to sd. Harris by Arthur Dobbs & wf Justina 10 Feb 1765 also 240 A granted to Harris by Abner Nash & wf Justina 5 Feb 1771 and another tract granted by Nash 5 Feb 1771, 112 A...William Harris (Seal), Martha Harris (Seal), Wit: John Ouicry, Alexdr. Finney. "We saw Martha Harris sign this deed: Will White, James Ross" Prov. by William White, July Court 1774.

Pp. 365-366: 18 Dec 1769, John Mitchel & wf Elisabeth to Archibald Ramsay of Meck., for ₤ 33 proc. money, land on a branch of Coddle Creek, adj. John Findley, Meloney, granted to Ambrose Harding...Wit: Patrick Carr, Joseph Patterson, Samuel Wilson. Rec. July Court. Prov. by Samuel Wilson

Pp. 366-368: 1 Jan 1774, John Barkley & wf Agnes of St. Marks Parish, Craven Co., S. C., Yeoman to Archibald Cousard of same, Yeoman, by a granted 25 Sept 1763(?), unto William King, 640 A and conveyed to Andrew Nutt, then to John Barkley, for ₤ 500...155 A on N side Waxhaw Creek, on both sides of the waggon Road, part of sd. 640 A grant...John Barkley (Seal), Agness Barkley (O) (Seal), Wit: James Kill, ___ seph McMeen, ___ bert Barkley. Prov. by James Kill in Craven County, 1 Jan 1774, before James ___.

Pp. 369-370: 12 July 1773, Thomas Polk, Abrm Alexander & Jeremiah McCafferty of Meck., to William McAlwell, for ₤ 4 proc. money, lot in Charlotte, No. 133-141, on W side Traid St., near an acre, Wit: Zebulon Alexander, ___ Scot. Prov. by Zebulon Alexander, Oct. Sessn. 1774.

Pp. 370-372: 16 June 1768, Robert Caldwell of Meck., to George McWhorter of same, for ₤ 65...land on E side Cataba River on waters of Waxaw Creek, by virtue of a patent 3 Feb 1754, adj. Samuel McAlvenys...Robert Caldwell (RC) (Seal), Wit: Jno Crocket, Samuel Lessley, James Waughop. Prov. in open court by James Waughop, Oct. Sessn 1774.

Pp. 372-373: 18 Oct 1774, John Howey & wf Ann of Meck., to Jacob Secres of same, for ₤ 5 proc. money, 125 A adj. Crocket, 226 A...John Howey (Seal), Ann Howey, Wit: John McCorkel, John McNelley. Prov. by John McCorkel, Oct. Sessn. 1774.

Pp. 373-375: 18 Oct 1774, Andrew Baxter & wf Francis of Meck., to John Baxter of same, for two guineys sterling...land on waters of Shugar Creek, in the old line which was Ezekiel Alexander and out of the Indian line, 200 A...Andrew Baxter (Seal) Frances Baxter (G) (Seal), Wit: James Potts, John McCain. Prov. by James Potts, Octr. Sessn. 1774.

Pp. 375-377: 27 Sept 1774, James Carruth & wf Margaret of Roan Co., Farmer, to Mary Craighead of Meck., Farmer, for ₤ 35 proc. money, 225 A, granted to sd. Carruth 10 Feb 1769, adj. Thomas Ferguson...James Carruth (Seal), Margaret Carruth (Seal), Wit: Hannah Creaghead, Elisabeth Creaghead. Prov. by Hannah Creaghead Oct. Sessn 1774.

Pp. 377-378: 19 Oct 1774, David Hay & wf Jean of Meck., to Hugh Reed of same, for ₤ 200...land on N side Catawba River, granted 17 May 1754 to Samuel Young, 300 A and conveyed by deed to ___...David Hay (Seal), Jean Hay (Ihn) (Seal), Wit: Thos Polk, James Neal (X). Prov. by James Neal, Oct. Sessn 1774.

VOLUME 6

Pp. 378-379: 16 Apr 1771, Thomas Polk, Abraham Alexander & Jeremiah McCafferty of Meck., to Samuel McCombes of Charlotte town, for Ł 50 proc. money, lots #66 & 74 on S side Tryon St., near an acre...Wit: Mathew Stewart, Samuel Jack.Prov. Oct. Sessn 1774.

Page 380: 19 March 1773, John Graham & wf Jean of Meck., to Thomas Thomson for Ł 100 proc. money, land on N side Cataba River on the head drafts of Rocky River, 240 A...John Grimes (Seal), Jean Grime (X) (Seal), Wit: Samuel Gingles, John Brown (X). Prov. by Samuel Gingles, Oct. Sessn 1774.

Pp. 381-382: ___ 1774, John McColloh of Meck., to John Hagans of same, for Ł 40 proc. money, 300 A on E side Catabo River on both sides of Seder fork of 12 Miles Creek above Robt Ramsey, 100 A...John McColloh (Seal), Wit: Hugh Huston. Rec. Oct. Sessn. 1774. Ack. in open court.

Pp. 382-383: 15 Oct 1774, Martin Fisher of Meck., to Frederick Fissher Junior of same, for Ł 200 proc. money, 149 A on the rights between Cold water and Adams Creek, granted to sd. Martin Fisher by Fraderick Fisher by deed 15 July 1767...Martin Fissher (Seal), ___ (Probably German signature), John Barringer, Peter Rape. Prov. by Peter Rape, Oct. Sessn. 1774.

Pp. 383-384: 14 Jan 1767, James Johnston of Meck., to Henry E. McColloh of Hallifax Co., for Ł 31 s 4 d 9, land adj. Samuel Wilson, 120 A granted ___ Jan 1770...James Johnston (I) (Seal), Henry E. McColloh (Seal), Wit: John Frohock, Thomas Polk, Prov. by John Frohock. Sd. Mortgage ack. by Henry E. McCulloh.

Pp. 385-386: 19 Aug 1774, Abraham Cook & ___ his wife of Meck., to Michell Leggett of same, for Ł 5 proc. money, 300 A in Meck. on the lick Branch adj. John Osburns, James McClure, Abraham Cook (Seal), Mary Cook (X) (Seal), Wit: George Walker, William Young. Prov. by William Young, Octr. Sess. 1774.

Pp. 386-388: 8 Jan 1767, John Garrison to Henry E. McColloh, ___ A, granted 8 ___ 1770...mortgage. Wit: John Frohock, Thomas Polk. Prov. by John Frohock before Richd Henderson, Salisbury.

Pp. 389-390: ___ June 17--, Robert Dickson of Duplin Co., to Jacob Ormands of Meck., for Ł 45 proc. money, land on E side Cataba including Noble Osburns Cabbin, surveyed for James & John Osburn, adj. William Osburns, granted to sd. Dickson 16 Dec 1769...Robt Dickson (Seal), dated 22 June 1774. Wit: Joseph Dickson, Thally, ___ abin Ormand. Prov. by Benjamin Ormond, Oct. Sessn. 1774.

Pp. 390-391: 30 Nov 1773, William Wotherford & wf ___ to Peter Kiser of Meck., for Ł 16 proc. money, 80 A on Rocky River...William Witherfo--, Sarah Witherfo (*), Wit: William Mitchel, Peter Cisfer (+), Prov. by Peter Ki---, April Court 1774.

Page 392: Book No. 19th.

END OF VOLUME 6.

VOLUME 7

Pp. 1-2: 10 Feb 1775, Alexander McRee (McKee?), to Michal Stivison, for ₺ 260 proc. money, land on waters of Sugar Creek, granted ___ 1754, and conveyed to sd. McKee, Willm Pattan, ___ Mar 1773(?)...Alexander McKee (A) (Seal), Wit: Thos Polk, Samuel McCombs. Acknowledged in open Court April Session 1775.

Pp. 2-4: 10 Oct 1773, Thos Polk, Abram Alexander, Jeremiah McCafferty, of Meck., to Zablun Alexander of same, for ₺ 6 proc. money, lots #182 & 183 in Charlotte on S side Tryon St., Wit: James Foster, Saml Jack. Ack. in open court by grantors July Session 1775.

Pp. 4-5: 10 Aug 1773, Thos Polk, Abrm Alexander, Jeremh McCafferty to Zabulon Alexander, for ₺ 3 proc. money, lots in Charlotte, No. 178 near half an acre, on W side Tryon St., Wit: Saml Jack, James Foster. Ack. in open court July Sessn 1775.

Pp. 5-7: 10 Oct 1775, Aaron Huston & wf Margret of Meck., to Mathew Patton of same, for ₺ 40 proc. money, land on N side Catawba River on N fork Twelve Mile Creek, granted to David Houston, late of Rowan Co., decd., 31 Mar 1753, 203 A.... Aaron Houston (Seal), Margret Houston (Seal), Wit: John Knighten, Robert Stewart, Will Matthews. Prov. by Robert Stewart, Oct. Sessn. 1775.

Pp. 7-9: 5 Feb 1771, A Nash of Hallafax Co., to John Lemonds of Meck., for ₺ 10, 82 A in Tract #2, waters of Caldwells Creek adj. Lucky, Harrison, Wit: R. Smith. Prov. Oct. Sessn 1775 by Robt Smith.

Pp. 9-10: 18 Oct 1775, John Hood of Meck., to Jonathan Buckaloo of same, for ₺ 2 proc. money, 50 A including part of Jonathan Buckaloos Improvement....John Hood (Seal), Wit: Will Wylie, David Harrison. Prov. by John Hood, Oct. Sessn 1775.

Page 11: 5 Dec 1772, Saml Jack of Meck., to Patrick Jack of same, for ₺ 50 proc. money, land on both sides of McCalpins Creek, adj. Robt Elliot, Samuel Jack, whereon the sd. Patrick Jack now lives, 150 A....Saml Jack (Seal), Wit: Will Barnet, Joseph Scott, John Jack. Prov. by Will Barnet, Oct. Sessn 1775.

Pp. 12-13: 17 Feb 1775, James Duglas & wf Hannah of Meck., to Aaron Huston, for ₺ 63 proc. money, 200 A on both sides of six mile Creek adj. Donalson, John Sloan, Benjabin Lowry, John McCance, granted to a certain William Lofton, 30 Oct 1765 and conveyed to Jacob Secrift by Margaret Loften and Samuel Lofton, by deed 17 Sept 1772, and then to sd. Douglas 18 Apr 1774...James Duglas (Seal), Hannah Duglas (Seal), Wit: James Tate, Oughtrey McKibben, Jurate., Andrew Dunn. Prov. by Oughtree McKibben, Oct. Sessn. 1775.

Pp. 13-14: 17 Aug 1775, Michael Kline & wf Katherina of Meck., to Jacob Misinhimer, for ₺ 36 proc. money, 170 A on the head branches of Adam Creek, granted to sd. Michael Kline by deed from Arthur Dobbs 25 June 1764...Michael Klein (German signature (Seal), Catherina Kline (X), Wit: John Phifer, Jurat, _____ (German signature), Martin Pfifer, Prov. by Phifer Oct. Sessn 1775.

Pp. 15-16: 15 Oct 1775, James Linn & wf Sarah of Meck., to Thomas Paxton of same, for Ł 100 proc. money, land on N side Cautaba River on N fork Twelve Mile Creek, known as Six Mile Creek, part of a grant to Johnathan Lewes; 12 Aug 1762 conveyed to sd. James Linn...James Linn (Seal), Sarah Linn (1) (Seal), Wit: Benjabin Lowrey, William Mathews. Prov. by James Linn, Oct. Sessn 1775.

Pp. 16-17: 4 Aug 1770, George Augustin Selwyn of Mahon, Gloucester County, Great Britain, to James Maxwell of Meck., for Ł 10 proc. money, land in Meck. Co....Wit: John Black, Jurat, Willm Alexander. Rec. Oct. Sessn. 1775.

Pp. 17-19: 20 Oct 1773, Andrew Shields & wf Sarah of Meck., to Robert Barkley, Capt. of Rowan Co., for Ł 50 proc. money, land in Meck. Co., one half of the Plantation where Moses White now Decd formerly used to live, and willed from him to his daughter Sarah...Andrew Sheilds (Seal), Sarah Shields (Seal), Wit: James McDowell, Archibald Houston, William Panney(?), Prov. by Archibald Houston, Oct. Sessn. 1775.

Pp. 19-20: 10 Feb 1769, John Mitchel & wf Elisabeth of Salisbury, to John Newman of Meck., for Ł 15 proc. money, 182 A granted to Ambrose Harding....Wit: Willm McDowell, David Wilson. Prov. by David Wilson, Oct. Sessn 1775.

Pp. 21-22: 17 Dec 1770, Thomas Yewings & wf Sarah of Barkley County, Prov. of South Carolina, to Hugh, Robt & Andrew Jackson of Mecklenburg Co., North Carolina, for Ł 14 Currant money of NC...200 A on the waters of Twelve Mile Creek on Leggits Branch, granted 21 Sept 1766...Thomas Ewing (Seal), Sarah Ewing (Seal), Wit: Joseph Adams, Benjamin Cregg, James Crafford, Jurat. Prov. by James Crafford, Oct. or April Sessn. 1775.

Pp. 22-23: 23 Apr 1774, Willm Eliott of Meck., to James Jack of same, for Ł 50 proc. money, lot in Town of Charlotte, #27 on N side Traid St., near half an acre...Will Eliotte (Seal), Wit: William Barnet, George Nichalson. Prov. April Sessn 1775 by oath of Grantor.

Pp. 24-25: 1 Dec 1774, Paul Barringer & Anless his wife of Meck., to Henry Sosamonhouser of same, for Ł 200 proc. money ...land on both sides of Duch Buffalo Creek, a branch of Rocky or Johnston River, 182 A...Paul Barringer (Seal), Angles Barringer (X) (Seal), Wit: _____ (German Signature), Jacob Eagner, Jacob Egner, Jurat. Prov. by Jacob Agner July Sessn 1775.

Pp. 25-26: 16 Jan 1772, James Thomson & wf Precilla of Meck., to Jennins Thompson of same, planter, for Ł 16 proc. money...48 A on Rocky River...James Thompson (I) (Seal), Prissilla Thompson (X) (Seal), Wit: Charles Pollock, John Pollock. Prov. by John Polk, July Sessn 1775.

Pp. 27-28: 1 Apr 1774, Thos Polk, Abram Alexander, Jermiah McCafferty, Isaac Alexander and William Pattesson, Commissioners, Directors and Trustees of the Town of Charlotte, to Waightstell Avery, for Ł 9 s 15 proc. money...lots in Charlotte, #156, 157, 158, 159, 160, 161, 207, 208, 209, 210, 211, 212, 213 on the Right hand of the Road leading from the Court House to the Tuckasejah Ford, 6½ A...Wit: Eph Bravard, Hugh

VOLUME 7

Pollock. Prov. by Ephraim Bravard, April Sessn. 1777.

Pp. 28-30: ____ 1774, Thomas Polk, Abraham Alexander, Isaac Alexander, Jeremiah McCafferty, and William Patesson, Commissioners Etc. of Charlotte, for L 7 s 10 to Waighstell Avery...lots #162, 214, 316, 317, 319, 320, 321, 322, 323, 5 A ...Wit: John Pfifer, Jurat; William Haggans. Prov. by John Pfifer, April Sessn. 1775.

Pp. 30-32: 24 Oct 1774, James McElwee of Long Cane Settlement, South Carolina, for L 3 proc. money, to Tunas Hood of Meck., land conveyed to James McElwee, 22 May 1772 on the watters of McCalpins Creek, adj. his own and James Crocks land (later appears to be Clark), 31 A...James McElwee (Seal), Wit: Haz Alexander, Jurat., Frederick Shaver (F). Prov. April Sessn 1775 by Hezekiah Alexander.

Pp. 32-33: 12 Apr 1772, David McCord of Meck., to Robt Mitchell of same, for L 15 proc. money...115 A adj. David McCord, Shipley, on the head of the Muddy branch, granted to Frances Beaty for 640 A 21 Dec 1763, and conveyed to sd. McCord by L & R, 4 & 5 July 1766...David McCord (Seal), Ann McCord (Seal), Wit: Robt McCord, Jurat. Prov. by Robt McCord, April Sessn 1775.

Pp. 33-34: 17 Apr 1775, William Smith & wf Jennet of Meck., to James Boyes of same, for L 60 proc. money...land on waters of McCalpins Creek adj. Flannigan, 121 A...Will Smith (Seal), Jennet Smith (Seal), Wit: Will Black, John Smith. Prov. April Sessn 1775 by Will Black.

Pp. 35-36: 27 Mar 1775, Andrew Greer of Meck., to Col. Robt Harris, Esqr., of same, for L 20 proc. money, 35 A on Branches of Mudy creek, waters of Rocky River, granted to sd. Andrew Greer by Andrew Nash, 25 Mar 1772, also 640 A on Caldwells Creek, granted to Greer by Nash, 25 Mar 1772...Andrew Greer (Seal), Wit: John Alexander, Jurat; Mary Huston. Prov. by John Alexander, April Sessn 1775.

Pp. 36-37: 17 Feb 1775, Col. Robt Harris of Meck., to Andrew Crocket, planter, of same, for L 60 proc. money... land on waters of Twelve Mile Creek on Turkey branch, 151 A adj. to the Indian Line, Andrew Crocks (sic), granted to sd. Harris by patent...Robt Harris (Seal), Wit: John McKean (X), Marry Huston. Prov. by grantor April Sessn. 1775

Pp. 37-38: 19 Apr 1775, William Givens of Meck., to John McColloh of same, for L 50 proc. money, land on waters of Six Mile Creek in New Providence, adj. Hugh Juston, 80 A granted to sd. Givens 25 Apr 1767...Will Givens (Seal), Wit: None. Acknowledged in open court April Session 1775.

Pp. 39-40: 9 Sept 1772, Griffeth Rutherford of Rowan Co., to Will Reed of Meck., for L 100 proc. money, land on both sides Pickens Creek, a branch of Twelve Mile Creek, granted to sd. Griffeth Rutherford & William Pickens, 28 Sept 1754, and conveyed to Martin Pfifer by deed 17 Jan 1770...Griffeth Rutherford (Seal), Wit: John Graham, Abraham Taylor, Jurat; Prov. by Abraham Taylor, April Sessn 1775.

Pp. 40-41: 11 Apr 1775, Margret Donalson of Meck., to Andrew

Donalson, land on the Head of Kings Branch, adj. John Taylor, part of Selwyn tract, 160 A...Margret Donalson (X) (Seal), Wit: Robt Campbell, Robt Donalson. Prov. by Robt Campbell, April Sessn.1775.

Pp. 42-43: 8 Apr 1775, Jacob Kline & wf Cathrain of Meck., to Peter Stigenwalt of same, for Ł 77 proc. money, 191 A...Jacob Kline (X) (Seal), Catherine Kline (X) (Seal), Wit: John Pfifer, Jurat; _____ Dart. Prov. Oct. Sessn. 1775 by John Pfifer.

Page 44: 20 Mar 1772, Barnet Miller & wf Catron of Meck., to George Eagle of same, for Ł 30 proc. money...200 A on a branch of Duch Buffalo adj. Waddle, Brandon, Gov. Dobbs line ...Barnet Miller (X) (Seal), Catron Miller (X) (Seal), Wit: Michal Goodman, Jurat, Joseph Shinn. Prov. by Michal Goodman July Sessn. 1775.

Pp. 45-46: 10 Feb 1769, John Mitchel & wf Elizabeth of Rowan Co., to Samuel Alexander of Meck., for Ł 10 proc. money... land adj. James Barr, part of a grant to Ambrose Harding...Wit: William Sheilds, Jas Wishart. Prov. by William Shields, April Sessn. 1775.

Page 46: 2 Oct 1773, John Anderson of Meck., to Thomas Polk of same, for Ł 70 proc. money...Negro Dick...John Anderson (Seal), Wit: Willm Pattesson, Sam McCree. Prov. Jan. Sessn. 1776 by William Patteson.

Pp. 47-48: 25 Sept 1773, Thomas Polk, Abraham Alexander & Jeremiah McCafferty of Meck., to Joseph Wishart, for Ł 10 proc. money...Lot on N side Tryon St., Lot #38...Wit: James Foster, Saml Jack. Ack. in open court by the Commissioners, Jany Sessn. 1776.

Pp. 48-49: 13 Apr 1775, Joseph Galbreath of Meck., to Thomas Polk of same, for Ł 50 proc. money...land on N side Goos Creek, and N side Crocket Creek, granted to sd. Galbreath by deed from Abner Nash 25 Mar 1772...Joseph Galbreath (Seal), Thomas Polk (Seal), Wit: Jeremiah McCafferty, Joseph Harris. Prov. Jan. Sessn. 1776 by Jeremiah McCafferty.

Pp. 49-50: 15 Dec 1774, Edmon Bearden of Ninty Six Districk, South Carolina, to Benjamin Alexander of Meck., for Ł 25 proc. money of NC...land in Meck., adj. his own lands, 317 A granted to sd. Edmon Bearden 16 Dec 1769...Edmon Beardon (Seal), Ann Bearden (Seal), Wit: William Hemphill, Andrew Alexander. Prov. Jany. sessn. 1776 by Andrew Alexander.

Pp. 51-52: 4 Apr 1775, William Gillaspy of Meck., to Thomas Wallace of same, for Ł 100 NC money...land on both sides of the Six Mile Creek including the surplus land of John Clarks Survey, adj. Hugh Houston, Robeson, 70 A granted to sd. Gillaspy 4 May 1769...William Gillaspy (Seal), Wit: John McColloh, Joseph Stevenson. Prov. April Sessn. 1775 by John McCuloh.

Pp. 52-53: 18 Jan 1774, John Keeloh of Meck., to Thomas Polk of same, for Ł 50 proc. money...land on M'Michael Creek adj. John Swan...John Kelloh (Seal), Wit: Saml Spencer, Dun Ocheltree. Prov. Jany Sessn. 1776 by Duncan Ochiltree.

VOLUME 7

Pp. 53-55: 23 __ 1774, Henry Eustace McColloh to Tunas Hood Senr, for ₺ 60 proc. money...land onwaters of McCalpins Creek adj. John Holas___(?), 145 A, Wit: John Foard, Tunas Hood Junr. Receipt wit. by Valt Beard, Richard Shafer. Prov. by Tunas Hood Junr. Jan. Sessn. 1776.

Pp. 55-56: 20 Apr 1775, Mathew Cook of Meck., to William Mason of same, for ₺ 12 proc. money...land on both sides McMichaels Creek and between Doctr. Carrols and Robt Barnets lands, granted 4 May 1769, 86 A...Nathaneil Cook (X) (Seal), Wit: Will Reed, John Bally. Prov. April Sessn. 1775 by Will Reed.

Pp. 56-57: 18 Feb 1775, Robt Patteson of Meck., to Joseph Hart of same, for ₺ 30 proc. money...104 A part of 500 A granted to Samuel Bigham, 21 Dec 1763, conveyed by him to John Giles 1 Apr 1767, and to Henry McMurdy, 2 May 1770 and to Robt Patterson, 5 July 1771...Robt Patteson (Seal), Wit: William Bigham, James McCord. Prov. Jan. Sessn. 1776 by grantor in person.

Pp. 58-59: 12 Dec 1772, Henry Estace McCulloh to Tunas Hood Senr for ₺ 100 proc. money, land on waters of McCalpins Creek adj. John Culbertson, granted by deed from John Johnstone 9 Dec 1772...Wit: John Ford, Jurat. Tunas Hood Junr. Prov. by Tunas Hood Junr., Jan Sessn. 1776.

Pp. 60-61: 20 Dec 1772, Henry Eustace McCulloh to Tunas Hood Senr for ₺ 59 s 10, 127 A on waters of McCalpins Creek...Wit: John Ford, Tunas Hood. Wit. to receipt Valt Beard, Richard Shaver. Prov. by John Ford, Jany Sessn. 1776.

Pp. 62-63: 10 Oct 1773, James Way of Meck., to Thomas Polk of same, for ₺ 102 s 10...land on both sides of the fore Mile Creek adj. Henry Downs, Thomas Harris, and Negro Jack about 22 years old bought of Robt Alexander (?)...apparently a mortgage due 10 Oct 1778...James Way (Seal), Thomas Polk (Seal), Wit: Will Pattison, Robt Alexander. Prov. Jan. Session 1776 by William Patteson.

Pp. 64-66: 5 Dec 1772, William Scot of Meck., to David Purvance of same, for ₺ 72 s 2 proc. money...land on the Ridges between English Buffalo and Coddle Creek, by the waggon Road leading to Capt. Phifers, by virtue of a will executed by James Scott, decd, 8 Dec 1771 wherein the sd. William Scot is appointed sole Exr., land granted to sd. James Scot by deed from John Hughs 20 Aug 1768 and conveyed to Hugh by Gov. Dobbs 25 June 1764, 123 A...William Scott (Seal), Wit: James Russal, Alexander Forguson. Prov. by James Russal, No date given.

Pp. 66-68: 17 Jan 1775, Robt Rodgers,Yoman, of Meck., to David Purvance for ₺ 200, 138 A between Codle and Bufilo Creek...Robert Rodgers (Seal), Mary Rodgers (O) (Seal), Wit: James Black, John Kean or Kearr. Prov. April 1775 by Kearr (Kean?).

Pp. 68-69: Thomas Sharp of Tryon Co., for ₺ 385 pd. by Joseph Kennedy of Meck., a warrant of 300 A now lying in the Land Office in Philadelphia, the land which the Warrt. contains lyes in Lancaster County within about 10 miles from John Harrisses Ferry, the land warrant was obtained by Thomas Sharp, father to the above mentioned Sharp, adj. James Dickon, John Frenchland or (John French land), Archibald McCelenvy...Thomas

Sharpe (Seal), Wit: George Montgomery, Agness Graham (O). The Clerks records of the probate of this Deed is lost.

Pp. 69-70: 14 Feb 1775, Jeremiah Harris of Meck., to George Harris of same, for Ł 30 proc. money...land on Crooket Creek adj. William Shelbin, 88 A, granted to sd. Jeremiah Harris by Abner Nash & wf Justina 5 Feb 1771...Jeremiah Harris (Seal), Wit: James Wilson, James Orr. Prov. by James Orr, April term 1776. Dun. Ochiltree, Clk C.

Pp. 71-72: 16 Jan 1776, Henry Eustace McCulloh to John Wood, for Ł 15, land on waters of beard branch, 75 A... Wit: Richd. Mason, Wm Patteson. Prov. Jan Sessn. 1776 by William Patteson.

Pp. 73-74: 15 Sept 1775, Mary Mason and Richard Mason, Exrs. to the estate of Charles Mason deceased of Meck., to Joseph Kennedy of same, for Ł 60 proc. money, land on E side Cataba River, on waters of paw Creek, 200 A, granted to Robert Sloan by patent 29 Apr 1768, and conveyed to Charles Mason... Mary Mason (X) (Seal), Richard Mason (Seal), Wit: Robert Green, John Green. Prov. by John Green, July Sesn. 1776.

Pp. 74-75: 21 Mar 1776, John Fransischo & Rebeca his wife of Meck., to George Herron of same, for Ł 175 proc. money...land in the fork of Little Bear Creek, 280 A plantation whereon John Fransischo now lives, part of a tract of land conveyed from John Mitchel to George Maggone and from him to Charles Thompson MillRight and then to John Fransischo...John Fransischo (+) (Seal), Rebeca Fransischo (+) (Seal), Wit: Paul Barringer, John Barringer. Prov. by Paul Barringer April Term 1776.

Pp. 76-77: 6 Feb 1775, Jacob Kook & wf Ann of Craven County, South Carolina, to Jacob Kline of Meck., for Ł 88 proc. money of NC, land on County of Mecklenburg formerly Anson, 288 A adj. Christofel Bliss...Jacob Kook (Seal), Ann Kook (AK) (Seal), Wit: Christ. Lewis, Bostain Kook (BK). Prov. by Christopher Lewes, April Sessn 1775.

Pp. 78-79: 15 Sept 1775, Mary Mason & Richard Mason Exrs. of Charles Mason decd., of Meck., to Joseph Kennedy, for Ł 178 proc. money...350 A including the sd. Mary Masons and Richard Masons improvements adj. the land that Francis Beaty sold to Robt McCord, adj. John Cathey, near to Tools Road, said land formerly conveyed to John Sloan by a deed from Hugh Beatey 22 Feb 1768, and afterwards conveyed to Charles Mason...Mary Mason (+) (Seal), Richard Mason (Seal), Wit: Robt Green, John Green. Prov. by John Green July Sessn. 1776.

Pp. 79-80: 17 Apr 1776, Saml Wilson of Meck., to Joseph Kennedy of same, for Ł 30 proc. money...Lot #3 on S side Trade St., adj. John Springsteen, Daniel Okain, near half an acre... Sam Wilson (Seal), Wit: Charles Comins, Joseph Nicklson. Prov. by Joseph Nickilson, January Sessn. 1777.

Pp. 80-81: James Foster of Meck., appoint Joseph Kennedy my lawful attorney to recover debts...4 May 1774...Jas Foster (Seal), Wit: Thos Polk, Sam Martin. Prov. by Samuel Martain, Jany Sessn. 1777.

VOLUME 7

Pp. 81-82: 6 April 1774, James Foster, of Meck., to George Reed of same, for Ł 30 proc. money...land adj. his own and Benjamin Alexanders land, John Sh---- corner, 240 A...James Foster (Seal), Wit: Ezekiel Alexander, Joseph Mitchell. Prov. by Joseph Mitchell, Jany Sessn 1776.

Finis Book No. 20th

Page 83A: Book No. 21st
J McK A to James McElwee
90 Acres part of the 300 Acres pattent in page 43
N. B. No other Deed in the alphabets from J McK Alexr to James McElwee or any other persons for any part of his grant of 55 Acres thus:
a Kings pattent Viz a 2 that tract or above

Books 21 and 22 and 24
bound together by J McK Alexander
October 28th 1809

Page 83B: 13 April 1779, James Jack of Meck. in the town of Charlotte, for Ł 200 pd. by Joel(?) Bravard, lot #8 in Charlotte adj. Joseph Nickelson...(signature and wit. not legible)

Pp. 84-85: 7 Apr 1779, Thos Polk, attorney for David Oliphant of Meck., for Ł 35 proc. money...land on waters of Rocky River, 72 A...Thos Polk (Seal), Wit: Wm Polk, Philip Miller. (No rec. date)

Pp. 85-86: 9(?) June 177-, Thos Polk attorney for David Oliphant, to John Dickson...(deed very dim)...David Oliphant (Seal), Thos Polk (Seal), Wit: Thos Rodgers, James Nash.

Pp. 86-88: 20 May 1779, Thos Polk and David Oliphant of Meck., to Rees Shalbey of same, for Ł 46 proc. money...land on E side Rocky River, adj. John Powel, 90 A...David Oliphant by Thos Polk (Seal), Wit: Wm Polk, Wm. Haynes. (No rec. date)

Pp. 88-90: 8 Apr 1779, Thos Polk attorney for David Oliphant, to David Shelby, for Ł 22 proc. money, land on W side Rocky River...Thos Polk (Seal), Wit: John Polk, Wm Polk. (No rec. date)

Pp. 90-91: 28 March 1779, Thos Polk to Rees Shelby, planter, for Ł 50 proc. money, land in the Great Tract #2...Wit: Wm Polk. (No rec. date).

Pp. 91-93: 24 May 1779, Thos Polk attorney for David Oliphant to William Lemonds, land on waters of Clear Creek, adj. John & Philip Millers corner, 22 A...Wit: Wm Polk, Robt Hope. (No rec. date).

Pp. 93-94: 13 May 1779, Thos Polk attorney for David Oliphent, to Richard Trimble, land on both sides of Crooked Creek, joyning William Culberson, 20 A...Wit: Wm Polk, Saml Smith. (No rec. date).

Pp. 94-95: 20 May 1779, Thos Polk attorney for David Oliphant, to Joseph Galbreath, land on north sides of God's Creek, a branch of Rockey River...Wit: Hugh Pollock, Joseph Harris. (No rec. date).

Pp. 95-96: 20 May 1779, Thos Polk attorney for David Oliphant to Joseph Galbreath for ₤ 68 proc. money...53 A on both sides Gap (Goss?) Creek...Wit: Hugh Polock, Joseph Harris. (No rec. date).

Pp. 97-98: 20 May 1779, Thos Polk attorney for David Oliphant to Joseph Harris Junr for ₤ 56 proc. money...90 A on both sides Crooked Creek...Wit: Wm Polk, Joseph Galbreath. (No rec. date).

Pp. 98-99: 12 May 1779, Thos Polk attorney for David Oliphant to William Hayns, for ₤ 16 proc. money...28 A on both sides Muddy Creek...Wit: Wm Polk, Rees Shelby. (No rec. date).

Pp. 99-100: 20 May 1779, Thos Polk to Joseph Harris Junr, for ₤ 24 proc. money...62 A on both sides Crooked Creek ...Wit: Wm Polk, Joseph Galbreath. (No rec. date).

Pp. 100-102: 14 Aug 1779, Thos Polk & wf Susannah of Meck., to Charles Commins of same, for ₤ 95 proc. money... land on waters of Sugar Creek granted to Hugh Berry 14 April 1761, adj. Saml Young, 300 A...Thos Polk (Seal), Susannah Polk (S) (Seal), Wit: John Sterat, Major Femster(?). (No rec. date).

Pp. 102-104: 7 Apr 1779, Thos Polk attorney for David Oliphant to Joseph Ford of Meck., for ₤ 30 proc. money... 66 A on both sides Muddy Creek...Thos Polk (Seal), Wit: Wm Polk, Philip Miller. (No rec. date).

Pp. 104-105: 3 April 1779, Thos Polk attorney for David Oliphant to Michal Yearman of Meck., for ₤ 62 proc. money... 143 A...Wit: Wm Polk, Wm Hanna(?). (No rec. date).

Pp. 105-106: 5 June 1779, Thos Polk attorney for David Oliphant of Meck., for ₤ 30 proc. money...land on waters of Andersons Creek, adj. Great Tract No. 5, 49 A...Wit: Wm Polk, John Coruthers. (No rec. date).

Pp. 107-108: 12 May 1779, Thos Polk attorney for David Oliphant to John Lowrey of Meck., for ₤ 25 proc. money... 33 A on waters of Goose Creek...Wit: WM Polk, Robt Esteven. (No rec. date).

Pp. 108-109: 13 Apr 1779, Thos Polk attorney for David Oliphant to Harden Warner of Meck., for ₤ 20 proc. money ...176 A on waters of Muddy Creek...Wit: Philip Miller, John Nelson. (No rec. date).

Pp. 109-110: 5 Sept 1776, Andrew Baxter attorney for Mathew Caldwell of Meck., to Thos Polk of same, for ₤ 100 ...land on waters of Kings branch of Sugar Creek 155 A...Andrew Baxter (Seal), Wit: Ezekiel Polk, Edward Sharp. (No rec. date).

Pp. 110-112: 7 Apr 1779, Thos Polk attorney for David Oliphant to John Nilson for ₤ _____ ...135 A on waters of Muddy Creek,,,Wit: Wiliam Polk, Phi͞l͞ip Miller (No rec. date).

VOLUME 7

Pp. 112-113: 16 April 1779, Thos Polk, Eph Bravard and James Jack of Meck., to Petter Mathews of same, for Ł 140 proc. money...Lot # 68 on S side Tryon St in Town of Charlotte...Wit: Ad Osburn, Archabald Huston. (No rec. date).

Pp. 113-115: 4 June 1778, John Anderson of Meck., to Thos Polk of same, for Ł 77-15-8...land on both sides Long Creek, 640 A granted to John Anderson 28 Oct 1755...John Anderson (a) (Seal), Wit: Ezek. Polk, Dun Ochiltree. (No rec. date).

Pp. 115-116: 13 May 1779, Thos Polk attorney for David Oliphant to Joseph Galbreath for Ł 18 proc. money...37 A on waters of Goos Creek adj. John Hall...Wit: John ____, Wm Polk. (No rec. date).

Pp. 116-117: 7 Apr 1779, Thos Polk attorney for David Oliphant to John Culberson for Ł 55 proc. money...102 A on waters of Goos Creek...Wit: John McCoy, Wiliam Blair. (No rec. date).

Pp. 117-119: 14 May 1779, Thos Polk attorney for David Oliphant to Wm Murphey for Ł 41 proc. money, 82 A on E side Rocky River...Wit: James Jack, Wm Polk. (No rec. date).

Pp. 119-120: 17 Apr 1779, Thos Polk attorney for David Oliphant to Moses Culberson, for Ł 100 proc. money...271 A adj. John Culberson...Wit: John Culberson, Rees Shalbey. (No rec. date).

Pp. 120-121: 13 May 1779, Thos Polk attorney for David Oliphant to Robert Stevens, for Ł 110 proc. money...252 A on both sides Crooked Creek...Wit: Wm Polk, John Lowrey. (No rec. date).

Pp. 122-123: 5 June 1779, Thos Polk attorney for David Oliphant to John Caruthers, for Ł 90 proc. money...51 A on both sides Muddy Creek...Wit: Wm Polk, Thos McFadon. (No rec. date).

Pp. 123-124: 16 Oct 17_8, William McCafferty of Meck., to James Orr of same, for Ł 800 proc. money...lot # 10 on E side Traid St...Wm McCafferty (Seal), Wit: Thos Polk, Hugh Polock. (No rec. date).

Page 125: 14 Apr 1779, James Cook Senr of Meck., to William Crye of same, for Ł 5 proc. money...300 A on a branch of 12 Mile Creek, adj. Robert Davies...James Cook (Seal), Wit: James Paxton, John Howey. (No rec. date).

Pp. 125-127: 13 Jan 1779, John McKnit Alexander of Meck., to James McElwee, for Ł 80 proc. money...land grante to sd. Alexander 26 Oct 1767, adj. William Brown, Henry's...John McNit Alexander (Seal), Wit: William McElwee, Martha McElwee. (No rec. date).

Pp. 127-128: 30 June 1779, Robert Rodgers & wf Frances of Meck., to Hugh Rodgers of same, for Ł 100 proc. money...116 A confirmed to Robert Rodgers by John Moloney, to Moloney by a certain John Moore, to said Moore by Capt. Robt Tenman...Robert Rodgers (Seal), Frances Rodgers (X) (Seal), No wit. (No rec. date).

VOLUME 7

Pp. 128-129: 14 Apr 1779, Robert Graham of Meck., to James Sharp of same, for ₤ 200...land on the dividing Ridge between Shugar Creek and McMichels Creek, 145 A...Robert Grahms (Seal), Wit: Ezekiel Polk, Robt Hunter. (No rec. date).

Pp. 129-131: 18 Jan 1779, John Kook of Meck., to Nicklas Flin of same, for ₤ 25....50 A on Mallard Creek adj. Buchanan, McClearys, granted to Michael Shaver 30 Jan 1773 and sold by Shaver to Kook 26 Jan 1774, 35 A...John Kook (Seal), Barbra Kook (X) (Seal), Wit: John McT----(?). (No rec. date).

Pp. 131-132: 13 June 1779, Robert Rodgers and wf Frances of Meck., to Hugh Rodgers of same, for ₤ 100 proc. money...land including the improvements now in possession of the sd. Robt Rodgers on the west side of Codle Creek adj. land he now lives on, adj. Joseph James, Taner(?)...90 A...Robt Rodgers (Seal), Frances Rodgers (X) (Seal), Wit: Joseph Taner, John lane. (No rec. date).

Pp. 132-134: 20 Oct 1778, William Lemonds of Meck., to James McComb(?) of Tryon Co., for ₤ 30 proc. money...45 A adj. John Wiley...William Lemond (Seal), Wit: Saml McComb, Wm Wylie. (No rec. date).

Pp. 134-135: 3 Feb 1775, James Gilmore & wf Margret of Meck., to Nathaniel Gilmore of same, for ₤ 100 proc. money... 40 A, part of 12,600 A granted to Ambros Harden, consigned to John Michel by James Wyle Sheriff, and by Michel to John Gilmore deceased and bequeathed to sd. James Gilmore...James Gilmore (Seal), Margrat Gilmore (Seal), Wit: Zaccheus Wilson, John Wilson. (No rec. date).

Pp. 135-137: 21 Oct 1777, John Johnston of Township of Lingrain(?), County of Cumberland, Prov. of Pa., yeoman & wf Ruth, to Isaac Ray, yeoman Township of Fannel, in the county afsd., for ₤ 60 Pa. money...land in Meck., 100 A, conveyed by Abner Nash 5 Feb 1771...John Johnston (Seal), Ruth Johnston (Seal), Wit: Mathew Henderson, Adam Cuningham, Isabella McGumery. (No rec. date).

Pp. 137-138: 29 April 1779, James Dunn of Meck., to Robt Dunn of same, for ₤ 50...land on S side Twelve Mile Creek, 112 A...James Dunn (Seal), Martha Dunn (X) (Seal), Wit: John Robison, Andrew Dunn. (No rec. date).

Pp. 139-140: 20 Aug 1774, John Maloney of Meck., to Robert Rodgers of same, for ₤ 70 proc. money...land including the improvements now in possession of sd. John Maloney, on N side Cataba River, on waters of Coddle Creek, 116 A, part of tract confirmed to sd. John Moloney by John More and to sd. More by Robert Tennan, and to him by a patent...John Moloney (I) (Seal), Wit: Thos Thompson, John Tennan. (No rec. date). Mary Moloney (R) relinquished dower, Wit: John Martin, Robt Patton.

Pp. 140-142: 13 Aug 1777, John Beats & wf Margrat of Meck., to William McDowel of same, for ₤ 150...130 A on waters of Kings Branch, adj. Margrat Donelson, David Davis, granted to sd. John Beats by deed from George Selwyn, 19 Jan 1767...John Bates (↳) (Seal), Margaret Bates (O) (Seal), Wit: Will Reed, Robert Campbell. (No rec. date).

Pp. 143-144: 17 May 1779, Thos Polk attorney for David Oliphant for ₤ ___ ...to Robt Caruthers, land on Caldwells Creek., on Stoney Hill...Wit: Tho McFadon, Leany Rant(?). (No rec. date).

VOLUME 7

Pp. 144-146: 15 Sept 1779, Samuel Sprot of Meck., to Joseph Garbreath of same, for ₤ 100...130 A on both sides Long Creek, adj. John McFarlan, below John Moores old mill, granted to Francis Beaty 6 Apr 1765...Samuel Sprot (Seal), Wit: John Knighton. (No rec. date).

Pp. 146-147: 13 May 1779, Thos Polk attorney for David Oliphant to John Power of Meck, for ₤ 10 proc. money...land on W side Rockey River...Wit: John Springs, Wiliam Polk. (No rec. date).

Pp. 147-148: ___ Oct 1779, Nathaniel Alexander of Meck., to Samuel Lusk of same, for ₤ 25...80 A adj. John Clark, John Hagens...Nathaniel Alexander (Seal), Wit: John Wylie, John Sillman(?). (No rec. date).

Pp. 149-150: 2 May 1779, James Blackwood of Meck., to Thos Polk of same, for ₤ 60...land on waters of Sugar Creek, adj. Joseph Galbreath, Ferguson, 177 A...James Blackwood (seal), Wit: Joseph Nichelson, Robt McDowel. (No rec. date).

Pp. 150-153: 28 Aug 1779, Archy McCurdy & wf Margaret of Meck., to William Lemmonds of same, for ₤ 275 NC money...land on head waters of Caldwells Creek, 140 A...Archibald McCurdoy (Seal), Margret McCurdoy (Seal), Wit: Adam Alexander, Francis Miller. (No rec. date).

Pp. 153-154: 20 May 1772, John Braton, Black Smith, of S. C., Craven County, to James Corrygin of Meck., for ₤ 100 NC money...164 A in Meck. Co., granted to Robert Tennan, 30 March 1753, conveyed to Allen Alexander 23 Feb 1761, then to John Bratton 4 Feb 1769...John Bratton (Seal), Wit: James Robinson, John Robinson. (No rec. date).

Pp. 154-157: 1 Oct 1779, John Robinet & wf Mary of Meck., to John Hood of same, for ₤ 400...land on the Ridge between McCalpins Creek and Gooss Creek adj. Joseph Robb, Gov. Dobbs line, conveyed by John Ford to sd. Robenet and sd. Robinet conveyed a part of tract to Joseph Robb....John Robenet (Seal), Mary Robenet (1) (Seal), Wit: Wm Ramsey, Zebulon Ford. (no rec. date).

Pp. 157-159: ___ Feb 1779, Hugh Nealy & wf Ann of Meck., to William Shields of same, for ₤ 340...land on branches of Mallard Creek adj. Andrew Robison, Samuel Hogshead, 98 A granted to sd. Neely by deed from Andrew Robison 17 July 1778...Hugh Nealy (Seal), Ann Nealy (Seal), Wit: Joseph Mitchel, Saml Beaty. (No rec. date).

Pp. 159-161: 17 July 1779, William Alston of Orange Co., N. C., to John McFarling of Lincoln Co., N. C., for ₤ 150 proc. money of NC...land in Meck., on E side Cataba River, 100 A part of a grant to John Scot 10 Apr 1761, conveyed to Moses Scott by deed...William Alston (Seal), Wit: John McCall, Benjamin Newton. (No rec. date).

Pp. 161-162: 28 July 1778, James Huston of Meck., to Robert Bratney of same, for ₤ 100 NC money...150 A on waters of ___ mile Creek, adj. Thos Polk, Thos Black...James Huston (Seal), Wit: Hugh Huston, John Gabb(?), _____. (No rec. date).

VOLUME 7

Pp. 162-164: 5 Aug 1779, Jacob Secrest & wf Barbra of Meck., to Robert McCrorey of same, for Ł 5 proc. money...225 A adj. Crockets line...Jacob Secrist (O) (Seal), Barbra Secrist (+) (Seal), Wit: John Howey, John Secres. (No rec. date).

Pp. 164-165: 17 Sept 1779, Samuel Smith of Rowan Co., to Joseph Shinn of same, for Ł 700....200 A in County of Craven formerly Mecklenburg, now provance of South Carolina, on the waters of Turkey Creek, between loves and burlesons fork adj. Thomas Garven, adj. Loves land...Samuel Smith (Seal), Wit: David Huston, John Walker (I). (No rec. date).

Pp. 165-167: 23 Aug 1779, Robert Barkley of Rowan Co., to John Baker of same, for Ł 90...land on Buffelo Creek of Rocky River, to the dividing line between John Baker and Absalom Baker to the Earl of Granvils line, 42 A...Robt Barkley (Seal), Wit: Charles Baker (C), Joseph Shinn. (No rec. date).

Pp. 167-169: 22 Sept 1779, Robert Barkely of Rowan Co., to Absolam of same, for Ł 30...18 A on West side Buffelo Creek, adj. John Baker...Robt Barkley (Seal), Wit: James Brown, Jason Fresel. (No rec. date).

Pp. 169-171: 12 Oct 1779, John Robenet and wf Mary of Meck., to John Hood of same, for Ł 1200...land on waters of McCalpins Creek part of a larger tract conveyed by John Ford to John Robenet by deed 10 Oct 1771...John Robenet (Seal), Mary Robenet (1) (Seal), Wit: Wiliam Ramsey, Zebulon Ford. (No rec. date).

Pp. 171-172: 17 Oct 1779, Joseph Taggart of Meck., to David Freeman of same, for Ł 115...land on waters of Shugar Creek adj. Samuel Bigams old place, 200 A granted to John Taggert by patent, 25 July 1774...Joseph Taggert (Seal), Wit: James Taggert, John Nichelson. (No rec. date).

Pp. 173-174: 12 Oct 1779, Wiliam Gardnor of Meck., planter, to John Kennady, carpenter, for Ł 1310...73 A on waters of Sugar Creek...William Gardnor (Seal), Wit: Wiliam McKee, Reece Price, Robert Paterson. (No rec. date).

Pp. 174-176: 12 Aug 1779, Archabald Henderson of Meck., to William Henderson of same, for Ł 100...100 A granted by deed to Archabald Henderson, 17 June 1776, half of 200 A granted 30 Aug 1753 to George Renick, father to John Renick who conveyed it to sd. Henderson...Archabald Henderson (Seal), Wit: Fra. Bradley, George Elliot, John McKnit Alexander. (No rec. date).

Pp. 176-178: 16 Nov 1778, William Gardnor of Meck., to John Johnston of same, for Ł 900 procl.money...200 A on waters of Sugar Creek adj. Samuel Roach, Robert McCreek, Robert McCleary ...William Gardnor (Seal), Wit: Thos Patterson, George Calhown, James Patterson. (No rec. date).
                    Book No. 21st
                    Finis.

Pp. 179-180: 23 Nov 1778, Michael Ligget of Meck., to John Rodgers of same, for Ł 50 proc. money...300 A on a branch of 12 Mile Creek...Michael Ligget Senr (Seal), Wit: Francis Bassett, John McCorket, Jurate. (No rec. date).

VOLUME 7

Pp. 180-182: 16 Oct 1777, James Findley, Husbandman, of Meck., to Thomas Findley of same, farmer, for ₺ 40 proc. money ...193 A on Rocky River, part of 12,500 A granted to Ambrose Harding...James Findley (Seal), Margaret Findley (Seal), Wit: Robert Findley, Joseph Findley, Jurat. (No rec. date).

Pp. 182-183: 8 May 1778, William McKinley & wf Margaret of Meck., Gent., to Moses Sharply of same, farmer, for ₺ 40... part of 600 A on both sides of Paw Creek, granted to John Davis by patent 10 Apr 1761, conveyed to Matthew Patton 19 July 1763 and one moiety of which was sold ro Robert McKinley 18 Apr 1764, and by said Robert McKinely deceased to sd. William McKinley, by deed 13 June 1770...William McKinley (Seal), Margaret McKinley (Seal), Wit: James Neil, Robt Migchell, William Hay. (No rec. date).

Pp. 184-186: 20 Apr 1779, Thomas Harris Esqr, Sheriff of Meck., to Adam Alexander Esqr. of same, by judgment obtained in the Court of P & QS for Meck. Co., in July 1772 at suit brought by Matthew Stuart and Adam Alexander against John Warden deft., for ₺ 20...145 A sold by a writ of fiere facias...Thos Harris Shff. (Seal), Wit: Sam Martin. (No rec. date).

Pp. 186-188: 14 Nov 1778, Joseph McCane of Meck., to Robert Craighead of same, for ₺ 100 proc. money of NC...100 A on waters of Rockey River on both sides John McKnit Alexanders Waggon Road adj. Williams...Joseph McCain (Seal), Jane McCane (O) (Seal), Wit: Willm Alexander, Nath. Alexander. (No rec. date).

Pp. 188-190: 10 Apr 1779, Thomas Polk & wf Susannah of Meck., to John McGinty of same, for ₺ 55 North Carolina Currency ...land on waters of McCauplins Creek adj. William Miller, granted to sd. Thomas Polk, 230 A, 4 March 1775...Thomas Polk (Seal), Wit: Ezek. Polk, Neil Morrison (No rec. date).

Pp. 191-193: 13 July 1779, Samuel Fleniken of Meck., to William Hagins of same, for ₺ 50 proc. money...land on N side Waxhaw Creek near Robert Davis Senr, 250 A granted to Robt McCallin 28 March 1755...Samuel Flenniken (Seal), Wit: Jo. Douglass, David ____. (No rec. date).

Pp. 193-194: 12 Oct 1779, Nathaniel Alexander of Meck., to Thos Carter for ₺ 225...150 A adj. McCollocks line, Clarks line...Nathaniel Alexander (Seal), Wit: John Wylie, John Robinson(?). (No rec. date).

Pp. 194-195: 10 July 1779, James Sawyers of Meck., to Thos Polk of same, for ₺ 600 proc. money...137 A...James Sawyer (Seal), Wit: Robt Scott, John McKoy. (No rec. date).

Pp. 195-196: 7 April 1779, Thos Polk attorney for David Oliphant to William Barker of Meck., for ₺ 15 proc. money... 25 A   both sides Muddy Creek...Wit: William polk, Eph Barker. (No rec. date).

Pp. 197-198: 7 Apr 1779, Thos Polk attorney for David Oliphant to Daniel Barker of Meck., for ₺ 47 proc. money...72 A Wit: Jordan(?) Barker, William Polk (No rec. date).

Pp. 198-199: 7 Apr 1779, Thos Polk attorney for David Oliphant to Christopher Ryan of Meck., for ₺ 13 proc. money...

22 A on waters of Andersons Creek...Wit: Eph Brevard, William Polk (No rec. date).

Pp. 199-201: 23 Jan 1779, John McKnit Alexander of Meck., to Nathaniel Johnston of same, for Ł 500...222 A on both sides Long Creek, part of 12,500 A granted to Jeremiah Joy ...John McKnit Alexander (Seal), Jean Alexander (Seal), Wit: David Hays, Margaret Smith (M).(No rec. date)

Pp. 201-203: 17 Aug 1779, Francis Beaty, Cooper, of Tryon Co., to David Robison of Meck., for Ł 200...land on Paw Creek adj. John Cathey, Elis McGee, John Beaty, 280 A... Francis Beaty (Seal), Wit: Robt Beaty, Mathew Robison, Alexr. Robison. (No rec. date).

Pp. 203-204: 13 Oct 1779, Alexander McKee of Meck., to Robert Walker of same, for Ł 25 proc. money...land on waters of Sugar Creek, 25 A...Andrew McKee (Seal), Wit: Thos Walker. (No rec. date).

Pp. 204-206: 4 Oct 1779, John Johnston of Meck., to Hugh Harris of same, for Ł 300 NC money...land on waters of Big Sugar Creek adj. Samuel Roch, Robert McKee, Robert McCleary, 188 A...John Johnston (Seal), Wit: Joseph Hampton, John Province. (No rec. date).

Pp. 207-208: 9 December 1769, John Mitchell & wf Elisabeth of Rowan Co., to Ezekiel Sharp of Meck., for Ł 5 proc. money... 128 A...Wit: None. Rec. Jan. term 1770.

Pp. 208-210: 9 Dec 1779, John Mitchell & wf Elisabeth to James Cannon of Meck., for Ł 10 proc. money...124 A on Long Creek...Wit: Isaac Mitchell, Jno. McKnitt Alexander. Rec. Jan. term 1770.

Pp. 210-211: 9 Dec 1769, John Mitchell & Wf Elizabeth to John Smith of Meck., for Ł 10 proc. money...106 A on waters of Long Creek adj. James Bradley...Wit: Isaac Mitchell, Jno McKNitt Alexander. Rec. Jan. term 1770.

Pp. 211-213: 9 Decm 1769 John Mitchell & wf Elisabeth to Hugh Barnit, for Ł 8 proc. money...100 A adj. John McRee ...Wit: Isaac Mitchel, Jno McKnitt Alexander. Rec. Jan. term 1770.

Pp. 213-215: 9 Decm 1769, John Mitchell & wf Elisabeth to John McClure of Meck., for s 5 proc. money...land on waters of Sugar Creek, 256 A, Wit: Max Chambers, Jno McKnitt Alexander. Rec. Jan. term 1770.

Pp. 215-216, 9 Dec 1769, John Mitchell & wf Elizabeth to Robert McEntire of Meck., for s 5 proc. money...land on waters of Sugar Creek adj. James Reed, 40 A...Wit: Max Chambers, Jno McKnitt Alexander. Rec. Jan. term 1770.

Pp. 217-218: 9 Dec 1769, John Mitchell & wf Elizabeth to James Allen of Meck., for s 5 proc. money...40 A on waters of Long Creek adj. his own line...Wit: Max Chambers, Jno McKnitt Alexander. Rec. Jan. term 1770.

VOLUME 7

Pp. 218-220: 18 Dec 1769, John Mitchell & wf Elisabeth to Samuel Willson of Meck., for Ł 75 proc. money...255 A on Rocky River adj. Jonathan Newman...Wit: Samuel Pickens, James Gilmore. Rec. Jan. term 1770.

Pp. 220-221: 18 Dec 1769, John Mitchell & wf Elisabeth to Jonathan Newman of Meck., for Ł 100 proc. money...280 A on Clarks Creek adj. John Gillmore, Saml Willson...Wit: Samuel Pickens, James Gillmore. Rec. Jan. term 1770.

Pp. 222-223: 18 Dec 1769, John Mitchell & wf Elisabeth to James Gillmore of Meck., for Ł 35 proc. money...103 A on Rocky River, adj. Robert Smith...Wit: Jos Barr, Samuel Pickens. Rec. Jan term 1770.

Pp. 223-225: 18 Dec 1769, John Mitchell & wf Elisabeth to Samuel Pickens of Meck., for Ł 95 proc. money...land on Clarks Creek on Rocky River, adj. Joseph Patterson, 472 A... Wit: James Gilmore, James Barr. Rec. Jan. term 1770.

Pp. 225-227: 18 Dec 1769, John Mitchell & wf Elisabeth to Nathaniel Gilmore of Meck., for Ł 40 proc. money...land on Rocky River, 141 A...Wit: Samuel Pickens, James Gilmore. Rec. Jan. term 1770.

Pp. 227-229: 18 Dec 1769, John Mitchell & wf Elisabeth to John Gilmore of Meck., for Ł 45 proc. money...140 A on Clarks Creek adj. Robert Smith...Wit: Samuel Pickens, James Gilmore. Rec. Jan. term 1770.

Pp. 229-229B: 18 Dec 1769, John Mitchell & wf Elisabeth to Robert Harris of Meck., for Ł 30 proc. money...160 A adj. Samuel Pickens, Joseph Patterson...Wit: James Gilmore, Samuel Pickens. Rec. Jan. term 1770.

Pp. 229B-231: 13 March 1769, Benjamin Ford of Meck., to Richard Henderson of Granville Co., prov. aforesd., for Ł 20 proc. money...100 A on Millstone Branch of Twelve Mile Creek on the waggon road...Benjn. Ford (Seal), Wit: Ant: Newman, Waightstill Avery. Rec. Jan. term 1770.

Pp. 231-232: 23 Dec 1768, John Henry & wf Martha of Meck., to John Bigham, Robert Birgham Junr., & James Bigham of same, for Ł 90 NC money...land on north branch of Steel Creek, above William Barnet's, granted to sd. John Henry by deed 21 Dec 1763...John Hendry (Seal), Martha Hendry (ᘛ) (Seal), Wit: William Brownfield, John Brownfield. Rec. Jan. term 1770.

Pp. 232-234: 1 Feb 1767, Henry E. McCulloh to Abraham Caradine of Meck., planter, for Ł 40 proc. money...land in Meck., where he now lives, adj. Arthur Donolson, 254 A...Wit: Willm. Giles, William Ffrohock. Prov. by William Giles 8 March 1770.

Pp. 234-236: 7 Feb 1768, Edward Givens & wf Agness of Meck., to Samuel Givens of same, for Ł 5...part of a grant to Edward Givens 24 Apr 1762, 49 A...Edward Givens (O) (Seal), Agness Givens (O) (Seal), Wit: William Drew, William Caldwell. Ack. in open court by Edward Givins. Rec. Jan. term 1770.

VOLUME 7

Pp. 237-238: 6 Feb 1768, Edward Givens & wf Agness of Meck., to Samuel Givens, for Ł 5...part of grant to sd. Edward Givens 8 Oct 1751, 92 A. (Same signature and wit. as preceding deed). Ack. in open court by Edward Givens. Rec. Jan. term 1770.

Pp. 239-240: 18 Jan 1770, Thos Polk, Abraham Alexander & George Allen of Meck., to Samuel Willson for s 40 proc. money...lot #3 in Charlotte in S side Trade St...Wit: Alex Martin, Saml Willson. Rec. Jan. term 1770.

Pp. 241-242: 30 Aug 1769, Georg Cathey of Meck., to William Moore of Rowan Co., for Ł 100 proc. money...land in forks of McDowells Creek, being part of tract of 710 A, 263 A....Geo Cathy (X), Wit: Matthew McClure, Jno McK. Alexandr. Rec. Jan. term 1770.

Pp. 243-244: 16 Jan 1770, Joseph Cannon of Meck., Cooper, to James Cannon of same, Taylor, for Ł 8-6-6 proc. money of NC...land on waters of Long Creek, part of tract granted by John Mitchell to sd. Cannon 9 Dec 1769, adj. Wm Samples...Joseph Cannon (Seal), Ann Cannon, Wit: Jos. Young, Jno Mck. Alexd. Rec. Jan. term.

Pp. 244-246: 30 Sept 1767, Henry E. McCulloh to Moses Alexander for Ł 15 proc. money...land on waters of Mallard Creek on both sides of Stony Creek including the forks adj. Joseph Mitchell...Wit: James Townsley (D), Ths. Frohock. Prov. by Thomas Frohock 8 March 1770.

Pp. 246-247: 2 Sept 1760, Joseph Cannon of Meck., to John McKnight Alexander of Meck., for Ł 5 proc. money...land on both sides Rudesels Creek in Tryon Co., above Rudisels land, 200 A granted to JosephCannon 26 Oct 1767...Joseph Cannon (Seal), Wit: John Moffet, Jam Alexander. Rec. Jan. term 1770.

Pp. 248-250: 1 May 1765, James Alexander of Lancaster Co., Pa., to John Ramsey & Alexander Baldridge both of Lancaster Co., Pa., yeoman, for Ł 53 PA money...land in Meck. on West side Catawba River on Crowders Creek adj. Allisons corner, 346 A granted to James Alexander 1752...James Alexandr. (Seal), Eliz. Alexandr. (X) (Seal), Wit: Thoams Buffington, Samuel Scott. Prov. by Saml Scott in Lancaster County 2 Oct 1769 before Jos. Bickham, J. P.
Edward Shippen, Clerk of Court of Quarter Sessions and prolontary of the Court of Common Pleas for Lancaster Co., Pa., certify that James Bickham is a J. P., 2 Dec 1769.
Rec. Jan. term 1770.

Pp. 251-255: 9 Jan 1770, Willm Pickins of Meck., planter, to William Black of same, Distiller, for (lease s5, release 30 pistoles)...162 A, part of Tract #3...William Pickens, Wit: James Tate, John Black, Willm Flenniken. Ack. in open Court. Rec. Jan. term 1770.

Pp. 255-257: John Potts for love, goodwill & affection to son Robert Potts of Meck., farmer, 636 A adj. Robt Brevard, 16 Jan 1770. John Potts (O) (Seal), Wit: Alexandr. Osburn, Agness Osburn, Thos Alexander. Ack. in open court. Rec. Jan. term 1770.

VOLUME 7

Pp. 258-259: 7 Jan 1769, Thomas Dearmond of Meck., to Peter Johnston of same, for s5 ster. money...land on both sides Mc-Colpins Creek adj. Wm Flenagens survey, 182 A by deed 10 Jan 1767 ...Thomas Dermond, Wit: Thomas Polk, George Dodd. Rec. Jan. term 1770.

Pp. 259-261: 28 Dec 1769, Edmond Bearden of Meck., planter, to Benjamin Alexander, of same, planter, for ₺ 71 proc. money...220 A in Meck., granted by deed from Henry E. McCulloh to sd. Bearden 27 Jan 1767...Edmund Bearden (Seal), Ann Bearden (Seal), Wit: John Allen, James Scott. Rec. Jan. term 1770. Rec. Jan. term 1770.

Pp. 261-263: 18 Jan 1770, Abm Alexander, Thoams Polk & George Allen of Meck., to Robert Elliott of Meck., for ₺ 2 proc. money, lot #19 in Charlotte.Wit: Saml Willosn, John Springstee(n). Rec. Jan. term 1770.

Pp. 263-264: 25 Aug 1767, Samuel McCleary & wf Deborah of Meck., to Robert McCleary for ₺ 24 proc. money...150 A on East side Sugar Creek, granted to sd. Samuel McCleary 25 Apr 1762 .. Samuel McCleary, Deborah McCleary, Wit: Thoms. Polk, Ezekiel Polk. Rec. Jan term 1770.

Pp. 265-266: 9 Jan 1770, John McKain of Meck., to Andrew Crockett of Augusta Co., Va., for ₺ 90 proc. money of NC... land on west side Six Mile Creek, adj. James Potts, William Donolson, James Tate, Brice Millar, 140 A...John McKain (8) Wit: Archibald Crocket, John Rea, James Cochran. Rec. Jan. term 1770.

Pp. 266-267: John McKain of Meck., for ₺ 92-10-0 proc. money to Wm King of same...bay mare brander on the shoulder MK one gray horse branded shoulder & buttock MK and one Dople Gray Horse branded on the shoulder & buttok MK and one brown horse branded on the should & Buttock MK & one bay mare brander on the shoulder & Buttock MK & one bay Mare branded on the shoulder H & on the buttock M and one bright bay mare branded on the Should & Buttock MK & dark gray horse colt branded on Shoulder Buttock MK & one black Cow marked on the right ear with a crop & half moon under in the left with a slit, seven red & white Coloured Cows marked said mark, to one black & white Cow marked said mark, one bull marked said mark, four two year old marked said mark, to six year old marked to twelve Sheep marked said mark...9 Jan 1770. John McKain (O) (Seal), Wit: Archd Crockett, Andrew Crockett, Mary Crockett. Rec. Jan. term 1770.

Pp. 268-271: July 15th 1769, Mecklenburg County.
Came before me one of his Majestys Judtices for said County Benjamin Wallace & declares upon oath that last Satterday he heard Colonel Moses Alexander say he thought it was a damn'd scandal to send a man to the house of assembly that cant neither (sic) read nor write; and whichwise that he heard said Moses Alexander say that Martin Phifer had a bill drawn at the last assembly to Eastablish Mr. Samuel Suter Reader of the Parish of Mecklenburg and that said Suter sho'd be allowed one hudnred and thirty six pounds anuly for said Service & said Moses Alexander said, that if Capt. Thoams Polk and him had not interposed, that said bill wou'd have past.
                                                Benjamin Wallace (✓)
Sworn before me
David Rees.

205

North Carolina
Mecklenburg County) This day personally appeared John Dellinger before me one of his Magestes Justices of the peace for said County & made oath...that on or about 16 March last he saw at the house of Collonel Alexander in Company Capt Thomas Polk & Colonel Moses Alexander, and the subject of there discourse was in Major Martin Pfifers acting at the last assembly which seemed to him in gennal (sic) Injurous to Major Fifer's Charector & in particular he heard them say that Major Fifer did bring a bill into the house of assembly to Establish a Church Minister or Reader in the said County and if Capt. Thomas Polk had not opposed said bill it would have pass'd & said Deponant farther saith that in or about the last of may or the first of June at the above said Moses he also heard the said Captn. Thomas Polk & Coll Alexander enter on the same Kine of discourse & in particular about the said Bill....

                  John Dellinger

Sworn & signed before me
this 2 day of Sept. 1769
David Rees, J. P.

North Carolina) This day personally appeared John McGinty before
Rowan County) me one of his Majestys Justices of the peace for
      said County & made oath on the holy Evengelist of Almight God that on or about the 9the of July 1769, he heard Robt Erwin Sadler say at his the said Deponents own House that Major Fifer had brought a bill in to the House of Assembly, to get a minister to preach to his people & have his pay lifted by a County Tax annually & Capt. Polk being in the House of Assembly at the same time as Capt. the Bill & when Major Fifer did not get the said Bill answered to his mind, the next Day he put in another bill to the House in order to get a man to read to his people as the (sic) were poore and not able to pay a Minister & Thirty pounds was to be lifted yearly of the County for that service...a Bill for Mecklenburg to have a Reader for the Dutch people & thirty pounds to be lifted of the county...
Sworn before me October seventh day   John McGinty
1769 John Ford (?)

North Carolina
Whereas Major Martin Fifer late one of the Representatives of the County of Mecklenburg has been very much aspersed in his Publick Character as a member of Assembly of the said Province, as may appear by the many untruths and insinutations of his Enemies as set forth in the Papers & Depositions hereunto annexed, all which appear to us to have been maliciously & scandalously uttered, with an Intent to lessen the said Martin Fifer in the good opinion of the Freeholders of his County.

We the subscribers members of his Majesty's General Assembly of the said Province, in Justice to the said Martin Fifer Do hereby certify that the Charges and such aspersions mentioned in the annexed Depositions & Papers...are false & scandalous...31 October 1769.
John Woodhouse, John Ashe, John Harvey Speaker, Wm Eray(?), Com. Harnett, Richd Ward Beard, Henry White, Jacob Blount, John Kinner, Henry Desoran(?), Aquila Sugg, Jos Bell, Felix Kenan, Abm. Sheppard Jur.

(Another similar statement) signed by John Harvey, Richd Caswell, J. Moore, Abm. Sheppard Junr., Felix Kenan, Andrew Knox, Joseph

VOLUME 7

Jones, John Simpson 3 years John Speir has known him. John Kinner has known him 2 years. Edw. Veil.

Pp. 271-272: 4 July 1778, William Porter of Meck., to Alexander Porter of same, for Ł 10 proc. money...49 A on E side Catabo River on S side Paw Creek, part of 500 A granted to Samuel Bigam(?) 21 Dec 1763...William Porter (Seal), Wit: Joseph Hart, Davis Hart, James Hart. (No rec. date).

Pp. 273-274: 16 Sept 1777, William Henry to Richard Springsteen, for Ł 215...land on waters of McMichels Creek adj. David Vance and John (sic), 175 A granted to sd. Henry by deed from H. E. McCulloh 1767...Wiliam Henerey (Seal), Wit: John Spring, Sarah Springs. (No rec. date).

Pp. 274-276: 17 June 1777, John Murphey to James Neal, both of Meck., for Ł 215, land granted to Henry Henry 27 Sept 175- sold to John Dunn, then to John Davies 27 Sept 1759, then to Murphey and James Kerr 20 Oct 1765, 228 A on Thoms McCowns line, on both sides Codle Creek, below Joseph Lemons bridge...John Murphey (X) (Seal), Wit: Thos McQuown, Robert Carlile, Thos Benson. (No rec. date).
Book No 22. 22d Book
Finis.

Book No. 33d

Pp. 277-278: 30 Sept 1775, Charles Fisher & wf Barbara of Meck., to Phillip Lideker, for Ł 320 proc. money...227 A on both sides Adams Creek a branch of Rockey or Johnston River, also 80 A on both sides Adams Creek adj. other tract, conveyed to sd. Fisher by Gov. Dobbs 25 June 1764...Chs. Fisher (Seal), Barbara Fisher (B) (Seal), Wit: John Fifer & a Name wrote in Dutch. Rev. Oct. Court 1777.

Pp. 279-280: 16 June 1775, Peter Keeler of Meck., to Frony Bluer of same, for Ł 100 proc. money...166 A on both sides Dutch Buffilow Creek, granted to sd. Peter Keeler by deed from Gov. Dobbs 2 March 1764...Peter Keeler (Seal), Wit: John Fifer & a Name wrote in Dutch. Rec. July Sessn. 1775, prov. on oath of John Fifer.

Pp. 280-281: 17 Jan 1775, John Wallace & wf Mary of Meck., to Joseph Wallace his son of same, carpenter, for Ł 20 ...116 A conveyed to John Wallace by Henry E. McCulloh by deed 28 Jan 1767...John Wallace (Seal), Mary Wallace (X) (Seal), Wit: John Wilson, Benj. Wallace. Rev. Jan. Sessions 1776. Proved by Benj. Wallace.

Pp. 282-283: 13 Jan 1775, Robert Dowdle & wf Jane of Meck., to John Wallace Senr of same, planter, for Ł 30...land the sd. Dowdle now lives on adj. Barthw Johnston & Mathew McCorkle ...100 A granted to James Marble by patent 17 May 1754, and conveyed to John Burnet, and by him to John Dowdle 25 Feb 1763...the above land and premises conveyed by John Dowdle to Robert Dowdle by deed bearing date 14 July 1770...Robt Dowdle (Seal), Jane Dowdle (P) (Seal), Wit: Joseph Wallace, Benj. Wallace, Bartholomew Johnson. Prov. by Joseph Wallace Jany Sesn. 1776.

VOLUME 7

Pp. 283-284: 25 March 1774, John Phifer of Meck., to John Baker of Rowan County, for ₺ 10 proc. money...land on Buffelow Creek, a draft of Rockey River 200 A, granted to sd. Phifer 22 Dec 1768...John Pifer (Seal), Wit: Sam: Martin, Prov. by Samuel Martin, April Sessn. 1775.

Pp. 284-285: 2 June 1773, Joseph Kerr to James Todd, for ₺ 57 proc. money...land on head branches of Sugar Creek, adj. John Boot, 374 A...Joseph Kerr, Wit: Joseph Moore. Prov. by Joseph Moore April term 1776.

Page 286: 27 Dec 1774, Jacob Cline & wf Catrin of Meck., to Jacob Suit of same, for ₺ 20 proc. money...130 A on Lick branch...Jacob Cline (+) (Seal(, Catrin Cline (+) (Seal), Wit: Michal Goodnight (M), Robt McPherson, and two Names wrote in Dutch. Rec. April term 1776.

Pp. 287-288: 3 Oct 1775, Moses Swan Senr of Paxton Township, Lancaster County, Pa., and wf Margaret to Moses Swan Jr. of Meck., for ₺ 1 Pa money...200 A on SW of a small Path leading to Widow Armours from Johnys town in Mecklenburg Co., part of grant to Samuel Knox 19 Apr 1763 and transferred 1 May 1770 to sd. Moses Swan...Moses Swan (Seal), Margaret Swan (4) (Seal), Wit: Joseph Johnston, Richard Graham. Acknowledged in open court in Lancaster County, 3 Oct 1775 before Timy. Green. Prov. by Joseph Johnston in Mecklenburg Co., April term 1776.

Pp. 289-290: 3 Oct 1775, Moses Swan of Paxton Township, Lancaster Co., Pa & wf Margaret to Joseph Swan of Meck., Cordwiner, for ₺ 100 PA money...200 A, 1/2 of 400 A, on SW of a small path to Widow Armours from Johns Town, granted to Samuel Knox....(Same wit and rec. dates).

Pp. 290-292: 17 Jan 1775, Thomas Polk, Abraham Alexander, Isaac Alexander, Jeremiah McCafferty and William Patterson, Commissioners, Directors and Trustees of Charlotte to Robert Harris, Richard Barry, Adam Alexander and Hezekiah Alexander, and other Justices of the Inferior Court of Pleas and Quarter Session for Meck., for s 20 proc. money...lot # 37 whereon the Public Goal for Meck. was heretofore built and hath been used to the day of this date, Wit: Sam Martin, Jno McK. Alexander. Prov. in open court by Sam Martin, April Session 1775.

Pp. 292-294: 22 Aug 1773, John Flemming and wf Grizzy of Meck., to James Sloan of same, for ₺ 42 NC money...250 A on waters of Paw Creek including the improvement of said Flemming adj. David Hay, John Hunter...John Flemming (Seal), Grizzy Flemming (O) (Seal), Wit: William Berryhill, Josias Cathey, George Morrow. Prov. in open court by William Berrehill, Jan. Sessn 1776.

Pp. 294-296: 22 Nov 1775, John Giles of Meck., to William Henderson son in law to sd. John Giles, weaver, for ₺ 5 sterling...250 A on E side Cataba River asdj. line the Samuel Allen sold to Francis Beaty, part of 938 A granted to James Carter and John Linn, 9 Apr 1753, sold to Edward Hughs then to James Carter, and by sheriff's deed to John Brandon then to Samuel Allen, then to John Gilles (sic)...John Giles, Wit: William Hendreson, John Henderson, James Henderson. Prov. by William Henderson in April 1776.

VOLUME 7

Pp. 297-300: 26 July 1777, Paul Barringer of Meck., planter, & Barbara Hernhart, heretofore Barbara Haygler, Extx of the L. W. & T. of John Gaygler, late of Meck., planter, decd., to Charles Darr of same, planter...whereas the sd. John Haygler by the L. W. & T. dated on or about 29 May 1771, will and directed that if his wife Barbara should intermarry again his Executors whould sell and dispose of his lands, and sd. Haygler nominated Paul Barringer an Exr., and the sd. Barbara afterwards intermarried with Philip Hernhart of Rowan Co., planter, whose wife she still is, for ₤ 250...land on Dutch Buffalow Creek, 250 A, conveyed to Haygler by Arthur Dobbs...Paul Barringer (Seal), Barbara Hernhart (Seal), Wit: Jacob Dun, Matthias Beaver. Prov. by Mathias Beaver Oct. Sessn 1777.

Pp. 300-301: 9 Jan 1777, Andrew Logan of Granvil Co., S. C., to William Spear of Meck., for ₤ 130 NC money...400 A on both sides of a branch of Rockey River called Reedy Creek, land granted to Logan 18 May 1756...Andrew Logan (Seal), Wit: Archable Edger, James Ross, Adam Edger. Prov. by Adam Edger Oct. Sessn 1777.

Pp. 302-303: 17 Oct 1777, Matthew Bigger & wf Ann of Craven Co., S. C., to Joseph McKinley of Meck., for ₤ 200 NC money...part of tract where on John Bigger now lives, conveyed to him by James Bigger who obtained the same by patent...Matthew Bigger (Seal), Ann Bigger (O) (Seal), Wit: Thomas Bogs (+), Wm Kerr, Samuel Chambers. Prov. by Thomas Boggs, Oct. Sessn 1777.

Pp. 304-305: 2 Oct 1777, William Sawyer of Township of London Derry, Lancaster County, Pa., yeoman & wf Sophia, to James Sawyer of Meck., yeoman, for ₤ 100 Pa. money...land on waters of Sugar Creek adj. Joseph See, James Moore, land made over to James McCord Junior by his father James McCord Senr 9 Jan 1767, and to William Sawyer by sd. McCord Jr., 29 Sept 1772 ...William Sawyer (2) (Seal), Sophiah Sawyer (8) (Seal), Wit: Willia- Whiteside, Moses Swan. (No rec. date).

Pp. 305-306: 22 Oct 1777, James Stafford of Meck., planter, to James Britain of same, Black-Smith, for ₤ 100 proc. money...land on waters of Twelve Mile Creek on a branch called Cedar Creek above Nathl. Alexander, adj. Francis McCalls, 150 A ...James Stafford (Seal), Wit: William McKee, Robert Philips. (No rec. date).

Pp. 306-307A: 1 April 1776, David Smith of Meck., to Moses Steel of same, for ₤ 20 proc. money...106 A adj. the land he lives on...David Smith (Seal), Wit: Dunn Ocheltree, Joseph Nicholson, Peter Johnston. Prov. by Joseph Nickelson, before Eph Bravard. Prov. in open court Oct. Sessn 1777 by Duncan Ochiltree.

Pp. 307B-308: 17 June 1776, John Rennick of Craven Co., S. C. to Archibald Henderson of Meck., for ₤ 20 NC proc. money...land on N side Catawba, 100 A, part of 200 A granted to George Rennick 30 Aug 1753...John Rennick (Seal), Wit: Dun Ochiltree, Peter Johnston, Adam Stewart. Prov. by Peter Johnston, Oct. Sessn 1777.

Pp. 309-310: 30 Aug 1777, William King & wf Mary Ann of Meck., to Daniel Cavin of same, for ₤ 110 proc. money...320 A, part of 640 A on N side Waxaw Creek adj. John Crocket, Archd.

Crockett...William King (Seal), Mary Ann King (O) (Seal), Wit: Wm McCulloh, Andrew Crockett, Alexr Carns. Prov. by Alexr Carne, Oct. Sessn 1777.

Pp. 310-311: 22 Aug 1777, William Wallace & wf Sarah, planter, of Meck., to Marthew Balch, Relick of the Rev. Hezekiah James Balch, decd, of Meck., for ₤ 200...162 A on S side of Coddle Creek, adj. Zacheus Wilson...Will Wallace (Seal), Sarah Wallace (8) (Seal), Wit: David Reese, David Wilson. Prov. by David Reese October Sessions 1777.

Pp. 311-313: 21 Feb 1776, Henry Cromley & wf Sarah of Meck., to James Cook of same, for ₤ 5...land including his own improvement adj. William McCorkle, 200 A, granted May 1772 to sd. Henry Cromley...Henry Crumly (Seal), Sarah Crumbly (S) (Seal), Wit: John McCulloh, John Howey. Prov. by John Howey Oct. Sessn 1777.

Pp. 313-315: 13 Dec 1774, William Sawyer of Derry Township, Lancaster Co., Pa., yeoman, to James Sawyer, of same, (one of the sons of the sd. William Sawyer),...whereas John Garrison of Meck., by indenture 1 July 1771, did sell unto sd. Wm. Sawyer, land on waters of Sugar Creek adj. Moses Steel, 400 A and Thomas Polk on 20 Oct 1772, did confirm unto sd. Wm. Sawyer 68 A adj. sd. Thomas Polk, Garrison, Harriss, now for natural love & affection to James Sawyer...these two tracts...William Sawyer (2) (Seal), Wit: William Whiteside, Moses Swan. Rec. Oct. Session 1777. Prov. by William Whiteside.

Pp. 316-317: 9 Dec 1769, John Mitchel & wf Elizabeth to Robert Kerr, for s 5 proc. money...39 A on waters of Long Creek...Wit: William Henry, Jno McK. Alexander, James Reid. Prov. Oct. Session 1777 by James Reed.

Pp. 317-319: 6 Sept 1777, Asmus Binager and wf of Meck., farmer, to Charles Saverett of same, for ₤ 18 proc. money... land on a small branch of Dutch Buffalow Creek, 9 A...Asmus Binager (Seal), Susan Binager (+) (Seal), Wit: Jason Frissell, & Two Names Wrote in Dutch. Prov. by Jason Frissell Oct. Sessn 1777.

Pp. 319-321: 13 Jan 1778, Hugh Park Senr & wf Margaret of Rowan Co., Farmer, to John Park, son of sd. Hugh Park Senr., for s 10 proc. money...land on both sides N fork Sugar Creek, 325 A, part of 689 A granted to sd. Hugh Park Senr 23 Jan 1754...Hugh Park (Seal), Margret Park (?) (Seal), Wit: Alexander McQuown, Henry Fleming. Prov. by Alexander McQuown, Jan. Sessn 1778.

Pp. 321-322: 13 Jan 1778, Hugh Park Senr & wf Margaret of Rowan Co., to Hugh Park Junr, son of sd. Hugh Park Senr., for s 10 proc. money...land on both sides N fork of Sugar Creek, 325 A, part of 689 A...(Same wit and rec date).

Pp. 323-324: 4 Sept 1777, Asmus Binager of Meck., farmer, & wf Susanna to John Duke of same, weaver, for ₤ 100 proc. money...land on E side Dutch Buffalo Creek, 100 A...Asmus Binager (Seal), Susanna Binager (Seal), Wit: Jason Frissell and Two Names Wrote in Dutch. Prov. by Frissel Oct. Sessn 1777.

Pp. 324-325: 6 Sept 1777, John Duke of Meck., weaver & wf Margret to Charles Saverett of same, farmer, for ₤ 50 proc. money...land on a branch of Dutch Buffalow Creek, adj. John Young

VOLUME 7

...John Duke (Seal), Margaret Duke (+) (Seal), Wit: Jason Frissell and Two Names wrote in Dutch. Prov. by Frissell, Oct. Sessn 1777.

Pp. 326-327: 14 Nov 1775, Martin Phifer Senr of Meck., to John Holbrook of same, for ₺ 40 proc. money...200 A on head of Armstrongs Branch...Martin Phifer and wf Margaret... Martin Phifer (Seal) Margaret Phifer (-) (Seal), Wit: Martin Phifer, Caleb Phifer. Prov. by Caleb Phifer, Oct. Sessn 1777.

Pp. 328-329: 3 Sept 1777, Jacob Kline & wf Catharine of Meck., to Christopher Bliss, of same, for ₺ 3 proc. money... 16 A on the line that divides Mecklenburg and Rowan Counties, on Buffalow Creek...Jacob Kline (I) (Seal), Catharine Kline (+) (Seal), Wit: Jason Frissell and Two Names wrote in Dutch. Prov. by Frissell Oct. Sessn 1777.

Pp. 330-331: 13 Sept 1777, Michael Shever of Meck., to Francis Lock of same, for ₺ 144...land on Bufflow Creek adj. Matthew Locks, Francis Lock, conveyed to Michal Shever by Joseph Rodgers and David Russell 15 Jan 1775, 144 A...Michl Shaver (M) (Seal), Wit: Joseph Rogers, John Thomson, Caleb Phifer. Prov. by Caleb Phifer, Oct. Sessn 1777.

Pp. 332-333: 21 Oct 1777, Moses Steel of Meck., to Henry Mitchell of same, for ₺ 25 proc. money...land on waters of McCalpins Creek adj. the land David Smith lives on, granted to David Smith 4 March 1775, conveyed to sd. Moses Steel 1 Apr 1776 ...Moses Steel (Seal), Wit: Sam Martin. Prov. by Grantor Oct. Sess 1777.

Pp. 333-334: 11 Feb 1777, Thomas Frohock of Rowan Co., to Duncan Ochiltree & Comrs of Charlotte, for ₺ 80 proc. money ...all that peace of a lot adj. lot sold to William Patterson on Tryon St., # 17...Tho: Frohock (Seal), Wit: John Jack (+), Adam Stewart. Rec. Oct. Sessn 1777. Prov. by Adam Stewart.

Pp. 335-336: 1 Sept 1777, Duncan Ochiltree & Compy. of Meck., to James Jack of same, for ₺ 765 currency of NC...land on Tryon St., ...Wit: David McKee, Peter Johnston, Adam Stewart. Prov. by Adam Stewart Oct. Sessn 1777.

Pp. 336-337: 14 Sept 1776, William Elliot of Meck., merchant, to James Gardner of same, Shoemaker, for ₺ 130...lot on West sd of Trade St., in Charlotte, # 19...Wm Elliot (Seal), Wit: Dun. Ochiltree, Peter Johnston. Prov. by Peter Johnston, Oct. Sessn. 1777.

Pp. 338-339: 3 Dec 1773, William Beard & wf Mary of Meck., to John and Francis Cummins of same, for ₺ 5 proc. money... land on waters of Long Creek adj. John Moore, John Boyd, 200 A... William Beard (3) (Seal), Mary Beard (M) (Seal), Wit: Charles Cummins, Elizabeth Cummins. (No rec. date).

Pp. 339-341: 25 Jan 1777, Jerom Miller & wf Rachel of Meck., to Thomas Cochram Junr of same, for ₺ 20...land on waters of Twelve Mile Creek, 300 A including the big Glade and Colhouns improvement, granted to Peter Johnston 4 May 1769...Jerom Miller (Seal), Rachel Miller (a) (Seal), Wit: James Cochrane (I), John Lawson. Prov. by James Cochran, Oct. Sessn 1777.

VOLUME 7

Pp. 341-343: 19 Sept 1770, Moses Andrew and wf Martha of Meck., to William Penney of same, for L 15-10-0...land on E side Caudle(?) Creek adj. Zebulon Brevard, part of grant to Ambrose Harding...Moses Andrew (Seal), Martha Andrew (M) (Seal), Wit: Archibald Houston, James Osbonr(???). Prov. by Houston, Oct. Sessn 1777.

Pp. 343-344: 7 Oct 1777, Philip Walker of Meck., to William Hasler of same, for L 5...land on the dividing ridge between the Waxhaw and Cane Creek including the improvement William Hasler now lives on, 200 A, granted to sd. Philip Walker, 4 March 1775...Philip Walker (Seal), Wit: Jas. Cook, Thomas Walker. Prov. Oct. Sessn 1777 by James Cook.

Pp. 345-346: 13 Feb 1777, Robert Patterson and wf Margaret of Meck., to William Whitsitt, Blacksmith, for L 50 proc. money ...land on waters of Paw Creek and Bever Dam, granted to Robt Patterson 4 March 1775, 200 A...Robert Patterson (Seal), Margret Patterson (X) (Seal), Wit: William Patterson, John Jack. Prov. by John Jack Oct. Sessn 1777.

Pp. 346-348: 10 June 1777, Richard Sanders and wf Ann of Meck., to John Helms, of same, farmer, for L 45...land on both sides Indian Creek, including sd. Sanders improvement, granted to Richard Sanders 2 Feb 1774, 150 A...Richd Sanders (R) (Seal), Wit: James Harris, George Helms. Prov. by Geroge Helms, Oct. Sessn 1777.

Pp. 349-350: 11 Apr 1778, John Richey Senr of Meck., planter, to John Richey Juner, for L 100...land on E side Catabo River above the land where sd. John Richey now Dwels on, 400 A granted to William Watson, 28 Feb 1754, and conveyed by Stanly to More and then to Richey Senr....John Richey (Seal), Wit: Robt Beaty, James Richey (No rec. date).

Pp. 351-352: 15 July 1778, Thos Polk of Meck., to George Allen of ___, for L ___, 70 A on Michals Creek adj. John Allen, John Spring...Thos Polk (Seal), Wit: Ezekiel Wallace, John Ford. (No rec. date).

Pp. 352-353: 16 Dec 1778, Adlai Osborn and Moses Winsely of Rowan Co., to William Patterson of Meck., for L 600... lot in Town of Charlotte, on Tryon St., # 17... Ad Osburn (Seal), Moses Winsely (Seal), Wit: Eph Bravard, Dun Ochiltree. (No rec. date).

Pp. 354-355: 7 Nov 1778, John Davies & wf Elizabeth of Meck., to Thos Greer of same, for L 400...328 A adj. Henry Nealy, John Price, Saml Allen, Wm Beaty, near the River bank, granted to Alexander Dobbins by patent 6 March 1754, conveyed to Hugh Couthers (Caruthers?), 11 July 1763, then to Thos Polk, 5 June 1773, then to John Davies 23 Jan 1778...John Davies (Seal), Elisabeth Davies (Seal), Wit: Robt Erwin, Rees Price. (No rec. date).

Pp. 356-357: 19 Jan 1779, James Davieson of Meck., to Samuel Davison of same, for L 50 proc. money...one tract including his improvement he now lives on, part of 377 A granted by Abner Nash to William Thompson 5 Feb 1774, 149 A; also a tract part of 88 A granted by sd. as above, 22 A, adj. Benj. Brown... (deed very confusing) total 179 A...James Davison (Seal), Jean

VOLUME 7

Davison (X) (Seal), Wit: Hugh Bryson, John McK. Alexander. (No rec. date)

Pp. 358-359: 26 Nov 1778, Thos Polk, Abram Alexander, and Eph Bravard to James Jack, for ₤ 100 proc. money... lot # 24 in Charlotte...Wit: Eph Bravard, Mark Alexander. (No rec. date).

Pp. 359-361: 11 Aug 1778, Elizabeth Lusk and John Lusk of Meck., to George Harkness, for ₤ 300 proc. money...land on McAlpins Creek adj. surveys formerly made for Smith and Critenden 137 A adj. John Lusk, John Slone, John Wilson, Brice Miller... Elizabeth Lusk (Seal), John Lusk (Seal), Wit: Henry Downs, George Hogans(?), Daniel John. (No rec. date).

Pp. 361-363: 10 Oct 1778, Robert Slone & wf Margret to James McGee, Adam McGee, Wiliam McGee and Thomas McGee, for ₤ 150...land on both sides Paw Creek adj. Mathew Robison, John Slone, 200 A, part of grant to Charles Beaty 30 Aug 1753, conveyed from beaty to Young 18 March 1762 and from Young to Slone 27 Nov 1762...Robert Slone (Seal), Margrat Slone (+) (Seal), Wit: John Slone, Alexander Porter, Wiliam Porter. (No rec. date).

Book No. 24th

Pp. 364-365: 21 Oct 1767, John Hill of Meck., to John McKnitt Alexander for ₤ 5...200 A granted to Hill 27 Sept 1766...John Hill (Seal), Wit: Samuel Sharp, William Steel. (No rec. date).

Pp. 366-367: 7 Oct 1773, Thomas Polk of Meck., to Jeremiah McCafferty of same, for ₤ 60 proc. money...land on waters of Garrison Creek, adj. Thomas Polk, 142 A deed by Selwyn to James Moore, then to Henry E. McCulloh, then to Polk...Thomas Polk (Seal), Wit: John Davies, Ack. in open court by Polk, April Court 1774.

Pp. 367-368: 29 Oct 1773, Thos Polk, Abraham Alexander & Jeremiah McCafferty of Meck., to Daniel Huey of same, for ₤ 15 proc. money...lot # 39 on W side Tryon ST...Wit: Saml Jack, James Foster. Prov. by Foster April court 1774.

Pp. 369-370: Francis Yeast of Meck., to Paul Yoast my now youngest son by my lawful espoused wife Christian Yoast, whose maiden name was Christian Heart to said son Paul (now about 8 years old)...land on waters of Duch Buffalo Creek adj. Andrew Presleys line, 252 A, granted to Benjamin Robison 17 March 1752, purchased by Yoast from Benjamin Robinson of Rowan Co., 3 Feb 1762...Francis Yost (X) (Seal), _____ (German signature) (Seal), Wit: George Henry Berger, John Leper. Prov. by George Henry Yoast, April Court 1774. (N. B. The clerk likely misread a German signature of George Henry Yoast as George Henry Berger.)

Pp. 370-371: 21 Oct 1772, James Cook of Meck., to William Hester of same, for ₤ 5 proc. money...150 A adj. Jacob Gray, being the land the said William Hester now lies (sic) on... James Cook (Seal), Wit: John Davis, Joseph Greer. Prov. by John Davis, April Court 1774.

VOLUME 7

Pp. 371-373: 15 May 1773, Henry Eustace McCulloh to Jeremiah McCafferty of Meck., for ₤ 164 proc. money...land on both sides Sugar Creek, adj. Saml Carrol...Wit: Thos Polk, Thos Frohock. Prov. Thomas Polk April Court 1774.

Pp. 374-375: 6 Feb 1774, James Case of Meck., planter, to John Lusk of same, planter, for ₤ 55 proc. money... land on waters of Sugar Creek adj. John Lusk, John Stone, John Wilson, and Brice Miller, 127 A...James Case (X) (Seal), Abigail Case (A) (Seal), Wit: John Dermand, Richard Lansdall, Roger Cunningham. Prov. by Roger Dunningham, April Court 1774.

Pp. 376-377: 20 Sept 1773, John Hill of Meck., to David Parks of same, for ₤ 5 proc. money...26 A adj. Alexander McGinty, on waters of Sugar Creek...John Hill (Seal), Wit: Thos Polk, James Foster. Prov. by Thos Polk April Court 1774.

Pp. 377-378: 18 Jan 1773, John Howey & wf Ann of Meck., to John McNeely of same, for ₤ 5 proc. money...75 A adj. sd. John McNeely, Jacob Gray...John Howey (Seal), Ann Howey (X) (Seal), Wit: Abraham Cook, John McCorkle. Prov. by Abraham Cook April Court 1774.

Pp. 378-379: 20 Dec 1773, Michael Legett & wf Margeret of Meck., to Abraham Cook of same, for ₤ 5 proc. money... 300 A on the High side of the Lick Branch, adj. James McLure... Michal Leget (Seal), Margret Leget (8) (Seal), Wit: John McCorkle, John McNeeley. Rec. April Court 1774, prov. by John McNeely.

Pp. 379-380: 10 Oct 1772, Brice Miller of Meck., to Andrew Baxter of same, for ₤ 100 proc. money...land on waters of Sugar Creek on the Indian Line, in the old line which was Ezekiel Alexanders...Brice Miller (B) (Seal), Jane Miller (0) (Seal), Wit: Henry Downs, Archd. Crocket, James Jack. Prov. April Court 1774 by Henry Downs.

Pp. 381-382: 25 Feb 1774, Andrew Baxter of Meck., to Roger Cunningham of same, for ₤ 150 proc. money...land on Reedy branch of Sugar Creek, adj. Mary Jones, 350 A...Andrew Baxter (Seal), Francis Baxter (D) (Seal), Wit: William Reed, John Jack. Prov by William Reed, April Court 1774.

Page 382: 2 Nov 1770, William Hester & wf Sarah of Meck., to John Howey of same, for ₤ 5 proc. money...150 A adj. John McNeeley, Jacob Gray...William Hester (X) (Seal), Sarah Hester (X) (Seal), Wit: John McNeeley, John McCorcle. Prov. by John McNeely April Court 1774.

Pp. 383-384: 31 July 1773, Brice Miller of Meck., planter, to John Bruster of same, for ₤ 10 proc. money...land on S side McCalpins Creek adj. John Bruster, Walter Davis, & Ye Indians lands, part of 160 A granted to sd. Brice Miller May 1772...Brice Miller (B) (Seal), Wit: Henry Downs, Isaick Fitter, George Archer. Prov. by Henry Downs, April Court 1774.

Pp. 384-385: 20 April 1774, John Newman of Meck., to Robt Hoop of same, for ₤ 50 proc. money...200 A granted to Newman by deed from H. E. McCulloh 12 ___ 1767...John Newman (Seal), Wit: Thos Polk, Jurate. Henry Verner. Prov. by Thos Polk April Court 1774.

VOLUME 7

Pp. 385-386: 10 Jan 1774, Joseph Gant of Meck., to William Mitchell of same, for Ł 12 proc. money...68 A granted by Abner Nash & wf Justina Feb 1771...Joseph Gant (S) (Seal), Susana Gant (S) (Seal), Wit: Peter Guizen (X), Moses Burlansen (X) Prov. by Peter Guizen, April Court 1774.

Pp. 386-388: 1 April 1773, Saml Jack of Meck., to Andrew Baxter, for Ł 13 proc. money...land on N side McCalpins Creek, adj. William Flanagans Corner...Saml Jack (Seal), Wit: John Jack, Patrick Jack, Patrick Jack. Prov. by Patrick Jack, April Court 1774.

Pp. 388-389: 19 Oct 1772, Hugh Wilson of Meck., to Andrew Baxter for Ł 100 proc. money...land on Reedy Branch of Sugar Creek including William Credittons improvements, 50 A...Hugh Wilson (Seal), Mary Wilson (O) (Seal), Wit: Henry Downs, Jurat, James Tate, Phillip Weeks (P). Prov. by Henry Downs, April Court 1774.

Pp. 389-391: 30 Nov 1773, William Weatherford & wf Sarah to Peter Kizer of Meck., for Ł 16 proc. money...80 A on a branch of Rockey River...William Weatherford (Seal), Sarah Wetherford (X) (Seal), Wit: William Mitchel, Peter Kizer (+). Prov. April Court 1774 by Peter Kizer.

Pp. 391-392: 13 May 1773, Henry E. McCulloh to Andrew Baxter, for Ł 35-18-0 proc. money...land on both sides McMichals Creek, 95 A adj. Kings line...Wit: Thos Polk, Thos Frohock. Prov. by Thos Polk, April court 1774.

Pp. 393-394: 14 May 1773, Henry E. McCulloh to Josiah Alexander, for Ł __ proc. money, part of land surveyed for John Bohannon 24 April 1766, 225 A...Wit: Thos Polk, Thos Frohock, Prov. by Thos Polk, April Court 1774.

Pp. 394-398: 30 Jan 1767, George Augustus Selwyn to Andrew Baxter of Meck., 159 A...Wit: Thos Frohock, William Frohock Prov. April Court 1774 by Thos Frohock.

Pp. 398-399: 16 Jan 1767, William Beaty of Meck., to Henry Eustace McCulloh...271 A adj. Thos Polk in the forks of Reedy Creek...Wit: John Frohock, Thos Polk. Prov. April Court 1774

Pp. 400-401: 21 Jan 1767, Arthur Garrison to Henry E. McCulloh, Ł 43-16-0...181 A...Wit: John Frohock, David Robison. Rec. April Term 1774.

Pp. 402-403: 11 Jan 1767, William Flannagan to Henry E. McCulloh, for Ł 63-6-0 proc. money...240 A...Wit: John Frohock, Thos Polk. Rec. April Term 1774.

Pp. 404-405: 13 Mar 1767, Noble Osborn to Henry E. McCulloh, for Ł 32-4-8... __ A (torn)...Wit: John Frohock, George Alexander. Rec. April Term 1774.

Pp. 406-407: 14 Jan 1767, John Ramsey of Meck., planter, to Henry E. McCulloh, Ł 82-5-6...land on four Mile Creek, including plantation & Improvements whereon sd. John Ramsey now lives, 312 A...Wit: John Frohock, Thos Polk. Rec. April term 1774.

VOLUME 7

Pp. 408-409: 21 Jan 1767, Isaiah Parker of Meck., to Henry E. Mc-
          Culloh, for ₤ 50-0-0 proc. money...300 A adj. John
McK. Alexander...Wit: John Allen, John Frohock. Rec. April term
1774.

Pp. 410-411: 16 Jan 1767, Walter Beaty of Meck., planter, to Henry
          E. McCulloh, for ₤ 65-2-6 proc. money...246 A...
Wit: John Frohock, Thos Polk. Rec. April Term 1774.

Pp. 412-413: 10 Jan 1767, William Black of Meck., planter, for ₤
          40...147 A Abraham Miller "including the dam Mill
Plantation..." Wit: John Frohock, Thos Polk. Rec. April term 1774.

Pp. 414-415: 9 Jan 1767, John Swann of Meck., planter, to Henry
          E. McCulloh for ₤ ___...534 A adj. Henry's Line...
Wit: John Frohock, Thomas Polk. Rec. April term 1774.

Pp. 416-417: 17 Jan 1767, George Ross of Meck., planter, to Henry
          E. McCulloh for ₤ 25-14-6...land including
plantation where George Ross now lives, 100 A...Wit: John Frohock,
Thos Polk. Rec. April term 1774.

Pp. 418-419: 16 Jan 1767, John Black of Meck., planter, to Henry
          E. McCulloh, for ₤ 36-5-0...137 A adj. Henry Hendry...
Wit: John Frohock, Thos Polk. Rec. April term 1774.

Pp. 420-421: 3 Feb 1767, Alexander Monteith of Rowan Co., to
          Henry E. McCulloh, for ₤ 44-16-0... 225 A adj. George
Cathey, Sharps Branch...Wit: John Frohock, William Frohock. Rec.
April term 1774.

Pp. 422-423: 16 Jan 1767, William Pickens of Meck., planter, to
          Henry E. McCulloh for ₤ 27-7-4...101 A...Wit: John
Frohock, Thos Polk. Rec. April term 1774.

Pp. 424-425: 15 Jan 1767, Jane Flanagan of Meck., planter, to
          Henry E. McCulloh, for ₤ 121-9-6...288 A on E side
McCalpins Creek...Wit: John Frohock, Thos Polk. Rec. April term
1774.

Pp. 426-430: 22 April 1767, John Russell of Rowan Co., to Robert
          Walker of Meck., for (lease s5, release ₤80)...
land above John Willsons Entry in the big Creek of Litle River
waters of Broad River, granted to sd. Russell by deed from Arthur
McClure, 27 Oct 1766...John Russell (Seal), Wit: Will: Reed,
Robt Campbl., Sam. Crawford. Prov. by Will Reed, July Term 1774.

Pp. 430-431: 5 Feb 1770, Thos Polk, Abm. Alexander and George
          Allen of Meck., and John Frohock of Rowan Co., to
Alexr. Martin of Rowan Co., for ₤ 1 proc. money...lot in Char-
lotte...Wit: Isaac Jetten, Robt Pown(?). Prov. by Isaac Jetten
July Court 1774.

Pp. 431-433: 7 June 1768, George Cathey, of Meck., planter, to
          William Willson of Meck., cooper, for ₤ 5 proc.
money...land on E side Catabo River on waters of Shugar Creek,
adj. Henry Walker, 300 A granted to sd. Cathey 27 Oct 1767...
George Cathey (+) (Seal), Wit: Jane Alexander, Jno McK. Alexander.
Rec. July Term 1774.

VOLUME 7

Pp. 433-435: 10 May 1773, Samuel Harris & wf Martha of Meck., to Andrew Miller of same, for L 350 proc. money...land conveyed to sd. Harris by Arthur Dobbs 24 June 1762, 453 A... Samuel Harris (Seal), Martha Harris (O) (Seal), Wit: James Harris, Alexander Phiney, James McCall. Prov. by James McCall, July Court 1774.

Pp. 436-438: 10 May 1773, Samuel Harris & wf Martha of Meck., to Andrew Miller of same, for L 170 proc. money...land conveyed to Harris by Agner Nash 5 Feb 1771, part of Tract # 2, 50 A...Saml Harris (Seal), Martha Harris (M) (Seal), Wit: Jams. Harris, Alexandr. Finney, Jams. McCall. Prov. by Jams Harris and Jams. McCall, July Court 1774.

Pp. 438-440: 5 June 1773, Hugh Carothers of Meck., to Thomas Polk of same, for L 300 proc. money...land granted to Alexr Dobbins 6 March 1754, and conveyed to sd. Carruthers 11 Feb 1763, 550 A...Hugh Carothers (C) (Seal), Wit: Jerom: McCafferty, Francis Ross. Prov. by Francis Ross, July Court 1774.

Pp. 440-441: 21 Aug 1772, William Cronical of Tryon Co., to Thomas Polk of Meck., for L 100...land on waters of Steel Creek, adj. John Henry, Samuel Knox, John Davies, 600 A...William Chronicill (Seal), Wit: William Patterson, James McKee. Prov. by Paterson, July Court 1774.

Pp. 441-443: 14 May 1773, Elijah Alexander of Meck., to Thomas Polk, for L 55 proc. money...132 A part of tract where sd. Alexander now lives, adj. Thomas Polk, Shugar Creek... Elijah Alexander (Seal), Wit: John Potts, Benjamin Alexander. (No rec. date).

Pp. 443-445: 14 May 1773, Henry E. McCullock to Thomas Polk, for s 5...53 A adj. Thomas Polks line and the Town land ...Wit: T Frohock, Benjn. Alexander. (No rec. date).

Pp. 445-447: 6 Nov 1772, Ezra Alexander of Meck., to Thomas Polk for L 55 proc. money...land on midel fork Sugar Creek adj. Arthur Alexander, Samuel McCleary, John Barnet, 100 A... granted to sd. Ezra 16 Dec 1769...Ezra Alexander (Seal), Wit: Wm Patterson, Joseph Nickelson. Prov. July Court 1774 by Wm Paterson.

Pp. 447-448: 20 July 1774, William Sterat of Meck., to Andrew Baxter of same, for L 45...land including the mouth of four mile Creek, 487 A granted 21 Dec 1763...Wiliam Sterret (W) (Seal), Wit: Nathaniel Cook (X), William Reed. Prov. by Wm Reed, July Court 1774.

Pp. 448-449: 30 July 1773, Brice Miller of Meck., to Andrew Baxter of same, for L 20 proc. money...land at the Indean line, John Bruster, 90 A granted to Brice Miller, part of 160 A ...Brice Miller (B) (Seal), Wit: John Baxter, Mary Linn. Prov. by John Baxter, July Court 1774.

Pp. 450-451: 23 July 1774, John Davies of Meck., planter, to Andrew Baxter, for L 80 proc. money...190 A granted to John Killian 13 Apr 1771, on the ridge between McMichals Creek and McCapins Creek adj. Baxter, Frohock, conveyed to John Davies by deed 27 Apr 1774...John Davies (Seal), Wit: Thomas Polk, Wm Reed. Prov. by Wm Reed, July Court 1774.

VOLUME 7

Pp. 451-453: 1 July 1774, James McCrakan of Meck., to David McCree of same, for Ł 200 proc. money...land on waters of Shugar Creek, 308 A, adj. Robert Elliot, McRee...James McCrakan (8) (Seal), Wit: John McClure (McCree?), Peter Johnston. Prov. by John McKee, July Court 1774.

25th Book

Pp. 454-455: 4 April 1777, Alexander Lewis of Meck., & wf Hannah to Benjamin Wallace, for Ł 74 NC money...land near Edward Givens, 300 A, granted to Alexander Lewis, 9 Apr 1753... Alexr Lewis (Seal), Hannah Lewis (X) (Seal), Wit: Thos Wallace, Benj. Lewis. Prov. by Thos Wallace, April Session 1778.

Pp. 455-457: 10 March 1777, John McKnit Alexander of Meck., to James Akin of same, for Ł 25...land adj. William Bigham, Samuel Bigam, granted to Robert Carruth 20 Oct 1765, conveyed to sd. Alexander 13 Aug 1772...John McKnit Alexander (Seal), Wit: Hez. Alexander, Jno Patterson. Prov. by Hez. Alexander Esqr, April Sess. 1778.

Pp. 457-459: 10 May 1773, Henry E. McCollok to Robert Arthur of sd. province, for Ł 15 proc. money...land adj. James Norris, William and Alexander and John Alen(?), 74 A... Wit: Thos Polk, Thos Frohock. Prov. by Thos Polk, April Sess. 1778.

Pp. 459-461: 18 Mar 1778, Thos Shields & wf Margret of Meck., to Henry Shool of same, for Ł 500 proc. money... land adj. McQueston, Saml Pickens, Joseph Paterson, 465 A... Thos Shields (Seal), Margret Shields (S) (Seal), Wit: John Grime, Saml Pickens. Prov. by Saml Pickens, April Sessn. 1778.

Pp. 461-463: 7 Oct 1777, John Henry of Meck., to Charles Cummine of same, for Ł 33 proc. money...land on waters of Clim Davies branch, granted to Walter Davies, 23 Dec 1768...179 A... John Henry (Seal), Wit: France Cumins, John Cummins. Prov. by Francis Cummins, April Session 1778.

Pp. 463-465: 11 Dec 1776, James McCall & wf Elizabeth to William McCall, for Ł 100 proc. money...182 A, part of Tract #2, on S side Goose Creek...James McCall (Seal), Wit: Joseph Harris, Francis McCall, Thomas Harris. Prov. by Thom Harris, April Session 1778.

Pp. 466-467: 19 April 1777, Samuel Bigham of Meck., to Alexander Porter, for Ł 45 proc. money...200 A on waters of Paw Creek, adj. George Cathey, James Sloan, granted to Samuel Bigham, 12 March 1774...Samuel Bigham (Seal), Wit: James McKee, William Porter. Ack. by grantor, April Sessn. 1778.

Pp. 467-468: 10 Feb 1778, Thomas Polk to Robert Grahm, for Ł 60 proc. money...land adj. William Wilson, James Wilson, John McElwee, 170 A...Thos Polk (Seal), Wit: Adam Alexander, Robt smith. Prov. by Adam Alexander Esqr., April Session 1778.

Pp. 468-470: 21 July 1777, Samuel Bigham, farmer, to John Bigham, planter, for Ł 40 proc. money...land adj. John Bigham, 41 A...Samuel Bigham (Seal), Wit: Andrew Bigham, Patrick Brown (S). Prov. by Patrick Brown, April Session 1778.

VOLUME 7

Pp. 470-472: 16 June 1773, George Alexander of Meck., to Sarah Alexander, for ₤ 20 proc. money...land granted from James Carter and Hugh Foster to Nathaneil Alexander Esqr by deed 29 March 1755, lot # 19 in West Square...George Alexander (Seal), Wit: Rebekah Walker, Robt Harris. Prov. by Robt Harris April sess 1778.

Pp. 472-473: 3 April 1778, Thomas Polk of Meck., to Joseph Galbreath, for ₤ 66 proc. money...land on Goss (sic) Creek, 55 A granted by Abner Nash 25 March 1772 to sd. Joseph Galbreath, and by Thos Polk 13 March 1775...Wit: Mathew Stewart, Eph Bravard. Prov. by Mathew Stewart, April Sess 1778.

Pp. 474-475: 16 Jan 1778, Benjamin Walace & wf Mary of Meck., to Robert Kerr, for ₤ 46 NC money...land on waters of Long Creek 125 A, granted by deed from Patrick Kerr & wf to Robert Kerr, 26 Sept 1772, and to Benjamin Wallace, 22 Jan 1773... Benjamin Walace (Seal), Mary Walace (M) (Seal), Wit: John Walace, John Carr. Prov. by John Carr, April Sess 1778.

Pp. 475-477: 10 Aug 1776, John Ford of Meck., to John Roberts of same, for ₤ 20 proc. money...land on ridge between McAlpins Creek and Gooss Creek adj. his own corner, Gov. Dobbs line, 150 A granted March 1775 to John Ford...John Foard (Seal), Wit: Zebulon Ford, John Wofice(?). Ack in open court April Sessn 1778.

Pp. 477-478: 10 Oct 1778, Robt Harris Esqr of Meck., to Thos Rodgers of same, Blacksmith, for ₤ 75...land on head waters of Muddey Creek, 35 A, land conveyed by Abner Nash 25 March 1775 to Andrew Greir, and to Robt Harris 27 March 1775...Robt Harris (Seal), Wit: James Black, Robert Harris, Jurat. (No rec. date).

Pp. 478-480: 13 March 1772, Abner Nash to Robert Freear, son of Richard Freear of Town of Halifax, for ₤ 20 proc. money, 91 A on waters of Clear Creek...A. Nash (Seal), Wit: M. Moore.

Pp. 481-483: 13 March 1773, Abner Nash to Robert Freear, son of Richard Freear, for ₤ 20 proc. money...land on S fork Rockey Creek adj. Diserts (Dysarts?) line, 75 A...Wit: M. Moore.

Pp. 483-485: 20 May 1773, Waightstill Avery of Meck., attorney at law, to William McCafferty and James Mccafferty of same, for ₤ 30 proc. money...1/2 of lot # 9 in Charlotte... Waightstill Avery (Seal), Wit: Joseph Moore, Robt Scott...Prov. by Robert ____, July Term 1778.

Pp. 485-486: 9 Jan 1778, Joseph Walace & wf Jean of Meck., to Arthur Starr of same, farmer, for ₤ 90...land adj. Gilmore, Wolfs, 116 A conveyed to sd. Joseph Wallace from John Wallace, 7 Jan 1775...Joseph Walace (Seal), Jean Walace (Seal), Wit: John Walace, John Cunaughy. Prov. by grantor in open court July 1778.

Pp. 486-488: 26 Sept 1777, Robert McKee of Meck., to Samuel McCleary of same, for ₤ 10...land on a branch of Bigg Sugar Creek on the Road from Charlotte to Cataba Ford, 20 A... Robt McKee (Seal), Wit: Ezek. Polk, Tho: Alexander. Prov. by Tho:

VOLUME 7

Alexander, 1778 (No term given.)

Pp. 488-489: 25 April 1777, William Hay and wf Rebeca of Meck., to William Porter Senr for Ł 50 proc. money...250 A on E side Catabo on S side of Paw Creek adj. John Giles, part of 500 A, granted to Samuel Bigham 21 Dec 1763...Wiliam Hay (Seal), Rebecah Hay (Seal), Wit: Samuel Bigham, Saml McCombe, Alexander Porter. Prov. by Saml Bigham, July 1778.

Pp. 490-491: 14 July 1778, John Wood of Meck., to John McCreaven of Rowan Co., for Ł 170...land on waters of Berds Branch near Samples line, 75 A...John Woods (Seal), Lattes Woods (Seal), Wit: Sam Martin. Ack in open court by grantor, July term 1778.

Pp. 491-493: 14 July 1778, John Woods of Meck., to John McCreaven of Rowan Co., for Ł 170...land on waters of McCalpins and Four Mile Creek including Erwins improvement, adj. John Osburn, 200 A bearing date 20 May 1772 (grant?)...John Wood (Seal), Lettes Wood (Seal), Wit: Saml Martin. Ack in open court by grantor July Term 1778

Pp. 493-494: 5 July 1778, Patrick McDonald of Meck., to John Garison of same, for Ł 20 NC money...lots #206-335-336 on N side Tryon St., near an acre and a half...Patrick McDonald (X) (Seal), Wit: Robt Hope, John Allen. Prov. by John McDonald, July 1778.

Pp. 495-496: 2 April 1770, John Phifer of Meck., to David Wilson cooper, for Ł 15 proc. money...200 A on both sides Cane Creek between John Currey, and Moses Shelby...John Phifer (Seal), Wit: James Walace, Archbald Huston. Prov. by Archbald Huston, July term 1778.

Pp. 496-498: 15 July 1778, James Huston and Isbel Stewart Exrs. of L. W. & T. of Robert Stewart deceased, to William Mathews, for Ł 150...land on both sides of Glady Fork of 12 Mile Creek adj. above land survey'd for William Legat, 150 A, originally granted 13 Oct 1765...James Huston (Seal), Isbel Stewart (Seal), Wit: Henry Downs, Alexander Inglis, Mathew Paton. Prov. by Henry Downs, July Term 1778.

Pp. 498-500: 27 May 1778, Thos Polk, Eph Bravard, and James Jack of Meck., to Patrick McDonald, for Ł 12 proc. money ...lot #104-335-336 on N side Tryon St...Wit: Dun Ocheltree. Prov. by Thos Polk, July Term 1778.

Pp. 500-502: 22 June 1778, William McElwee, eldest son and Heir of John McElwee, carpenter, to James McElwee, brother of sd. William, for Ł 50...70 A, part of 80 A granted by deed to John McElwee decd, by H. E. McCollock 24 Feb 1767...William McElwee (Seal), Wit: Andrew McRee, Robert Graham. Prov. by Robert Graham, July 1778.

Pp. 503-505: ___ 1777, John Ford of Meck., planter, and wf Cathrean to Hugh Caragan of same, for Ł 27-10-0 proc. money... land on waters of McAupins Creek adj. John Robnette, Mathew Walker, granted to Ford 30 Jan 1773...John Ford (Seal), Catherine Ford (Seal), Wit: William Morris, Joseph Robb. (No rec. date.)

VOLUME 7

Pp. 506-508: 7 Oct 1778, John McCall & wf Jean of Meck., to William Watson of same, for ___...75 A on waters of Clear Creek...John McCall (Seal), Jean McCall (1) (Seal), Wit: Thos Ree, Robt Donelson, William Wylie. (No rec. date).

Pp. 508-510: 27 Aug 1774, James Wallace of Meck., to Zaccheus Wilson of same, for Ł 3 proc. money...28 A part of grant to James Wallace adj. David Rese...James Wallace (Seal), Jean Wallace (Seal), Wit: Thos Harris, David Wilson. Prov. by David Wilson, July Term 1778.

Pp. 510-512: 15 April 1778, Adam Carruth of Tryon Co., planter, to James Reed of same, for Ł 273...200 A on waters of Sugar Creek including Adam Carruths improvement, on the line between Adam Carruth and John Carruth, granted to Francis Beaty 23 Apr 1762 and # 64...Adam Carruth (Seal), Elizabeth Carruth (Seal), Wit: John Carruth, John Slone. Prov. by John Carruth July term 1778.

Pp. 512-512B: 19 May 1773, Abraham Alexander Esqr. of Meck., to William McCafferty of same, for Ł 30 proc. money... lot #10 in Charlotte...Abraham Alexander (Seal), wit: Waightstill Avery. Prov. by Avery July term 1778.

Pp. 512B-513: 10 July 1778, Thos Polk, Ephm Bravard and William Paterson of Meck., to Patrick McDonald, for Ł 15 proc. money...lots #202 and 203 in Charlotte on W side Tryon St. Wit: Andrew Cathey, James Armstrong. Prov. July term 1778 by Thos Polk.

Pp. 514-515: 16 June 1778, Thos Polk, Ephm Bravard and James Jack of Meck., for Ł 12 to Patrick Mcdoneld...lots 46, 47 on W side Tryon St., Wit: James McRee, _____. Prov. July term 1778 by Thos Polk.

Pp. 515-517: 22 June 1778, Thos Polk, Eph Bravard, James Jack of Meck., to William Davidson of Rowan Co., for Ł 60... lots # 30-32-52 in Charlotte, Wit: James McKee, ____. Ack. in court July term 1778.

Pp. 517-519: 10 July 1778, John Ritchey of Meck., planter, to William Ritchey of same, for Ł 15 proc. money...land on E side Catabo River adj. McCord, half of 400 A granted to William Wilson 28 Feb 1754, conveyed to Benjamin Hardin, then to Joseph Killer(?)...John Ritchey (~~111~~)(Seal), Wit: James Nealy, John Richey. (No rec. date).

Pp. 519-521: 14 July 1778, John McCall and wf Jannet to William Cuthbertson of same, for Ł 30 proc. money...92 A on S side Crocket Creek...John McCall (Seal), Wit: Samuel Montgeromy, George Finley (J). Prov. by John McCall, July Term 1778.

Pp. 521-523: 14 July 1778, Christofer Irwin of Meck., to John Swan of same, for Ł 45 proc. money...land on both sides McMichaels Creek adj. John Swan, Petter Johnston, granted to sd. Irwin by patent 105 A, 30 Jan 1773...Christopher Irwin (M) (Seal), Wit: Sam Martin. Prov. by Irwin in Court, July Term 1778.

Finis of book No. 25. by Robt Harris register in 1778.
(END OF VOLUME 7)

VOLUME 8

(N. B. The first few pages of this volume are badly mutilated.)

Pp. 1-3: 5 Feb 1771, Abner Nash & wf Justina to Burdy Howel, for ₤ 10 proc. money...68 A...Wit: Clement Nash. Prov. by Clement Nash, 9 Feb 1771.

Pp. 3-5: 5 Feb 1771, Abner Nash and wf Justina for ₤ 26 proc. money, to John Davis...38 A in the welsh track...Wit: Clement Nash. Prov. by Clement Nash 9 Feb 1771.

Page 6: Blank

Pp. 7-9: 24 Apr 17__, James Bigger to Matthew Bigger, for ₤ 40... 320 A on E side Cataba River, above the mouth of Crowders Creek granted 21 Sept 17_3...James Bigger (Seal), Wit: William Elliott, Jurat, Mathew Knox, Wm Kerr. (No rec. date).

Pp. 9-14: 13 Jan 1767, Selwyn to William Wylie of Meck., planter, ...land on waters of Sugar Creek adj. Alexander Erwin, 125 A Wit: John Frohoc, Thos Polk. (No rec. date).

Pp. 14-16: 26 March 1772, Robert Harris Junr & wf Martha to Andrew Miller, late of Cumberland Co., Pa., for ₤ 20 proc. money...225 A on watters of reedy Creek adj. Gov. Dobbs, granted 1771 from Selwyn, adj. David Sloughs and Tract #2...Robert Harris Jnr (Seal), Martha Harris (Seal), Wit: William Miller, Robert Robison, Robert Harris Senr. Prov. Jany Term 1773 by Robert Harris Esqr.

Pp. 16-19: 23 Oct 1772, Moses Alexander of Meck., & wf Sarah to Alexander F. Phiney of same, for ₤ 60 proc. money... 83 A on a branch of Clear Creek, sold by Gov. Dobbs & wf to sd. Alexander...Moses Alexander (Seal), Sarah Alexander (Seal), Wit: Abraham Alexander, Ezra Alexander. Ack. in court by Moses Alexander Jany. term 1773.

Pp. 19-21: 6 Feb 1772, Abraham Miller of Meck., to John Frohoc of Rowan Co., for ₤ 100 proc. money...241 A...Abraham Miller (Seal), Wit: Hez. Alexander Jurat, John Cowan. Prov. by Hez. Alexander, Jan. term 1773.

Pp. 21-23: 8 Dec 1772, Robert Barnet of Meck., to Thomas Polk for ₤ 30 proc. money...200 A by deed from H. E. McCulloh 20 Feb 1767...Robert Barnet (Seal), Wit: Alexander Eakin, Moses Craig, Jurat. Rec. Jan. term 1773.

Pp. 23-24: 22 Oct 1772, Samuel McCleary of Meck., Blacksmith to Thomas Polk of same, for ₤ 10 proc. money...60 A... Samuel McCleary (Seal), Wit: John Dunn, Jurat., Jeremiah McCafferty. Rec. Jan. term 1773.

Pp. 25-26: 20 Oct 1772, John Davis & wf Elizabeth of Meck., to Thomas Polk, for ₤ 100 proc. money...413 A, part of two grants to James Davis 16 Nov 1763 and John Davis 1762...John Davis (Seal), Elizabeth Davis (1) (Seal), Wit: Wm Patteson, John McGinty, Jurat. Rec. Jan. term 1773.

Pp. 27-28: 22 Oct 1772, Samuel McCleary of Meck., Blacksmith, to Thomas Polk for ₤ 200 proc. money...100 A...Wit: John Dunn, Jurat., Jeremh. McCafferty. Rec. Jan. term 1773.

VOLUME 8

Pp. 29-31: 21 Jan 1767, David Davis of Meck., planter, to Henry E. McCulloh, for ₺ 63-17-6...240 A. Rec. Jan. term 1773, Wit: John Frohock.

Pp. 31-34: 14 Jan 1767, James Tate of Meck., to Henry E. McCulloh for ₺ 59-10-0...220 A including the plantation & improvements...Wit: John Frohock, Thomas Polk. Rec. Jan. term 1773.

Pp. 34-37: 10 Jan 1767, John Darmon of Meck., to Henry E. McCulloh for ₺ 37-7-8...land on McMichaels Creek including plantation and improvements...144 A...Wit: John Frohock, Thomas Polk. Rec. Jan Court 1773.

Pp. 37-39: 23 Jan 1767, Peter Garrison of Meck., to Henry E. McCulloh, for ₺ 42...land adj. Arthur Garies(?) corner 163 A...Wt: John Frohock, John Fifer. Rec. Jan. 1773.

Pp. 40-42: 15 Jan 1767, Arthur Alexander of Meck., to Henry E. McCulloh for ₺ 65 proc. money...268 A...Wit: John Frohock, Thomas Polk. Rec. Jan. term 1773.

Pp. 42-44: 15 Jan 1767, Joseph Lee of Meck., planter, to Henry E. McCulloh for ₺ 48 proc. money...185 A...Wit: John Frohock. Rec. Jan 22d 1773.

Pp. 45-47: 15 Jan 1767, Jonathan Buckalew to Henry E. McCulloh for ₺ 44-13-6 proc. money...land on both sides McCapins Creek...Jonathan Bucklew (O) (Seal), Wit: John Frohock, Thomas Polk. Rec. Jan. term 1773.

Pp. 47-50: 12 Jan 1767, George Allen of Meck., planter, to Henry E. McCulloh, for ₺ 97-15-6 21(?) A Wit: John Frohock, Thomas Polk.

Pp. 50-52: 9 Dec 1772, David Garison of Prov. of South Carolina, Granville(?) Co., to John Wire(?), land on W side Abraham Alexanders Mill Creek adj. Alexander Sterat, William Wilson, John Mal___, 257 A...David Garison, Isabela Garison (O); Wit: ___Blyth, ___Garrison. (No rec. date).

Pp. 52-55: 10 Jan 1767, Robert Parks of Meck., planter, to Henry E. McCulloh, for ₺ --...462 A...Wit: John Frohock, Thomas Polk. Rec. Jan. Court 1773.

Pp. 55-57: 12 Jan 1767, John Carson of Meck., planter, to Henry E. McCulloh for ₺ 54-7-6...land adj. John Tygart... John Carson (O) (Seal), Wit: John Ffrohock, Thomas Polk. Rec. Jan. term 1773.

Pp. 58-60: 17 May 1765, Thomas McCall of Meck., to Henry E. McCulloh for ₺ 117-17-1 proc. money...485 A...Wit: J. Frohock, Jurat. Rec. Jan. term 1773.

Pp. 60-65: 9 Jan 1767, George Augustus Selwyn to John Allen of Meck., planter, for ₺ 50 sterling...land on waters of Sugar Creek adj. John McK. Alexander, Joseph Sample...Wit: Thomas Parfer(?), John Frohock. Rec. Jan. term 1773.

Pp. 66-68: 5 Feb 1771, Abner Nash & wf Justina to Thomas Shelby for ₺ 18 proc. money...50 A in Tract #2, adj. sd. Shelby...Wit: Clement Nash. Prov. 9 Feb 1771.

VOLUME 8

Pp. 69-70: 21 Jan 1773, Elijah Davis & wf Elizabeth of Meck., to Francis Herrin of same, Blacksmith, for ₺ 5 proc. money...100 A granted to David Davis, by Selwyn 17 Jan 1767, and conveyed to sd. Elijah Davis by deed 12 March 1770...Elijah Davis (Seal), Elizabeth Davis (X) (Seal), Wit: Robert Paterson, Robert Campbell, Jurat. Rec. Jan. term 1773.

Pp. 71-72: 10 June 1769, Moses Alexander & wf Sara to Samuel Smith of Meck., for ₺ 30 proc. money...76 A on both sides of Duck Creek...Moses Alexander (Seal), Sarah Alexander (Seal), Wit: Dan Alexander, William Blair. Ack in open court by grantor Jan. 1773.

Pp. 72-73: John Saddler for ₺ 40 proc. money of NC to David Keneday, 70 A on waters of Shugar Creek adj. James Kennedy...John Saddler (Seal), Janet Sadler (/) (Seal), Wit: Joseph Moore, Jurat. James McColoh. Prov. by Moore Jan. term 1773.

Pp. 73-74: 29 July 1772, James Neisbett & wf Ann of Tryon Co., to Hugh Houston of Meck., for ₺ 20 proc. money... land on waters of Twelve Mile Creek adj. Jas. Linn, Francis McCall, 200 A granted to sd. James Neisbett 25 Sept 1766...James Neisbett (C4) (Seal), Ann Neisbett (N) (Seal), Wit: Samuel Neisbett, Thomas Penny (X), Jerema Neisbett, Jurat. Prov. by Jeremiah Neisbett, Jan. term 1773.

Pp. 75-76: 15 Jan 1773, Samuel McCord Senior of Barkly Co., S.C., to James McCord Jr. of same, for ₺ 20 proc. money... 100 A on waters of Shugar Creek, adj. Lee's corner...James McCord (Seal), Wit: John Moore, Jurat; Joseph Beley. Prov. Jan. term 1773.

Pp. 77-78: 3 Apr 1771, Joseph Lee of Meck., to Nathaniel Irwin for ₺ 40 proc. money...land in Meck., on Garisons Creek, adj. James McCord, John Henry, 185 A, by deed from McCulloh 14 Jan 1776 (sic)...Josh. Lee (Seal); Thomas Polk, Jurat, Alex. Stuart (A). Prov. by Polk Jan. term 1773.

Pp. 78-80: 20 Nov 1772, Robert Harris Junr & wf Martha of Meck., to Robert Harris Senr, for ₺ 50 proc. money...land on Duch Buffalo Creek, conveyed from Robert Harris Eqr. & wf Francis of Anson Co., to sd. Robt Harris Jun, 12 June 1762...Robert Harris (Seal), Martha Harris (Seal), Wit Robert Robinson, Jurat, Wa. Cowdon. Rec. Jan. term 1773.

Pp. 80-82: 18 Jan 1773, Robert McCord of Meck., planter, to James McCord of same, for ₺ 34 proc. money...land adj. John Richey, Charles Mason(?), on Paw Creek, 150 A, conveyed from Francis Beaty to Robt McCord, 4 & 5 July 1766, granted to sd. Beaty, 21 Dec 1763...Robert McCord (Seal), Wit: Sam Martin, Joseph Galbreath. Ack. in open court by McCord, Jan. term 1773.

Pp. 82-83: 10 Sept 1772, Archibald Gilleland of York Co., Pa., to John Clark of York Co., Pa., for ₺ 40 Pa. money...land near a springhead of Paw Creek adj. Hugh Berry, formerly surveyed for James McConnel, originally granted to Francis Beaty, 15 Feb 1764, conveyed to Gilleland 24 & 25 March 1765...Archibald Gilleland (Seal), Wit: James Pally, Robt Kennaday Clark, Jurat. James Leeper. Prov. by Robert Kenneday Clark, Jan. term 1773.

VOLUME 8

Pp. 84-86: 4 Nov 1772, Alexander Lewis of Meck., to Hanah Miller, the wife of John Miller of same, for ₺ 28...land adj. E side Cataba River, Alexander Caths, 315 A, granted to James Armor by Lease and Release 16 July 1752, it being the plantation the sd. Hanna Miller now lives on, also a tract adjoining it and the mill place 212 A granted to Andrew Armour by patent 10 Apr 1761, and conveyed to John Miller...Alexander Lewis (Seal), Hanna Lewis (Seal), Wit: Richard Berry, Jurat; Joseph Keller. Prov. Jan. term 1773.

Pp. 86-88: 18 Jan 1773, Samuel Wilson of Meck., to Hannah Miller, wife and relict of John Miller decd., for ₺ 20 proc. money...land granted to James Armour by L & R 16 July 1752, to John Miller by L & R __ Aug 1757, 315 A, also 215 A adj. to it (appears to be same tracts as preceding deed!)...Saml Willson (Seal), Margret Wilson (Seal), Wit: Richd Berry, Jurat, Robert Erwin. Rec. Jan. term 1773.

Pp. 88-90: 6 Nov 1772, John Wilson of Meck., farmer, to Samuel Blyth of same, for ₺ 75...land on N side Cataba River adj. Richd Graham, James Armour, Geo Renix, Malion(?) Hammilton, including ye place on which Adnw Arwin did live, 400 A, granted to Thomas Price 3 Oct 1754, and conveyed by Andrew Irwin to John Wilson 12 Nov 1771...John Wilson (Seal), Wit: Thos Polk, Andrew Greer, Jurat. Rec. Jan. term 1773.

Pp. 90-92: 5 Feb 1771, Abner Nash & wf Justina to John Powel of Meck., planter, for ₺ 10 proc. money...land on S side Rockey River...50 A...Wit: Clement Nash. Prov. 9 Feb 1771.

Pp. 93-95: 5 Feb 1771, Abner Nash & wf Justina to John Powell, for ₺ 10 proc. money...70 A on N side Muddy Creek...Wit: Clement Nash. Prov. 9 Feb 1771.
Finis.
End of Book 26.

Pp. 96-100: Blank.

Page 101: 27th Book (also a plat or beginning of a plat of land of John Knox).

Pp. 102-103: 31 July 1773, Richard Stevenson & wf Hannah of Meck., to John Buchanan of same, for ₺ 25 proc. money...land granted to sd. Richard Stevenson 28 Oct 1765 adj. his own line, Mr. Joyes barony, at a corner of hopewell meetinghouse land... Richard Stevenson (Seal), Hannah Stevenson (8) (Seal), Wit: Richard Barry, Samuel Buchanan. Prov. by Richard Barry, July Court 1774.

Pp. 103-105: 28 Feb 1771, Thomas Wiggins to William Haggans and James Huston, for ₺ 20...land on back Creek or Six Mile Branch of Twelve Mile Creek, granted to B. Lowery 6 Apr 1765, conveyed to James Brice 19 July 1765, then to Wiggins 29 Sept 1765 ...Thomas Wiggins (Seal), Prov. by Joseph Kenady, July Court. (Wit not listed).

Pp. 105-107: 2 July 1774, Daniel Hay of Meck., to Joseph Kenedy Esq., of same, for ₺ 30 proc. money...land granted to Thos Polk and Abraham Alexander by deed from Selwyn 15 Jan 1767 ...Daniel Henry (Seal), Margret Hay (Seal), Wit: Wit: Samuel Kenedy, Robert Quarel (X). Prov. by Quarel, July Court 1774.

Pp. 107-109: 20 July 1774, John Price & wf Mary of Meck., to Isaac Price of same, for L 30 proc. money...land on E side Catauba River, adj. Isaac Prices plantation, granted to John Price 9 Nov 1764...John Price (Seal), Mary Price (O) (Seal), Wit: William Bamel(?), Benjamin Onnan. Ack in open court July Court 1774.

Pp. 109-110: 5 Dec 1772, John Jack of Meck., to Samuel Roach of same, for L 20 proc. money...land on both sides Sugar Creek adj. Elijah Alexander, John Davis, granted 24 Dec 1770... John Jack (Seal), Wit: Samuel Jack, William Reed. Ack by John Jack, July Court 1774.

Pp. 111-112: 23 Jan 1773, James McCord Jr. of Meck., to James Sawers, for L 30 proc. money...land on waters of Shugar Creek, adj. the land where sd. McCord formerly lived, 100 A granted to James McCord and from him to sd. McCord Junr...James McCord (Seal), Wit: John Pattison, Thos Polk. Prov. by John Pateson, July Court 1774.

Pp. 113-114: 5 Dec 1772, Samuel Jack of Meck., to Samuel Roach of same, for L 20 proc. money...land adj. John Jack, part of a larger tract conveyed to sd. Samuel Jack by deed from Thomas Polk 10 Aug 1769, 88 A...Samuel Jack, Wit: John Jack, Will Reed. Prov. by David Reed., July Court 1774.

Pp. 114-116: 25 June 1774, James McCall & wf Elizabeth of Gradvill (Granville) County, S. C., to Hugh McQuown of Meck., for L 65 proc. money...184 A on Reedy Creek on McKinley branch, deeded to Thomas McCall from Selwyn 15 May 1765...James McCall (Seal), Elizabeth McCall (E) (Seal), Wit: Thomas McCall, Nathan Orr. Prov. by Nathan Orr, July Court 1774.

Pp. 117-118: 13 Apr 1774, Thomas Polk, Abraham Alexander and Jeremiah McCafferty of Meck., to John Patterson & Will Patterson junr of same, for L 2 proc. money...lots # 197 & 194 on N side Tryon St., in Charlotte...Wit: Is. Alexander, David McRee. Prov. April Court 1774 by David McRee.

Pp. 119-121: 28 May 17 73, George Neel of Meck., planter, to Oughtry McKibbin of same, for L 80 proc. money... land on Sedar fork of Twelve Mile Creek, granted to John Hagins by Gov. Thomas Boone of South Carolina, 20 Dec 1762, and conveyed by sd. Hagans & wf Elizabeth his wife 19 Obr 1766...George Neel (Seal), Wit: Wm Haggans, Archb. Crockett, Robt Stuart, Jur. Prov. by Robert Stuart, April Court 1774.
(For an explanation of the grant from South Carolina, see "Some South Carolina Land Grants in North Carolina," in The North Carolina Genealogical Society Journal, Vol. I, No. 4 (Oct. 1975)

Pp. 121-123: 23 Apr 1772, Thos Polk, Abraham Alexander & Robt Ellot of Meck., to Marry Curran of same, for s 20 proc. money, lot # 91 on W side Traid St., in Charlotte...Wit: Adam Alexander, Will Patteson. Prov. by Adam Alexander April Court 1774.

Pp. 123-125: 10 Oct 1773, Thos Polk, Abm Alexander, & Jmh. McCafferty of Meck., to William Patteson of same, for L 5 proc. money...lots # 135 & 145 on Traid St., in Charlotte... Wit: James Foster, Saml Jack. Prov. by Foster April Court 1774.

VOLUME 8

Pp. 125-127: 26 Nov 1773, Robt Ellot & wf Martha of Meck., to Thomas Polk & Abrm. Alexander, for ₺ 20 proc. money... lot # 19 on N side Traid St., by deed from Selwyn to sd. Polk & Alexander...Robt elliot (Seal), Martha Elliott (N) (Seal), Wit: Wm Pattesson, Will Elliott. Prov. by Will Patteson, April Court 1774.

Pp. 127-129: 29 Nov 1773, Thomas Polk, Abraham Alexander & Jeremiah (McCafferty) all of Meck., to Wm Patteson of Charlotte Town, for ₺ 19 proc. money...lot where on his house is now built...Wit: Dun Ocheltree, Hugh Polloch. Prov. by Pollock April Term 1774.

Pp. 130-132: 1 Feb 1772, Thomas Polk, Abraham Alexander and Robt Elliot of Meck., to Mary Couran of same, for s 30 proc. money...lot # 83 in Charlotte...Wit: Adam Alexander, William Patesson. Prov. by Alexander April Court 1774.

Pp. 132-134: 18 Aug 1773, Thomas Polk, Abraham Alexander and Jeremiah McCafferty of Meck., to David McRee of same, for s 10 proc. money...lot # 28 on N side Traid St in Charlotte. Wit: John Brown Skrimshire, Wm Little. Prov. by Wm Little, April Court 1774.

Pp. 135-137: 24 Nov 1773, Thomas Frohock Esqr. of Roan Co., to Wm Patteson of Meck., for ₺ 15 proc. money... lot # 17 on W side Tryon St. in Charlotte, Wit: Thomas Polk, Henry Verner. Prov. by Col. Thomas Polk, April Court 1774.

Pp. 137-138: 19 Apr 1774, David Kenedy of Meck., to Robert Mountgomery of same, for ₺ 28 proc. money...land on waters of Sugar Creek, 106 A, granted to sd. Kenedy 22 Dec 1768...David Kenedy (Seal), Martha Kenedy (M) (Seal), Wit: Will Berryhill, John Parker. Prov. by William Berryhill, April Court 1774.

Pp. 138-140: 17 April 1771, Thomas McClure & wf Agness of Meck., to Robt McCleary of same, for ₺ 30 proc. money... land on branches of Mallard Creek adj. Parker, Russell, McClure, 200 A granted to Thomas Boal 22 Dec 1768, and conveyed by his L. W. & T. to Thomas McClure & John Boal...Thos McClure (Seal), Agness McClure (A) (Seal), John Cole (Seal), Margaret Bole (M) (Seal), Wit: Will Alexander, David Robinson. Prov. by David Robinson, April term 1774.

Pp. 140-142: 30 Jan 1773, Robert Parks & wf Marry of Meck., to Garret Wilson of same, for ₺ 133 proc. money...200 A on waters of McCalpins Creek, and waters of Camples Creek, adj. Ezekiah Wallace & Henry Mitchel...Robt Parks (Seal), Mary Parks (M) (Seal), Wit: Sam Martin, Hez. Alexander. Prov. April term 1774 by Samuel Martin.

Pp. 143-144: 5 July 1773, Isaiah Parker & wf Katherine of Meck., farmer, to William McClure of same, for ₺ 12 proc. money...300 A granted by deed from John Camble to sd. Parker, 20 Jan 1767, 16 A (part of 300 A)...Isaiah Parker (I) (Seal), Katherine Parker (X) (Seal), Wit: Robt Crocket, Jno McK. Alexander. Prov. by Alexander, April term 1774.

Pp. 145-147: 2 Jan 1773, Thomas Black and Josiah Black, both of Roan Co., to Archibald Henerson (sic) of Meck., for ₺ 210...land bequeathed to sd. Thomas and Josiah by will their father John Black, 300 A, granted to Peter Ellot, conveyed to George Renex 13 April 1742, then to John Black 3 Oct 1754... John Black, Elener Black (X), Josiah Black, Jean Black (I), Wit: John Black, Elizabeth Oglethorpe (X), Mat McClure. Prov. by John Black, April Court 1774.

Pp. 147-149: 1 Dec 1773, John Lucky & wf Mary of Meck., to George Findly of same, for L 100 proc. money...168 A on S side Caldwells Creek...John Lucky (Seal), Mary Lucky (O) (Seal), Wit: John McCracken, wamuel Montgomery. Prov. by Montgomery April term 1774.

Pp. 149-151: 4 April 1772, Hezekiah Alexander of Meck., to James Alexander of Cecil Co., Md., for L 100 proc. money... land on both sides Long Creek adj. John McNitt Alexander, 370 A, conveyed to sd. Haz. Alexander 23 April 1771...Hezekiah Alexander (Seal), Wit: Abrm Alexander, W. Avery, Robt Marin. Ack in open court, April Court 1774.

Pp. 152-153: 27 Dec 1770, George Denny & wf Jean of Tryon Co., NC, to Frances Baity of Meck., for L 165 proc. money...tracts in Meck (1) on N S Catawba one or two miles above Leepers or McDowels Creek, 175 A, granted to Robert Renex 30 Sept 1749, and conveyed to sd. Denney 7 Sept 1756 (2) land on E side Catawba, 150 A granted to sd. Denney __ Dec 1770, 375 A... George Denney (G) (Seal), Jean Denney (Seal), Wit: John Smith, Mat McClure. Prov. by McClure, April term 1774.

Pp. 154-155: 21 April 1773, Richard Stillwell to William Smith, for L 29 proc. money...58 A in Tract #2...Richard Stillwell (2) (Seal), Margret Stilwell (M) (Seal), Wit: Joseph Harris Jur., John Robinet. Prov. by Joseph Harris, April term 1774.

Pp. 156-157: 18 Apr 1774, Jacob Secris & wf Barbra of Meck., to James Duglas of same, for L 60 proc. money...land adj. Donalsons line, John Sloan, Benjabin Lowre, on Courtneys branch, 200 A, granted to Wm Loftin 13 Oct 1765...Jacob Secris (N) (Seal), Barbra sacris (X) (Seal), Wit: John Howey, Jacob Gray. Prov. by Jacob Gray, April Court 1774.

Pp. 158-160: 3 June 1773, James Ormond of Meck., to James Witherspoon of same, for L 30 proc. money...land on waters of McCappains Creek, adj. Dermond, granted to James Ormond 4 May 1769, 250 A...James Ormond (Seal), Wit: Thos Polk, Saml Blyth. Rec. Apl Court, 1774, prov. by Thomas Polk.

Pp. 160-163: 14 July 1773, William Booth & wf Martha of Meck., to Daniel England of same, Millwright, for L 69 proc. money...214 A on both sides Coddle Creek, granted to Wm Booth by deed from Gov. Dobbs 22 Jan 1764...Wm Booth (J) (Seal), Matthew Booth (B) (Seal), Wit: Smith, George Alexander,Jur. Prov. by Alexander April term 1774.

Pp. 163-165: 20 Apr 1774, Hugh Barnet of Meck., to Andrew Neel of same, for L 19 s 5 proc. money...part of a track on waters of 12 Mile Creek adj. James McClure, 200 A, granted to Barnet by deed from Zebulon Alexander 22 Oct 1768...Hugh Barnet (Seal), Elizabeth Barnet (C) (Seal), Wit: Sam Martin. Ack. in open court, April Term 1774.

VOLUME 8

Pp. 166-167: 18 Dec 1769, John Mitchell & wf Elizabeth of Salisbury, to James Barr of Meck., for Ł 55 proc. money... land on waters of Rocky River...Wit: Samuel Pickens, James Wishart. Rec. April Term, prov. by Samuel Pickens.

Pp. 168-169: 19 Apr 1774, Abraham Miller & wf Jannet of Meck., to John Woods of same, for Ł 35 NC money...200 A on waters of McCapins Creek and four mile Creek including Irvins improvements, adj. William Black, granted to sd. Miller 20 May 1772...Abraham Miller (Seal), Jennet Miller (8) (Seal), Wit: Adgin Pucon(?). Rec. April term 1774.

Pp. 169-172: 18 Jan 1774, Ebenezer Newton & wf Elizabeth of Meck., to Robt Phillips of same, for Ł 200...243 A granted to John Selwil (Selwyn?)...adj. David Garrisons, John McElwees, on waters of Sugar Creek, also adj. George Allon, near the race paths...Ebenezer Newton (Seal), Elizabeth Newton (O) (Seal), Wit: Hez: Alexander, James Wilson, Willm. Alexander. Prov. by Hez. Alexander, April Court 1774.

Pp. 172-174: 25 May 1773, John Flanikin of Meck., to Hezr. Alexander of same, for Ł 70 proc. money...land conveyed to John Flaniken by deed 14 Jan 1767, by Selwyn...John Fleniken (Seal), Wit: Robt Maclain, Henry Parson. Prov. by Flanihan, April term 1774.

Pp. 174-177: 19 Apr 1773, John Davis & wf Mary & Moses Davis & wf Jean of Cravan Co., South Carolina, to Robert Davis, of Meck., for Ł 100 proc. money...land adj. Beards, on both sides Waxhaw Creek, 380 A, granted 12 Sept 1752...John Davis (Seal), Mary Davis (Seal), Moses Davis (Seal), Jean Davis (Seal), Wit: George Davis, John Pickens, John Davis. Prov. by John Pickens April term 1774.

Pp. 177-180: 10 Nov 1773, David Wilson & wf Jean of Meck., to Stephen Alexander of same, for Ł 40 proc. money... land on W side Caudle Creek, adj. Frohock...David Wilson (Seal), Jean Wilson (Seal), Wit: John Hamilton, Mar__ _____. Prov. by John Hamilton, July Court 177_.

Pp. 180-182: 21 July 1774, Margaret Donaldson of Meck., to William Baird of same, ...land on E side Catawba River above Carters and Bighams, 300 A...Margret Donaldson (X) (Seal) Wit: James Stafford, William Barnet. Ack in open court July court 1774.

Pp. 182-184: 1 Feb 1770, Thomas Polk, Abrm Alexander & George Allen to James Kerr of Roan Co., for s 30 proc. money... lot # 98 in Charlotte...Wit: Isaac Jitton, Robt Burns. Prov. by Burns, 8 April 1770 before Richard Henderson.
       Book No. 27th

Pp. 185-188: Blank

Pp. 189-190: (these pages are quite badly torn and fragmentary; contain a deed from Abner Nash & wf Justina to John _____).

Pp. 191-193: 5 March 1772, Abner Nash & wf Justina to Henry Talley of Meck., for s 10 proc. money...70 A on N

VOLUME 8

side Rocky River...Wit: R Smith. Prov. by Robt Smith (No date).

Pp. 194-196: 25 March 1772, Abner Nash & wf Justina to Thomas Hall of Meck., for d 4 proc. money...15 A on waters of Duck Creek...Wit: R. Smith, Jurat. Prov. by Robt Smith (No date).

Pp. 197-199: 25 March 1772, Abner Nash to Peter Kizer of Meck., 30 A on N side Rocky River, for L 3 proc. money... Prov. by Robt Smith (No date).

Pp. 200-202: 25 March 1772, Abner Nash to Francis Glass of Meck., for s 25 proc. money...22 A...Wit: Robt Smith. (No rec or prov. date).

Pp. 203-205: 12 Jan 1767, Robert Leeper & wf Katrin of Meck., for L 40 proc. money, pd. by John Buchannan...350 A on W side Cataba River on Mill Creek, granted to sd. Robert Leeper, and adj. land said Leeper sold to William McCulloh... Robert Leeper (Seal), Katrin Leeper (K) (Seal), Wit: Robert Johnson, Andrew Armor. Prov. by Andrew Armor (No date).

Pp. 205-207: 15 Sept 1772, William McCulloh of Meck., to Daniel OCain, for L 10 proc. money...lot # 67 on E side Tryon St., ½ acre...William McCulloh (Seal), Wit: Thos Polk, Jno Paterson. Prov. by Paterson (No rec. date).

Pp. 208-210: 25 March 1772, Abner Nash to Peter Kyzer, for s 15 proc. money...33 A on a branch of Rocky River...Wit: R Smith. Prov. by Robt Smith. (No date).

Pp. 211-213: 25 March 1772, Abner Nash to John Morrison of Meck., for s 50 proc. money...41 A on Reedy Creek adj. Abner Windes(?)...Wit: R. Smith. Prov. by Robert Smith (No date).

Pp. 214-216: 25 March 1772, Abner Nash to John Polk of Meck., for s 20 proc. money...78 A on waters of Goose Creek... Prov. by R Smith (No date).

Pp. 217-219: 25 March 1771, Abner Nash of Halifax Co., to Robert Glass of Meck., for s 20 proc. money...18 A on S side Middle fork of Goose Creek...Wit: R. Smith. Prov. by Robert Smith (no date).

Pp. 220-222: 25 March 1772, Abner Nash to Andrew Greer for s 50 proc. money...35 A on the head spring of Muddy Creek ...Prov. by R. Smith (No date).

Pp. 223-225: 25 March 1772, Abner Nash to Andrew Greer of Meck., for L 12 proc. money...land on Caldwells Creek, 140 A...Prov. by Robt Smith (No date).

Pp. 226-228: 25 March 1772, Abner Nash to Johnathan Query of Meck., for L 7 proc. money...62 A between the two middle forks of Duck Creek...Wit: R. Smith. Prov. by Smith. (No date).

Pp. 229-231: 25 March 1772, Abner Nash to Samuel Harris of Meck., for L 4 proc. money...56 A on waters of Clear Creek ...Prov. by Robt Smith (No date).

VOLUME 8

Pp. 232-234: 25 March 1772, Abner Nash to Alexander Finney of Meck., for Ł 5 proc money...60 A on waters of Clear Creek...Wit: R. Smith. Prov. by Smith (no date).

Pp. 235-237: 25 March 1772, Abner Nash to John McCall of Meck., for Ł 5 proc. money...168 A on waters of Clear Creek...Wit: R. Smith. (No rec. date).

Pp. 238-240: ____ 1772, Abner Nash to James Wilson of Meck., for Ł 7 proc. money...70 A on head waters of Goose Creek Wit: R. Smith (No rec. date).

Pp. 241-243: 29 April 1772, James Biggar of Tryon Co., to Joseph (?) Biggar of Meck., for Ł 50 NC money...320 A on E side Cataba River opposite to the mouth of Crowders Creek, granted to sd. James Biggar 21 Dec 1763...James Biggar (Seal), Wit: William Elliott, Jurat. Mat Knox, Wm Kerr. (No rec. date).

Pp. 243-245: 28 Apr 1772, James Bigger of Tryon Co., to John Bigar of Meck., for s 5 sterling (apparently the lease with the foregoing deed)...Rec. July term 1772(?).

Pp. 245-249: 25 March 1772, Abner Nash to John Davis of Meck., for Ł 8 proc. money...86 A in the Welsh Tract...Wit: R. Smith (No rec. date).

Pp. 249-252: 25 March 1772, Abner Nash to David Flough of Meck., for Ł 3 proc. money...land on waters of Clear Creek, 47 A...Wit: R. Smith (No rec. date).

Pp. 252-255: 1 Sept 1771, Joseph Kenedy of Meck., to John Montgommery of same, for Ł 18 proc. money...100(?) A, granted to sd. Kenedy 24 ____ 1770...Joseph Kenedy (Seal), Easter Kenedy (Seal), Wit: David Smith, James Kenedy, Jurat. Prov. by James Kenedy, July Term 1772.

Pp. 255-258: 25 March 1772, Abner Nash to John Polk for Meck., for Ł 10 proc. money...125 A on Rocky River.... Wit: R. Smith (No rec. date).

Pp. 258-261: 25 March 1772, Abner Nash to John Query of Meck., for Ł 5 s 10 proc. money...55 A on waters of Goose Creek. Prov. by Robert Smith (No date).

Pp. 261-264: (this deed badly mutilated), 25 March 1772, Abner Nash to William Lemmons(?)...45 A....

Pp. 265-268: 25 March 1772, Abner Nash to William Query of Meck., for Ł 12 proc. money...136 A on waters of Goose Creek. Prov. by Robt Smith (no date).

Pp. 268-271: 9 July 1772, Andrew Barns & wf Susanna of Meck., to William White, weaver, of same, for Ł 50 proc. money ...75 A on back Creek a branch of Rocky River, by deed from Gov. Dobbs to John Caldwell 24 Nov 1772, then to William Campbell 2 Aug 1763, and by said Campbell to Andrew Barnes, 18 March 1769... Andw Barns (Seal), Susana Barns (X) (Seal), Wit: Isaac Barns, Thomas Neely. Prov. by Isaac Barns (no date).

VOLUME 8

Pp. 271-274: 4 March 1772, Ginnings Thomspon & Elizabeth of Meck., to John Phillip Weeks, planter, for Ł 16 proc. money ...48 A on Rocky River...Jinnings Thomson (X) (Seal), Elizabeth Thomson (C) (Seal), Wit: Thomas Dove (D), Jurat; John Coruthers. Prov. in open court July Term 1772.

Pp. 274-277: ___ 1772, William McKorkle & wf Ester of Meck., to Robert Crockett of same, for Ł 60...230 A, the uppermost of the plantation I now live on, 600 A, which was granted in my father's name, which became my right after his Disease by being his heir the Land on the twelve mile Creek... Wm McKorkle (Seal), Esterh McKorkle (E) (Seal), Mit: Henry J. Foster, Andrew Nell, Wm Davis, jurat. (No rec. date).

Pp. 277-280: 29 Aug 1772, William White of Meck., & wf Margaret to James Morrison of same, for Ł 50 proc. money... 161 A on English Buffalo Creek, a branch of Rocky River adj. Alexander Ferguson, originally granted by Gov. Dobbs 25 June 1764 to William White...William White (Seal), Margaret White (Ø) (Seal), Wit: Andw Barns, Jurat, John White. Prov. by Andrew Barns (no date).

Pp. 280-283: 25 June 1772, Robt Davis Senr of South Carolina of Long Cain Settlement to James Davis of Meck., for s 5 proc. money...200 A on N branch of the Waxhaw Creek, granted 6 Apr 1763...Robt Davis (Seal), Wit: Wm Davies, Jurat, John McElroy. Prov. by Davies (No date).

Pp. 283-285: 28 Apr 1772, James Biggar of Tryon Co., planter, to Matthew Biggar of Tryon Co., planter, for s 5 proc. money...300 A on E side Cataba above the mouth of Crowders Creek, granted to sd. James Biggar 21 Dec 1763...James Biggar (Seal), Wit: Wm Elliot, Jurat. Matthew Knox, Wm Kerr. Prov. July term 1772.

Finis.

END OF VOLUME 8.

VOLUME 9

29th Book.

Pp. 1-3: 20 June 1769, John Miller of Meck., planter, to John Buchannan of same, for ₤ 15 proc. money...land on E side Cataba River on waters of Gum Branch of Long Creek adj. John Boyd, 150 A, granted to sd. Miller 20 April 1768...John Miller (Seal), Elizabeth Miller (O) (Seal), Wit: William Ramsey, John Long (X). Prov. Oct. term 1771.

Pp. 3-5: 15 Aug 1771, Alexander McKee of Meck., to William Clark of same, for ₤ 100 proc. money...land on waters of Sugar Creek, 200 A granted to sd. McKee, 21 Dec 1763...Alexander McKee (A) (Seal), Wit: James Hope, Jno Mck. Alexander. Prov. Oct. term 1771.

Pp. 5-7: 20 Sept 1771, John Slone Junior & wf Jean of Meck., for ₤ 90 proc. money...350 A on both sides Paw Creek including sd. Sloans improvement, adj. land that Francis Beaty sold to Robert McCord, conveyed to sd. John Slaon by deed from Hugh Beaty 22 Feb 1768...now sold to Charles Mason...John Sloan (Seal) Jane sloan (O) (Seal), Wit:Joseph McCinley, Joseph Galbreath. Prov. October term 1771.

Pp. 7-9: 30 Dec 1767, William Hall & wf Elizabeth of Rowan Co., to John Graham and wf Jean of Meck., for ₤ 60... part of a grant to William Hall 24 Sept 1754...William Hall (Seal) Elizabeth Hall (Seal), Wit: William Brown, James Hall, James Dysart. Prov. Oct. term 1771

Pp. 10-11: 15 Sept 1767, Thomas Houston of Meck., to Doctr. Joseph Kenedy of same, for ₤ 25 proc. money...land on saw mill Branch of McCorpins Creek knwon as the Brown Bottom, 85 A...Thomas Houston (Seal), Agness Hueston (O) (Seal), Wit: Henry Downs, John Keliah, Wm Flenneken. Prov. Oct. term 1771.

Pp. 12-13: 20 March 1771, William Adams to Moses Shelby, for ₤ 12...land on waters of Reedy Creek, 100 A...William Adams (O) (Seal), Wit: F. Nash, _ Alexander. Prov. Oct. term 1771.

Page 14: Robert Burns of Meck., for ₤ 70 pd. by Josiah Alexander sell negro woman Hanah...24 Aug 1771...Robert Burns (Seal), Wit: Jer: McCaferty. Prov. Janyr. Term 1772.

Pp. 14-15: Richard <u>Reigns</u> of Meck., for ₤ 150 pd. by Josiah Alexander ...negro fellow Ned...17 Dec 1771(?)...Richard Raines (Seal), Wit: Joseph Sample, John Walter Gibbs. Rec. Jan. term 1772.

Pp. 15-17: 26 Aug 1771, Samuel Jack of Meck., to Philip Weeks of same, for ₤ 20 proc. money...land on E side McMichaels Creek, 250 A granted to sd. Samuel Jack, 9 April 1770...Samuel Jack (Seal), Wit: Samuel Fleniken, Mc McMurey. Prov. Jan. term 1772.

Pp. 17-19: 22 Jan 1772, David Miller of Meck., to Samuel Barnet of same, for ₤ 50 proc. money...land on E side Cataba River adj. John Scott, Johnston, 360 A, granted to Robt Miller 6 March 1765...David Miller (Seal), Wit: Robt Harris Junr., John McKnit Alexander. Rec. Jan. term 1772.

VOLUME 9

Pp. 19-21: 13 July 1770, John Davies of Meck., to Samuel Bigam of same, for Ł 20 proc. money...land on north of Steel Creek adj. John and Robert Bigams line, Robert Maxwells, 260 A, granted to James Davies and Francis Beaty 21 Apr 1764...John Davies (Seal), Wit: Petter Johnston, Robert Maxwell. Rec.Jan. term 1772.

Pp. 21-22: 25 Dec 1771, John Fifer & wf Cathrian of Meck., to Samuel Morton of same, for Ł 30 proc. money...181 A adj. John Frohock, granted to sd. Samuel Morton by patent 18 Apr 1771...John Fifer (Seal), Cathrian Fifer (Seal), Wit: James Killpatrick, Peter Morton, Christopher Walbert. Prov. Jan. term 1772.

Pp. 23-24: 17 Jan 1771, Henry McMurdy of Meck., to John Sloan of Meck., for Ł 25 proc. money...land on both sides a branch of Shugar, adj. James Taggert, granted to sd. McMurdy 16 Dec 1769, 200 A...Henry McMury (1) (Seal), Wit: John Fleming, Edward White, Walter Brown (W). Prov. Jan. term 1772.

Pp. 25-26: 11 Sept 1771, James McCord to James McCord Jr., for Ł 60 proc. money...137 A on waters of Shugar Creek, adj. Joseph Lee, James Moor...James McCord (Seal), Wit: Thomas Polk, Robert Finely. Rec. Jan. term 1772.

Pp. 26-28: 14 Jan 1772, William Henry of Meck., farmer, to James Henry of same, farmer, for Ł 20 proc. money...land on both sides Long Creek, adj. Alexander, Erwin, 129 A, part of 300 A, granted to William Henry by John Mitchell by deed 9 Dec 1769...William Henry (Seal), Elizabeth Henry (Seal), Wit: James Bardley, John McKnit Alexander. Prov. Jan. term 1772.

Pp. 28-31: 2 Nov 1771, John Beaty of Tryon Co., to Mary Armstrong wife(?) of Mathew Armstrong, and daughter of sd. Beaty, and her son John Armstrong, both of Meck., for s 5 sterling...land on N side Cataba River, 300 A including part of an Island, granted to John Beaty 3 Jan 1754...John Beaty (Seal), Elizabeth Beaty (.) (Seal), Wit: Wiliam Herdney (O), Sarah Petty (X). Rec. Jan. term 1772.

Pp. 31-33: 13 Dec 1771, Alexander Barryhill of Prov. of Georgia, planter, to Mary Graham of Meck., widow, for Ł ...land on E side Catabo on waters of Paw Creek, adj. Archd. Gilliland, near Joseph Mores, 200 A, granted to sd. Berryhill, 26 Apr 1767...Alexander Berryhill (Seal), wit: David Hay, John Cathey. Prov. Jan. term 1772.

Pp. 33-35: 22 Jan 1772, Moses Steel of Meck., to John Beaty of same, for Ł 40 proc. money...land on waters of Shugar Creek adj. ___, 50 A also 84 A, total 134 A...moses ___ Wit: Peter Johnston, William Ster __ (W), John Davies. Rec. Jan. term 1772.

Pp. 35-36: 7 Aug 1771, Wiliam Query & wf Margaret to John Reed of Meck., for s 2 proc. money...30 A in Tract #2... Wiliam Query (Seal), Margret Query (4) (Seal), Wit: James Wilson, James Richardson. Prov. Jan. term 1772.

Pp. 36-38: 10 July 1771, Samuel Bigham to William Bigham Junr, for Ł 70...250 A on waters of Rockey Shugar Creek, adj. John McDowell, part of two grants to James Aston and Samuel Bigham... Samuel Bigham (Seal), Wit: Peter Johnston, Samuel Bigham. Rec. Jan. term 1772.

VOLUME 9

Pp. 38-40: 22 Jan 1772, Joseph Paterson of Meck., to George Ross for ₺ 30 proc. money...196 A on Rocky River, conveyed by John Mitchell & wf Elizabeth of Salisbury...Joseph Paterson (Seal), Wit: John Wyly. Rec. Jan. term 1772.

Pp. 40-42: 17 Apr 1771, John Dermond of Meck., planter, to James Yandell of same, for ₺ 20 proc. money...105 A on waters of Shugar Creek...John Dermond (Seal), Wit: Andrew Baxter, Wiliam Flenicken. Rec. Jan. term 1772.

Pp. 42-45: 2 Sept 1771, James Caldwell & wf Elizabeth of NC, to James Love & John Meachim, for ₺ 30 proc. money...140 A on a branch of Rocky River...James Caldwell (Seal), Elizabeth Caldwell (U) (Seal), Wit: James Harris, Robert Harris. Rec. Jan. term 1772.

Pp. 45-48: 12 Oct 1766, William White of Meck., & wf Margaret to James Morrison of same, Plr., for ₺ 13 s 12 proc. money ...136 A on Caldwells Creek...William White (Seal), Margaret White (O) (Seal), Wit: James Scott, Allan McLean. Rec. Jan. term 1772.

Pp. 48-50: 5 Nov 1770, John Frohock of Rowan Co., to Ephraim Farr of Meck., for ₺ 48 sterling...land on both sides a branch of Coddle Creek, adj. James Martin lives, 280 A, granted to sd. Frohoc by deed from H. E. McCulloh...John Frohoc (Seal), Wit: Abraham Jones, Thomas Frohock. Rec. Jan. term 1772.

Pp. 50-52: 5 Sept 1771, William Miller of Lancaster Co., Pa., to David Millar of Meck., for s 5 sterling...360 A adj. John Scotts line including John Hardens impruvments, adj. McCartey, granted to Robert Miller by patent 6 Apr 1761...William Miller (Seal), Wit: William Johnston, John Robinson. Rec. Jan term 1772.

Pp. 52-53: 20 May 1771, George Wilham & wf Eve of Meck., to Jacob Pence of same, for ₺ 32 proc. money...land 285 A, granted to Philip Miller for 580 A, 10 Apr 1753, then sold to John Leppard, then to George Wilham...George Wilham (Seal), Eve Willim (O) (Seal), Wit: _____, ___ Phifer Junr. Rec. Jan. term 1772.

Pp. 54-57: 2 March 1764, Arthur Dobs & wf Justina to Christopher Walbert of Meck., for ₺ 5 proc. money...50 A on Great and Little Cold Waters, waters of Rockey or Johnston River... Wit: Martin Fifer, Richd Barry. Rec. Jan. term 1772.

Pp. 57-59: 21 July 1770, Hugh McKnight of Rowan Co., farmer, to James McKnight, farmer, of same, for ₺ 200 proc. money ...land on E side Cataba River, at the mouth of Morrisons Branch, a grant # 268 by Gov. Dobbs to William Morr---, 13 Oct 1756... Hugh McKnight (Seal), Wit: John Kerr, William Byers, Stephen Potts. Rec. Jan. term 1772.

Pp. 59-62: __ Aug 1770, Charles Hart & wf Clera of Meck., to Charles Feagle, for ₺ 50 proc. money...115 A on waters of Rocky River...Charles Hart (M) (Seal), Clera Hart (A) (Seal) Wit: John Phifer, Ru--- Hart (D), _____. Rec. Jan. term 1772.

Pp. 62-63: 24 Jan 1772, Charles Purvaince of Rowan Co., to Robt Allison of same, for ₺ 5 sterling...200 A near Jeremiah Joys...Charles Purviance (Seal), Wit: Thos Polk, Robt Burns. Rec. Jan. term 1772.

Pp. 63-65: 20 Sept 1771, Charles Thomson of Roan Co., millright, to Peter Lance of Meck., for ₤ 26 proc. money...land on E side Little Bear Creek, 200 A conveyed from John Mitchell to George Magoune, and then to sd. Thomson...Charles Thomson (X) (Seal), Wit: Jas Craige, Mortnir (?) Berber (German signature), Matts. Beaver. Rec. Jan. term 1772.

Pp. 65-67: 23 Jan 1772, William Elliott of Meck., to John Watterson for s 40 proc.money...lot # 31 on N side Traid St., in Charlotte...Wit: Ths Polk, John Davies. Rec. Jan. term 1772.

Pp. 67-68: 20 Sept 1771, Charles Thomson of Rowan Co., Millright, to Peter Lance, for ₤ 25 proc. money...land on E side Little Bear Creek, 160 A...Charles Thomson (X), Wit: Matthias Binber, Matts. Beaver. Rec. Jan. term 1772.

Pp. 69-70: 17 Sept 1771, Charles Thomson of Rowan Co., to John Francises of Anson Co., for ₤ 30 proc. money...land in the fork of Little Bear Creek, 280 A...Charles Thomson (Seal), Wit: Jas Craige, Matthias Binber, Matts. Beaver. Rec. Jan. term 1772.

Pp. 71-73: 6 Feb 1770, Hance McWhorter of Tryon Co., to David Waddle of Meck., for ₤ 46 proc. money...200 A adj. Reese Morgan, Richard Graham, Thomas Irwin, formerly surveyed for Thomas Irvin, on E side Cataba River, granted 16 Feb 1754 to James Ormond and sold to Hance McWhorter...Hance McWhorter (Seal), Wit: John Davison, Jonathan Potts. Rec. Jan. term 1772.

Pp. 73-75: 20 Jan 1772, William Barnet & wf Agnes of Craven Co., South Carolina, to John Barnet of Meck., for ₤ 20... land on S side Waxhaw Creek, 200 A granted 1754 to Andrew Nutt and sold by Andrew Nutt & wf Margaret of William Barnet... William Barnet (X) (Seal), Agnes Barnet (X) (Seal), Wit: Matthew Patton, James Barnet, Joseph Barnet. Rec. Jan. term 1772.

Pp. 76-77: 13 Sept 177-, Benjamin Cohorn of Meck., to Henry Watts of same, for ₤ 50 proc. money...land on E side Cataba on waters of Armor Millbranch, adj. Downs, Miller, 100 A granted 25 Apr 1767 to Thomas Jarret, then sold to Amos Alexander, 3 Nov 1767, then to Benjamin Cohorn 26 Dec 1767... Benjamin Cothran (Seal), Wit: _ Cathey, _ Martin. Rec. Jan. term 1772.

Pp. 77-79: 10 Dec 1771, Benjamin Cohorn of Meck., to Henry Watts for s5 (apparently the lease for the above land).... Wit: John Cathey, John Martin.

Pp. 79-81: 22 _ 1772, William McClure and wf Elizabeth of Meck., to Isaac Williams, for ₤ 50 proc. money...land on Little Sugar Creek adj. Adam Carruth, James Tagerty, Thomas Polk, David Hays Senr., 100 A granted to William McClure 22 Dec 1768...William McCluer (Seal), Elizabeth McClure (C) (Seal), Wit: Richard Mason, William Sims. Rec. April term 1772.

Pp. 81-83: 16 Apr 1772, John Reed of Meck., weaver, to James Wilson, planter, for ₤ 13 proc. money...land in Tract #2, sold by William Query & wf Margaret, ____ 1771...John Reed (H) (Seal), Wit: James Orr. Rec. April term 1772.

VOLUME 9

Pp. 83-84: 22 Jan 1772, John Davis of Meck., to John Weeks of same, for L 50 proc. money...land adj. James Johnston, the indian line, 100 A on waters of Sugar Creek...John Davis (Seal), Wit: Thomas Polk, Peter Johnston. Rec. April term 1772.

Pp. 84-86: 4 Jan 1772, Thomas Polk, Abraham Alexander and Robert Elliot of Meck., to Thomas Bond of Tryon Co., for L 2 proc. money...lots # 82 & 98 in Charlotte on W side of Tryon St., Wit: W. Avery, Jurat., Ezekiel Polk. Rec. April term 1772.

Pp. 86-87: 14 Feb 1771, Thomas Bond of Tryon Co., to Ezekiel Polk of same, for L 30 proc. money...lots # 82 & 98 in Charlotte...Wit: Samuel Milson, Jurate, Alexander Henry. Rec. April Term 1772.

Pp. 88-90: John Polk and wf Elinor for L 25 proc. money, to Jones Bradley, 100 A on both sides south fork of Crooked Creek, including Jacob Pauls improvements...(no date). John Polk. (Seal), Elinor Polk (e) (Seal), Wit: Joseph Moore, jurate, Thomas Magby. Rec. April term 1772.

Pp. 90-91: 20 April 1772, James Wilson of Meck., & wf Elizabeth to James Richardson, Shoemaker, for L 19 proc. money ...land conveyed by Abner Nash & wf Justina 15 Feb 1771, on N side Goose Creek...James Wilson (Seal), Elizabeth Wilson (Seal), Wit: William Ramsey, Jurat., John Reed (H). Rec. April term 1772.

Pp. 92-93: 22 April 1772, Patrick Kerr of Meck., to William Allen of same, for L 25 proc. money...land on both sides Gum branch of Long Creek, adj. John Allen, James Brown, 101 A part of 126 A granted to Patrick Kerr 4 May 1769...Patrick Kerr (Seal), Mary Kerr (ᴍ) (Seal), Wit: Joseph Kerr, John Sloan. Rec. April term 1772.

Pp. 94-95: 21 April 1772, William McCulloh & wf Elizabeth for s 1 proc. money, and for paternal love to our son in law John Sadler of same...70 A adj. James Kaneday... William Mcculloh (W) (Seal), Elizabeth McCulloh (O) (Seal), Wit: John McCord, Jurate, David Kenedy. Rec. April term 1772.

Finis.
Book No. 29th

Pp. 96-100: Blank.

30th Book

Pp. 101-102: 23 April 1771, John Davis of Meck., to Thomas Polk of same, for L 5 proc. money...land on waters of Sugar Creek adj. elijah Alexander, Saml McClery, 50 A, conveyed by deed from Henry E. McCulloh, 24 Feb 1767...John Davis (Seal), Wit: Adam Alexander, John sloan, Jurate. Rec. July term 1772.

Pp. 103-104: 19 Feb 17--, Samuel Lofton & wf Sarah of Meck., to Aaron McWhorter of same, for L___ proc. money... land on waters of Twelve Mile Creek, adj. Donalson, Alexander, ___ & Mary Johns lines, 160 A granted to sd. Samuel Loftain... Saml Lofton (Seal), Sarah Lofton (S) (Seal), Wit: Andrew Crocket, William Robison, Hugh Barnet, Jurate. Rec. July term 1772.

VOLUME 9

Pp. 105-107: 13 April 1772, William Hagans & wf Mary of Meck., to Robert Hogston of Rowan Co., for ___ pistoles...land on both sides Twelve Mile Creek, 160 A...William Hagans (Seal), Mary Haggans (ɟ) (Seal), Wit: Frans. Mc____, ____. Rec. July term 1772.

Pp. 108-110: 22 March 1768, William Adams of Meck., planter, to James Stafford of same, for ₺ 1-- proc. money... 330 A on Redy Creek (later appears to be 180 A)...Wiliam Adams (ɟ), James Stafford, Wit: Robt Harris, Moses Alexander. (No rec. date).

Pp. 110-113: 16 __ 177-, Alexander McKee of Meck., planter, to Henry Neel of same, for ₺ 340(?), land granted to Frances Nickoles by patent 23 Apr 1762, and conveyed to Alexander Nicols and then to Alexander McKee, 17 Oct 1771, adj. Widow Armor, 356 A...Alexander McKee (X) (Seal), Wit: Frances Harron, Robt Brownfield Jur. (No rec date).

Pp. 113-116: 12 Nov 1771, Andrew Erwin now of Pennsylvania to John Wilson of Prov. of NC...for 100 A in the County of Cumberland made over to him with a warrant from the Office and ₺ 5...land on Meck on N for the Cataba River adj. Richard Graham, James Armor, Geo. Rennicks, Malcon Hamilton, including the place on which the said Erwin did live, 400 A, granted to William Price decd father of Thomas Price, 3 Oct 1765, conveye'd by sd. Thomas Price to Andrew Irwin 26 Feb 1762...Andrew Erwin (Seal), Wit: Richard Barry, Geo. Elliot, Andrew Wilson. Prov. by Richard Barry (no date).

Pp. 116-118: 9 Jan 1772, David Wilson of Meck,, cooper, to Ephraim Farr of same, planter, for ₺ 18 proc. money...94 A adj. John Frohock, Turner...David Wilson (Seal), Wit: Wm Wallace, Jurat; Wm Gardner. (No rec. date).

Pp. 118-121: 25 June 1772, Robert Davis of Cravan Co., NC, joiner, to Phillip Walker of Meck., for ₺ 20 proc. money... 200 A on both sides Waxhaw Creek, part of tract that the sd. Robert Davis formerly livd on, granted 6 Apr 1753...Robert Davis (Seal), Wit: James Wauhup, John Davis, Robert Davis, Jurat. (No rec date).

Pp. 121-122: 28 Jan 1767, Henry E. McCulloh to Benjamin Alexander of Meck., for ₺ 4 proc. money...45 A on Mallard Creek, adj. Moses Alexander Junior...Prov. by John McKnitt Alexander. (No date).

Pp. 123-126: 24 March 1772, Abner Nash to Jno Hall of Meck., for s 20 proc. money...13 A on Goose Creek adj. his own line... Wit: Robt Smith, Jurat. (No rec date).

Pp. 126-127: 18 Aug 1772, John Lance & wf Catherine of Meck., to Paul Barringer of same, for ₺ 200 proc. money... 106 A adj. Jacob Smiths mill place, on Dutch Buffaloe Creek, conveyed by deed from Gov. Dobbs & wf Justina 25 June 1764... John Lance (2) (Seal), Wit: John Fifer, David Hart (D). (No rec. date).

Pp. 128-131: 25 March 1772, Abner Nash to James Orr of Meck., for ₺ 5 proc. money...92 A...Wit: R. Smith (No rec. date)

VOLUME 9

Pp. 131-134: 25 March 1771, Abner Nash to Joseph Galbreath for s5 proc. money...55 A on N side Crooked Creek...Wit: R. Smith, Jurat. (No rec. date).

Pp. 134-137: 25 March 1772, Abner Nash to Josiah Alexander of Meck., for Ł 25 proc. money...130 A on Beaver Dam branch of Rockey River...Wit: Robt Smith, Jurat. (No rec. date).

Pp. 137-139: 22 Jan 1772, John Cooper of Tryon Co., to Thos Polk of same(!), for Ł 50 proc. money...land on the waters of King branch, adj Robert Campbell, 138 A by deed from Henry E. McCulloh 12 Jan 1767...John Cooper (Seal), Wit: John Beard, John Davis. Prov. by Davis (No date).

Pp. 139-142: 3 Oct 1772, Francis Johnston of Meck., to Samuel Knox for Ł 100...150 A on E side Cataba adj. Buckannan, Walker, conveyed to sd. Johnston by Moses Ferguson and Samuel Knox who purchased the same from John Farmer to whom it was granted 29 Apr 1768...Francis Johnston (Seal), Wit: Frances Moore, Hugh Herron, Matthew Knox, Jurat. (No rec. date).

Pp. 142-143: 8 Oct 1772, John Pfifer of Meck., & wf Catherine to William Osburn of same, for Ł 5 proc. money...150 A above Andrew Neels plantation, being the same on whom (sic) the said William Osburn now lives...John Pfifer (Seal), Catherine Fifer (Seal), Wit: John Osburn, John Foster, Jurat. (No rec date).

Pp. 144-145: 18 Sept 1772, Jacob Moyar & wf Margaret of Meck., to Jacob Swink of same, for Ł 50 proc. money...122 A on both sides Shinwolf Creek, a branch of Rockey River...Jacob Moyars (Seal), Margaret Moyers (M) (Seal), Wit: John Pfifer, Paul Berringer, Jurat. (No rec. date).

Pp. 146-148: 8 Nov 1770, Robt McMurry & wf Elinor of Meck., to Isaac Borns, planter, of same, for Ł 60 proc. money ...155 A the place where he lives on S side Rocky River, granted to Gov. Dobbs to McMurry 25 June 1764...Robt McMurry (Seal), Eliner McMurry (O) (Seal), Wit: Andw Borns, William White. Prov. by William White (no date).

Page 148:   24 Aug 1772, John Moore of Tryon Co., to David McCoard of Meck., for Ł 100 proc. money...200 A.... (apparently six pages of the original missing at the time the present numbering system was added. See below).

Pp. 149-150: to Jeremiah McCafferty, 91½ A, a part of the tract where William McCulloh now lives, granted to him by deed from Selwyn by H. E. McCulloh ___ Jan 1767...William McCulloh (Seal), Elizabeth McCulloh (O) (Seal), Wit: Thos Polk, Peter Johnston. Ack. in open court by grantors (no date).

Pp. 151-159: 3 July 1772, Robert Davis of South Carolina, to John McElroy of Meck., for s5...240 A on N side Cataba River on a north branch of the Waxhaw Creek, granted ___ July 1753...Robt Davis (Seal), Wit: Wm Davis, James Davis, Jurat, Rebekkah Green. Prov. by George Davis (no date.)

Pp. 153-154: (remainder of deed from John Moore to David McCoard on p. 148)...land on both sides Long Creek, granted to John Moore by patent 4 Dec 1763...John Moor (Seal), Wit: Robert

VOLUME 9

McCoard, William McCleary. Prov. by Robert McCoard (no date).

Pp. 154-156: 16 March 1772, Alexander McCee (McKee) of Meck., to Henry Neal for s 5 sterling...256 A granted unto Francis Nichols 23 Apr 1762, and sold to sd. McKee 17 Oct 1771... Alexander McKee (A) (Seal), Wit: Francis Herron, Robert Brownfield, Jur. Ack. by sd. McKee (no date)

Pp. 156-158: 26 Sept 1772, Patrick Kerr of Meck., to Robert Kerr Jr., of same, for Ł 8 proc. money...land on Long Creek of Cataba, 120 A, conveyed by John Mitchell & wf to Kerr, 9 Sept 1769...Patrick Kerr (Seal), Mary Kerr (X) (Seal), Wit: Joseph Kerr. Ack. in open court by grantor.

Page 158: (see Pp. 149-150), 7 Aug 1772, William McCulloh & wf Elizabeth of Meck., to Jeremiah McCafferty, for Ł 50 proc. money....

Pp. 160-161: 29 July 1772, Matthew Brown of Tryon Co., to David McChord of Meck., for Ł 20 proc. money...112 A on E side Cataba River on a small branch of Paw Creek, adj. Matthew Patton, granted to Matthew Brown by patent 11 Dec 1770... Matthew Brown (Seal), Wit: Robert Shipley, George Shipley, Jurat. (No rec. date).

Pp. 162-163: 20 Oct 1772, Thos Polk of Meck., to William Sawyers of Lancaster Co., Pa., for Ł 15 proc. money...64(?) A adj. Thos Polk...Wit: Alex Martin, David Haynes. Prov. by Martin (no date).

Pp. 164-167: 5 March 1772, Abner Nash to John Morrison of Meck., for s 35 proc. money...land on waters of Reedy Creek adj. his old line, 23 A...Wit: R Smith, Jurat. (No rec. date).

Pp. 167-169: 10 Feb 1769, John Mitchell & wf Elizabeth of Salisbury, to James Carruth of Meck., for Ł 15 proc. money... 225 A...Wit: ez. Alexander, __ as Alison. Prov. by Hezekiah Alexander (no date).

Pp. 169-171: 21 Oct 1772, Henry Downs of ___ Co., NC, to John McCreavy(?) of ___, for Ł 24 NC money...200 A, part of a patent dated 18 April 1772...Henry Downs (Seal), Francis Downs (Seal), Wit: None. Ack in open court (no date).

Pp. 171-174: 20 Oct 1772, David Garison & wf Mary of Meck., to Benjamin Alexander of same, for Ł 60 proc. money... 50 A adj. his own and Moses Alexander Jr., granted 4 May 1769... David Garrison (Seal), Mary Garrison (M) (Seal), Wit: James Alexander, William Alexander, Jurat. (No date of rec.).

Pp. 174-176: 13 Sept 1772, Moses Ferguson of Tryon Co., to Samuel Knox of Meck., for Ł 100 NC money...150 A on E side Cataba River, adj. Biggar, Walker...lawfully made over to Samuel Knox and Moses Ferguson from John Farmer, to whom it was granted 29 April 1768...Moses Ferguson (Seal), Samuel Knox (Seal), Wit: Frans.(?) Moore, Matthew Knox, Jurat. Prov. by Knox (No date).

Pp. 176, 13 Aug 1772, Robert Caruth of Rowan Co., to Jno Mc-
187-188: Nitt Alexander of Meck., for Ł 5 proc. money...

VOLUME 9

land adj. Samuel Allen, William Bigham, 200 A granted to Robert Caruth 28 Oct 1765...Robert Caruth (Seal), Wit: Hez Alexander, Jurat., Jas. Alexander. (No rec. date).

Pp. 186, 177, 178: 16 Oct 1772, Isaac Harlan of Meck., to George Bacor Junr, for Ł 30 proc. money...(later George Baker)...land on waters of Sugar Creek adj. George Bacor Senior, part of tract sold by Thoms Polk to Isaac Harland, 21 Aug 1767, 100 A...Isaac Harlan (Seal), Wit: Threehas Alexander, George Baker (B). (No rec. date).

Pp. 178, 189, 190: 16 Oct 1772, Isaac Harlan of Meck., to George Baker Sr, for Ł 75 proc. money...land on waters of Sugar Creek including Thomas Dolromples Improvements, conveyed to Harlan by Thos Polk, 31 Aug 1767...Wit: George Baker, Jurat, Phinehas Alexander. (No rec. date).

Pp. 179-181: 12 July 1771, Samuel Bigham of Meck., to Wm. Bigham & his son Samuel, for Ł 70 proc. money...land on N fork Steel Creek adj. Hugh Park, James Carter, Samuel Bigham, 200 A, granted 26 Oct 1767...Samuel Bigham (Seal), Wit: Peter Johnston, Alexander Porter, William Porter. Ack in open court (no date).

Pp. 181-183: 10 Feb 1769, John Mitchell & wf Elizabeth to Robert Anderson of Meck., for Ł 13 proc. money...land adj. John Paterson, John McCuistions, 143 A...Wit: Paul Berringer, Jurat; George Henry Berger(?). (No rec. date).

Pp. 184-186: 17 Oct 1771, Francis Nickols of Meck., to Alexander McKee of same, for Ł 50 proc. money...land adj. Alexander Dobbins, Widow Armors,256 A, granted to sd. Nickols, 23 Apr 1762...Francis Nickles (O) (Seal), Wit: William Berryhill, Jurat, John Fri___(?). Prov. by Berryhill (No date).

Pp. 190-193: 29 Sept 1772, James McCord Junior, of Meck., to William Sayers of Lancaster Co., Pa., for Ł 70 proc. money...137 A on waters of Sugar Creek adj. Joseph Lee, James Moor, granted to James McCord Sr., and made over to his son James 9 Jan 1767...James McCord (Seal), Sarah McCord (X) (Seal), Wit: David Garrison, David Haynes. Ack. in op. court (No date.)

Pp. 193-195: 22 Oct 1772, Samuel Wilson Senior of Meck., to Samuel Wilson Jr., of Craven Co., SC., Mercht., for Ł 10 proc. money of NC...land on N side Cataba adj. George Cathey Senr., 300 A...Sam: Wilson (Seal), Thos Polk, Jurat, Ezek Polk. Prov. by Thos Polk (no date).
                              Finis.

Page 196: Book No 30th.
         NB about the fourth part through this Book is a Deed
            from Robt Davies to Phillip Walker 200 Acres Waxaw

Pp. 197-200: Blank.

Pp. 201-202: 8 July 1778, Moses Scot & wf Sarah of Tryon Co., to Edward Shipley of Meck., for Ł 80 currency...161 A on E side Catabo River including Moses Scot's improvements, 86 A of which was granted to John (More) by patent 16 Nov 1764 and conveyed to Scott 8 Oct 1771, and 76 A granted to Moses Scot 25 July 1774...Moses Scott (Seal), Sarah Scott (∠) (Seal), Wit:

241

VOLUME 9

Pp. 203-205: 1 Jan 1775, Robert Craford of Craven Co., South Carolina & wf Jean to Hugh White of same, for ₤ 200 ...land in NC on the Waxaw Creek, 163 A, part of 300 A patent by Wiliam Beard 23 Feb 1754...Robt Craford (Seal), Jean Craford (+) (Seal), Wit: Thos Craford, Nathaniel Barnet. (No rec. date).

Pp. 206-208: 16 March 1778, David Reess Senr of Meck., yeoman, to David Reese Junr., for ₤ 50 s 10...159 A, part of 259 A conveyed by Doobs to David Reese 27 Dec 1763(?)... David Rees (Seal), Wit: Willm Sharpe, George Rees (No rec. date).

Pp. 208-210: 4 Jan 1774, James Flanigen of Meck., cooper, to John Flenigan, for ₤ 25...land on waters of McColpins Creek, 175 A adj. John Swan, John Clark, Thos Dermond...James Flenigan (Seal), Wit: John Flenigen, Saml Flenigan. (No rec date).

Pp. 210-212: 24 Jan 1777, Thos Polk, Abraham Alexander and Wiliam Paterson of Meck., to Samuel Flenigan of same, for ____ ...lot #4 in Town of Charlotte on E side Tread St...Wit: Eph Bravard, Thos Harris. (No rec. date).

Pp. 212-213: 23 Oct 1777, Joseph Wishhard of Meck., to Patrick McDonald, for ₤ 20 proc. money...lot # 38 on N side Tryon St...Joseph Wishard (Seal), Elizabeth Wishard (X) (Seal), Wit: John Herron, Robt Barnet. (No rec. date).

Pp. 214-215: 16 Apr 1778, Charles Keagle & wf Mary Ann of Meck., to Elizabeth Miller, Relick of John Miller, late of Sd. County and State, decd., for ₤ 350 currency...land on the fork of plum Branch and hamberg(?) Run of Rockey River, 115 A... Charles Keagle (Seal), Maryan Keagel (X) (Seal), Wit: John McKnit Alexander, Nathan Orr. (No rec. date).

Pp. 215-217: 3 Feb 1775, James Gilmore of Meck., planter, to Wiliam Johnston for ₤ 160 proc. money...203 A... James Gilmore (Seal), Wit: John Wilson, David Wilson (No rec. date).

Pp. 217-220: 24 March 1777, John Wallace & wf Marey of Meck., to Andrew Barns of same, for ₤ 180 proc. money... 122 A on waters of Rockey River...John Wallace (Seal), Mary Wallace (X) (Seal), Wit: Robt Smith, John Harris. (No rec. date).

Pp. 221-222: 1 June 1778, Thos Polk, Ephm. Bravard and James Jack of Meck., to Richard Meason of same, for ₤ 120 proc. money...lots #145-153 in Charlotte...Wit: Sam Martin, Dun Ocheltree. (No rec. date).

Pp. 223-225: 30 May 1778, Thos Polk, Eph Bravard & James Jack to Easter Kennady of Meck., for ₤ 100 proc. money... lot #4 on S side Tread St in Charlotte...Wit: Richard Meason, ____. (No rec. date).

Pp. 225-227: 11 July 1778, Wiliam Hagens of Meck., to Joseph Dugless of same, for ₤ 50 proc. money...land on waters of Twelve Creek, 276 A, adj. province line...William Hagens (Seal), Wit; Benj. Lowery, John Dunn. (No rec. date).

Pp. 228-230: 4 June 1778, William Johnston of Meck., to Charles Caldwell, late of Caswell Co., NC, for ₤ 270...

VOLUME 9

land on waters of Rockey River, 203 A, sold by Mr McCollock to
James Gilmore, then to William Johnston...Wiliam Johnston (Seal),
Wit: Richard Barry, John Wallace, Adam Meek. (No rec. date).

Pp. 231-233: 26 Dec 1774, Joseph Alexander, Minister of the Gospel,
of Meck., to Samuel Davies of same, for L20 proc.
money...land conveyed by McCulloh to James Orr, 2 Jan 1767,
then to sd. Alexander 20 July 1769, 50 A...Joseph Alexander (Seal),
Wit: Saml Martin, James Cannon, George Huston. (No rec. date).

Pp. 233-235: 25 May 1777, Hugh Carrigan & wf Mary to William Love
& wf Sarah, 78 A...Hugh Curigan (H), Mary Curighan
(E) (Seal), Wit: James Glass,Wm Query, Robt Donelson. (No rec.
date).

Pp. 235-237: Saml Younge of Rowan Co., for L 49 proc. money pd. by
John Morrow...land granted to sd. Young 20 May 1754,
adj. John Bravard, Zebulon Bravard, 300 A...6 Aug 1777...Saml
Young (Seal), Wit: Robert Morrow, Ricahrd Morrow. (No rec. date).

Pp. 237-239: 30 May 1778, Thos Polk, Eph Bravard and James Jack
to John Garrison, for L 12 proc. money...lots #
201-330-331 in Charlotte on N side Tryon St...Wit: Dun Ocheltree,
Wm Polk (No rec. date).

Pp. 239-241: 3 June 1778, Robt Smith & wf Sarah of Meck., to
Ezekiel Sharp of same, for L 20...land on both sides
Coddal Creek- adj. John Alexander, 254 A graned by deed to Abra-
ham Carriden, 1 Feb 1767 by McCulloh, and since conveyed by deed
to Sarah Alexander, widow of Moses Alexander but now wife of Robert
Smith, 19 Nov 1773...Robt Smith (Seal), Sarah Smith (Seal), Wit:
Edward Giles, William Alexander. (No Rec. date.)

Pp. 241-243: 23 Nov 1772, Andrew Neal of Colloton County, South
Carolina, to John Foster of Meck., for seven pistoles
...land on waters of Twelve Mile Creek, adj. Michal Ligget,
granted to Andrew Neal 25 Oct 1771...Andrew Neal (Seal), Wit:
James Tate, Moses Crassels, Moses Craige. (No rec. date).

Pp. 243-244: 16 June 1778, Ezekel Polk of Meck., to Samuel Roch
of same, for L 200...land on waters of Shugar Creek,
277 A...Ezekiel Polk (Seal), Wit: Thos Polk, Eph Bravard. (No
rec. date).

Pp. 245-247: 3 Jan 1778, Thomas Dove & wf Dorathy to George Garman
for L 54...land at the mouth of meadow Creek, 48 A...
Thomas Dove (TD) (Seal), Dourity Dove (O) (Seal), Wit: George
Kiser, Archb. White. Prov. by George Ciser, April Sessn. 1778.

Page 248: Blank.

Pp. 249-250: 25 March 1772, Abner Nash to Mathew Stewart of Meck.,
for L 10 proc. money...land on N side Goose Creek...
Wit: R Smith. Rec. Jany. Sessn 1776, prov. by Robert Smith.

Page 252: Blank.

Pp. 253-254: 10 Oct 1773, James Way of Meck., Silver Smith, to
Thomas Polk of same, for L 102 s 10 proc. money...
land on both sides four mile creek, adj. Henry Downs, Thomas Harris
and Craig, also a negro Jack aged 22, bought of Robert Alexander...

243

James Way (Seal), Thos Polk (Seal), Wit: William Patterson, Robt Alexander. (apparently a mortgage).
Recd 7 Sept 1778 from Robert Arthur the sum of Ł 129 currency for full satisfaction. Thomas Polk (Seal), Wit: Peter Johnston. (No rec. date).

Pp. 255-256: 9 Feb 1778, William Barnett & wf Jane of Meck., to Robert McCleary for Ł 18...land on a branch of big Sugar Creek adj. William Barnett, Robert McCleary, 18 A...William Barnett (Seal), Jean Barnett (Seal), Wit: Ezekiel Polk (No rec. date).

Pp. 256-258: 6 March 1775, Robert Greer of Meck., planter, to Hugh Cummings of same, planter, for Ł 31 s 5 proc. money...land on S side McCees Creek, 90 A, sold by Abner Nash 5 Feb 1771...Robert Greer (Seal), Wit: George Davis, Jurat; John Burns. (No rec. date).

Pp. 258-260: 3 Oct 1778, William McCafferty of Meck., to Thomas Polk of same, for Ł 5500...land on both sides Sugar Creek including a Grist and Saw mills said land was formerly deeded to Joseph Galbreath and reconveyd by him to Henry E. McCulloh, adj. William McCulloh, 420 A...William McCafferty (Seal), Wit: Peter Johnston, Joseph Nickelson. (No rec. date).

Pp. 261-263: 14 Oct 1778, James Jack of Meck., to Adlai Osburn and Moses Winslow of Rowan Co., for Ł 1500...part of a lot in Charlotte on Tryon St...Wit: R. Smith, Dun Ochiltree, Jurat. (No rec. date).

Pp. 263-265: 16 Jan 1778, Thomas Polk, Jeremiah McCafferty, and William Patterson of Meck., to William McCulloh of same, for Ł 2 proc. money...lot # 18 on W side Trade St...Wit: Wm Reed, Hugh Pollock, Jurat. (No rec. date).

Pp. 265-268: 11 Jan 1779, Thomas Gribble & wf Sarah of Meck., to Davis Harrisson of same, for Ł 50 proc. money...land granted to sd. Gribble 25 July 1778, 58 A adj. John McGintys, Frohocks, on waters of McCaupins Creek...Thomas Gribble (Seal), Sarah Gribble (P) (Seal), Wit: Tunas Hood, Jurat. John Ford. (No rec. date).

Pp. 268-270: 2 May 1778, William Thomson of Meck., weaver, to James Davison of same, for Ł 105...land on waters of Rockey River, (1) 370 A (2) 88 A (3) 22 A adj. Benjamin Brown, Osburn, granted by deed from Abner Nash to Thomson 5 Feb 1771...William Thomson (Seal), Wit: Jno. JcKt. Alexander, Hugh Bryson. (No rec. date).

Pp. 270-272: 27 Feb 1775, William Starrit & wf Ruth of Meck., to Andrew Sprott of same, for Ł 25 proc. money...part of a grant to William Starrit by Selwyn...William Starritt (W) (Seal), Wit: Ruth Starritt (X) (Seal), Wit: Robert Donaldson, John Newton, John Carson. (No rec. date).

Pp. 272-274: 13 Jan 1779, James Davison of Meck., to Hugh Bryson of same, for Ł 60 proc. money...377 A where sd. Bryson now lives, granted by Nash to William Thomson 5 Feb 1771, then sold to Davison 2 May 1778, adj. Ben. Brown, also 10 A adj. to it, part of 22 A granted by Nash to Thomson 5 Nov 1771, and then to Davison 2 May 1778...James Davison (Seal), Jane Davison

(O) (Seal), Wit: Samuel Davison, Jno McK. Alexander. (No rec. date).

Pp. 274-277: 26 Nov 1778, James Alexander of Cissil (sic) Co., Maryland, to Ezekiel Alexander of Meck., for ₺ 200 ...land on both sides Long Creek, adj. John Smith, John McKnitt Alexander, 300 A...James Alexander (A) (Seal), Wit: Amos Alexander, Jos. Gilhim, Beaty McCay, Jurat. (No rec. date).

Pp. 277-279: 28 Oct 1777, John Fleniken of Meck., to Samuel Fleniken, planter, for ₺ 50 proc. money...land adj. James Witherspoon, James Wagsland, Frohock, granted to John Fleniken by patent 18 June 1775, 150 A...John Flenikin (Seal), Jane Fleniken (T) (Seal), Wit: James Witherspoon, Robert Osburn. (No rec. date).

Pp. 280-282: 12 Oct 1778, Robert Sloan & wf Margaret of Meck., to John Sloan of same, for ₺ 150...land on N side Cataba above the mouth of Paw Creek adj. Matthew Robinson, James Adams, William and Thomas McGees, granted to Charles Beaty by patent 30 Aug 1753, conveyed to James Young 17 & 18 May 1762, then to Robert Sloan by deed 27 Nov 1768...Robert Sloan (Seal), Margaret Sloan (X) (Seal), Wit: Alexander Porter, William Porter, Alish Mage (A). (No rec. date).

Pp. 282-283: 10 Feb 1769, John Mitchell & wf Elizabeth to John Gilmore of Meck., for ₺ 6 proc. money...66 A, adj. John Gilmore...Wit: Samuel Wilson, Nathaniel Gilmore (No rec. date).

Pp. 284-286: 16 Sept 1778, Samuel Flanikin & wf Mary of Meck., planter, to James Flenniken of same, cooper, for ₺ 25 proc. money...land granted to sd. Samuel 4 March 1775, 198 A...Samuel Flenniken (Seal), Mary Flenniken (Seal), Wit: John Flennikin, James Flannikean. (No rec. date).

Pp. 286-287: 14 Sept 1778, James and Margaret Waughoup of Meck., to John Rogers of same, for ₺ 100 NC money...120 A on N side Waxhaw Creek adj. Robert Calwell, James Waughup... James Waughup (Seal), Margaret Waughup (Seal), Wit: John Pickens, James Davis, Samuel Waughup. (No rec. date).

Pp. 288-289: 1 Sept 1778, John Wallace & wf Mary of NC, Meck., to Anthony Hammond of Rowan Co., for ₺ 55...land originally granted to James McClelan, 17 May 1754, conveyed to John Barnet, then to John Dowdle 25 Feb 1763, then to Robt Dowdle, 14 July 1770, then to Wallace 13 Jan 1775...John Wallace (Seal), Mary Wallace (O) (Seal) Wit: Bartholomew Johnson, Samuel Givens. (No rec. date).

Pp. 290-291: 6 Aug 1776, Thomas Polk of Meck., to Doctor Ephraim Brevard of Meck., for ₺ 350 proc. money...lot # 1 on S side Tryon St in Charlotte...Thos Polk (Seal), Wit: William Patterson, James Bane. (No rec. date).

Pp. 292-293: 4 Feb 1771, Duncan Ochiltree of Meck., to William McCulloh, planter, for ₺ 52 proc. money...lot # 17 in Charlotte adj. lot of William Pattison on Tryon St....Wit: Robert Scott, Richard Mason. (No rec. date).

VOLUME 9

Pp. 294-295: 12 Nov 1778, Richard Perry & wf Elizabeth of Meck., to Hugh Gallaugher of Rowan Co., for L 117...land on little Coldwater Creek, 200 A...Richard Perry (R) (Seal), Elizabeth Perry (E) (Seal), Wit: John Nuchberry(?), John Hugs(?), John Campbell, Jurat. (No rec. date).

Pp. 295-296: 4 Feb 1777, John McReavy of Meck., to William Robinson of same, yeoman, for L 35 proc. money...land on both sides of the old Sawmill path, 200 A granted to Henery Downs 18 Apr 1771, conveyed to sd. John McCreavy...John McReavy (Seal), Mary McReavy (Seal), Wit: Archibald McReavy, Jurat; Archibald Crockett, James Lymon. (No rec. date).

Pp. 297-298: 19 Dec 1778, James Martin of Meck., planter, to Richard Martin, son of James Martin, of same, planter, for love and fillial regard...land subdivided from the place sd. James now lives on, on Astons branch of Coddle Creek, 81 A adj. John Allison, David Reese...James Martin (Seal), (C) (Seal), Jane Martin (A) (Seal), Wit: David Wilson, Jurat, Zacheus Wilson. (No rec. date).

Pp. 299-301: 16 Dec 1778, William Pattison of Meck., to Adlai Osburn, Duncan Ochilltree and Samuel Martin of same, Merchants, for L 2000...part of lot # 17 on Tryon St. in Charlotte ...Wit: Moses Wnysley, Eph Brevard. (No rec. date).

Pp. 301-302: 10 Sept 1778, Nathaniel Irvin of Meck., to Samuel McComb of same, for L 700 NC currency...land on waters of Garrisons Creek adj. James McCord, John Henery, 185 A deeded to sd. Irvin from Joseph Sul(??), 3 Apr 1771...Nathaniel Irvin (Seal), Wit: Alexander Starret, Dun. Ochilltree. (No rec. date).

Pp. 303-305: 5 Feb 1771, Abner Nash to William Thomson of Meck., for L 4...22 A in Welsh Tract including the Big Hill, part of 377 A...Wit: Hezekiah Alexander, Jurat; Zacheus Wilson. (No rec. date).

Pp. 305-307: 16 Oct 1778, Richard Springs of Meck., to John Springs for L 300...land adj. Vance, sold to William Henry by H. E. McCulloh 9 Jan 1777...Richard Springs (Seal), Wit: Adam Alexander, Jurat. (No rec. date).

Pp. 308-309: 3 Feb 1775, Nathaniel Gilmer & wf Jean of Meck., to James Gilmer of same, for L 100 proc. money... land on Rockey River, 141 A...Nathaniel Gilmer (Seal), Jean Gilmer (Seal), Wit: David Wilson, Samuel Wilson. (No rec. date).

Pp. 310-311: 22 Feb 1779, Nathaniel Cook of Meck., to John Wilson, of same, Blacksmith, for L 300...land adj. William McCafferty, 50 A, adj. Nathaniel Irwin...Nathaniel Cook (X) (Seal), Wit: Ezekiel Polk, John Betty. (No rec. date).

Pp. 311-312: 19 June 1778, Arthur Starr of Meck., to Samuel Kealah of same, for L 300...land adj. Gilmores, Wolfs, 116 A conveyed to Starr by Joseph Wallace, 9 Jan 1778...Arthur Starr (Seal), Hannah Starr (Seal), (No rec. date).

Pp. 312-313: 20 Jan 1779, William McCulloh of Meck., planter, to Samuel Martin & Adlai Osburn, Merchants, for L 500... lot #18(?) in Charlotte on Trade St...William McCulloh (Seal), Wit: Eph Brevaird, William Pattison (No rec. date).

VOLUME 9

Pp. 314-315: 25 Feb 1779, Samuel Wilson of Frederick Co., Maryland, administrator and heirs at law to the Real Estate of Garret Wilson deceased, to Ezekiel Wallace of Meck., for ₺ 400... land on Cambles Creek, waters of McCawpins Creek, adj. Ezekiel Wallace, Henry Mitchell, 200 acres...Sam: Wilson (Seal), Wit: Hezekiah Alexander, jurat; A. Raander(?) (No rec. date)

Page 216: Book N. 31st
           M. County N. Carolina

END OF VOLUME 9

ERRATA:

Page 12 (Pages 285-287) should read, 3 & 4 Nov 1765, Thomas Allison of Rowan Co., to Pattrick Duncan of Martick Township, Lancaster Co., Pa....

Page 53 (Pages 361-364): should read, 12 & 13 Jan 1764, Isabel E'Sleven, widow of William E'Sleven

Pages 248-249, captions are reversed on plat maps.

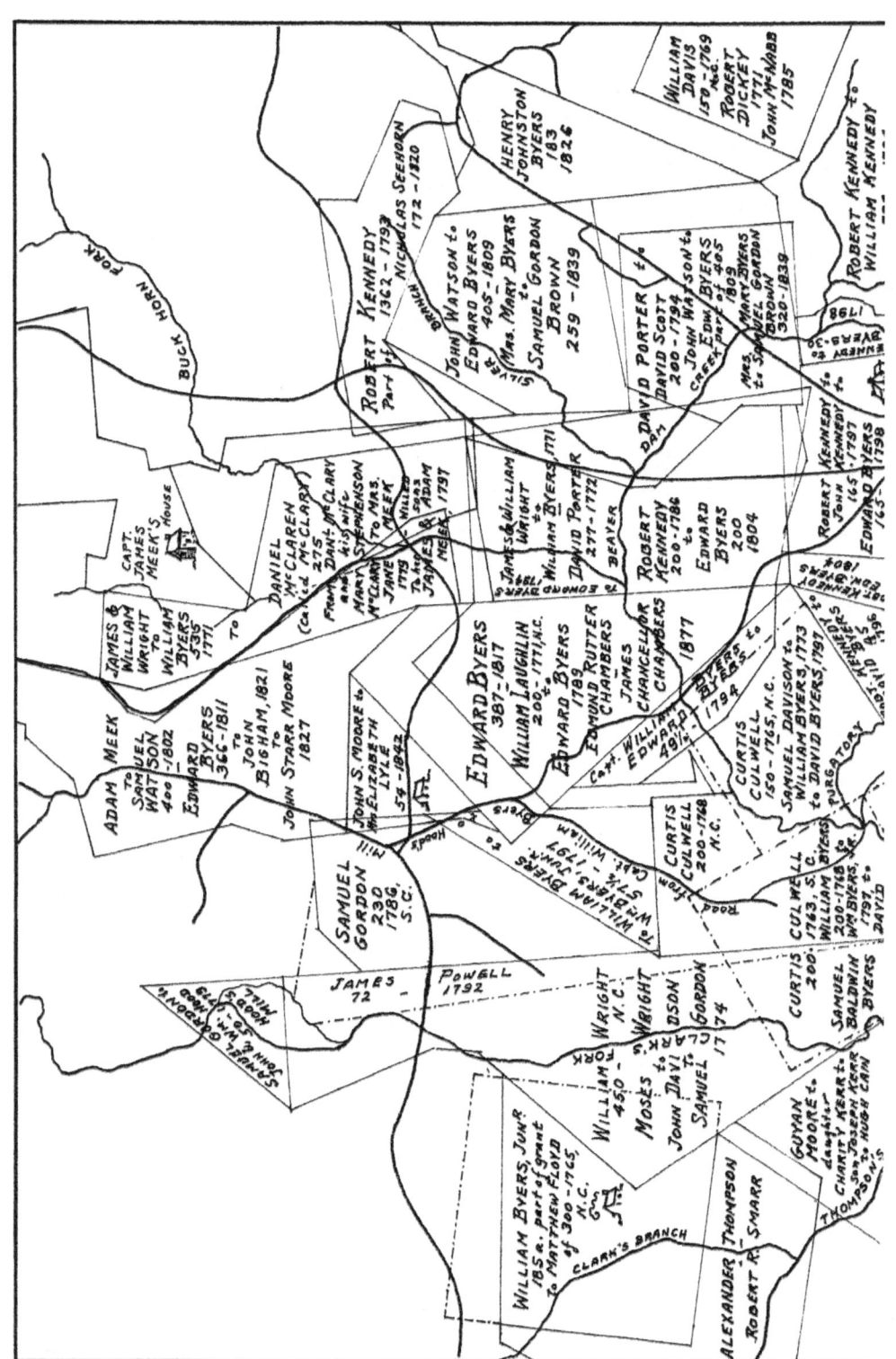

North Carolina Land Grants on the Headwaters of Bullock's

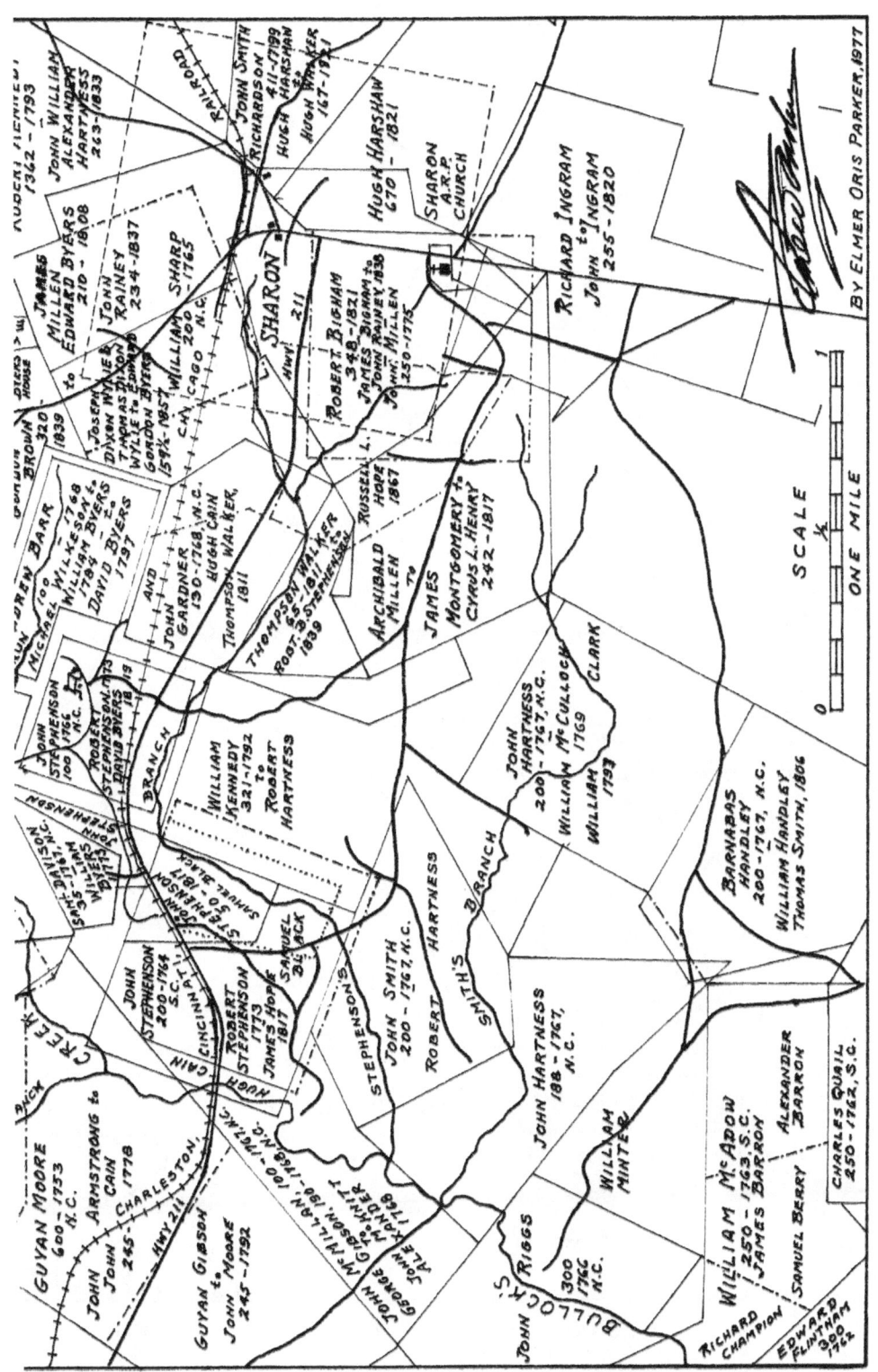

and Allison's Creeks in present York County, S. C.

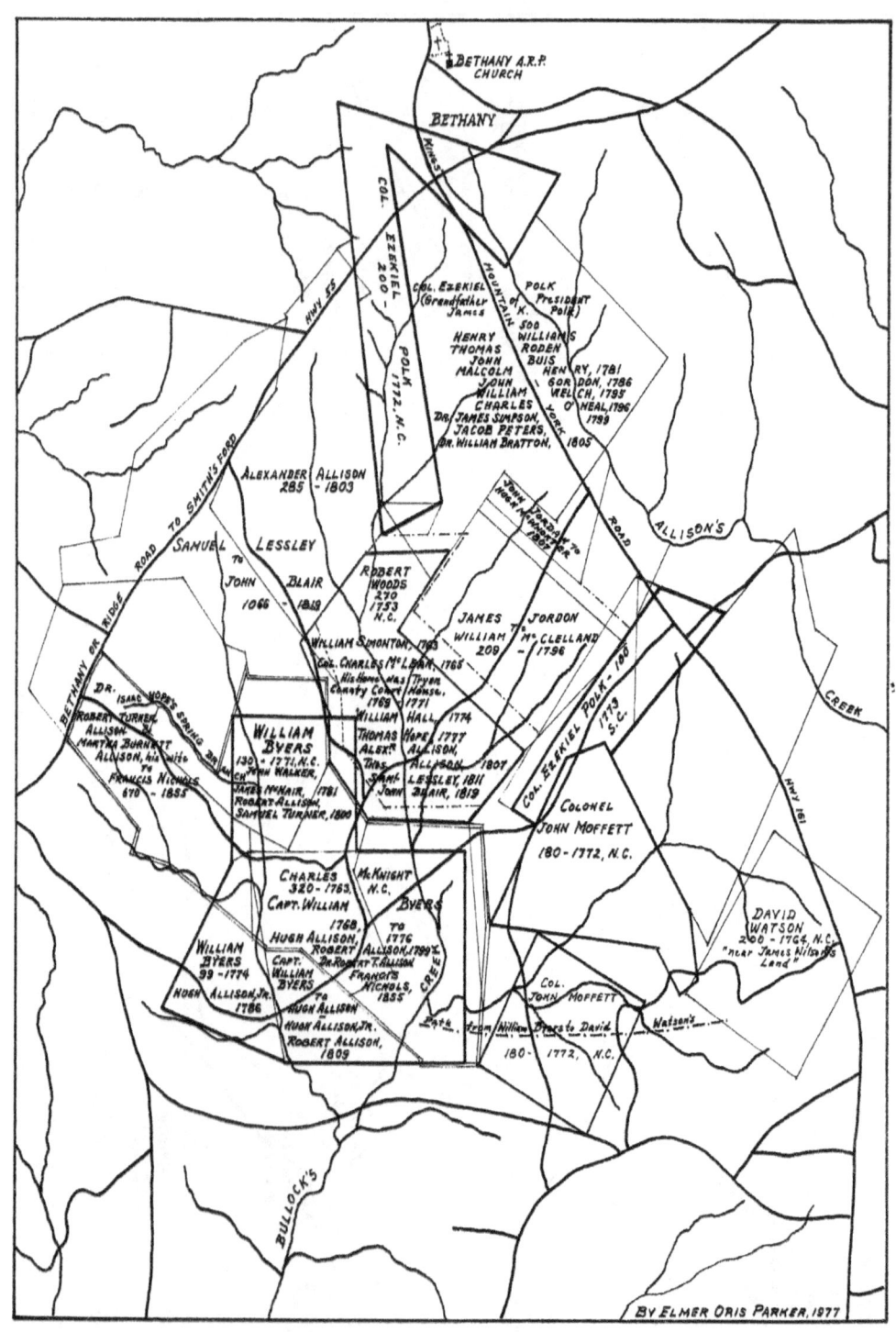

Bullock's Creek area near Sharon, S. C. showing Eighteen North Carolina Land Grants in Mecklenburg County, N. C., now York County, S. C.

INDEX

Prepared by
Flora C. & John W. Curd

Aarney,Robert 56
Abernathy,
  James 73,108
  Robert 116
Acre,
  Christian 24,25,38
  Eve 38
  Peter 24
Adair,William 132,133
Adcock,
  Ann 79
  Tobias 79
Adear,
  James 135
  Mary 27,135
  William 27
Ader,William 26
Adrian,David 78
Afee,James 136
Agner,Jacob 51,190
Ahart,Abraham 19
Akin,James 218
Aldrey,William 34
Alen,
  Alexander 218
  John 218
  William 218
Adams,
  Agness 12
  David 101,116,118
  Francis 141
  James 245
  Jean 39
  Joseph 190
  Robert 19,52,110
  William 3,12,24,34,74,
    132,233,238
Alexander,
  Aaron 31,104,132,134,138
    160,161,185
  Abigail 122
  Abraham 25,69,70,80,81,
    82,83,88,91,101,127,
    129,138,144,151,152,
    153,155,160,161,163,
    165,166,173,164,177,
    178,180,181,183,185,
    187,188,189,190,191,
    192,204,205,208,213,
    216,221,222,223,225,
    226,227,228,237,242
  Capt. 41,94
  Adam 2,12,35,46,53,65,
    69,97,127,136,138,140,
    144,162,167,173,176,
    182,183,185,199,201,
    208,218,226,237,246
  Allen 4,5,50,58,62,199
  Allon 5
  Amos 102,132,134,236,
    245
  Andrew 48,192
  Ann 5,81,175,185
  Archibald 90
  Aron 163
  Arthur 86,121,150,217,
    223
  Benjamin 15,69,93,106,
    115,127,139,142,144,
    176,185,186,192,195,
    205,217,238,240
  Charles 1,6,44,87
  Dan 225
  Daniel 16,28,69,151,155,
    186
  David 41,42,48,50,72,73,
    102,117,143,161

  Davis 132
  Ebenezer 4,112
  Elenor 2
  Elias 163,174,175,185
  Elijah 101,145,159,217,
    226
  Elizabeth 7,16,18,77,135,
    137,204
  Eza 142,217
  Ezekiel 45,58,87,92,94,
    121,130,135,137,159,
    161,162,173,174,187,
    195,214,245
  Ezra 85,86,121,150,151,
    222
  George 4,16,18,40,47,
    72,96,97,98,112,123,
    144,151,178,184,186,
    215,219,228
  Hannah 123
  Hezekiah 12,21,61,84,
    101,103,122,135,144,
    161,162,164,182,183,
    191,208,218,222,227,
    228,229,240,241,246,
    247
  Isaac 181,184,185,186,
    191,208,226
  Jam? 204
  James 29,41,44,45,69,93,
    104,118,135,137,140,
    143,144,161,162,204,
    228,240,241,245
  Jane 15,92,182,216
  Jean 16,51,102,175,202
  John 7,26,42,75,77,92,
    118,138,183,191,243
  John McKnitt 8,15,16,21,
    23,40,41,42,44,46,51,
    64,73,91,92,93,96,98,
    102,104,106,114,116,
    117,118,119,122,124,
    125,126,128,129,134,
    135,139,143,148,151,
    153,157,159,166,175,
    178,182,184,185,195,
    197,200,201,202,204,
    208,210,213,216,218,
    223,227,228,233,234,
    238,240,242,244,245
  Joseph 21,123
  Joseph,Rev. 243
  Josiah 102,151,160,161,
    215,233,239
  Margaret 82,87,89,184,
    185
  Mark 213
  Martha 135
  Mary 12,97,109,163
  Morgan 82
  Moses,Jr. 238,240
  Moses,Col. 6,7,16,18,
    21,28,40,41,42,44,47,
    48,58,62,64,72,74,77,
    78,93,94,98,118,123,
    143,180,183,185,204,
    205,206,222,224,238,
    243
  Nancy 50
  Nathaniel 2,3,4,6,7,15,
    16,18,28,29,30,31,34,
    41,42,44,46,47,54,58,
    61,69,199,201,209,219
  Oliver 2
  Phinehas 241
  Rachel 121
  Robert 48,56,109,193,

(Robert con't) 243,244
  Samuel 192
  Sarah 183,185,186,219,
    222,224,243
  Sophia 72
  Stephen 159,186,229
  Susannah 69,106,139,142
  Thomas 159,176,204,219,
    220
  Threehas 241
  "Widow" 130
  Will 99,186,227
  William 15,42,48,53,58,
    61,83,92,94,99,114,
    118,121,130,137,139,
    140,148,155,156,162,
    164,166,177,190,201,
    229,240,243
  William Jr. 48
  William B. 80
  Zebulon 84,101,123,130,
    175,183,187,189,228
Alison,
  Ann 54
  Robert 54
Allain, Samuel 39
Allcorn,
  Catren 101,102
  James 20,101,102,106,
    132
  Katin 101,102
Allen,
  Agness 131,132
  George 10,28,40,43,83,
    89,127,129,139,145,
    150,153,155,173,177,
    204,212,216,223,229
  James 107,125,152,202
  John 7,20,55,84,94,101,
    131,132,144,148,176,
    205,212,216,220,223,
    237
  Patience 96
  Samuel 96,105,172,208,
    212,241
  Sarah 10,189
  "Widow" 59
  William 237
Allison,
  Adam 5,53
  Andrew 3,19,25,37,53,
    63
  Elizabeth 53
  John 246
  Margaret 3
  Robert 24,235
  Rockey 10
  Thomas 12
Allon,George 229
Alston,William 160,197
Ambrose,Thomas 8,11
Anderson,
  Charles 18,30,53,54
  Cornelius 54
  Elizabeth 18
  Elloner 102
  James 48,73
  John 21,28,43,45,49,
    105,113,127,160,166,
    173,192,197
  Margaret 21,28
  Robert 176,241
  Samuel 43
  Thomas 103
  William 102
Andrew,
  Martha 212

Andrew(con't)
  Moses 212
  Robert 179
Andrews,Moses 152,154,175,
  179
Anthony,
  Paul 73
  Philip 72,104
Archer, George 214
Arkins,Thomas 13
Armor,
  Andrew 162,165,230
  James 2,34,225,238
Armour,
  Andrew 7,19,25,28,29,
    34,51,64,70,75,106
  James 3,25,28,53,64,75,
    106,113,114,121,134,
    142,225
  Jane 127
  Jean 157
  Jennet 106,115
  "Widow" 122,208
Armstrong,
  Agness 10
  Benjamin 64
  Elizabeth 72,74
  Francis 133
  James 30,36,47,50,72,74,
    98,108,109,221
  John 4,15,18,20,24,27,
    28,34,38,46,50,78,98,
    100,102,116,133,234
  Joseph 108
  Lancelot 21
  Margaret 57,113
  Martin 4,18,53,74
  Mary 27,34,53,74,100,
    115,234
  Matthew 7,29,64,78,234
  Robert 5,7,10,17,18,19,
    36,37,54,57,101,218
  William 57,113
Arnolpender,John 34
Arthur,Robert 244
Ashe,John 206
Ashmore,James 135
Ashybranner,Orpha 116
Aston,
  James 49,52,55,234
  Mary 52
  Thomas 62
Avery,
  W. 163,228,237
  Waightstell 190,191,203
    219
  Waightstill 221
  Wrightstutt 61,154
Baber, John 11
Bacor, George 241
Baghensmark,Joseph 21
Bahanon,
  Ann 74
  John 75
Baily,John 69
Baird,
  Adam 114
  James 122
  John 3
  William 229
Baities,Charles 68
Baity,Frances 228
Baker,
  George 164,241
  John 200,208
  Joseph 116
  Ralph 6,16,70,78,113
Balch,
  Hezekiah James 118,210
  Matthew 210
Baldridge,
  Alexander 113,204
  John 100

Ball,____ 118
Bally,John 193
Bardley,James 234
Baret,John 60
Barker,
  Jordan 201
  Michael 101
  William 201
Barkley,
  Absolam 200
  Agnes 187
  John 156,187
  Robert 187,190,200
Barnel,William 226
Barnet,
  Abraham 173
  Agnes 236
  Alexander 49
  Catherine 164
  Elizabeth 228
  Hugh 83,93,106,122,123,
    140,184,228,237
  James 31,236
  John 2,32,100,131,140,
    154,156,157,178,217,
    236
  Joseph 10,11,236
  Margaret 173,183,184
  Martha 100
  Nathaniel 242
  Robert 1,29,87,131,164,
    178,193,222,242
  Samuel 2,233
  Thomas 183,184
  Will 189
  William 3,39,64,141,164,
    173,179,183,184,190,
    203,229,236
Barnett,
  Alexander 8,11
  Elizabeth 164
  Hugh 164
  Jane 244
  John 159
  Joseph 11
  Robert 132
  William 10,55,132,153,
    154,178,184,244
Barnhart,
  Charles 49
  Christian 65
Barnit,Hugh 202
Barns,
  Andrew 180,231,232,242
  Isaac 231
  Susanna 231
Barr,
  Caleb 152,153,168
  James 152,171,178,192,
    203,229
  John 38,50,126
  Joseph 203
  Margaret 9,28
  Thomas 9,28,38
  William 101
Barringer,
  Angles 190
  Anless 190
  Antis 126
  Georg 165
  John 188,194
  Market 120
  Martin 23
  Mathias 35,71,75,76,104,
    114,116,119,120
  Matthias 105
  Paul 9,11,13,23,29,33,49,
    64,72,96,120,126,157,
    185,190,194,209,238
Barry,
  Andrew 5,18,176
  Ann 3,18,72,136
  Hugh 12,18,27,72,76,78,

Barry(con't)
  Hugh(con't) 99,116,176
  John 10,64,68,72,96,99
  Margaret 176
  Richard 2,3,5,7,11,12,18,
    21,22,25,26,27,29,34,
    38,40,42,43,44,45,46,
    47,49,51,52,55,58,106,
    107,113,122,123,127,
    136,160,176,180,208,
    225,235,238,243
  William 44
Barryhill,Alexander 234
Barten,Samuel 6
Bassett,Frans. 183
Bates,
  John 145,198
  Margaret 198
Batty,Hugh 116
Bauford,
  Ann 24
  Thomas 24
Bauhannon, John 106
Baxter,
  Mr. 186
  Andrew 187,196,214,215,
    217,237
  Francis 187,214
  John 187,217
Beaird,James 6,60
Bear,
  Jean 13
  William 13
Beard,
  Balentine 112
  Edmund 26,51
  Frances 23
  James 69,98
  Jean 13
  John 23,78,98,138,239
  Mary 211
  Richard Ward 206
  Valt. 193
  William 13,23,154,177,
    211,242
Bearden,
  Ann 192,205
  Edmond 192,205
Bearing,Edmond 92
Beates,John 87
Beatey,
  Charles 27
  Francis 105,115,121,129,
    130,183
  Hugh 115,194
  James 183
  John 153,118,123,139
  Robert 160,175
  Samuel 17,28
  Thomas 113,123
  Walter 82,149
Beats,
  John 198
  Margaret 198
Beatty,
  Charles 25
  Hugh 23
  John 96
  William 149
Beaty,
  Agness 43
  Charles 7,29,73,176,213,
    245
  Elizabeth 63,234
  Francis 7,8,9,17,18,19
    20,21,22,23,24,25,26,
    27,28,30,32,34,36,37,
    43,45,50,55,57,59,74,
    75,76,78,94,96,97,98,
    99,100,101,102,103,
    105,107,109,116,117,
    133,158,160,172,173,
    175,191,194,199,202,

Beaty(con't)
  Francis(con't) 208,221,
    224,233,234
  Francis Jr. 176
  Hugh 8,19,24,27,36,37,
    45,57,75,102,107,135,
    233
  James 5,17,18,19,22,25,
    28,32,36,37,54,55,96,
    101,102,133,173
  John 8,9,20,63,91,96,100,
    107,108,173,176,183,
    202,234
  Margaret 29,74
  Martha 8,9,18,20,28,45,
    55,98,100,102,103,107
  Robert 172,202,212
  Samuel 199
  Thomas 6,28,29,34,36,63,
    73,74,82
  Wallace 175
  Walter 216
  William 212,215
Beaver,
  Mathias 71,126,163
  Matthias 209,236
Beckmman,Christopher 180,
Beech,Justice 179
Beley,Joseph 224
Bell,
  George 53
  James 182
  Joseph 206
  Samuel 116
  Thomas 111
  Zachariah 139
Benben,Mathias 153
Benson,Thomas 54,207
Berber,Mortinir 236
Berger,George Henry 213,241
Bent,Justie 172
Berringer,Paul 155,174,239
  241
Berry,
  Hugh 98,136,165,196,224
  Jean 136
  Richard 76,138,177,225,
  William 19,43,72,108
Berryhill,
  Abram 176
  Joseph 37,160
  Samuel 2,156,160
  William 181,208,227,241
Bery,
  Hugh 28
  Richard 28
Beson,Samuel 103
Bess, Boston 100
Best,
  Bostan 100
  Lesecat 100
  Liestat 100
Betty,
  Charles 26
  John 246
Bevers,Matthias 120
Becor,Matthus 162
Bickham,James 204
Bigam,
  John 234
  Robert 234
  Samuel 207,218,234
Bigar,
  John 231
  Mathew 53
Bigem,Samuel 1
Biger,James 179
Biggar,
  James 156,165,231,232
  Joseph 231
  Mary 179
  Matthew 52,179,232
  Moses 1

Bigger,
  Ann 209
  James 52,179,209,222
  John 52,156,179
  Matthew 69,209,222
  Moses 52,182
Biggers,
  James 17
  Matthew 162,
Biggerstaff,
  Aaron 45,50,121
  Benjamin 37
  Elizabeth 37,115
  Samuel 28,37,55,94
  "Widow" 45
Bigham,
  Andrew 218
  James 28,29,203
  John 79,203,218
  Mary 2,28,29,39
  Robert 177
  Samuel 2,3,10,17,25,28,
    29,39,51,52,74,79,105,
    115,127,154,162,164,
    165,177,184,193,200,
    218,220,234,241
  Samuel Jr. 17,51
  Samuel Sr. 105,178
  Sarah 164
  William 1,2,39,132,162,
    164,165,184,193,218,
    241,234
Binager,
  Asmus 210
  Susan 210
Binber,Matthias 236
Binegar,Martin 126
Binghart,Andrew 12
Billings,Joseph 79
Bird,Amos 76
Birgham,Robert Jr. 203
Bishop,
  Elizabeth 134
  Lucy 140
  Robert 134
  William Glover 140
Black,
  David 34,52,88,149
  Edward 186
  Elener 52,59,228
  James 127,166,193,219
  Jean 166,228
  John 23,34,38,46,51,59,
    60,65,76,84,86,129,
    149,154,155,156,166,
    172,190,204,216,228
  Josiah 172,227,228
  Josias 38,72
  Margaret 59,129
  Rebecca 186
  Robert 53
  Thomas 16,27,52,53,57,
    84,85,127,141,146,149,
    172,181,199,227,228
  Will 191
  William 34,46,51,78,86,
    131,147,164,178,180,
    204,216,229
Blackburn,Robert 20,104,119
Blackwelder,
  Adam 67
  Caleb 4,68
Blackwell,Joel 21,142
Blackwood,James 199
Blair,William 167,171,172,
  197,224
Blake,John 56
Blarlord,Henry 72
Bliss,Christofer 194
Blith,Samuel 172
Blount,Jacob 206
Bluer,Frony 207
Blyth,

Blyth,
  James 142
  Samuel 36,225,228
Boal,
  John 1,124,153,227
  Thomas 227
Boals,
  John 122
  Susannah 70
Bochanan,John 74
Bogan,William 136,
Boggs,
  Joseph 137
  Thomas 209
Bogs,
  John 4,33,45
  Thomas 209
Bohannan,Ann 74
Bohannon,John 136,215
Boldridge,John 100
Bole,Margaret 227
Boles,John 41,152
Bond,Thomas 237
Bones,Andrew 122
Bonham,Absolem 95
Boogs,John 5,30,42
Boone,Gov.Thomas 226
Boot,John 208
Booth,
  Martha 228
  Marthew 228
  William 64,228
Borns,
  Andrew 239
  Isaac 239
Bost,
  ____ 116
  Bastian 33
  John 1,68
  Katharine 33
Bouchanan,John 121
Bougher,Abram 45
Bound,____ 117
Bourns,Robert 173
Bowers,John 64,107
Bowhannon,
  Ann 159
  John 159
Bowls,Susannah 76
Bowman,Andrew 92
Bowmar,Andrew 92
Boyd,John 76,166,211,233
Boyl,Edward 45,71
Boyles,James 191
Bradley,
  Fra. 20
  Francis 157
  Hannah 157
  Henry 124
  James 125,152,157,202
  John 104,106
  Jones 237
  Rebecca 106
Bradford,David 175,176
Bradner,
  Joseph 23
  Margaret 76
Brady,John 27
Braly,
  Jaohn 39
  John 39,52,59,128,165
Brandon,
  Christopher 20
  Elizabeth 39,158
  Isaac 163
  John 1,20,24,29,34,39,69,
    105,135,158,208
Branham,Jean 139
Brantney,Robert 199
Braton,John 199
Brattain,Hugh 71
Bratton,
  John 50,199

Bratton(con't)
  Robert 107
  William 17
Bravard,
  Ephraim 190,191,197,209,
    212,213,219,220,221,
    242,243,246
  Hugh 129
  Jane(Jean) 128
  Jean 28
  Joel 195
  John 28,57,128,243
  Robert 102,204
  Zebulon 212,243
Bredmore,Joseph 76
Breedmore,
  Joseph 76
  Margaret 76
Bresson,John 30
Brevard,
  Eph. 159,202
  Jojm 21
  Robert 161
Brian,John 58
Brice,James 19,20,36,225
Bridges,
  James 21
  John 37
  Wm.(Lord Mayor of London)
    56
Bigham,
  John 178
  Samuel Sr. 180
Britain,James 209
Britton,
  John 116
  Thomas 116
Bropots(Probst?),Lewis 9
Brown,
  Agness 44
  Alexander 42,44,148
  Ann 24,179
  Benjamin 55,172,179,212,
    244
  Eve 95
  George 63,95,138
  Jacob 10,26,32,64
  James 107,182,200,237
  John 24,174,188
  Mathew 181,240
  Patrick 218
  Richard 177
  Robert 74,91,151
  Samuel 41,99,117,143,164
  Walter 234
  William 89,97,140,147,
    197,233
Brownfield,
  John 203
  Robert 164,182,240
  Robert Jr. 238
  William 203
Bruster,John 214,217
Bryson,
  Hugh 213,244
  John 53
Buccaloo,Jonathan 183
Buckaloo,Jonathan 189
Buchanan,
  Ann 120,139
  John 17,19,58,78,87,90,
    102,103,120,139,145,
    151
Buchannon,John 135,225,
    230,233,244
Buckalew,Jonathan 223
Buckelew,
  Jonathan 85,150,223
  Richard 85,89,131,150
Buckellew,Richard 149
Buckhannon,John 154
Buffington,Thomas 204
Bullinger,Henry 14,119

Bullion,Thomas 102
Bullock,Zachariah 16,78,79
    138
Bumgardner,John 28,56
Bumgarner,
  John 77
  Mary 116
  Peter 116
Bunten,John 101
Burk,Thomas 140
Burlansen,Moses 215
Burnet,
  John 32,57,129,207
  Mary 32,57
Burnett,Samuel 6,57
Burns,
  Mary 162
  Robert 85,129,140,151,
    153,155,162,165,229,
    233,235
Butner,Adam 4
Buzzard,John 153,163
Byares,James 135
Byars,James 3
Byers,
  David 38
  James 103,121
  William 79,235
Byrd,
  Amos 13,43,72
  Sarah 72
C--cket,John 30
Cahoon,Thomas 106
Cain,John 51
Cairns,
  Alexander 155,159
  Daniel 159
Calaham,Timothy 32
Caldwell,
  Charles 242
  David 58,170
  Elizabeth 13,235
  James 31,235
  John 13,127,231,246
  Margaret 116
  Mathew 196
  Robert 4,8,116,187
  William 203
Caley,Robert Sponey 140
Calhoon,George 17
Calhoun,
  Elizabeth 179
  George 179,
  George Jr.178
  Samuel 179
  Thomas 9
Calhown,George 200
Camble,John 227
Campbell,
    96
  Agness 97
  Alexander 82
  Andrew 104,111,112,116
  James 11,24,25,37,42,76,
    104,106,143,180
  Jane 123
  Jean 111,122,123
  Jennet 104
  John 31,40,42,44,45,48,
    56,93,94,98,118,122,
    129,135,137,162,184
  Margaret 133
  Moses 97,100
  Richard 26
  Robert 15,60,81,83,97,
    100,105,117,133,134,
    145,147,155,175,186,
    192,198,224,239
  William 26,31,83,122,
    123,231
Cample,
  Andrew 52
  James 52

Jennet 52
John 44
Moses 68
Robert 66-216
Cameron,Joseph 92
Canner,Joseph 44
Cannon,
  Ann 139,204
  James 134,135,138,152,
    159,202,204,243
  Joseph 12,122,124,125,
    138,139,204
  Russell 140
  Simcock 140
Cannos,Joseph 126
Cansillor,Phillip 16
Caradine,Abraham 117,164,
    183,203
Caragan,Hugh 169,200
Carins,Alexander 157
Carithers,
  Hugh 141
  John 141
Carlile,Robert 207
Carloh,Conrod 158
Carmichael,
  John 71
  Thomas 20
Carmilian,John 19
Carnahan,____ 119
Carne,Alexander 210
Carniham,John 19
Carnes,Alexander 210
Carothers,
  Hugh 68,212,217
  James 178
  John 174,179
  Robert 179
Carpenter,Christian 25
Carrathers,Hugh 26
Carouth,Walter 135
Carpenter,
  Peter 106
  Woolrick 141
Carr,
  James 77
  John 50,55,56,219
  Patrick 179,182,187
  Robert 61
  William 94
Carrel,
  Jean 32
  John 3,108
  Joseph 3,4,32,136
  Mary 108
  Thomas 4
Carriden,Abraham 243
Carrigan,
  Hugh 243
  Mary 243
Carrol,
  Dr. 193
  Joseph 74,80,108
  Richard 26
  Samuel 80,85,214
Carroll,
  Joseph 116,165
  Samuel 82,83,87,147,159
  Thomas 116,165
Carrot,Samuel 183
Carrothers, Hugh 55
Carruth,
  Adam 59, 117,158,159,160,
    177,221,236
  Elizabeth 117,221
  James 59,152,165,177,178,
    187,240
  John 59,158,221
  Margaret 187
  Robert 59,218
  Walter 25,106,107,158
Carry,John 169
Carson,

Carson,
  Charles 177
  Jane 160
  John 80,147,148,135,183,
    184,223,244
  Mary 132
  Walter 43,45,158
  William 132,181
Carswell,Andrew 53
Cartee,James 39,127
Carter,
  James 20,33,69,79,105,
    208,219,241
  Thomas 201
Caruth,Robert 240
Caruthers,Robert 198
Case,
  Abigail 214
  James 214
Cash,James 13
Caster,Christian 80
Castor,Jacob 65,80,115
Castolo,
  Ellener 22
  John 22
Cashwell,Richard 206
Cathey,
  Alexander 39,75,121
  Andrew 20,26,47,64,121,
    162,221
  Archibald 20,103,121
  George 7,8,14,23,31,49,
    52,58,78,92,95,96,106,
    114,121,143,204,216,
    218
  George Sr. 241
  James 99,155
  John 26,39,45,47,52,70,
    75,76,101,102,132,134,
    155,194,202,234,236
  John Jr. 70,158
  John Sr. 158
  Josiah 208
  Margaret 7
  Martha 26,64
  Mary 52,155
  Rebecca 20
  William 32,99
Caths,Alexander 225
Cathy,
  Archibald 100
  John 3,29,71,135
  Mary 101
Cavin,Daniel 209
Chadwick,Thomas 111,119,164
Chadwock,Thomas 78
Chambers,
  Mr. 152
  Maxl. 48,125.126,163,
    180,202
  Michael 158
  Samuel 182,209
Chames,William 97
Cherry,
  David 74,95
  Robert 95
Christman,
  Elizabeth 158
  Michael 158
Chittim,John 27
Chronicle,
  William 158
  William Jr. 158
Chronow,William 79
Ciser,George 243
Cisfer,Peter 188
Claig,Samuel 172
Clark,
       121
  Agness 105
  Elizabeth 109
  Henry 73,103
  James 44,49,82,84,93,

James(con't) 114,135,150
  176,191
  John 17,18,26,30,32,46,
    51,53,57,61,69,74,77,
    97,112,123,133,137,151,
    160,192,199,224,242
  Jon 21
  Jonathan 99
  Joseph 3,17,49,103,109,
    165
  Margaret 49
  Martha 46
  Nathaniel 72,73,78,104
  Reyerius 78
  Robert Kennady 224
  Thomas 9,19,28,38,50,105
  William 30,61,176,233
Clegge,
  Jean 99
  Samuel 47,99
Cleghorn,
  Lettice 22,27
  William 22,27,31,53,64,
Clemence,Mathias 15
Clement,Mathew 71
Clemons,
  Abram 137
  John 27
Cline,
  Boston 119
  Catherina 42
  Catrin 208
  Jacob 119,208
  John Martin 42
  Margaret 119
  Michael 67
Clingan,
  Catherine 24
  William 24
Clining,Thomas 46
Clob,Peter 27
Clony,Samuel 141
Cloud,Joseph 27
Cloues,Mathias 33
Clouse,Mathies 5
Clow,Mathias 19
Clows,Matthew 28,77
Club,
  Margaret 138
  Peter 22,118,138
Clue,Gasper 77
Coborn,Samuel 106
Cobrun,
  Jacob 18,133,134
  Samuel 7
Coburn,
  Jacob 24,31,34,63,72
  John 13
  Judith 27
  Samuel 27,72
  Thomas 25,46
  William 33
Cochram,Thomas Jr. 211
Cochran,
  Benjamin 138,158
  James 205
  Robert 12
Cochrane,James 211
Cockran,Thomas 14
Cochrean,Benjamin 180
Cockren,Benjamin
Cohorn,Benjamin 134,136
Cokune,Thomas 103
Cohune,Thomas 104
Colbrith,Robert 184
Coldwell,
  David 25,65
  Elizabeth 31
  John 3,65
  William 160
Cole,
  John 227
  William Temple 49

Coleman,William 13,14
Coles,William Temple 123,
  135,136
Collins,Robert 26,51
Collson,Mary 132
Colquehoun,
  Charles 127
  George 127
Colson,
  John 132
  William 132
Colter,Martin 100
Coltener,Andrew 14
Colwell,John 31
Comins,Charles 194
Commins,Charles 196
Conaldson,Margaret 102
Conder,George 67
Coningham,Samuel 53
Conjines,John 12
Conkran,Thomas 13
Connelly,
  Bryan 95,105
  John 63,95
  Mary 105
Conner,John 122
Connor,James 163
Conyers,David 156
Cook,
  Abraham 188,214
  Benjamin 120,121
  Jacob 37
  James 73,109,116,118,
    120,121,128,129,175,
    177,210,212,213
  James Sr. 197
  John 44
  Lucy 118,120,121,177
  Mary 188
  Mathew 193
  Nathaniel 193,217,246
  Nicholas 65,66
  Roger 10,37,73,75,133
  Thomas 112
Cooper,John 83,117,147,239
Coot,Francis 95
Copland,Maryan 20
Corbely,John 140
Corborn,Samuel 4
Cordin,Abraham 42
Corrygin,James 199
Coruth,Margaret 177
Coruthers,John 196,232
Couran,Mary 227
Cousard,Archibald 187
Corzines,Nicholas 66
Cost,
  Francis 138
  Thomas 13
Costner,Jacob 27
Cotton,James 17
Cottrell,John 56
Coulter,Archibald 59
Cowan,
  John 222
  Robert 140
Cowdon,
  Robert 36,54,56
  Walter 56
  William 36,224
Cox,
  Elizabeth 141
  George 141
  Thomas 14
Coyl,Thomas 130
Coyle,Thomas 6
Crafford,James 190
Craford,
  Jean 242
  Robert 30,242
  Thomas 242
Crafts,Edward 68
Crage,James 5

Craig,
    James 33,70,100
    John 32,52
    Moses 85,150,151,222
    Samuel 5,32,216
Craige,
    James 112,236
    Moses 89,91,243
Craighead,
    Alexander,Rev. 21
    Jane 88,161
    Mary 187
    Robert 161,201
Crassels,Moses 243
Crawford,
    Agness 154
    Elenor 100
    George 68,100
    James 43,117
    John 101
    Joseph 6,45,97,154
    Oliver 23,24
    Robert 6,45
    Samuel 216
    William 23,24
Creaghead,
    Elizabeth 187
    Hannah 181,187
    Jean 181
    Robert 181
Creditton,William 215
Cregg,Benjamin 190
Cresimore,Jacob 70
Crewsell,Matthew 101
Crissmore,Jacob 103,104
Crittenden,William 58
Crittes,Devalt 33
Crock,James 191
Crocket,
    Andrew 191,237
    Archibald 117,214
    Arem-- 184
    John 54,97,109
    Magel 128
    Margaret 97,157
    Mary 54
    Robert 93,227,232
Crockett,
    Alexander 161
    Andrew 161,164,183,184,
        205,210
    Archibald 37,38,42,161,
        164,183,184,205,210,
        226,246
    James 161
    Jean 38,68
    John 4,37,68,155,157,187
    Margaret 37,50
    Mary 37,183,184,205
    Rachel 61
    Robert 6,14,37,38,41,61,
        68
Crofer,Ralph 107
Crofts,Edward 68,138
Croham,William 43
Cromikel,William 10
Cronicle,William 118
Cromall,William 17
Cromley,
    Henry 210
    Sarah 210
Cronical,William 217
Crosimore,Jacob 70
Crosley,George 155
Crowder,Ulrick 96
Crowel(1),
    Betty 49
    Catherine 33
    Elizabeth 174
    George 156,169
    Jamima 156
    Peter 33
    Samuel 170,174

Crowel(1) (con't)
    Simon 49
Crown,William 112
Crumley,Henry 210
Crunbly,Sarah 210
Crye,William 197
Crymble,Mary 56
Culberson,
    John 167,197
    Moses 197
    William 195
Culbertson,John 81,193
Culp,
    Casper 30,43,54
    John 165
    Peter 14,39
Culverson,John 154
Cumins,France 218
Cummie,Charles 218
Cummings,
    Charles 211
    Hugh 244
Cummins,
    Elizabeth 211
    Francis 211
    John 211,218
Cunningham,
    ___ 100,198
    Adam 198
    James 76,116,133,139
    Roger 124
Cunntz,___ 33
Cuntz,Nicholas 46
Curran,Mary 226
Currey,John 154,220
Curron,Mary,Mrs. 61
Curry,
    Charles 158
    Edward 177
    John 122
    William 103
Cuthberson,John 97
Cuthbertson,William 221
Darr,Charles 209
Darmon,John 223
David,James 120
Davidson,
    Benjamin 78
    George 31,50,75,76
    James 109
    John 50,108
    Margaret 50
    William 221
Davies,
    Clim 218
    Daniel 14,178
    David 119,154,179
    Elijah 154
    Elizabeth 31,154,212
    James 110,120,122,234
    John 31,95,110,120,212,
        213,217,234,236,239
    Joseph 54
    Margaret 31,110
    Moses 1
    Robert 154,197,241
    Samuel 243
    Sarah 95
    Walter 20,31,107,218
    William 154,156,232
Davieson,James 212
Davis,
    Andrew 65
    Ann 11
    Daniel 47,168,177,180
    David 64,81,83,87,119,
        127,130,141,145,198,
        223,224
    Elijah 175,224
    Elis 31
    Elizabeth 17,130,222,224
    George 12,95,229,239,244
    Hugh 98

Davis(con't)
    James 13,29,106,119,120,
        122,130,142,222,232,
        239
    Jean 229
    John 7,13,17,26,28,29,31
        32,37,46,47,51,61,73,
        74,101,106,117,120,121
        127,130,157,159,172,
        176,179,180,182,213,
        222,226,229,231,237,
        238
    John Jr. 7,11,12,13,22,
        35,36,62,64,65,66,67,
        68,97
    Margaret 52,130
    Mary 229
    Mildred 95
    Moses 229
    Rebecca 79,106
    Robert 1,95,128,229,238,
        239
    Robert Sr. 201,232
    Samuel 160
    Thomas 22
    Walter 7,58,74,79,101,
        102,106,165,175,214
    William 10,11,34,64,117,
        232,239
Davison,
    David 121
    George 3,9,30,52,53
    James 244
    Jane 244
    Jean 213
    John 8,33,48,49,62,113,
        127,236
    Katherine 53
    Margaret 9,30
    Samuel 8,9,53,212,245
    Violet 8
    William 3,11
Daviss,
    Jean 1
    Moses 1
Dawson,Bartholomew 117
Day,Robert 137
Dean,John 154
Dearmon,Mr. 131
Dearmond,
    John 85,101,147
    Thomas 84,143,156,205
Deel,William 119
Delaney,Deus 75
Dellinger,John 206
Dempsey,Margaret 61
Dennis,John 117
Denenny,Samuel 24
Denney,George 38
Denny,
    ___ 114
    George 25,136,228
    Jane 25
    Jean 228
Dermand,John 214
Dermond,
    John 235
    Thomas 242
Derrick,George 33
DeRosset,Lewis 91
Desar,John 98
Desoran,Henry 206
Dick,
    George 32
    Mary 32
    Mathias 32,33
Dickerson,William 18
Dickey,
    John 34,117
    Margaret 31,52
    Moses 9,50,53,57
    William 3,11
Dickie,___ 79

Dickson,
  Alexander 92
  Arthur 135,137
  David 24
  Edward 92
  James 193
  John 195
  Jo 73,74,138
  Joseph 92
  Michael 141
  Robert 70,71,92,188
  Sarah 141
  Thomas 104,109
  William 17,23,33,38,54,
    73,74,92,100,110,137,
    138
Dicky,George 107
Dill,John 114
Dillinger,
    22
  Fanny 18
  Hannah 21
  Henry 21,24
  John 17,19,21
Dinn,James 36,115
Dismut,William 73
Dobbins,Alexander 6,26,96,
    112,212,217,241
Dobbs,
    11,12,47,62,65,66,
    67,68
  Arthur 1.2.7.12.13.21.22.
    23,25,26,29,31,32,35,
    36,40,45,51,52,55,58,
    64,80,96,97,98,99,107,
    122,126,127,136,154,
    155,162,173,180,185,
    187,189,209,217,235
  George 42
  Governor 146,154,177,192
    193,199,207,223,228,
    238
  Justina 7,13,34,35,36,40
    58,80,97,98,136,155,
    187,235,238
Dobrum,Samuel 72
Dodd,George 205
Doherty,
  James 68
  John 126,132
Donaldson,
  Arthur 7,40
  Margaret 82,87,145,191,
    229
  Robert 244
  William 117,118,123,183,
    184
Donalson,Andrew 192
Donelson,
  Margaret 198
  Robert 221,243
  William 164
Donolson,
  Arthur 203
  William 205
Doudle,
  Elenor 129
  John 57,129
  Robert 129,185
Douglas,George 4,5
Douglass,
  James 166
  Jo. 201
Dove,
  Dorathy 243
  Dourity 243
  Thomas 174,232,243
Dover,John 138
Dowdle,
  Jane 207
  John 207
  Robert 207
Downes,Hendry 14

Downs,
  Andrew 104,158
  Ann 158
  Francis 58,181
  Henry 8,13,30,74,82,83,
    85,87,88,120,129,146,
    150,161,173,181,185,
    186,193,213,214,215,
    220,233,240,243,246
  Henry Jr. 161,173
  Joseph 58
Dozer,
  John 73
  Leonard 73,142
  Mary 73
Draper,William 55
Drennan,John 14
Drew,William 7,38,47,49,
    136,203
Drue,William 18
Dry,George 66
Duff,James 134
Duglas,
  Hannah 189
  James 189,228
Dugless,Joseph 242
Duhart,John 64
Duke,
  John 210,211
  Margaret 210,211
Dulkwalk,Sarah 127
Dun,Jacob 209
Duncan,
  David 5
  Francis 115
  John 11,12,38
  Peter 43,57,142
  Vilatt 76
Dunlap,
  Mary 64
  Samuel 31,64
Dunlop,
  Mary 62
  Samuel 62
  William 15,63,108
Dunn,
  Andrew 102,173,189,198
  Elizabeth 47
  James 20,47,118,129,173,
    198
  John 8,48,49,69,94,125,
    135,136,138,152,180,
    207,222,242
  Martha 198
  Robert 198
Dunningham,Roger 214
Dunns,James 123
Dur,George 78
Dyer,Dennis 142
Dysart,
  James 62,153,162,169,
    176,233
  John 93
Dyzart,
  James 164,179
  Margaret 164
Eagan,
  Barnaby 58
  Rachel 14,58
Eadey,William 6
Eagle,George 192
Eagner,
  Jacob 51,95,190
  Mary 51
Eakee,Alexander 87
Eakin,Alexander 146,222
Earick,Philip 5
Earington,Philip 5
Earle,Joseph 31
Earnharts,Philip 11
Eberhart,Jacob 77,116
Edger,
  Adam 209

Edger,
  Archable 209
Edwards,
  Is.(Isaac?) 48,86
  James 151
  John 171
  Mark 32
Egner,
  Jacob 113,119,190
  Mary 113,119
Elder,John 56,106
Eliot,
  George 47,127
  Robert 52,181
Eliott,William 190
Elliot,
  Archibald 32,113
  Andrew 98
  George 18,28,99,200,238
  James 57,164,
  John 79,110
  Patrick 172
  Robert 52,53,56,57,62,
    81,86,144,164,165,166,
    174,189,218
  William 164,177,211
Elliott,
  Andrew 7,16,25,99,143
  John 109,110
  Martha 227
  Peter 22
  Robert 82,161,205
  William 165,222,227,231,
    232,236
Ellot,
  Peter 228
  Robert 226
Els,John 105
Emanuel,David 22,53,63,114
England,Daniel 228
Ewart,Robert 51,55,107
Eray,William 206
Ervin,Nathaniel 102
Erwin,
  Alexander 222
  Andrew 2,25,238
  Christefor 61
  Jacob 18
  James 32
  Joseph 109
  Robert 212,225
  Samuel 35
  Thomas 56
  William 37,94
Erwyn,William 111
Esbell,Zachary 49
Esteven,Robert 196
Evans,
  Jabez 20,78,175
  James 152
  Robert 123
Ewart,Robert 11,47
Ewing,
  George 115
  Nathaniel 100
  Sarah 190
  Thomas 190
Exevyor,William 86
Fall,Andrew 133,134
Falls,
  Andrew 18
  Galbresth 63
  John 46
  William 37
Fannin,James 140
Fanning,
  Edmond 1,24,48,52,64,95,
    96,112
  James 138
Faris,
  James 74
  John 74
Farmer,John 108,128,239,240

Farr,
  Ephraim 235,238
  John 158
  William 139
Fashparmon,Henry 176
Fashpermon,Christiana 176
Faver,Theophilus 17
Feagle,Charles 235
Felmming,Ralph 133
Fearil,John 17
Femster,
  Joseph 53
  Major 196
  Samuel 53
Ferguson,
  Alexander 12,39
  Charles 23
  Henry 101,102
  Martha 157
  Moses 1,2,3,12,13,17,22,
    25,28,29,31,51,55,56,
    62,64,69,79,80,115,
    127,135,136,157,239,
    240
  Robert 79
  Thomas 187
  William 76
Ferral,Thomas 30,54
Ffier,John 78,80,107,114,
    135,144
Ffrock,William 203
Ffrohock,
  John 44,45,47,48,80,81,
    92,93,94,95,98,143,
    144,145,146,147,148,
    149,150,151,152,153,
    155
  Thomas 130
  William 76,130,143
Fields,
  John 71,80,114,117
  Sarah 117
Fifer,
  Capt. 31
  Catherin 234
  John 77,78,79,177,207,
    223,234,238
  Martain 4,12,34,46,47,
    68,69,75,114,120,235
File,George 157
Findlay,Samuel 63
Findley,
  George 180
  James 201
  John 187
  Joseph 201
  Margaret 201
  Robert 21,201
  Samuel 25,36
  Thomas 201
Findly,George 228
Finely,Robert 234
Finley,
  George 221
  James 152
  John 152,154,162,163,
    175
Finney,
  Alexander 180,187,231
  James 180
Fishar,
  Jacob 107
  Sevely 107
Fisher,
  Capt. 68
  Archibald 54,62
  Barbara 207
  Charles 36,64,66,72,207
  Fraderick 188
  Frederick 67,107
  Jean 54
  John 119
  Malcom 62

Fisher(con't),
  Malkam 54,
  Martin 188
Fissher,Frederick Jr 188
Fitten,Isaiah 103,105
Fitter,Isaiah 214
Flanagan,Jane 150,216
Flanajen,John 154
Flanekin,Samuel 154
Flanican,James 184
Flanigen,James 242
Flaniken,
  Jane 183
  Mary 245
  Sarah 183
  William 143,174,204
Flenagen,William 205,215,
Fleniken,
  John 183,229
  Samuel 201
Flannagan,
  Jean 83
  William 84,85
Flannakan,James 81
Flannakin,James 151
Flanney,Thomas 52
Flannigan,John 82
Flanniken,William 156
Fleet,John 15
Fleming,
  Grizzy 208
  Henry 210
  John 208,234
  Ralph 103,105,133,139
Flemming,John 68
Flenigan,
  John 242
  Samuel 242
Fleniken,
  Jane 245
  John 245
  Samuel 233,245
Flenneken,William 233
Flenniken,
  James 245
  John 182
  William 135,235
Flentham,Edward 26
Fletchall,Thomas 49
Flin,Nicklas 198
Flintham,Edward 51
Flough,David 129,140,231
Floy,Daniel 152
Floyd,
  Matthew 7,17,21,23,71,75,
    103,109,111,112,116,
    136,137,139
  Sarah 17
Foard,
  John 59,165,193
  Zebulon 59
Fondren,
  Alender 13
  Elinore 7
  John 6,7,8,11,13,17,68,
    73,74,79,80,95,101,
    109,110,138,
Fondron,John 77,137
Ford,
  Benjamin 97,203
  Cathrean 220,
  Frederick 50,62
  John 59,85,131,157,165,
    183,193,199,200,206,
    212,219,220,244
  Joseph 196
  Katherine 157
  Zebulon 199,200,219
Forden,
  Ann 99
  James 99
Forgison,Moses 29
Forguson,

Forguson,
  Alexander 193
  Charles 126
  Thomas 152,182
Forney,
  Jacob 19,29,33,51,108
  Mary 29,108
Forrer,Henry 72
Forster,
  Henry 57
  James 15,16
Forsyth,
  James 70,77,80,112,166
  Mathew 43
Foster,
  Andrew 181
  Ann 5,30,54
  Arthur 5
  Henry 4,5,30,54,
  Henry J. 232
  Hugh 219
  James 70,77,81,106,127,
    140,141,143,151,174,
    181,183,184,185,186,
    189,192,194,195,213,
    214,226
  Jacob 54
  John 239,243
  Moses 141
  William 128
Franklin,John 104,117
Fransischo,
  John 194
  Rebecca 194
Francises,John 236
Fraser,Donald 45
Frazer,James 178
Freeear,
  Richard 219
  Robert 219
Freeman,David 200
French,John 193
Frenchland,John 193
Fresel,Jason 200
Frey,Leasalet 119
Friday,Nicholas 142
Frissell,Jason 180,210,211
Frohoc,John 222
Frohock,
  Col. 130
  John 7,8,9,15,16,40,41,
    42,58,88,89,90,91,99,
    101,106,111,118,127,
    155,165,173,180,188,
    216,223,234,235,238
  T. 217
  Thomas 76,89,95,96,100,
    101,111,115,204,211,
    214,218,227,235
  William 76,89,90,95,96,
    100,101,111,114,115,
    215,216
Fronoburger,William 38
Fry(Frey),
  Gabriel 105
  Magdalena 75
  Nicholas 76
  Niklos 75
Fryday,Nicholas 18
Frye,Nicholas 57,119
Fulton,Thomas 34
Furgoson,Moses 180
Gabb,John 199
Gabbie,Robert 115
Gabby,
  Joseph 115
  Robert 74,109
Galbreath,Joseph 85,88,
    91,147,157,192,195,
    196,199,219,224,233,
    239,244
Gallaugher,Hugh 246
Galts,Robert 51

Gambell,
  James 101
  William 30
Gamon, William 99
Gant,
  Joseph 215
  Susana 215
Gardner,
  Jacob 14,58,92,104,139,
    166
  James 99,211
  Sophia 182
  William 94,98,107,238
Gardiner, William 37
Gardnor, Wm. 200
Garies, Arthur 223
Garison,
  Arthur 89
  David 223
  Hannah 130
  Isabela 223
  John 130,220
Garlaugh,
  Cunrad 186
  Mary 186
Garner, Sophia 157
Garret, Joseph 174
Garril, Thomas 102
Garrison,
  Arthur 87,147,215
  David 42,82,83,131,142,
    148,151,176,229,240,
    241
  Hannah 161
  John 84,86,119,146,160,
    161,165,176,188,210,
    243
  Mary 240
  Peter 83,87,144,223
Garven,
  John 17
  Martha 17
  Thomas 200
Garvin,
  John 63
  John Jr. 17
  Thomas 33
Gatchell, Jeremiah 140
Gault, Robert 42
Gay, Samuel 13,16,17,75,107
Gaygler, John 209
German, George 67
Gerrel,
  Mary 138
  Thomas 138
Gerrett, Robert 130
Gerrison, John 181
Gesander, Robert 50
Gibbons, John 184
Gibbs, John Walter 233
Gibley, Robert 10
Gibson,
  George 103
  James 103
Gilbert, Telix(?) 39
Giles,
  Edward 6,18,40,243
  John 58,105,127,162,193,
    208,220
  William 203
Gilham, Charles 132
Gilhim, Joseph 245
Gilkey, Samuel 102,104
Gill, George 73,74
Gillaspie,
  Henry 57
  Thomas 57
Gillaspy, William 192
Gilleland,
  Alexander 72
  Archibald 5,32,37,224
  Thomas 140
Gillespie,

Gillespie,
  Joseph 21
  Mathew 6
  Thomas 45
  William 105
Gillespy,
  Joseph 115
  Thomas 71
Gilham,
  Elizabeth 114
  Ezejiel 114
  Thomas 114
Gillham, Charles 114
Gilliland, Archibald 234
Gilmer,
  James 162,246
  Jean 246
  Nathaniel 246
Gilmore,
  _____ 42
  James 153,162,178,179,
    182,186,198,203,242,
    243
  John 6,16,152,203,245
  Margaret 198
  Nathaniel 178,198,203,
    245
Gindley, John 179
Gingles, Samuel 69,78,174,
    188
Given,
  Edward 47,76
  Samuel 76
Givens,
  Agness 203,204
  Edward 160,175,185,203,
    204,218
  John 160
  Margaret 160
  Samuel 203,204
  Thomas 160
  "Widow" 158
  William 118,160,181,191,
Gizer, Peter 68
Glaghorn, _____ 100
Glass,
  Francis 171,230
  James 243
  Robert 168,230
Glimp, Abraham 13
Glover,
  John 39
  Robert 39
  William Bishop 140
Goforth,
  Andrew 28
  Preston 2,46,104
  William 77
Goldman, Henry 67
Goodman,
  Christopher 186
  Michael 158,192
  William 14
Goodnight,
  George 186
  Jacob 208
  Marry 185
  Mary 185
  Michael 185,186
Gordan, Robert 3
Gorden, _____ 74
  James 99
Gordon,
  Ann 99
  Benjamin 107
  David 78
  George 62
  James 72
  John 118
  Robert 57
  William 136
Gorright, Fight 163
Gould, George 56

Graham,
  Agness 194
  James 1,2,6,135
  Jean 2,6,69,188,233
  John 2,103,188,291,233
  Mary 234
  Richard 2,208,225,236,
    238
  Robert 198,220
  William 57,69,160
Grahm,
  Richard 56
  Robert 218
Grhame,
  Jean 69
  William 69
Grairel,
  Dietrich 76
  George 76
  William 76
Grant, William 26,34,63
Granville, Earl 2,32
Gray,
  Jacob 13,118,120,175,213,
    214,228
  Robert 36
Greay, Jacob 128
Green,
  Ann 58
  Andrew 34
  George 29
  John 194
  Joseph 25,38,49
  Mary 25
  Rebekkah 239
  Robert 194
  Timy. 208
  William 21,45,58,112
Greer,
  Andrew 166,179,191,225,
    230
  Joseph 213
  Robert 244
  Thomas 212
Gribbill, Thomas 89
Gribble,
  Sarah 244
  Thomas 60,149,244
Grier, Thomas 172
Grigg,
  Abner, Sr. 137
  Burrel 112
  Jess 137
Grime, John 218
Grimes, William 30
Grims, Patrick 113
Grindal,
  Esther 107
  John 107
Grover, John 39
Grubb, Benjamin 72
Grundel, John 107
Guiss, Christopher 77
Guizen, Peter 215
Gullick,
  John 18,45,102,161
  Jonathan 5
Guy, Samuel 140
Haberty, William 108
Hackey, John 14
Hag, William 127
Hagan,
  Hugh 3
  John 20
  William 14,161
Hagans,
  Elizabeth 15,226
  John 6,15,129,188
  Mary 129,238
  William 18,129,130,238
Hagar, Elizabeth 38
  John 29
  William 29,38

Hagarty,
　Sarah 96
　William 96
Hagens,
　John 199
　William 242
Hager, William 25,38
Hagertie, William 70
Haggan,
　Elizabeth 20
　John 20
Haggans,
　John 94
　Mary 9
　William, Capt. 9
　William 191,225
Haggars, William 173
Haggartis, William 137
Haggarty, William 74
Hagger, William 142
Haggerty, William 63
Haggin, John 32
Haggins,
　Elizabeth 13
　John 13
　Mary 6,14
　William 6,14,161
Hagins,
　John 226
　William 201
Hairston, William 87
Hales, J.H. 5
Hall,
　Elizabeth 184,233
　James 84,233
　John 157,184,197,234
　Thomas 12,170,230
　William 233
Hally, John 48
Hambright,
　Frederick 2,7,27,37,73,
　　75,76
　Sarah 27,37
Hamer, John 69
Hamilton,
　Hugh 164
　John 59,60,173,229
　Malcom 238
　Malion 225
Hampton,
　Andrew 26,31,53,56,72,
　　132,135
　Joseph 202
　Katherine 132
Hamright,
　Frederick 133
　Sarah 133
Hamston, Melion 2
Handle,
　David 137
　Catherine 137
　John 137
Haney, John 140
Hankins, John 142
Hanna,
　James 74,108,110,118
　William 118,196
Hannagen, William 131
Hannah,
　James 16,18,20,46,68,
　　70,71,78,80
　Jean 18
　John 13
Hannas, James 137
Harans, William 185
Harch, John 14
Hardan,
　Benjamin 79
　John 80,138
Harden,
　Alexander 19,49
　Ambrose 151,198
　Benjamin 2,10,23,36,

Harden(Con't)
　Benjamin(Con't)37,63,73,
　　75,76,99,101(Capt.),
　　102,116
　Catherine 23
　Elizabeth 132
　John 17,36,49,54,102,132,
　　235
　Joseph 10,37,73,79,109,
　　133
Hardin,
　Benjamin 43,221
　John 137
　Joseph 23,158
Harding,
　Ambrose 127,128,135,152,
　　153,154,159,162,176,
　　178,179,187,190,192,
　　201,212
　Benjamin Jr. 52
　Joseph 10,43,118,173
Hardlocker, Christopher 66
Harind, Joseph 32
Harkness, George 213
Harlan,
　Isaac 241
　Joel 175
Harland, Isaac 132,241
Harnett, Com. 206
Harrahas, Martin 33
Harpell, Peter 116
Harper,
　Alexander 70
　Mary 74
　Peter 115
　Robert 70,74,104,140
Harphill, ___ 70
Harrel, Richard 23
Harris,
　Charles 41,45,48,63,99,
　　128,143,153,173
　Colonel 66
　Dinah 50
　Elender 60
　Elizabeth 55
　Francis 1,69,118,224
　George 194
　Hugh 202
　James 12,31,32,34,43,45,
　　50,55,61,65,66,74,100,
　　103,128,129,139,167,
　　169,173,212,217,235
　James Jr.63
　John 50,60,100,167,169,
　　173,242
　Joseph 60,130,192,195,
　　196,218
　Joseph Jr. 196,228
　Laird 162
　Margaret 1,12,100
　Martha 187,217,222,224
　Mary 45,103,139,173
　Mathew 129
　Rebecca 2
　Robert 1,3,9,12,13,21,
　　25,29,31,32,33,40,41,
　　44,46,50,55,57,61,62,
　　63,64,69,71,74,78,79,
　　99,100,106,118,127,
　　129,132,139,152,163,
　　167,177,179,191,203,
　　208,219,221,235,238
　Robert Jr. 1,2,12,13,16,
　　22,26,30,31,33,36,48,
　　50,54,55,96,97,99,100,
　　127,130,141,156,166,
　　182,185,222,224,233
　Robert Sr. 185,222,224
　Samuel 2,12,45,139,163,
　　167,168,171,217,230
　Samuel Jr. 12
　Susannah 71
　Thomas 1,60,74,82,91,102,

Harris(con't)
　Thomas(con't) 103,127,
　　131,150,151,193,201,
　　218,221,242,243
　Tyla 47
　Tyry 46
　Will 8,16,58,99,163
　William 6,11,32,34,37,
　　70,139,185,186,187
Harrison,
　David 189
　Davis 244
　Jeremiah 31,194
　William 24,33
Harrod, Thomas 137,138
Harron,
　Frances 238
　Hugh 136
Harshea, Conrad 33
Hart,
　A. 19
　Charles 11,71,233
　Clera 235
　David 238
　Davis 207
　James 207
　Joseph 162,193,207
　Kelra 71
Hartsel, Leonard 67,174,186
Hartsell, Easter 174
Hasell, James 71
Hasler, William 212
Harvey,
　John 206,
　Robert 183
Hatherly, Ewings 95
Havener,
　Peter 142,
　Teter 95,116
Hawkins, Thomas 6,79,110
Hay,
　Daniel 225
　David 1,13,19,184,208,
　　234
　Jean 13,187
　Margret 225
　Rebeca 220
　William 159,201,220
Haygler, Barbara 209
Haynes,
　David 86,240,241
　William 195
Hayns, William 196
Hays,
　David 51,124,145,152,
　　184,202
　David Sr. 13,236
　Jean 13
　Thomas 14
　William 65,96
Hayward, Samuel 100
Heager, Elizabeth 38
Heaker, William 38
Heart, Christian 213
Hecker, William 142
Hegler, John 67
Heitower, John 160
Helms,
　George 212
　John 212
Hemphill,
　Alexander 10,11
　W. 41,45,141
　William 44,192
Henderson,
　Archabald 172,200,209
　Daniel 20
　James 27,107,109,208
　John 38,72,208
　Kairns 93
　Kern 41
　Mathew 198
　Nathaniel

Henderson(con't)
  Nathaniel 5,70,114,136,139
  Philip 97
  Richard 44,51,52,70,77,94,109,145,167,188,203,229
  Robert 99
  William 38,59,169,172,200,208
Hendres,John 179
Henerson,Archibald 227
Henery,John 246
Hendrie,John 140
Hendry,
  ___ 114
  Esabella 109
  Henry 8,9,39,48,49,50,102,105,185,216
  Henry Jr. 105,155
  Henry Sr. 155
  Isabel 48,109
  James 50
  John 6,11,20,50,106,109,165
  Martha 106,119
  Thomas 109
  William 109
Henry,
  Alexander 126,237
  Daniel 225
  Elizabeth 234
  Henry 207
  James 57,234
  John 5,10,11,17,29,85,88,89,95,102,130,147,203,217,218,224
  Martha 11,203
  Thomas 25,133
  William 4,25,39,56,87,124,125,134,138,139,148,152,163,207,210,234
Henty,John 101
Herdney,William 234
Herkey,Martin 120
Herion,Andrew 87
Hernhart,Barbara 209
Heron,Andrew 90
Herrin,Francis 224
Herring,Francis 130
Herron,
  Andrew 10,165
  Charles 106
  Francis 130,177,240
  George 194
  Hugh 239
  James 178
  John 242
Heslop,
  Andrew 47
  Katherine 47
Hester,
  Sarah 214
  William 213,214
Hetherington,James 70
Hickcock,John 33
Hide,Benjamin 57
Hider,Benjamin 132,135
Jies,Heirge 14
Higgison,Ann 127
Hildebrand,Henry 142
Hilf,John 45
Hill,
  Jean 10,11
  John 10,11,32,43,58,64,138,147,213,214
  Thomas 95
Hillhouse,Mr. 134
Hindry,John 58
Hise,
  George 174
  Mary 174

Hitchcock,John 32
Hix,Richard 140
Hobbs,Joseph 185
Hobles,Joseph 111
Hogan,John 77
Hogans,George 213
Hoghead,Elizabeth 115
Hogshead,
  Samuel 199
  Walter 40
Hogston,Robert 238
Hoil,Michael 37
Holbrook,John 211
Holdman,Henry Jr. 70,106
Holland,James 90,114
Hollingsworth,
  Elias 13,14
  Joseph 13,14
  Martha 14
  Thomas 13,14
Hollman,Henry 141,142
Holloway,John 84,90,131,150
Holly,Matthew 174
Hood,
  John 189,199,200
  Tunas 191,193,244
  William 64
Hoop,Robert 214
Hooper,
  Enos 109
  Thomas 109
  William 155
Hope,
  James 233
  Robert 195,220
Hort,
  Margaret 114
  Simon 114
Hose,Jacob 22
Hoss,Jacob 22
Hough,David 173,181
House,Mark 65
Houston,
  Aaron 2,3,22,105,112,118,124
  Agness 30,74,233
  Archibald 15,18,94,120,177,190,212
  David 2,3,6
  Hugh 22,192,224
  James 118,124,185
  Levinas 99
  Livinus 164
  Margaret 18,120,124
  Mary 2,3
  Sevinis 99
  Stephen 16
  Thomas 19,30,75,86,161,233
  William 2,3,148
Hover,
  Gesper 108
  George 113
  Jasper 108
  Margaret 108
How,
  Catherine 7
  William 7
Howard,
  James 137,
  M. 89,90,91
  Samuel 14
Howe,
  Catrin 7
  Joseph 49,139
  William 7,47
Howel,
  Burdy 222
  Joseph 174
  Margaret 174
Howell,
  Beadig 170,174
  Catherine 6
  William 6

Howey,
  Ann 187,214
  John 177,187,197,200,210,214,228
Hoyl,
  Jacob 133
  Peter 52
Hoyle,Michael 133
Huddleston,
  David 78,127
  William 78
Hudson,
  D. 151
  Daniel 79,81
  John 108,112
Huey,
  Daniel 213
  James 56
  John 139
Huff,
  Jonathan 75
  Thomas 75
Huggins,
  Elizabeth 50
  John 133,160
  William 50,65,162
Hughes,
  Edward 33,38,208
  John 68,175
  Sarah 175
  Thomas 175
  Will 58
Hughey,James 26,51
Hughs,
  Edward 105
  John 193
  Samuel 10,152
Hughston,Davis 28
Hugs,John 246
Huie,
  George 78,79
  Mary 78
Hull,
  Agness 4
  James 84
  William 4
Humphrey,John 22,39
Humphries,
  John 12
  Joannah 63
  Samuel 108,109
Hunter,
  John 1,208
  Robert 30,198
Huston,
  Aaron 124,189
  Agness 30
  Archibald 39,197,220
  David 39,189,200
  George 243
  Hugh 39,188,199
  James 129,199,220,225
  Margaret 189
  Mary 191
  Marry 191
  Thomas 186
Hutchins,Andrew 21
Hutchison,___ 20
Hymes,David 86
Iher,Joseph Jr. 153
Inglis,Alexander 220
Irvin,
  Jane 155
  Nathaniel 246
  Robert 151,178
  Samuel 162
  William 129
Irwin,
  Andrew 225
  Christofer 221
  Edward 126
  Hugh 70,98,108
  Jean 70,76
  Jennet 134

Irwin(con't)
  John 5,98
  Mary 177
  Nathaniel 135,224
  Robert 50,76,120,137,177,
    178,180
  Sarah 60,130
  Thomas 63,99,236
  William 60,129,130
Irwyn,
  Nathaniel 94
  William 113
Itchel,Henry 227
Jack,
  Frances 182,183
  James 103,161,190,195,
    197,211,213,214,220,
    221,242,243,244
  John 159,189,211,212,214,
    215,226,
  Patrick 180,181,182,189
  Samuel 157,159,162,181,
    182,183,185,188,189,
    192,213,215,226,233
Jackson,
  Andrew 190
  Hugh 190
  Mary 185
  Robert 190
James,Joseph 198
Janes,
  Barry 174
  Thomas 22,50
Jarrel,
  Mary 104
  Thomas 104,134
Jarret,Thomas 236
Jeans,Thomas 3
Jerrel,Thomas 138
Jetten,Isaac 216
Jetton,
  Abraham 166
  Elizabeth 166
  Isaac 153,166
  John 166
  Lewis 166
Jinkins,David 137,138
Jinnings,Robert 57
Jitton,
  Isaac 229
  John 185
John,
  Daniel 213
  David 63,72
  Mary 237
Johnson,
  Ann 60
  Bartholomew 104
  Francis 129
  Henry 110
  Isaac 13,14,104
  Jacob 73
  John 60
  Napilot 54
  Peter 112
  Robert 19,230
  Samuel 107,108
  Thomas 57,86,132
Johnston,
  Alexander 157
  Brartholomew 129,138,207
  Francis 16,157,182,239
  Henry 49,74
  Isaac 17
  James 47,49,83,87,89,
    105,110,120,146,166,
    169,173,177,188,237
  John 81,149,169,183,198,
    200,202
  Joseph 60,157,208
  Mary 112,138
  Mary Ann 166
  Nathaniel 182,184,202

Johnston(con't),
  Peter 60,120,154,156,
    158,163,164,165,174,
    176,184,205,209,211,
    218,221,234,237,239,
    241,244
  Ruth 198
  Samuel 109,138
  William 75,93,104,139,
    166,182,184,235,242,
    243
Johnstone,John 193
Jolley,
  Joseph 72,73,119
  William 73
Jones,
  Abraham 235
  Adam 19,20
  Adam Crain 18,19,20,98
  John 72,183
  Joseph 53,207
  Mary 98,214
  Molly 19,20
  Nathaniel 19
  Richard 19
  William 69
Jordon,John 76
Joy,
  Mr. 7,107
  Jeremiah 20,56,61,107,
    124,136,152,153,156,
    182,186,202,235
Julian,George 137
Julien,Rene 132
Juston,Hugh 191
Kaler,Peter 120
Kaneday,James 237
Kar,Henry 72,73
Karcher,Conrode 49
Karr,
  James 39,142,185
  Joseph 152
Keagle,
  Charles 242
  Mary Ann 242
Kealah,Samuel 246
Kealer,
  Anamore 157
  Peter 157
Kean,John 193
Kearr,John 193
Keeler,Peter 52,207
Keer,John 45,71
Keliah,John 233
Kellar,Joseph 133
Keller,
  John 26
  Joseph 23,75,225
Kelloh,John 192,
Kelly,
  James 108
  William 22
Kelso,John 42,141
Kelsy,John 141
Kenady,Joseph 225
Kenan,Felix 101,111,206
Kenedy,
  David 130,224,227,237
  Easter 231
  James 231
  Joseph 231
  Joseph,Dr. 233
  Martha 227
  Samuel 225
  Thomas 135
Kennady,
  Easter 242
  John 200
  Joseph 74
Kennedy,
  David 81,89,146,154,237
  Elizabeth 105
  Felix 44

Kennedy(Con't)
  James 130,224
  John 105,160
  Joseph 60,85,127,146,181,
    194
  Joseph,Dr. 21
  Martha 154
  Thomas 83,127,146
  William 24
Kenor,John 113
Keny,Henry 50
Kepple,Peter 49
Ker,James 8
Kere,Joseph 237
Kerr,
  David 52
  James 20,29,124,152,207,
    229
  John 20,53,62,80,100,235
  Joseph 115,125,152,208,
    240
  Joseph Jr. 61
  Joseph Sr. 61
  Mary 240
  Patrick 219,237,240
  Robert 125,152,210,219,
    240
  Walter 101,151
  William 179,209,222,231,
    232
Kerrel,
  John 42
  Joseph 47
Kersey,John 185
Kill,James 187
Killen,
  Andrew 8
  Mary 8
Killer,Joseph 221
Killian,
  Ann 9
  John 9,10,217
  Lenard 29,57,95
Killion,
  Andrew 102
  John 32,64
  Leonard 63,69,108
Killpatrick,James 180,234
Kilogh,Isaac 46,136
Kilough,Mary 46
Kilpatrick,
  Andrew 137
  John 105
  Thomas 90
Kilpattrick,Alexander 97
Kinkaid,John 102
Kinkead,John 120
King,
  John 142,161
  MaryAnn 105,209,210
  William 105,187,205,209,
    210
Kinnedy,Joseph 193
Kinner,John 206,207
Kirkendall,Cobus 43
Kiser,
  George 243
  Peter 188,230
Kitchen,Charles 70
Kittchens,Thomas 16
Kizer,Peter 174,215
Kline,
  Catherine 96,192,211
  Jacob 96,192,194,211
  Katherina 189
  Michael 189
Knight,Peter 116
Knighten,
  John 189
  Thomas 177,178
Knighton,John 199

Knox,
  Andrew 206
  John 225
  Mary 127,156,157,166
  Mathew 3,136,180,222,231,
    232,239,240
  Pattrick 172
  Samuel 10,17,28,29,58,79,
    115,127,156,157,166,
    179,208,217,239,240
Kook,
  Ann 194
  Barbara 198
  Bostain 194
  Jacob 194
  John 198
Köslr,Johann Petter 157
Kress,Nicholas 126
Krotz,Voluntine 77
Kries,Peter 77
Krowl,
  Betty 49
  Catharine 33
  Simon 49
Kur,
  John 9
  Robert 16
Kuykendal,James 74
Kuykendall,
  Abraham 29,45,69,74,115
  Alisabeth 45
  Cobus 78,80
  Elizabeth 29,45,74
  James 62,108
  John 2,10,37,57,73,98,
    102,113,132,133
  Mary 8,26,53,108
  Matthew 26,64,107
  Peter 64
  Rebecca 98
  Sarah 20
Kuykendalls,Peter 7,8,9,
  25,26,29,36,45,74,79
Kyzer,Peter 230
Lacey,
  Edward 94
  Samuel 20,27
Lach,John 30
Lacky,Alexander 52
Lacy,
  Edward Jr. 107
  Jane 107
Lagardere,Elias 56
Lahiff,John 173
Laird,
  Loudwick 20,62
  Nathaniel 98
Lamkin,William 105
Lamkins,George 73,75,105,
  160
Lance,
  Catherine 238
  John 238
  Peter 236
Land,
  Eleanor 156
  James 59
  Thomas 156
Lane,John 198
Lanham,John 64,105,107
Lansdall,Richard 214
Large,John 73,142
Larimore,James 11
Larrimore,James 10
Lata,
  Elizabeth 54
  John 54
Latta,
  Elizabeth 54
  John 42
Laughlin,John 141
Launce,John 30
Lawing,

Lawing,
  Jane 153
  William 153
Lawson,
  John 211
  Roger 42
Leaney,Andrew 120
Leany,Titus 164
Leard,
  John 6,19
  William 62
Leaper,Robert 33
Learges,John 73
Lee,
  ___ 77
  Edmond 113
  Joseph 79,87,89,119,131,
    147,149,223,224,234,
    241
Leech,Margaret 54
Leeper,
  Catherine 5,19,25,48
  Hugh 19
  James 2,7,37,224
  Katherine 70,78
  Katrin 230
  Nicholas 7,36,107
  Robert 5,6,7,10,22,25,
    27,28,38,48,51,70,78,
    96,100,120,230
  "Widow" 133
Leepers,Nicholas 20
Legat,William 220
Legett,Margaret 214
Legget,Michael 66,188,214
Leinberger,Peter 137
Leinburger,John 29
Leman,John 184
Lemmond,William 163,183
Lemmonds,William 199,231
Lemon,Joseph 207
Lemonds,
  John 189
  William 195,198
Leonard,
  Davis 62
  Thomas 62
  William 32
Leper,
  John 213
  Robert 19
Leppard,
  James 10
  John 235
Leoerd,Robert 100
Leppart,John 9
Lessebee,Daniel 50
Lessley,Samuel 187
Lessly,Samuel 116
Lethen,David 159
Leufever,John 119
Lewes,Jonathan 190
Lewing,William 108
Lewis,
  Alexander 5,6,14,21,22,
    25,29,39,43,47,69,101,
    102,105,134,137,159,
    171,177,218,225
  Bartholomew 112
  Benjamin 6,14,22,43,50,
    71
  Christopher 45,194
  Evan 53
  Hannah 6,43,218,225
  Isaac 126
  James 141
  John 174
  Jonathan 6,32,103
  Josiah 53
  Mary 53
Lideker,Phillip 207
Ligget,
  Michael 136,160,200,243

Ligget(con't)
  Michael Jr. 98
  Michael Sr. 129,200
  William 129
Ligtle,John 32
Limmond,William 168
Lindsay,Walter 58
Lindsey,
  John 24,34
  Walter 112
Lineberg,Seville 115
Linee,John 7
Lineberger,
  Esbel 114
  John 114,115
  Ludwick 114
Lingell,Lorentz 158
Linn,
  James 15,22,77,190,224
  John 32,52,105,163,208
  Mary 217
  Sarah 190
  William 53,97
Lipe,
  Barbara 71
  Godfrey 66,71
Lippard,
  Catherine 13
  John 13
Lippert,Catherine 9
Littel,Daniel 33,174
Little,
  Archibald 2,4,95,105,142
  Elizabeth 105
  Jennet 2,4
  John 2,4,73
  Thomas 103,105
  William 227
Lizzenbey,Daniel 141
Lock,
  Andrew 127
  Francis 211
  Mathias 38
  Matthew 158
Lockerd,John 161
Lockert,Alexander 104
Lockart,
  Ann 76
  Robert 84,144
Lockhart,
  Alexander 42,73,76,102
  Arthur 104
Loftain,Samuel 9,118,120
Loftin,
  Margaret 185,189
  Samuel 185
  William 228
Lofton,
  Samuel 89,105,189,237
  Sarah 237
  William 112,189
Logan,Andrew 209
Long,
  Agnis 172
  John 172,233
Love,
  Alexander 8,9,98,107
  Benjamin 57
  James 61,235
  John 23,103
  Martha 103
  Robert 57
  Sarah 243
  Wi;;iam 103,243
Low,John 63
Lowery,
  B. 225
  Benjamin 242
  Robert 42
Lowing,William 172
Lowre,Benjamin 228

Lowrey,
  Benjamin 190
  John 196
  Thomas 197
Lowry,
  Benjamin 19,20,185,189
  Robert 9,25,96
Lucky,
  Andrew 74
  John 228
  Mary 228
Luckey,
  Andrew 114
  William 53,114
Lundes, Abraham 73
Lusk,
  Elizabeth 213
  James 10,21,26
  John 120,174,213,214
  Samuel 112,199
Lust, John 20
Lynn,
  Andrew 128
  James 6,103,105,163
  John 6
  Sarah 103,105
Lyon, William 26
McCain,
  Eleanor 161
  Hugh 161
  John 161,187
McCalin, Andrew 156
McCall,
  Elizabeth 218,226
  Jannet 221
  James 20,58,59,99,168,
    169,217,218,226
  Jean 221
  John 199,221,231
  Margaret 59,99
  Thomas 59,86,99,143,155,
    223,226
  William 218
McCallen, James 116
McCallin, Robert 201
McCamey, George 105,156
McCance, John 189
McCane,
  Jane 201
  John 8
  Joseph 160,201
McCanley, Samuel 135
McCarnes, John 185
McCarter,
  Alexander 78
  William 97
McCartey,
  Agness 24
  Daniel 4,24
McCarty,
  Agness 43
  Alexander 133
  Daniel 32,43
  David 24
  James 44
  William 188
McCasland, ___ 115
McCaul,
  Francis 174
  James 99,163
  Thomas 163,
McAdau, William 175
McAdow, William 176
McAfall, Denis 93
McAfee,
  James 45,46,49,103,104,
    106,132
  Margaret 103,104,106
McAferson, Robert 77
McAin, Ebenezer 70
McAlluly, Alexander 49
McAlveny, Samuel 187
McAlwell, William 187

McBrayer, Mr. 134
McBride, Francis 52
McCacklin, John 61
McCafferty,
  James 60,184,219
  Jereh 60
  Jeremiah 61,160,161,166,
    178,180,181,183,185,
    187,188,189,190,191,
    192,208,213,214,217,
    222,226,227,233,239,
    240
  William 60,160,197,219,
    221,244,246
McCay, Beaty 172,245
McCinley,
  Joseph 179,233
McChord, David 240
McClain,
  Archibald 156
  Ephriam 113,132
  James 63,68
  William 97
McClaine, Archibald 107
McClary,
  Robert 120
  Samuel 150
McClean,
  Charles 50,109
  John 98
  Susanna 109
McCleary,
  Abigail 130
  Deborah 205
  Robert 200,202,205,227,
    244
  Samuel 120,159,205,217,
    219,222,
McCleery, Robert 130
McClery, Samuel 237
McCleland, James 128,129
McClellan,
  James 129
  Rebecca 158
  Robert 35,54,158
McClelland, Robert 77
McClenackan, Robert 105
McClenachan,
  Elizabeth 5
  Fenney 14
  John 47
  Robert 1,4,5,8,14,18,30,
    32,33,34,37,38,39,42,
    43,45,47,49,50,51,52,
    53,54,59,62,68,69
McClenahan,
  Ann 14
  Thomas 14
McClenechan, Robert 22
McClennan, James 50,104
McClenningham, Robert 156
McClenry, Damist 141
McClenvy, Archibald 193
McClery, Samuel 86
McCloy, Neal 5
McClure,
  Agness 227
  Arthur 13,216
  Elizabeth 173,236
  James 19,20,36,77,115,
    181,185,188,228
  John 84,85,88,90,146,
    147,176,202,218
  Margaret 36,115
  Mat. 16.204,228
  Matthew 8,88,127
  Matthus 92
  Nat. 13
  Thomas 98,130,227
  William 13,141,166,173,
    176,227,236
McCiord, David 239
McCoord, Robert 240

McColoh,
  Henry Eustace 59
  James 224
McColloh,
  H.E. 220,235
  Henry E. 188,218
  John 181,188,191,192
McComb,
  James 198
  Samuel 198,246
McCombe, Samuel 220
McCombes, Samuel 188
McCombs, Samuel 189
McCome, James 8,9
McConnal, James 165
McConnell,
  James 37,224
  William 50,63
McConnels, Alexander 63
McCool,
  Adam 23
  Thomas 23
McCooll, Adam 24
McCord,
  Ann 173,181,191
  David 8,9,173,178,181,
    191
  James 63,87,89,91,145,
    193,209,224,234,246
  James Jr. 163,224,226,
    234,241
  James Sr. 163,226,241
  John 83,124,125,144,239
  Robert 8,9,75,181,191,
    194,224,233
  Samuel Sr. 224
  Sarah 341
McCorkel, John 187
McCorket, John 200
McCorkle,
  Ester 157
  Jean 175
  John 214
  Mathus 207
  Matthew 160,175,185
  Thomas 160
  William 157,210
McCormic, Matthew 185
McCormick, Dennis 115
McCown,
  Alexander 117
  Thomas 207
McCoy,
  Beary 126
  Daniel 53,97
  John 197
  Martha 97
McCrakan, James 218
McCracken, Hugh 160
  James 86
  John 178,228
McCracklin, Hugh 173
McCreaven, John 220
McCreavy, John 240
McCree,
  David 164,218
  Hannah 163
  Hug 177
  John 163
  Richard 160
  Robert 177
  Sam 192
McCreek, Robert 200
Mccrorey, Robert 200
McCrum, Samuel 127
McCrury, Samuel 8
McCuistion, John 241
McCulloch,
  Alexander 32
  Henry E. 7
  James 32
  John 25,32,37,62
  William 25,38,86

McCuloh, William 161
McCulloh,
  B. 111
  Elizabeth 10,237,239,240
  Eustice 43
  H.E. 205,207,222,237
  Henry 41,56
  Henry E. 203,204,207,213,
    215,216,217,223,238,
    239,244,246
  Henry Eustace 8,9,15,16,
    40,41,42,44,47,48,56,
    71,77,80,92,93,94,95,
    96,98,99,106,111,114,
    118,142,143,144,145,
    146,147,148,149,150,
    151,153,155,161,180,
    182,183,184,193,195,
    214
  James 135
  John 6,7,9,19,38,49,56,
    76,79,104,105,109,110,
    134,181,210
  Pennelope 90,135
  Thomas 73,185
  William 10,23,48,79,82,
    83,85,94,105,120,143,
    147,152,159,161,177,
    183,210,237,239,240,
    244,246
McCullough
  H.E. 120
  Isaac 4
  John 23
  Sam 20
  Samuel 113
  Thomas 49
McCurdy,
  Archy 199
  Archibald 199
  Margaret 199
McCurry, Robert 100
McDada, Pattrick 73
McDavid, Patrick 100
McDonald, Patrick 220,221,
  242
McDowel,
  Ann 3,43,44,
  Archibald 31,113,117
  John 3,8,9,14,22,24,34,
    44,47,49,58,92
  Margaret 34
  Matthew 3
  Robert 199
  William 198
McDowell,
  Archibald 160
  Charles 14,58
  James 190
  John 184,234
  Joseph 24,34
  Mary 52,154
  Mary (Margaret) 24
  Rachel 58
  Robert 2,3,26
  William 19,23,98,190
McElmorry, John 132
McElmurry, William 50
McElroy,
  101
  John 108,232,239
McElwain, James 71,78
McElwee,
  Elizabeth 166
  ames 84,149,191,195,
    197,220
  Jean 142
  John 59,131,142,148,152,
    218,220
  Martha 197
  William 197,220
McElwees, John 229
McEntire,

McEntire,
  John 124,125,157
  Robert 152,202
McFadien, John 54
McFadon, Thomas 198
McFarlan, John 199
McFarling, John 199
McGee,
  Adam 213
  Elis 202
  James 213
  Thomas 180,213,245,
  William 213,245
McGin, James 125
McGinty,
  Alexander 88,89,145,214
  John 88,201,206,222,244
McGloughlan, Daniel 5,30
McGough, Robert 181
McGradgn, John 137
McGuire, James 152
McGummery, Isabella 198
McGunagle, John 109
McKain,
  Hugh 74,161
  John 164,205
McKay,
  Arthur 11,12,26,35,36,
    64,65,66,67,68,74
  Nathan 4
McKean, John 191
McKee,
  Alexander 136,181,189,
    233,238
  Ambrose 117,178
  David 61,150,211
  James 79,217,218
  John 1,15,43,119,218
  Mary 1,83,89,127,144
  Robert 33,202,219
  Samuel 43
  William 43,59,200,209
McKelmurry, William 7
McKelwee, John 82,83,86
McKimmins, Daniel 129
McKendrick, Sarah 27
McKenny,
  Barbara 43
  William 43
McKey, David 82
McKibben, Oughtry 189
McKibbin, Oughtry 226
McKiblin, Aughtrey 112
McKindly,
  Elizabeth 182
  William 179
McKinley,
  Joseph 102,157,182,209
  Margaret 201
  Robert 47,127,179,201
  William 15,127,201
McKinney,
  George 8
  William 50
McKirly, William 166
McKlevney,
  Margaret 4
  Samuel 4
McKlewain, James 5
McKnight,
  Charles 5,33
  Hugh 3,184,235
  James 1,235
  John 4,38
  Robert 1
  Thomas 34,115
  William 3,33,50
McKnitt, John 148
McKorkle,
  Ester 232
  Mathew 128,129
  William 232
McKown,

McKown,
  Snoddy 124
  William 104,136
McKowns, Hugh 12
McKoy, John 201
Maclain, Robert 229
McLean,
  Alexander 20
  Allan 235
  Charles 11,76,134
  Elizabeth 11
  Ephraim 15,20,113,118
  Susannah 11
McLehany,
  Margaret 31
  Robert 31
McLilly, John 115
McLure, James 214
McManus, James 56
McMeen,
  James 57
  Joseph 187
McMichen, David 80
McMickin, David 116
McMickons,
  David 136
  Mary 136
McMillan,
  John 139
  William 71
McMillen,
  Andrew 19,78
  John 70,78
McMillin,
  John 109
  William 109
McMulin, John 17
McMullan, William 103
McMullen, John 71
McMurdy, Henry 193,234
McMurray, Robert 66,67
McMurry,
  Elinor 239
  Robert 239
McNabb, Andrew 15,51,113,
  117,137
McNall, Andrew 137
McNeal,
  Archibald 136
  Edward 78
McNeall, Archibald 39,118,
  154
McNealy, John 177
McNeely,
  James 160
  John 214
McNelley, John 187
McNight,
  Charles 11
  Robert 17
McNil, John 81
McNelley, John 120
McOntire, Robert 160
McPherson, Robert 25,208
McQuown,
  Alexander 210
  Hugh 33,48,59,226
  James 59
  John 59
  Thomas 8,12,48,207
McRay, William 18
McReavy,
  Archibald 246
  John 246
  Mary 246
McRee,
  Alexander 189
  Andrew 220
  David 185,226,227
  John 124,183,202
  Richard 160
  Robert 132
  William 80,179

McSwains,Francis 14
McThibben,Oughtery 37
McWhorter,
　George 187
　Hace 72
　Hance 36,49,56,236
　Jean 21
　John 174
McZacklin,James 75
Macilmurry,John 79
Mackay,Arthur 2,7,22,55,
　62,98
Mecklemarry,William 2
Mackelmorry,William 7
Mackelmurry,John 49
Macklehany,Robert 6
Mackelwain,Francis 3
Mackelwean,Francis 47
Mackey,David 70
Macklemory,
　Samuel 38
　William 9,109
Macky,
　Alexander 58
　John 140
Macklewean,Francis 100
Magby,Thomas 237
Mage,Alish 245
Mageum,William 15
Maggone,George 194
Magoune,George 236
Maloney,
　Edward 154
　John 198
　Mary 198
Malony,John 58
Marchbank,William 137
Marble,James 207
Marin,Robert 228
Markle,Lorance 113
Martain,Samuel 194
Martin,
　Alexander 32,166,177,
　　204,216,240
　Jane 246
　James 94,111,182,235,
　　246
　John 7,71,120,132,134,
　　138,198,236
　Mary 177
　Richard 246
　Sam 201,208,211,220,221
　　224,227,228,242
　Samuel 59,60,61,158,160,
　Thomas 37,158
　William 65,177
Martindale,Thomas 154
Mason,
　Charles 157,194,224,233
　Mary 194
　Richard 194,236
　Samuel 177
　William 193
Massey,
　Elijah 75
Joseph 37
Master,Michael 138
Mathews,
　Petter 197
　William 190,200
Matinges,Henry 4
Matthews,Will 189
Mauney,
　Jacob 37
　Valentine 27,106
Maxwell,
　Benjamin 158
　James 87,90,99,144,155,
　　173,190
　Joseph 159
　Robert 234
Mayes,James 141
Mayr,Franz 77

Mays,James 71
Meachim,John 235
Means,James 54
Meason,Richard 242
Mecullah,William 68
Meek,
　＿＿ 69
　Adam 15,38,40,47,48,58,
　　243
　Andrew 69
　Elizabeth 38,47,58
　James 64
Menzen,James 164
Merryhill,William 34
Mexwell,Robert 115
Nichel,John 198
Miffitt,John 19
Migchell,Robert 201
Milar,David 30
Miles,
　James 75,76
　Thomas 31
Milikon,Joseph 73
Mill,William 20
Millar,
　Brice 205
　David 235
　James 30,104
　Texanna 30
Millbranch,Armor 236
Miller,
　Abraham 46,60,85,86,88,
　　131,147,161,182,216,
　　222,229
　Andrew 217,222
　Barnet 192
　Brice 173,174,183,213,
　　214,217
　Catron 192
　Charles 118
　David 45,115,138,233
　Elizabeth 45,242
　Francis 199
　Hannah 75,225
　Jacob 76,119
　James 14,15,18,32,37,38,
　　47,54,68,78,102,134,
　　138,214
　Jannet 229
　Jerom 211
　John 2,3,22,23,26,32,38,
　　47,51,75,78,111,174,
　　180,195,225,233,242
　John Barnett 155
　Mary 3,38,47
　Michael 51,57
　Nathaniel 45,141
　Patrick 184
　Phillip 9,195,196,235
　Rachel 38,211
　Richard 21,23,58
　Robert 3,38,47,51,78,95,
　　102,141,143,184,233,
　　235
　William 201,222,235,
Millican,James 98,109
Millikan,
　James 23,50,63,107
　Jean 63
　Joseph 36
Milliken,
　Joseph 64
　William 64
Millikin,
　＿＿ 45
　Edward 141
Millright,Charles Thompson
　　194
Mills,
　Ann 42
　Blaney 107
　Bleney 2,23,25,63
　Jeane 42

Mills(con't)
　Sarah 42
　Will 42
Miiisap,Thomas 55
Milner,Benjamin 176
Milson,Samuel 237
Minter,
　Martha 75
　William 17,21,75,76
Minzes,James 132
Misinhimer,Jacob 189
Mitchel,
　Agnes 30
　Alexander 124,125
　Elizabeth 39,127,178,179,
　　182,186,187,190,192
　George 181
　James 5
　John 39,112,127,178,179,
　　182,186,187,190,192,
　　194
　Joseph 195,199
　Thomas 30
　William 188
Mitchell,
　Alizabeth 16
　Andrew 152
　Elizabeth 61,124,125,126,
　　128,152,153,162,163,
　　165,176,202,203,210,
　　229,235,240,241,245
　Henry 87,131,147,211,247
　Isaac 124,125,202
　James 15
　Joab 101
　John 33,48,61,124,125,
　　126,128,135,136,151,
　　152,153,157,159,162,
　　163,164,165,176,202,
　　203,204,210,229,234,
　　235,236,240,241,245
　Joseph 16,44,204
　Matthias 179
　Robert 181,191
　Thomas 57
　William 215,
Mitchener,Luke 178
Mitcher,Mathias 40
Mitler,George 55
Moffat,David 172
Moffet,
　John 168
　Robert 152,153,154
Moffett,John 204
Moffit,David 12
Mole,John 34
Moloney,John 197
Monteith,Alexander 95,216
Monteeth,Henry 95
Montieth,Alexander 143
Montgomery,
　George 194
　Hugh 49,162
　John 154,186,197,198,199,
　　231
　Robert 227
　Samuel 60,221,228
Mony,Jacob 63
Moor,
　Aaron 106
　James 10,116,234,241
　William 48,49,56
Moore,
　＿＿ 113
　Aaron 97,106
　Ann 10,63,99
　Anna 166,183
　Charles 3,12,29,42,43,44,
　　47,51,76,102
　David 83,131,146,167,183
　Elizabeth 8,11
　Frances 180,239,240
　Francis 162

Moore(con't),
  J. 206
  James 17,22,27,44,76,87,
    94,113,119,149,209,213
  John 4,16,17,27,44,58,63,
    79,94,99,102,113,127,
    141 153,166,183,184,
    211,224,239
  Joseph 1,20,43,60,107,
    108,111,127,156,165,
    172,208,219,224,237
  M. 219
  Margaret 11
  Martha 159
  Mary 15,70
  Maurice 21,22,26,97,98
  Michel 31
  Moses 12,27,39,44,50,57,
    97,108,124,141,155
  Rebecca 159
  Rachel 17,113
  Robert 159,178
  Sal. 133
  Thomas 8,11
  William 10,15,18,20,22,
    27,34,39,53,70,73,75,
    98,100,102,107,109,115,
    127,155,157,159,204
More,
  Aaron 106
  James 29
  John 241
  John Jackson 185
  Joseph 31,234
  Rachel 106
  Samuel 22
Morgan,
  Rees 39,43,56,236
  Thomas 74
Morr,Anna 157
Morris,
  James 166
  Mary 74
  Robert 74,113
  William 59,168,220
Morrison,
  Andrew 169
  James 167,170,232,235
  John 13,170,171,230,240
  Neil 201
  Robert 144,170
  Samuel 171
  William 34,50
Morrow,
  George 208
  John 243
  Richard 158,243
  Robert 243
Morton,
  Japheth 141
  Peter 234
  Samuel 234
Mouat,John 111
Mouney,Jacob 58
Moyar,
  Catherine 239
  Jacob 239
Moyart,
  Jacob 79
  Margaret 79
Muckols,John 114
Muckelhaney,Robert 14
Mungen,Joseph John 13
Murphey,John 207
Murphy,
  James 71
  John 8
  William 174,197
Muse,Hopkins 33
Muskelly,James 17
Müssler,Matthaus 158
Myers,
  Catherine 46

Myers(con't),
  Henry 46
  Jacob 35
Mylrite,
    46
  Catherine 46
Nagel,Johannes 32
Nash,
  A. 96,189
  Abner 167,168,169,170,
    171,172,173,177,178,
    179,180,181,187,192,
    194,198,212,215,219,
    222,223,225,229,230,
    231,237,238,239,240,
    243,244,246
  Agner 159
  Andrew 191
  Clement 167,222,223,225
  F. 233
  James 195
  Justina 167,168,169,170,
    171,172,178,187,194,
    215,222,223,225,229,
    230,231,237
Neal,
  Ann 21
  Andrew 243
  David 49
  George 226
  Henry 240
  James 48,187,207
  Jean 49
  John 9,87,120
  Thomas 32,48,49
Neale,Archibald 174
Nealy,
  Ann 199
  Elizabeth 29
  Henry 29,212
  Hugh 199
  James 221
  John 49
  Thomas Jr. 180
Neally,Samuel 43
Neel,
  Andrew 184,228,239
  George 13,14
  Henry 238
  James 6,12
  John 86,131,143
  Thomas 3,5,9,19,78,106
Neeley,
  Elizabeth 49
  Henry 77
  John 49
  Samuel 112
Neely,
  Hugh 157
  Jackson 58
  John 164
  Thomas 102,118,157,164,
    231
  William 29,77,113
Neichler,John 118
Neil,
  Andrew 77
  James 204
Neilly,Thomas 101
Neily,Henry 113
Neisbett,
  Ann 224
  James 224
  Jerema 224
  Samuel 224
Nell,Andrew 232
Nelley,Hugh 77
Nelson,
  John 196
  Samuel 85,87,89,146
Nesbitt,William 152
Nesh,
  Abm. 60

Nesh,Justina 60
Nesmith,Thomas 104
Newell,John 145
Newman,
  Anthony 203
  John 80,82,84,87,135,
    147,183,190,214
  Jonathan 18,23,136,203
Newton,
  Abenr. 59
  Benjamin 199
  Ebenezer 82,83,148,229
  Elizabeth 229
  John 244
Nichalson,George 190
Nichelson,
  Culbert 125
  John 200
  Joseph 97
Nicholas,Joseph 97
Nicholes,John 70
Nicholson,
  Cutbert 82,149
  Joseph 209
Nichols,
  Francis 240
  Jacob 109
Nickelson,Joseph 217
Nickell,
  Alexander 19
  James 19
Nickelson,Jospeh 244
Nicklson,Joseph 134,195
Nickoles,Framces 238
Nickols,
  Francis 241
  Jon. 106
Nicoll,John 139
Nicols,Alexander 238
Niehler,John 48
Nilson,John 196
Nisbet,
  Agnes 53
  Alexander 53,113
Nocks,J. 24
Norris,James 44,82,218
Nuchberry,John 246
Nuckols,John 7,77
Numan,
  Jonathan 3
  Rebecca 3
Nusman,Jonathan 10
Nutt,
    14
  Agness 155,157
  Andrew 10,105,156,187,
    236
  George 14
  John 155,157
  Katherine 155,157
  Margaret 10,156,236
  William 37,68,155,157
Oar,Nathan 181
O'Cain,Daniel 230
Ocheltree,
  Duncan 192
  Dunn 209,220,227,242
Ochiltree,Dun. 194,197,
  209,211,212,243,244,
  246
Odare,
  Robert 16
  Susannah 16
Ofle,John 129
Ogle,
  Hon 21
  John 128
Oglethorpe,Elizabeth 228
Okain,Daniel 194
Oliphant,
  David 195,196,197,198,
    199,201
  John 25

Oneal,Henry 47
Onnan,Benjamin 226
Orman,James 37
Ormands,Jacob 188
Ormond,
  Benjamin 161,188
  James 80,84,144,150,228,
    236
Ormund,James 56
Orr,
  James 81,90,148,163,194,
    197,236,238
  John 78
  Nathan 81,83,88,90,148,
    226,242
  Nathan Jr. 90
  William 81,83
Osborn,
  Adlai 89,212
  Alexander 47,112
  James 212
  Noble 215
  Samuel 2
Osborne,
  John 180
  William 180
Osburn,
  Adlai 21,69,90,197,244,
    246
  Agness 21,69,204
  Alexander 21,46,69,102,
    161,174,204
  Collonel 19,103
  James 60,188
  John 46,188,220,239
  Noble 89,131,151,188
  Robert 245
  "Widow" 161
  William 46,188,239
Ovenshire,Christian 2
Ownsby,George 65
Oyster,
  Julianna 38
  Michael 38
  Peter 38
Paff,George 32,33
Palley,
  Agnes 179
  James 175,179,183
  Thomas 130
Pally,James 224
Panney,William 190
Parfer,Thomas 223
Park,
  David 78
  George 26
  Hugh 52,154,164,241
  Hugh Jr. 210
  Hugh Sr. 210
  John 71,210
  Margaret 21,154
  Robert 147
Parke,John 131
Parker,
  Elizabeth 61
  Isaac 61,94,139
  Isaiah 216
  Isiah 227
  John 22,227
  Katherine 227
  Thomas 14,41,144
Parks,
  David 34,51,82,101,214
  Hugh 79,124
  James 90
  John 83,89,131
  Mary 227
  Marry 227
  Robert 28,86,87,223,227
Parsons,Henry 229
Patan,Samuel 68,185
Paten,Thomas 15
Paterson,

Paterson,
  John 230,241
  Joseph 218,235
  Robert 200,224
  William 174,221,242
Patison,William 181
Paton,Mathew 220
Patrick,
  John 7,37
  Mary 50
  Robert 7,49
  William 12,22,27,37,50,
    79,119
Pattan,
  Samuel 185
  William 189
Patterson,
  Arthur 54,120
  James 127,200
  John 32,176,218,226
  Joseph 152,153,179,187,
    203,
  Margaret 212
  Robert 7,16,18,50,63,212
  Thomas 200
  William 59,60,61,133,159,
    162,165,185,208,211,
    217,244,
  Will Jr. 226
Patteson,
  John 129
  Robert 193
  William 194,222,226,
Pattesson,William 190,191,
  227
Pattison,
  John 226
  Will 193
  William 246
Pattin,Matthew 179
Patton,
  ___ 114
  Anna 117
  Benjamin 4,66,97,117
  Charles 126,152
  Elizabeth 181
  James 18,30,32,54,79,105
    112
  James Sr. 33
  Jane 25,112,127
  Jean 47
  John 2,23,25,32,45,56,
    76,79,103
  Matthew 30,31,33,37,47,
    54,102,105,127,189,201
    236
  Michael 33
  Rebecca 105
  Robert 105,112,198
  Samuel 23,71,117,120,126,
    153,163
  Thomas 181
  William 181
Pattons,Mathew 9
Pattrick,
  Andrew 70,136
  William 117
Pattson,William 166
Paul,Jacob 237
Paxton,James 197
  Thomas 190
Peal,James 92
Pearson,
  John 19,65
  Henry 84
Peeples,Isom 135
Pelle,James 111
Pence,Jacob 235
Penenton,Beanige 104
Pennington,
  Benige 104
  Elizabeth 104
  Jacob 76

Penny,
  Elizabeth 180
  John 114,120,
  Margaret 120
  Thomas 133,224
  William 65,180,212
Perry,
  Elizabeth 246
  Richard 246
Perviance,Charles 156
Petty,Sarah 234
Pfifer,
  Caleb 180
  John 163,164,180,191,192,
    239
  Margaret 164,239
  Martin 164,189,191
  Martin,Major 206
Phifer,
  Capt. 175,193
  Caleb 211
  John 6,39,55,71,96,117,
    118,120,126,176,189,
    208,220,235
  Margaret Martin 211
  Martain 2,4,11,12,25,29,
    31,32,39,40,45,47,51,
    52,55,57,58,64,96,117,
    135
  Martin 176,205
  Martin Jr. 176
  Martin Sr. 211
Philer,Henry 35
Philips,
  Robert 209,229
  William 186
Phillips,
  Ben 6
  Benjamin 79,137
  Rachel 79,137,
  Reuben 186
  Stephen 138
Phiney,Alexander 217,222
Phyfer,Martin 6
Pickens,
  Andrew 10,11,37,45,64,
    68
  Elizabeth 9
  James 165
  John 4,11,24,54,229
  Joseph 4,45
  Samuel 120,152,153,162,
    203,218,229
  "Widow" 1,13
  William 4,9,84,85,148,
    150,191,204,216
Pickett,James 153,163
Pifer,John 114,155,158,
  185
Pigg,Hezekiah 135
Pistenbustill,
  Henry Funt 155
  Saffey 155
Plat,George 80
Plummer,Daniel 54
Plummers,William 5
Plunket,James 55
Plyler,Henry 72,
Poff,George 19
Polk,
  Charles 55,66,67,171
  Elenor 55
  Elinor 12,55,237
  Ellener 55
  Ezekiel 55,77,144,151,
    159,166,196,197,198,
    201,205,219,237,241,
    243,244,246
  Hugh 172
  John 2,12,55,64,169,174,
    190,230,231,237
  Susannah 196,201
  Thomas

Polk(con't)
  Thomas 14,15,16,17,30,51,
    59,60,61,77,80,81,82,
    83,85,86,88,91,93,94,
    101,102,103,106,110,
    117,118,127,129,130,
    135,139,142,143,144,
    145,146,147,148,149,
    150,151,152,153,155,
    156,157,159,160,161,
    162,163,165,166,173,
    174,175,176,177,180,
    181,182,183,184,185,
    186,187,188,189,191,
    192,193,194,195,196,
    197,198,199,201,204,
    205,206,208,210,212,
    213,214,216,217,218,
    219,220,221,222,223,
    235,236,237,239,240,
    241,242,243,244,245
  Will 159
  William 195,196,199,201,
    202,217,243
Pollock,
  Charles 154,190
  Hugh 77,138,191,195,227,
    244
  John 190
  Mary 154
Pollinger,Henry 100
Polock,Hugh 155,196,197
Pooff,George 118
Poovey,Boby 114
Pope,
  Christiana 73
  George 73
Porter,
  Alexander 207,213,218,
    220,241,245
  David 109
  Samuel 74,113
  William 184,207,213,218,
    241,245
Portman,
  John Sr. 140
  John Jr. 140
Pots,
  James 69
  Sarah 69
  Stephen 162
Pottesory,William 184
Potts,
  Ann 9
  Devault 51
  George 9,29,51,204
  Henry 58,112,174
  James 1,30,36,50,54,183,
    187,205
  Jeremiah 25,27
  John 8,14,104,117,166,
    204,217
  Jonathan 116,141,236
  Margaret 112
  Mary 14,15
  Sarah 30
  Stephen 235
  Thomas 73
Povey,
  Conrade 114
  Magdalen 114
Powell,
  John 12,195,199,225
  William 4,31,32
Pown,Robert 216
Presley,
  Andrew 213
  Thomas 157
Price,
  Eleanor Alexander 2
  Isaac 175,176,226
  Isabel 113,114
  Isabella 62

Price(con't)
  James 18,23,39,43,45,
    120,166
  John 6,10,23,27,43,75,
    108,166,212,226
  John Jr. 176
  John Sr. 175,176
  Joseph 100
  Margaret 23,166
  Mary 23,45,166,226
  Rachel 23,166
  Rees 3,5,25,47,172,200,
    212
  Reese 126
  Samuel 75
  Sarah 3
  Thomas 2,3,53,62,112,
    113,114,132,225,238
  William 2,23,33,38,43,
    45,47,62,68,238
Prichard,
  Daniel 16,23
  Mary 23
Priest,
  Joseph 84,148
Probst,Matthias 73
Proclus,Robert 106
Province,John 202
Pucon,Adgin 229
Puliam,Thomas 97
Purvance,David 193
Purvaince,Charles 235
Pursley,James 115,119
Quall,Robert 69
Quanton,Jacob 73
Quarel,Robert 225
Quarles,Moses 78
Queery,
  Margaret 129
  William 129
Query,
  John 65,168,231
  Jonathan 230
  Margaret 234,236
  William 65,168,231,234,
    236,243
Quin,Hugh H. 6
Quinn,
  Hugh 17,77,95
  Margaret 17
Quire,Christop 77
Raidy,Hannah 136
Raines,Richard 233
Rainey,
  Benjamin 113
  Samuel 113,118
  Thomas 113,137
Rains,
  Lucy 184
  Richard 184
Ramsey,
  Archibald 152,187
  James 8,9,43,45,113,140
  John 8,9,83,84,89,102,
    131,146,173,204,215
  Margaret 69,113
  Robert 31,42,62,64,69,
    113,159,181,188
  William 39,105,166,199,
    200,233,237
Ramsoeur,
  Jacob 43,141,142
  Darrick 16,45
Ramsour,
  David 70,98
  Daniel 18
  Derrick 18,141,142
  Jacob 70,106
  John 70
Randall,Jacob 132
Raney,
  Agness 6,17
  Ann 6,137
  Benjamin 17

Raney(con't)
  Thomas 6,17
Rankin,
  David 57
  Samuel 72
Rant,Leany 198
Rape,Peter 188
Ratchford,
  Mary 3
  William 3,23,52,63,107
  Willm 77
Ray,
  Isaac 198
  Thomas 51,73,
  William 6,72,132,134
Rayne,Thomas 13,71
Rayney,Thomas 79
Raynolds,
  Hannah 137
  Thomas 127
  William 137
Rea,
  Andrew 88,89,146,184
  John 91,144,205
Read,
  Andrew 184
  George 132
  John 73
Ready,Thomas 136
Ree,
  Thomas 60,221
  William 120
Reed,
  Daniel 70,71,75,76,107,
    154,226
  George 139,195
  Hugh 187
  James 125,152,154,159,
    202,210,221
  John 95,234,236,237
  Martha 95
  Mary 6
  Rebecca 70,76
  Will 2,5,38,39,57,59,70,
    79,103,104,106,108,112,
    113,136,155,161,178,
    191,193,198,216,226
  William 6,56,91,145,214,
    217,226,244
Rees,
  David 28,34,48,77,96
  George 56,242
  James 120,164
  Thomas 69
Reese,
  David 94,210,246
  David Jr. 242
  David Sr. 242
Reid,
  Adolph 9
  James 124,210
  John 95,142
Reip,Adolph 141,
Renex,
  George 228
  Robert 228
Renick,
  George 200
  John 172,200,209
  Mary 69
Renicke,George 33
Renicks,George 172
Renix,George 225
Rennick,George 2,38,47,69,
  209,238
Rese,David 221
Reynhart,
  Andrew 13,58,
  Hannah 13
Reynold,
  Henry 108
  Thomas 108
  Thomas Jr. 108

Reynolds,
  Elizabeth 75
  Henry 112
  John 108,112
  Richard 68,75
  Thomas 112
  Thomas Jr. 112
  Thomas Sr. 112
Riall,Phin. 31
Rian,James 14,19
Richardson,
  ___ 114
  Daniel 139
  James 234,237
  John 17
  Samuel 17,95,97,134
  William 31,64
Richey,
  Catherine 154,155
  Jacob 154,155
  James 95,115,212
  John 75,118,173,224
  John Jr. 212
  John Sr. 212
  Thomas 94,99,115,117,125
Richman,
  John 45,74,115
  Sarah 115
Rickey,
  Jacob 68
  James 138
Ridley,Bromfield 156
Riggs,John 134,135
Rile,Thomas 49
Rine,Jacob 52
Rion,James 36,37
Risk,James 10
Ritchey,
  John 221
  William 221
Ritzhaupt,Johan 95
Ritzhoup,John 115,132
Roach,Samuel 159,200,226
Road,
  Lewis 49,65
  Ludwig 49
Roaddy,Thomas 66
Roan,Matthew 31
Robb,
  Joseph 199,220
  Robert 88,145
  William 172
Robenet,
  John 200
  Mary 200
Roberts,
  Benjabin 186
  Benjamin 25,30,161
  Ellinor 30
  Josiah 77,88,150
  John 219
  Mary 77
  William 85,144
Robertson,
  Alexander 62,98
  James 14,73
  John 72,99
  Jonathan 137
  Jonathon 73
  Robert 70
  Samuel 7
  Thomas 70
Robeson,
  Joseph 173
  Israel 112
  William 125
Robinet,
  John 199,228
  Mary 199
Robinette,John 157,220
Robinson,
  Alexander 1,39
  Archibald 93

Robinson(con't)
  Andrew 22,118
  David 140,144,227
  Hugh 52
  James 2,13,14,17,23,34,
    45,46,51,103,119,174,
    199
  James Jr. 36,115
  Jean 1
  John 2,52,99,115,163,
    199,201,235
  Jonathan 63,104,117
  Matthew 245
  Robert 86,156,224
  Thomas 27,47,52,115
  William 39,96,143,246
Robison,
  Andrew 162,163,199
  Benjamin 213
  David 202,215
  James 42,155
  John 4,97,198
  Mathew 41,172,202,213
  Moses 41
  Richard 93,105
  Robert 222
  William 237
Roch,Samuel 202,243
Rockey,John 99
Roddy,
  Francis 136
  Hannah 136
  Thomas 136
Roden,___ 117
Rodgers,
  Frances 197,198
  Hugh 197,198
  John 67,200
  Joseph 211
  Mary 193
  Robert 61,107,158,177,
    193,197,198
  Thomas 195,219
Rogers,
  John 127
  Robert 4,97
Rosh,Samuel 70
Ross,
  Anthony 176
  Elizabeth 118,135
  Francis 33,132,136,139,
    140,217
  George 76,93,144,176,216
    235
  Hamilton 24,54
  James 137,161,187,209
  John 76
  Joseph 176
  Nicholas 66
  Rebecca 178
  Reuben 177
  William 35,118,135
Rotch,Samuel 70
Rottes,Mary Barbara 49
Routh,
  Elizabeth 133
  Jeremiah 82
  Zachariah 133
Rowan,Matthew 9,181
Rudasel,Mary 52
Rudasul,Phillip 52
Rudisal,Michael 19
Rudisale,Michael 9
Rudisall,Phillip 24
Rudisail,
  Elizabeth 18
  Phillip 18
Rudisally,Gerick 24
Rudisalo,Michael 132
Rudisil,___ 22
Rudisill,Michael 96
Rudisilly,
  Gerick 24

Rudisilly,
  John 24
Rudisily,Phillip 24
Rudsil,
  James 34
  Robert 23
Rufer,Caleb 96
Run,Matthew 153
Rush,James 32
Rusk,James 23,25,28,36
Russ,Hezekiah 133
Russal,
  James 193
  Robert 53
  William 53
Russel,
  David 48,65,118,211
  John 13,78,96,216
  Matthew 105,173
Russell,
  James 39,51,97,98,117,
    182
  Jane 160
  Jean 39
  Matthew 160
  Robert 39
Ruth,
  Jeremiah 25,109
  Margaret 25
  Zacheus 109
Rutherford,
  Elizabeth 9
  Griffith 9,191
Rutledge,
  George 64,107,108
  James 108
  Thomas 96
Ryan,
  Christopher 201
  James 129,173
Sadler,
  Henry 98
  Janet 224
  John 116,224,237
  Richard 6,7,71,116
  Robert Erwin 206
Sailor,___ 113
Salby,Lusart 13
Salles,James 13
Salter,Thomas 115
Sample,
  Benjamin 138
  Joseph 84,88,90,91,142,
    145,148,223,233
  William 124,135
Samples,
  Joseph 144
  William 152,204
Sanders,
  Ann 212
  Daniel 172
  Richard 212
Sartain,John 77,109
Saunders,
  ___ 113
  Lemuel 19
  Samuel 77
Saverett,Charles 210
Sawers,James 226
Sawyer,
  James 209,210
  Sophia 209
  William 209,210
Sawyers,
  James 201
  William 130,240
Sayers,William 241
Saylor,Leonard 108
Schocher,George Sr. 156
Scotcher,George Jr. 156
Sconnel,John 182
Scot,
  John 199

Scot(con't),
　Joseph 163,164
　Moses 241
　Sarah 241
Scote,John 165
Scott,
　Abraham 26,33,62,64
　Alexander 25
　James 23,45,96,99,100,
　　126,132,152,158,175,
　　193,205,235
　John 2,24,35,51,75,79,
　　92,94,95,117,127,158,
　　162,233,235
　Joseph 62,120,183,189
　Moses 94,95,158,160,166,
　　199
　Patrick 158
　Robert 44,60,201,219
　Sarah 160
　Samuel 204
　Thomas 29,34,39,109
　William 97,100,117,175,
　　193,
Sealer,
　Geo.Leonard 96
　Peter 96
Secres,
　Barbara 228
　Jacob 187,228
　John 200
Secrest,
　Barbara 200
　Jacob 200
Secrift,Jacob 189
Secrist,Jacob 185
See,Joseph 209
Seids,Jacob 73
Seigel,Elizabeth 33
Seil,Georg 126
Seits,Jacob 27
Sellars,John 54
Seller,
　Geo.Leonard 32
　John 33
Sellers,
　Elizabeth 53
　Isaac 180
　John 22,53
Selvy,Geo.Augustus 114
Selway,Geo.Augustus 40
Selwyn,
　___ 100,101
　George 198
　Geo.Augustus 7,41,44,48,
　　56,60,76,80,81,82,83,
　　84,85,86,87,88,89,90,
　　91,115,129,130,131,
　　153,155,156,157,165,
　　183,186,190,215,223
　John 44,56,183,229
Seman,John 161
Semple,
　Jennet 185
　Joseph 185
　William 134
Setsner,Jacob 114
Shafer,Richard 193
Shalbey,Rees 195
Shalby,Rees 197
Shambley,John 49
Shanks,James 186
Shannon,Hugh 53
Sharp,
　Edward 181,196
　Ezekiel 202,243
　James 198
　Jamima 41,126,159
　Samuel 213
　Thomas 193,194
　Walter 142
　"Widow" 95,96,143
　Willis 142

Sharp(con't),
　William 15,16,21,58,71,
　　107,109,112,114,117,
　　132,133,134,135,138,
　　139,142,
Sharpe,William 242
Sharply,Moses 201
Shaver,Frederick 191
Shavers,Michael 198
Shaw,
　Benjamin 50,107,108,141
　Robert 10
Sheals,John 144
Shearman,Phillip 76
Sheild,John 127
Sheites,Thomas 178
Shelbey,Moses 65
Shelby,
　David 195
　Isabel 161,162
　Moses 97,161,162,167,
　　171,220,233
　Rees 2,12,55,195,196
　Thomas 223
　William 194
Shephard,Abm.Jr. 206
Shepherd,Henry 134
Sherell,William 104
Sherill,William 13,63
Sherril,
　Moses 63
　William 63
Sherrill,
　Aventon 73
　William 14,72,137
Shever,Michael 211
Shields,
　Agnes 175
　Andrew 190
　John 16,127,152,153,162,
　　175
　Margaret 175,218
　Sarah 190
　Thomas 152,153,154,159,
　　182,218
　William 192,199
Shin,Abgal 179
Shine,Isaac 75
Shinn,
　Abigail 40
　Isaac 179
　Joseph 179,192,200
Shipe,George 79
Shipley,
　Edward 241
　George 240
　Robert 176,240
Shoefoot,John 137
Shoofoot,George 112
Shuford,John 17,100
Shutts,Martin 46,96
Sides,
　Adam 73
　Andrew 153
　Christian 153
　George 73
　Susannah 73
Sights,Jacob 9,22
Sigle,John 33
Sigmon,Stofal 75
Sillman,John 199
Simmerman,Christian 37
Simms,William 118,124,134
Simonson,Magnus 13
Simonton,William 5,11
Simpson,
　Hugh 134
　John 207
Simral,
　James 134,135
　Violet 134,135
Sims,
　___ 114

Sims(con't),
　William 95,109,173,236
Simson,James 173
Sinclair,Samuel 56
Sisson,William 134
Sites,Andrew 114,162
Sits,Andrew 71
Sitton,Abraham 18
Slemon,J.F. 161
Siegel,John 33
Skrimshire,Jno.Brown 227
Skool,Henry 218
Sloan,
　Henry 54
　James 208
　Jean 178
　John 11,20,27,36,37,54,
　　59,75,157,174,177,178,
　　189,194,234,237
　John Jr. 7,55
　Robert 7,10,27,36,76,
　　116,157,176,194,245
Slone,
　David 180
　James 55,129,160,169
　Jean 233
　John 213,221
　John Jr. 233
　Margaret 213
　Robert 180,213
Sloon,
　James 218
　John 228,245
　Margaret 245
Sloughs,David 222
Small,W. 88
Smart,
　Isabella 112
　William 112
Smith,
　Abraham 111
　Amy 103
　Andrew 49
　Arthur 31
　Cadarina 104
　David 156,209,211,231
　Edward 31
　Ema 78
　Ezekiel 138
　George 104
　Henry 78,103,111,116,
　　119,139
　Hugh 7,77
　Jacob 238
　James 11
　Jennet 191
　Jenry 78
　John 18,32,43,126,127,
　　129,132,138,140,152,
　　154,182,191,202,228,
　　245
　Margaret 202
　Mary 32
　Patrick 31
　R. 172,177,178,179,181,
　　189,240,244
　Robert 40,143,152,163,
　　167,185,189,203,218,
　　230,231,238,239,242,
　　243
　Roger 8,10,11
　Sarah 243
　Samuel 168,195,200,224
　Thomas 172
　Vill 132
　William 21,60,88,102,
　　146,157,163,182,183,
　　191,228
　Willis 164
Smitz,Georg 155
Snapp,Lawrence 73
Snford,Isaeri 164

Snider,
  Hance Adam 100
  Sarah 100
Sosamonhouser, Henry 190
Sparks,
  James 82
  Robert 82
Spear, William 209
Speek, David 6
Speeks, David 23
Speers, William 35
Speir, John 207
Spencer, Samuel 24,133,192
  Thomas 177
Spring, John 207
Springer, Aron 134
Springs,
  John 199,246
  Richard 246
  Sarah 207
Springstan, John 177
Springsteen,
  John 147,162,165,194,205
  John Jr. 161,184
  Richard 161,184,207
Springstell, John 70,87
Springstree, John 160
Sproot,
  Martha 1
  Matthew 1
  Thomas
Sprot,
  Andrew 10,11,86
  James 154
  Samuel 17,199
  Thomas 32,154
  William 92,141
Sprots, James 73
Sprott,
  Andrew 66,82,85,244
  James 101
  Martha 100,101
  Samuel 1
Sprotts, James 184
Spurlock, Robert 72
Stafford,
  James 22,26,74,81,209,
    229,238
  Turner 66
Stallings,___ 74
Stallinger, John 114
Stalfinger, John 129
Staly, David 133
Standley,
  David 36,43,63,98,138
  Hannah 138
Standford, Isaac 169
Standly, David 183
Stanford, John 109,135
Stanlee, David 63
Stanley,
  David 36,99,109
  Hannah 63
Starens, Lennard 71
Starr,
  Arthur 161,219,246
  Hannah 161,246
  John 84,86,88,91,148,161
Starrans,
  Catherine 175
  Joseph 175
Starret,
  Alexander 60,81,246
  Ruth 60
  William 60,81
Starrett,
  Alexander 82,85
  William 85
Starring,
  Anna Catherine 120
  Leonard 120
Starrit,
  Ruth 244
  William 244

Stater, Ross 172
Steel,
  Aaron 36
  James 80,150
  Martin
  Moses 81,84,85,146,209,
    210,211,234
  Thomas 62
  William 87,155,156,213
Steen,
  James 108,112
  John 45
Stell, Moses 130
Stenson, John 49
Stephens, Abraham 136
Stephenson,
  James 74
  William 19
Sterat,
  Alexander 223
  John 196
  William 217
Sterns, Joseph 13
Sterratt, William 186
Sterret,
  Abigail 162
  Alexander 162
  Ruth 162
  William 162
Steven, William 114
Stevens,
  Isabel 53
  Robert 197
  William E. 53
Stevenson,
  David 74
  Hannah 225
  James 140
  Joseph 192
  Richard 225
  William 59,104
Stewart,
  Adam 209,211
  Isbel 220
  John 89
  Mathew 67,170,188,219,
    243
  Robert 189,220
Sties, Henry 114
Stigenwalt, Peter 192
Still, William 150,173
Stillwell,
  Margaret 60,228
  Richard 60,228
Stilt, Thomas 62
Stitwell, Richard 170
Stivison,___ 189
Stokes, Henry 154,177
Stone,
  John 214
  Thomas 128
Story, George 78
Stotler, Peter 116
Strain, David 53
Stratford, James 7
Sticken, Moses 175
Stroud,
  John 73,138,142
  Martha 142
Stuart,
  Alexander 166,224
  Hugh 120
  John 132
  Matthew 201
  Robert 163
  Robert Jr. 226
Sturgeon, John 184
Stuts, Peder 116
Stutt, William 150
Sugg, Aquilla 206
Suin, William 99
Suit, Jacob 208
Sul, Joseph 246
Sulls, Jno. Martin 21

Summerman,
  Catherine 17
  Jacob 17
  Peter 17
Summy, Peter 116
Sumrall, Andrew 32
Suter, Samuel 205
Suther, Rev. Samuel 158
Swan,
  John 221,242
  Joseph 208
  Margaret 208
  Moses 209,210
  Moses Jr. 208
  Moses Sr. 208
Swann,
  John 84,87,148,150,192,
    216
  Moses 156
Swearingam, Joseph 161
Sweringame, Joseph 30
Swink, Jacob 239
Swinny, William 132
Sytes, Christian 35
Tagart, James 156
Tagert, John 114,136,140,
    185
Tagerty,
  James 236
  John 108
Taggart,
  James 23
  John 74,79,100,148
  Joseph 200
Taggert,
  James 200,234
  John 71,200
Tagget, Jacob 96
Tally, Henry 159,229
Tallinger,
  Mary 19
  Martin 19
Tankersley, William 118
Taner, Joseph 198
Tanner,
  Joseph 8
  William 177
Tate,
  Ann 173
  James 14,15,19,20,36,45,
    83,97,118,124,146,173,
    181,183,189,204,205,
    215,223,243
  Lazarus 14
  Robert 26,57
Tay, John 82
Taylor,
  Abraham 155,191
  John 145,155,192
  Margaret 56
  Michael 78
  William 24,43,50,54
Temple, Major 127,130
Templeton, Robert 50
Tenan, Robert 4
Tenman, Capt. Robert 197
Tennan,
  John 198
  Robert 198,199
Terrence, Hugh 111
Thallman, Elizabeth 98
Thelby, James 50
Thom,
  James 166
  Sarah 166
Thomas,
  Jean 73
  John 6,7,13,16,17,18,20,
    22,23,25,26,27,29,32,
    62,63,68,73,74,75,79,
    113,138,142
Thomasson, John 72
Thomason, John 13,14,43,62,
    65,166

Thompson,
  Alexander 52
  Charles 174
  Elisha 133
  Elizabeth 232
  Gideon 99,139
  Ginnings 232
  James 39,49,190
  Jennins 190
  M. 61
  Moses 26
  Precilla 190
  Samuel 8,10,11,14,53,54,
    62,69,75,134
  Sarah 52,139
  Thomas 188,198
  William 92,102,129,161,
    172,212
Thomson,
  Charles 236
  James 110
  John 110,211
  Thomas 153
  William 244,246
Tillinger,
  John 118
  Martin 19
  Mary 118
  Philip 118
Timings,Thomas 42
Tindsley,James 167
Tinnen,Robert 50
Titus,Dennis 155
Tobinson,Thomas 44
Todd,
  James 208
  John 20,107
  John Jr. 107
Tom,
  James 166
  Sarah 166
Torrance,Adam 75
Townsend,
  Mary 8,61
  Moses 147
  Repentance 8
Townsley,James 204
Trammell,Thomas 45
Travish,Francis 115
Trimble,Richard 195
Trum,Nickles 21
Truom,Nickles 18
Tryon,
  Gov. 140
  William 88
Tucker,George 120,158
Turner,
  John 15,182
  Thomas 15
Tuts,Dennis 157
Tygart,John 64,65,68,223
Vaird,William 1
Vance,
  David 132,148,165,178,
    207
  Ruth 178
Varner,Henry 81,83
Varnor,Henry 87,183
Vel,Leonard 73
Venables,Jojn 11,109
Verner,Henry 80,214,227
Vernon,
  Alexander 78
  Henry 133,147,159
  James 139
Vernor,
  Barbara 55,62
  Henry 22,55,62
Verry,Hugh 135
Waddele,Davis 236
Waddell,Joseph 19
Wade,
  John 112,118,136

Wade(con't),
  Thomas 119,136
Wadington,William 67
Wagsland,James 245
Wahop,James 23
Walbert,Christopher 29,
    234,235
Walker,
  Elizabeth 34,52,100
  Ellenor 100
  Francis 96
  Fromey 96
  George 63,188
  Henry 59,142,155,165,
    166,216
  James 59,139,140,170
  Jean 30
  John 24,27,31,34,39,52,
    63,64,72,114,134,200
  Matthew 170,220
  Nathaniel 51
  Phillip 30,51,54,212,
    238,241
  Rebecca 219
  Robert 53,96,216
  Thomas 27,163,202,212
  William 59,142,164
Walkup,James 1,9
Wallace,
       96
  Alexander 141,159
  Benjamin 205,207,218,
    219,
  Ezekiel 28,63,82,87,89,
    147,155,212,227,247
  Hugh 70,100
  James 15,18,41,48,77,80,
    98,117,137,164,220,
    221
  John 92,93,98,100,137,
    207,219,242,243
  Joseph 118,207,219,246
  Marey 242
  Mary 207,219,242
  Oliver 18,116
  Sarah 182,210
  Thomas 169,192,218
  William 40,42,99,143,
    144,180,182,210,238
Wallas,Thomas 154
Waller,
  James 91
  Robert 31,96
Wallis,
  James 182
  Jo. 152
  John 18
  Thomas 103,127
Walter,Robert 31,34
Walton,William 25
Ward,Richard 43
Warden,John 163,171,201
Warlick,
  Daniel 95
  Maria Barbara 95
Warlock,Daniel 20,45,104,
    106,116
Warlocks,Daniel 25
Warner,Harden 196
Warnock,John 140
Watkins,
  John 63
  Rachel 63
  Robert 95,138
  Samuel 137
Watson,
  Allsey 109
  David 30
  James 12,19,30,109,141
  Jean 12
  Samuel 10,30
  Villiam 50
  Violet 39,49,76

Watson(con't)
  William 5,8,9,10,11,12,
    19,39,49,63,75,76,104,
    109,115,137,212,221
Watterson,John 236
Wattesson,William 192
Watts,Henry 236
Wattson,
  John 13,19,
  Vilatt 76
  Violet 137
  William 76,99,136,137
Waughop,James 187
Waughup,James 4,62,116
Wauhup,James 238
Way, James 6,82,85,91,109,
    118,136,150,151,181,
    193,243,244
Weatherford,
  Sarah 215
  William 156,215
Weathers,Zebulon 164
Weaver,Valentine 96
Weeks,
  John 237
  John Phillip 159,232
  Phillip 215,233
Wel,Leonard 73
Welch,
  John 77
  Nicholas 46,73,76,77,127
  Sarah 73
Wells,Elijah 140
Welsh,
  John 20
  Margaret 20
  Nicholas 20,45
  Niclas 42
  Robert 16
  William 42,49,73,79
Wharrey,John 48
Whill,Timothy 70
Whisenant,Adam 70
Whistenhunt,Paul 9
Whistlehunt,Nicholas 51
White,
  Agness 4,44,62,73
  Archibald
  Bartholomy 51
  Edward 234
  George 69
  Henry 17,44,69,206
  Hugh 30,73,242
  James 15,36,60,66
  James Sr. 180
  John 127
  Joseph 6,52,131
  Leady 51
  Margaret 180,232,235
  Moses 190
  Sarah 190
  Stephen 4,44,62
  Timothy 131,151
  Will 187
  William 13,15,35,180,
    187,231,232,235,239
Whitely,
  Alexander 13,14,72
  Moses 51
Whiteside,William 209,210
Whitesill,   79
Whitsitt,William 212
Whiticar,Charles 44,
Whitner,
  Henry 21,34
  Michael 21
Whitsell,
  James 178
  Rachel 180
Whitsill,John 180
Wicks,David 178
Wiggins,Dr.Thomas 20,225
Whilham,

Whilham,
    Eve 235
    George 235
Wiley,
    Mary 162,198
    Oliver 162
    William 170
Wilkes,John 57
Wilkins,
    John 30,43,49,57,63
    Jonathan 45,58
    Rachel 63
    Rebecca 49
    Samuel 17,69,112
    William 44,58,112
Will,Gerhardt 108
Willcocks,William 137
Willhany,Jacob 2
Williams,
    Andrew 156
    Edward 43,76
    George 9
    Henery 70
    Isaac 236
    John 109,154
    John Jr. 51,77
    Jonathan 16
    Patrick 89,145
    Thomas 22,53,141
Williamson,
    James 98,133
    Jonathan 16
Wills,Samuel 10
Willson,
    Benjamin 75,95
    James 26,99,106,177
    James Jr. 26
    John 67,76,79,216
    Samuel 76,96,203,204,205
    Thomas 129,177,184
    William 78,216
Wilson,
    Andrew 238
    Beersheba 22
    Benjamin 140
    David 94,113,120,140,
      190,220,221,229,238,
      242,246
    Elizabeth 237
    Frances 178
    Francis 116,178
    Garret 227,247
    Hugh 6,30,174,186,215
    Jacob 103
    James 3,12,23,25,45,46,
      50,61,90,103,104,109,
      129,130,151,163,169,
      176,179,181,194,218,
      229,231,234,236,237
    Jane 120,163
    Jean 113,229
    John 3,10,11,15,53,63,
      137,141,160,164,174,
      183,184,198,207,213,
      214,225,238,242
    Joseph 159
    Margaret 140,225
    Mary 186,215
    Mathew 45,46,95
    Robert 13,102,104,139,
      177,178,179,181
    Samuel 8,9,10,18,22,49,
      75,81,101,102,140,152,
      160,176,177,178,182,
      186,187,188,194,225,
      241,245,247
    Samuel Jr.241
    Sarah 47
    William 3,17,61,74,82,
      165,174,176,218,221,
      223
    Zaccheus 54,177,178,179,
      198,210,221,246

Wilson(con't),
    Zacheus 72,132
Wimpson,Samuel 141
Winde,Abner 230
Winsely,Moses 212
Winslow,Moses 244
Wire,John 223
Wisenant,Nicholas 76
Wise,Frederick 116
Wishard,
    Elizabeth 242
    Joseph 115,242
Wishart,James 192,229
Wisenhunt,
    Jacob 95
    Nicholas 113
Wishinhunt,Jacob 105
Witherow,James 57,103
Witherspoon,James 228,245
Wnysley,Moses 246
Wofice,John 219
Wolcher,Adam 154
Wolfang,Jacob 21
Wood,
    John 194,220
    Margaret 5
    Robert 5
Woodhouse,John 206
Woods,
    Andrew 156
    James 156,157
    John 20,29,142,229
    Lattes 220
    Robert 11,106
Wotherford,
    Sarah 188
    William 188
Wray,
    John 37
    William 106
Wright,
    James 141
    John 137
    Martha 101
    Moses 141
    Thomas 53,101
    William 141
Wyatt,James 9
Wyle,James 198
Wyley,James 40,86,99,114,
    143
Wylie,
    John 163,199,201
    Moses 36,63
    Oliver 139,140,168,172
    Will 189
    William 171,198,221,222
Wyly,
    James 118,130,135,136,
      144,152,154,156,159,
      162
    John 170,235
    Oliver 129
Wylly,James 97
Yancey,William 17
Yancy,William 112
Yandell,James 235
Yarbrough,Henry 157
Yarborough,Humphrey 157
Yates,Thomas 26,27
Yearman,Michael 196
Yeats,Thomas 2,5,34,75
Yelton,Isaac 129,173
Yeward,Joseph 172
Yewings,Sarah 190
    Thomas 190
Yoast,
    Christian 213
    Francis 213
    Geo. Henry 213
    Paul 213
Yost,Francis 213
Yother,Conrad 21,34

Yottle,Jacob 52
Youn-,Gottlieb 18
Youart,Robert 51,55
Young,
    ___ 113
    Ann 11,23
    Alexander 129
    Elizabeth 47
    James 27,45,62,64,70,74,
      80,115,137,176,245
    John 11,23,62,64,126,210
    Joseph 204
    Samuel 10,26,32,37,42,47,
      54,56,133,187,196,243
    William 78,127,176,188
Younge,Samuel 243
Youte,Godfrey 67
Zach,Samuel 29
Zicklagg,Samuel 28
Zicklegg,Samuel 139
Ziklagg,Samuel 153
Zimmerman,Jacob 52

ADDENDA

Leech,John 54
Ouicry,John 187
Spreech,David 126
Walace,Jean 219
Wallice,James 42
White,Archibald __

SLAVE INDEX

Dick, 192
"Fellow" 139
Hanah 233
Jack 193,243
Kate 122
Ned 233
Rachel 127
Warrick 123

www.ingramcontent.com/pod-product-compliance
Lightning Source LLC
Chambersburg PA
CBHW020644300426
44112CB00007B/230